2

The Age of Nelson

also by G. J. Marcus

A NAVAL HISTORY OF ENGLAND, 1
The Formative Centuries

in preparation

A NAVAL HISTORY OF ENGLAND, 3
The Empire of the Ocean

A NAVAL HISTORY OF ENGLAND

2

The Age of Nelson

G. J. MARCUS

London
GEORGE ALLEN & UNWIN LTD

FIRST PUBLISHED IN 1971

© *G. J. Marcus 1971*

ISBN 0 04 359006 3

PRINTED IN GREAT BRITAIN
in 11 on 13pt Imprint
BY C. TINLING AND CO. LTD
PRESCOT

TO ROBERT GREENHALGH ALBION

CONTENTS

		PAGE
Preface		9
I	THE FRENCH REVOLUTION	15
II	JERVIS IN THE MEDITERRANEAN	59
III	THE NAVAL MUTINIES	82
IV	THE WAR ON TRADE, 1793–1802	102
V	THE CAMPAIGN OF THE NILE	124
VI	THE WESTERN SQUADRON	153
VII	'OF NELSON AND THE NORTH'	170
VIII	LAND POWER AND SEA POWER	193
IX	NAPOLEON AND GREAT BRITAIN	214
X	THE CAMPAIGN OF TRAFALGAR	244
XI	THE CONTINENTAL SYSTEM	295
XII	THE PENINSULAR WAR	331
XIII	THE WAR ON TRADE, 1803–15	361
XIV	THE CRISIS OF THE COMMERCIAL WAR	406
XV	THE UPRISING OF THE NATIONS	426
XVI	'MR. MADISON'S WAR'	452
XVII	THE HUNDRED DAYS	485
Bibliography		505
Index		521

MAPS

PAGE

The English Channel 24

Western Approaches 32

Bantry Bay 45

The Mediterranean 60

St. Vincent, 14 February 1797 76

The North Sea 93

The West Indies 109

Indian Waters 112

The Nile, 1 August 1798 133

Approaches to Brest 161

The Battle of Copenhagen, 2 April 1801 186

The British Attack at Trafalgar, 21 October 1805 278

Spain and Portugal 333

The Walcheren Campaign 342

The Baltic Sea and the North 371

The Coasts of Europe in 1810 408

The Eastern Seaboard of North America 454

The Blockade of American Ports 464

No living man has known the Royal Navy in the age of its greatest power and glory. The last surviving officer of Trafalgar died more than eighty years ago. A full half-century has passed since the death of 'Jacky' Fisher, who received his nomination for the Navy from the last of Nelson's captains. Notwithstanding that until comparatively recent times this country retained her old pre-eminence at sea, she did not do so in anything like the same degree as in the period under review; her maritime ascendancy in 1906 could not, in fact, be compared for a moment with that in 1806.

When Great Britain had to meet the challenge of the French Revolution and Empire, our Navy was, perhaps, the most formidable fighting force on earth. The past fifty years had seen a steady and sustained improvement both as regards the personnel and *matériel* of the Service. To Admiral Lord Anson belongs the credit of having evolved a powerful and well-trained Western Squadron, raised the standard of British naval construction, and overhauled the organization of the Fleet; to Admiral Sir Charles Middleton (later Lord Barham), of having achieved a much-needed reform of the dockyards, raised the efficiency of the Admiralty staff-work to an unparalleled level, and formulated the strategy for the decisive campaign of 1805. Even more significant, in some respects, was the general improvement in the morale and efficiency of the Service, especially among the officers. A cardinal factor, whose importance can scarcely be set too high, was the living tradition of naval warfare inherited by these sea-officers of Howe's and St. Vincent's generation; many of whom had had experience, not only of the War of American Independence, but also of the Seven Years' War.

At the same time the military power and prowess of the French Republic, and later of the Napoleonic empire, were similarly un-exampled in previous generations. Every state in Europe, save Great Britain only, was sooner or later forced into this hegemony. It is scarcely

too much to say that by the turn of the century the conflict had resolved itself into a duel between Land Power and Sea Power; and it
was a struggle to the death. The whole matter, indeed, was on a
tremendous scale, calling to mind the well-known lines of Livy in
Book XXI of the *Historia*, prefacing his epic narration of the Second
Punic War. 'Never,' Livy recounted, 'did any other states and peoples
of greater strength and resources engage in war against each other;
nor were these states at any other time possessed of such reserves of
strength and power.'

The Great War (as it used to be known to our forbears) which,
with one brief intermission, continued from 1793 to 1815 abounded
in supremely important lessons for the Navy of the early twentieth
century. Problems of blockade; the right use of Intelligence; defence
against invasion; the conduct of conjoint operations; the various
measures of commerce protection and commerce attack—on all
these, and others besides, much light is shed by the history of the
French Revolutionary and Napoleonic Wars.

In the long general peace, however, virtually no attempt was made
by the Admiralty to digest the lessons of this mighty struggle. The
only full-scale, professional study of the greatest fighting admiral in
history was the work of a captain of the United States Navy. The
first attempt to compile a real Staff history of the campaign of Trafalgar
was the achievement of a French army officer. In consequence of
this long-continued official lethargy and neglect most of the lessons
of the Great War were, for all practical purposes, wasted and forgotten—those relating to trade defence in particular; and that vital
element of our maritime ascendancy already referred to, *the living,
continuous tradition of naval warfare*, was lost, never again to be fully
recovered.

The loss of that tradition might have been repaired in some degree
by the careful and systematic study of naval history. Thus on the
other side of the North Sea the treatises of Clausewitz on the Napoleonic War had been turned to good account by the Prussian General
Staff, who looked to military history as 'the most effective means of
teaching war during peace' and had set up a special department for
its study. But over here the official attitude to naval history, both
inside and outside the Service, has been usually, to say the least of it,
half-hearted. 'You wouldn't call history *work*,' one of the illuminati

of the Naval Education Department was heard to declare during the last war; 'not *real* work, like mathematics.' 'We were not instructed in naval history,' an officer of his own generation informed the present writer more recently. 'We were only given "pep talks".' The criticism was well founded. The instruction imparted to the future officers of the Service in those days might with justice have been described as the literary equivalent of a 'hurrah cruise'; and the pompous, avuncular, semi-jocose style of approach adopted in the official text-books must have done much to prejudice them against naval history permanently.

The universities, more especially the ancient universities, have seldom revealed any interest in naval history. It is not without significance that so many maritime historians of note, from Michael Oppenheim to J. A. Williamson, have in some way or other been snubbed or cold-shouldered by the academic tribe. 'The clever men at Oxford Know all there is to be knowed'; and, consequently, anything which they do not happen to know, such as naval history, is plainly not knowledge. It was this supercilious, condescending, and occasionally downright discourteous attitude of the dons which soured Oppenheim's temper and turned him from the task that should have been his lifework, with the result that he presently abandoned his *History of the Administration of the Royal Navy* after completing only one volume; and when, shortly before his death, he was setting his affairs in order, he left instructions for all his notebooks to be destroyed, observing that if these were made available to the learned, 'some damned fool would make a mess of the business'. Oppenheim knew his dons. Some damned fool probably would.

In the circumstances it is scarcely surprising that the naval side of the War of 1793–1815 has never been fully and comprehensively treated. The second work in Mahan's classic trilogy on Sea Power, *The Influence of Sea Power upon the French Revolution and Empire*, ends in effect with the action of Trafalgar; the remaining ten years of the war being covered only in outline.

The lack of an authoritative and comprehensive narrative of the war at sea from 1805 to 1815 has for long been a major handicap to the proper knowledge and understanding of the Napoleonic era; and has inevitably resulted, in certain general, national, and military histories of this period, in many a hiatus in the chain of causation. Notwithstanding that the Peninsular War may be considered the greatest combined operation in our history, all too often the crucial factor of Sea Power has been overlooked in the conclusions of scholars. No more than the Duke of Wellington in his day (as will afterwards appear) has the academic tribe ever properly comprehended the realities of the 'sea affair'—the interrelation of stations, bases, and distances; the imperative duty of trade protection; the dependence of effective naval strength on hygiene and supply; the diverse problems posed by navigational conditions in the various theatres of the war; the vital importance of seamanship in connection with convoy, reconnaissance, the blockades, conjunct expeditions, the enforcement of our maritime rights, and 'the dangers of the sea'; the calamitous consequences of 'old lady captains' and their hangers-on; the deflection of naval strategy by petticoat influence (Lady Hamilton was by no means the only offender in this respect: merely the most notorious); and, last but not least, the fell significance of what was likely to occur on the day 'when it was Buggins's turn'.

Assuredly, this is an era worthy of the most sustained and concentrated study; for, taken all in all, the achievement of the British Navy and mercantile marine in the War of 1793-1815 may be accounted a supreme example—to quote Liddell Hart—'of Britain's sea power, her historic weapon, the deadliest weapon which any nation has wielded throughout history'.

Hartland, North Devon
1970

ACKNOWLEDGMENTS

My grateful thanks are due to the following for advice and assistance on particular points: Professor R. G. Albion, Skipper Thomas Alchorn, Captain A. G. Course, Captain John Creswell, R.N., Captain H. A. Jewell, Professor David Joslin, Professor C. C. Lloyd, Dr. J. J. McCusker, Professor W. E. Minchinton, Captain Bertram Pengelly, R.N., the late Mr. A. B. Rodger, Mr. A. N. Ryan, Captain W. J. Slade, the late Captain Carl V. Sölver, Rear-Admiral A. H. Taylor, the late Skipper J. H. Tonkin, Mrs. E. Tucker, Lieut.-Commander D. W. Waters, R.N., and the late Dr. J. A. Williamson.

I have also to thank the Staffs of the Admiralty Library, the Bodleian, the Reading Room, Manuscripts Room, and Map Room of the British Museum, the National Maritime Museum, the National Portrait Gallery, the Public Records Office, the Tate Gallery, the University of London Library, and the West Sussex County Library for their kind and patient help.

I should also like to thank the Editor of the *Royal United Service Institution Journal* for allowing me to make use of material which has already appeared in his journal.

ABBREVIATIONS

Add. MSS. Additional manuscripts in the British Museum.
A.M. Archives de la Marine, Paris.
Adm. Admiralty Papers in the Public Record Office.
Captains' Letters. From the National Archives, Washington, U.S.A.
F.O. Foreign Office Papers in the Public Record Office.
H.M.C. Historical Manuscripts Commission.

There were giants in those days, not necessarily because they were more favoured at birth than the men of our generation, but because many of them had experience of two or even three wars and each man was carrying on a living tradition from the generation before him. CAPTAIN JOHN CRESWELL, R.N., *Naval Warfare* (1942).

II

The French Revolution

I

On Saturday, 29 December 1792, the *Childers* sloop-of-war, Captain Robert Barlow, left Plymouth Sound to reconnoitre Brest. After ten years of peace, our relations with France were again becoming critical; and the Admiralty desired early intelligence of the state of the squadron in Brest roads.

In the afternoon of the Wednesday following, having entered the Iroise, the *Childers* stood with a moderate north-east breeze within three-quarters of a mile of the batteries guarding the entrance to Brest harbour. Her colours were not then hoisted; the batteries on the southern shore of the Goulet fired a shot, which passed over her; whereupon the *Childers* hoisted the British colours, and the battery ran up the republican tricolour: after which, according to the *Exeter Flying Post*, 'without the least reserve' two other batteries also opened fire on her. The wind falling light, and the flood setting her within half a mile of the French batteries, the sloop came under a heavy cross-fire; and Barlow ordered the sweeps to be got out. Later a westerly breeze sprang up, and the *Childers* made sail. Presently the firing ceased. Only one shot had actually struck the vessel, piercing her side and deck and splitting a gun; without, however, injuring any of the crew. The sky, which from the early hours of the morning had been overcast, darkened with the approach of nightfall, and the breeze continued. By midnight the *Childers* was some nine miles to the eastward of St. Mathieu Point.[1]

Next day the *Childers* stood over to the English shore, and, after weathering a hard northerly gale, anchored, on the evening of 4 January, in Fowey harbour. Barlow at once set off express for London, and duly delivered both his report, and the French shot, to the Admiralty. More than twenty years were destined to pass before the

[1] Adm. 52/2859, 3 January 1793.

reverberations of the fateful cannonade in the entrance to Brest harbour, on that dark January afternoon, finally died away.

When the Revolution broke out in France in 1789 Great Britain had for long held aloof from the alliance which was formed for its suppression. The prime minister, William Pitt the younger, was committed to a policy of peace and retrenchment; the task which he had set himself was to encourage commerce and industry and to repair the national finances after the ravages of the late war; he regarded the disturbances in France as a matter which concerned the French alone. As late as February 1792, when the Revolution was nearly three years old, he continued, in pursuance of this policy, to reduce the Army and Navy; and in his budget speech on the 17th looked forward with confidence to a large standing surplus of revenue over expenditure.

'Unquestionably,' Pitt declared, 'there never was a time in the history of this country, when, from the situation of Europe, we might more reasonably expect fifteen years of peace, than we may at the present moment.' During the last few years Great Britain had successfully weathered one major crisis in the Netherlands, and another, in the year of the 'Spanish Armament', over the Nootka Sound imbroglio with Spain. Our historic rival and antagonist, France, was to all appearances paralysed by the Revolution. At home, the previous decade had been a period of steadily mounting prosperity: prosperity which, moreover, had apparently come to stay. 'From the whole result,' the prime minister continued, 'I trust I am entitled to conclude that the scene which we are now contemplating is not the transient effect of accident, not the short-lived prosperity of a day, but the genuine and natural result of regular and permanent causes. The season of our severe trial is at an end, and we are at length relieved, not only from the dejection and gloom which, a few years since, hung over the country, but from the doubt and uncertainty which, even for a considerable time after our prospect had begun to brighten, still mingled with the hopes and expectations of the public.'[1]

Among those who sat listening to Pitt that day in the Commons there can have been few who realized that so far from the worst of the nation's troubles being over the severest ordeal of all was yet to come and that even now the inhabitants of these islands were on the verge of the most arduous, most protracted, and most desperate struggle for

[1] *War Speeches of William Pitt*, ed. Coupland (1940), pp. 16, 22.

survival in their history. The present preoccupation of the prosperous country gentlemen who filled so many of the benches in the House was with the revolution in English agriculture, rather than with that in the French polity. What chiefly concerned them during the following months was not so much the excesses of the mob in Paris as the effect of a wet and sunless summer upon the harvest—'the worst of all summers,' observed Horace Walpole, who earlier in the year had watched his hay spoiling under the endless downpour. On the river that flowed beneath the windows of their ancient chamber plied the busiest and most lucrative traffic in the world: every week on average there were forty-four ocean-going and 200 coasting vessels lying in the waterway; London at this time carried more than half the total commerce of the kingdom; goods to the value of £60 million annually entered and left the Thames. British merchant shipping was actually three times more numerous than the French. The rising mercantile and industrial community of Great Britain was absorbed in developing and expanding the various branches of our overseas trade and in exploiting the invention and application of machinery. 'Our good old island,' Aukland had remarked to Grenville a few weeks earlier, 'now possesses an accumulation of prosperity beyond any example in the history of the world.' For both landed and moneyed interests, in fact, the prospect had never seemed so fair.

Then in Paris, on 10 August, the mob stormed the Tuileries and slaughtered the King's Swiss Guard. On our side of the Channel, also, ideological passions began to rise. Crowds gathered outside the print shops and gazed their fill on the cartoons of Gillray and others. The pamphlets of Burke and Paine were read with avidity. Notwithstanding the growing horror and indignation excited by the September Massacres, however, the government still clung to neutrality. Until almost the end of 1792 Pitt's purpose continued unshaken. All this time some of the most promising officers in the Navy were vainly seeking employment.

'God knows when we shall meet again,' Collingwood wrote despondently to Nelson in November, 'unless some chance should draw us again to the Sea-shore.' 'If,' the latter, already unemployed for five weary years, entreated the Admiralty, 'your Lordships should be pleased to appoint me to a *cockle-boat*, I shall feel grateful.' Throughout the summer and autumn Pellew, impatient for a frigate, had been importuning his noble patron, Lord Falmouth, to press his claims at the Admiralty.

But in the autumn and winter the situation rapidly deteriorated. The French presently annexed Savoy and overran much of the Rhineland. The invasion of the Austrian Netherlands by the Republican forces, their victory over the Austrians on 6 November, and the opening of the Scheldt on the 16th, were events which directly concerned the vital interests of these islands in the Netherlands. The desire of revolutionary France to use the North Sea coast as an invasionary base in the imminent struggle against Great Britain was well understood on both sides of the Channel. *'Prenons la Hollande,'* declared Danton in 1793, *'et Carthage est à nous!'* The opening of the Scheldt violated a whole series of international settlements; the determination of France to dominate the Low Countries aroused the implacable hostility of Great Britain; and, over and above all this, the exponents of the 'armed doctrine' had proffered their aid to all peoples that should rise against their governments.

Events now moved inexorably towards the ideological conflict which Pitt had struggled so long to avert. In December the militia were called out, and there was general talk of war in England. Early in the new year, on the execution of Louis XVI, M. de Chauvelin, the French minister in London, was ordered to leave the kingdom. About the same time the republican government prepared to mobilize their fleet and ordered the fitting out of thirty sail of the line and twenty frigates. In the British dockyards, too, all was bustle and activity. One after another ships were being commissioned. Things were beginning to move at last, it appeared to half-pay officers fretting on the beach.

'After the clouds comes sunshine,' Nelson wrote exultantly to his wife. 'The Admiralty so smile upon me, that really I am as much surprised as when they frowned. Lord Chatham yesterday made many apologies for not having given me a ship before this time, and said, that if I chose to take a sixty-four to begin with, I should be appointed to one as soon as she was ready; and whenever it was in his power, I should be removed into a seventy-four. Everything indicates War.'[1]

On 26 December orders were received at Plymouth dockyard for the artificers in every department to work 'double tides'; while the greatest

[1] Nicolas, *Nelson's Dispatches*, I, 297.

exertions were used to get the ships ready for sea. Day after day, in all the great naval ports, the work went steadily on. At Portsmouth a few weeks later, to the strains of 'God Save the King' played by the Marine band, and watched by admiring crowds lining the ramparts, a famous flagship of the previous war, the *Victory*, 100, stood out of harbour to the anchorage at Spithead.[1] Nelson—his long days of anti-chambering at the Admiralty now over—was back again in his father's parsonage in Norfolk, endeavouring to raise men for his new command, the *Agamemnon*. Soon he was to leave Burnham Thorpe forever. Among a good many other officers who were returning eagerly to the service from 'that peaceful country life for which a sailor always longs, and with which a sailor is never satisfied' were Thomas Troubridge, who as a youngster had been with Nelson in the gunroom of the *Seahorse*; Cuthbert Collingwood, another of his friends, from his Northumbrian home; Edward Pellew, from his Cornish farm, Treverry, and James Saumarez, from his native Guernsey.

All over the kingdom feeling was rising rapidly against the revolutionaries and their British sympathizers; liberal views were to be out of fashion for almost a generation: the parliamentary reformers had become the object of bitter public attack, and Tom Paine was burnt in effigy on countless village greens. Finally, on 1 February 1793, war was declared by the French Convention, which was already at odds with Austria, Prussia, and Sardinia, against Great Britain and Holland.

On the 12th, a cold, gusty day with heavily clouded skies, Pitt addressed a packed and anxious House of Commons at the second reading of the Militia Bill. Scarcely twelve months before, he had confidently predicted long years of peace and prosperity for this country. Since then the prospect had ominously darkened. 'A sad spring, summer, and autumn,' noted Parson White of Selborne; the harvest of 1792 had failed; the price of bread was continually rising, and rioting broke out in some of the manufacturing areas. What would

---

[1] Laid down in the Year of Victories, 1759, with many years of service to her credit in the American War, flying the flags successively of Admirals Keppel, Hardy, Geary, Hyde Parker, Kempenfelt, Howe, and Hood, the *Victory* was still fitted with her original open stern galleries and her ornate figurehead—a group comprising the bust of King George III, with Britannia on his right, and the British Lion crouching behind her, and, on the opposite side of the King, Victory holding out a crown of laurels, followed by Fame with her trumpet.

be the outcome of the cataclysm on the Continent no man could foresee. But the die was cast, and England must face the issue.

'When war was declared and the event no longer in our option,' observed Pitt, 'it remained only to be considered, whether we should prepare to meet it with a firm determination, and support His Majesty's Government with zeal and courage against every attack. War now was not only declared, but carried on at our very doors; a war which aimed at an object no less destructive than the total ruin of the freedom and independence of this country.'[1]

2

In the opening phase of the war, torn by faction within and menaced by a ring of formidable foes without, the infant Republic appeared doomed to dissolution. But the jealousies and dissensions of the Allies—Austria, Prussia, Spain, Piedmont, Holland, and Great Britain—afforded France a short breathing-space in which to restore order out of chaos and to improvise armies from the raw and ragged levies sent to defend her frontiers. Fired with the spirit of the Revolution, commanded by young and able generals, these troops fought with such daring and *élan* that the professional armies of the *ancien régime* were presently forced back across their borders. At Valmy, in the wooded line of hills known as the Argonne, between the Meuse and the Aisne, a Prussian army, under the Duke of Brunswick, which had captured Verdun and was advancing on Paris, was, on 20 September 1792, successfully held by the republicans and obliged to retreat. Next day France declared a republic. Soon the enemy gave way all along the line. Within a month the French Army of the Rhine had marched into Mainz and Worms; in the north, Dumouriez crossed the Belgian frontier, and overthrew the Austrians at Jemappes. In the course of the campaigns of 1793 and 1794 the number of men under arms in the revolutionary forces rose to 700,000; Carnot skilfully planned their strategy; and the prowess and efficiency of the republican army rapidly increased. 'Everywhere', J. M. Thompson sums up, 'the regular troops of old Europe seemed to be falling before the volunteers of new France. Everywhere the Rights of Man were eclipsing the Divine Right of Kings.'

[1] Coupland, *op. cit.*, p. 54.

With the French fleet, however, it was a very different matter; for a navy, unlike an army, cannot be extemporized. The continuous tradition handed down from generation to generation of officers, the professional training and experience, the rigorous discipline of the old royal navy of France, its high, keen *esprit de corps*, were forever extinct. About three-quarters of the officers of the fleet had either perished by the guillotine or else had gone into exile. Squadrons were commanded by promoted lieutenants, and ships of the line by sub-lieutenants and mates.[1] The corps of highly trained seamen-gunners had been abolished on the general grounds that 'it savoured of aristocracy that any body of men should have an exclusive right to fight at sea'. The revolutionary leaders were profoundly ignorant of the conditions of sea life. Everywhere was carelessness, incompetence, disorder, and neglect. The warships were dirty and ill-found. Victuals, sails, rigging, timber, and naval stores alike were lacking. During the first years of the war against the French Republic Great Britain, with Russia's support, succeeded in intercepting most of the grain and naval stores bound to the enemy's ports from the Baltic. The republican crews counted many sick, and they were without proper clothing. Their pay was continually in arrears. A spirit of indiscipline developed into insubordination, and insubordination into something resembling anarchy. As early as the latter half of 1789 disturbances had occurred in all the naval ports of France. On the outbreak of hostilities against Great Britain, a mutiny broke out in Brest. In the great Mediterranean arsenal of Toulon conditions were as bad, or worse. In short, during the first twelve months of hostilities the republican navy, comprising about eighty of the line (of which less than thirty were in commission) was an all but negligible factor in the struggle.

On this side of the Channel, notwithstanding the drastic economies effected by Pitt during the previous decade, the Navy had by no means been neglected. The alarms excited successively by the Dutch, Russian, and Spanish armaments had served to keep the administration up to the mark. The strength of our peace-time establishment was due in large measure to Pitt's concern for the efficiency of the service and to his firm support of the Comptroller, Sir Charles Middleton. No less than

---

[1] Most of the French admirals, however, were of the old royal navy of France; and Morard de Galles, Villaret-Joyeuse, and Bouvet had all served under the brilliant Bailli de Suffren in the previous war.

thirty-three new sail of the line had been added to the Fleet, and the dockyards were well supplied with naval stores.

On the French declaration of war there was a substantial force already in commission, comprising twenty-five sail of the line, nearly fifty frigates, and thirty lesser vessels; and more than double that number were in process of being prepared for sea: for, in consequence of Sir Charles Middleton's measures for allocating an ample reserve of stores to each vessel, large numbers of ships could be fitted out with extraordinary rapidity. As the year advanced, vessel after vessel was brought forward from ordinary and prepared to receive men, took on board her boatswain's and carpenter's stores, completed her water and provisions, then weighed and made sail, and dropped down towards the fleet anchorage.

Portsmouth in ordinary workaday times had been described by a visitor as a 'dull, inanimate place'. With the outbreak of the war it suddenly came to life. Every morning hordes of dockyard mateys— those highly skilled if occasionally difficult subjects—shuffled in through the great gates of the dockyard where, beside the spacious, bottle-shaped harbour, lay the mast-houses, the rope-houses, the workshops, the offices, the mould and sail lofts, the mills, building slips, and anchor-forge. Every evening, after a more strenuous day's work than had been their lot for many a long year, saw them depart. Not since the 'Spanish armament' of 1790 had there been such scenes of bustle and excitement as those which accompanied the assembly of the large trading fleets awaiting convoy at Spithead. The streets, shops, markets, and taverns of Portsmouth were then thronged with seamen and passengers, as well as with all the wagons, carts, and hand-barrows loaded with baggage and provisions. Once again, as in the last war, the long High Street presented an ever-changing kaleidoscope of naval and military uniforms and the George, Fountain, and other leading hostelries swarmed with officers.

'The Channel and North Sea full of frigates,' wrote one of his friends to Rear-Admiral Cornwallis. 'Rear-Admiral McBride commands in the Downs, and has the management of the cruising frigates. . . . The fleet fitting out with the greatest exertion; every town in England granting bounty to seamen and vieing with each other who can obtain the greatest number.'[1]

[1] *Life and Letters of Admiral Cornwallis*, ed. G. Cornwallis-West (1927), p. 249.

To find the necessary complements was, as usual, a far more urgent problem than to find the ships. The bait of bounty brought in a certain number of men: but by no means enough. Recourse was then had to impressment, reinforced by the new and far more efficient organization of the Impress Service. ('Without a press', Nelson declared, 'I have no idea how our Fleet can be manned.') In the latter half of February the press was out in London River; and large numbers of seamen were taken out of the incoming merchantmen and colliers. It was the first of many such visitations. One after the other the great trading fleets arrived in London and the other great ports. Towards the end of April, in 'the hottest press ever remembered', nearly all the vessels in the Thames were boarded and stripped of their hands. It was not, however, until nearly six months after the war had begun that most of the men-of-war in home waters could be fully manned.[1] While the heavy ships remained in harbour, frigates watched the enemy's ports.

By certain orders in council of February and March 1793 all un-armed ocean-going merchant vessels were prohibited from sailing 'until such time as the Naval preparations now carrying on, shall be sufficiently advanced to afford them adequate protection'. At the same time frigates were sent out to warn homeward-bound merchantmen. By March protection could be provided for all the ships in the coasting trade, though not for all the colliers; and later in the spring the first foreign-going convoys began to sail, and in September escorts were provided for the Yarmouth herring fishery.[2]

The first task of the Navy thereafter was to secure the safe passage of the outward convoys through the Western Approaches or across the North Sea; and similarly of the homecoming convoys through the soundings or back across the North Sea. The trades, or fleets of merchantmen, would assemble at a specified place and time and proceed together under escort of a force of warships sufficient to repel any threatened hostile attack. These escorts were generally cruisers; but occasionally ships of the line were employed on convoy duty. When a

---

[1] The drain of personnel from the mercantile marine was so heavy and so sustained that by the following January *The Times* observed: 'Sailors are so scarce that upwards of sixty sail of merchants' ships bound to the West Indies and other places, are detained in the river, with their ladings on board; seven outward-bound East Indiamen are likewise detained at Gravesend for want of sailors to man them.'

[2] Adm. 2/1097, *passim*.

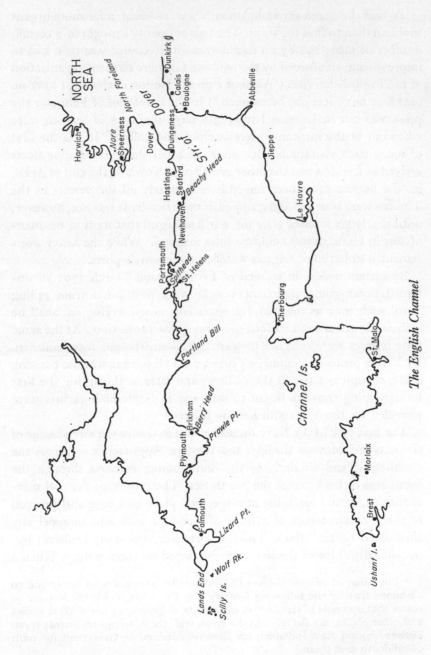

NORTH SEA

Dunkirk

North Foreland

Calais
Boulogne

Abbeville

Harwich

Nore

Sheerness

Dover

St. of Dover

Dungeness

Jeppe

Hastings
Seaford
Beachy Head
Newhaven

Le Havre

Portsmouth
Spithead
St. Helens

Cherbourg

Portland Bill

St. Malo

Channel Is.

The English Channel

Brixham
Berry Head
Prawle Pt.

Morlaix

Plymouth

Falmouth
Lizard Pt.

Brest

Wolf Rk.

Lands End
Scilly Is.

Ushant I.

warship was ordered away on any mission whatever it was required to convoy the trade during all or part of its voyage. Additional protection would be given when the need arose. Thus on occasion the battle fleet or a strong squadron would escort the outward-bound trade clear of the Channel or stretch to the westward to meet a homecoming convoy. The cruisers stationed in the Western Approaches would also reinforce the convoy escorts while passing through their area. In accordance with a long-standing practice it was customary to combine two or more of these convoys during the passage through the danger zone on both the outward and homeward journeys; the trade eventually broke up into its component parts, each part proceeding, under the protection of a small escort, to its destination. Throughout the war the bulk of the long-distance trades was carried on by convoys. The coastal trade also occasionally 'snowballed' into convoys of several hundred sail, especially on the east coast. This practice is mentioned in the earliest issue of the King's Regulations and Admiralty Instructions, which appeared in 1731—'When convoys bound to different ports sail at the same time, or when they meet at sea, they are for the better protection of the whole, to keep company together as long as their respective courses allow them . . . and Merchant ships of one convoy [being] kept from mixing with those of another to prevent as much as possible all mistakes and confusion when the convoys separate.'[1]

The convoy system was supplemented by large numbers of cruisers of all sizes which patrolled the Channel, the Irish Sea, and other focal areas. Excise cutters which formerly pursued English smugglers now hunted hostile privateers. This second method of trade defence was the one relied upon to protect ships sailing independently of—as well as those which, for various reasons, had become separated from—convoys.

The first notable engagement of the war was that which won Captain Edward Pellew of the *Nymphe*, 36, his knighthood. As a youngster he had distinguished himself in the previous war in the action on Lake Champlain; he was well known in the service for his extraordinary activity and daring, his shrewd judgment and prompt decision, and, above all, his superb seamanship. 'In every undertaking by sea or land,' wrote the Cornish antiquary, Polwhele, 'his whole mind was in it.' Off Prawle Point, at daybreak on 18 June, Pellew, who had just left

[1] *Q*. D. W. Waters, *Notes on the Convoy System of Naval Warfare*. Admiralty MS.

Falmouth, fell in with the *Cléopatre*, one of the crack frigates of the French navy, then under the command of Captain Jean Mullon, who had served under the illustrious Suffren. The two vessels were fairly equally matched. The *Nymphe*'s gun-power was somewhat superior to that of her opponent: but her crew was far inferior in numbers, and most of them—including eighty Cornish tin-miners—were raw and untrained. Pellew knew that, though his people could not manœuvre, they could certainly fight. Just as the stars were paling in the eastern sky he bore down on his enemy; and then, as the two frigates ran side by side before the wind, engaged her broadside to broadside for about three-quarters of an hour, when, most of her crew having run below, the enemy surrendered. This success was in large measure due to the skilful gunnery of Israel Pellew, the captain's younger brother, who first shot down four of the enemy's helmsmen, then shattered the wheel itself, and finally brought down the mizenmast; as a result of which the *Cléopatre* fell on board of her opponent. 'We dished her up in fifty minutes,' Pellew wrote proudly to one of his relations, 'boarded, and struck her colours.'

On the outbreak of the war Captain James Saumarez was appointed to the *Crescent*, 36, and dispatched to cruise in the Channel. Whilst engaged in this service he learned that a French frigate was in the habit of stealing out of Cherbourg under cover of darkness, snapping up one or two British merchantmen in the offing, and returning to port with her prizes the following morning. Saumarez resolved to intercept her. Early on 20 October the *Crescent*, under reefed topsails, was close in with the lighthouse off Cape Barfleur when she sighted the *Réunion* frigate and a cutter. About daybreak the wind, which had been westerly during the night, came south, making it impossible for the Frenchman to fetch back to Cherbourg, and enabling the *Crescent* to weather and get inshore of the enemy. 'We were on the larboard tack with the wind off shore,' declared Saumarez; 'I was happy in being able to keep between them and the land. When about two miles from us, the frigate tacked with all her sail set, and the cutter made sail to windward: we edged down to her, and at a cable's distance, at half-past ten, began the action which continued with scarcely any intermission two hours and ten minutes.' There was little wind and the sea was calm. The *Crescent*, clean from the dockyard, was the faster sailer, and far more skilfully handled than her opponent. Both frigates were soon cut up in their sails and rigging. The French, as usual, fired so high that scarcely any shot struck the hull of the British frigate and not a man of Saumarez's crew was hit. Despite the loss of her foretopsail-yard and foretopmast, the *Crescent* was presently manœuvred by her captain into a position— under the stern and on the larboard quarter of the enemy—from which he had the *Réunion* at his mercy. 'Our guns,' recorded Saumarez, '. . . were so well served that the French ship soon became unmanageable, and enabled us to rake her fore and aft; in which situation she struck her colours.' Such was the overwhelming superiority of British gunnery and seamanship, that, while the *Réunion* had sustained a loss of 120 killed and wounded, the *Crescent* had not lost a single man.

The successful issue of these and other single-ship engagements during the first year of the war appeared to confirm the historic ascendancy of Great Britain at sea, and served as a happy augury for the long years of conflict which lay ahead.

At the outbreak of the war our squadrons on foreign stations were numerically weak. In the Mediterranean, we had only one 50 and a couple of frigates; on the North American station, one 50 and two frigates; in the West Indies, three 50s and five frigates; on the coast of Africa, one 44, and in the East Indies, one 50 and two frigates. It was imperative to reinforce them at the earliest opportunity. Accordingly one of the first measures taken by the Admiralty was to dispatch a squadron of seven of the line, under Rear-Admiral Alan Gardner, to the Caribbean.

At the beginning of 1793 the French had a large fleet in Toulon. To hold it in check successive detachments were sent out that spring to the Mediterranean, under Rear-Admiral John Gell, Vice-Admiral Phillips Cosby, and Vice-Admiral William Hotham; and finally Vice-Admiral Lord Hood, flying his flag in the *Victory*, with a squadron of eight of the line, left Portsmouth on 22 May, and, after covering the passage up-Channel of a substantial home-coming convoy, shaped course for the Mediterranean to join forces with a Spanish squadron, under Admiral Langara, off Minorca. In August the British fleet consisted of twenty-two sail of the line and a number of cruisers.

The command of the Channel squadron was entrusted to the veteran Admiral Lord Howe. Reputedly the first sea-officer of his day, he was immensely popular with the Fleet, and implicitly trusted by the Cabinet. Now approaching his seventies, he had given a lifetime of service at sea. More than half a century had passed since Howe, as a youngster of eighteen, had sailed with Anson in his famous voyage round the world; as captain of the *Magnanime*, he had led the British line at Quiberon Bay; in the American Revolutionary War he had greatly distinguished himself against d'Estaing off the North American coast in 1778 and again at the third relief of Gibraltar in 1782. To Howe, in collaboration with Kempenfelt, belongs most of the credit for the revolutionary improvement in our system of signalling towards the close of the eighteenth century.

His courage and his taciturnity were legendary. Howe has been well described by Horace Walpole as 'undaunted as a rock and as silent'. His dour, forbidding demeanour and harsh, unsmiling countenance belied a humane and compassionate disposition. 'There was a shyness and awkwardness in Lord Howe's manner which made him apparently difficult of approach,' wrote Codrington, who knew him well, 'and gave him a character of austerity which did not really belong to him.'[1] Since the far-off days when, as captain of the *Magnanime*, he introduced the custom of granting leave of absence to the whole crew, watch by watch, and was noted for his kind attentions to the wounded, Howe had been the idol of the lower deck. 'With this good and great man,' Dr. Trotter declared, 'the health and comfort of his people were his first objects.' From his strongly marked features and swarthy complexion he was known to the seamen as 'Black Dick'. 'I think we shall have the fight today,' one of them is reported to have said on the morning of the Glorious First. 'Black Dick has been smiling.'

In the middle of July Howe at last got the Channel fleet, numbering fifteen of the line, to sea. Several weeks earlier a hostile squadron approximately equal in numbers to his own had taken up its station off the south Brittany coast in order to prevent assistance from reaching the insurgents in that province. During the remainder of 1793 the Channel squadron spent much of its time at sea, though often obliged by stress of weather to find shelter in Torbay.[2] From time to time they sighted

---

[1] Bourchier, *The Life of Sir Edward Codrington* (1873), p. 12.

[2] It was on one of these occasions that James Bowen, the master of Howe's flagship, the *Queen Charlotte*—'the skilful Palinurus of the fleet', as Captain Ekins called him—saved the squadron from imminent disaster, when, after several days of navigation by dead reckoning in thick south-westerly weather, he volunteered to take the fleet into Torbay. 'After a little consideration Lord Howe replied, "You shall try it, sir." Both Sir Roger Curtis and Captain

detachments of the French fleet on the horizon, but they never succeeded in overhauling them. As a result of his failure to bring the enemy to action there was strong and by no means unjustified criticism of Howe in the press. It was suggested in fact that if the Admiral had spent more of his time off the French coast and less in the anchorage at Torbay he would have stood a better chance of securing a decision.

Unlike his old commander, Sir Edward Hawke, Howe was no believer in the close blockade. He preferred to sacrifice the strategic advantages to be gained by the close investment of the enemy's ports to what was, in his view, the paramount necessity of preserving his own force in good condition. Lying at anchor in the sheltered waters of Torbay it would be saved the ceaseless strain and buffeting to which a fleet must be exposed cruising continuously off the enemy's coast. It followed that during these months his ships' companies saw a good deal more of Brixham pier and the long, curving sands between Paignton and Tor Quay than they did of Ushant, La Parquette, and the other isles and rocks in the approaches to Brest so familiar to Hawke's men in the close blockade of 1759.

The case that may be made out for the open blockade is, in fact, at first sight sufficiently plausible. It would after all seem not unreasonable for a commander-in-chief to wish to preserve his squadron in good order against the day of battle. In the previous war Keppel had declared that

---

Christian remonstrated with Bowen on the impossibility of his knowing exactly where we were, and on the probability of his making a mistake and losing the whole fleet in Whitsund Bay. Bowen's answer was, "We shan't make any mistake." Sir Roger Curtis then added, "But if you do make a mistake, recollect you will be the loss of the whole fleet." Bowen replied, "The fleet won't be lost." And then, as desired by Lord Howe, he directed the course for Start Point [10 a.m.]. The *Phaeton* frigate was directed to keep on the lee bow of the *Queen Charlotte* as far forward as she could go without losing sight of her. The *Black Joke* lugger was directed to do the same by the *Phaeton*. In this way the fleet continued, the *Queen Charlotte* leading under all the sail she could bear. At about 4 o'clock p.m. the *Black Joke* was seen to haul short up on the starboard tack, having run very close to the breakers of the Start, and the *Phaeton* to follow her example. And the *Queen Charlotte* kept steadily to the course on which she had started, by which she just cleared the Start Point so as to keep away for Bury Head; and thus the whole fleet were conducted into a snug anchorage in Tor Bay by the confidence and skill of James Bowen, the master' (Bourchier, *op. cit.*, pp. 16–17). This appears to have occurred in the early winter of 1793: cf. Howe's *Journal*, Adm. 1/391, 11 December, and the logs of the *Queen Charlotte, Phaeton, Phoenix*: Adm. 52/3196, 52/3284, 52/3288, 10–12 December 1793.

no large fleet could remain at sea for more than about six months and winter cruising he unreservedly condemned; 'Indeed wisdom must direct the ships into port as soon as the bad weather months come on'; and again: 'Suppose the enemy should put to sea with their fleet—a thing much to be wished for by us. Let us act wiser, and keep ours in port; leave them to the mercy of long nights and hard gales.' In the present war Howe continued opposed to the whole system of blockading the enemy's ports. According to his biographer, Sir John Barrow, he was decidedly averse to keeping ships at sea in all weathers, blockading a port from which, he declared, 'the enemy can always be in readiness to escape after a gale of wind, by which the blockading squadron has been driven off and dispersed, the ships much damaged in their masts, sails, and rigging, and their crews disheartened and disgusted.'

In practice, however, the policy favoured both by Howe and his successor, Lord Bridport,[1] was open to serious objections. For much of the year the Channel squadron was based on Spithead, which was far in rear of the enemy's point of departure. The advantages to be gained by keeping their ships in port during 'the bad weather months' by no means justified the choice of so unfavourable a strategic position. The preservation of the fleet in good order was on the whole a consideration of inferior consequence to taking up the best strategic position, which must necessarily be either before, or else within effective striking distance of, the hostile arsenals. Moreover, a fleet lying up for weeks, and even months, in some secure anchorage would never acquire the intimate knowledge of the enemy's coast or attain to anything like the same high level of seamanship which belonged to a squadron which was constantly on its blockading station.

The policy of open blockade, in fact, played into the hands of the enemy. A handful of frigates cruising off the Brittany ports was no substitute for an advanced squadron properly supported.[2] As a result of

[1] I am unable to follow P. G. Mackesy (*The War for America*, p. 519) in his assertion that, when Bridport succeeded Howe in the command of the Channel squadron, he 'instituted the close blockade of Brest which became the foundation of subsequent success'. Indeed, any such suggestion that 'the old lady Bridport' was capable of closely blockading Brest—or, for that matter, anywhere else on a dead lee shore—must surely have caused St. Vincent to turn in his grave. See *infra*, pp. 42, 144, 159 *et passim*.

[2] 'Frigates are not worth a pin off Brest,' St. Vincent informed Spencer in 1800; 'the enemy out-numbers them and drives them off at will' (*Spencer Papers*, III, p. 376).

these dispositions Howe ran the risk of allowing the French to get away to sea without his knowledge, until too late to intercept—which would have been almost impossible under the system of close blockade. Another serious disadvantage of this policy was that it tended to lower the fleet's morale and did nothing to hinder the depredations of hostile cruisers in the Western Approaches. Moreover, though Howe frequently exercised his force in sail-drill and manœuvres, he failed to impose proper discipline upon his captains, who had very little idea, in the early years of the war, of station-keeping during the night and in blowing weather. In the middle of December he finally returned to port, leaving the frigates to watch off Brest, and there remained until the following May.

3

Owing largely to this ultra-cautious policy of Howe's, and also to the demoralized state of the republican navy, it was not until the early summer of 1794 that the first fleet action of the war was fought.

At Christmas 1793 Rear-Admiral Vanstabel had left Brest with a squadron comprising two sail of the line and three frigates to bring home a large grain convoy, the safe arrival of which was vital to stave off an impending corn famine in France. The convoy, which was presently joined by the French West Indies trade, lay in Hampton roads. There Vanstabel arrived on 12 February, sailing again for France on 11 April. On the same date another French squadron of five of the line, under the daring and resourceful Rear-Admiral Nielly, was sent out from Brest to a station 100 leagues west of Belle Ile to meet the homecoming convoy. A few weeks later Nielly fell in with our Newfoundland convoy, capturing the escort, the *Castor* frigate, together with a great many of the merchantmen. Then, as the summer approached and the emergence of the British Channel squadron was to be apprehended, a great fleet under Villaret-Joyeuse sailed from Brest to join forces with Nielly off Belleisle, under orders to cover the approach of the grain convoy at all hazards.

In the spring of 1794 the Channel squadron was charged with two main duties: the first, to escort a great trading fleet safely out of the English Channel,[1] and the second, to intercept the enemy's grain convoy. The cardinal error on the British side was in not arranging for

[1] See *infra*, p. 118.

Western Approaches

the convoy to be intercepted at the point of departure—Chesapeake Bay. As it was, Howe sailed on 2 May from Spithead with thirty-two of the line, and, after detaching eight of his ships off the Lizard to escort the trade as far southward as the latitude of Cape Finisterre, stood over to France and looked into Brest. Finding the enemy's fleet still there, he stood to the westward in hopes of intercepting the grain convoy. After parting company with the trade off Cape Finisterre, six of the line under Rear-Admiral Montagu proceeded, in pursuance with their orders, to cruise between Cape Ortegal and the latitude of Belle Ile, to intercept the enemy convoy. On his return to the Brittany coast on 19 May, Howe again looked into Brest and discovered that the birds were flown—Villaret-Joyeuse had got away into the Atlantic with twenty-six of the line.

For eight days Howe, ignorant alike of Villaret-Joyeuse's position and of the course of the homecoming convoy, quartered the ocean in vain. At last on the 28th, when some 400 miles to the west of Ushant, his look-out frigates signalled a fleet to windward. It was blowing fresh from the south-west, with squalls and a great head sea. The French fleet, recorded the twelve-year-old William Parker, a midshipman on board the *Orion*, 'was keeping close up to the wind to prevent us getting the weather-gauge of them. We carried a great press of canvas, notwithstanding it blew very hard, to get to windward of them. At nine we beat to quarters.'[1] Late in the evening 'Admiral Pasley got within gun-shot of the enemy's rear, and gave them a very warm and fierce reception, which the enemy returned with great vivacity. The whole of our Fleet were now carrying all the sail they could to get up with, and bring the French Fleet to action. The night being very dark, it afforded a grand and awful sight from the flash of the guns. At nine-thirty the firing ceased, owing to the wind blowing very hard and a rough sea prevented our ships from getting up with and bringing the enemy to action.'[2]

At dawn on the 29th the rival fleets, standing to the westward, were about six miles apart, with the French on the weather bow of the British. For forty hours Howe clung to the enemy's tail, and by skilful manœuvring succeeded in forcing several ships out of their line and gaining the wind. During the night, however, a thick mist with drizzling rain descended. The two fleets stood on in close company, invisible to each other except for fleeting glimpses, through rifts in the fog-bank, of shadowy spars and sails. From time to time the sound of the bells struck on board the French ships was clearly audible to the British. Villaret-Joyeuse's one aim was to draw Howe's fleet out of the track of the oncoming convoy. On the 29th, though he had lost the weather-gauge, he found himself to the north of his opponent, and stood to the northward and westward during the two following days. During the fog, as if by a miracle, Nielly's squadron suddenly joined Villaret-Joyeuse, bringing his strength up to twenty-six of the line. Throughout the night of the 31st both squadrons held a westerly course under a heavy press of sail.

[1] A. Phillimore, *The Life of Sir William Parker* (1876), I, p. 51.
[2] *Ibid.* I, pp. 51–2.

Sunday, the Glorious First of June, dawned fine and clear, with a moderate southerly wind, the sea fairly smooth, and a long Atlantic swell. The two fleets, under single-reefed topsails, were still standing to the westward, the French some four miles to leeward of the British. Howe chose his position and formed his line with extreme precision; and then, shortly after eight o'clock, stood slowly down for the enemy. While his ships were clearing for action, he made his final preparations for the attack. 'And now, gentlemen,' observed the Admiral, closing his signal-book; 'no more book, no more signals.'[1] His plan was to 'divide the enemy, at all points, from to windward.' Each British vessel was to cut through under the stern of her opposite number in the enemy's line and engage her from to leeward. The advantages of this manœuvre, if successful, were, in the first place, that his ships would be able while passing through the enemy's line to pour a heavy raking fire into the hulls of their opponents, and, secondly, that the retreat of disabled Frenchmen would thereby be cut off, since a crippled ship could only retire to leeward. In the event the seamanship of most of the British fleet was not equal to this manœuvre, and the intervals between certain of the enemy's ships were in any case too narrow; moreover, the *Caesar*, leading the van, instead of running down to her appointed place in the French line, backed her main topsail and hauled to the wind, which checked the British advance: only seven of Howe's ships out of twenty-six, in fact, succeeded in piercing the enemy's line. Even so, this sufficed to bring on a desperate mêlée and prevented the French from disengaging.

At about ten o'clock the *Queen Charlotte*, steering to cut the enemy's line astern of the flagship *Montagne*, came under heavy fire from the *Vengeur* and *Achille* before she finally accomplished her purpose; she thereupon flung a raking broadside into the *Montagne*, shattering her stern and killing three hundred of her crew. 'The smoke was so thick', observed William Parker, 'that we could not at all times see the ships engaging ahead and astern. Our main-topmast and main-yard being carried away by the enemy's shot, the Frenchmen gave three cheers, upon which our ship's company, to show they did not mind it, returned them the three cheers, and after that gave them a furious broadside.'[2] To quote the flagship's log:

[1] Bourchier, *The Life of Sir Edward Codrington* (1873), I, p. 31.
[2] Phillimore, *op. cit.*, I, p. 54.

We reserved our fire and set the foresail and topgallantsails; passing the second ship, received and returned her fire, and ran close to the French Admiral's stern, when we began to engage; but his second astern made sail and closed with his Admiral, which prevented us from getting alongside to leeward; immediately put our helm up and raked him fore and aft, keeping up a most tremendous fire right into him and his second astern, who bore up and ran away to leeward. We then sheered to port and got between him and his Admiral, engaging on both sides. In luffing up alongside of the French Admiral we lost our fore topmast. He then made sail and ranged from us, leaving us engaged between his two seconds, not being able to keep way with him, we soon dismasted one of his seconds on the larboard side.[1]

Soon the engagement became general all along the line. As has already been said, seven of the British ships cut through the enemy's line and engaged their opponents to leeward. The remainder hauled up to windward and opened fire at varying distances. The French line dissolved into scattered groups of vessels, smothered in smoke, striving furiously with their assailants.

The most remarkable of these fights was the duel between the *Brunswick* and the *Vengeur de Peuple*. The *Brunswick*, which was the *Queen Charlotte*'s second astern, was endeavouring to break the French line ahead of the *Vengeur*, when the *Brunswick*'s starboard anchor became hooked in the *Vengeur*'s fore chains. The master of the *Brunswick* proposed to cut her free. 'No,' replied the *Brunswick*'s captain, 'as we've got her we'll keep her.' Locked together in desperate combat, the two ships fell off the wind and went away to leeward. The crew of the *Brunswick* alternately raised and depressed their pieces, so that at one discharge the shot tore through the Frenchman's decks, while at the other they plunged to the bottom. About an hour after their fight began the *Brunswick*, while engaging the *Vengeur* to leeward, compelled the *Achille*, to windward, after exchanging half a dozen broadsides, to strike her colours. At the end of some three hours' fighting several other British ships came to the *Brunswick*'s aid; and the *Ramillies* poured two terrific broadsides into the *Vengeur*. Dismasted, and with torrents of water flooding in through her shattered hull, the *Vengeur* hauled down her colours and shortly afterwards sank, carrying down with her more than half the crew. Some time later the *Brunswick*, being to leeward of

[1] Adm. 52/3333, 1 June 1794.

35

the enemy with her mizen-mast gone, was obliged to make sail to the northward; she subsequently returned safely to port.

Another of Howe's ships which greatly distinguished itself on 1 June was the *Marlborough*. Breaking the line astern of the *Impétueux*, the *Marlborough* ranged up alongside of her to leeward. The two presently fell on board each other, and a fierce fight ensued. As a result of her previous encounters with the *San Pareil*, *Mucius*, and *Montagu*, the *Marlborough* had been dismasted and severely damaged in other ways; her captain and first lieutenant had been badly wounded; and there was apparently some talk of surrender, for one of the lieutenants exclaimed, 'I'll be d – d if she shall ever surrender: I'll nail her colours to the mast.' About the same time a cock which had escaped from a battered coop nearby suddenly perched himself upon the stump of the mainmast, clapped his wings, and delivered himself of a rousing crow. The ship's company thereupon gave three hearty cheers, and there was no more talk of surrender. The *Marlborough* at last succeeded in dismasting both the *Impétueux* and *Mucius*.[1]

But long before this the fate of the battle had been decided. The French crews, though they put up a stubborn resistance, were no match for the British in seamanship and gunnery. Howe must have reckoned on this inferiority when he ordered his own vessels to approach the enemy in line abreast in order to cut through the French line at a number of points. In the close fighting of the 'Glorious First', the heavy-shotted carronades of the British vessels wrought havoc among their opponents, whose casualties were far heavier than ours. The *Jacobin* ran down to leeward out of the fight, and the *Montagne* stood out of range of the *Queen Charlotte*'s fire. Their example was presently followed by many other of the French ships and the enemy's line fell into confusion. Howe made the signal for a general chase.

'In less than an hour after the close action commenced in the centre,' he observed in his dispatch, 'the French Admiral engaged by the *Queen Charlotte* crowded off; and was followed by most of the ships of his van, in condition to carry sail after him: leaving with us, about ten or twelve of his crippled or totally dismasted ships exclusive of one sunk in the engagement.'[2] Close fighting in a strong breeze had brought about heavy losses of masts and other spars. Nearly all the logs of the

[1] Adm. 51/1151, 1–2 June 1794.
[2] Adm. 1/101, 3 June 1794.

ships closely engaged report this severe damage to masts, sails, and rigging. The *Marlborough* and the *Defiance*, which had been in the thick of the fighting, were totally dismasted; the *Queen Charlotte* had lost her topmasts. 'Several of the enemy's ships dismasted and lying mere wrecks all round us,' records the log of Howe's flagship, 'the remainder of their fleet forming to leeward on the starboard tack.' 'We had only four killed and about thirty wounded,' states the log of the *Bellerophon*. 'But masts, sails, and rigging were cut to pieces; even the boats and spars on the booms were all destroyed with shot.' 'Saw several of their ships with all their masts shot away,' runs the log of the *Culloden*. '. . . On the smoke clearing up saw six or seven of their ships dismasted, and two three-deckers with only their fore masts standing.'[1]

Several of the French ships of the line which had been dismasted managed to sail back to their own fleet under their spritsails, while three of their hulks were taken in tow by two enemy frigates and a brig. That these vessels were not also taken was largely owing to the physical condition of the ageing Howe, who during the previous five days had been continuously on deck and was by this time so exhausted that he had almost to be carried below. The *Thunderer* and *Queen* were recalled by Howe's orders when just about to take possession of two dismasted Frenchmen, which consequently escaped. The French Commander-in-Chief skilfully disposed his force to protect his crippled ships. Eventually he escaped to the north-west. Strategically, the French fleet had achieved its object. For though defeated in this, the first great action at sea of the Revolutionary War, Villaret-Joyeuse had successfully drawn his enemy away from the rendezvous appointed for the convoy.[2] In the meantime Montagu, having failed to discover either the convoy or his Admiral, had put back into Plymouth.

Many years afterwards Villaret-Joyeuse informed Captain Brenton, the naval historian, that Robespierre had warned him that he would be guillotined should the grain convoy fall into the hands of the enemy. Therefore his chief object was to draw Howe out of the track of the

[1] Adm. 52/3333, 51/1162, 52/3014, 1–2 June 1794.
[2] 'It is a singular and instructive fact that from first to last not a single British ship appears to have laid eyes on the convoy from America. Ships both of commerce and war, belonging to other bodies, were taken and re-taken in the Bay of Biscay; but those coming from America wore invisible garments' (Mahan, *The Influence of Sea Power upon the French Revolution and Empire*, I, p. 159).

convoy. He declared that the loss of a few ships was of relatively small consequence. 'While your admiral amused himself refitting them, I saved my convoy, and I saved my head.'

Instead of sending his frigates to search for the convoy as it stood towards its destination Montagu, who had already retired before Villaret-Joyeuse's crippled but numerically superior force, on 10 June bore up for the Channel. On the night of the 12th Vanstabel, fearing that he would find a hostile force guarding the Iroise, had steered for the Penmarcks further down the coast and thence stood through the Raz de Sein into the Bay of Brest. Two days later the convoy and Villaret-Joyeuse's squadron entered Brest together; and Great Britain's opportunity of dealing the young Republic a mortal blow had been lost.

These considerations were, however, wholly forgotten in the universal applause and congratulation which followed upon the arrival in London, on the night of 9 June, of Sir Roger Curtis with Howe's dispatches. At the Opera the performance was abruptly broken off as the orchestra struck up 'Rule, Britannia' and the prima donna 'joined in the general joy and sang "God Save the King"', the rejoicings continued for several nights, the finest of the illuminations being on the 13th ('not the hasty blaze produced by alarm of broken windows,' as the *London Chronicle* observed, but a most lavish and impressive exhibition of lights and decorations), and the principal streets were thronged with strollers until dawn. On the same day Howe had arrived at Spithead with his battle-scarred squadron and his prizes, and landed at the sally port to the strains of 'See the Conquering Hero Comes' and the thunder of artillery; as in London, at Portsmouth that night there was a general illumination—'the whole town seemed in a blaze'. The King and his daughters drove down to Portsmouth and dined with Howe on board his flagship, and large sums of money were subscribed by a grateful public for the relief of the widows and orphans of those who had fallen in the action.

With this triumph of the Glorious First, Howe's career as a fighting admiral was virtually at an end. Later in the summer he cruised between Ushant and Scilly; until, towards the end of October, he was driven into Torbay by bad weather. He again put to sea for a few weeks in November. He stayed ashore on leave during most of the winter of 1794–5. Towards Christmas, in wild weather, the enemy fleet, comprising over thirty battleships and several frigates, sailed out of Brest.

The cruise came to nothing, and the French suffered severely, as long ago Keppel had prophesied they would: over and above all the heavy damage throughout their fleet, they lost five ships of the line. But the news that the enemy were at sea brought Howe hastily down to Torbay. He hoisted his flag in the *Queen Charlotte* and would have put to sea, had not the wind suddenly shifted to S.S.E., which was a dangerous quarter for that bay. The gale threw in a heavy sea, and in the face of that and a strong ebb-tide the fleet could not get out. The bad weather continued for a week or more. After a spell of strong westerlies there was a brief lull—followed, in the early morning of 13 February, by a violent south-easterly gale, during which the large squadron anchored in Torbay was in imminent peril of destruction. In a swirling confusion of sleet and snow, with a rapidly rising sea, a number of Howe's ships parted their cables. According to Captain Brenton:

> The fate of England now depended on our anchors and cables; to a seaman and friend of his country the scene was awful. The *Queen Charlotte* was dipping the sea into her wardroom windows, and every pitch was expected to break adrift; nine sail of the line parted their cables, but providentially brought up before they got foul of any other ships, or in shoal water; and the fleet rode out the gale without further damage.[1]

Towards noon on the 14th it moderated somewhat, though the sea still ran high. In the late afternoon, with a fresh north-easterly wind and hazy weather, the squadron weighed and stood out of the bay under double-reefed topsails.[2] Having seen the East and West Indies and other convoys safely out of the Channel, and gained certain intelligence that the French fleet was again in Brest, Howe returned to Spithead, and soon after relinquished the command. During the ensuing months the protection of trade was entrusted to squadrons of frigates which effectively held the enemy's cruisers in check.

4

In December 1794 Lord Spencer, one of the Portland Whigs who had lately joined Pitt's ministry, was appointed First Lord in succession to the incompetent Lord Chatham; and early the following year Howe— though he still continued nominally in command—was succeeded by

[1] Brenton, *Naval History of Great Britain* (1823), I, p. 366.
[2] Adm. 52/3333, 13–14 February 1795.

another elderly Commander-in-Chief, Admiral Lord Bridport. Under the latter the Channel fleet spent rather more of its time at sea during the summer months; and a small squadron of half a dozen sail of the line cruised continuously in the soundings. In other respects, however, there was little improvement in the strategic dispositions of the Channel fleet; the same lax and easy-going system was followed, and the effective blockade of Brest was never attempted.

As before, the crux of the whole matter lay in the investment of Brest. In this port lay what was by far the largest and most powerful detachment of the enemy's fleet. To prevent the combination of the ships at Brest with those in any other of the enemy's naval ports was therefore of great consequence to the British Admiralty. Nevertheless, the Channel fleet continued to be based on Spithead: an anchorage which lay too far to leeward, in the westerly winds which prevailed, for the proper blockade of Brest; there was ample time after a westerly gale for the enemy to get out of Brest before the British blockading fleet could return to its station from Spithead; and, to make matters worse, the main body of the fleet was kept in port during the winter months. The consequence was that on successive occasions the enemy were able to slip out past Bridport's guard while Duncan, off the Texel (and, in later years, St. Vincent off Cadiz), were keeping their opponents effectively blockaded.

The summer of 1795 saw two minor engagements in the Bay of Biscay.

In the morning of 16 June 1795, with the wind westerly, a strong French squadron under Villaret-Joyeuse, while working off the land near Penmarck Point in the Bay of Biscay, sighted a small British squadron of five of the line and three frigates under Vice-Admiral William Cornwallis directly to windward. The French squadron was sailing close-hauled under a press of canvas; and, as soon as he realized the enemy's strength—twelve of the line and fifteen frigates—Cornwallis stood away under all sail. Some three hours later the French squadron separated into two divisions; and presently the wind shifting to the northward greatly aided the pursuit. 'In the afternoon,' wrote Cornwallis, 'the wind fell and came to the northward off the land, and of course brought those ships of the enemy which had tacked to windward, and the other ships laid up for us.'[1]

[1] Adm. 1/103, 19 June 1795.

Cornwallis's retirement was seriously retarded by his two worst-sailing ships, the *Bellerophon* and *Brunswick*, both of which were obliged that night to cut away their anchors and jettison a large quantity of provisions and gear in order to hasten their progress. At daylight on the 17th the enemy's ships were seen coming up very fast on both quarters of Cornwallis's squadron; the French weather division being already abreast of the British rear. It was at this stage that the frigate *Phaeton*, which was detached several miles ahead of the British force, pretended to be in communication with an imaginary fleet over the horizon. The *Phaeton* continued making these signals throughout the day. According to James, this ingenious strategem eventually caused Villaret-Joyeuse to break off the action.[1]

At about 9 o'clock the enemy's leading ship opened fire on the rearmost British ship, the *Mars*; while the French frigate *Virginie* at the same time ran up on the lee quarter of the *Mars* and also harassed her. Shortly after Cornwallis ordered one of his 'lame ducks', the *Bellerophon*, to pass ahead: the order of the British line being now the *Brunswick*, *Bellerophon*, *Royal Sovereign* (flagship), *Triumph*, and *Mars*. Several other French ships came up in succession; and by noon all the British ships were engaged, each of them firing her stern and quarter guns as they could be brought to bear on the enemy. In the evening the French pressed their attack on the *Mars*, whose sails and rigging were already seriously damaged. Four of the leading Frenchmen had borne up to secure the crippled ship; when the *Royal Sovereign*, closely followed by the *Triumph*, ran down to support her and flung several raking broadsides into the bows of the leading Frenchmen. Their steady and destructive fire caused the French to haul to the wind, and saved the *Mars*.[2] 'This was their last effort, if', Cornwallis added acidly, 'anything they did can deserve that appellation.' A desultory fire was kept up for about two hours longer; but the enemy made no further effort to close and before sunset had gone about and were standing away from the British squadron.

Cornwallis, now in his middle fifties, was a veteran of the two previous wars. This bold manœuvre of 17 June established his reputation. 'In less skilful hands that squadron must have been lost,' commented Sir Charles Middleton, 'and which points out the necessity of

[1] W. James, *Naval History* (1837), I, p. 268.
[2] Adm. 52/3191, 52/3379, 52/3507, 17–18 June 1795.

sending these squadrons under experienced flags, and the ships as far as can be of an equal rate of sailing.'[1]

In the same month a British squadron commanded by Commodore Warren escorted an expedition of Royalist exiles to the Quiberon peninsula, a large proportion of whose inhabitants were hostile to the Republic, while the Channel fleet, under Bridport, cruised in the Bay. On the 22nd, Villaret-Joyeuse with nine of the line encountered Bridport with fourteen (of which eight were three-deckers) and retreated towards L'Orient. Bridport made the signal to chase; and early on the 23rd the leading British vessels overtook the French rear off Ile Groix. Villaret-Joyeuse's squadron was not only heavily outnumbered, but his ships were ill-found and poorly manned, and his officers did not know their business. He was unable to bring his vessels into line; and those of them which were engaged resisted feebly. The result was that three—the *Alexandre*, *Tigre*, and *Formidable*—successively struck. Despite his greatly superior strength, Bridport made no attempt to secure the others. The two fleets were now close in with Groix, and he threw out the signal to discontinue the action. He stood away with his prizes to the south-west, while the the French, after making several tacks, took refuge between Groix and L'Orient. A few days later the *émigrés* safely disembarked. But their leaders quarrelled and the republican government sent strong forces against them, and the rising was quickly suppressed.

The laxity of the British blockade of Brest was glaringly revealed in the French expedition against Ireland in 1796–7. About one-half of the Channel squadron was two hundred miles away in its winter quarters at Spithead, and its elderly Commander-in-Chief was still further off. Apart from its distance from Brest, Spithead laboured under another serious disadvantage as a blockading base which played an important part in the events about to be related: for, when the wind came easterly and gave the French their opportunity, it was foul for Bridport's ships endeavouring to work up the stretch of three miles between Spithead and St. Helens. The force cruising off Ushant, under Rear-Admiral John Colpoys, was not distinguished either for vigilance or good discipline. In short, what was in years to come a cardinal and decisive factor in the grand strategy of the war against Napoleon's

[1] *Spencer Papers*, I, p. 49.

empire had yet to be achieved—namely, the effective blockade of the enemy's chief naval arsenal.

Stimulated by reports of grave and growing discontent in Ireland, especially in the Protestant North, the attention of the French government had lately been drawn to the prospects of a surprise descent upon that troubled country; and, since the summer of 1796, secret preparations had been in train to fit out an expedition from Brest.

'To detach Ireland from England', had declared the Directory in June, 'is to reduce the latter to the level of a second-rate Power; it will, besides, rob her of a substantial part of her supremacy at sea. It is needless to relate the advantages that will result to France if Ireland's independence is assured.'

The moment seemed opportune for such an attempt. For more than a century that unhappy land, still preponderantly Catholic and Gaelic, had endured the worst evils of alien misrule. Irish industries had been ruthlessly sacrificed to English commercial interests. The more rigorous parts of the penal laws against Catholics had only lately been abrogated and political rights were still denied to them. Grattan had failed to procure either parliamentary reform or Catholic emancipation. The hopes of the Catholics, momentarily raised by the appointment, in 1794, of the liberally minded Lord Fitzwilliam as Lord Lieutenant, were dashed by his abrupt recall soon after. Fitzwilliam's successor, Lord Camden, fell back on a policy of merciless repression.

Towards the close of the century, Irish national feeling began to revive. In the northern counties Catholics and Dissenters alike were disaffected towards the despotic regimen of Dublin Castle. Wolfe Tone, who in 1791 had founded the Society of United Irishmen, with their headquarters in Belfast, to unite his countrymen against English exploitation, was now a refugee in Paris. But the French Revolution had caught the imagination of Irishmen; bonfires were lit on Ulster hills in honour of republican victories, and there were rumours of an impending invasion. The North began almost openly to arm and drill; and the Society of United Irishmen, reorganized on a new and revolutionary basis, advanced from strength to strength. Inadequately garrisoned as the island was, it was confidently reckoned in France that the landing in Ireland of an invasionary force would be the signal for a prompt and general insurrection.

True to their favourite policy of evasion, the French expected to

avoid Colpoys by slipping out through the Passage du Raz and to deceive any British frigates by steering a false course until their fleet was
well out to sea. On the dark and squally evening of 16 December 1796
the French fleet, with some 20,000 troops on board, got under way. The
squadron was commanded by Admiral Morard de Galles, and the troops
by the young and ardent Lazare Hoche; in the flagship of the second-
in-command, Admiral Bouvet, was the Irish leader, Wolfe Tone.
However, in consequence of a sudden shift of the wind, the plan was
changed at the last moment; and the result, in the gathering darkness,
was utter chaos. The raw and ill-trained ships' companies were not
equal to the task of manœuvring together in such perilous waters, and
the fleet became separated. Some got out through the rock-bound
Passage du Raz, and others through the Iroise Channel. Pellew
increased the confusion by accompanying the enemy's van through the
Raz, and firing off rockets and blue lights. Two of their ships collided.
The *Séduisant*, 74, ran on a rock and became a total wreck. Worst of all,
the frigate *Fraternité*, which carried de Galles, Hoche, and Bruix,
became separated from the main body of the fleet.[1]

After Pellew had looked into the Bay of Brest early on the 16th, he
dispatched a lugger to warn Colpoys. In the afternoon he sent a
frigate to warn the Admiral that the enemy were now at sea, before
working up towards the French fleet. Colpoys, however, was not on the
rendezvous when the frigate came to seek him, nor was he anywhere
in the vicinity when Pellew searched for him the same night, and
throughout the following day. On the 18th the latter stood over to
Falmouth to warn the Admiralty.

On the same day the two separated divisions of the French fleet
came in sight of each other, but the *Fraternité* was still missing. 'I
believe', wrote Wolfe Tone, 'it was the first instance of an admiral in a
clean frigate, with moderate weather and moonlight nights, parting
company with his fleet.'[2] Early the following morning most of the
French ships, under Admiral Bouvet, arrived safely off the entrance
to Bantry Bay, at the head of which the landing was to be made. During
the whole of the passage the wind had continued easterly, with fog;
but when the French turned northward to close the land they made so

[1] A.M. BB4, 103, *Rapport de Morard de Galles*.
[2] *Autobiography of Theobald Wolfe Tone*, ed. W. B. O'Brien (1893), II,
p. 165.

much leeway that they arrived off Dursey Island instead of Mizen Head, their intended landfall: but for this they might have hauled close round Mizen Head and so reached a safe anchorage.

As it was, the whole of the 21st and the following morning were spent in continuously tacking to enter the bay; and the task of working up the long, narrow waters within in the face of the strong easterly winds sweeping down from the rocky, precipitous southern shore

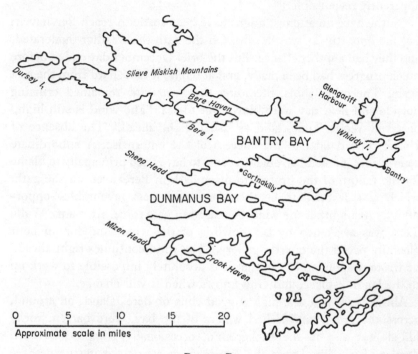

Bantry Bay

proved too much for the capabilities of the unseasoned French crews. The bay was no more than from three to four miles wide; and the head of it was eighteen miles distant. From time to time heavy squalls burst over the lofty mountain-ridge to the southward. Nor for a moment did the wind let up. During the rest of the 22nd Bouvet's vessels continued vainly beating to windward. 'We have been tacking ever since eight this morning,' Wolfe Tone recorded in his journal early in the

45

afternoon, 'and I am sure we have not gained one hundred yards; the wind is right ahead.'

Late in the evening Bouvet anchored, with eight of the line and seven other vessels, off the eastern end of Bere Island in mid-channel, instead of the anchorage mentioned in Bruix's instructions, in Bere-haven.[1] In the former anchorage, he was exposed to the full force of the easterly winds; in the latter, he would have been both well sheltered and close up to the landing-place. For this his Irish pilots were apparently responsible.

On the 23rd an attempt might have been made to reach Berehaven; but the opportunity was let slip. On the 24th the weather moderated, and they had another chance. But the brief December day ended before much progress had been made, and at 6 p.m. it blew hard from the east again. The other ships, including the *Fraternité*, remained cruising outside and next day were blown out to sea. 'The wind is still high,' observed Wolfe Tone, 'and as usual, right ahead.' The absence of Hoche proved fatal to the success of the enterprise. A subordinate commander, General Grouchy, seems to have been principally to blame for the failure of the French to disembark in Berehaven on the 24th, which was destined to be their last—and most favourable—opportunity.[2] At nightfall the wind increased to gale force. At 2 a.m. Wolfe Tone was awakened by the howling of the wind, and for an hour gloomily paced the quarter-gallery. 'The wind continues right ahead,' he wrote despondently, 'so that it is absolutely impossible to work up to the landing-place, and God knows when it will change.'

Above them rose the high rugged cliffs of Bere Island; all around, across the grey, wind-lashed waters of the bay, were barren, rocky hill-slopes; and in the background, occasionally glimpsed between flurries of whirling snow, the mountain-crests on the northern shore showed up dark against the wintry sky. The gale continued throughout the 25th and 26th, with squalls and driving snow; and disembarkation was out of the question.

'All our hopes are now reduced to get back in safety to Brest,' declared Wolfe Tone, 'and I believe that we will set sail for that port the instant the weather will permit. I confess, myself, that I now look upon the expedition as impracticable.' He added, 'This infernal wind

---

[1] A.M., BB4, 103, *Journal de Bouvet*; cf. *ibid.* 104 (Bruix's Instructions).
[2] See E. H. Stuart Jones, *An Invasion that Failed* (1950), pp. 139–44.

continues without intermission, and now that all is lost I am as eager to get back to France as I was to come to Ireland.'[1]

Several ships dragged their anchors, and the cable of Bouvet's flagship parted. Finding himself driving on Bere Island, Bouvet cut his cable and stood out to sea, where he cruised around for three days and then returned to Brest.[2] In Bantry Bay, the wind and sea continuing unfavourable, one after another several other ships also stood out to sea. Finally, on the morning of the 27th, Commodore Bedout in the *Indomptable* left the bay with seven of the line and one frigate which still remained there. The following night this force was scattered by a hurricane and returned to Brest. A number of Bouvet's vessels shortly after straggled back to Bantry Bay and lay at anchor for several days, when they also steered for Brest.[3]

The last to return, a ship of the line called the *Droits de l'Homme*, had the misfortune to fall in with Pellew in the *Indefatigable*, accompanied by another British frigate, the *Amazon*, some 150 miles southwest of Ushant. It was blowing hard from the west, with hazy weather. The two frigates, which were inshore of her and to leeward, at once made sail to head her off. The chase continued throughout the afternoon. An hour before the action the *Droits de l'Homme* was severely damaged by a squall that carried away her fore and main topmasts, which not only reduced her speed and power of manœuvre, but also caused the vessel to roll so heavily that her main battery was rendered useless. Closing with the enemy shortly after dark, the two frigates stationed themselves one on either bow of her, whence they alternately raked her, damaged her severely during a long night action, and eventually became embayed with her in Audierne Bay.[4] Early the next morning, on sighting the land first on his lee bow and later on his weather bow, Pellew wore his ship to the southward, and just after

[1] O'Brien, *op. cit.*, II, pp. 171, 174.
[2] A.M., BB4, 103, *Rapport de Bedout*.
[3] *Ibid. Journal de Bouvet.*
[4] Pellew's letter to Spencer after the action is worth quoting as an illustration of 'the living tradition', which might be said to have inspired the whole corps of our officers. 'I fear your lordship will think me rather imprudent on this occasion, but what can be done if an enemy's coast is always to frighten us and give them protection as safely as their ports? If Lord Hawke had no fears from a lee shore with a large fleet under his charge, could I for a moment think of two inconsiderable frigates?' (*Spencer Papers*, I, pp. 379–81). See the present writer, *Quiberon Bay* (1960), pp. xiv, 145–8, 161–2.

seven o'clock saw 'the enemy on her broadside without masts, the surf breaking over her'. The *Amazon*, like the *Droits de l'Homme*, went ashore in Audierne Bay and was wrecked. The *Indefatigable* was saved by a sudden shift of wind and skilful seamanship. By strenuous exertions, after wearing twice, she just managed to clear the land. 'Exhausted as we were with fatigue,' Pellew informed the Admiralty, 'every exertion was made and every inch of canvas set that could be carried and at 11 a.m. we made the breakers and by the blessing of God weather'd the Penmark Rocks about half a mile.'[1]

Notwithstanding the misfortune which deprived the French fleet of their two commanders-in-chief, the Irish expedition had come within an ace of success. 'We had', wrote Beresford to Auckland, 'two days after they were at anchor in Bantry Bay, from Cork to Bantry, less than 3,000 men, two pieces of artillery, and *no magazine of any kind, no firing, no hospital, no provisions*, &c., &c., No landing was made,— Providence prevented it; if there had, where was a stand to be made?'[2] Such troops as were stationed in Munster could never have withstood Hoche's veterans. 'Upon a naval defence alone the safety of Ireland was staked,' the Marquis of Abercorn declared in the House of Lords. 'To place it in a state of internal preparation, no exertion had been made.'[3] But for the fatal error in navigation which brought the enemy's ships to Dursey Island instead of Mizen Head, and the failure to anchor in Berehaven, a substantial proportion of his troops would probably have got ashore; and the capture of Cork—wherein was stored the better part of the Navy's victuals for 1797—must have followed. 'We purpose to make a race for Cork, as if the devil were in our bodies', Wolfe Tone had written in his journal.

The responsibility for the strategical failure to post a superior force at the point of departure lies squarely at the door of the Admiralty. It was the result of a fallacious and long-continued policy which, time and again, had allowed the enemy to get away from Brest. Mahan thus sums up the situation: 'An inadequate force at the decisive point, inadequately maintained, and dependent upon a reserve as large as itself, but unready and improperly stationed—such were the glaring

---

[1] Adm. 1/107, 15 January 1798.
[2] Q. W. E. H. Lecky, *History of Ireland in the Eighteenth Century*, (1892), iv, p. 3.
[3] *Parliamentary History*, xxxiii, p. 112.

faults of the strategic disposition.'[1] For a fortnight (with the exception of one day, 28 December) the enemy's ships had anchored in Bantry Bay. It was all too apparent that the British owed their salvation on this occasion, not to their own efforts, but to the winds and to the inefficiency of the hostile navy.

Of Bridport's part in this sorry affair all that need be said is that it stands as a classic example of what might be expected to happen on the day 'when it was Buggins's turn'. The Admiral was living ashore at the time, and had to be flushed from his rural retreat—appropriately named 'Cricket Lodge, near Chard'—by special Admiralty messenger. At the news that the French were at sea Bridport on 21 December intimated that 'he would be ready to sail in four days'. His fleet lay in two divisions, one at Spithead and the other at St. Helens; his flagship, the *Royal George*, being at the former. When at last he did attempt to sail it was blowing hard from the east. Instead of directing the division at St. Helens to run down to Spithead and then taking the whole force out through the Solent, Bridport actually endeavoured to work up to St. Helens. Four of his ships were in consequence damaged by collision, and another went aground. Since he declined to sail without them, another delay ensued. On the 27th the Admiralty dispatched an urgent order by the manual telegraph: 'Lord Bridport to sail without waiting for the *Prince*.' The Admiral replied that the tides were against him. On the 29th, when at last his ships arrived, he was obliged to report, 'though I have gained the ships, their Lordships will perceive I have lost the wind, which blows now at S.S.W.'[2] Bridport eventually got away on 3 January 1797, by which time the French were on their way back to Brest. After looking into the roadstead to make sure that the enemy fleet had really returned, he went back to Spithead and resumed his former easy-going method of blockade.

Why Colpoys was not on the appointed rendezvous at the crucial moment is not easy to explain. For days the wind had been easterly— fair for a fleet sailing from Brest. He had, moreover, received a succession of reports from Pellew which could mean but one thing: the enemy were coming out. Yet on 16 December, though he had been informed that another report would be arriving later in the day, he

[1] Mahan, *The Influence of Sea Power upon the French Revolution and Empire*, I, p. 366.
[2] Add. MSS., 31, 159, 21, 27, 29 December 1796.

quitted the rendezvous before this intelligence could reach him.[1] The generally accepted explanation is that he was forced off his station by an easterly gale. According to James: 'A strong north-east gale drove [Admiral Colpoys] from his station, and enabled the Brest fleet . . . to put to sea from Bertheaume Bay.' This is simply moonshine. In point of fact, it was blowing no more than a topsail breeze; and it was not till midnight that the *London* got down her topgallant-yards. With 'fresh breezes at S.E. by E.' he should never have drifted out to a position over forty miles to the west of Ushant. It is hard to dispel the suspicion that Colpoys was something of a 'shy cock'. That, at any rate, was the idea commonly held on the lower deck; and it may be reckoned among the lesser contributory causes of the great mutiny which broke out at Spithead a few months later.

After the abortive attempt of 1796–7, the situation in Ireland steadily deteriorated. The North was on the edge of revolt. The opposing religious factions carried on a savage guerrilla warfare, with mutual atrocities. Law and order were everywhere breaking down. From Ulster the new revolutionary spirit spread southward. Hatred of the historic enemy who had exploited and oppressed the 'most distressful country' was fast reviving among a downtrodden peasantry who for long had remained sunk in seemingly hopeless apathy. Presently the belief arose among the people that deliverance would come to Ireland— apostrophized as the *Shan Van vocht*, 'the poor old woman'—in the guise of an army from France.

> Oh! the French are on the sea,
> Says the *Shan Van vocht*;
> Oh, the French are on the sea,
> Says the *Shan Van vocht*.
> Oh! the French are in the bay,
> They'll be here without delay,
> And the Orange will decay,
> Says the *Shan Van vocht* . . .

'As long as the war last, I fear I cannot promise your Grace any settled tranquillity in Ireland,' wrote Camden to the Duke of Portland in November, 'and if the French shall be able to effect a landing, I apprehend much blood will be shed and many atrocities committed.' By the spring of 1798 there was general expectation that England's

---

[1] *Spencer Papers*, I, pp. 368–71.

danger would be Ireland's opportunity. But the authorities in Dublin Castle struck suddenly, arresting the Irish rebel leader, Lord Edward Fitzgerald, and seizing a great quantity of arms, with the result that the long-expected general insurrection never materialized; and though in Co. Wexford some 30,000 peasants rose under the leadership of one of their priests, Father Murphy, routing the local militia and slaughtering the Protestants of Enniscorthy, the rebel army was unsupported, and the rising, after several anxious weeks, was suppressed at Vinegar Hill.

When the French, a few months later, did make a further descent on Ireland, it was too late. Bonaparte with the Toulon squadron and the flower of the French army had already sailed for Alexandria; and no large-scale expedition was possible. In August a small squadron of four of the line, carrying 1,150 veteran troops under General Humbert and a large quantity of arms, got away from Rochefort and landed the troops in Killala Bay in Co. Mayo. Near Castlebar the French routed a body of over 2,000 regular troops; but later at Ballinamuck they were surrounded by a vastly superior British force and obliged to surrender.

In September another expedition, under Rear-Admiral Bompart, comprising the *Hoche*, 74, and eight frigates, with a reinforcement of 3,000 on board, slipped out of Brest through the Passage du Raz while Bridport was in Torbay. On the following day the squadron was sighted by Keats in the *Boadicea*, who at once made sail for the fleet in Torbay to raise the alarm. Meanwhile Bompart shaped a course for the entrance of Lough Swilly in the north of Ireland. On the last two occasions the enemy had succeeded in reaching the south coast unopposed: but this time, thanks to Keats's promptitude, they were intercepted. Within view of the rugged cliffs of Tory, Bompart's force was sighted, at midday on 11 October, by a superior British squadron, comprising three 74s and five frigates, under Rear-Admiral Sir John Warren.

The French were hopelessly outmatched. Bompart hauled closely to the wind and Warren threw out the signal for a general chase. With a rising gale and a great hollow sea, the chase was continued during the rest of the 11th and the following night. In the early morning of the 12th the enemy were sighted at a short distance to windward; the leading British frigate, the *Anson*, having carried away her mizen-mast, which in its fall brought down the other topmasts, and one of the French frigates having sprung a dangerous leak. Action was joined soon after

7 a.m.; and at 11 the *Hoche*, after a gallant resistance, struck her colours.

'The frigates made sail from us,' wrote Warren in his dispatch, 'the signal to pursue the enemy was immediately made, and, in five hours afterwards, three of the frigates hauled down their colours also; but they, as well as the *Hoche*, were obstinately defended, all of them being heavy frigates, entirely new, full of troops and stores, and everything necessary for the establishment of their plans in Ireland.'[1] On the following day three more of the hostile frigates were taken; only two ever returned to France.

With the surrender of Bompart's squadron perished the last hopes of the Irish revolutionaries. For with Bompart on board the *Hoche* had sailed the great rebel leader, Wolfe Tone. He was taken to Dublin, tried by court-martial, and sentenced to death. Tone cut his throat while in prison. The wound was not immediately fatal; but after lingering for several days he expired on 19 November.

5

At the outset of the war Pitt, relying over much on the economic strength of Great Britain, had greatly underrated the latent power of a nation in arms. Observing that France was already on the verge of bankruptcy, he thought that the war would be over 'in one or two campaigns'; and he considered that the most effective policy would be to weaken the enemy by destroying her overseas trade and by capturing her colonies. With greater perspicuity Burke was prophesying that it would be 'a long and dangerous war—the most dangerous we were ever engaged in.' And the event proved Burke right. Contrary to Pitt's expectations, so far from being speedily suppressed, the revolutionary forces in the course of the next few years overleaped the frontier and swept like wildfire through the adjacent territories, the rotten fabric of the *ancien régime* everywhere crumbling before their victorious onset. Himself wholly ignorant of war, Pitt could expect little help from his colleagues in the Cabinet; and his government pursued, with calamitous consequences, a policy of drift, delay, and improvisation, dissipating its resources over a wide range of different and unrelated enterprises.

Pitt had counted over-optimistically on the naval assistance of our

[1] Adm. 1/111, 20 October 1798.

Spanish allies for operations in the Mediterranean and off the Atlantic coasts of Spain. Admittedly, the Spanish bases were admirably situated for intercepting the enemy's trade; but Pitt does not seem to have taken into account the inherent incapacity of the Spaniards for sea warfare (Nelson and his brother-officers entertained no such illusions); it is difficult, if not totally impossible, to imagine a Spanish squadron cruising continuously off Finisterre.

It was Pitt's intention to use such small British military forces as were available to operate in the West Indies in conjunction with the Navy. Accordingly in the spring of 1794 a small conjunct expedition, under Vice-Admiral Sir John Jervis and Lieutenant-General Sir Charles Grey, successively captured Martinique, St. Lucia, and Guadeloupe. But the British blockade of the enemy's ports was so laxly maintained that 6,000 troops arrived from Brest and reconquered Guadeloupe before the end of the year; and native risings were fomented by republican agents in the British, as well as in the French, West Indian islands. Meanwhile a British descent on Haiti had disastrously failed, and yellow fever had broken out among our forces. The war in the West Indies was badly directed from home; Pitt had nothing like the knowledge of local conditions in these islands that his father had possessed of those in French North America; and his failure to dispatch adequate reinforcements in time not only cost us several of our recent conquests, but gave the French a valuable base from which to attack British trade. The situation was to some extent restored by the arrival in 1796 of a large force under Admiral Christian and General Sir Ralph Abercromby. But disease exacted an ever-increasing toll; and within a few years the West Indian campaign had cost our Army more in casualties (40,000 dead, and about the same number rendered unfit for further service) than the entire Peninsular War. 'They poured these troops into these pestilential islands, in the expectation that thereby they would destroy the power of France, only to discover, when it was too late, that they had practically destroyed the British army.'[1]

Though the West Indian campaigns deprived France of an important part of her overseas trade and revenue, they had not succeeded in crippling the young Republic financially or diminishing its powers of resistance. The French treasury was, in fact, amply replenished by the abundant contributions levied from the lands overrun by her

[1] Fortescue, *History of the British Army*, IV, 385.

victorious generals. On land the enemy carried all before them. On the seas the *guerre de course* soon attained menacing proportions.

On the other hand, it may be said in defence of this part of Pitt's war policy that the safety of the British West Indies was in his generation essential to the economic stability of Great Britain. These West Indian islands were considered to be 'the principal source of the national opulence and maritime power'[1] of the kingdom, and the mainstay of the national economy: for on their rich plantations depended more than a quarter of the total overseas commerce of the country, which was, after all, vital to the successive alliances that she headed against the French Republic. Moreover, though it was soon apparent that Pitt had inherited little of his father's genius for conjoint strategy, his conduct of the war at sea stood on an altogether higher plane than his military policy. It was Pitt who chose Spencer as First Lord during the years which saw some of the greatest victories in our naval history. It was due to Pitt's care and foresight that our country was in 1796 replenished with adequate naval stores.[2] It was Pitt whose courage and constancy were unshaken during the worst months of 1797. Lastly, it was Pitt who was insistent for the return of the fleet to the Mediterranean in 1798.

On the Continent, Pitt looked to our allies to carry on the invasion of France; but these soon proved a broken reed. The armies of Spain were speedily chased over the frontier. Austria, Prussia, and Russia were ready enough to accept British subsidies; but their main preoccupation was with the third partition of Poland. Before the end of 1794, the Austrian, Prussian, British, and Dutch forces operating on the eastern frontier of France had been soundly beaten; and the republican armies then proceeded to occupy the Austrian Netherlands, as well as parts of Holland and the Rhineland. The remnant of the British expeditionary force was embarked at Bremen and Cuxhaven. On 20

---

[1] See Bryan Edwards, *History of the British West Indies* (1793).

[2] When war with Spain was imminent, and an eventual rupture with the Northern kingdoms was apprehended, our government proceeded to import ship timber from the Adriatic, masts and hemp from North America, and naval stores, tallow, hemp, iron, and corn from the Baltic. In one year no less than 4,500 British merchantmen passed through the Sound, laden for the most part with naval stores, iron, hides, and corn. At the same time the strictest economy was enjoined both in the dockyards and in the ships of war. It was through these measures that the Navy was equipped to meet the coming storm.

January 1795 the French entered Amsterdam and proclaimed a republic. By the spring the Dutch fleet had been captured by a French flying column galloping across the frozen Zuyder Zee; and the allied armies had been chased out of Holland.

In northern Europe the war was over. The whole continental coast-line facing England was now in the hands of the French; and when on 16 May the Batavian republic declared war on Great Britain, the fifteen battleships and thirty smaller vessels belonging to Holland were carried over to the naval forces of the enemy. This entailed an additional heavy burden on our already over-strained resources. As the Dutch fleet in the Texel not only constituted a threat to our Baltic trade but might also be used to convoy a hostile expedition north-about to Ireland, the Channel fleet had to be weakened in order to supply a squadron to blockade the Texel and to protect our Baltic convoys.

The command of this squadron was given to Vice-Admiral Adam Duncan, who with exiguous forces was responsible for an immense area extending from the Orkney Islands to the Nore. Despite the incessant demands of the numerous convoys and other services in this region, Duncan continually maintained a rigorous blockade of the enemy squadron in the Texel. Almost every day one or more of his cutters or luggers looked into the anchorage and brought back a report on the number and condition of the enemy ships. His luggers also proved their worth in pushing close inshore to prevent coasters from entering the Texel.[1]

A Russian squadron, under the orders of Vice-Admiral Peter Hanikoff—later described by Duncan's second-in-command as 'a curious Squad'—which was attached to his force in the summer of 1795, often proved more of a liability than an asset. The Russian ships spent a good deal of their time in port undergoing repairs, while their crews were ill-fed and sickly. 'I wish to the Lord', his exasperated second-in-command, Vice-Admiral McBride, complained to Duncan a year later, 'you would get them altogether out of our way and let his Excellency Hanikoff show himself with them off the Texel, he will frighten the Dutch men out of their Wits.'[2]

During the summer of 1796 McBride thus summarized the method of blockade:

[1] Adm. 51/4012, 52/3447, 52/3448, *passim.*
[2] *Q. E. Turner in Mariner's Mirror, Vol. 49, pp. 216–17.*

the cutters as near the Texel as they can safely get, the frigates next them, then two line of battle ships to cover them, and the rest of us without and still farther off so as to be seen from their look-out. This keeps them in suspense as to the amount of our force.[1]

The North Sea squadron was kept constantly on the alert by reports of the Dutch fleet having put to sea and Spencer's exhortations on the need for vigilance. When from time to time the main body of the squadron was obliged to return to England to revictual or refit, the frigates and smaller cruisers remained on their post to keep watch on the enemy. For this work the luggers (craft which had already proved their worth in the revenue service) were particularly useful, admirably adapted as they were to working in shoal water close inshore. In the autumn of 1796 McBride, whose health had broken down, was relieved by Vice-Admiral Richard Onslow. The situation in the North Sea continued more or less unchanged from the autumn of 1795 to the spring of 1797.

At the same time Pitt's government took the courageous decision to send out of the country a substantial part of its diminished military forces to safeguard the sea-route to the east. A squadron under Sir George Elphinstone (later Lord Keith) joined hands with another under Commodore Blankett in Simon's Bay, near the Cape of Good Hope, in June 1795. The landing of the troops, commanded by Major-General James Craig, was virtually unopposed. After protracted but unsuccessful negotiations Craig's troops, reinforced by a large detachment of seamen and marines, forced the pass at Muizenberg, on the road to Cape Town; the enemy offering little resistance. Shortly after, on 15 August, the governor capitulated; and the whole colony passed into British keeping. Cape Town, situated at the head of Table Bay, consisted at this time of about 1,100 houses, 'disposed in straight and parallel streets, intersecting each other at right angles, kept in very good order'. The Cape was visited by increasing numbers of ships in the last two decades of the century, which was a time of great prosperity for the colony. The climate was a genial and healthy one, so that the sick sent ashore there often made a rapid recovery. Ample supplies of livestock, corn, butter, vegetables, and fruit were available to the shipping. Henceforward the Cape would not only cease to supply Mauritius and

[1] Adm. 1/523, 23 August 1796.

Bourbon Island, but would also serve as a base for the British block-ading force there.[1]

The following year a small Dutch squadron which had broken out of the Texel with the object of recapturing the Cape was caught by a greatly superior British force in Saldanhe Bay, and obliged to capit-ulate.

The destruction of a large part of the Toulon fleet had so far increased the margin of British superiority in European waters as to make it possible for reinforcements to be sent out to India. In May 1794 a small squadron under Commodore Peter Rainier sailed from Spithead with the Channel fleet, with which he presently parted company off the Lizard, finally reaching Madras in September. There the news reached him that the British blockade of Mauritius, or the Isle of France (as the French called the island), had been broken up by a small force, under Captain Jean Renaud, which drove off our frigates in a minor engagement on 22 October. In the months which followed Rainier had not enough ships to resume the blockade. As in previous wars, the hostile privateers, based on the secure and spacious harbour of Port Louis in Mauritius, levied a heavy toll on British shipping in the Indian Ocean. During this time the French also had a strong force of frigates in eastern waters; but, notwithstanding that they met with little opposition, these achieved practically nothing.

Rainier's first major objective was Trincomali, which the experience of the last war had shown could be, in French hands, a serious threat to our East Indies squadron. The Dutch garrison of the port, which was in no condition to resist, capitulated on 31 August 1795. A fortnight earlier a small force under Captain Newcome had captured Malacca. The purpose of both these conquests had been to prevent the Dutch bases from falling into the hands of the French. The following year, on 16 February, Rainier landed and occupied Amboyna, capital of the Moluccas. Banda was captured early in March.

To prevent its recovery by the Dutch it was deemed necessary to

---

[1] Though the Cape was chiefly valued as a place of refreshment on the passage to India, the anchorage in Table Bay was a bad one. The holding ground was poor, and ships were liable to be driven on shore in a north-westerly gale. 'The Cape may be a capital colony,' observed Captain Beaver somewhat later, 'but its bay is an infernal one; it is safe against no wind, and its sea is worse than the wind.' It was in the neighbouring Simon's Bay that the naval base was situated.

station a powerful squadron at the Cape. This was a far more formidable
force than that stationed in Indian waters. For a time the Admiral at
the Cape commanded both squadrons. Mauritius, which in the later
years of the war was in danger of a hostile descent, was saved, first, by
an unsuccessful Dutch attempt on the Cape, and, second, by Napoleon's
Egyptian expedition.

II

Jervis in the Mediterranean

I

In the opening phase of the struggle the outlook for Great Britain in the Mediterranean was deceptively fair; for, soon after the arrival of Hood and his fleet, the leading citizens of Toulon invited him to take possession of the great French arsenal in the name of Louis XVII.[1] But Hood only held Toulon for six months before he was driven out by republican forces of greatly superior strength whose artillery was under the command of the youthful Napoleon Bonaparte. Three of the French force in Toulon were then carried off by Hood, and ten of the line and several cruisers were destroyed in time by Captain Sir William Sydney Smith; but the remainder, comprising fifteen of the line, thirteen frigates, and nine corvettes, fell into the hands of the republicans, to constitute the nucleus of a powerful fleet. Most of these vessels were destined to form part of the squadron which, in 1798, accompanied Bonaparte to Egypt.

After the evacuation of Toulon, Hood selected Corsica, with its fine anchorage of San Fiorenzo Bay, as his base. San Fiorenzo was admirably situated to serve as a base for operations on the Riviera, which would fulfil the double purpose of severing French communications with their army and protecting British trade. Our possession of the island would, moreover, deprive Toulon of the important reserves of timber and naval stores which it had formerly been accustomed to draw from the forests of Corsica. The island had been sold to France twenty-five years before by Genoa; but the inhabitants were bitterly hostile to French rule, and the fortresses of Calvi and Bastia surrendered to the British after a close blockade and a series of vigorous conjoint operations in which Nelson in the *Agamemnon* played a distinguished part. Hood was then succeeded by Vice-Admiral William Hotham, who, though a

[1] Adm. 1/391, 29 August 1793.

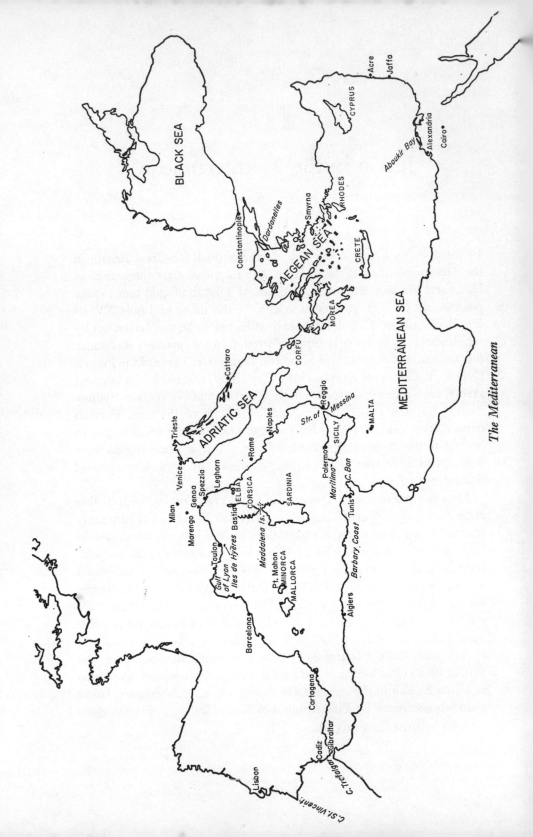

The Mediterranean

BLACK SEA

MEDITERRANEAN SEA

AEGEAN SEA

ADRIATIC SEA

Acre
Jaffa

CYPRUS

Alexandria
Cairo

Aboukir Bay

RHODES

Smyrna

CRETE

Dardanelles

Constantinople

MOREA

CORFU

Cattaro

Reggio

Str. of Messina

MALTA

Trieste

Naples

SICILY

Palermo

C. Bon

Maritimo

Venice

Rome

Leghorn

Milan

Genoa
Spezzia

Marengo

SARDINIA

Tunis

ELBA
CORSICA

Bastia

Barbary Coast

Toulon
Gulf of Lyon
Iles de Hyères

Maddalena Is.

Pt. Mahon
MINORCA

Algiers

MALLORCA

Barcelona

Cartagena

Gibraltar
Cadiz
C. Trafalgar

Lisbon

C. St. Vincent

good officer and sufficiently reliable in a subordinate capacity, showed himself quite unequal to the high strategic and political responsibilities of the Mediterranean command. 'It has been said he was not fit to command in chief,' Gardner related, 'but very able as a second.'[1] Much of his time Hotham spent lying peacefully at anchor in Leghorn and San Fiorenzo Bay. As might be expected, the investment of Toulon during this stage of the war was no more effective than that of Brest.

The chief duties of the Mediterranean fleet were to control the sea for the protection of commerce and to assist on shore our continental allies in the war against the Republic. The active support of our fleet was essential to the allied cause in southern Europe: without it there could be no effective combination, or unity of action. Hitherto little had been attempted on the Italian front by the armies on either side. The French, whose forces were much the weaker, were obliged to stand on the defensive. Then in June 1795 the Austrians launched a determined offensive against the republicans, driving them back across the Apennines and securing the important anchorage of Vado. But this allied success was not followed up; and their chance of destroying the Army of Italy before it became a force to be reckoned with was thus thrown away. During the summer the French, having disposed of Holland, Prussia, and Spain, turned their attention to Italy. They substantially reinforced their forces there, and in November, under General Schérer, heavily defeated the Austrians at Loano. This was the decisive action of the campaign. Loano gave the French the Ligurian passes.

When in March, 1795, the enemy's fleet put out from Toulon with the intention of retaking Corsica it was intercepted on the 14th by the British—inferior in numbers, but greatly superior in quality—in the Gulf of Genoa. The southerly wind was light and fitful, and the rival fleets were drawn out in long scattered lines. In the course of the action one of the ships in the French rear, the *Ça Ira*, 84, colliding with her next ahead, carried away both fore and main topmasts and fell astern of her fleet; whereupon Captain Thomas Fremantle of the *Inconstant* frigate, 'who was then far advanced on the chase', bore down on her and engaged her closely, inflicting a good deal of damage; when the

[1] *Above and under hatches (Recollections of James Anthony Gardner)*, ed. C. C. Lloyd 1957), p. 110.

Inconstant was finally obliged to retire she was succeeded by the leading ship of the British line of battle, the *Agamemnon*. Nelson's tactics were to keep astern of the huge *Ça Ira* so that she could not bring her broadside to bear; and his crew manœuvred the *Agamemnon* about her stern and quarters, as their captain afterwards said, 'with as much exactness as if she had been working into Spithead.' Approaching to within a hundred yards' range, the *Agamemnon* yawed and, with every gun double-shotted, poured a raking broadside into the Frenchman's stern. Immediately afterwards she turned and stood after the *Ça Ira* again, closing the enemy and repeating her attack. This went on for more than two hours, 'never allowing the *Ça Ira* to get a single gun from either side to fire on us,' as Nelson declared; 'and at the end of which, the *Ça Ira* was a perfect wreck, her sails hanging in tatters, mizen topsail, and cross jack yards shot away.'

Next morning there was a fresh breeze at N.W. and the British had the weather-gauge. The *Ça Ira* had been taken in tow by another ship of the line, the *Censeur*. From eight o'clock to ten the two fleets, sailing in line ahead, engaged each other at long range. The British squadron succeeded in cutting off the *Censeur* and the *Ça Ira* from the main French body; and in the action which followed both these ships were dismasted and compelled to strike. They were taken possession of by the *Agamemnon*, which happened to be the nearest British vessel. Early in the afternoon the French fleet bore away towards Toulon. 'I have good reason to hope,' wrote Hotham complacently in his dispatch, 'from the enemy's steering to the westward after having passed our fleet, that whatever might have been their design, their intents are for the present frustrated.'[1]

This was Nelson's first action. Already he was recognized as a man of whom great things might be expected. The dates of his commissions reveal how swiftly he rose in the service. He had passed for lieutenant when he was under nineteen; he was commander of the *Badger* at the age of twenty. He was now thirty-six—soon he would be entering upon the final decade of his life, the ten crowded, glorious years that were to render his name immortal. In this encounter with the *Ça Ira* the characteristic Nelsonic qualities of instant decision, unfailing resource, unshakeable tenacity of purpose, brilliant tactical insight, swift and audacious action—combined with the all-consuming, over-

[1] Adm. 1/393, 16 March 1795.

mastering urge towards victory—were made manifest to all the squadron. It was the opening of what Mahan has truly described as 'Nelson's page in history'.

There followed four months of inactivity, after which another opportunity of engaging the enemy fleet was similarly thrown away by Hotham. The Commander-in-Chief had been joined some weeks before by a reinforcement from home, under Rear-Admiral Robert Man, bringing his total strength up to twenty-three of the line. His opponent, Martin, had only seventeen. On 14 July, off the Hyères Islands, action was joined with the hostile fleet. The westerly wind was light and failing; the rival fleets, as in the earlier engagement, were dispersed over a wide area; the Admiral himself had his flag in one of the worst sailers in the squadron, the *Britannia*, which lay about seven miles astern of his van. Early in the afternoon the best-sailing ships of the squadron, Nelson's *Agamemnon* and five others, came up with and engaged the rear of the enemy. The *Alcide*, 74, struck her colours, but shortly afterwards caught fire and blew up. Then, just as the *Cumberland* and *Agamemnon* were getting into close action, Hotham signalled retirement, 'the wind being directly into the Gulf of Fréjus'.[1]

'Had the wind lasted ten minutes longer,' observed Nelson regretfully, writing to his old captain, William Locker, 'the six Ships would have each been alongside six of the Enemy . . . but the west wind first died away, then came east, which gave them the wind, and enabled them to reach their own Coast, from which they were not more than eight or nine miles distant.'[2]

The truth was, neither Hotham nor Martin was really willing to fight a decisive action but wished to gain some trivial advantage at no risk. Though Hotham enjoyed a substantial superiority over his opponent, he had first taken his squadron into action in bad order, and later forfeited his chance of a limited success. 'The scrambling distant fire was a farce,' Nelson declared; and he went on to observe that 'Hotham has no head for enterprise, perfectly satisfied that each month passes without any losses on our side.'

Moreover, the chance of large-scale amphibious operations against the enemy's vulnerable line of communication between Nice and Genoa

[1] Adm. 1/393, 16 July 1795.
[2] *Nelson's Dispatches*, II, pp. 50–1.

had been thrown away.[1] Though Nelson during the summer and autumn of 1795 was detached with a small squadron to support the Austrian army on the Riveira, his force was not strong enough to cut the French line of supply. 'My command here', he wrote to his friend Collingwood, 'is so far pleasant as it relieves me from the inactivity of our Fleet, which is great indeed, as you will soon see.'

Hotham's failure to bring the enemy's fleet to decisive action was destined, indeed, to have disastrous consequences for the Allied cause and the British Mediterranean squadron. The capture of a large number of French seamen would have severely impeded the operations of the flotilla from Toulon which supplied their Army of Italy with ammunition, guns, and stores. The Austrians not unreasonably protested that they had received little support from the fleet; and Nelson later attributed the remarkable advance of the Army of Italy under Bonaparte's command to Hotham's failure to use British sea power in the Mediterranean to the best advantage. Hotham's successor likewise censured this lax and lethargic strategy. 'Had the squadron resorted to Vado Bay', Sir John Jervis was later to complain to Lord Spencer, 'instead of Leghorn, and vigorous measures been pursued, the enemy never would have penetrated Piedmont coastwise.'[2]

2

The appointment of Admiral Sir John Jervis to the command of the Mediterranean squadron marked an era in the history of the Navy. As a youngster, he had received both his nomination and his commission from Anson. In the Seven Years' War he had been with Saunders at the capture of Quebec. The ship that he commanded in the War of American Independence, the *Foudroyant*, had been renowned throughout the service as a model of discipline and good order; he had been Keppel's next astern in the indecisive action of 1779, and off Ushant in 1782 he had distinguished himself by taking the *Pégase* without the loss of a single man, for which he had been rewarded with a baronetcy

[1] The Maritime Alps and the Apennines, descending nearly to the shore, left only the long, narrow line of communication by way of the Corniche road, in many places within cannon-shot of the sea and described by the French historian Jomini as *l'horrible route de la Corniche sous le feu des cannonières anglaises* (*Q.* J. Holland Rose, *Life of Napoleon I* (1929), I, p. 258).

[2] *Spencer Papers*, II, p. 240.

and the Order of the Bath. The West Indian expedition of 1795 had been remarkable for the unusually harmonious relationship which existed between the naval and military commanders-in-chief. ('Good Lord deliver us from all conjunct expeditions,' remarked Jervis in retrospect, 'unless they are commanded by Sir Charles Grey or Sir Charles Stuart.') His notions of discipline, system, and efficiency were on an altogether higher plane than those of Lord Howe. In character and demeanour also the two men were strikingly dissimilar. 'Where Howe was patient, gentle, indulgent, and kind, by which he won the attachment of both officers and seamen,' observed Barrow, '[Jervis] was rigorous, peremptory, and resolute, rigidly maintaining that the life and soul of naval discipline was obedience—his favourite word was *obedienza*.'[1]

Jervis came out in the *Lively* frigate; and, finding Rear-Admiral Man —a vital link in the chain of communications with England—at Gibraltar, immediately ordered him back to his post off Cadiz.[2] He joined his squadron anchored in San Fiorenzo Bay on 3 December 1795; and for the first time since the outbreak of the war the investment of Toulon became a reality. The following year Jervis with the main body of the fleet blockaded Toulon without a break for nearly 150 days, while a detached division under Nelson assisted the allies in the Gulf of Genoa.[3]

On Jervis's arrival our Mediterranean fleet could boast of a galaxy of fine sea-officers such as England had never known before or was ever to know again; a galaxy which included the illustrious names of Nelson, Collingwood, Troubridge, Foley, Berry, Hardy, Hallowell, Hood, Miller, Thompson, and Fremantle. 'Great Captains they assuredly were,' writes Tucker; 'bright they have made our annals; each ship was a perfect school.'[4] The good material certainly was there; but the standards of leadership, discipline, health, seamanship, and gunnery were, in the majority of cases, far too low. The men were badly led, ill-fed, sickly, and rebellious. The ships were short of their proper complements, and many of them were in bad repair. There was a chronic shortage of naval stores and, indeed, stores of every kind. Jervis

---

[1] Barrow, *Life of Richard Earl Howe* (1838), p. 427.
[2] Adm. 1/393, 23 November 1795.
[3] Adm. 1/395, 11 May–6 October 1796; 51/1126 *passim.*
[4] J S. Tucker, *Memoirs of the Earl of St. Vincent* (1844), I, p. 152.

effected a transformation: and the 'Mediterranean discipline' became a byword in the Service.

'Our fleet is in excellent order,' declared Collingwood, 'well provided with everything, in which our Admiral, Sir John Jervis, takes wonderful pains, and the consequence is we are remarkably healthy after being twenty-eight weeks at sea.'[1]

He established method and order, put down mutiny, and disciplined his whole squadron—officers and men alike—with a firm hand. He organized a sound commissariat. He restored the crews to health. Slowly but steadily he raised the level of seamanship and gunnery throughout the whole fleet. It was, taken all in all, an astonishing achievement. 'Of all the fleets I ever saw,' wrote Nelson in October 1796, 'I never saw one in point of officers and men equal to Sir John Jervis's.' Not only did he hold rigidly in check the dangerous disaffection existing among his crews, but out of the heterogeneous elements under his charge he created the finest fleet Great Britain had ever possessed: the fleet with which Nelson, his favourite pupil, was soon to achieve one of the most brilliant victories of all time.

The inshore squadron, comprising four or five of the line, was stationed at the very entrance of the harbour, while the main fleet, sailing in two columns, with the *Victory* on the weather bow to observe slack station-keeping, cruised continuously in the offing. During the spring and summer of 1796 a series of standing orders reflected the steadily rising standard of discipline and seamanship throughout the squadron, of which the following are significant examples: 'The Commander-in-Chief requests the attention of the Captains to the expediency of watching the motions of the *Victory*; and when the signal is made to tack or wear, every yard of plain canvas should, in moderate weather, be spread instantly, more particularly in the rear ships, they having most way to make.' A subsequent order directed that, when sailing in close order, 'the ships should keep the masts of their leading ships in one, and so calculate their rate of sailing as to be able to reduce it to the hauling down or hoisting a stay sail; and the backing a mizen-topsail should be studiously avoided, as it always throws the ship to leeward of her station in the line.'[2]

[1] *The Private Correspondence of Admiral Lord Collingwood*, ed. E. A. Hughes (1957), p. 39.
[2] *Ibid.*, I, pp. 177–8, 189.

As the French advance continued and the problem of stores became daily more serious and pressing, Jervis showed himself possessed of a gift for economical management and ingenious improvisation that amounted almost to genius. By precept and practice he constantly instilled the lesson of strict economy in the consumption of supplies; and in particular he gave orders that boatswain's and carpenter's stores were to be expended with the 'utmost frugality'. 'As the stores brought out in the storeships,' he wrote, 'will be inadequate to the demand of the fleet, without the most scrupulous attention in the officers ordered on surveys, I desire you will direct the masters so ordered on boatswain's stores to be very particular in describing the defects they find, and whether the topsail haulyards, braces, lifts, and tacklefalls may be converted into a jib or staysail, haulyards, sheets, etc.; and when the carpenters are so ordered they are to be as circumspect as possible in their duty, reporting to you whether the lower masts, topmasts, and yards they survey, can by any artificial means be made serviceable; or if not, their opinion of the use to which the same may be best converted.'[1]

A few months after Jervis's arrival in the Mediterranean, Bonaparte was appointed to command the French Army of Italy. After months of stagnation things suddenly began to move. The opening phase of his first Italian campaign must be accounted one of the classic examples of great generalship. Animating his ragged, half-starved troops with the hope of glory and spoil, he at once prepared to take the field. Though the French were heavily outnumbered by their enemies, in several successive encounters Bonaparte, exploiting to the full the immense possibilities opened up by surprise and speed, repeatedly achieved a superior concentration in the attack by a series of rapid marches. Striking northwards on 9 April 1796 from the Riviera, he speedily drove a wedge between the Austrians and their Piedmontese allies, and, forcing them further and further apart, within a fortnight compelled the latter to sue for an armistice. His flank thus secured, Bonaparte turned into Lombardy. On 10 May his troops forced the bridge of Lodi; the Austrians fell back in headlong retreat, and, five days later, the young commander entered Milan in triumph.

By the end of May he had resumed his eastward march across the richest plain in Europe. Crossing the Mincio, he laid siege to Mantua;

[1] *Ibid.*, II, pp. 171–2.

and then, at the orders of the Directory, turned southward down the Italian peninsula. One after another the neighbouring States abandoned the struggle and came to terms. Deprived of Mediterranean depots by the arms and diplomacy of France, Jervis's squadron found itself living a hand-to-mouth existence. 'The enemy possessing themselves of Leghorn', Nelson declared, 'cuts off all our supplies such as fresh meat, fuel and various other most essential necessaries; and of course our fleet cannot always in that case be looked for on the northern coast of Italy.'

Towards the end of June 1796 the threat to Leghorn suddenly materialized. On receiving news of the French advance through Tuscany, Nelson had sailed southward from Genoa; but the wind being light for his passage, he did not make Leghorn till the 25th, when Bonaparte's troops were already in the town and the British colony and its property were being evacuated by Captain Thomas Fremantle of the frigate *Inconstant*, under whose escort a convoy of some forty merchant vessels was working slowly seaward as Nelson stood in in the *Captain*.

Among the refugees was a well-to-do English family, the Wynnes, who were later carried in Fremantle's frigate to the fleet off Toulon and there transferred to the *Britannia*. Two of the daughters— Betsey and Jenny, aged seventeen and sixteen years respectively— kept a diary; and in that diary is conjured up, as seen through the eyes of two young English girls, a picture which is fresh and intimate to an extraordinary degree, of the Mediterranean fleet in this most brilliant era of our naval annals.

'Nothing so fine as the sight of this Fleet always under sail,' Betsey exclaimed, 'and so near Toulon that you may easily see the town and the French shipping.'[1] It was radiant summer weather. Northward across the azure sea lay the entrance to the blockaded port, with the craggy heights of Mount Faron towering in the background. To and fro before Cape Sepet and the outer harbour—beyond which rose the serried masts and spars of the enemy fleet, under shores bristling with cannon and the massive fortifications of Vauban's great arsenal— cruised the two long columns of British line-of-battle ships, 'the wooden walls of Old England'; their dark hulls majestically rising and falling with the motion of the sea, and their triple pyramids of trim white

[1] *The Wynne Diaries*, ed. A. Fremantle (1937), II, p. 109.

canvas gently swaying against the dark blue sky. On the weather bow, in her usual station, sailed that veteran first-rate, the *Victory*, flagship of so many famous commanders, conspicuous by her elaborate figure-head and her beakhead richly adorned with carven mermaids and dolphins, with her Admiral's flag at the main-topgallant masthead. If the sight of the fleet moored in the anchorage at Spithead had power to move the onlooker to wonder and admiration, how much more must the spectacle of this fine squadron of Jervis's, cruising proudly before the enemy's very threshold, have stirred the hearts of these two impressionable maidens, who now beheld, for the first time in their lives, the power of England on the sea.

On fine moonlight nights, with the wave-crests glistering in the silver radiance as the great ships glided smoothly on their course down the dark mountainous coast, in the matchless order and dressing that was the product of Jervis's assiduous sail-drill, the prospect was, per-haps, even more impressive. 'We spent the evening,' wrote Betsey on 16 August, 'chattering in the Stern Gallery and admiring the moon and beauty of the night'.

The advent of the Wynnes infused new life into the somewhat jaded social round of the Mediterranean squadron. To many of the young officers, long exiled from their country and kin, the presence of such a family in their midst must, indeed, have come as a magical glimpse of England, home, and beauty. 'To have ladies on board is thought quite a rarity; every minute we have a new visitor and we are looked upon like curiosities.' Betsey took to the life on shipboard as a duck to water, while their hosts, from the Admiral downwards, spared no effort, 'to make it pleasant and comfortable to the Damsels'. There was music, there was dancing, and there were supper-parties on decks 'most elegantly dres't up, all the guns being removed'.[1] One after another the captains of the squadron hastened on board to pay their respects to Mr. and Mrs. Wynne—and to Mr. and Mrs. Wynne's young daughters: Robert Calder, the Captain of the Fleet; Captains George Grey, George Cockburn (the future scourge of the Chesapeake and Napoleon's gaoler), Richard Bowen, Richard Dacres, Lord Garlies, Thomas Sotheby; and not a few of the 'band of brothers', shortly after to immortalize their names at the Nile: the recent captor of the *Ça Ira* —'old Nelson', as the Wynne girls called him, Benjamin Hallowell,

[1] *Ibid.*, pp. 101–2.

James Saumarez, Thomas Troubridge, Samuel Hood, Ralph Miller, and Thomas Foley. 'All these gentlemen are equally complaisant and good-natured,' recorded Betsey admiringly; 'they live like brothers and give all they have.'[1] Before very long, as may be seen from the increasing number of entries in her journal concerning the young captain of the *Inconstant*, she was head over heels in love with Thomas Fremantle. 'How kind and amiable Captain Fremantle is, he pleases me more than any man I have yet seen. . . . Every body agrees to say that his ship is one of the best kept in the Mediterranean. Indeed, he is very far advanced for his age and has reason to flatter himself that he will reach to the highest, for he is on a very good way.'[2] But there were difficulties in the path of the young lovers. Fremantle had a formidable rival in the tall, grizzle-haired, middle-aged captain of the *Goliath*, Thomas Foley, who just then, apparently with her parents' approval, had begun to press his unwelcome attentions on the eldest Miss Wynne. 'I must be kind and civil to this old fool,' was Betsey's comment, 'whom I cannot bear since he has so plainly given us to guess his plans and these are so contrary to my wishes.' Foley, who stood high in the opinion of his Admiral, was only just short of forty; in other respects, however, he might have been regarded as a more eligible match than Fremantle. So, it would seem, thought the elder folk. 'Mamma', Betsey wrote plaintively, 'says that I am not in the least engaged to Fremantle and that the matter is far from settled.'[3]

The Wynnes were presently invited on board the flagship to dine with the Admiral, whom all the ladies of the party were in turn required to embrace ('the old Gentleman is very partial to kisses,' noted Betsey). After dinner her sister and she were persuaded to sing a duet—'It was a large party and we were very gay'.[4] Old Jarvie plainly approved of the Wynnes. He dubbed them 'the Amiables' and made them free of his squadron; he informed the delighted Betsey that she would make the best wife in England, and from that time on exerted himself to forward the match. 'Nothing can express how kind, gallant and friendly the Admiral was to us,' Betsey declared, 'he is a fine old man, though past seventy he is fresh and brisk as if he was only thirty.'[5] Early in the

[1] *Ibid.*, II, p. 101.
[2] *Ibid.*, II, p. 93.
[3] *Ibid.*, II, pp. 121, 126.
[4] *Ibid.*, II, p. 118.
[5] *Ibid.*, II, p. 113.

following year Betsey and her Fremantle were married in the British Embassy at Naples.

During the summer of 1796 the food supplies of Jervis's squadron were gravely threatened by the continued advance of Bonaparte's forces down the Italian peninsula. With the ports of Tuscany, Naples, and the Papal States closed to his squadron, and our former ally, Spain, becoming hostile, Jervis's position in the Mediterranean was growing increasingly precarious. The welfare of his ships' companies was his constant preoccupation. Hitherto, by a judicious system of victualling, Jervis had successfully ensured a continual supply of fresh provisions for the fleet. 'From the failure of the supplies of live cattle since the enemy has been in possession of Leghorn,' he observed, 'I have been under great apprehensions of a return to the scurvy.'[1] Despite difficulties that might well have appeared overwhelming he persevered in his unremitting and, in the main, successful exertions to keep the crews healthy. 'I am confirmed in an opinion that I have long entertained', he noted on another occasion, 'that, next to fresh animal food, onions and lemons are the best antiscorbutics and antiseptics;' and he added that 'no price is too great to preserve the health of the fleet.'

The loss of the important naval and commercial facilities of Leghorn had been a heavy blow to British interests in the Mediterranean. It gave the French, moreover, a secure base for their projected attempt on Corsica, which Jervis took immediate steps to prevent. On 9 July Nelson accordingly arrived off Elba with a small squadron, and on the 10th landed troops which at once took possession of Porto Ferrajo. In the meantime the blockade of Leghorn continued. 'This blockade', wrote Nelson to Collingwood on 1 August, 'is complete, and we lay very snug in the North Road, as smooth as in a harbour.'[2] The watch maintained on Leghorn, together with the occupation of Elba, appears to have effectually prevented any large body of French troops from getting across to Corsica.

Presently Naples withdrew from the coalition and concluded a French alliance. Piedmont had already yielded up Savoy and Nice to France. 'All our expected hopes', observed Nelson, from Leghorn roads, to Jervis, 'are blasted, I fear, for the present . . . Austria, I

[1] Tucker, *op. cit.*, I, p. 204.
[2] *Nelson's Dispatches*, II, p. 224.

suppose, must make peace, and we shall, as usual, be left to fight it out.'[1] During the months which followed, the struggle for northern Italy centred on the key-point of Mantua, which was strongly held by 13,000 Austrians. After repulsing four successive armies sent to relieve the city, Bonaparte finally secured its submission on 4 February 1797. With this last obstacle removed, the victorious republicans swept eastward and northward across Lombardy. Spain had already forsaken the coalition and was soon to make her peace with France. The British Viceroy of Corsica was threatened with a dangerous rising.

The position of our Mediterranean squadron was becoming untenable. The attitude of Spain, lying as she did on the line of its communications with England, had become the crucial factor. The danger was that Jervis might be caught between the French and Spanish fleets. To the Toulon fleet and the French division in Cadiz might presently be joined the main Spanish fleet, which was also in Cadiz, as well as a squadron of seven Spanish sail of the line in Cartagena. At any moment the odds against the British in the Mediterranean might well be overwhelming. True, the capacity of the Spaniards for sea warfare was not rated high by their opponents. 'I know the French long since offered Spain peace for fourteen Sail of the Line fully stored,' Nelson declared in August 1795; 'I take it for granted not manned, as that would be the readiest way to lose them again.' 'Be assured,' wrote Jervis to the First Lord, 'I will omit no opportunity of chastening the Spaniards, and if I have the good fortune to fall in with them the stuff I have in this fleet will tell.' It was in the autumn that the long-awaited blow fell. Spain signed a treaty of alliance with France on 19 August and declared war on Great Britain in October. Rear-Admiral Robert Man, who had been blockading the French division in Cadiz with seven of the line, was attacked on the 2nd by the main Spanish fleet, under Admiral Langara, to the east of Gibraltar, and instead of rejoining Jervis, in accordance with his instructions, lost his nerve and retired precipitately to England.[2] On the 24th Langara's fleet entered Toulon. Thus, when he was already so heavily out-

---

[1] *Ibid.*, II, p. 248.

[2] Jervis had for long entertained misgivings about Man. 'Poor Admiral Man', he wrote to Spencer, 'has been afflicted with such a distempered mind during the last nine months that imaginary ills and difficulties are continually brooding in it. . . . When the Blue Devils prevail, there is an end of resource and energy' (*Spencer Papers*, II, p. 42).

numbered, Jervis found himself deprived of a third of his force. The Navy was strained to the utmost in fulfilling its other commitments at home and overseas; and it was altogether out of the question to provide a fleet strong enough to face the combined forces of France and Spain.

The Cabinet also feared for the safety of Ireland. They determined to stand on the defensive in Europe and to concentrate their forces for the protection of the British Isles and of their more important colonial possessions. They therefore sent orders for Corsica to be evacuated and for the fleet to withdraw from the Mediterranean.[1] On 19 October Nelson, who had been entrusted by Jervis with the task of evacuating Corsica, took off the last of the troops; and carried them, together with the British viceroy, to Elba. Jervis held on in San Fiorenzo Bay to the last possible moment, in the hope that Man might yet join him; but by 2 November his stores were so depleted that he could remain there no longer and sailed, with the whole squadron, for Gibraltar. During the following year no British ship of the line, and only an occasional frigate, passed within the Straits; and British merchant traffic in the Mediterranean had practically ceased to exist.

3

After a long and difficult passage on short rations, Jervis anchored, on 1 December, in Gibraltar Bay, his hopes of gaining a decisive victory over the enemy frustrated and his Mediterranean strategy calamitously defeated; shortly after the first of a series of disasters befell the fleet. One of his vessels, the *Courageux*, dragging her anchors, was carried out of Gibraltar Bay by a terrific gale and wrecked on the African coast with heavy loss of life. A number of other vessels had also been driven out to sea, as Jervis reported to the Admiralty: 'The *Gibraltar* struck twice on Cabrita Point in getting out of the bay after parting her cables; her foretopmast was carried away by the shock, but she does not make water. . . . The *Zealous* struck twice on the reef off Cape Malabata and makes a little water. . . . The *Andromache* is returned with a sprung bowsprit and the *Niger* without any injury except the loss of two anchors'.[2]

After this disastrous gale he received orders to take the fleet to

[1] J. Holland Rose, *William Pitt and the Great War*, pp. 258, 275.
[2] Adm. 1/395, 15 December 1796.

C*

Lisbon to strengthen and encourage the Portuguese government, which was under the threat of a Franco-Spanish invasion. The limits of his station were extended to Cape Finisterre. Before sailing, Jervis sent Nelson back into the Mediterranean with two fast-sailing frigates, the *Minerva* and *Blanche*, to evacuate the garrison and naval stores from Elba, the abandonment of which had lately been determined on. In entering the Tagus he lost another of his ships, the *Bombay Castle*, 'the wind blowing at right angles with the bar', on a sandbank, as a result of the failure of the British minister to procure pilots;[1] the *Gibraltar* and *Culloden* were driven ashore; a few days afterwards the *Zealous* struck a rock in Tangier Bay, following which she was found to be leaking so badly that she had to be laid up for repairs.

At his anchorage in the Tagus Jervis grappled determinedly with the manifold deficiencies of Lisbon as a base and strove to keep the men out of mischief. 'To avoid dissentions and quarrels with the Portuguese which always terminate in assassinations,' and moreover to prevent 'straggling and desertions', he gave orders that no boat should be sent on shore unnecessarily.[2] Repairs were hurried forward; stores and provisions materialized by hook or by crook; the shortages of men were somehow made good; the naval hospital was drastically overhauled. Nevertheless, Jervis was anxious to be off: 'I will not stay here a moment longer than is necessary to put us to rights,' he declared; and added that 'inaction in the Tagus must make us all cowards.'[3]

On his departure from the Tagus, on 18th January, the *St. George* ran aground and had to be abandoned; ten days later the *Meleager* sprang her bowsprit and was forced to return to Lisbon for repairs: the result was that Jervis's force was reduced to ten of the line. Off Cape St. Vincent on 6 February, however, he was joined by a reinforcement of five of the line under Rear-Admiral Sir William Parker which had been sent out from England after the abatement of the Irish alarm.

Meanwhile on 20 December Nelson, on his passage from Gibraltar to Elba, had encountered off Cartagena, in thick and blowing weather, two Spanish frigates; he promptly engaged them, and captured one of them. Proceeding on his hazardous mission, he reached Porto Ferrajo

---

[1] Adm. 1/395, 22 December 1796.
[2] Brenton, *Life and Correspondence of St. Vincent* (1838), I, p. 277.
[3] Tucker, *op. cit.*, II, p. 252.

on the evening of Christmas Day. There, finding the seasonal festivities in full swing, he escorted Jenny Wynne and her sister Betsey (now married to his friend, Captain Fremantle) to the ball, entering the assembly rooms to the triumphal strains of 'Rule, Britannia' and 'See the Conquering Hero Comes'. The Commander-in-Chief of the military forces refused to leave the island; but Nelson embarked all the naval stores in Elba and on 29 January 1797 sailed again to rejoin Jervis.

Early in the new year, preparatory to an intended descent on Ireland, the French and Spanish fleets were ordered to concentrate at Brest. The Toulon fleet had succeeded in passing through the Straits of Gibraltar in the same easterly gale which had cost us the *Courageux*. But some weeks later, when the Spanish fleet from Cartagena was preparing to follow, Jervis, with his squadron of fifteen of the line, was cruising in readiness off Cape St. Vincent. Emerging from the Straits and making for Cadiz, the Spaniards were blown far out into the Atlantic and were sailing on an easterly course, with the wind astern, when their approach was reported to Jervis. On 13 February he was rejoined by Nelson in the *Minerva*—who, having reached Gibraltar four days after the Spaniards, was obliged to sail right through them before he could get clear.[1] The commodore now shifted his broad pendant from the frigate to the *Captain*, 74. Before sunset signal was made to keep close order and to prepare for battle. Jervis entertained several of his captains to dinner that evening and as the party broke up the toast was drunk: 'Victory over the Dons in the battle from which they cannot escape to-morrow!'

During the hours of darkness the British squadron held on its course in two columns, in close order; the weather was misty, and throughout the night the signal-guns of the Spaniards were heard to windward drawing nearer and nearer. In the grey dawn of St. Valentine's Day the Commander-in-Chief paced the quarter-deck of the *Victory* in his usual stern silence. 'A victory is very essential to England at this moment,' he was heard to declare. The Spaniards were sighted from the leading ships of the British columns about fifteen miles to the south-west—'thumpers,' the signal-lieutenant of the *Barfleur* recorded, 'they loom like Beachy Head in a fog'. It was a raw, foggy morning; as the day advanced the mists began to disperse; and Sir Robert Calder,

[1] Adm. 51/1186, 11–13 February 1797.

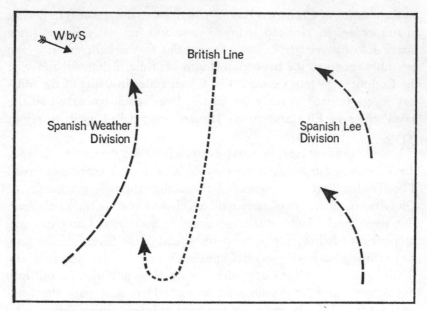

St. Vincent. The action of 14 February 1797, about 11 a.m.

the Captain of the Fleet, reported the hostile numbers to Jervis with growing concern.

'There are eight sail of the line, Sir John.'

'Very well, Sir.'

'There are twenty sail of the line, Sir John.'

'Very well, Sir.'

'There are twenty-seven sail of the line, Sir John; near double our own!'

'Enough, Sir,' was the sharp reply, 'no more of that: the die is cast; and if there are fifty sail of the line, I will go through them,' added Jervis, to the delight of the huge New Englander, Captain Hallowell, who was standing beside the Admiral.

'That's right, Sir John; that's right,' he exclaimed, and in his enthusiasm actually clapped his Admiral on the back—'By G – d we shall give them a d – d good licking.'[1]

About ten o'clock the fog lifted, and during the next hour or so it cleared completely. It was an almost perfect fighting day. There was no

[1] J. S. Tucker, *Memoirs of Earl St. Vincent* (1844), I, p. 255.

sea, and no more wind than to allow the ships to go into action under topgallant sails. The enemy fleet, heading E.S.E., was seen stretching in two straggling bodies across the horizon, while Jervis's squadron, close-hauled on the starboard tack, still sailing in two columns in 'admirable close order', was shaping a southerly course roughly at right angles to that of the Spaniards. Jervis's plan was that his van should attack the weather division of the Spanish fleet, while his rear prevented their leeward division from coming to the assistance of their consorts. Presently in response to the Admiral's signal his two columns merged into one perfect, ordered line, heading for the gap between the enemy divisions, which were vainly endeavouring to re-unite.[1] Led by Captain Thomas Troubridge in the *Culloden*, one of the finest fighting ships in the Navy, the British column came on under a press of sail, while the main body of the Spaniards stood to the northward in increasing disorder on a course nearly parallel to the British. A heavy cannonade ensued. 'We gave them their Valentines in style!' wrote a seaman of the *Goliath*. Jervis's next signal was to tack in succession in pursuit of the main body of the enemy to windward. Anticipating the order, Troubridge had already repeated the signal and the *Culloden* luffed up into the wind: to the huge satisfaction of the Commander-in Chief. 'Look at Troubridge,' Jervis cried exultantly, 'he tacks his ship to battle as if the eyes of all England were upon him! and would to God they were!' Ship after ship of the British line thereupon went about in rapid succession and stood on in pursuit of the enemy; at the same time those to the rearward on the original course were still interposed between the two hostile divisions. Suddenly the enemy's lee division, endeavouring to join their consorts to windward, put about in order to cut the British line. Their attempt failed. A huge three-decker, the *Principe de Asturias*, the flagship of the Spanish vice-admiral, in trying to force her way across the British line of advance was heavily raked by the *Victory*'s broadside, and drifted out of the fight with riven sails and shattered topmasts.

Shortly after one o'clock came the crisis of the action. As one after another Jervis's vessels swept through the gap and bore up, they left the sea clear in their rear. Now was the Spaniards' opportunity, and they

[1] The enemy's intention was to protect a valuable mercury convoy which had become separated from the main body of their fleet. See Rear-Admiral A. H. Taylor in *Mariner's Mirror*, Vol. 40, pp. 228–30.

took it. Hauling their wind on the larboard tack, the leading ships of the main or weather division steered to pass astern of the British line and thus join their ships to leeward. Jervis in the *Victory* was at this moment far ahead in the billowing smoke-bank of the cannonade. It is doubtful whether he realized what was happening; at any rate he made no signal. The leading Spaniards were rapidly approaching the tail of the British line, and their ships were newer and faster than ours: they were in fact on the point of achieving their purpose when Commodore Nelson, seeing what was about to happen, ordered the *Captain* (the third ship from the rear in the British line) to be immediately wore, and, steering between the *Diadem* and *Excellent* astern of him, laid his ship directly in the track of the three great Spanish three-deckers, the *Santissima Trinidad*, 130, the *Salvador del Mundo*, and *San Josef*, each of 112 guns; beside which were the *San Nicolas*, 84, and *San Isidro*, 74. The *Captain* was enveloped in a hail of fire. She lost her foretopmast; her sails and rigging were slashed to pieces, and her wheel was shot away. But Nelson's brilliant manœuvre had effectually frustrated the Spanish design: 'we turned them,' declared his flag-captain, 'more like two dogs turning a flock of sheep than anything else I know of'; abandoning all hope of joining their consorts, the enemy ships resumed their northerly course. The mêlée thus brought on was the turning-point of the action.

The *Captain* was speedily joined by the *Culloden*; and for the best part of an hour the two 74s engaged three Spanish first-rates and two sail of the line. Actually the odds were not quite so desperate as they might at first sight have appeared: the Spanish ships were sailing in close, confused order and had difficulty in pointing their guns without hitting one another; their gunnery, too, was contemptible; otherwise the *Captain* might well have been blown out of the water. Somewhat later the *Blenheim* came up from astern and Jervis, having signalled to Collingwood in the *Excellent* to support Nelson, was himself beating back into the fray. For an hour Saumarez in the *Orion* engaged the great three-decker *Salvador del Mundo* before she finally surrendered; and the *San Isidro* struck to Collingwood; who, said Nelson, 'disdaining the parade of taking possession of beaten enemies, most gallantly pushed up, with every sail set, to save his old friend and messmate, who was to appearance in a critical state.' The *Blenheim* had fallen to leeward, while the *Culloden* was crippled and astern. The *Excellent* ranged up within ten feet of the *San Nicolas*, pouring in 'a most tremendous fire', and then standing on for the *Santissima Trinidad*. The tumult and the fighting swept on and away from the *Captain*, as she lay practically disabled; and presently occurred one of the most dramatic incidents in our naval history.

The *San Nicolas*, which was already badly damaged, fell aboard the *San Josef*, which was in no better condition: whereupon Nelson had the battered *Captain* laid alongside the nearest enemy—the *San Nicolas*—her spritsail yard hooking in the mizen shrouds of the Spaniard; then while some of the *Captain*'s people swarmed up her spritsail yard and dropped from it on to the enemy's deck, Captain Berry[1] made a leap for the mizen-chains of the *San Nicolas* and Nelson led a boarding-party into her starboard quarter. Berry was supported by a stream of boarders dropping down from the spritsail yard and swarming up on the poop. After a brief tussle Nelson and his men pushed through to the quarter-deck, where they found Captain Berry in possession of the poop, and the Spanish ensign hauling down. Some of the enemy opened fire on them from the stern gallery of the *San Josef*; following which Nelson, shouting to his flag-captain to send more men into the *San Nicolas*, and posting sentinels over the hatchways of their prize, ordered his party to board the *San Josef*. Berry immediately helped him into the main chains. But at this moment a Spanish officer, looking down from the quarter-deck rail, cried out that the *San Josef* had surrendered; and Nelson went up with his men on to the quarter-deck of the great three-decker, where the Spanish captain, on bended knee, presented him his sword. Surrounded by a group of old 'Agamemnons', the Commodore then received the swords of the Spanish officers, handing them to William Fearney, his coxswain, who stuffed them 'with the greatest sangfroid under his arm'. As the *Victory* at that moment sailed past them she saluted with three cheers, 'as did every Ship in the Fleet'. 'It was at this moment also', relates an eye-witness, 'that an honest Jack Tar, an old acquaintance of Nelson's, came up to him in the fulness of his heart, and excusing the liberty he was taking, asked to shake him by the hand, to congratulate him upon

---

[1] Berry was at the time a passenger in the *Captain*, which was commanded by Captain Miller, who was, like Hallowell, a New Englander by birth. Essentially a man of action—impulsive, daring, and headstrong—Berry was in his element in this fight.

seeing him safe on the quarter-deck of a Spanish three-decker.'[1] This remarkable feat—which from beginning to end had occupied rather less than fifteen minutes—caught the imagination of the lower deck, and was acclaimed throughout the squadron as *'Nelson's Patent Bridge for boarding First-Rates'*. After making a prize of the *Salvador del Mundo* Saumarez stood after the *Santissima Trinidad*, and, closely engaging her, compelled her to strike. Before he could take possession of this splendid prize, however, Jervis signalled the fleet to wear and come to the wind; with the result that the *Santissima Trinidad*—the largest vessel then afloat—escaped to fight again eight years later at Trafalgar.

Late in the afternoon Jervis interposed his squadron in line between his four prizes and the defeated Spaniards—still seventeen to Jervis's fifteen (the six other Spanish ships comprised the mercury convoy). While the British shaped a course for Lagos, the Spanish fleet withdrew under cover of night to Cadiz and were there blockaded by the victors.

Tremendous enthusiasm was aroused at home by the news of the victory; for, coming as it did when the outlook was black indeed, it put new life into the British people. The year 1796 had closed disastrously for the Allies, and 1797 looked like being little better. Great Britain herself showed signs of cracking under the strain. Consols had dropped to 51—a figure lower than any recorded in the disastrous American War. In the Navy discontent was rife and was on the point of coming to a head. The peace negotiations which had recently been begun with the French Republic had resulted in the British envoy being ordered out of France.

Now the sky suddenly lightened. The superb fighting efficiency of Jervis's fleet, and the inferiority of Spain at sea, were alike made manifest. The entire scheme of French naval strategy had collapsed; and all fear of an overwhelming hostile concentration and invasion was at an end. The battle of St. Vincent possibly saved England. It certainly saved the Government. The Cabinet's relief was reflected in the profusion of honours and awards which were presently showered upon the principal commanders. Parliament formally voted them its thanks. Jervis was raised to the peerage as the Earl of St. Vincent with a pen-

[1] Col. John Drinkwater, *A Narrative of the Battle of St. Vincent* (1840), p. 45.

sion of £3,000 a year.[1] The subordinate admirals were made baronets.

Nelson, who on 20 February had been promoted to the rank of rear-admiral, was invested with the Order of the Bath. From this time on his name was a household word among his fellow-countrymen. The fame he had so ardently desired was his in full measure. 'My reception from John Bull has been just what I wished', he confessed to St. Vincent. About this time Nelson assumed the appearance made familiar to us by the most famous of his portraits—the slight, eager figure, the empty right sleeve, the shock of rumpled white hair, the pouting lips, the strangely blue eyes. Even the failure of the heroic attempt, in mid-July, on the great island fortress of Teneriffe, which had lost Nelson his right arm and very nearly cost him his life, only served to enhance his renown both at home and overseas. Accompanied by his servant, Tom Allen—an old retainer of the Nelsons, who had followed him to sea in '93—he set off by post-chaise, on his return home six weeks later, to join his wife and father at Bath.

[1] The government had actually decided on this honour a fortnight before the action, on Spencer's representation that 'the economy with which this fleet has been conducted, and above all the perfection of efficiency and order to which it had been disciplined, had never been rivalled in the British Navy'. Seldom, indeed, was a peerage better deserved than that conferred upon St. Vincent.

III

The Naval Mutinies

I

Despite the victory of St. Valentine's Day, the year 1797 has sometimes been described as the darkest hour in our history. On land, France was everywhere victorious. The British Army had been driven off the Continent, leaving the great ports of the Scheldt and Rhine in enemy hands. The British Navy had been obliged to abandon Corsica and the Mediterranean. Austria, the last of our Allies, was about to lay down her arms. The West Indian islands taken by Jervis and Grey had been lost. A formidable army of invasion was encamped by the Texel ready to be ferried across to the British Isles under convoy of the Dutch fleet. 'Nothing talked of at present', wrote Parson Woodforde that spring, 'but an Invasion of England by the French.' Ireland, smouldering with rebellion, could scarcely be held if ever the enemy landed in force. Now it was no longer France, but Great Britain, that stood alone against Europe. Once again the harvest had failed. The National Debt had risen by the then enormous sum of £135 millions. The Bank of England had recently suspended payment in gold. British shipping losses this year reached the alarming total of 949 vessels—more than 11 per cent. of our foreign-going shipping; the national finances were strained by unprecedented taxation; the invasion alarm had occasioned a run on the banks. And on the morning of 17 April the news reached London that the whole Channel fleet had mutinied.

To some extent the genesis of the insurrection is, even to this day, shrouded in mystery. Conditions on the lower deck, bad as they were, were certainly no worse than before: on the contrary, they had somewhat improved. It is significant, moreover, that mutiny broke out spontaneously at a number of places, both at home and overseas, at about the same time and after the same period of fomentation. It apparently took the government by surprise. For this there was no justification, for, after all, they had had ample warning. Two years earlier Rear-Admiral Philip Patton had addressed a memorandum on the subject of the seamen's grievances to Spencer, who showed it to some of his colleagues. Again, towards the close of 1796 Captain Pakenham had warned the First Lord that the pay of A.B.s was grossly insufficient. Above all, anonymous petitions, in sufficient number to suggest that a storm was gathering up, had been received by Howe (still the nominal Commander-in-Chief of the Channel squadron) while he was on sick leave at Bath, and by him forwarded to the Admiralty,[1] where they were examined and discussed at the next Board meeting. There followed genteel murmurings about 'the risk of unpleasant consequences' and the matter was shelved. By the spring of 1797 a general and deep-rooted discontent pervaded the lower deck in relation to the scale and time of payment, prize-money, food, clothing, leave, and discipline. The seamen's grievances were unquestionably known to Codrington (first lieutenant of the *Queen Charlotte*), as well as to various other officers, to the Admiralty, and to the Cabinet. They had one and all been ignored. Finally, when Bridport came up to town on private business he had failed to inform the Admiralty of all the gathering unrest and of the indignation meetings held almost daily in the squadron; and, on his return to Spithead to assume the command, he had omitted to inform even his subordinate admirals.

The early years of Spencer's term of office as First Lord were by no means so successful as the later ones. He was young, capable, energetic, and conscientious; he had brought new standards of method and punctuality to the administration of the Admiralty: but he lacked ministerial experience and knew little of naval affairs; he was, besides, arbitrary and incautious, and over-confident in his own powers; in the past few months he had managed to fall out with Sir Charles Middleton, for many years the real power behind the throne at the Admiralty— with the result that the latter at last resigned; and he had driven into retirement several of our most distinguished admirals. By the time of the mutinies, however, he may be said to have found his feet at the Admiralty; and if the crisis was unfortunately handled in its initial stages much of the credit for the ultimate settlement of the affair belongs to Spencer.

With the wind at south-west, Bridport was instructed by the

[1] Adm. 1/107, 15 April 1797.

Admiralty to send Gardner's squadron down to St. Helens. The order to weigh precipitated the outbreak; at sunrise the crew of the flagship *Queen Charlotte* suddenly manned the shrouds and gave three defiant cheers, their example being followed by the crews of the surrounding ships. The ringleaders then put off in a boat and toured the fleet, requesting each crew to send two delegates to the flagship that evening. The delegates were duly elected and assembled in council in Howe's cabin on board the *Queen Charlotte*.

During the next few days, though the normal routine of the ships was observed, the men refused to weigh anchor until their grievances had been redressed 'except the enemy are at sea and a convoy wanted'. As they declared in a public petition to the Commons on the 18th, they had already 'laid their grievances before the Honourable Earl Howe, and flattered ourselves with the hopes, that his Lordship would have been an advocate for us'. Their principal demands were for a rise in pay (this was still on the same scale as that obtaining in the reign of Charles II, while the pay of the merchant seaman was no less than four times the naval rate), a more equitable division of prize-money, better victuals, and more humane treatment for their sick and wounded. The insurgents were unanimous and determined. Marines as well as seamen took an oath to support the uprising—the very patients in Haslar hospital broke into cheers at the news of the mutiny. Strict discipline prevailed among the revolting crews, and officers were treated with obedience and respect.[1] The delegates were no scallywags. They were prime seamen—in fact, the *élite* of the lower deck, A.B.s and petty officers to a man; and the whole fleet was behind them. There is no evidence whatever to support the view that the mutiny was politically inspired. The General Assembly continued to meet in the great cabin of the *Queen Charlotte*; yard-ropes were rove at the fore yard-arm of each vessel; and at eight o'clock every morning and at sunset the crews manned the yards and cheered.

Though Spencer hurried down to Portsmouth on the night of the

---

[1] Some of the more unpopular officers, however, were ordered out of their ships. Thus the captain and six other officers of the *Hind* frigate received the following anonymous note: 'Gentlemen, it is the request of the ship's company that you leave the ship precisely at eight o'clock. . . . As it is unanimously agreed that you should leave the ship we would wish you to leave it peaceable or desperate methods will be taken' (Manwaring and Dobrée, *The Floating Republic*, p. 86).

17th with two junior Lords and the Secretary of the Admiralty, he was at first disposed to underrate the gravity of the crisis. But on the 20th, after a long consultation with Bridport, three other admirals, and sixteen captains, who urged the immediate concession of the men's demands, the Admiralty party agreed to most, though not all, of the provisions in question. At a stormy meeting with the delegates on board the *Queen Charlotte*, Gardner, losing his temper, strode up on the forecastle and told the indignant seamen that they were 'skulking fellows, who knew the French were ready for sea, and yet were afraid of meeting them; that their reasons for disobedience were mere pretences; their conduct sheer hypocrisy; for that cowardice, and cowardice alone, had given birth to the mutiny'. Following this imprudent and quite groundless accusation, the angry old man was hustled out of the ship. The red flag was then hoisted, and the General Assembly presently informed their Lordships that it had been resolved, until there was full concessions of all their demands, 'the grievances of private ships redressed, an act passed, and His Majesty's gracious pardon for the fleet now lying at Spithead be granted, that the fleet will not lift an anchor: and this is the total and final answer'.

Once more, confronted with a major crisis, Spencer acted promptly. He set out from Portsmouth at midnight on the 21st, and, arriving in town at nine o'clock the next morning, went to Pitt and demanded an immediate Cabinet council. In the afternoon, accompanied by Pitt and the Lord Chancellor, he drove down to Windsor to secure the King's pardon, which was read out on board the fleet on the 23rd. This terminated the first phase of the mutiny; and the following day most of the vessels dropped down to St. Helens to await a fair wind for Brest. There the trouble might have ended if only Bridport could there and then have got the fleet to sea. But while the ships lay windbound in the roads the suspicions of the crews were once more awakened by the dilatory procedure of Parliament and certain ill-advised actions on the part of the Admiralty; so that when the wind became fair on Sunday, 7 May, and Bridport made the signal to sail, the seamen once again manned the shrouds and cheered.[1]

The second phase of the mutiny was accompanied by violence and bloodshed. The *London*, with two other ships, under the command of Rear-Admiral Colpoys, was still at Spithead. Colpoys having

[1] Adm. 1/107, 7 May 1797.

determined to maintain his authority by force, a savage scuffle ensued, in the course of which several seamen were mortally wounded, and the Admiral narrowly escaped hanging. Colpoys, his flag-captain, and the first lieutenant (who had been in the thick of the fighting) were led off to their cabins and kept under close arrest. The Admiral's flag was struck and the 'bloody flag of defiance' run up in its place. Fortunately for the imprisoned officers the news reached the *London* shortly after that the House of Commons had passed the 'seamen's bill'; and on 10 May the three officers were put ashore. On the 7th and several succeeding days a considerable number of officers were ordered to leave their ships.[1] They were taken ashore and unceremoniously dumped, together with their belongings, on the quay-side.

Gloom and foreboding lay heavy upon the inhabitants of Portsmouth. They assembled in hundreds on the ramparts and beaches to watch the coming and going of boats laden with officers who had been summarily dismissed their ships, guarded by piratical figures each armed with a brace of pistols and a cutlass. Courts and side-streets which had once resounded with the halloing of jovial tars and their Polls were now ominously silent. The gates of the military garrison at Portsmouth were shut and the drawbridge was hauled up; guns were planted at the Point gates to command the landing-place at the new sally port. The workaday life of the great arsenal was overshadowed by the dread fact of the mutiny. 'The horror and confusion of this town are beyond description,' recorded the *Morning Post*; and added later: 'The whole town wears a most gloomy appearance and every countenance betrays the most evident anxiety'.

Meanwhile the conflagration had spread to other ports. On 26 April, as the result of representations from the fleet at Spithead, mutiny broke out at Plymouth. Throughout the crisis the seamen of the two ports were in close communication; and the mutineers at Plymouth followed the same policy as their brethren at Spithead. On 30 April there was a minor outbreak on board the *Venerable*, the flagship of the North Sea squadron, at Yarmouth. It was quickly settled; the men were questioned about their grievances, and then, on receiving satisfactory assurances, returned at once to their duty.

By this time the 'seamen's bill' had been hurriedly passed through both Houses of Parliament. The Royal assent had been given, and a

[1] *Ibid.*, 8 May 1797.

number of copies printed forthwith for distribution in the fleet. To the King and Spencer belongs the credit of dispatching Howe, at this critical juncture, to Portsmouth as the government's emissary and plenipotentiary. 'Black Dick' was without doubt an ideal choice for such a mission. Both as captain and admiral he had been adored by the men under his command. He was trusted by the lower deck as was no other flag officer. He arrived at Portsmouth on the 11th and at once had himself rowed across the Solent to St. Helens, where he boarded in turn the *Royal George, Queen Charlotte*, and *Duke*, addressed the ships' companies, and later met the delegates of the other ships. During the next few days Howe set to work, with infinite tact and patience, to convince the crews that the official promises would be made good, and the general amnesty strictly observed. He made no attempt to talk down to the men, as had the authorities in the early stages of the mutiny: but dealt with them freely and frankly, as was 'Black Dick's' way, as man to man. In spite of his age and infirmities he proceeded to visit each vessel in turn, making long speeches to the crews, and also had several meetings with the General Assembly.

One of the urgent problems he had to solve lay in the persistent refusal of the crews to take back the more unpopular characters among the large number of officers that they had sent out of the ships. 'However ineligible the concession,' Howe declared, 'it was become indispensably necessary.' And 'applications being made,' he continued, 'on the part of the officers themselves, entreating that they might not be required to resume their command over men who had taken such exception to their conduct, I judged fit to acquiesce in what was now the mutual desire of both officers and seamen in the fleet.'[1] About one half of the officers who had been set ashore were, however, permitted to return.

On the return on the 13th of Sir Roger Curtis's squadron from Plymouth, Howe at once boarded these ships also and satisfied their crews. Next day the signal was made by Admiralty telegraph that the amended royal pardon was on its way; and great were the rejoicings ashore and afloat. May 15 was a gala day. Portsmouth, Gosport, and Southsea were in holiday mood and the beaches thronged with spectators. In the early morning a large number of ships' boats arrived at the sally port; and the delegates marched in procession up to the Governor's House with the massed bands of the fleet playing alternately, 'God Save

[1] Adm. 1/4172, 16 May 1797.

the King' and 'Rule, Britannia'. They were invited inside to partake of refreshments, and later appeared on the balcony to the unrestrained delight of the multitude below. Shortly after, an imposing procession of boats, composed of Lord and Lady Howe, the Governor and his lady, the delegates, and a great many officers, set out for the anchorage at St. Helens and the final act of reconciliation. Going on board the *Royal George*, Howe stood on her quarter-deck and read out the royal pardon in its amended form to the assembled ship's company, holding up the document so that all could see the royal seal. Three tremendous cheers were given. Then the yard-ropes were taken down and the red flag replaced with the royal standard. All the other ships followed suit. The afternoon was spent in a tour of Curtis's squadron. On their return to Portsmouth the procession was greeted by wildly cheering crowds and the *feux de joie* of the military. The now exhausted Admiral was borne shoulder high—with the Union Jack waving triumphantly above him—up to the Governor's House, where the day's jubilations ended with a grand banquet given to the delegates by Lord and Lady Howe, with loyal toasts and speeches. On the following day the Channel fleet put to sea.

2

The most dangerous outbreak of all occurred on 12 May at the Nore, and continued for several weeks after the general settlement had been reached at Spithead. At the height of the mutiny no less than twenty-four line-of-battleships were involved, in addition to a good many lesser vessels. The same forms and ceremonies were observed as at Spithead—the cheering, the hoisting of yard-ropes and red flags, and the election of delegates. Every day the mutineers landed in large numbers at Sheerness and marched through the streets in procession or rowed around the harbour with brass bands playing 'Rule, Britannia', 'God Save the King', and 'Britons, Strike Home'. Most of the officers were either imprisoned on board the ships or sent ashore.

The mutineers at the Nore, unlike those at Spithead, had no clear objective in view and never put forward any specific demands. They were led by an ex-officer, Richard Parker, one of the crew of the *Sandwich*, who showed none of the moderation and restraint which had marked the conduct of the delegates of the Channel fleet. Parker and his principal lieutenants, believing that the government would in the end be obliged to concede their demands, conducted themselves with extreme insolence. They presently informed Vice-Admiral Buckner that 'no accommodation could take place until the appearance of the Lords of Admiralty at the Nore'. On 23 May Buckner's flag was struck, and a red flag hoisted at the fore on board the flagship *Sandwich* and other mutinous vessels. On the 24th Parker again refused the Admiralty's offer of a conditional pardon. When Spencer and two of his colleagues arrived in Sheerness to negotiate with the mutineers, they found that they could do nothing in the face of Parker's intransigence; using old Admiral Buckner as their intermediary, on the 27th they informed the delegates that they could only be admitted to an interview if they came to make their submission and to ask for pardon; by this time Spencer had gained some insight into the minds and behaviour of the seamen, and he made no mistake in his policy; his colleagues and he refused to make any further concessions, and in the end returned to London.

Towards the end of May mutiny broke out in the North Sea squadron. The outbreak started on board the flagship; there it failed owing to the forceful character and great personal popularity of the commander-in-chief, old Admiral Duncan, a veteran of more than fifty years' service,[1] and the staunchness of the marines under Major Trolloppe. The crew of the *Venerable* had given the usual signal for mutiny by breaking into three defiant cheers. The uproar brought the Admiral instantly to the break of the quarter-deck. Descending wrathfully and unhesitatingly into their midst, he first rated them severely and then dismissed them. 'In all my service', he later declared, 'I have maintained my authority, which I will not easily part with.' Shortly after there was another outbreak on board the *Adamant*. Duncan immediately boarded the ship, hoisted his flag, and mustered the ship's company. In response to his demand whether any man among them presumed to challenge his authority, one of the crew stepped forward and gruffly replied, 'I do'. Old Duncan at once seized him by the collar and held him suspended at arm's length over the side, crying, 'My lads, look at this fellow, he who dares to deprive me of the command of the

[1] 'They say as how they are going to make a Lord of our Admiral. They can't make too much of him. He is heart of oak; he is a seaman every inch of him, and as to a bit of a broadside,' wrote one of Duncan's seamen after Camperdown, 'it only makes the old cock young again' (Q. Earl of Camperdown, *Admiral Duncan* (1898), p. 359).

fleet!' Thereafter there was no more trouble on board either the *Venerable* or *Adamant*, the crews remaining staunch and obedient to their officers. But the rest of the squadron were on the brink of mutiny. 'Yarmouth', wrote one of the midshipmen in the *Nassau*, 'is at present in an uproar: the seamen committing depredations, beating & evil treating all the inhabitants & breaking windows etc. so that no people venture out after dusk.' When Duncan gave the order to weigh nearly all his ships left him and returned to the Nore 'to redress their grievances'.[1]

'They now muster 15 sail of the line & 9 frigates and God knows where it will end,' related the midshipman quoted above. 'His Majesty will not give pardon until the heads are given up to the law, but the seamen will not hear of anything of the kind. Their cruelties to the officers are shocking in most ships. In one they tarr'd & feathered the surgeon & sent him on shore in that state, & in another they flogged the midshipman and a second master, shaved their heads & left one lock of hair in the crown of the head to be hauled up (as the Turks have it) by Mahomet, & then towed them round the fleet playing the Rogues' March as they went along & many other disgraceful punishments that I cannot relate without shuddering. They have hung Wm. Pitt in effigy in all the ships.'[2]

Though the delegates had in no way abated their truculent and aggressive demeanour, the mutiny at the end of the month seemed bound to collapse in a matter of days; but the arrival of most of the ships of Duncan's squadron had greatly heartened the mutineers, whose strength was thereby more than doubled. The effect of these reinforcements was to prolong and intensify the struggle.

In the first week of June an address in the form of a stern remonstrance 'from the Seamen at Spithead' was dispatched to 'their Brethren at the Nore' and must have given the cooler heads among the latter, at least, much food for thought.

> *Brother Sailors*: It is with the utmost concern we see that several ships' companies continue in a state of disaffection and illegal proceedings, notwithstanding every demand made by our Brethren in Lord Bridport's fleet have been most graciously granted to Us by his Majesty and both Houses of Parliament assembled. ... We have wrote these lines while

[1] *Q. C. C. Lloyd in Mariner's Mirror*, Vol. 46 (1960), pp. 287–8.
[2] *Ibid.*, p. 292.

unmooring, and preparing to go out to sea to face our enemies, and to protect the Commerce of our Country, which as Seamen it is our duty to encourage to the utmost of our power. We have a full reliance that all our Brother Seamen who labour under any grievances will make no unreasonable demands, nor delay an amicable settlement by standing out for trifling objects.[1]

The attitude of the government hardened; Rear-Admiral Lord Keith and General Sir Charles Grey were sent down to Sheerness to concert naval and military measures for the suppression of the mutiny: but with so many officers still held by the rebels as hostages, the authorities were naturally reluctant to proceed to extremes. However, public opinion turned decisively against the mutineers, and the provisions of the ships at the Nore were stopped. On 2 June by way of reprisals the rebels blockaded the Thames and plundered a number of merchantmen and fishing vessels attempting to enter or leave the river. The trade of the Port of London was for a time suspended and 3 per cent. consols dropped to $45\frac{1}{2}$—the lowest in their history. The government thereupon had all the buoys and beacons in the estuary removed, which effectually cut off the retreat of the rebel fleet; the forts at Tilbury, Gravesend, and Sheerness were provided with furnaces for red-hot shot; a flotilla of gun-boats was prepared; communication with the revolting crews was forbidden; and calling on the aid of the military, the merchants, and such ships as had continued loyal, the government was eventually able to blockade and isolate the ships containing the ringleaders. 'We are here as in a besieged town,' wrote a correspondent of the *Oracle and Public Advertiser* from Sheerness; 'no vessel, not even a wherry, is allowed to pass from the river; row-boats, and patrols of soldiers, are out day and night.' The growing bewilderment and frustration of the rank and file was well expressed in a letter addressed to the Admiralty by one of the ship's company of the frigate *Champion*.

Dam my eyes if I understand your lingo and long proclamations, but, in short, give us our due at once, and no more of it, till we go in search of the rascals the enemys of our country.

It was apparent that the men were not unanimous and discontent with their leaders grew. On 6 June the government formally declared the mutineers rebels, though still holding out its offer of conditional pardon. On the 9th, when Parker proposed to take the fleet over to the Texel,

[1] *The Times*, 4 June 1797.

the crews refused to sail.[1] The *Repulse* and *Leopard* were recaptured by their officers, ran down through the fleet, and, though a good deal damaged, sought refuge under the guns of Sheerness. In many ships quarrels and fights broke out among the crews, in the course of which a number of lives were lost. The mutiny was now fast breaking up: the desire of the majority was to make their peace with the authorities; most of the ships were short of food and water; the delegates found that their influence was passing from them; the mutinous faction put up a desperate but unavailing resistance, and were ultimately overpowered. During the next few days a number of the mutineers got away to France and Holland, including some of the principal ringleaders. On the 10th several ships hauled down their red flags, and the river traffic was again permitted to pass. Keith went on board some of the ships and made numerous arrests. By the 12th the mutiny was virtually ended. One by one the ships struck the red flag, slipped their cables, and sailed off to surrender to the authorities. Before nightfall on the 13th the bulk of the revolting crews had signified their willingness to submit if a general pardon were granted. Finally the crew of the *Sandwich* returned to their duty and handed over Parker to the military. The mutineers having been obliged to surrender unconditionally, Parker and twenty-eight other leaders were tried, found guilty, and hanged. A number of others were flogged round the fleet.

3

The menace from the Texel had overhung England all through the summer of 1797. In the Board Room at Admiralty anxious glances were directed at the wind-dial mounted on the north wall whenever the wind happened to hang in the east. Month after month Adam Duncan had maintained an unrelaxing blockade of the hostile invasion base. After the desertion of almost his entire squadron, the old Admiral in his flagship, the *Venerable*, together with the *Adamant*, continued to blockade the enemy. 'Shall therefore', he informed Spencer, 'continue off the Texel and make up as well as I can for the want of my fleet by making a number of signals as if the fleet was in the offing. . . . I

---

[1] It is said that when the crew of the *Nassau* heard of the proposal to escape to Holland, they all replied, 'No, we'll be damned if we leave Old England whatever happens to us' (Conrad Gill, *The Naval Mutinies*, p. 232).

never was closer in. As the wind favoured going along the shore, I was not a mile from the break in the land.'[1] So long as the wind was easterly and favourable for the escape of the Dutch, he anchored in the narrow channel off the Texel and kept his men at quarters. His small force was ordered to fight to the last. If the worst came to the worst, he told them, 'the soundings were so shallow that his flag would still fly above the shoal water after the ship and company had disappeared'. When the wind shifted to the west, he stood out to sea again. He thus maintained the blockade with only two of the line, signalling, as has been said, to an imaginary squadron below the horizon. However, he was not left

The North Sea

[1] *Spencer Papers*, II, p. 147.

long unsupported. Not many days later Sir Roger Curtis was ordered to join him with six ships of the Channel fleet; and other ships were sent out to him, including the small Russian squadron. The worst of the danger was over when these reinforcements arrived. When the mutiny was finally put down, the rest of Duncan's squadron returned to their station off the Texel.

In July, the wind coming east, the enemy's troops actually began to board their transports: but navigational conditions that summer were usually unfavourable to the Dutch design: the essential combination of wind and tide was lacking, and a long spell of westerly winds ensued. On board one of the Dutch vessels was the Irish leader, Wolfe Tone: 'Wind foul still,' he recorded in his journal on 19 July; '. . . I am to-day eighteen days on board', he added on the 26th, 'and we have not had eighteen minutes of fair wind.' On the 30th: 'In the morning early the wind was fair, the signal given to prepare to get under way and everything ready, when, at the very instant we were about to weigh anchor and put to sea, the wind chopped about and left us'.[1]

While the stormy westerly weather continued the blockading squadron was hard put to it to remain on its station, and to take on board provisions and water from the victuallers: which at times, indeed, proved impossible.

'We have sent you out wine, fresh meat and water', wrote Spencer to Duncan towards the end of July, 'and will continue to supply you with those necessary refreshments on every opportunity, as it would be wrong to quit your station at present.' A fortnight later Duncan was able to reassure him. 'We have got the oxen, sheep, &c., and water; they joined yesterday about mid-day, and will this day be all cleared. . . . I expect we will be able to hold out as long as the weather is favourable.'[2]

During this long delay Hoche died; and with him perished all hope of a successful *coup* in Ireland. In August the Irish project was abandoned in favour of a large-scale raid against the sister island. Apparently out of national pique, de Wynter was ordered to sea to engage the British should there be any reasonable prospect of success.

With the approach of autumn came a succession of westerly gales. The sails and rigging of Duncan's squadron suffered severely, as he presently informed the Admiralty; moreover, after a cruise lasting

[1] *Autobiography of Theobald Wolfe Tone*, II, pp. 244, 246, 247-8.
[2] *Spencer Papers*, II, pp. 186, 190.

nineteen weeks symptoms of scurvy had begun to appear in the fleet.

On Friday night last a strong gale of wind came on at WNW, and for sixteen hours blew a mere hurricane, during which period the *Agincourt* and *Warrior* made the signal of distress. . . . The *Inflexible* is very leaky her main and mizen mast sprung. The *Naiad*'s foremast and bowsprit badly so. The *Circe* carried away most of her main shrouds, and the *Venerable* two of hers, which are replaced with others. I have had no return from the other ships and therefore cannot say what state they are in. The wind has shifted to the SE with every appearance of a gale. Indeed it is blowing so hard at present that I am under the necessity of putting this letter into a keg, in order to convey it on board the lugger.[1]

On 14 September the weather moderated, but it was so hazy that Duncan could only count seventeen sail in company. The Admiralty ordered him to return with the squadron to Yarmouth roads, to refit and complete stores and provisions, and then to proceed to sea again as expeditiously as possible. On 1 October, the wind south-westerly, 'with every appearance of continuing', Duncan accordingly crossed to Yarmouth, ready to return to the Texel, where his frigates and cutters kept vigilant watch over the Dutch fleet, 'the moment the wind shall change to the eastward.'[2]

A few days after the wind at last came east. The *Venerable* was taking in provisions in Yarmouth roads, on the morning of 9 October, when a lugger appeared at the back of the sands and signalled that the enemy were coming out: whereupon Duncan, with eleven of the line, instantly weighed and stood over to the Dutch coast, leaving the rest of his squadron to follow.[3]

As soon as de Wynter put to sea on the 6th, our small inshore squadron, under the command of Captain Trolloppe of the *Russell*, had cleared for action, and, having early secured the weather-gauge, hung for the next three days on the enemy's flank.[4] On the morning of the 11th, with a lumping sea rising under the dark, heavily overcast sky, and the wind variable and moderate, the hostile fleet bore S. by W., distant about four miles. Duncan joined hands with Trolloppe; at noon threw out the signal for close action; and, shortly after, brought the enemy to action three leagues N.W. of Camperdown.

[1] Adm. 1/524, 11 September 1797.
[2] *Ibid.*, 1 October 1797.
[3] *Ibid.*, 13 October 1797.
[4] Adm. 51/1235, 6–10 October 1797.

The rival fleets numbered sixteen sail of the line on either side; but the Dutch ships were lighter and less powerful than Duncan's. The latter, having the wind, steered between the enemy and the shore, in order to cut off his line of retreat. 'At nine o'clock in the morning of the 11th,' wrote Duncan in his dispatch, 'I got sight of Captain Trolloppe's squadron, with signals flying for an enemy to leeward; I immediately bore up, and made the signal for a general chace, and soon got sight of them forming in a line on the larboard tack to receive us, the wind at N.W. As we approached near I made the signal for the squadron to shorten sail, in order to connect them; soon after I saw the land between Camperdown and Egmont, about nine miles to leeward of the enemy, and finding there was no time to be lost in making the attack, I made the signal to bear up, break the enemy's line, and engage them to leeward, each ship her opponent, by which I got between them and the land, whither they were fast approaching.'[1]

De Wynter lay so close to the shoals that Duncan, to close the enemy without delay, approached in two columns, each comprising eight ships, sailing in line ahead, almost at right angles to the Dutch line.[2] With the enemy's fleet thus 'crossing his T', Duncan ran the risk of having his ships heavily raked by the Dutchman's fire. But he achieved his purpose. His second-in-command, Vice-Admiral Richard Onslow, in the *Monarch*, outsailed his admiral and cut the enemy's line, bringing nine ships against five of the Dutch. Shortly after the *Venerable*, leading the lee division with the *Triumph* and *Ardent* in close support, engaged the enemy's flagship, the *Vrijheid*, lying fifth from the van. For a while the *Venerable*, surrounded by several of the enemy's ships of equal strength, was in extreme peril. Other ships arrived to her assistance, however, and achieved a concentration similar to that which had already developed on the Dutch rear. 'I began a close action', wrote the Admiral, 'with my division on their van, which lasted near two hours and a half, when I observed all the masts of the Dutch Admiral's ship go by the board.'[3] The rest of Duncan's vessels gradually came up, broke through the line—thereby dividing the Dutch fleet into three roughly equal

[1] Adm. 1/524, 13 October.
[2] 'There was no time for tactique or manœuvre,' observed Captain Hotham of the *Adamant*: 'the day was advanced, the wind on shore, the water shoal; and hence the charge against him of going down in some confusion on the enemy's fleet' (Q. Camperdown, *Admiral Duncan* (1898), p. 223).
[3] Adm. 1/524, 13 October 1797.

groups—and, gaining the leeward berth, closely engaged the enemy.

Throughout the action the Dutch fought with the stubborn courage and grim tenacity of their race. Their first two broadsides inflicted terrible losses on board Duncan's fleet: but afterwards the British gunnery showed itself markedly superior. As on the Glorious First, the powerful armament of carronades carried on board the British ships gave them a substantial advantage over the Dutch, who had none. The action lasted for three and a half hours. Ship after ship of de Wynter's fleet struck. His own flagship—surrounded by foes, her hull riddled with shot, her masts trailing over her sides, and her scuppers streaming blood—fought until de Wynter himself was the only un-wounded man on deck. The carnage on board the *Venerable* was hardly less terrific. 'The pilot and myself', Duncan recorded in his dispatch, 'were the only two unhurt on the quarterdeck left alive.'[1] On the Dutch side, the *Jupiter*, *Hercules*, and the *Monnikendam* frigate also distin-guished themselves. Eight more of de Wynter's ships, besides the *Vrijheid*, finally struck their colours. Each one of these was dismasted and practically a wreck; two of them sank on the way to England. The gathering dusk, the strong wind, and the vicinity of a dangerous lee shore prevented Duncan from pursuing the remaining Dutch ships, which eventually escaped into port.

The evening of 11 October set in with a rising gale and heavy rain-squalls. Across a dark and foam-flecked sea rolling shoreward under the stormy, lowering sky lay the long flat coastline of Holland, broken here and there by a steeple or windmill. Duncan's ships found themselves in but nine fathoms of water and within five miles of the land. During the next few days they were much dispersed by the gale. The admirable seamanship of the captains and crews enabled them with difficulty to keep off the shore and to work to seaward. On the 13th the wind, which had been blowing hard from W.S.W. to W.N.W., shifted at last to the north; and the battered squadron struggled home across the North Sea. Within six weeks of the mutiny at the Nore had come this resounding victory, which destroyed the formidable Dutch fleet and eliminated the threat from the Texel.

[1] *Ibid.*

4

From the mutinous squadrons at Spithead and the Nore the infection spread to St. Vincent's force blockading Cadiz. Mutiny broke out in the Mediterranean squadron on almost the same day which saw the red flag hoisted on board the *Queen Charlotte*. St. Vincent's difficulties were greatly aggravated by the incompetence and unreliability of his flag officers, several of whom had presently to be sent home. The suppression of these sporadic outbreaks was due in part to the stern discipline imposed by St. Vincent and in part to his unremitting attention to the health and welfare of his men. It was not without justification that he later informed Spencer that his squadron was 'the only part of His Majesty's fleet to be relied on'.

In the meantime the investment of Cadiz was carried on by two divisions—the inshore squadron being composed of the *élite* of the fleet: the nocturnal bombardment of Cadiz by the inshore squadron serving (as the Commander-in-Chief remarked with grim satisfaction) to occupy the minds of the seamen to the exclusion of mutinous inclinations. 'We are carrying on the most active desultory war against the port and town of Cadiz', he observed on 4 July 1797, '*to divert the animal* from these damnable doctrines which letters from England have produced.' Nelson was in his element. 'We are in advance day and night,' he wrote, 'prepared for battle; bulkheads down, ready to weigh, cut, or slip, as the occasion may require.' At the same time St. Vincent had to resist the Government's constant desire to reduce the force under his command by detaching ships and squadrons. There were between thirty and forty of the line in Cadiz, and the Spanish admiral was making strenuous efforts to fit them for sea. 'It is the more necessary', St. Vincent reminded the Admiralty, 'I should be on my guard, nothing being so dangerous as holding an enemy too cheap, and there can be no doubt the Spanish fleet is much better commanded than when I met it last.'

It was during these critical months that he made the strongest representations concerning the delays in the payment of prize money and the too-frequent deficiencies in the supply of food and clothing. He laboured unceasingly to improve the living conditions of the ships' companies: not always with the cooperation of his commanders. For the rest, communication between ship and ship was forbidden except with the express permission of the Commander-in-Chief; and the marines, in whom St. Vincent put great reliance, were ordered to be berthed apart from the seamen. 'I assembled all the Captains of Marines on board the *Ville de Paris*', he wrote later, 'under pretext of informing them about the uniformity of dress, in exercise, and in economy; but really to give them some sense about keeping a watchful eye, not only upon their own men, but upon the seamen. I directed that a subaltern should visit them at their meals; I exhorted them to keep up the pride and spirit in their detachments; to prevent conversation being carried on in Irish, and to call the roll at least twice a day.'

A revealing anecdote related by Captain Edward Brenton serves to show how strong was the impression made on the lower deck by St. Vincent's iron discipline. To one of his seamen lying drunk by the roadside at Gibraltar, the Admiral said gruffly, 'Come, get up; and go on board your ship.' 'No, I shan't,' was the wily response; 'for if I goes on board drunk, that old rascal will hang me.' 'What old rascal do you mean?' asked the Admiral, with a grim smile. 'Why, old Jack, to be sure,' rejoined the culprit—to the secret delight of the Commander-in-Chief.[1]

When the crisis came during this same July, St. Vincent was ready for it. About this time a serious mutiny had broken out in the *St. George*. The four ringleaders were seized and marched on board the flagship, tried and found guilty, sentenced to death, and then, in defiance of all precedent, hanged on the following day, which happened to be a Sunday.[2] The prisoners had begged for five days in which to prepare; but this respite St. Vincent would by no means allow. In five days, he declared, the men would have hatched 'five hundred plots'. It is clear that Nelson completely concurred in this decision. 'We know not what might have been hatched by a Sunday's grog,' was his comment; '*now* your discipline is safe.' Vice-Admiral Thompson publicly protested and was in consequence recalled by the Admiralty. 'I hope I shall not be censured by the Bench of Bishops,' St. Vincent wrote to Spencer, 'as I have been by Vice-Admiral Thompson for profaning the Sabbath.' At the end of the month mutinies in the *Alcmene* and *Emerald* were sternly suppressed and the

---

[1] Brenton, *Life and Correspondence of . . . St. Vincent* (1838), I, p. 380.
[2] Adm. 1/396, 5 and 9 July; 51/1219, 9 July 1797.

ringleaders hanged. 'At present', Jervis observed to Captain Lord Garlies, 'there is every appearance of content and proper subordination.' During the autumn and winter of 1797–8 the Admiral kept vigilant watch over the Spanish squadron blocked up in Cadiz and never for an instant relaxed his rigorous precautions for the discipline and well-being of his ships' companies.

The final struggle occurred in the last week of May 1798 when St. Vincent had just detached ten of his best vessels for service under Nelson in the Mediterranean and he was left blockading Cadiz with a squadron heavily outnumbered by that of the enemy and with several of his ships newly joined from England in a state of almost open mutiny. As a result of his prudent preparations the mutinous ships found themselves anchored in the centre of the fleet; an immediate trial was ordered, and a seaman of the *Marlborough* was found guilty. The Commander-in-Chief ordered him to be hanged on the following morning, 'and by the crew of the *Marlborough* alone, no part of the boats' crews from the other ships, as had been usual on similar occasions, to assist in the punishment'.

The captain of the *Marlborough*, Captain Ellison, having demurred at these measures, was admonished by St. Vincent as follows: 'Captain Ellison,—you are an old Officer, Sir,—have served long— suffered severely in the service, and have lost an arm in action,—and I should be very sorry that any advantages should now be taken of your advanced years. That man *shall* be hanged—at eight o'clock to-morrow morning—*and by his own ship's company*—for not a hand from any other ship in the Fleet shall touch the rope. You will now return on board, Sir; and, lest you should not prove able to command your ship, an Officer will be at hand to you who can.'[1]

The following morning the prisoner was hanged as St. Vincent had decreed;[2] and, though outbreaks of insubordination continued to occur, henceforward the issue was scarcely in doubt. The capital sentence was repeatedly inflicted: in all cases of mutiny the crews were invariably the executioners of their own rebels: and never again was the power of the law doubted by anyone. To a plea for mercy on the grounds of good character, urged by the mutineer's own commander, St. Vincent turned a deaf ear. 'Those who have suffered hitherto', he replied, 'have for

[1] Tucker, *op. cit.*, I, pp. 303–9.
[2] Adm. 51/1200, 29 May 1798.

the most part been worthless fellows; I shall now convince the seamen that no character, however good, shall save a man who is guilty of mutiny.' The lesson was well learned. It was the newcomers on the station, not the old Mediterranean crews, who had yet to learn that rebels would receive short shrift. When the *London* arrived in the Tagus fresh from Spithead, a man in her captain's barge called to a seaman peering out from one of the lower-deck ports in the flagship: 'I say, there, what have you fellows been doing out here, while we have been fighting for your beef and pork?' To which the old hand in question quietly replied: 'If you'll take my advice, you'll just say nothing at all about all that here; for by G – d if old Jarvie hears ye he'll have you dingle dangle at the yard-arm at eight o'clock to-morrow morning.'[1]

[1] Tucker, *op. cit.*, I, p. 312.

IV

The War on Trade, 1793–1802

I

Under the Directory the state of the French fleet, both *matériel* and personnel, was such as to determine France finally to abandon all attempt to dispute the control of the sea with Great Britain; and this policy remained unchanged during the years which followed. The French at this stage resorted to the historic strategy of the *guerre de course*, in which they had for long excelled, and sent out small squadrons of ships of the line and frigates, under some of their most enterprising commanders, to assail our shipping and harass our colonies. Ganteaume in the Levant, Allemand off the west coast of Africa, Richery in North American waters, Leyssègues in the Caribbean, and Sercey in Indian seas, achieved greater or lesser success.

Of all the French admirals Joseph de Richery was the most successful in his attacks on British trade, and to the day of his death skilfully eluded the vigilance of our squadrons. Early in October 1795, with a force of three of the line and six frigates, he attacked our Smyrna convoy out in the Atlantic off Cape St. Vincent, and captured one of the three escort vessels, the *Censeur*, 74, together with thirty out of thirty-one richly laden merchantmen. About the same time a division of French frigates captured eighteen ships of the Jamaica convoy; and more than forty prizes were taken off the Madeiras. During the summer of 1796 Richery fell upon the British Newfoundland fishery and accounted for about 100 fishing vessels, while a division detached under Allemand captured a rich convoy off the coast of Labrador.

As a result of the disappearance of French merchant shipping from the high seas, large numbers of ships and seamen were released for the war on British trade. In innumerable ports, large and small, along the Channel and Atlantic coasts of France, ships were either newly built or else hurriedly adapted and equipped for privateering, and sent to prey on British shipping. These vessels were nearly always fast sailers. Their commanders were selected both for their seamanlike qualities and for their knowledge and experience of the English coast and its traffic. There was at this time no lack in France of such daring and resourceful seamen, who eagerly took great risks in order to gain rich prizes, and yet, by one stratagem or another, managed to avoid capture by the numerous British cruisers. For years to come, indeed, privateering was to be a staple occupation of the French seafaring community.

As Fayle has pointed out, between 1774, just before the outbreak of the War of American Independence, and 1792, on the eve of the French Revolutionary War, the clearances of British vessels at ports in Great Britain had nearly doubled in number. They now amounted to 1,563,744 tons. The total British exports and imports in 1792 had reached the unexampled figure of more than £44½ millions.[1] 'The target which British trade and shipping exposed to attack during the Revolutionary and Napoleonic Wars was far greater than in any earlier conflict. Its defence, too, was of greatly increased importance, owing to the rapid growth of industry, bringing with it increased dependence on overseas sources of supply and foreign markets.'[2]

The port of London handled at this time more than one-half of the total commerce of Great Britain; over and above its extensive overseas trade it was the main centre of a teeming coastal traffic. It has been estimated that the average number of entries and departures of shipping from the Thames amounted to something between 13,000 and 14,000 annually; of this enormous volume of traffic, nearly two-thirds had to pass through the narrow waters of the Channel, while the remainder, comprising all the trade to Holland, North Germany, and the Baltic, as well as the swarming east coast traffic of Great Britain, was only too vulnerable to attack from Boulogne, Calais, Dunkirk, and the Netherlands ports.

In the age of sail, seamanship was a factor of governing importance in a maritime war. This was exemplified to an impressive degree in the *guerre de course* of 1793–1815, especially in the Channel. The superior

[1] This was in terms of 'official values' which had been assigned to specific goods a hundred years before; in terms of 'real values', calculated from current prices, they must have been at least 70 per cent. higher. See Mahan, *The Influence of Sea Power upon the French Revolution and Empire*, II, p. 229 n.

[2] C. E. Fayle in *The Trade Winds*, ed. C. Northcote Parkinson (1948), p. 26.

seamanship and daring of the French privateersmen made it possible for the enemy to inflict grievous and continued blows on the immense seaborne trade of Great Britain. The vast numerical preponderance of the Navy would by no means suffice to protect us against a run of heavy losses; for, however numerous were the British cruisers, they could not be everywhere at once: while the corsairs could almost always choose the place and moment of attack. They would stand off and on along the English coast, in severe or hazy weather, awaiting their opportunity, emerging suddenly from one blinding rain-squall and disappearing in another. The lifelong familiarity of their commanders and crews with the navigational conditions on our side of the Channel—the outlying rocks, sands, and other dangers; the tides and winds, and signs of the weather—would usually give these raiders a decisive advantage over their adversaries.

The fine-lined, three-masted lugger that was becoming increasingly common on the opposite side of the Channel had amply proved its worth as a privateer in the previous war. Short and light as were its masts, they carried a remarkably large area of canvas; and the dipping lug could be reckoned one of the handiest and the most weatherly of rigs. With its light draught, the lugger could sail in shoal water close in to the shore where neither cruisers nor merchantmen dared venture. The privateersmen were well aware that a cutter could never catch a lugger where there was room to work their vessel. The dipping lug was *par excellence* the fishermen's rig; and, as was only to be expected, a large proportion of these privateersmen were fishermen, with an intimate knowledge of our southern coast which their descendants possess to this day.

Winter was the great season for the privateersmen. Their winter campaign may be said to have lasted from the late autumn to the following spring; though November and December were generally the busiest months. It was then that the privateers were out in their maximum strength and brought in the greatest haul of captured vessels. The long moonless nights of winter which favoured the escape of their prizes, the frequent mists and fogs, and the spells of bad weather which dispersed the convoys and made the stragglers an easy prey were the great allies of the marauder. Privateers sailing at sunset with a fair wind from St. Malo and the neighbouring ports would arrive on their cruising grounds before daybreak in the long nights of winter. They would usually make for some headland or other chosen vantage-point, whence they might pounce on their quarry. The favourite hunting-grounds were off the great Channel promontories—Dungeness, Beachy Head, Portland Bill, Start Point, the Lizard, and Land's End; out in the Atlantic off the Isles of Scilly, up the Bristol Channel, and in the Irish Sea.

Perhaps the most lucrative station of all for the privateers in home waters was in the vicinity of Beachy Head, at the eastern extremity of the long range of high chalk cliffs rising at Black Rock, near Brighton. The bold *massif* of this 500-foot headland, coupled with the distinctive profile of the neighbouring Seven Sisters cliffs, made Beachy Head an unmistakable mark, familiar in peace and war alike. Here one or more of these marauders, sometimes for days and even weeks on end, would be lying in wait for the unwary merchantman. Beyond the cliffs, a gleaming, dazzling white in fair weather, the swift cloud-shadows chased one another across the bare, windswept South Downs, where large flocks of sheep moved slowly from slope to slope, and practically nothing else stirred. No less familiar to these raiders was the towering front of the great headland looming in a sea-mist, when the water was often as smooth as a mill-pond, and a becalmed merchantman would drift helplessly to his doom. (A major advantage from the privateers-men's point of view was that in hazy weather they could frequently distinguish the base of the cliffs, while their ship was wholly invisible from the signal station above, enveloped as it was in mist.) Nor would they readily be driven from their post by strong westerly winds, with the foam-capped seas rolling shoreward under a lowering sky and heavy sprays rising all along the foot of the cliffs. In these skilfully prepared ambuscades the tidal streams off Beachy Head, and between Pevensey Bay and the Royal Sovereign shoals to the eastward, the sudden sharp gusts from the high chalk cliffs above, and the roadstead off Langney Point near Eastbourne—where our smaller cruisers were accustomed to anchor—in relation to the privateers' station in the prevailing westerlies, played a crucial part.

The short distance of the hunting-grounds from their home ports naturally enhanced the weight of their attack. Under such favourable conditions a single privateer was able to do as much damage as ten which had to make a longer run. Another important advantage of the short run was that it enabled a whole fleet of quite small vessels to assist in these operations. The majority of the enemy privateers, after all, had neither the necessary sea-keeping qualities, nor were they equipped or provisioned, for lengthy periods at sea. Most of the Malouins, indeed, seldom ventured out beyond the Channel and its approaches.

For the summer campaign the procedure was somewhat different. Many of the privateers then preferred to avoid the Channel, which was apt to be full of British cruisers; besides which the long periods of daylight would render escape difficult or even impossible for themselves and for their prizes. In the summer season, therefore, the Norman and Breton privateers often chose to operate in the soundings.

As the war continued privateers swarmed all along the enemy's coast between the Texel and St. Malo. They ranged from small rowing-boats manned by a dozen or so men armed with muskets to comparatively powerful vessels manned by 150 men and carrying twenty guns. Towards the bottle-neck of the Channel the small privateers of Calais and Boulogne were particularly active between 1796 and 1802. In these years they inflicted damaging losses on British commerce at comparatively little cost to themselves. By way of reprisals the British cut to pieces the local fishing fleets. At the other end of the Channel the hardy Malouins exacted a heavy toll on the shipping in the soundings and off the Cornish and Devon coasts.[1] They would cruise far out in the Atlantic within sight of the low-lying Isles of Scilly and within easy striking distance of traffic entering the soundings. They would lie in wait off the dark, rugged cliffs of the Lizard, and, during a gale, run for shelter to some cove to which the Breton fishermen still resort. They would hover off the lonely Eddystone Rock and under the lofty crags of Prawle Point. It has been estimated that, in the winter of 1800, there were more than eight privateers operating from the larger Channel ports of France alone, as well as considerable numbers of fishing vessels and other small craft especially fitted out for the *guerre de course*, under commanders who were intimately acquainted with navigational conditions on the other side of the water. In a vivid passage Mahan summarized their tactics:

> Innocent-looking fishing-boats, showing only their half-dozen men busy at their work, lay at anchor upon, or within, the lines joining headland

[1] The privateers belonging to St. Malo usually operated from ports to the westward, such as Batz and Abervrach.

to headland of the enemy's coast, watching the character and appearance of passing vessels. When night or other favourable opportunity offered, they pulled quickly alongside the unsuspecting merchantmen, which, under-manned and unwatchful, from the scarcity of seamen, was often first awakened to the danger by a volley of musketry, followed by the clambering of the enemy to the decks. The crews, few in number, poor in quality, and not paid for fighting, offered usually but slight resistance to the overpowering assault. Boarding was the corsair's game, because he carried many men.[1]

One of the most renowned privateersmen of those years was Jean Blanckmann, of Dunkirk. Blanckmann, who had been constantly at sea from his boyhood, was possessed of a phenomenal knowledge of our east coast and of the teeming coastwise traffic, which he had acquired, many years earlier, as a fisher boy.[2]

His knowledge was improved to a perfection scarcely credible, by his being, in the beginning of the late and present wars, in a small Privateer that kept constantly close in with our coast. The trade from London to Berwick, in the Smacks, were his favourite objects, not only from the value of their cargoes, but because they required only a few hands to man them, and were besides almost sure, from their good sailing, to escape our cruizers, and get in safely to the ports of France or Holland. He was equally well acquainted with the Baltic and coal trade: light Colliers he was averse to take possession of, unless the wind was fair for France, on account of being encumbered with prisoners, and besides parting with his own men.[3]

Blanckmann had first made a name for himself when in command of the *Anacreon* brig. At a time when France could lay claim to few naval successes, and those few of but minor importance, the *Moniteur* was ready enough to laud the numerous prizes taken by the *Anacreon* in 1799. Blanckmann was one of those resourceful privateersmen who would daringly and successfully assail British convoys. Bearing down on a convoy escorted by several men-of-war, he audaciously hung on their flanks, and then, swooping on one of the duller sailers, attacked and quickly carried it out of reach of the escorts; he repeated this

[1] Mahan, *The Influence of Sea Power upon the French Revolution and Empire*, II, pp. 208–9.
[2] As St. Vincent had observed to Spencer in the autumn of 1800: 'Your Lordship is aware that the Dutch and Flemish fishermen are better acquainted with our sands then we are' (*Spencer Papers*, IV, p. 20).
[3] *Naval Chronicle*, XII, p. 454.

manœuvre several times over, and in three days succeeded in capturing no fewer than six large merchantmen richly laden. A month later the *Anacreon* was back again on the English coast and harrying our commerce. In the final year of the war, in the *Bellone* and afterwards in the *Chasseur*, Blanckmann managed to secure another rich haul of prizes. According to the following account in the *Naval Chronicle* in 1804:

> He constantly boasted, that with a Fishing Smack not worth 600 l. he would at any time take an English Merchantman worth as many thousands; and that, therefore, he little regarded being taken (which he was three times last war) and remaining in an English prison two or three months, particularly as he could depend upon his partners at home, that they would make the most of the prizes which he sent in; the number of which, during the last war, amounted to thirty-four, of different descriptions.[1]

Louis Leveille, also of Dunkirk, was another leading privateersman, who from 1795 on was well known on both sides of the Channel. Like Blanckmann, he had spent his entire life at sea, in traders, fishing craft, and smugglers, and possessed an intimate knowledge of our south coast. In the 220-ton *Vengeance* he ranged the Channel during 1795 and 1796, making more than forty prizes, including a number of richly laden Indiamen. Like Blanckmann, too, he was responsible for some daring attacks on convoys. In March 1796 he fell in with a convoy which had just come out from Spithead. Taking advantage of the confusion which generally prevailed during a convoy's first few hours at sea and observing the slack supervision exercised by the escorts, Leveille presently boarded and carried off no less than five prizes.

French privateers were also active on the eastern side of the North Sea. Some of these vessels, based on Norwegian ports, committed numerous depredations on our Baltic trade. One of the enemy's favourite cruising grounds was off the Naze, which our merchantmen were obliged to pass on their passage in and out of the Kattegat. The privateers would be lurking behind some rocky islet or up some hidden cove, ready to slip out, by day or night, and by boarding suddenly, carry off their prey within some inaccessible anchorage.

The privateers of Bordeaux, Nantes, and the other French Atlantic ports usually operated far out in the ocean. For this kind of service their vessels needed to be large and seaworthy, and provisioned and

[1] *Ibid.*, p. 457.

equipped for a long cruise in the open Atlantic. They were amply manned and strongly armed. Their quarry was the heavily laden merchantmen homeward-bound from the Mediterranean, or the East or West Indies, whose track lay far from the coast. They were accustomed to cruise out there as long as possible: for the greatest risk they ran was in either leaving or returning to their home ports.

Another highly important field of privateering activities was in the West Indies. The recapture by the enemy, in 1794–5, of Guadeloupe and other islands once more gave the French cruisers and privateers a

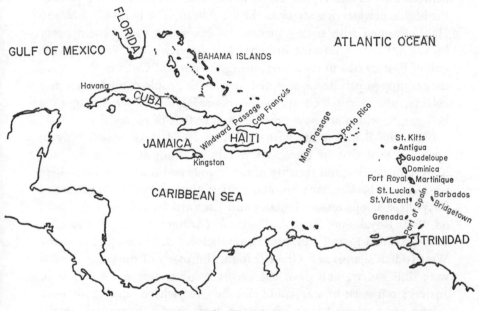

The West Indies

secure base of operations, of which they were prompt to take full advantage. Particularly in the early years of the war, British commercial interests sustained severe losses from these depredations.

Though our naval supremacy in the West Indies was undisputed throughout the war, the protection of commerce from the hostile privateers that swarmed all over the Caribbean presented serious difficulties. The conditions that obtained in this area were peculiarly favourable to the marauder. The trade of the West Indies fell under two main categories. First, there was the large and highly profitable commerce with Europe (several hundred West Indiamen arrived annually in the Thames alone). Second, there was an extensive local traffic. The privateers which operated against the former were for the most part fast-sailing brigs or schooners; for operations against the inter-island trade rowing-boats and other small craft were usually employed.

As a result of the alliance in 1796 between France and Spain, the ports belonging to the latter in the West Indies served not only to shelter the Spanish privateers, but also to extend the range of French depredations in this region. As in home waters, 1797 saw the peak of the hostile privateering attack in the Caribbean. The ports of Cuba and Haiti swarmed with enemy privateers. According to a contemporary historian, Captain Edward Breton: 'The activity of the French in the gulf of Florida was unremitting; using the ports of Cuba as their own, they equipped privateers, manned them with people of all nations and colours, and carried on the same depredations under a flag of a belligerent, which are now practised under that of piracy'.[1]

Since the British trade with the West Indies was second only in importance to that in European waters, a strong force was assigned 'for the protection and security of the islands and trade'. In 1800 there were six of the line, one 50, and no less then forty-five frigates and forty-three sloops on the Jamaica and Leeward Islands stations based on Port Royal and English Harbour (Antigua) respectively. The convoys sailed to and fro, with comparatively little loss, between the West Indian islands and Great Britain. But many of the older vessels were dull sailers, and gave the escort commanders a good deal of anxiety; our men-of-war could not be everywhere, and there were certain areas where the merchantmen were especially exposed to the risk of attack. Ships bound to the West Indies from Europe were accustomed to run down the parallel of their destination until they made the land; and all the corsairs had to do was to station themselves in the vicinity of these latitudes and await the arrival of their prey. The more powerful privateers cruised to the westward of the Windward Islands in the track of outward-bound shipping. The important traffic of Jamaica could be intercepted on its outward passage as it ran down the southern coast of Haiti, while the homeward-bound vessels could be attacked both in the Windward Passage between Cuba and Haiti and

[1] Brenton, *Naval History of Great Britain*, II, pp. 427–8.

in the Gulf of Florida by privateers based on the numerous ports in those islands.

Small forces only were assigned to, or in fact were required on, the North American station, whose main duty was to provide convoys for the trade to and from Europe. In the year 1800 Halifax had no more than four frigates and a couple of sloops, while Newfoundland had only two frigates and four sloops. A frigate had to be sent with the homeward-bound trade from Quebec to the Banks of Newfoundland, and, in the same way, to escort the outgoing convoy between Anticosti and Quebec. Sometimes the resources of the small division stationed at Halifax would be stretched to the limit to guard the vital mast ships safely through the danger zone.

In the early phase of the war British shipping in the Indian Ocean was left almost unprotected, and in consequence suffered severely. In the ensuing years squadrons of French frigates, supplemented by a far more numerous force of privateers, under the leadership of some of the most daring and resourceful seamen that ever came out of France, assailed the East India Company's ships, the country ships, and smaller vessels, British or neutral, which, being laden with British goods, were also liable to capture. In 1795 the conquest of Holland by the French secured the ports of the Dutch East Indies as bases for their cruisers on the flank of the great trade route between China and Europe.

British attempts to blockade the enemy's base, Mauritius, had broken down for want of ships. On his arrival at Madras in September 1794 Commodore Peter Rainier was petitioned by the merchants for more adequate naval protection in the Straits of Malacca through which most of the trade between India and China had to pass. The problem of commerce protection was, in fact, the main preoccupation of the commander-in-chief on the East Indies station for the rest of the war.

Already in 1793 the name of the Malouin François Lemême had become only too familiar to the British mercantile community in India. In his fast-sailing privateer, the *Hirondelle*, Lemême would overtake our merchantmen and elude our cruisers. He became one of the most distinguished and successful commanders in the eastern seas and accumulated an immense fortune.

Greatest of all the privateersmen of Mauritius was another celebrated

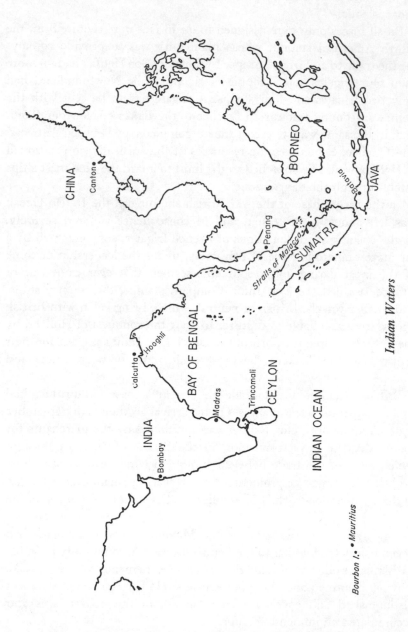

Malouin, Robert Surcouf, 'the king of corsairs.' A specialist in disguise, surprise, and other stratagems of the privateersman, Surcouf was at this time in his early twenties. At the beginning of 1796 he arrived in the *Emilie* off the mouths of the Hooghli: it was during the north-east monsoon, a season when no enemy privateers were expected there. Before long he had captured two merchantmen and a pilot brig, the *Cartier*, to which he instantly transferred himself and his crew. 'In the brig *Cartier* Surcouf had the perfect privateer,' Parkinson observes: 'perfect, at least for the station on which he was now cruising. . . . In a pilot brig off the Sandheads Surcouf was disguised to perfection. Not only was his appearance above suspicion, he could also be sure that his victims would seek him out.'[1] On 29 January, by an ingenious and daring stratagem, Surcouf with the *Cartier*, which mounted only four guns and carried only seventeen men, seized a large Indiaman, the *Triton*, armed with twenty-six guns and manned by 150 men.'[2]

Later in the war, in 1799, Surcouf cruised in the *Clarisse* in the Bay of Bengal and in neighbouring waters, taking a large number of prizes and practically blockading Calcutta. In 1800, having taken the *Clarisse* to Mauritius to refit, he accepted the offer of the *Confiance*. With a large crew—160 of them Europeans—Surcouf lay off the south-east coast of Ceylon, where, presently chased by a British cruiser, he was saved by his vessel's superior speed; after which, despite the weather— it was the time of the south-west monsoon—he returned to his old hunting ground in the Bay of Bengal. There he seized more than a dozen prizes in quick succession, including the East India Company's ship, the *Kent*. By this time Surcouf had gained an almost legendary fame; he was dreaded by the merchants for his amazing skill as a corsair; he was admired, by friend and foe alike, for his resource and daring, his unquenchable gaiety, and his unfailing consideration and courtesy to prisoners.

During the last three years of the war there appear to have been about a dozen privateers operating in Indian waters. Second in renown only to Robert Surcouf was Jean Dutertre of the *Malartic*. Dutertre was a rough old sea-dog, much in the Jean Bart tradition. Since 1796

[1] C. N. Parkinson, *War in the Eastern Seas, 1793–1815* (1954), p. 108.
[2] Strictly speaking, this amazing exploit (subsequently described by the *Madras Courier* as an 'extraordinary capture') was, in fact, an act of piracy; Surcouf having no commission to attack British vessels.

he had made a series of cruises, profitable both to himself and to Mauritius; eventually he was captured and taken to England, where he remained a prisoner of war until released by the Peace of Amiens in 1802. Another famous privateersman was the Malouin, Mallerousse of the *Iphigénie*, who actually engaged and sank one of our warships, the sloop *Trincomalee*, before his own vessel blew up and went to the bottom.

Since a really effective blockade of Mauritius presented almost insuperable difficulties, the only lasting remedy would have been either the provision of frequent and regular convoys through the danger zone, or the reduction of the enemy's base.[1] The latter was only attempted in part, and the latter not at all. The British merchants in Bengal, unlike those of Bombay, remained, for reasons of their own, consistently opposed to the convoy system. As early as 1799 Rainier had, without success, 'frequently taken occasion to point out to the merchants the security that would result to their trade from their ships sailing with convoy'. Throughout the war the corsairs exacted a heavy and continuous toll, despite the overwhelming superiority of the British squadron in Indian waters. Nevertheless it has to be remembered that insurance premiums at no time rose to the sums demanded by underwriters during the memorable campaign of the Bailli de Suffren in the last war.

The French attack on British commerce came to a head in 1797. In that year our shipping losses reached their peak. The enemy's privateers displayed phenomenal activity alike in European seas and in the Caribbean, which was evidenced in the long columns of captured vessels published in *Lloyd's List* and the *Moniteur* and in the frequent jeremiads which appeared in the British press. Our cruisers in the Channel and elsewhere were manifestly unable to hold them in check. The corsairs hovered off the Naze, Cape Clear, Cape Finisterre, the Isles of Scilly, Land's End, the Lizard, Beachy Head, and other Channel headlands; the severe weather of that winter, as usual, greatly aiding

[1] 'The Mauritius is the only place in these parts in the possession of the French, its present utility to them is therefore considerable, and affords every refuge and shelter to their Cruizers in these Seas, by which the British Commerce is greatly annoyed; upon these grounds the subduction of it becomes an important value to His Majesty's Service' (Vice-Admiral George Elphinstone to the Admiralty, 30 July 1796; Q. C. N. Parkinson, *War in the Eastern Seas, 1793–1815*, p. 88).

these depredations. Within the Straits of Gibraltar the French were assisted by the Spaniards and Italians—among the latter Bavastro had won fame as the 'Surcouf of the Mediterranean'. Across the Atlantic the marauders cruised off Cape Henry and waylaid the trade with Europe, while from the French and Spanish ports of the West Indies Pierre Leroi and his brethren levied an increasing toll on the shipping of the Caribbean. From their strong island base athwart the trade-routes to Europe, the Breton and creole privateersmen of Mauritius sallied forth against the rich traffic of the Bay of Bengal, the Straits of Malacca, and other focal regions. It was this alarming intensification of the attack on trade, which, coming on top of earlier losses[1] and an unparalleled closure of the markets of the Continent to British commerce, gravely threatened the already overstrained national economy. Both at home and abroad 1797 was the worst year of the war. Not only was grave discontent rife in the lower ranks of the Navy, but the wholesale capture of British merchant shipping also involved the seizure of large numbers of our seamen—on whom, in the last resort, the Sea Power of Great Britain depended—as prisoners of war. The rising toll of losses pointed to disastrous gaps in the existing system of trade defence. In too many cases vessels were wont to sail when it suited their owners' interests, and not under the protection of convoy; and when they did sail in convoy, they had little hesitation in parting company in order to steal a march on their rivals. Within the next twelve months steps were taken to close some of these gaps.

2

It was because of the secure bases which the enemy possessed in the Caribbean and Indian Ocean that they had been able to inflict such havoc on British trade in those regions. It followed that one of the most effective counter-measures which could be taken by Great Britain in the *guerre de course* was to seize the overseas bases upon which the raiders depended. Deprived of their own or friendly harbours to which they could resort to refit or conduct their prizes, the activities of the privateers in those areas would be effectually checked. Thus within a few months of the outbreak of war two small French islands situated

---

[1] British shipping losses throughout the war averaged about 500 a year.

off the coast of Newfoundland, St. Pierre and Miquelon,[1] as well as Pondicherry in India, were taken by the Navy. In the next few years several of the West Indian islands, in addition to the Cape of Good Hope and Ceylon, passed into British keeping.

In the course of successive wars waged between Great Britain and other maritime Powers the twofold system of commerce protection upon which the Admiralty relied—namely, patrolled areas and convoys —had been progressively developed and expanded. The patrol system, as it may be termed, was employed in great focal areas like the Channel approaches and other regions of the sea where the trade-routes converged and the traffic was thickest. Similarly, at the terminal ports overseas—e.g. in the Caribbean—cruisers were usually detached for this duty by the squadron stationed there. By this means a measure of protection was provided for merchantmen which, through stress of weather or for any other reason, had parted company with their convoy, as well as for independent sailers or 'runners'.[2]

The organization of the convoy system was materially improved by the Convoy Act of 1793 and the Compulsory Convoy Act of 1798, which imposed heavy penalties on vessels that broke convoy and made such convoy obligatory, with certain limited exceptions, for all foreign-going commerce. The exceptions were East Indiamen, the Hudson's Bay Company's ships, ships bound for Irish ports, and certain fast and well-armed ships known as 'runners'. Under the new measures, masters were to be denied clearance papers until they had given a written undertaking not to sail independently and not to separate from the convoy. If they disobeyed the orders of the commander of the convoy, they became liable to severe punishment. (Complaints of ill-disciplined ships were, however, noticeably less frequent than in previous wars.) If their vessels were in danger of being boarded by an enemy, they were to signal to the rest of the convoy; and, if boarded, to destroy the secret instructions. The Act of 1798 also required

[1] St. Pierre and Miquelon, though virtually barren rocks, possessed good natural harbours.

[2] It is to be noted that the patrol system proved far more efficacious under the conditions of the French Revolutionary and Napoleonic Wars than it did under those of the First World War with the new situation created by the introduction of submarine warfare. In the former case a fair proportion of the prizes taken by the enemy were afterwards recaptured by our cruisers; but in the latter this was unlikely to happen, as the victims were usually dispatched out of hand by the U-boats.

owners to contribute towards the cost of their protection. Throughout the war there was close and continuous cooperation between the Admiralty and the Committee of Lloyd's over the regulation of the convoy system, which was strongly supported by the underwriters. To the influence of Lloyd's, indeed, the introduction of the new Convoy Acts may in large measure be attributed. The efficacy of these measures was soon shown by a significant reduction in the insurance rates of vessels under convoy.

This is not to deny that the drawbacks of the convoy system were many and onerous. Much time was necessarily lost in assembling such large fleets of merchantmen; progress was inevitably retarded by the dullest sailers among them; moreover, the simultaneous arrival of large quantities of the same goods tended to depress prices. The result was that a good many owners, trusting to the speed of their vessels and willing to take a great risk in the hope of making a great profit, preferred their vessels to sail without convoy.

The pros and cons of convoy had given rise to endless controversy in this and previous wars; but the overwhelming consensus of opinion —above all, that of the underwriters, who were manifestly in a position to know—came down unhesitatingly on the side of convoy. The evidence of the statistics is irrefutable. Not until more than a century later was British commerce permitted to sail in war-time without the provision of convoy: a calamitous innovation which came near to losing us the First World War.

Not only was the convoy system organized, during the French Revolutionary War, far more elaborately and comprehensively than ever before, but individual convoys sometimes attained very large proportions. The strength of the escort force was proportionate to the size and value of the convoy and the degree of danger to be apprehended in the area through which the convoy was passing. Generally speaking, larger convoys and stronger escort forces were the rule than in the previous war.[1]

---

[1] 'The reason for smaller relative losses in big convoys is probably due to the fact that the perimeter of a large convoy is only slightly larger than that of a small one, because the area occupied by the ships increases as the square, while the perimeter is directly proportional to the length, of the radius. Hence the number of escort vessels needed to watch the perimeter of a big convoy is almost the same as that needed to watch the perimeter of a small convoy' (J. G. Crowther and R. Whiddington, *Science at War*, p. 101).

Thus in September 1793 Rear-Admiral Gardner sailed for England from the West Indies in the *Queen* with a small squadron, having under convoy a fleet of nearly 150 merchant vessels. Their passage, he informed the Admiralty, was 'very tedious, owing to the very light breezes of wind, and several heavy sailing vessels, which the squadron have been under the necessity of towing'. He presently detached Captain Alan Gardner (his son) in the *Heroine* and sent him on ahead to Portsmouth with his dispatch, himself remaining with the convoy. 'As I consider the safety and protection of so large a convoy to be an object of the first consideration, and of the greatest importance to the common interests of the Country, I have determined not to quit them, but to see them safely up the Channel as far as Spithead.'[1]

A much larger convoy than this is recorded by Midshipman William Parker of the *Orion* in February 1794.

We left Torbay on the 13th, Saturday, and the next day were off Plymouth, where the convoy came out to us. It was the grandest sight ever was, a convoy of 600 sail, besides 36 line-of-battle ships. The wind was quite fair and a fine evening; as soon as the convoy were all out, it came on so fine a breeze that we went eight miles an hour, without a stitch of sail set; in fact, in three days they were so far to the southward that they were out of all danger; and so we hauled off, and the next day made Cape Turrana, Port of Spain; we were so far to the southward that it was more than a great coat warmer than in England. We stood off from the land directly, and the wind came right fair, with a good breeze from the south-west, brought us home right before it, so that we anchored here the day before yesterday, after having been out ten days. Captain Duckworth says that if I live to be one of the oldest commanders it is ten thousand to one if ever I see so large a convoy carried out so far to the westward, and without the least accident, and the wind fair enough to bring us back again in so short a time; and that he never saw such providential winds since he has been to sea, which is thirty-five years.[2]

Some of the convoy commanders were accustomed to enforce their orders with a high hand. Commander James Anthony Gardner (then acting as signal officer in the *Gorgon* frigate) recounts such an experience, in the summer of 1794, when his ship was sent as a whipper-in among a large convoy bound for England from Gibraltar. 'Our admiral (Cosby) was a glorious fellow', wrote Gardner, 'for keeping the

[1] Adm. 1/316, 11 September 1793.
[2] A. Phillimore, *The Life of Sir William Parker* (1876), pp. 39–40.

convoy in order, and if they did not immediately obey the signal, he would fire at them without further ceremony.' The testimony of the future Captain Crawford shows how skilfully the commanders of some of the smaller cruisers engaged in escort duties went about their business. (This occurred while a couple of sail of the line and the *Gannet* brig were escorting a large convoy of transports, bound for Sicily, early in the Napoleonic War). 'We found the *Gannet* very useful in keeping the convoy together,' Crawford declared. 'Captain Bateman, her commander, moving from flank to flank with wonderful celerity; and like an experienced whipper-in, who always has the dogs so that a sheet might cover them, by his great diligence and watchfulness he prevented straggling, and kept the fleet in compact order.'[1]

An important fact which should never be overlooked is that in comparison with the immensity of the sea there is scarcely any significant difference between the size of a convoy and the size of a single vessel. A compact, well-disciplined convoy had almost as much chance of slipping by unseen as a single ship. It followed that vessels thus concentrated in space and time were far more likely to pass unobserved by the enemy than the same number sailing independently and scattered over wide areas of the seas and oceans.

Convoy, then, was the main and fundamental factor in the British defence of trade; it provided effective protection for the vital long-distance trades, on which so much of our commerce with Europe also depended. A really destructive attack on one of our convoys, during the French Revolutionary War, was quite exceptional. The few cases that occurred have already been mentioned—on each of these occasions the escorts were overwhelmed by greatly superior forces and the convoy snapped up without opposition. To these must be added the fairly frequent successes scored by privateers. The more skilful and successful of the enemy privateersmen would sometimes take as many as five or six prizes from a single convoy. But, throughout the years under survey, British commerce sustained no such disastrous blow as the capture of the East and West Indies convoy by Cordova in the last war. For the overseas trades convoy, after 1798, was compulsory; for the swarming coastwise traffic of Great Britain frequent and regular

---

[1] *Above and under hatches* (*Recollections of James Anthony Gardner*), ed. C. C. Lloyd (1957), p. 119; A. Crawford, *Reminiscences of a Naval Officer* (1851), p. 270.

convoys were instituted by the Admiralty: but there was no compulsion on vessels to sail in them. However, the powerful influence of the Committee of Lloyd's was always—both before and after the passage of the Compulsory Convoy Act—exercised strongly in support of convoy, which was regarded as the only effective security for shipping in time of war.

All this time the demand for British goods was rapidly increasing and there were not enough of either ships or seamen available to meet that demand. Year after year the drain of men away from the merchant service into the Navy continued; and it often happened that vessels were unable to sail for want of crews. As early as April 1793 the Navigation Act had been so modified as to allow three-quarters of the crews of British ships to be foreigners. Another significant development was the growing use of neutral bottoms to carry British goods; so that the proportion of neutral shipping to our own used in British overseas trade actually increased from 13 per cent. in 1792 to nearly 34 per cent. in 1800.

> The demands of the navy for seamen, the risks of capture, the delays of convoy, entirely arrested, and even slightly set back, the development of the British carrying trade; while at the same time the important position of Great Britain as the great manufacturing nation, coinciding with diminution in the productions of the Continent, consequent upon the war, and a steadily growing demand for manufactured goods on the part of the United States, called imperiously for more carriers. The material of British traffic was increasing with quickened steps, at the very time that her own shipping was becoming less able to bear it. Thus in 1797, when the British navy was forced to leave the Mediterranean, all the Levant trade, previously confined to British ships, was thrown open to every neutral. In 1798, being then at war with Spain, the great raw material, Spanish wool, essential to the cloth manufactures, was allowed to enter in vessels of any neutral country.[1]

A rapidly increasing share of the world's carrying trade was now passing into the hands of the American merchant marine. The long trade depression of the 1780s was a thing of the past. Already by the outbreak of the present war New England had not only recovered much of her former West Indian connection, but was also tapping important new sources of profit. The New England trading system came to

[1] Mahan, *The Influence of Sea Power upon the French Revolution and Empire*, II, pp. 228–9.

embrace most of the major ports of Europe and of the Near East from Archangel to Smyrna. Above all, it was the oriental commerce which amply restored the prosperity of New England.

During the war years the maritime expansion of New England continued without a break. Freights had risen to unexampled figures. By far the greater part of the important traffic between Great Britain and the United States was carried in American bottoms; and New England, as well as Great Britain, was active in Hamburg and the Baltic. The British government as yet made no attempt to hinder the American carrying trade in European waters. The vessels of New England rounded the bleak cliffs of Cape Horn and sailed up the Pacific coasts of South and North America. Presently the masters and shipowners of Boston developed the North-West fur trade for the sake of an invaluable medium of exchange in the markets of Canton. To obtain sandalwood for the same purpose they sailed to the Hawaii Islands. Meanwhile Salem traders voyaged to the Fiji group to procure the edible bird's-nests, tortoiseshell, and sea-cucumbers to import to China in exchange for tea and textiles. Nantucket whalers were active in the South Pacific. Braving the perils of the Sandheads, Yankee shipping penetrated the intricate channels of the Hooghli; and merchants from New England set up business in Calcutta and other cities of British India. Throughout the French Revolutionary War the British government placed no restrictions on this American trade with the Orient. Before the turn of the century Boston and Salem had become entrepôts of world commerce. In fishing and whaling, as well as in seaborne trade, the gain of the war years had been immense: the aggregate tonnage owned by Boston was second only to that of New York. These were 'boom' years also for Salem and Newburyport. It was on all this accumulated wealth, derived from the high freights of the neutral carrying trade, that the future industrial structure of New England was laid.

During the French Revolutionary War the perennial problem of neutral rights recurred with increasing urgency. In the past the lesser maritime powers had endeavoured, without success, to establish a positive code of neutral rights based on the doctrines of effective blockade, limited contraband, and *free ships, free goods*. The matter became more and more pressing as a result of the ever-increasing share of the world's carrying trade borne by the United States. The Americans alone could compete with Great Britain in the continental market as carriers of colonial produce. Since the outbreak of the war they had been constructing new ships by the score, and were employing about 600,000 tons in foreign trade. American vessels were now finding their way to the most distant parts of the earth. Both Great Britain and France were only too glad to avail themselves of their services.

The President of the United States, George Washington, holding resolutely to a policy of strict neutrality, issued his famous declaration, in the spring of 1793, of his country's firm intention to pursue 'a conduct friendly and impartial towards the belligerent Powers'. But as the war continued difficulties arose. The British proclaimed a blockade of the enemy's ports and added corn to the list of contraband. In November 1793 our government ordered the seizure of 'all ships laden with goods the produce of any colony belonging to France, or carrying provisions or other supplies for the use of any such colony'. This order was based on the Rule of the War of 1756. Several hundreds of American ships were then seized and taken into West Indian ports by British cruisers. To resolve the growing differences between Great Britain and the United States the President in 1794 appointed John Jay, Chief Justice of the Supreme Court, as his Envoy Extraordinary to London. In November of the same year there was signed the Treaty which is known by his name. The terms finally agreed to were largely in accordance with the suggestions that had been made by Alexander Hamilton, at that time the leading member of Washington's cabinet, whose recently devised credit system depended upon tariff revenues; by far the greater part of which came from those on British imports. This credit system would have collapsed in the event of war or even suspension of trade with Great Britain; entailing, in all probability, the speedy disintegration of the young Republic. Though it was widely denounced in the United States as a surrender, it is difficult under the circumstances to see what better settlement could have been arrived at. Jay's Treaty was, in effect, a victory for British diplomacy; for though American shipping was henceforward permitted to engage in direct traffic between the United States and British possessions in the East and West Indies, they were still prohibited from carrying the produce of those colonies to foreign ports; and the Americans were obliged to acquiesce in the British doctrine of contraband. Moreover, the position as regards the impressment of seamen remained unchanged; and herein lay the seeds of future strife. Nevertheless, for close on a decade relations between the two governments were placed on a comparatively settled basis, and Anglo-American trade prospered exceedingly, to the mutual advantage of both countries; for, whatever grievances the British and Americans had got against each other, the fact remained that the United States were Great Britain's best customer, and the Americans were still largely dependent upon British manufacturers.

Soon after the Americans had obtained this settlement with Great Britain, they experienced even more serious difficulties with France. The Directory presently arrogated powers in excess of any that Great Britain had ever claimed; relations between the two countries continued to deteriorate; and at last, in June 1798, hostilities broke out at sea, though war was never formally declared, and lasted for about eighteen months. The actual hostilities did little harm to France. The cessation of the American carrying trade, however, was a severe blow to her rapidly diminishing commerce.

V

The Campaign of the Nile

I

In the spring of 1798 the British Cabinet, with the object of ending the strategical stalemate and of reviving the alliance against revolutionary France, decided to send a squadron within the Straits of Gibraltar again. Already the Austrian government had been pressing for the return of a British fleet to the Mediterranean; and it was in any case becoming apparent that, should southern Europe fall completely under French control, St. Vincent would be unable to maintain his station off Cadiz. Another important consideration was the formidable armament reported to be preparing in Toulon, whose objective was unknown. Along the Mediterranean coast of France, and in Genoa, Civita Vecchia, and Corsica, troops and transports were assembling in large numbers. Only by watching this armament at its point of departure could the danger be countered. There were risks, indeed, in weakening our forces at home and in Spanish waters while enemy squadrons lay in Brest and Cadiz, and the French were threatening to invade Ireland. Spencer doubted if the extra ships could be found; observing that only thirty-four of the line were available to guard the entrance of the Channel and Ireland, and no more than twenty-four remained for the Mediterranean. Three more of the line were refitting for sea, and eight, under construction, were nearing completion. But, as usual, the chief difficulty was in seamen, another 8,000 being needed. Pitt, however, resolved that these risks must be run in order to wrest the initiative from France in the Mediterranean.[1]

Orders were therefore dispatched to St. Vincent on 2 May to detach part of his force for service in the Mediterranean; his squadron watching Cadiz was shortly to be reinforced by eight vessels withdrawn from

[1] H.M.C., *Dropmore Papers*, IV, p. 166; *Pitt Mss.*, 108: Spencer to Grenville, 6 April 1798; F.O., *Austria*, 51: Grenville to Eden, 20 April 1798.

Irish waters; and at the same time it was recommended that the command of this detached division should be entrusted to Nelson, who, having now recovered from his wound, was back again in the Mediterranean. 'When you are apprized', Spencer wrote to St. Vincent, 'that the appearance of a British squadron in the Mediterranean is a condition on which the fate of Europe may at this moment be said to depend, you will not be surprised that we are disposed to strain every nerve and incur considerable hazard in effecting it.'[1]

By a curious coincidence, on the very day that this letter was written St. Vincent, aware of the powerful armament that was assembling in the Provençal and Italian ports, had sent Nelson with a small squadron, comprising the *Vanguard, Orion,* and *Alexander,* together with three frigates, within the Straits to watch the hostile fleet in Toulon and, if possible, to discover its objective. On 20 May, however, Nelson's flagship was dismasted in a heavy gale. With the assistance of the *Orion* and *Alexander* she was brought safely into the anchorage of San Pietro, on the south coast of Sardinia, where, after four days' strenuous exertions, she was refitted and actually at sea again 'with a main topmast for a fore-mast, and a topgallant-mast for a top-mast, and everything else reduced in proportion'.[2] A much worse misfortune was the loss of their scouting force. Nelson's three frigates had parted company in the gale and when on 4 June his squadron returned to the rendezvous in the Gulf of Lyon were nowhere to be seen; for, having witnessed the disaster of 20 May, and incorrectly concluding that the *Vanguard* would be obliged to go into dock at Gibraltar, they had presently returned there themselves.

Meanwhile, convinced that France could not at present contest the command of the sea with her enemy and that without it a descent upon the British Isles was impracticable, Bonaparte was preparing to strike at Great Britain in the Levant and threaten her interests in India. This touched the British economy in a vital spot. Great Britain's industry and commerce were now closely bound up with Asia. Her Indian possessions were not only important in themselves, but India was also the citadel and 'place of arms' of British power in the East. Deprived of these territories, she could not have carried on her rich commerce with the East Indian archipelago and China. The eastern

[1] *Spencer Papers*, II, p. 438.
[2] *Nelson's Dispatches*, III, p. 19.

trades were in fact almost essential to her survival as a first-class Power. Bonaparte planned eventually to found a great French empire in the East on the ruins of the British. Though he kept up the pretence of invading these islands to the last possible moment he had ordered preparations on the largest scale to be made secretly in the south of France for an expedition against Egypt.

From his earliest youth Bonaparte had been powerfully attracted by the lure and mystery of the East. 'This little Europe is too small a field,' he told his secretary, Bourrienne, on 29 January 1798. 'Great renown can be won only in the East.' The scheme was not a new one. Long before, the famous German philosopher Leibnitz had called on the French to conquer Egypt. Choiseul's thoughts had turned in the same direction. Bonaparte now saw himself a second Alexander. He trusted in his destiny. The Directorate had readily accepted the project.

By this time St. Vincent had received his instructions from the Cabinet, and, notwithinstanding his precarious situation before Cadiz, and the mutinous state of a number of the crews, proceeded to detach ten of his best ships—*Culloden*, Captain Thomas Troubridge, *Goliath*, Captain Thomas Foley, *Bellerophon*, Captain Henry Darby, *Minotaur*, Captain Thomas Louis, *Majestic*, Captain George Westcott, *Defence*, Captain John Peyton, *Audacious*, Captain Davidge Gould, *Zealous*, Captain Samuel Hood, *Theseus*, Captain Richard Miller, and *Swiftsure*, Captain Benjamin Hallowell—'the *élite* of the Navy of England', to send to Nelson off Toulon, under Troubridge's command, directly the promised reinforcement from home arrived. It is recorded by Berry that on 24 May 'as soon as Sir Roger Curtis with the squadron under his command from England was visible from the masthead of the Admiral's ship, Captain Troubridge with his squadron put to sea, and was actually out of sight on his course to the Straits of Gibraltar, before the former cast anchor at the British station off Cadiz Bay.'

About the same time as the disaster to the *Vanguard*, the Toulon fleet had put to sea. It comprised thirteen sail of the line, including three three-deckers, and seven frigates, under the command of Admiral Brueys, assisted by Rear-Admirals Ganteaume, Decrès, and Villeneuve; and under its escort were three hundred transports carrying an army of nearly 36,000 war-seasoned troops under the leadership of Bonaparte and some of the most skilful generals of the Republic—Berthier, Marmont, Lannes, Murat, Desaix, Reynier, Caffarelli, Andreossy, Junot, Davout, and Kleber. Besides the troops, the transports carried some 160 guns and 1,200 horses. The expedition was amply equipped, not merely for conquest, but also for colonization; for along with the army sailed an illustrious corps of engineers, mathematicians, geologists, chemists, artists, naturalists, and antiquarians, to assist in the foundation of the new State. To the last moment Bonaparte had succeeded in keeping the destination of the expedition a close secret.

To commit this splendid host to the passage of an uncommanded sea was, perhaps, the most hazardous enterprise of Bonaparte's career. The expedition would be obliged to travel the entire length of the Mediterranean and would be at sea for several weeks. The chances of evasion and of interception would appear to have been about equal. As it was, it was only by the narrowest margin that a meeting was avoided between the greatest general and the greatest admiral in history —a meeting which could only have ended one way.[1] Much depended upon the wind, and even more upon fortune. In both regards the French were singularly favoured. The north-west wind which had forced Nelson off his station was fair for the passage to Egypt. The expedition stood to the eastward along the coast of Provence and then passed down the eastern shore of Corsica and Sardina. On 9 June they arrived off Malta. Three days later the Knights of Malta surrendered. The flag of the Order was thereupon run down, and the tricolour hoisted over Valetta. A rich haul of booty fell to the victors. The Order was dissolved. Malta was incorporated into France. A garrison of 3,000 troops was installed in the islands under the command of Vaubois.

At daybreak on the 19th the expedition again got under way. It was brilliant Mediterranean weather: the sun blazed down from a blue sky, the wind blew steadily from the north-west, and the sea was smooth. Hearts beat high with confidence and enthusiasm. The swift seizure of Malta had put everyone in a good humour. It was whispered among Bonaparte's staff that the conquest of Egypt would be as easy. Only the Admiral was anxious and preoccupied. So far their luck had held; but the chances of interception were increasing hourly as they

---

[1] 'It would have been my delight to have tried Buonaparte on a wind,' Nelson wrote regretfully to his wife, 'for he commands the Fleet, as well as the Army' (*Nelson's Dispatches*, III, p. 45).

approached their destination—the risk was perhaps greatest on 24–26 June—and no one knew better than Brueys what would happen if action were fairly joined. Encumbered as they were by the great convoy of crowded transports, his warships would stand little chance against the pursuing British squadron. The sooner they got to Egypt, and disembarked the troops, the better. Another reason for haste was the fact that, by August, the Nile would be in flood, and the inundation of the delta would impede the advance of Bonaparte's army upon Cairo.

For his part Bonaparte lost no time. Arriving in Aboukir Bay on 1 July, he hurriedly landed part of his army, which marched upon and seized Alexandria on the 2nd. Thereafter his progress was swift and triumphant. His transports disembarked the rest of the forces and their equipment in Alexandria; then, advancing eastward upon the capital, he routed the formidable Mameluke cavalry at the battle of the Pyramids on the 21st, and, only twenty-three days after landing, entered Cairo in triumph.

2

Meanwhile on 7 June Nelson had been joined by Troubridge's squadron and by the *Leander*, 50; and, after lying for several days becalmed, stood round the northern point of Corsica. He divided his force into three sub-squadrons: the *Vanguard*, *Minotaur*, *Leander*, *Audacious*, *Defence*, and *Zealous*, under himself; the *Orion*, *Goliath*, *Majestic*, and *Bellerophon*, under Saumarez; the *Culloden*, *Theseus*, *Alexander*, and *Swiftsure*, under Troubridge. Two of these sub-squadrons were to attack the hostile fleet, while the third was to pursue the transports, and to sink and destroy as many as it could.[1] Naples and Sicily had been mentioned in his orders as Bonaparte's most probable objectives. On the 14th he received intelligence that the French had been seen ten days before off the south-west shore of Sicily, standing to the eastward; whereupon his squadron stood after them under a press of sail, in accordance with Nelson's instructions 'to take, sink, burn, or destroy' the enemy wherever he found them. 'If they pass Sicily', he wrote to Spencer on the following day, 'I shall believe they are going on their scheme of possessing Alexandria, and getting troops to India—a plan

[1] *Ibid.*, III, p. 49.

concerted with Tippoo Sahib, by no means so difficult as might at first view be imagined.' 'The French have a long start,' he informed his Commander-in-Chief; and he added, 'you may be assured I will fight them the moment I can reach their Fleet, be they at anchor, or under sail.' Detaching the *Mutine*, a fast-sailing brig and the only single-decked vessel in the squadron, under the command of his friend, Captain Thomas Hardy, in search of intelligence, Nelson shaped course for Naples, where he learned that the French were at Valetta. On the 19th, again making all possible sail, they came in sight of the smoking cone of Stromboli. With a fair wind the squadron passed through the Straits of Messina; and off Cape Passaro, on the 22nd, Nelson had news from the British consul that Bonaparte had taken Malta, left a garrison there, and sailed on again. Rejecting the possibility that the enemy was bound for the western Mediterranean, he decided that he must be shaping a course to the eastward, and that Alexandria was his most likely objective. As he was later to observe, 'Spain, after Malta, or indeed any place to the westward, I could not think their destination, for at this season the westerly winds so strongly prevail between Sicily and the coast of Barbary, that I conceive it almost impossible to get a fleet of transports to the westward.'

Nelson was by now in such a state of nervous tension that long afterwards the slightest shock of pain or pleasure would set his heart feverishly pounding: and years later he was to recall with emotion the long-drawn-out strain and anguish of those weeks of cruel frustration, disappointment, suspense, and bewilderment. But his purpose held. There was never the least slackening of his stern determination to seek out and 'to take, sink, burn or destroy' the enemy fleet, the instant found. 'Be they bound to the Antipodes,' he had informed Spencer, 'your Lordship may rely that I will not lose a moment in bringing them to action.'

Crowding all sail, Nelson's squadron reached Alexandria in six days. But for lack of the missing frigates, 'the eyes of the Fleet', he twice failed to intercept the enemy: on the first occasion, during the hazy night of 25 June, when the French fleet heard the sound of the British signal guns in the mist and altered course to the northward; and on the second, on the 29th on Bonaparte's arrival at Alexandria, which occurred but a matter of hours after his own departure from that port. For the squadron had overrun its prey; and, finding no sign or news of the French in Egypt, Nelson, feverish with anxiety, at once stretched over to Asia Minor.

'If one-half the Frigates your Lordship had ordered under my command had been with me,' he declared in his dispatch to St. Vincent, 'I could not have wanted information of the French Fleet.' A fortnight later: 'To this day I am without the smallest information of the French Fleet since their leaving Malta,' Nelson informed the Commander-in-Chief. '. . . I have again to deeply regret my want of Frigates.'[1]

His one desire now was to get back to the westward. In the course of the next three weeks, while the French army was overrunning Egypt, Nelson was beating doggedly back to Sicily. Days of clear weather alternated with those of the hot Mediterranean summer haze. By 9 July the squadron was off Crete and working along the south side of the island, 'carrying a press of sail both night and day with a contrary wind; on the 18th we saw the Island of Sicily . . .'[2] At Syracuse, where they revictualled, there was still no news of the French; and he wrote on 20 July to Sir William Hamilton,[3] 'It is an old saying, "The Devil's children have the Devil's luck": I cannot find, or to this moment learn, beyond vague conjecture, where the French Fleet are gone to.'

On the 25th he sailed for the south of Greece and a few days later learned from some Greek fishermen that the French fleet had been seen off Crete about a month before, standing to the south-east. With every inch of canvas set, he bore up once again for Alexandria. Before a freshening north-westerly wind he made rapid progress, and three days later was nearing his destination. The squadron's health was good and its morale high. 'At this moment', Nelson observed, 'we have not one sick man in the Fleet.' 'The officers and crews in the several ships are all in the highest spirits', Saumarez had remarked, 'and I never remember going into action with more certain hopes of success.'

During these final weeks of the long and anxious pursuit the crews were being continually drilled and exercised for the coming battle; every man was ready to start to his post at a moment's notice; the decks of all the ships were kept cleared for action night and day; the captains would assemble on the quarter-deck of the *Vanguard*, whenever the weather and circumstances would permit, to learn from Nelson

---

[1] *Nelson's Dispatches*, III, p. 42.
[2] Berry, *An Authentic Narrative . . . of the Nile* (1798), p. 13.
[3] The British minister at Naples.

of his plans and intentions, which he explained to them 'with such perspicuity, as to render his ideas completely their own'. Preparation was made for every possible combination of circumstances in which the French might be encountered. In the words of Captain Berry, 'There was no possible position in which they could be found that he did not take into his calculation, and for the most advantageous attack of which he had not digested and arranged the best possible disposition of the force which he commanded'.[1]

3

The first of August was a brilliant summer's day with light breezes and clear weather; just before noon the look-outs sighted the Pharos of Alexandria, and some time later the white domes and minarets of the city beyond and the low-lying, sandy coast of the Nile delta rose above the horizon. Though there were apparently no French men-of-war in the harbour, the tricolour could be seen waving on the neighbouring ramparts: and at 2.45 p.m. the *Zealous*, cruising eastward along the coast, suddenly sighted the topmasts of the enemy fleet across the low shores of Aboukir Bay. Saumarez has described the dramatic scene in the wardroom of the *Orion* when the news was made known to the officers at table—the swift transition from despondency and gloom to the wildest jubilation.

> I do not recollect to have felt so utterly hopeless, or out of spirits, as when we sat down to dinner; judge then what a change took place when, as the cloth was being removed, the officer of the watch hastily came in, saying—'Sir, a signal is just now made that the enemy is in Aboukir Bay, and moored in a line of battle'. All sprang from their seats, and only staying to drink a *bumper* to our success, we were in a moment on deck.[2]

Nelson made the signal, *Prepare for battle*; and then, with a good appetite, sat down to his dinner. The fret and anguish of the long-drawn-out pursuit were over—so, too, were all doubts and misgivings. Throughout the squadron, in response to the urgent summons of the drums, the crews rushed to their appointed places and cleared for action. The hammocks were carried up from below and quickly stowed in the nettings around the upper deck. Down in the cockpit the surgeon and loblolly men were industriously spreading out bandages and

[1] Berry, *op. cit.*, p. 17.
[2] Q. Ross, *Life of Admiral Lord de Saumarez*, I, p. 215.

arranging their instruments. Presently, with bulk-heads down, battle-lanterns hung, ports open, matches lighted, and guns run out, the men stood at quarters, with their black silk handkerchiefs knotted round their heads and sleeves tucked up, cool, silent, and alert. There was general joy throughout the squadron at the prospect of a fight. As they stood by the guns, some of the men were talking hopefully of a 'bread-bag full of money' with which to buy a new outfit 'for Sundays and mustering days', and 'a d – d good cruise among the girls besides'. 'My station,' recounted John Nicol, a seaman on board the *Goliath*, 'was in the powder magazine with the gunners. As we entered the bay, we stripped to our trousers, opened our ports, cleared, and every ship we passed gave them a broadside and three cheers.'[1]

The French fleet, comprising thirteen of the line, lay anchored, in line ahead, close in with the shoals on the westward side of Aboukir Bay. The enemy's position was at first sight a strong one: their van was believed to be so well protected by the shoals and batteries of Aboukir Island that it would be altogether impossible for the British to pass inside their line; besides which they enjoyed a substantial superiority in guns and man-power.[2] It would be nearly dark before the British could work round the island and the outlying shoals and enter the bay; moreover, only eleven of Nelson's squadron were in company: his other three ships were far to the westward and would be unable to rejoin him until after nightfall. But Nelson, regarding the scene 'with the eye of a seaman determined on attack', did not hesitate; for 'it instantly struck his eager and penetrating mind, *that where there was room for an Enemy's Ship to swing, there was room for one of ours to anchor*.'[3] Hauling his wind, he signalled the *Alexandria* and *Swiftsure*, which had been acting as look-out ships, to rejoin him, and stood in to the land. The few guns which Brueys had mounted on the island proved virtually useless as a defence. Further, the leading French vessel was not anchored as close to the five-fathom line as she might have been;[4] nor

---

[1] Nicol, *Adventures of John Nicol, Mariner* (1822), p. 186.

[2] 'This situation of the Enemy seemed to secure to them the most decided advantages, as they had nothing to attend to but their Artillery, in their superior skill in the use of which the French so much pride themselves, and to which indeed their splendid series of Land Victories are in a great measure to be imputed' (Berry, *op. cit.*, p. 22).

[3] *Ibid.*, p. 22.

[4] A ship of the line drew nearly thirty feet in smooth water.

was she moored head and stern, but anchored only by the bows, and allowed to swing. The sea was calm, there was a good working breeze, and just two hours' daylight. Few signals had to be made, for Nelson's captains were already conversant with his plans for attacking the enemy 'whatever their position or situation might be, by day or by night'.[1]

The speed and ferocity of the British attack took the French by surprise. Many of their men were on duty ashore. Unprepared for immediate action, they had wholly neglected certain essential pre-

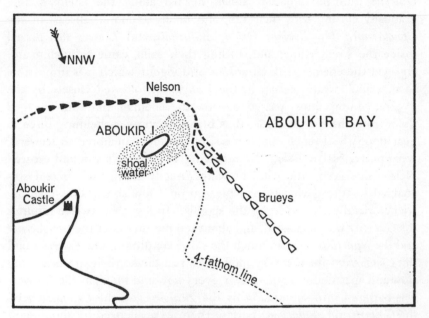

The Nile. The action of 1 August 1798

cautions: among other things, relying on the close proximity of the shoals to the head of their line, they had failed to clear their ships for action on the landward side, and the larboard batteries were in consequence cluttered up with stores. At five o'clock the British squadron bore up under a press of sail before the favouring northerly breeze, and, working round Aboukir Island, 'hauled well round all the dangers', and stood into the bay. As the blood-red sun sank towards the long flat horizon of the delta, the squadron steered unhesitatingly for the

[1] *Ibid.*, p. 21.

van of the French line, each ship sounding as she came on and gradually shortening sail as she closed with the enemy.

Just after 6.30, when the sun was setting, the *Goliath*, leading the British line, was fired on by the first two vessels in the French line, the *Guerrier* and the *Conquérant*. Without firing a shot in reply Captain Foley brought the *Goliath* 'in a very gallant and masterly manner' across the bows of the *Guerrier*, which he heavily raked with his larboard broadside, after which, steering for the narrow passage between the *Guerrier* and the adjacent shoal, he led along the enemy's line, gradually closing with their van, and finally anchored abreast of the *Conquérant*.[1] The *Zealous*, *Orion*, *Audacious*, and *Theseus* also passed inside the French line, and, furling their sails, came to anchor and engaged the enemy 'with an ardour and vigour which it is impossible to describe', while Nelson in the *Vanguard*, followed closely by the five remaining ships, passed outside the enemy's line and engaged them from the seaward side, thus bringing an overwhelming force to bear upon the French van, whose companions, anchored to leeward, were powerless to assist. 'By attacking the enemy's van and centre,' Nelson observed, 'the wind blowing directly along their line, I was enabled to throw what force I pleased on a few ships. This plan my friends readily conceived by the signals.' In less than twelve minutes the *Guerrier* was dismasted, and about ten minutes later the *Conquérant* and the *Spartiate* were in much the same condition. The *Guerrier* and the *Conquérant* made a very ineffective resistance, their fire becoming slow and spasmodic, a gun or two 'every now and then', as the *Guerrier* was battered into submission by the *Zealous*, and the *Conquérant* by the *Goliath* and *Audacious*; both of them were silenced by about eight o'clock. Just as the green afterglow was fading from the sky, and a pall of smoke began to spread itself above the bay, the *Spartiate*, already closely engaged on the larboard side with the *Theseus*, was engaged on the starboard by the *Vanguard*. For two hours the *Spartiate* put up a gallant resistance against the two British 74s, until, shortly after 8.30, she hauled down her colours. At about the same time the *Aquilon* also was silenced, with the loss of all her masts, by the fire of the *Minotaur* on her starboard, and that of the *Theseus* on her larboard, bow. The *Peuple Souverain* was entirely dismasted and silenced. In

---

[1] It is worth noticing that Foley was the only captain in the squadron who possessed a chart of Aboukir Bay.

short, half an hour after the *Goliath* had opened fire on the *Guerrier*, five French vessels found themselves engaged at point-blank range by eight British incomparably superior to them in point of gunnery, discipline, and leadership. The issue was already a foregone conclusion when Nelson, who, just before the *Spartiate* struck, had been severely wounded in the head by a fragment of flying iron, was penning his great dispatch to St. Vincent, 'Almighty God has blessed his Majesty's Arms. . . .'

But in the centre, where Brueys's strongest ships were placed, the issue of the action hung in the balance. The *Bellerophon*, dragging her anchors, came abreast of the 120-gun *Orient* and received the full force of the enemy flagship's broadside: dismasted, and almost a wreck, with her captain and a third of her people killed or wounded, she drifted helplessly out of the fight. The *Majestic*, following the *Bellerophon*, ran her jib-boom into the main rigging of the *Heureux* (the ninth vessel in the French line) and was fired into by both the *Heureux* and the *Tonnant*. After suffering severe losses (her captain, George Westcott, was almost the first that fell), she eventually got disentangled and brought her broadside to bear on the starboard bow of the *Mercure* (astern of the *Heureux*). Having laid that bow almost open, the *Majestic* at daylight had only a foremast standing. The arrival of the three remaining British ships came at an opportune moment. Bearing up to enter the bay, the *Culloden* had grounded on the tail of the shoal running out from Aboukir Island—where, notwithstanding the most strenuous exertions of Troubridge and his men, she remained immovable throughout the action; but the *Swiftsure* and *Alexander*, coming on swiftly and silently through the darkness, safely rounded the shoal, steered for the centre of the enemy's line, and engaged the *Orient* on the larboard quarter and starboard bow respectively. Later the *Peuple Souverain*, dismasted and silenced, drove to leeward of the French line and anchored about a cable's length abreast of the *Orient*. The *Franklin*, next ahead to the *Orient*, was thereby placed in extreme hazard. Into the space vacated by the *Peuple Souverain* presently glided the *Leander*, 'raking her with great success, the shot from the *Leander*'s broadside which passed that ship all striking *L'Orient*.'

It was now the turn of the French centre to be engaged by a superior concentration, and with decisive effect. The French made a brave fight of it, but the skill and intensity of the British fire was too much for them. The *Orient*, simultaneously engaged by the *Alexander*, *Swiftsure*, and *Leander*, was presently observed to be on fire. The blaze spread rapidly, the British vessels directing their fire at that part of the ship which was in flames. To avoid the threat of fire from the *Orient*, the *Tonnant*, her next astern, cut her cable and drifted to leeward. The *Leander* thereupon trained her guns on the *Tonnant*'s bow and raked her repeatedly. About the same time the *Heureux* and the *Mercure* likewise cut their cables, throwing the ships in the rear into such confusion that they began to fire into one another and to do one another considerable damage. The blazing flagship now illuminated the hostile fleets so brilliantly that the ensigns of both were clearly distinguishable. 'This circumstance Captain Berry immediately communicated to the Admiral, who, though suffering severely from his wound, came up upon deck, where the first consideration that struck his mind was concern for the danger of so many lives, to save as many as possible of whom he ordered Captain Berry to make every practicable exertion. A boat, the only one that could swim, was immediately dispatched from the *Vanguard*, and other ships that were in a condition to do so, immediately followed the example.' At a quarter to ten the *Orient* blew up with a tremendous explosion, after which, according to Captain Berry's account, 'An awful pause and death-like silence for about three minutes ensued, when the wreck of the masts, yards, &c. which had been carried to a vast height, fell down into the water, and on board the surrounding ships.'[1] By this time the moon had risen and shone down through a pall of dense black smoke upon the scene of strife and carnage.

With the destruction of the French flagship the action was virtually over. There was now no firing, except towards the enemy rear, and that broken and irregular. The *Franklin*, with two-thirds of her complement killed or wounded, fought on until shortly before midnight, when she also struck her colours. The remaining enemy ships had drifted far astern. As resistance in the centre collapsed, several of the British ships, in pursuance of Nelson's orders, passed down the line and engaged the rear. But many of the crews were utterly exhausted. Miller of the *Theseus* related: 'My people were also extremely jaded, that as soon as they had hove our sheet anchor up, they dropped under the capstan-bars and were asleep, in a moment, in every sort of posture, having been

[1] Berry, *op. cit.*, pp. 26–7.

working then at their fullest exertion, or fighting, for near twelve hours.' Ball of the *Alexander* said that his first lieutenant reported that the people 'were scarcely capable of lifting an arm', and, permission having been granted, flung themselves down by their guns and, for the space of twenty minutes, lay like the dead. One of the *Goliath*'s midshipmen fell fast asleep 'in the act of hauling up a shroud hawser'. In a short time the British concentration had obliged the *Heureux* and *Mercure* to strike. It was now sunrise. The *Généreux*, *Guillarme Tell*, and *Timoléon* got under way, and stood out of the bay in line of battle. The *Tonnant*, being dismasted, remained where she was. The *Timoléon* got ashore, and being abandoned by her crew, was set on fire with her colours flying, and soon blew up. The *Zealous* endeavoured to prevent the escape of the *Généreux* and *Guillaume Tell*, but as there was no other ship in a condition to support her, she was recalled.

With the full light of day it was seen that Brueys's line of battle had vanished overnight. The bay was strewn with varegated wreckage and scorched and mangled bodies. The whole of the enemy fleet, with the exception of the *Généreux* and *Guillaime Tell* and a couple of frigates that had also got away, were either British prizes or charred and smoking hulks. 'Victory is not a name strong enough for such a scene,' Nelson declared; he called it a conquest. 'We have left France only two sail of the line in the Mediterranean,' wrote Saumarez. 'A squadron of five sail leaves us masters of these seas.' The enemy's losses, 'taken, drowned, burnt and missing', were nearly six times greater than those of the British. Though the *Généreux* and *Guillaume Tell* had succeeded in escaping, they were taken off Malta eighteen months later. Brueys's fleet was thus annihilated.

Troubridge, having got his own ship off the sands, threw himself into the work of repairing the manifold damages sustained in the recent action; indeed, there was much to be done ('only two masts standing out of nine sail of the line'). 'Dear Troubridge,' said Nelson, 'the active business and the scolding he is obliged to be continually at, does him good.' 'I should have sunk under the fatigue of refitting the squadron,' the Admiral informed St. Vincent, 'but for Troubridge, Ball, Hood, and Hallowell. Not but all have done well: but these are my supporters.' Day by day the crews were employed in repairing the rigging and sails and fitting the ships for service again. At last, on 12 August, Nelson detached seven ships under Saumarez to escort the prizes to Gibraltar. This was a task which taxed all Saumarez's resource and seamanship: it took the battered squadron more than two months to reach the Straits. Then, leaving Hood with three of the line and three frigates to blockade Alexandria, Nelson sailed with his remaining ships to Naples.

For several nights after the action, bonfires had blazed on the sand-dunes around Aboukir Bay as the Bedouins rejoiced over the destruction of the hated enemy. The news spread far and wide across the delta. Wandering bands of partisans redoubled their guerilla attacks on the French. Far away in the desert Bonaparte, still occupied in parcelling out the provinces among his commanders following their triumphant entry into Cairo, learned of the destruction of Brueys's fleet. From that moment all his grandiose plans of eastern empire were doomed. Though he professed to make light of the British blockade, the fact remained that he and his army, encircled as they were by sea and desert, were virtually marooned. The Army of Egypt was thrown back on its own resources. For months to come neither supplies nor dispatches reached them from France.

4

At home uncertainty and gnawing suspense had prevailed all through the fine summer of 1798. 'By the publick Papers,' Woodforde wrote earlier in the year, 'every thing in them appears very distressing & alarming.' Nelson and his squadron had disappeared into the blue, and the Admiralty was severely censured for entrusting this important command to so young an admiral. A report of the enemy's having landed at Alexandria caused an immediate drop in the funds; and the public gloom was presently intensified by the news of a hostile descent on Ireland. 'The account of Bonaparte's arrival at Alexandria', wrote Pitt, 'is, I am afraid, true; but it gives us no particulars, and leaves us in entire suspense as to Nelson.' 'I have seldom', confessed Spencer, 'experienced a more severe disappointment than in the accounts which have lately reached us from the Mediterranean.'

The first rumours of a fleet action appear to have reached the Admiralty in the latter half of September. It was not, however, until 1 October, just two months after the action, that the earliest intelligence of Nelson's great victory was received in London, followed next day by the arrival of Captain Capel in the *Mutine* brig with the Admiral's dispatch. The news was immediately published in a *Gazette Extra-ordinary*. 'At last an official account has been received of Admiral Nelson's victory over the French Fleet,' Betsey Fremantle recorded in her diary on the 2nd, 'the most complete ever heard of.' The bells of London burst into joyful pealing; the guns in the Tower and Park fired a triumphal salute; the metropolis became 'one general blaze of illuminations', and the streets were crowded and uproarious to a late hour. It is related that at Drury Lane 'after the play the news of Admiral Nelson's glorious victory produced a burst of patriotic exultation that has rarely been witnessed in a theatre'. Carriages drove round the city to view the transparencies, and the 'Snug Little Island' was bawled till dawn. A wave of jubilation swept the country. Towards the end of the month Thomas Dibdin, who had celebrated the victory of Cape St. Vincent with *A Dose for the Dons*, hurriedly prepared a piece entitled *The Mouth of the Nile*, which enjoyed an enormous success at Covent Garden. In the *Annual Register* the victory was acclaimed as 'the most signal that had graced the British Navy since the days of the Spanish Armada'. In one of his most spirited cartoons Gillray depicted the one-armed Nelson slaying the French crocodiles of the Nile. Captain Berry's *Authentic Narrative* was selling like hot-cakes. The banqueting and junketing went on for weeks. 'Great Rejoicings at Norwich to day', noted Woodforde on 29 November, 'on Lord Nelson's late great & noble victory over the French near Alexandria in Egypt. An Ox rosted whole in the Market-Place &c.' Old Duncan celebrated the joyful occasion by a dinner with his officers at the Duke's Head, Yarmouth. Nelson was raised to the peerage with the title of Baron Nelson of the Nile and awarded a pension of £2,000 a year; from the East India Company, in gratitude for the protection of its Indian territories, he received a grant of £10,000; the King of the Two Sicilies later conferred on him the Duchy of Brontë; certain other sovereigns sent him handsome gifts; all his captains received gold medals, and their first lieutenants were promoted.

Nelson was now at the summit of his renown; year after year his star had been rising in the heavens; for the brief remainder of his life he was to be universally acknowledged as the greatest fighting admiral of his age. His genius for swift and audacious attack was comparable only to that of Bonaparte, as was also his faculty for exploiting to the full any success achieved over the enemy. By his whole-hearted insistence on, not merely the defeat, but the complete and utter destruction, of his antagonist, he had revolutionized the whole conception of a fleet action.

Moreover, from the campaign of the Nile arose a new tradition of leadership. This tradition, which was destined to be of incalculable value and importance, was the outcome of Nelson's independent service in the Mediterranean. Not a few of those '*élite* of the Navy of England' who had taken part in this campaign and in the crowning triumph of 1 August were companions who had assisted in the action of Cape St. Vincent the year before and had shared in the bitterness of defeat at Santa Cruz. 'I had the happiness to command a band of brothers,' he informed Howe after the victory. '. . . My friends readily conceived my plan.' Nelson's tactics were made possible, indeed, by the fine seamanship of his captains; every ship was fought with superb skill and courage. 'Never could there have been selected a set of officers better calculated for such a service,' Ross observes; 'Nelson was fortunate in commanding them and they in being commanded by him.' The action of 1 August, as Howe afterwards told Berry, 'stood unparalleled and singular in this instance, that *every Captain* distinguished himself.' 'God be praised!' exclaimed St. Vincent, 'and you and your gallant band rewarded by a grateful Country—for the greatest Achievement the history of the world can produce.' 'They are my children,' Nelson later remarked of his captains; 'they serve in my school, and I glory in them.' As at the Nile, the operation of this magical leaven was again to be a vital and decisive element in the victories of Copenhagen and Trafalgar.

5

The Nile completed the matchless roll of naval triumphs achieved during the administration of Lord Spencer, who, by his energy, zeal, and whole-hearted devotion to the business of the Navy, had become one of the ablest and most successful First Lords ever to preside over the Admiralty. No one before or since has held that office for a comparable period in war-time. The debt owed to Spencer by his country during these years of peril is almost incalculable. It was he who successively chose for their high commands Jervis, Duncan, and Nelson: with each of whom he kept up an intimate and regular correspondence. 'England,

Ireland, and India', his wife, Lady Spencer, declared, 'were all saved by victories won during his term of office.'

With the destruction of Brueys's squadron in Aboukir Bay the whole position in the great inland sea was changed. Great Britain found herself once more supreme in the Mediterranean; her influence revived all along its shores; its strategic islands and bases passed, one after the other, beneath her control; she was once more in close and constant touch with Russia; her lucrative commerce with Turkey entered upon a new lease of life; the threat to the Indian approaches had been dissipated, and Bonaparte's dreams of eastern conquest and empire had been brought to naught; the Russians and Turks were enabled to come out of the Dardanelles; and the continental enemies of France began to pluck up heart anew. The moral effect of the Nile can scarcely be set too high. 'It was this action', sums up Gravière, 'which for two years delivered the Mediterranean into the hands of the English and summoned thither the squadrons of Russia; which locked up our troops in the midst of a hostile population; which put India beyond the reach of our arms, and France in imminent jeopardy: for it rekindled the smouldering embers of strife with Austria, and brought Suvarov and the Austro-Russian army to our very frontiers.' The revolutionary navy never recovered from this calamitous blow; and the maritime ascendancy of Great Britain, which had been thus conclusively established, was to be the main and decisive factor in the long-drawn-out strife that lay ahead.

Largely through the instrumentality of the lavish subsidies provided by Pitt for the support of his allies, the Second Coalition now prepared to renew the war against revolutionary France. The moment seemed propitious for attack. Her strength rotted by corruption, her treasury empty, her armies outnumbered, France, to all appearances, was on the verge of collapse. During 1799 the Austrians and Russians overran most of Lombardy and Piedmont, and the French forces in Italy were in danger of encirclement. The French armies were also thrown back in Switzerland and southern Germany. Early in the same year a Russo-Turkish fleet entered the Mediterranean and took Corfu and Ancona.

On 7 November 1798 an expedition under Commodore Duckworth and General Sir Charles Stuart landed in Minorca; and in a little more than a week the entire island, with its important naval base of

Port Mahon, passed into British keeping. The conquest of Malta, however, proved a far more difficult matter. What had taken the French three days to achieve was to engage the British forces for more than two years.

That the victory of the Nile was not followed up with all possible dispatch was largely due to Nelson's illness resulting from the head-wound he had received in the action, which caused him to succumb all too readily to the corrupt influence of the Neapolitan Court: in his own significant words, he became *Sicilified*. 'Naples is a dangerous place,' he wrote soon after his arrival, 'and we must keep clear of it.' But he soon ceased to struggle against the strong spell that held him, and thereafter the war in the eastern Mediterranean languished.

At the end of October St. Vincent arrived at Gibraltar to supervise the preparations for the Minorca expedition. As soon as that expedition was on its way, he began the refitting of the vessels damaged at the Nile and the French prizes brought in next year by Sir James Saumarez. To this end each ship of the line engaged in blockading Cadiz was required to supply two shipwrights to the dockyard; and, thanks to the strenuous exertions of all concerned, the repairs were successfully completed without a single vessel having to leave the station.

During the winter St. Vincent turned his attention to the improvement of the docking and repairing facilities at Gibraltar, where he had found 'great want of vigour and exertion in the Dockyard'. He was of opinion that 'much more may be made of this Arsenal than I was aware of, until a three months' residence and unremitted attention to it showed me the means. Five or six ships of the line may be moored with safety in the Mole, and while we maintain our naval superiority in the Mediterranean with the additional works I have recommended, it will prove a very great resource.'[1] On Nelson's recommendation he had earlier appointed as Boatswain of the Yard one Joaquim, 'a Portugal then boatswain of the *Captain*', who had served under Nelson for many years and who latterly became known as Joe King. As usual, the squadron was starved of stores. To the Secretary of the Admiralty St. Vincent wrote, 'We are literally without a fathom of rope, yard of canvas, foot of oak or elem plank, board or log to saw them out of, have not a bit of iron, except what we draw out of condemned masts and yards, nor the smallest piece of fir plank.'[2] Nor was St. Vincent fortunate in some of

[1] Tucker, *op. cit.*, I, p. 472.
[2] Brenton, *op. cit.*, I, p. 498.

his subordinates. 'The promotion to the Flag,' he wrote caustically to Spencer in March 1799, 'has happily removed a number of officers from the command of ships of the line who at no period of their lives were capable of commanding them.'[1] Nevertheless, in spite of all difficulties, Gibraltar under his aegis developed into a major naval base, while Admiral Lord Keith, who had come out at the end of 1798 as his second-in-command, maintained a strict blockade of Cadiz.

Towards the end of 1798 the Cabinet sent Captain Sir William Sydney Smith with plenipotentiary powers to blockade the coast of Egypt, while the Turks bound themselves by treaty to send ships and troops against the French. In this way it came about that Bonaparte, advancing through Syria and capturing El Arish and Jaffa, found his path blocked by the fortress of Acre defended by the Turks and Smith's two ships of the line lying in the roadstead. To safeguard the French line of communications Acre must be taken before they could advance on Aleppo. It was at this crucial moment that Smith was fortunate enough to capture Bonaparte's siege train as it was ferried up the coast; and this was decisive. With the captured guns mounted on the walls of Acre and his ships enfilading the enemy's trenches Smith held out against Bonaparte's army, until the failure of the French assault and the arrival of the Turkish reinforcements, coupled with the onset of the plague, caused the siege to be raised on 20 May 1799, the French retiring during the night. Their dreams of eastern conquest shattered by the reverse, the enemy's forces retreated across the desert sands into Egypt. Many years afterwards Bonaparte informed Captain Maitland of the *Bellerophon* that, but for the English, he should have been Emperor of the East. 'But wherever there is water to float a ship,' he declared, 'we are sure to find you in the way.'

The fortunes of France had reached, perhaps, their lowest ebb when the Directory instructed Bruix, the youthful Minister of Marine, to take the Brest squadron down to the Mediterranean to the assistance of the French forces in Malta, Corfu, and Egypt. The preparations for this expedition occupied several months.

Notwithstanding the fact that the Admiralty had ample warning of a formidable armament fitting out in Brest (though not of its objective), they gravely miscalculated the situation. The result was that, as the crisis approached, there were by no means enough of our ships off that

[1] *Ibid.*, I, p. 472.

port. Bridport, moreover, had wholly failed to learn from experience: as usual, he was in no hurry to get to sea, and, when he finally did so, his plans miscarried ('a horrible bungling work,' was Collingwood's comment); back on his station, the few cruisers that he had with him were improvidently dispersed—and this despite the Admiralty's warning. Such was the laxity and inefficiency of his blockade that the lugger which was sent to mislead the British with false dispatches had to cruise for several days before she discovered a frigate obliging enough to capture her.

On 25 April, having looked into Brest and observed eighteen of the line ready for sea, Bridport, with the wind fair for the enemy's escape, stood out to a position four leagues W.S.W. of Ushant, where he dispatched an urgent request for reinforcements. Meanwhile Bruix, with twenty-five of the line and ten frigates, got safely away to sea, on a dark and foggy night, down the Passage du Raz. It was, perhaps, Bridport's crowning exhibition of incompetence.

Bridport then sailed for Ireland in accordance with standing orders to cover it against a possible descent. At the same time he sent word to Keith off Cadiz and St. Vincent at Gibraltar that the Brest fleet was out. Bruix stood to the southward. It was his intention to join forces with the main Spanish fleet and to effect an overwhelming concentration. Bridport's warning reached Keith in the Bay of Cadiz only one day before the enemy fleet appeared.

To leeward of the French lay Keith's blockading force of sixteen of the line, apparently at their mercy. Bruix's squadron prepared for battle. But the wind freshened, and his ships shortened sail. The strong westerly wind alike prevented his Spanish allies from putting to sea and gave the French enough to do to look after themselves. Bruix was no Hawke. He dared not attack on a lee shore with a wind blowing that would surely have taxed the abilities of seasoned crews. Keith boldly stood his ground. The wind increased to a gale. The large French squadron, under low sail, was in complete confusion. It was impossible for them to manœuvre. Bruix's only concern was for the safety of his ships. As soon as he had re-formed his squadron, he stood to the south-east and ran through the Straits. He arrived at Toulon on 14 May and remained there until the 14th.[1]

'Lord Keith', summed up St. Vincent in his dispatch, 'has shown

[1] G. Douin, *La campagne de Bruix en Méditerranée* (1923), pp. 100–7.

great manhood and ability, his position having been very critical, exposed to a hard gale of wind, blowing directly on shore, with an enemy of superior force to windward, and twenty-two sail-of-the-line ready to profit by any disaster that might have befallen him.'[1]

The sudden and unheralded arrival of Bruix with twenty-five of the line and ten frigates put the greater part of the British Mediterranean fleet, dispersed as it then was in half a dozen separate detachments, in extreme jeopardy. Our whole position in the Mediterranean was at once undermined. If Bruix sped eastward with the favouring wind he might attack and defeat in detail the scattered divisions lying at Port Mahon, Naples, Sicily, Malta, and Acre. This was his great opportunity. He had achieved a complete surprise over the enemy.

At this critical juncture, when a powerful enemy fleet was at large in the Mediterranean, Nelson's infatuation for Lady Hamilton rendered him an almost negligible factor in the complicated and constantly changing situation. The British Commander-in-Chief, moreover, was wholly mystified as to Bruix's intentions. Obliged through illness to relinquish his command, St. Vincent was succeeded by Keith, who failed to intercept Bruix when, on 6 June, he sailed for Cartagena. 'The Brest Squadron had such a game to play at Malta and Sicily,' St. Vincent observed to Spencer, 'that I trembled for the fate of our ships employed there and for the latter Island.'[2] But Bruix had thrown away his chance. He had achieved none of his objectives. He had done nothing about Duckworth's few ships stationed at Port Mahon. He had relieved neither Malta, Corfu, nor Egypt. All he did was to revictual Moreau's forces in Genoa and then return to Toulon. Then, on 22 June, he joined hands with the Spanish squadron, which, after a stormy passage, had arrived, badly damaged, at Cartagena from Cadiz. Bruix's one object was to get out of the Mediterranean with all possible speed. Early in July the combined French and Spanish squadrons returned through the Straits of Gibraltar. On the 21st Bruix's forty sail of the line sailed from Cadiz, and on the 30th Keith with thirty-one also passed through the Straits. With Keith hot on his heels, the enemy sailed northward for Brest. There they were promptly blockaded by the Channel fleet, now totalling more than fifty of the line, based on Torbay. With 'the whole naval power of France and

[1] Brenton, op. cit., II, p. 17.
[2] Ibid., II, p. 25.

Spain under lock and key', the threat of an overwhelming Franco-Spanish concentration had vanished.[1]

For Bruix's part, it may be said that his orders were badly framed—being based, apparently, on the erroneous belief that the numerically weaker British forces would simply take to flight on his arrival. It was yet another instance of the traditional French strategy of evasion, their perpetual preoccupation with ulterior objects.

St. Vincent's proposal had been to seize Malta from the French and to blockade Alexandria. But the first was partially, and the second wholly, neglected by Nelson, who remained preoccupied with Neapolitan affairs. The Admiral on his arrival at Naples had been given an overpowering reception by both Court and commonalty; the whole city was decorated in his honour; he was hailed as the saviour of their country and of the monarchy; day after day he was fêted and lionized; finally he had succumbed to the wiles of one of the most beautiful and fascinating women that have ever lived.

Meanwhile Hardy, who had succeeded Sir Edward Berry as Nelson's flag-captain, held aloof from the glittering gala scenes ashore; prepared the *Vanguard* for sea, and flatly refused to permit Lady Hamilton to interfere with the discipline of the ship. A close friendship had existed between the two men since 1796 when Nelson hoisted his broad pendant on board the *Minerva*, of which ship Hardy was the first lieutenant. From this time on their names were to be inseparably linked. Hardy, now in his thirty-first year, was one of the ablest and most devoted officers in the Service, and the Admiral came increasingly to rely upon him in all matters pertaining to the management of the ship. 'I never knew Hardy wrong upon any professional subject,' said Nelson; 'he seems imbued with an intuitive right judgment.'

In the middle of October Nelson sailed to Malta with the *Vanguard*, *Minotaur*, *Audacious*, *Goliath*, and *Mutine* brig; but leaving Ball in command of the squadron to blockade the island, he himself returned to Naples a few weeks later. In November he persuaded King Ferdinand to declare war on France, and himself sailed up the coast to capture Leghorn. But Austria failed to support the imprudent offensive; and at their first brush with the enemy the Neapolitan army, though far superior in numbers, turned about and fled. 'The Neapolitan officers have not lost much honour, for God knows', observed Nelson bitterly,

[1] Douin, *op. cit.*, pp. 223–30.

'they had but little to lose, but they lost all they had. Cannons, tents, baggage, and military chest—all were left behind.' Following this débâcle, the French began to advance upon Naples; the local Jacobins rose against Ferdinand, and the Admiral had to carry the Royal family off to Palermo, leaving their possessions on the mainland to be overrun by the enemy. Nelson fell more and more under the influence of Lady Hamilton and the Queen. 'I find', lamented the faithful Hardy to his brother-in-law in February 1799, 'the Admiral is not so anxious to quit this country as when I wrote you last.' The latter had, indeed, ceased to struggle against the strong ties, personal and political, which bound him to Sicily. He sent Troubridge with a few ships to blockade Naples and to assist the Royalist partisans on the mainland. The blockade of Malta dragged on; Gaeta was taken by Captain Louis of the *Minotaur*, and Naples was recaptured in May: a few weeks later, through the influence of Queen Caroline and Lady Hamilton, Nelson disobeyed orders and left his station off Maritimo to return to Palermo; he shifted his flag to a transport and lived ashore with Sir William and Lady Hamilton, while tongues wagged and the scandal grew apace. English visitors to Palermo told strange stories of how Nelson, after a heavy day's work, dragged off to gambling parties by Lady Hamilton, would fall fast asleep in his place beside his companion at the card table. For a period he made a not very creditable appearance in Neapolitan politics. In vain Admiral Lord Keith, who, to Nelson's disgust, had lately succeeded to the Mediterranean command, ordered him to send as many ships as could be spared from Naples.

Relations between Keith and Nelson continued to be strained during the long months when the *Foudroyant*[1] lay immobilized beside Palermo mole; until, on 12 February 1800, Nelson sailed with the Commander-in-Chief to Malta, where, ordered by Keith to chase to windward with four of the line in search of a French convoy which was reported to be making for Valetta, he succeeded in taking the *Généreux*, one of the survivors of Brueys's fleet at the Nile. Keith afterwards directed him to blockade Malta; but Nelson, pleading ill-health, once more returned to Palermo.

On the very day the *Foudroyant* returned to Malta without him the last of Brueys's battleships, the *Guillaume Tell*, suddenly weighed and

[1] Nelson had shifted his flag from the *Vanguard* to the *Foudroyant* early in June 1799.

ran out of Valetta harbour. Captain Henry Blackwood in the 36-gun frigate *Penelope* at once followed in pursuit and during the dark and squally night of 30 March rapidly overhauled her; the *Foudroyant* and the *Lion*, 64, had also joined in the chase. The Frenchman's only hope of safety was somehow to shake off the pursuing battleships before daylight. This hope was shattered by the bold and brilliant tactics adopted by Blackwood, as a result of which the *Guillaume Tell* lost both her main and mizen topmasts. On coming up with the chase, according to the *Penelope*'s log, Blackwood's frigate 'luffed under her stern, and gave him the larboard broadside, bore up under the larboard quarter and gave him the starboard broadside, receiving from him only his stern-chase guns. From this hour till daylight, finding that we could place ourselves on either quarter, the action continued in the foregoing manner, and with such success on our side that, when day broke, the *Guillaume Tell* was found in a most dismantled state.'[1] Throughout the engagement Blackwood manœuvred his frigate so skilfully that she sustained hardly any damage and had only one man killed, while her opponent suffered severely. At five in the morning the *Lion* and shortly afterwards the *Foudroyant* appeared on the scene; and, after a gallant but hopeless resistance, the *Guillaume Tell*, now totally dismasted and having suffered appalling casualites, was obliged to haul down her colours. That she had thus been brought to action and made a prize was entirely due to Blackwood's brilliant handling of his small vessel.

Nelson was off Valetta again in May, and was welcomed by several of the 'band of brothers'. Then he returned to Palermo; nor could the entreaties of Ball, Troubridge, and others of his old comrades ever draw him back again to Malta. The siege of Valetta dragged on for another nine months.

For some time disturbing rumours about Nelson had been reaching the Admiralty. Already his infatuation for Lady Hamilton had become the talk of London clubs and drawing-rooms, and the subject of 'unpleasant paragraphs in the newspapers'. 'They say here,' declared his friend Admiral Goodall, 'you are Rinaldo in the arms of Armida, and that it requires the firmness of an Ubaldo, and his brother Knights, to draw you from the Enchantress.' Towards the close of April, the First Lord had written to express his concern that the state of Nelson's health should have been such as to oblige him to quit his station off

[1] Q. *Blackwood's Magazine*, Vol. 34, p. 6.

Malta; and finally he took action. 'I am quite clear,' wrote Spencer significantly to the Admiral on 9 May, 'and I believe I am joined in opinion by all your friends here, that you will be more likely to recover your health and strength in England than in an inactive situation at a Foreign Court.'

The news reached Sir William Hamilton that he was about to be superseded by the Hon. Arthur Paget, who was already on his way out to Sicily to take up his appointment. Nelson and his friends had resolved to return home overland. On 10 June—the day of Marengo— he arrived at Leghorn, and a month later struck his flag and set out for Vienna in company with Queen Caroline and the Hamiltons. He remained in that city for about a month, and then resumed his journey— in part triumphal, in part ludicrous—across Central Europe with Sir William and Lady Hamilton. (It was at Dresden, where they passed a few days with the British minister, Hugh Elliot, that the latter made the caustic comment about 'Anthony and Moll-Cleopatra'.) There were those who would certainly have predicted that Nelson's professional career was at an end. 'He is covered with stars, ribbons and medals,' declared Sir John Moore, who had seen him that summer in Leghorn, 'more like a Prince of an Opera than the Conqueror of the Nile. It is really melancholy to see a grave and good man, who has deserved well of his country, cutting so pitiful a figure.' On all sides Nelson was received with applause and adulation, but none more fulsome than the flattery to which he was treated by Lady Hamilton. 'She puffs the incense full in his face,' observed Mrs. St. George, 'but he receives it with pleasure and snuffs it up very cordially.' 'Lady Hamilton was associated with all his ideal of Victory and triumph,' commented the Duchess of Devonshire long afterwards. 'She fed his vanity by every art that could gratify it.' After nearly a year's leisurely travel, the party at last reached England, where their reception was such as might have been expected. The scandal was considerable. The Hero of the Nile had not only lain in Circe's arms, but had insisted on bringing Circe home with him. The Admiral was loudly huzza'd by the mob: but the English ruling class tittered or frowned, and he was snubbed by the King. The break-up of Nelson's marriage soon followed.

6

The débâcle of the Nile, followed as it was by the disastrous Syrian campaign, represented the first serious reverse of Bonaparte's meteoric career. The latter, however, soon showed that he was a force still to be reckoned with. On 11 July a Turkish squadron arrived in Aboukir Bay escorting a convoy of troop-transports carrying a large army and accompanied by Sydney Smith with two of the line. The Turks disembarked and captured Aboukir Island. But on the 25th Bonaparte, having rapidly concentrated his forces in the vicinity of Alexandria, attacked the invaders on the Aboukir peninsula to such effect that the entire Turkish army was either killed, driven into the sea and drowned, or taken prisoner. Among those captured was the Turkish commander-in-chief, Mustapha Pasha. On 22 August, learning that Sydney Smith had temporarily raised the blockade of Alexandria, Bonaparte embarked with several of his principal generals in a frigate which, after a safe but tedious passage, arrived on 9 October off Fréjus in the south of France. He received an enthusiastic welcome and was carried ashore in triumph. All the way up to Paris admiring crowds pressed around his carriage and acclaimed him as the saviour of his country. He had appeared at an opportune moment. France was on the brink of anarchy. The Directory was by this time utterly discredited, while Bonaparte's brilliant military record had captured the French imagination. Within a month of his arrival at Fréjus he had overthrown the Directory and seized the supreme power in France, with the title of First Consul. By the following spring he had consolidated his position and could take the field again.

During the past year France had been assailed by a coalition comprising Austria, Great Britain, Russia, Naples, Portugal, and Turkey. Her armies in Holland, in Italy, and along the Rhine had been forced back with heavy losses. Later, in Germany, Moreau began to regain ground; but in Italy the French under Suchet found themselves heavily outnumbered and in danger of encirclement; while the Republic lay open to the threat of invasion through Provence. The French, however, possessed a strong central position in Switzerland, which exposed the Imperialist forces in Italy to a formidable blow from the rear. It was there that Bonaparte perceived his opportunity.

Crossing the Alps at the head of an army of 50,000 men, and making a hazardous flank march through Piedmont to Milan and then south to the Po Valley, Bonaparte cut through the enemy's communications, forcing him to retire, and finally overthrew the Austrians, on 4 June 1800, on the hard-fought field of Marengo. Desaix, whose providential arrival had saved the day for Bonaparte, perished on the battle-field; but the allied triumphs in Europe during the preceding year were nullified by this brilliant stroke. The following December Moreau destroyed another great Austrian army at Hohenlinden in southern Germany; moreover, the line of Austrian fortresses along the Mincio was turned by the passage of the Splügen in mid-winter by Macdonald—one of the finest achievements of the war.

Following on the collapse of the British campaign in the West Indies, the Cabinet in 1799 decided on a conjunct descent upon the Helder to expel the French from Holland. Under the terms of a treaty signed on 22 June with the Russians, the latter were to assist in this invasion, which was linked with a general offensive of the allied armies in the autumn. The expedition finally left England on 13 August; and, after being delayed by gales, the disembarkation of the advanced guard began at dawn on the 27th some four miles south of the Helder under cover of a heavy barrage from the guns of the North Sea squadron. The British troops under the command of Sir Ralph Abercromby successfully pushed back the French and Dutch; and on the 30th Rear-Admiral Mitchell, standing up the channel between the Helder and Texel Island, captured the whole Dutch squadron, comprising seven of the line and eighteen smaller craft, where they lay at anchor. But Abercromby failed to follow up his success in time; and the opportunity thus let slip was never to be regained. In the second week of September the invading force was reinforced by a large Anglo-Russian army; and the Duke of York arrived to take over the command. There were by this time more than 40,000 allied troops in Holland, three-quarters of them British. Attempting to fight their way through to Amsterdam, they were repulsed at Bergen on the 19th; after which the weather set in wet and stormy. The campaign now stagnated; and, the evacuation of the allied army having been decided upon, it was taken off by the fleet, with the loss of four ships and several hundred men, early in November. The vacillating and ill-coordinated strategy of the Cabinet, combined with the incompetence, jealousy, and dissensions of our allies, had frittered away the unique opportunities secured for us by the victory of the Nile.[1]

Shaken by the twin disasters of Marengo and Hohenlinden the Emperor sued for peace. On 9 February 1801 his government came to terms with Bonaparte in the Treaty of Lunéville, which restored to France the situation accepted four years earlier at Campo Formio. Once more the Hapsburgs were obliged to recognize the incorporation in France of Belgium and the Rhine frontier and the annexation of Savoy—as well as the Batavian, Helvetic, and Cisalpine Republics. Already the Tsar had abandoned the alliance; even the Kingdom of Naples was seeking peace with France and her young master; and finally Great Britain was left to carry on the war alone.

[1] Austria's stubborn refusal to take advantage of the amphibious power exercised by her British ally was in no small degree responsible for her overthrow at Marengo and the subsequent collapse of the Second Coalition.

VI

The Western Squadron

I

Though the Second Coalition was disintegrating and France had regained control of the Continent, the dominion of the sea still remained to Great Britain. Her maritime strength was further enhanced by the appointment, in the spring of 1800, of St. Vincent, whose health had lately somewhat improved, to the command of the Channel fleet, or Western Squadron. Despite the alarmed protests of his physician, the old Admiral prepared to hoist his flag once again. 'The king and the government require it,' he declared, 'and the discipline of the British navy demands it. It is of no consequence to me whether I die afloat or ashore.'

'You will', his pupil Nelson predicted, 'have an Herculean labour to make them what you had brought the Mediterranean fleet to.' But it was just this Herculean labour that St. Vincent proposed to undertake. At the outset he found the Channel fleet, as he later remarked, 'at the lowest ebb of wretched and miserable discipline'; the true cause of the trouble lying, in his estimation, in the 'licentiousness of the wardroom' and 'the old women, some of them in the guise of young men, I am burthened with.' 'Government', observed Troubridge, who early in the year had been appointed his Captain of the Fleet, 'would save much if these old women captains could be put safe on shore, it is what they are always expressing a wish for. I could give you a long list of these old ladies who have forgot everything they ever knew.'

It is said that when the news of St. Vincent's appointment reached the Channel fleet, the toast was given by one of the captains at Lord Bridport's own table: 'May the discipline of the Mediterranean never be introduced into the Channel Fleet!' According to his secretary, this gross breach of decorum evoked a swift reply from St. Vincent. "Bring me the Mediterranean order-books, Mr. Tucker," he said. And his Lordship at once issued every single order tending to enforce the discipline and general good management of the ships, establishing every restriction which had before been productive of such good effect. He at the same time addressed a courteous but firm letter to all the Admirals and Captains, requesting their cooperation.'[1]

'I am at my wit's end,' St. Vincent later declared, 'to meet every evasion and neglect of duty. Seven-eighths of the Captains who compose this fleet . . . are practising every subterfuge to get into harbour for the winter, and encouraging their carpenters to an exposition of defects, &c. &c.' Of Rear-Admiral Berkeley he wrote, 'He is now manœuvering to get to Spithead, and has called my old friend Lady Louisa Lennox to his aid, who, in a cunning, canting letter, described Mrs. Berkeley in such a way that she cannot live without seeing him now and then'. Similar disapprobation was visited upon the 'captains of frigates whose dilatory conduct in port annoys me beyond expression. All the married ones have their wives there, which plays the devil with them.' ('When an officer marries,' the Admiral declared, 'he is d – d for the service.') It is scarcely surprising in the circumstances that St. Vincent incurred the displeasure, not merely of the officers, but also of their families living ashore; and the story is told that on a festive occasion one good lady gave as a bumper toast: 'May his next glass of wine choke the wretch!'

St. Vincent's stern measures excited much resentment among his subordinate commanders; and several of these indignantly protested. To one of them the Admiral's secretary was instructed to reply, that, if he could not bear to be separated from his wife in war-time, 'it would be very unwise and unjust for him to delay for one day his intention of retiring.' Even so good and conscientious an officer as Collingwood was not immune from the prevailing discontent. 'I have been near five weeks in port,' declared Collingwood from Cawsand Bay, early in the following year, 'but I have little satisfaction here, for I have neither ate nor slept ashore. The Admiralty have given orders

[1] Not all the captains were opposed to the new Commander-in-Chief. Pellew, commanding the *Impétueux* off the Black Rocks, rejoiced most cordially 'in losing the old Lady Bridport': 'You will have heard that we are to have a new Commander-in-Chief, heaven be praised. The old one is scarcely worth drowning, a more contemptible or more miserable animal does not exist' (*Q*. C. N. Parkinson, *Edward Pellew Viscount Exmouth*, p. 228).

that no captain in this port shall sleep out of his ship.' 'This is the third summer that I have hardly seen the leaf of the trees,' he later lamented, 'except through a glass at the distance of some leagues.' To the remonstrances of Lord Spencer, who thought, perhaps, that these measures might have been carried too far, St. Vincent addressed a firm rejoinder: 'I have great confidence for your judgment,' he told the First Lord, 'but the *suaviter in modo* will not do here. I have tried it in vain.'[1]

A few, a mere handful, of the officers' wives came down to live in temporary quarters on the shores of Torbay, where from time to time their husbands might be able to see them without infringing the Admiral's rules. Mrs Collingwood and her small daughter, Sall, settled for several months in the pleasant village of Paignton, a few miles from Tor Quay; but her husband's fervent hope 'that some good gale might have driven us in there' was not to be fulfilled. Captain Markham of the *Centaur* rented Livermead Cottage, situated by the strand between Tor Quay and Paignton, for his wife Anne. Here Mrs. Markham dwelt with Bob, their dog, cultivated flowers and vegetables for her husband and his officers, went on Sundays to worship at Tor church, and climbed the neighbouring hills to catch a glimpse of the distant topsails of St. Vincent's fleet. In the month of July, when the *Centaur* was docked for necessary repairs, and also the following Christmas, when the squadron lay windbound in Torbay, Captain Markham was able to pass his leisure hours ashore in the day-time. Pellew's Susan was at Brixham. 'Summer is pleasant enough,' she declared; 'in June I have hopes we may all be . . . at Torbay, our cub is there.' But for the most part the officers of the fleet saw no more of their wives and children than did the men.

As in years gone by, the governing factors in the blockade of the enemy's ports—which put so heavy and continued a strain upon men and gear—were the health and morale of the ships' companies. the cleaning, refitting, and victualling of ships: and, last but not least, the weather.

2

During the months which followed the most careful attention was paid to the food, clothing, bedding, and general well-being of the

[1] *Spencer Papers*, IV, p. 12.

crews under St. Vincent's command. He revived the system of refit and maintenance developed by Sir Edward Hawke in the blockade of Brest in 1759.[1] Like his great antagonist, Napoleon, St. Vincent appreciated to the full the importance of the commissariat. Periodically the victuallers arrived from the English ports, bringing bread, beef, port, and pease, and bearing off the empty casks. It was the regularity and sufficiency of these supplies which made it possible for the hard-worked crews to remain so long at sea. 'I expect to be blockading for 20 weeks longer,' wrote Pellew in the spring of 1801. 'We make nothing now of a six months Cruise. We have only been 6 days in port for the last six months.'

In all these measures for the improvement of health and living conditions on the mess decks the Admiral was principally guided by the advice of his private physician, Sir Andrew Baird, whom he took to sea with him and who acted for some time as unofficial Physician of the Fleet. Room for improvement there undoubtedly was. 'Tho' poor,' Troubridge had observed while on the Mediterranean station under Nelson, 'I would sooner give up my commission than hold my ship as the captains of the Channel Fleet do, the men not half so comfortable as ours.' Under Bridport, moreover, the ships' surgeons had all too frequently neglected their duty, to the detriment of the health of the crews. 'The moment they obtain a diploma,' wrote St. Vincent to the Medical Board, 'they think themselves above the most ordinary and useful parts of their duty, play on the flute and at back-gammon the whole day and make their journals from Cullen and other medical authors which give them a reputation with your Board without the smallest title to it.' The period was one of steady progress in the medical service of the fleet.[2] For the future well-appointed sick-bays replaced the sluttish old sick-berths behind screens; scurvy was practically extirpated by the general use of lemon-juice, as well as by more regular supplies of fresh meat, fruit, and vegetables; all men who wanted it were to be vaccinated against small-pox; bedding was ordered to be regularly aired whenever the weather permitted it;

[1] See the present writer, *Quiberon Bay* (1960), pp. 58–69 *et passim*.

[2] The vitally important subject of medicine and hygiene in the Navy has only very lately received the attention that it deserves. See Lloyd and Coulter, *Medicine and the Navy*, 1714–1815, also E. Turner, 'Naval Medical Service, 1793–1815' in *Mariner's Mirror*, Vol. 46 (1960).

stoves and better methods of ventilation were introduced; and on the lower and orlop decks dry scrubbing with sand and holystone was substituted for washing. Such was the improvement in the health of the crews that a hospital ship was no longer required to accompany the fleet and when St. Vincent's ships returned to Spithead after their long vigil off Ushant only sixteen cases of scurvy were reported out of 23,000 men. 'Of all the services I lay claim to,' he observed in later years, 'the preservation of the health of our fleets is my proudest boast.' 'You taught us to keep the seamen healthy without going into port', declared Nelson, the greatest of his pupils, in congratulation, 'and to stay at sea for years without a refit.'[1]

3

Owing to the fallacious dispositions of his two predecessors, many of the advantages of a large Western Squadron had hitherto been lost. With more than fifty sail of the line under his command Bridport, as we have seen, had signally failed to prevent the escape of Bruix from Brest in 1799. Moreover, the laxity and indiscipline prevailing in the Channel fleet were becoming notorious. For the partiality of many of the senior officers for Bridport's system—or, rather, his lack of one —may be attributed quite as much to their marked aversion to the dangers and hardships of the close blockade as to any special concern for the good of their ships.

St. Vincent put a stop to all that. His orders exuded an energy and drive that the fleet had not known since the days of Hawke. 'While I command the Western Squadron,' he declared in the summer of 1800, 'no ships shall go to Spithead unless to dock or shift lower topmasts.' Henceforward ships normally went in to refit in Torbay or Cawsand Bay; and his orders to his second-in-command, when later left in charge off Brest, were 'on *no* account to authorize any ships to go to Spithead, unless by special orders from the Admiralty or from me.' 'The time for remaining in Plymouth Sound or Cawsand Bay,' St. Vincent directed, '*never* ought to exceed six days, unless a mast is to be shifted, and in that event not more than ten days.' 'A thousand thanks are due to you', he wrote to Rear-Admiral Whitshed, 'for the pains you have taken to dispatch the ships which were necessarily

[1] Tucker, *Memoirs of the Earl of St. Vincent*, II, p. 51.

sent into Cawsand Bay. Without such powerful aid, all my endeavours
to fulfil the wishes of the Cabinet would be in vain.' He sharply reminded one of his captains that 'a few sheets of copper off a frigate's
bottom is not a sufficient ground for remaining a day in port'; he gave
orders that leave was only to be granted between sunrise and sunset:
that no officer, from the captain down, should sleep ashore or go
further from the beach than Paignton or upper Brixham: that no
petty officer or man was to be allowed to leave his boat on any pretext
whatever: that no boats were to remain on shore after sunset; and he
directed all captains in turn to take guard-duty at Brixham watering-
place, assisted by a force of marines under their commanding officer,
'to prevent straggling and liquor being brought down to the beach'.
In these strictures he spared no one, however exalted the offender.
'As you know everything at your board, by hook or by crook,' he
wrote that summer to Nepean, the Secretary of the Admiralty, 'you
are probably informed that an Admiral was left behind when we last
sailed from Torbay,—half a dozen Captains, under the same circumstances, *has been* a trifle here!'[1]

Subordinate admirals who believed themselves to be above discipline; 'old lady captains' who were loth to quit the shore; uxorious
commanders who could scarcely bear to be parted from their wives
in war-time; dashing young frigate captains who vastly preferred to go
cruising after prizes to monotonous blockading duties; comfort-loving
commanders who abhorred the thought of turning out of warm beds
on to the windswept poop in the chill hour before dawn—all found
that they had met their match in St. Vincent.

Before many months were past St. Vincent's grim determination
and ruthless driving force had effected a great change, and this fleet,
like the Mediterranean, had been raised to the highest pitch of seamanship, discipline, and morale. Once more there was at sea a strong
and active Western Squadron, ably commanded, such as had brought
victory both in the war of 1739-48 and in the Seven Years' War. As in
earlier wars, this was the keystone of our naval strategy. Not for
nothing had this force been known from time out of mind as the 'Grand
Fleet'. St. Vincent's command comprised no less than forty sail of the
line, and five subordinate admirals. (It is no less significant that half
the captains in the squadron with which Nelson reduced the Danes

[1] *Ibid.*, II, pp. 14, 35, 78, 80.

at Copenhagen in 1801 were drawn from the revitalized Channel fleet.)

The blockade of the enemy's principal arsenal at Brest was maintained with a vigilance and efficiency undreamed of under the easygoing regimen of a Howe or a Bridport. The strength of the force on the blockading station was increased to between twenty-four and thirty of the line. Vessels went in to refit only when it was absolutely necessary, and then very few at a time. All St. Vincent's energies were directed towards expediting the refitting of vessels, prolonging their stay on their station, and keeping the largest possible force concentrated at the decisive point off Brest.

At the outset of St. Vincent's command the Channel fleet was dispersed by a violent gale. In the middle of May the fine weather broke up. The wind shifting from south-east to south-west, the weather became thick and hazy, with rain. During the night of 16–17 May 1800 the wind increased to gale force and next day shifted suddenly to north-west before the south-westerly sea had had time to subside. Towards noon, as the storm increased, with a heavy, breaking sea from the north-west, some of the vessels were 'labouring much and shipping much water'. The *Warrior*, being unable to weather Ushant, wore and stood to the southward; the *Montagu* lost all her masts; the *Ville de Paris* carried away her main topmast, the *Windsor Castle* her mainyard, and the *Prince*, *Hector*, and *Atlas* their main topmasts. Two sloops capsized and were lost with all hands. The *Ville de Paris* and a number of other ships having weathered Ushant scudded, under storm staysails, before the gale. By the afternoon of the 17th few of St. Vincent's ships were in sight of each other. During the absence of the squadron the *Beaulieu* frigate with a few small cruisers continued to cruise off the Brittany coast.[1]

On the 18th the *Ville de Paris* arrived in Torbay, where most of the

[1] From the log of the *Beaulieu*, 17 May 1800: A.M. Very sudden squalls and high sea. Split the main topsail by the sheet being carried away and the main sail blew to pieces in the act of setting. Furled the main topsail and sent down topgallantyards. Struck the masts and set the remains of the main sail adrift. ¼ before 2 wore ship and in fore top-sail. ¼ past up foresail and ranged the bower cables on deck. P.M. Hard gales and thick weather and a high sea. All hands empl'd bending another main sail. Reefed the course at 6. One cutter in sight. At 7 bore up for the Passage du Raz not being able to weather the Saints. Up main sail. Strong gales with heavy squalls and a high sea from the west (Adm. 51/1298, 17 May 1800).

squadron came to anchor. A few vessels took refuge in Cawsand Bay. In his dispatch to the Admiralty, St. Vincent reported that the flagship had 'lost her maintopmast and gaff, and had her fore and main courses, and main and fore staysails, split, and rendered useless. Observing on the morning of the 17th that the *Prince* and *Hector* had also lost their main topmasts, and the other ships of the squadron had suffered various damage, I judged it expedient to make the signal, to proceed to this rendezvous'.[1] But within a few days the squadron had regained their station off Ushant and there remained for nearly four months.[2] It is questionable whether anyone but St. Vincent could have accomplished such a feat.

The bay where in severe weather the Channel fleet was so often to anchor in the years to come lay about a hundred miles to the westward of Portsmouth. It was bounded on the north by Hope's Nose and on the south by Berry Head, the entrance being nearly four miles across. With the exception of the foul ground of the Ridge, the whole of Torbay afforded spacious and good anchorage, being well sheltered from the prevailing westerly winds. Strategically it was well situated for exploiting to the full the advantages that Great Britain always enjoyed over the enemy in the Channel. While Falmouth, lying a good deal further to the westward, was admirably suited for a rendezvous, it did not stand well as a port in the consensus of professional opinion; moreover, as Mahan has pointed out, 'ships running for refuge to Torbay would have the wind three points more free, an advantage seamen will appreciate.' By the end of October the seamanship and discipline of St. Vincent's force had improved to such a degree that, as he was presently able to inform the First Lord, the whole squadron could 'be got under sail and well out of the Bay in an hour and a half from the time of making the signal to unmoor.'[3]

4

The navigational conditions in the approaches to Brest rendered it impossible to maintain the main body of the squadron close in with the port. Brest road, which is entered by a long, narrow passage called

[1] Adm. 1/116, 18 May 1800.
[2] Adm. 1/116, 117, *passim*.
[3] *Spencer Papers*, III, pp. 377–8.

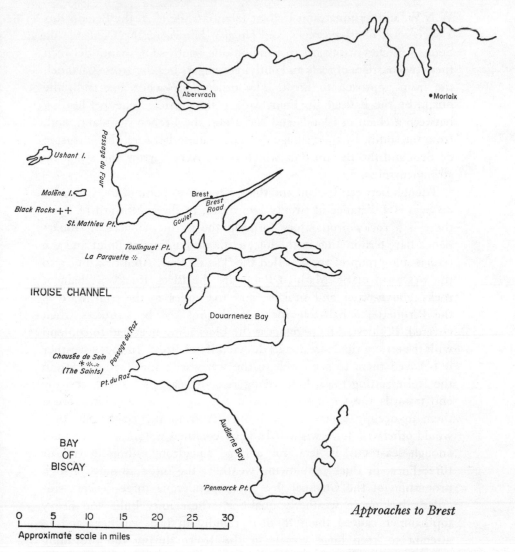

Aberⅴrac'h

•Morlaix

Ushant I.

Passage du Four

Molène I.

Black Rocks ++

St. Mathieu Pt.

Brest

Brest Road

Goulet

Toulinguet Pt.

La Parquette ⁙

IROISE CHANNEL

Douarnenez Bay

Passage du Raz

Chausée de Sein
⁘ ⁙...
(The Saints)

Pt. du Raz

Audierne Bay

BAY
OF
BISCAY

'Penmarck Pt.

Approaches to Brest

0   5   10   15   20   25   30
Approximate scale in miles

the Goulet, lies at the head of a deep indentation between St. Mathieu
Point and the Bec du Raz. Just outside the Goulet are two open
anchorages, Berthaume Bay to the north and Camaret Bay to the
south, in which the enemy's ships often used to assemble prior to
setting out on a cruise or when waiting for a wind. From both St.
Mathieu Point and the Bec du Raz a tongue of foul ground extends
for fifteen miles directly seaward; that from St. Mathieu Point trends

F

W.N.W. and terminates in Ushant Island, while from the Bec du Raz a succession of islets, reefs, and shoals—known as the Chaussée de Sein—stretches westward to a point due south of Ushant. Between these two barriers of reefs and outlying dangers lies the Iroise Channel, the main approach to Brest. The other approaches are, from the north, by the Passage du Four, a deep but intricate channel leading between a chain of islands and rocks and the French mainland, and, from the south, by the Passage du Raz, leading between the Chaussée de Sein and the Bec du Raz, which is also very narrow and swept by strong currents.

Though between Ushant and the westernmost point of the Chaussée de Sein is a distance of twenty-two miles, to the southward of Brest there is a rocky promontory forming the northern shore of Douarnenez Bay, terminating in the lofty cliffs of Toulinguet Point and the remarkable group of rocks called the Tas de Pois. About six miles to the westward of St. Mathieu Point are the Black Rocks, a chain of rocks, above-water and sunken; and five miles to the southward is the Parquette, a half-tide rock, usually marked by breakers when covered. Besides all these dangers the blockading fleet had to contend with the strong tidal streams in the vicinity of Brest. In foggy weather it behoved them to keep well to the westward—the flood stream in the Iroise setting towards the dangers south-east of Ushant, and the ebb towards the Chaussée de Sein. All these considerations forced them to occupy a station much further from the coast than they would otherwise have wished. In such confined waters there was not enough sea-room, in fact, for a large squadron, sailing in two or three lines, in thick or blowing weather: the more so since a high proportion of the Channel fleet were ponderous three-deckers singularly lacking in weatherly qualities, whose lofty hulls and heavy top-hamper caused them to drift rapidly in bad weather; and to attempt to keep huge vessels in the Iroise during the prevailing westerlies of the Bay of Biscay was to invite disaster. It was therefore imperative for the fleet to keep the English Channel open in case of heavy westerly weather. For this purpose the vicinity of Ushant—a flat, craggy island with granite cliffs, easily recognized—became the regular rendezvous of the Channel fleet.

As has been said elsewhere, the strategy of the close blockade of Brest was based on the fundamental fact that hard westerly gales which obliged the Channel squadron to bear up for Plymouth or Torbay would equally prevent the enemy from getting out of port; and that a shift of wind which enabled the French to leave Brest would also serve to bring the blockading force back on its station.

The seamanlike care and judgment with which St. Vincent disposed his force off the stormy Brittany coast excited the wonder and admiration of his contemporaries. These dispositions marked a return to the strategy inaugurated by Hawke in the Seven Years' War. The rendezvous of the main body of the Western Squadron was henceforth changed from eight leagues west of Ushant to 'well in with Ushant in an easterly wind'. The salutary effect of a Commander-in-Chief being continually at sea with his fleet was soon made manifest. 'Lord Howe,' Codrington related, 'by his forbearance, failed in obtaining that discipline, that perfection of manœuvre which the fleet ought to have attained; Lord St. Vincent obtained a strict and ready obedience by a severity which nobody could venture to resist.' In the ensuing weeks a transformation was wrought. In the middle of May the Commander-in-Chief took the opportunity of

expressing the satisfaction he derives from the zeal and activity shown in the squadron he has the honour to command; and has simply to recommend keeping the columns in compact order when wind and weather will permit, which can only be done by increasing sail, in small proportions, the moment the ship is perceived to drop, and when the ship is made to tack or wear, more particularly in succession, by every ship clapping on as much canvas as the distance from the file-leader will permit (and not to back, except to avoid an evident shock) and by not standing beyond the wake of the leader before she begins her movement. The officers commanding the Middle Watch are strictly enjoined to preserve close order at daybreak, to facilitate an immediate attack on falling in with the enemy, more especially on his coming out of port.[1]

'I never was on a station so readily, and with so little risk maintained as that off Ushant with an easterly wind,' St. Vincent remarked, 'owing to the length and strength of flood-tide'; and elsewhere he observed, 'If the flood flows strong, you will find *much shelter* between Ushant and the Black Rocks during the day'.[2]

To maintain this station, the ships were forced to tack or wear during the night. 'The principle upon which the squadron acts,' St.

[1] Add. MSS 31, 188, 10 May 1800.
[2] Tucker, *op. cit.*, II, pp. 14, 115.

Vincent explained, 'with the wind easterly, is to wear the sternmost and leewardmost first, which we are pretty expert in the practice of, even during the night, so as to be within a couple of leagues of Ushant at daylight in the morning.' This was an operation which, with so large a fleet and in the hours of darkness, required a high degree of seamanship and practice in sail-drill. One of St. Vincent's most stringent rules was that captains must be on deck while the evolution was in progress. 'The Commander-in-Chief', it was laid down in general orders, 'cannot suppose it possible that any Captain of a ship under his command is off the Quarter-deck or poop when any movement of the ship is made, night or day.' It is related by his secretary that one cold, rough November night, when the signal had been made 'to tack in succession', the old Admiral was discovered standing in the stern gallery of the *Ville de Paris*, clad only in his flannel dressing-gown and cocked hat, intently observing the movements of the fleet. 'When the secretary attempted to persuade him to return to his cabin, "Hush, Sir!" replied the Admiral: "I want to see how the evolution is performed in *such* a night of weather; and to know whether Jemmy [Captain James Vashon, of the *Neptune*, the second astern of the flagship] is on deck?" But the latter point being soon certified by Jemmy's shrill voice giving the usual warning, "Are you all ready forward there?"—"Ay", said the old Chief, "*that* will do"; and then the Secretary's entreaties were permitted to prevail.'[1]

5

The advanced squadron was anchored, in easterly winds, between the Black Rocks and Parquette Shoal—a station which soon gained a dread reputation as the 'New Siberia' and which, on some obscure *lucus a non lucendo* principle, St. Vincent was pleased to describe as the 'Elysian Lake'. In this post of peril, where long ago in 'the Great Fifty-nine' Augustus Hervey's small force had served as the eyes and ears of Hawke's fleet;[2] on the threshold of a hostile port containing more than two dozen of the line, which might at any moment slip out and attack a squadron of six; surrounded by dangers of every description and exposed to the full force of south-westerly winds, the

[1] *Ibid.*, II, pp. 40, 41–2, 114–15.
[2] Cf. *Quiberon Bay*, pp. 89–104.

advanced squadron was stationed to watch the motions of the enemy.

St. Vincent experienced the greatest difficulty in securing an admiral capable of commanding this force. 'It is evident', he informed Spencer that summer, 'that the man who faces a Frenchman or Spaniard with intrepidity does not always encounter rocks and shoals with the same feeling.' 'My *élève* Rear-Admiral Berkeley does not like the Black Rocks where I was obliged to pin him,' he observed on another occasion, 'for tho' when under sail with an easterly wind he was strictly enjoined to be close in with them at daylight every morning, I generally found him without me: probably not imagining that I was upon deck at 3 o'clock A.M.'[1]

'In the execution of this important service', St. Vincent informed Rear-Admiral Sir James Saumarez, who was in command of the inshore squadron during the later months of the blockade, 'the Line of Battle Ships, composing the advanced squadron, are to be anchored during an Easterly Wind, in the Iroise Passage, as well to support the look out Frigates, &c. as to intercept a Squadron of the Enemy which is held in constant readiness to slip out the very first opportunity that shall offer; and during a Westerly Wind, you are not to fail in making Brest every day, if possible, but at all events to take such precautions as will enable you to resume your former position in the Iroise, on the first appearance of Easterly Wind.' 'Inside,' he observed, 'between them and the Goulet, cruise a squadron of frigates and cutters plying day and night in the opening of the Goulet; and outside, between the Black Rocks and Ushant, three-sail-of-the-line cruise to support the five anchored.' The proper support of the inshore squadron was thus assured. 'Unless this is done', declared St. Vincent, 'the ships appointed to that important service may not feel the confidence necessary to keep them in their post—a failure in which has frequently happened before I was invested with this command.'[2]

The new dispositions ensured that the inshore squadron was close enough to Brest to watch the enemy's fleet; that it was strong enough not to be driven off without bringing on a general action; and that the main body was close enough in to lend the inshore squadron proper support.

[1] *Spencer Papers*, IV, pp. 6, 18.
[2] Ross, *Memoirs and Correspondence of Admiral Lord de Saumarez* (1838), I, p. 299, II. pp. 14, 88.

During Saumarez's period of command on the advanced station he was responsible for an important innovation. Towards the end of September a heavy gale came on, which obliged the force to abandon their post in the Iroise; but instead of bearing up for Torbay, as had been the practice hitherto, Saumarez put into Dournenez Bay, where he anchored with his whole squadron, just out of reach of the enemy's mortar batteries; and, striking topmasts and lower yards, rode out the equinoctial gales in safety.

'This is a most spacious bay', he observed in his dispatch, 'and may be considered safe anchorage in any weather: it lies about four leagues to the southward of Brest; from which port it is only separated about five miles by land, over a mountainous and hilly country. As the same winds that enable the enemy's fleet to put to sea, also lead out of this bay, we can always be in time for them; and this appears the most favourable position to prevent their coasting convoys coming from the southern ports.' 'I repose such unbounded confidence in your zeal and judgment,' St. Vincent informed Saumarez, 'that *I sleep as soundly as if I had the key of Brest in my possession.*'[1]

On 9 November, preceded by a spell of thick, hazy weather and an ominous swell from the westward, there came another heavy gale. The wind, which had been westerly, now backed to the S.W. and blew with increasing violence. The squadron lay-to under reefed foresail and storm-staysail. Though on the 10th the wind moderated, it soon freshened again and on the 12th shifted to the N.W., upon which Saumarez made the signal for the squadron to bear up for Torbay, where the main body of the Channel fleet was already at anchor. After three days in harbour, hard at work refitting and getting in fresh water and supplies, the squadron returned to its post. It has been claimed that during the whole fifteen weeks Saumarez commanded the advanced squadron, not a vessel either sailed from, or entered, the port of Brest.[2]

Collingwood did not care for the perilous station in the Iroise. 'It is a style of cruising unknown in any former period,' he wrote gloomily in later years. 'How very odd Lord Keppel's letter reads now! who thought he was near enough Ushant at 35 leagues.' The strain imposed by days and nights of fog in the vicinity of the Black Rocks,

[1] *Ibid.*, I, pp. 303, 305.
[2] *Ibid.*, I, p. 315.

where so many ships narrowly escaped shipwreck, and a number of them actually were wrecked, was also telling on the commander. 'Sir James Saumerez will never complain,' St. Vincent observed to the First Lord in September, 'but I am told he is as thin as a shotten red herring.'

Saumerez returned home in mid-December and was succeeded by Sir Edward Thornbrough. On 7 March 1801 he again assumed command of the advanced squadron and on the 20th sought shelter in his old refuge in Douarnenez Bay from a severe equinoctial gale, resuming his post off the Black Rocks on the 25th. During the next few weeks he was seldom more than three or four miles from the entrance to Brest roads.[1] On 1 June Saumarez was again relieved by Thornbrough.

Early in June 1800 Sir John Warren had been sent with a division to cruise off the Passage du Raz for the purpose of intercepting any ships or convoys of the enemy which might endeavour to push through. To prevent the improvident use of frigates, Warren was strictly enjoined 'under no account to suffer any of the ships or vessels under your orders to be led away from his important service by chasing or any other circumstances whatever'. At the same time frigates cruised all along the shores of the Bay of Biscay from Ile d'Yeu to Cape Finisterre to intercept coastal convoys carrying stores to the beleaguered arsenal. Since there were then at Brest no fewer than forty-eight of the line it was not long before that port was destitute of naval stores and all kinds of supplies; and Brest was practically paralysed as an arsenal and shipyard. 'The enemy appears so petrified by the change of system in approaching and scouring the coast', St. Vincent had informed Spencer in June, 'that the convoy of victuallers, afraid to attempt getting into Brest, is gone from Conquêt Bay to the eastward.' When early in 1801 Ganteaume managed to get away to sea with seven of the line, six of them were so badly damaged that they were unable to carry out their instructions. The condition of the blockaded fleet inevitably deteriorated. 'The *Argonaut*', wrote one of the officers of the *Impétueux* in April, 'appeared to be well manned, but by no means in good order; she was very dirty, and the sailors badly clothed, the quarter deck was at all times full of men of every description, and there seemed but little order and discipline

[1] *Ibid.*, I, p. 305.

kept up amongst them.' Just as St. Vincent kept his own ships' companies well fed and healthy, he successfully strove by his control of the Brest approaches to deny provisions to those of the enemy. There are repeated references in his correspondence with the Admiralty to the importance of cutting off all seaborne supplies to Brest. 'Your Lordship's apprehensions for the safety of the ships of the line before Brest are groundless', he assured Spencer, 'and if you mean to keep the enemy in check, and to prevent his supplies from entering Brest by sea, they must be kept there.' He returned to this point early in 1801. 'There is no doubt of their being able to man all their navy', he reported to the Admiralty; 'and if you will supply me with plenty of small craft they will find a difficulty in supplying them with victuals and drink.'[1] St. Vincent put no trust in conjunct attacks on the French coast. He believed that the proper strategy was rigorously to blockade the enemy in Brest in order to keep Keith in the Mediterranean 'on velvet'.

When winter and advancing years finally drove him ashore, St. Vincent exercised command from Torre Abbey, an ancient mansion belonging to his distant connections, the Carys, situated at the northern end of Torbay overlooking the anchorage. Here he superintended the system of reliefs, and the refitting and speedy dispatch of the ships sent in for repair. All his endeavours were directed towards keeping the ships out of the dockyard to the last possible moment and the squadron on its blockading station at full strength. By the close of 1800 the success of these measures had become manifest. As St. Vincent remarked to Keith, 'Our intelligence from France says that Bonaparte is coming to Brest to force the combined fleet to go forth and give us battle. *Nous verrons.* They had better have done it sooner, for beside having got this squadron into a healthy and well-arranged state as to the interior, our movements are improved to a degree that is really surprising for the time.'[2] 'The French at Brest,' Collingwood observed the following year, 'and indeed all along the coast as far as Bordeaux, never were more closely blockaded. The summer has been such as had admitted that service to be done well.'[3]

In February 1801 St. Vincent became First Lord of the Admiralty

[1] *Spencer Papers*, III, pp. 301, 342, 375–6.
[2] Tucker, *op. cit.*, II, p. 91.
[3] *Correspondence of Lord Collingwood*, ed. E. A. Hughes, p. 115.

in Addington's ministry, and the command of the Channel fleet devolved upon Admiral William Cornwallis, a commander after his own heart, under whom the blockade of Brest was carried on with the same unyielding and tenacious purpose.

VII

'Of Nelson and the North'

I

Following on the collapse of the Second Coalition, Great Britain found herself faced with a formidable new enemy. Despite the concessions wrung from this country by the Armed Neutrality of 1780, the new doctrine of neutral rights which had then been proclaimed was never established; and, on the outbreak of the French Revolutionary War, the belligerent rights claimed by Great Britain had received general acceptance. As Lord Grenville was to observe to the Danish and Swedish ministers in London, in January 1801: 'It was well known with what hostile intentions the attempt was made in 1780 to establish a system of innovations prejudicial to the most cherished interests of the British Empire. . . . This attitude has been completely abandoned, and at the beginning of the war the Court of Russia had formed ties with Great Britain which were not only inconsistent with the Convention of 1780, but entirely contrary to it.'[1]

But the war-time development of the carrying trade in the neutral Baltic States and the rapidly expanding commerce of Prussia and northern Germany had brought those countries into continual conflict with Great Britain. Enemy ships and cargoes had been protected in wholesale fashion by fictitious transfers to neutral subjects, who profited greatly in consequence. 'Merchants,' wrote James Stephen in 1805, 'who, immediately prior to the last war, were scarcely known, even in the obscure sea-ports in which they resided, have suddenly started up as sole owners of hundreds of ships, and sole proprietors of rich cargoes, which it would have alarmed the wealthiest merchants of Europe, to hazard at once on the chance of a market, even in peaceable times.'[2] The Danes had prospered exceedingly as

[1] Q. Phillips and Reade, *Neutrality* (1936), p. 104.
[2] James Stephen, *War in Disguise, or the Frauds of the Neutral Flags* (1917), p. 81.

a result of what Grenville, in 1794, described as 'the collusive and fraudulent commerce so openly carried on from the ports of the Baltic'. Even the coastal trade of France was to a large extent carried on under cover of the neutral flag. During the past half-century Danish commerce had attained the peak of its prosperity. Sweden had similarly prospered during the period for long remembered by her mercantile community as *den gode Tid*, 'the good time'.

In January 1798 a number of Swedish merchant vessels, laden with contraband of war, were, although under convoy of a Swedish man-of-war, seized by our Navy and condemned by our prize courts. The loss of these ships, valued at £600,000, gave rise to intense indignation in Sweden. Later in the war a number of Danish merchant vessels, under convoy of the frigate *Freja*, encountered a British squadron cruising in the Channel. Having resisted the British proposal to visit the convoy, the Danes, after a fight, eventually yielded to superior force and were escorted to the Downs. Later the *Freja* was released and a compromise agreement appeared to have been reached; but the question at issue was by no means resolved.

Towards the end of 1800 Bonaparte, playing upon the resentment of the Northern Powers at British interference with their trade, encouraged those States to revive the League of Armed Neutrality, which, comprising Russia, Sweden, Denmark, and Prussia, was pledged to resist the belligerent rights at sea claimed and enforced by Great Britain. The customary rights of search and seizure were boldly challenged.

The neutral rights now proclaimed struck at the very foundations of British naval power. 'Does he not know', Pitt later argued, in reply to one of the Opposition leaders, 'that the naval preponderance, which we have by these means acquired, has given security to this country, and has more than once afforded chances for the salvation of Europe? In the wreck of the Continent and the disappointment of our hopes there, what has been the security of this country but its naval preponderance?'[1] The leading principles affirmed by the League were that neutral vessels were free to engage in the coasting and colonial trade of belligerents; that enemy property carried in neutral shipping was not subject to seizure, nor were vessels under convoy of a man-of-war liable to the belligerent right of search; and that naval stores

[1] *War Speeches of William Pitt*, ed. R. Coupland, p. 300.

were to be excluded from the category of contraband. At the same time the Tsar arrested all British merchantmen in Russian ports and imprisoned their crews. Between them the Armed Neutrals disposed of a fleet of well over a hundred sail of the line, twenty-four of which were immediately available. The Armed Neutrality threatened both to disrupt the blockade of France and to close the Baltic to British commerce, thereby depriving this country of Baltic grain and the timbers and naval stores which were vital to the Fleet.

'Four nations', observed Pitt, early in February 1801, 'have leaguered to produce a new code of maritime laws, and in defiance of the most solemn treaties and engagements, which they have endeavoured to force arbitrarily upon Europe. . . . The question is whether we are to suffer blockaded fleets to be furnished with warlike stores and provisions, whether we are to suffer neutral nations, by hoisting a flag upon a sloop or fishing boat, to convey the treasures of South America to the harbours of Spain or the naval stores of the Pacific to Brest and Toulon.'[1]

In announcing their adherence to the Armed Neutrality the Swedes had declared that 'the Government which has so often tried to convince Europe of its pacific intentions now wants to begin a war for the enslavement of the sea, after having so often boasted that it was fighting for the liberation of Europe.' In rejoinder, Hawkesbury in a note to the Swedish government proclaimed 'the unalterable determination of Great Britain to uphold the accepted principles of maritime law, established by the experience of centuries, and perfectly adapted to secure the rights of neutrals and belligerents alike'. 'If we give way to them,' agreed his colleague Grenville, 'we may as well disarm our navy at once and determine to cede without further contest all that we have taken as a counter-balance to the continental acquisitions of France.'[2]

By this time Pitt was no longer at the helm. Following the Act of Union between Great Britain and Ireland, on New Year's Day, 1801, it had become imperative to concede some measure of Catholic relief. Pitt's attempt to make this concession broke down on the invincible obstinacy of the King; whereupon he resigned, and Dr. Addington,

[1] *Ibid.*, p. 299.
[2] Phillips and Reade, *op. cit.*, pp. 105–6; H.M.C., *Dropmore Papers*, VI, p. 400.

at the King's request, formed a government. Lord Hawkesbury (later Lord Liverpool) became Foreign Secretary and St. Vincent First Lord of the Admiralty.

Meanwhile St. Vincent, eager for action, was looking to ministers to 'make every exertion to put an extinguisher upon the northern confederacy by a great stroke at Copenhagen; and yet [he apprehended] so much time has elapsed since the event was known without any apparent preparation for a descent that I fear this weapon, so essential to final success, has met with insurmountable resistance in the Cabinet.'

In the end the ministry, after all, made up their mind. Rejecting the League's demands point-blank, they took the bold decision to send a fleet to the Baltic under Admiral Sir Hyde Parker, with Nelson as his second-in-command, to compel Denmark to break with her confederates, either by diplomatic pressure, or, if this should fail, by the bombardment of her capital. The fleet numbered eighteen sail of the line and thirty-five smaller vessels. The expedition finally left Yarmouth on 12 March.

It would scarcely have done so but for a timely communication from Nelson to his old chief, St. Vincent, via Troubridge. For Sir Hyde Parker, a slow, lethargic, oldish man, who had recently taken to himself a very young wife, was showing marked reluctance to quit the shore. He appears to have been waiting for a farewell ball which Lady Parker had arranged to give at Yarmouth on the 13th; or, as St. Vincent gruffly observed, 'to eat his *batter pudding*, as the fair Fanny is called'. Parker thereupon received a 'prog' from the First Lord couched in unmistakable terms. 'I have heard by a side wind that you have an intention of continuing at Yarmouth till Friday on account of some trifling circumstances. I really know not what they are, nor did I give myself the trouble of enquiring into them. . . . I have, however, upon a consideration of the effect your continuance at Yarmouth an hour after the wind would admit of your sailing, would produce, sent down a messenger purposely to convey to you my opinion, as a private friend, that any delay in your sailing would do you an irreparable injury.'

'Now we can have no desire for staying,' declared Nelson with satisfaction to Troubridge on the 10th, 'for her ladyship is gone, and the ball for Friday night is knocked up by your and the earl's unpoliteness to send gentlemen to sea instead of dancing with nice white gloves.' Earlier he had recalled the ribald comments which had been on the lips of half the old market-women of Yarmouth, 'Consider how nice it must be laying in bed with a young wife, compared to a damned cold raw wind!'

During the first part of the voyage, which was cold and stormy, the two Admirals were on decidedly distant terms. 'I have not yet seen my Commander-in-Chief', Nelson observed, 'and have had no official communication whatever. All I have gathered of our first plans, I disapprove most exceedingly.' It would appear that Parker, if left to himself, would never have entered the Baltic, but would have remained outside in the Kattegat; Nelson, on the other hand, was for proceeding with the utmost dispatch into the Baltic while the negotiations were in progress, off the Danish capital, where 'the Dane should see our Flag waving every moment he lifted up his head'. According to tradition, Nelson won over the Commander-in-Chief with the present of a fine turbot which he had caught while the fleet was passing over the Dogger Bank.[1] Shortly after, Nelson was invited to a conference on board the flagship *London;* and from that day onwards relations between the two Admirals markedly improved. The season was the worst in the year for a voyage to the Baltic: they stood across the North Sea, under lowering grey skies, against strong north-easterly winds, through fog, snow, and sleet; the spars and rigging of the ships were heavily coated with ice, and the men, many of them fresh from the Mediterranean, suffered severely. 'We have since we sailed experienced a second winter,' Captain Fremantle informed his wife; 'it has since snowed every day since, and the ship's company are hacking from morning to night with coughs.'[2]

2

The fleet, somewhat dispersed after a north-easterly gale on the 15th, did not reach the Naze until the 18th, and reassembled next day off the long, low, sandy promontory of the Skaw, the northernmost point of Jutland, where the Kattegat stretches southward to the island

---

[1] The story of how a turbot won the battle of Copenhagen is, however, believed to be a myth.
[2] *Wynne Diaries*, III, p. 31.

of Zealand—to the west, by way of the intricate channels of the Great Belt, and to the east, through the Sound. Though the north-west wind was fair for Copenhagen, Nicholas Vansittart, the government envoy on board the *London*, was sent ahead in a frigate, while Parker's second-in-command chafed at the delay. 'I hate your pen and ink men,' was Nelson's comment: earlier he had remarked that 'A fleet of British men-of-war are the best negotiators in Europe.'

On the afternoon of the 19th the fleet stood southward down the Kattegat, stretching over to the town of Varberg on the eastern shore, past the island of Anholt, and anchored on the evening of the 22nd, in thick south-westerly weather, off Nekke Head, towards the entrance of the Sound, where the smooth green slopes and extensive beech-woods on the Danish shore look over on the steep and rocky coast of Sweden—the channel gradually narrowing until, between the turreted and battlemented mass of Kronborg Castle and the old Swedish city of Helsingborg, the strait is only about three miles wide. Here Parker remained until Vansittart's return on the 23rd with the news that the British ultimatum had been rejected, when a council of war was held on board the flagship.

The council opened in gloom and apprehension. Vansittart had brought back alarming reports of the strength of the batteries at Elsinore and of the defences of Copenhagen. Hyde Parker, as has already been said, was reluctant to quit the Kattegat. While the council was deliberating, Nelson restlessly paced the cabin of the *London*, impatient for action. 'Lord Nelson is quite sanguine,' Fremantle informed his wife, 'but as you may well imagine there is a great diversity of opinion.' Parker's despondent outlook was shared by the Captain of the Fleet. Rear-Admiral Graves, too, feared they would be playing a losing game, attacking stone walls. Captain Murray of the *Edgar* saw no prospect of success, and was of opinion that if they once got into the Roads, they would be very glad to get back again. 'If I were to give an opinion on this business,' Fremantle concluded, 'I should say the Danes are exceedingly alarmed, but Delay gives them courage, and they will by degrees make Copenhagen so strong, that it may resist the attack of our fleet.'

For his part Nelson insisted that they should attack at once, following this up next day with a memorandum addressed to Sir Hyde Parker, which was a model of lucidity, sagacity, and strategic insight. 'The more I have reflected, the more I am confirmed in opinion that not a moment should be lost in attacking the enemy. They will every day and hour be stronger; we shall never be so good a match for them as at this moment.' Nelson was of opinion that they should strike straight at Russia, the head and heart of the Northern confederation; and he urged an immediate advance against the Russian squadron of twelve of the line at Reval while the wind was fair and the Russian fleet still remained ice-bound in Kronstadt. 'The measure may be thought bold, but I am of opinion the boldest measures are the safest.' As an alternative he suggested an immediate advance on Copenhagen, by way of the Hollænder Deep round the great shoal known as the Middle Ground, and back through the King's Deep, whereby the Danes would be taken in rear. 'It must have the effect of preventing a junction between the Russians, Swedes, and Danes, and may give us an opportunity of bombarding Copenhagen.'[1] Parker, apprehensive of leaving a hostile Denmark in his rear, rejected Nelson's proposal for an immediate advance on Reval, but eventually adopted his plan of attack against the Danish capital.

For the past few days the winds had been foul, with heavy showers of sleet and rain, and the weather raw and chill. Though in the afternoon of the 24th the wind came N.W. and fair for Copenhagen, and the general expectation was that the fleet should have sailed through the Sound on the following day, the alarming representations made by Vansittart as to the state of the batteries at Elsinore and Copenhagen induced the Commander-in-Chief to prefer the circuitous passage by the Great Belt. Nelson, as always impatient for action, was not much impressed by these formidable reports; his overmastering desire was to get to Copenhagen—'Let it be by the Sound, by the Belt,' he urged, 'or anyhow, only lose not an hour.' Early on the 25th the fleet accordingly weighed and stood to the westward, leaving astern the bleak, windswept moors above Nekke Head and the high black promontory of 'the Koll' across the water, towards Hessel Island and the entrance of the Great Belt. But, after proceeding for a few leagues along the Zealand coast, the plan was suddenly changed—apparently because of the navigational difficulties involved; and before sunset the fleet was back in its former anchorage.[2] It was then

[1] *Nelson's Dispatches*, IV, pp. 295–8; Adm. 1/4, 23–24 March 1801.
[2] Adm. 50/65, 25–26 March 1801.

decided to go by the Sound after all, and, on the evening of the 26th, with the wind blowing fresh from the south-west, the fleet moved nearer to Kronborg. 'We pass the Castle whenever the wind is anyway to the northward,' remarked Fremantle, 'so as to allow us to get through the channel without making a board.'[1] All these delays inevitably played into the hands of the Danes, enabling them still further to strengthen their defences before Copenhagen and increasing the danger of reinforcements arriving from their northern allies.

For three days tension heightened while the wind hung to the southward and the British fleet lay off the narrow entrance to the Sound, in those historic waters where from time immemorial the crown of Denmark had levied a toll on all the rich traffic passing in and out of the Baltic, in sight of the ancient town of Elsinore and Tycho Brahe's battlemented fortress with its memories of the ill-starred Queen Matilda and Shakespeare's Hamlet. The belief had long prevailed in Europe that the possession of this formidable stronghold gave the Danes an unchallengeable command of the passage of the Öresund: on approaching which the vessels of all nations lowered their topsails and paid their dues. Now that fighting was resolved upon, Nelson a few days earlier had shifted his flag from the *St. George* to a lighter ship, the *Elephant*, commanded by his old Mediterranean friend Thomas Foley, who had played so distinguished a part in the battle of the Nile; and on the following afternoon all the ships cleared for action.

At last, at daybreak on the 30th, it blew a topsail breeze from the N.W.; and the fleet weighed and made sail. In single column, with Nelson's division in the van, Parker's in the centre, and Graves's in the rear, the whole force, comprising fifty-two sail, entered the Öresund. The thundering peals of Kronborg Castle spread the alarm swiftly down the coast. As the leading ship, the *Monarch*, came within range, the batteries on the Zealand coast immediately opened fire. Not a shot, however, was fired from the further side of the straits; and our ships therefore stood over to the Swedish shore, with the result that though the batteries of Elsinore 'continued in one uninterrupted blaze during the passage of the Fleet' all their shot fell harmlessly 'at least a cable's length from our Ships'. The long procession of warships, each with its triple pyramid of lofty white canvas

[1] i.e. tacking.

shining in the sunlight, passed swiftly on and through the Sound. The fleet stood on to the southward, skirting on the starboard hand the wooded hills of Zealand, and to larboard the fertile plain of Skane with the steeples of Landskrona, Lund, and Malmö showing up in the clear air; past sombre winter beechwoods stretching down to the water's edge; past a panorama, extending as far as the eye could reach, of well-tilled fields and meadows, lofty windmills, white thatched farmhouses, manors, and ancient castles; past fine white sands, grass-grown dunes, and an occasional fishing-port; until presently in the widening channel appeared the low-lying isles of Saltholm and Amager, fringed with extensive sands and outlying rocks; while in the background rose up the stately spires of Copenhagen, one of the most imposing capitals in Europe, the fairest city of the North. The same afternoon the fleet anchored about midway between Hven Island and the city.

3

Meanwhile the Danes had taken advantage of all the delays to strengthen the defences of Copenhagen, which, combined with the navigational difficulties of the approaches, were now far more formidable than had been anticipated. 'We soon perceived', related Colonel Stewart, 'that our delay had been of important advantage to the enemy, who had lined the northern edge of the shoals near the Crown batteries, and the front of the harbour and arsenal, with a formidable flotilla.'[1] The whole front of the city was covered by an unbroken line of some twenty dismasted warships and floating batteries flanked and supported to the northward by the Trekroner Battery, and a smaller squadron of warships, which also guarded the entrance to the harbour. Before the British bomb-ships could be placed in the proper position to bombard the city, these defences would have to be wholly or in part destroyed.

At a second council of war, held in the afternoon of 31 March, the plan of attack suggested by Nelson had been finally adopted. Nelson proposed to take ten of the lighter ships of the line with all the frigates eastward of the Middle Ground[2] by the Outer Channel or Hollænder Deep

[1] *Nelson's Dispatches*, IV, p. 302.
[2] This shoal, which was of approximately the same extent as the seafront of the city, lay exactly before it, at a distance of about three-quarters of a mile.

and then to approach the city through the narrow and intricate channel of the King's Deep. The advantages of this plan were twofold. First, the Danish defences would be assailed from a wholly unexpected direction and at their weakest point, at the end of the long line of vessels stretching south-east from the Trekroner; and the same wind which brought Nelson's ships through the King's Deep would later enable them to rejoin Parker's division to the north of the city. Second, there was the supreme strategic advantage that by attacking from this direction the Danes would be cut off from their Russian and Swedish allies. Nelson's daring and ardent spirit had by now so wrought upon the Commander-in-Chief that the latter of his own accord added two further ships of the line to the ten originally requested.

The nights of 30 and 31 March were passed in sounding and buoying the channel round the Middle Ground. It was during these preparations for action that Captain Edward Riou of the frigate *Amazon* first became known to Nelson, who (according to Colonel Stewart) 'was struck with admiration at the superior discipline and seamanship, that were observable on board the *Amazon*'.

It was Riou's appearance, brief but glorious, on the stage of history. In that age of fine seamen this officer was, in truth, a prince among seamen. He had already made a name for himself in the Service when, as a lieutenant, he was in command of the *Guardian* frigate.[1] With his sombre, handsome features, and daring and resolution almost equal to his own, he was a captain after Nelson's own heart. Riou— who, had he lived, might well have been numbered among our most illustrious commanders—made so great an impression on Nelson that two days later he was appointed to lead the division in his frigate through the hazardous approach around the Middle Ground, and on the eve of the action he was kept on board the *Elephant* to assist Nelson in his dispositions for the attack.

The Hollænder Deep was little known, and extremely intricate; at one point it was only half a mile wide, the water shoaling suddenly

---

[1] In 1789 the *Guardian*, outward bound to Botany Bay, had collided with 'an island of ice' while sailing between the Cape and New South Wales. The frigate was so severely damaged that she was given up for lost by most of her company; but Riou, 'by well-nigh the most heroic feat of seamanship on record', as Fitchett truly says, succeeded at last in bringing her, waterlogged and sinking, safely back to Table Bay. On his return to England, Riou was promoted to commander and shortly afterwards to post-rank.

on the western side from $6\frac{1}{2}$ to $3\frac{1}{2}$ fathoms; all the buoys had been removed or misplaced by the enemy, who believed the channel impracticable for so large a squadron. On the 30th Hyde Parker, Nelson, Graves, Fremantle, Riou, and several other officers embarked in the *Amazon* to reconnoitre the Danish defences; and the following day Nelson carried out a further reconnaissance.

'During the interval that preceded the Battle,' recorded the surgeon of the *Elephant*, 'I could only silently admire when I saw the first man in all the world spend hours of the day and night in Boats, amidst floating ice, and in the severest weather; and wonder when the light showed me a path marked by buoys, which had been trackless the preceding evening.'[1]

On 1 April the whole British fleet stood over to the north-west end of the Middle Ground. About one o'clock, as Nelson in the *Elephant* made the signal to weigh, a great cheer went up from all the vessels of his division; and led by the *Amazon*, with a light but favouring wind, the long line of battleships and frigates stood slowly down the outer edge of the shoal. The passage of Nelson's division through the Hollænder Deep was a triumph of seamanship and cool nerve. By sundown all his ships had rounded the Middle Ground and anchored safely near its southern extremity to the south of the city, about two miles from the head of the Danish line. As the *Elephant* dropped anchor at nightfall, Nelson was heard to declare, 'I will fight them the moment I have a fair wind'.

As soon as the fleet was anchored, Nelson sat down to dinner in the great cabin of the *Elephant* with a large party of his senior officers, including Graves, Fremantle, Foley, Hardy, and Riou, together with 'a few others to whom he was particularly attached', wrote Stewart; adding, that from this party 'every man separated with feelings of admiration for their great leader, and with anxious impatience to follow him to the approaching Battle.' The cheerful lantern-light illuminated the little oasis of gaiety and good cheer amidst the encircling darkness and danger. Near by, though invisible in the night, were the grim line of enemy hulks, the great Trekroner Battery bristling with cannon, the crowded shipping lining the quays, and the towers and steeples of Copenhagen. As usual before an action, Nelson was in the highest spirits; and they all drank to a leading wind and

[1] *Nelson's Dispatches*, IV, p. 312.

victory over the Danes on the following day. Late that night Hardy took careful soundings round the head of the Danish line, while Nelson, assisted by Riou and Foley, prepared full instructions for the captain of every ship.[1] The leading British ships, after firing on the southernmost Danes, were to anchor opposite the fifth, sixth, and seventh vessels in the enemy line. The southernmost Danes, already damaged by the broadsides of the leading British ships, would then be beaten out of the fight by the fourth and fifth British vessels, which would thereupon cut their cables and drift north—thus bringing an overwhelming concentration to bear on the next part of the enemy line. The Danish fleet was, in effect, to be attacked and destroyed in detail.

By this time Nelson was so exhausted by the exertions of this and of the two preceding days that he was persuaded by his officers and his old Norfolk servant, Tom Allen, to lie down in his cot, which was placed on the cabin deck. From it, however, he still continued to dictate, occasionally calling on his clerks to hasten their work. Long before daybreak Nelson was up and making the last preparations. By eight o'clock on the morning of 2 April his captains had received their final instructions. The wind, which had veered during the night, came fair as S.S.E.; it was moderate and cloudy weather; and at half-past nine signal was made to weigh.

4

The seamanship of Nelson's squadron, on which everything depended, was now put to a hard test. The pilots of the squadron, for the most part mates of Baltic traders, with 'no other thought than to keep the ship clear of danger, and their own silly heads clear of shot', were unanimous in opposing the attempt to take vessels of deep draught down the channel. 'At eight o'clock in the morning of the 2nd April,' observed Nelson, 'not one pilot would take charge of a ship.' Finally the master of the *Bellona*, who had been master of the *Audacious* at the battle of the Nile, volunteered to lead the column.[2] He was ac-

[1] *Ibid.*, IV, p. 304.

[2] 'Brierly, who was Davidge Gould's Master in the *Audacious*, placed Boats for me, and fixed my order, saying, "My Lord, if you will command each Ship to steer with the small red house open with a mill, until such a Church is on with a wood, the King's Channel will be open"' (*Nelson's Dispatches*, IV, p. 499).

cordingly transferred to the *Edgar*, which was to lead. The second ship in the British line, the *Agamemnon*, on getting under way, ran almost immediately on the end of the Middle Ground. The *Bellona*, followed by the *Russell*, steering too close to the starboard shoal, also took the ground, and there remained—out of effective range—throughout the action. Thus, before the fight had fairly begun, Nelson had lost a quarter of his heavy ships. A still greater disaster was narrowly averted by his promptitude in having the *Elephant*'s helm put hard over and steering safely past the stranded *Russell* on the larboard side back into the proper channel. The signal to advance remained flying. The rest of the squadron, following in the wake of the *Elephant*, sailed clear of the shoal. At the head of the British line the *Edgar* steered through the intricate channel 'in a most noble manner' and anchored, according to plan, opposite the fifth ship in the enemy's line.

'A more beautiful and solemn sight I never witnessed,' wrote one of the midshipmen in the *Monarch*, describing the *Edgar*'s advance. '. . . We saw her passing on through the enemy's fire, and moving in the midst of it to gain her station. Our minds were filled with a sort of awe. Not a word was spoken through the ship save by the pilot and helmsman, and their commands, being chanted very much in the same manner as the responses in a Cathedral service, added to the solemnity.'[1]

The *Edgar* was fired at by the *Prövestein* as she came within range, but returned not a shot till she reached her allotted station. The *Elephant* came to anchor in the centre of the Danish line, about a cable's length opposite the flagship *Dannebrog*. 'The *Glatton* had her station immediately astern of us,' wrote Stewart; 'the *Ganges*, *Monarch*, and *Defiance* a-head; the distance between each not exceeding a half cable. The judgment with which each Ship calculated her station in that intricate Channel, was admirable throughout.'[2] The rest of the ships disposed themselves so as to fill up the gaps in their line left by the three which had gone aground. As each of the ships glided successively into place abreast of her opponent she anchored by the stern and, with the wind nearly aft, presented her broadside to the enemy.

[1] Q. E. Fraser, *The Sailors whom Nelson led* (1913), p. 185.
[2] *Nelson's Dispatches*, IV, p. 308.

The action began just after ten. Before half-past eleven the fighting had become general and lasted for nearly four hours. The Danes fought doggedly and well, so that for long the issue was uncertain. '*Here* was no manœuvring,' Nelson said afterwards, '*it was* downright fighting.' The British were severely handicapped by the stranding of the three battleships which were to have engaged the Trekroner Battery and the northernmost ships of the enemy line. The gallant Riou had thereupon endeavoured to fill their place with his squadron of frigates. The enemy's gunnery proved more formidable than had been expected, and the ships at the south end of their line, which Nelson had hoped to silence quickly, put up a stiff resistance; also the British vessels were anchored at too great a distance from their opponents on account of the pilots' apprehensions of shoaling their water on the larboard side. Furthermore, the Danes were able throughout the engagement to reinforce their crews with boatloads of men from the shore.

During the action the church-towers and roof-tops of Copenhagen were crowded with anxious spectators, who could see little of the long double line of fighting ships but the stabbing flash of the guns and the tops of Nelson's anchored squadron lifting above an impenetrable shroud of thick black powder-smoke. Later in the day the south-easterly wind slowly rolled the smoke-bank ashore, and over the quays and streets of the city.

The action reached its climax shortly after noon. Several of our ships were then hard-pressed. The *Monarch* and *Defiance*, related Fremantle, were 'dreadfully cut up, as they were exposed to the Crown batteries'. 'The *Monarch* was also suffering severely under the united fire of the *Holstein* and *Zealand*,' said Stewart; 'and only two of our Bomb-vessels could get to their station on the Middle Ground.' Both the *Isis* and the *Bellona* received serious damage by the bursting of some of their guns. The *Isis*, a small 50, was all but overwhelmed by the superior weight of the *Prövestein*'s fire. The former was to some extent relieved by the timely action of Captain Inman of the *Desirée* frigate, who, placing his vessel across the bows of the *Prövestein*, poured in a heavy raking fire. Certain of the Danes performed prodigies of valour. A seventeen-year-old lieutenant named Villemoes, who was in command of a small floating battery of twenty-four guns, manned by 120 men, succeeded in manœuvering this fragile craft under the very counter of the *Elephant* and firing point-blank into her towering sides until the cease-fire; by which time nearly every man of his force had been shot down.[1] The *Prövestein* fought until nearly all her guns were dismounted. The Danish commander-in-chief, Olfert Fischer, twice shifted his flag: first, to the *Holstein*, and, later, to the Trekroner Battery. After Fischer's departure the flagship fought on until her commodore lost his right hand and was succeeded by her flag-captain. Finally a renewed attack on her by the *Elephant* and *Glatton* not only completely silenced and disabled her, but, by the use of grape, killed nearly every man in the praams ahead and astern of her. 'I have been in a hundred and five engagements,' Nelson wrote after the battle, 'but that of today is the most terrible of them all.'

Meanwhile, on the other side of the Middle Ground Sir Hyde Parker's division had been unable, both the wind and the current being contrary, to get to Nelson's assistance; and shortly after one o'clock, while the cannonade was still at its height, the signal to discontinue the engagement was made on board the flagship. As soon as Riou saw the signal he repeated it to his frigates, and then withdrew with his whole squadron. As the *Amazon* turned with her stern to the Trekroner Battery she was heavily raked; and Riou with many of his men was killed. Nelson's second-in-command, Rear-Admiral Graves, also repeated the signal to his ships; but at the same time he kept the signal for close action still flying.

Nelson's reaction to the signal is well known. As the *Elephant* was closely engaging the enemy flagship *Dannebrog* and the two floating batteries ahead of her, he was walking with Stewart on the quarter-deck when a shot, striking the mainmast, scattered a few splinters about them. Nelson observed with a smile, 'It is warm work, and this day may be the last to any of us at a moment'; and then, stopping short at the gangway, he added, 'but mark you, I would not be else-where for thousands.' When the signal, No. 39 [to discontinue the engagement] was made, the Signal Lieutenant reported it to him. He continued his walk, and did not appear to take notice of it.

[1] After the action Nelson had young Villemoes introduced to him, and, greeting him with the utmost kindness, informed the Danish Crown Prince that so gallant a youth deserved to be made an admiral; to which the Prince gravely responded, that 'if he were to make all his brave officers admirals, he would have no captains or lieutenants in his service' (*Naval Chronicle*, Vol. 14, p. 398).

The Lieutenant meeting his Lordship at the next turn asked, 'whether he should repeat it?' Lord Nelson answered, 'No, acknowledge it.' On the Officer returning to the poop, his Lordship called after him, 'Is No. 16 [For close Action] still hoisted?' the Lieutenant answering in the affirmative, Lord Nelson said, 'Mind you keep it so.' He now walked the deck considerably agitated, which was always known by his moving the stump of his right arm. After a turn or two, he said to me, in a quick manner, 'Do you know what's shown on board of the Commander-in-Chief, No. 39?' On asking him what that meant, he answered, 'Why, to leave off Action.' 'Leave off Action!' he repeated, 'Now, damn me if I do.' He also observed, I believe, to Captain Foley, 'You know, Foley, I have only one eye—I have a right to be blind sometimes'; and then with an archness peculiar to his character, putting the glass to his blind eye, he exclaimed, 'I really do not see the signal.' This remarkable signal was, therefore, only acknowledged on board the *Elephant*, not repeated.[1]

By two o'clock most of the Danish line had ceased firing, and their flagship was seen to be drifting in flames before the wind, 'spreading terror throughout the Enemy's Line'. She fell away to leeward, and at about half-past three blew up. To quote the Danish Commander-in-Chief, Olfert Fischer, 'Thus the quarter of the line of defence from the Trekroner to the *Hjælperen* frigate, was in the power of the enemy; and the *Hjælperen*, thus finding herself alone, slipped her cables and steered to Stirbfen. The ship *Elven*, after she had received many shots in the hull, and had her masts and rigging shot away, and a great number killed and wounded, retreated within the Trekroner. The gun-boats *Nyborg* and *Aggershuus*, which last towed the former away, when near sinking, ran ashore; and the *Gernershe* floating battery, which had suffered much, together with the blockship *Dannebrog*, shortly after the battle, blew up.'[2]

Some of the Danish hulks renewed the fight after they had surrendered, and the shore batteries were firing on our boats which had been sent to take possession of the prizes. Nelson was naturally incensed at this and observed, 'That he must either send on shore, and stop this irregular proceeding, or send in our Fire-ships and burn them.' He accordingly retired into the stern-gallery and quickly composed an urgent letter to the Danish Crown Prince, with the address, '*To the brothers of Englishmen, the Danes*', declaring that,

---

[1] *Nelson's Dispatches*, IV, pp. 308–9.
[2] *Ibid.*, IV, p. 322.

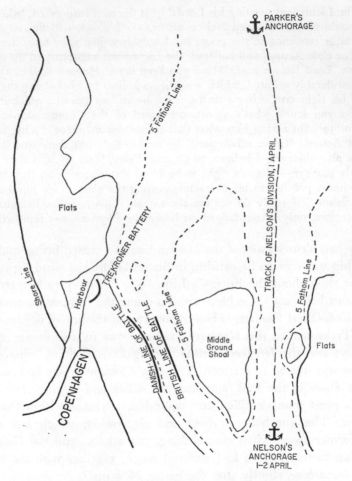

PARKER'S
ANCHORAGE

5 Fathom Line

Flats

Shore Line

Harbour

TREKRONER BATTERY

COPENHAGEN

DANISH LINE OF BATTLE

BRITISH LINE OF BATTLE

5 Fathom Line

Middle
Ground
Shoal

TRACK OF NELSON'S DIVISION, I APRIL

5 Fathom Line

Flats

NELSON'S
ANCHORAGE
I–2 APRIL

The Battle of Copenhagen, 2 April 1801

unless all firing ceased immediately, he would be forced to set on fire the prizes 'without having the power of saving the brave Danes who have defended them'. This letter was at once conveyed under a flag of truce to the Crown Prince near the sally port.[1]

The two leading ships of Sir Hyde Parker's division had by now arrived on the scene of action, with the result that all the Danes ahead of the *Elephant* struck their colours.

[1] *Ibid.*, IV, pp. 315–16.

While the parleying was in progress, Nelson seized the opportunity of getting some of his leading vessels, which were badly damaged, safely past the shoal under the guns of the Trekroner Battery. Upon the departure of the delegates to the flagship, signal was made for the *Glatton*, *Elephant*, *Ganges*, *Defiance*, and *Monarch* to weigh in succession. 'The intricacy of the Channel now showed the great utility of what had been done; the *Monarch*, as first Ship, immediately hit on a shoal, but was pushed over it by the *Ganges* taking her amidships. The *Glatton* went clear, but the *Defiance* and *Elephant* ran aground, leaving the Crown Battery at a mile distance; and there they remained fixed, the former until ten o'clock that night, and the latter until eight, notwithstanding every exertion which their fatigued crews could make to relieve them. Had there been no cessation of hostilities, their situation would certainly have been perilous.'[1] The same evening it was agreed that all the prizes were to be yielded up by the Danes; that hostilities were to be suspended for twenty-four hours, and the Danish wounded brought on shore. The prizes, with the exception of one 74 which was commissioned as a hospital ship, were presently all burned and sent to the bottom with their guns; and Nelson's squadron moved out of the channel to rejoin Parker. The city now lay open to bombardment; for it was possible to place the bomb-ships in the King's Deep.

'Considering the disadvantages of navigation,' observed Graves in his dispatch, 'the approach to the enemy, their vast number of guns and mortars on both land and sea, I do not think there ever was a bolder attack.' 'This day', wrote Stewart, 'was as glorious for seamanship as for courage.' The battle had been a desperate affair. Alone among the major actions fought by Nelson, it had come near to being lost. The British had lost nearly 1,000 killed and wounded; the Danes at least twice as many, 'The carnage on board the Danish vessels taken,' declared Fremantle, 'exceeds anything I ever heard of; the *Ça Ira* or Nile ships are not to be compared to the massacre on board them.' 'The French,' said Nelson, 'fought bravely; but they could not have stood for one hour the fight which the Danes had supported for four.' The issue of the action had perhaps hung in the balance, first, when Nelson's three battleships stranded on the Middle Ground, and, second, when Parker made the signal to discontinue the

[1] *Ibid.*, IV, p. 312.

engagement. In both cases it was Nelson's unerring and incomparable instinct for victory which had proved the decisive factor.

'We cannot deny it,' says the Danish historian Nieburh, who was himself an eye-witness of these events—'we are quite beaten; our line of defence is destroyed, and all is at stake, as far as we can see, without our being able to do much injury to the enemy, as long as he contents himself with bombarding the city, or especially the docks and the fleet.' Nieburh goes on to describe the scenes of grief and mourning in the stricken capital following the action. 'Every place was desolate; there was nothing to be seen in the streets, but wagons laden with goods to be carried to some place of safety, a silence as of the grave, faces covered with tears, the full expression of the bleeding wound given us by the defeat.'[1] Another eye-witness of the battle has vividly recalled all the white flags flying from the mastheads of the surrendered Danish vessels under a sullen, grey overcast sky.[2]

5

The truce agreed to after the action of 2 April had been continued from day to day. Finally, to save their city from bombardment the Danes, who in the meantime had received news of the Tsar's death, were induced by Nelson to consent to a permanent armistice whereby they undertook to suspend their alliance with the Russians and to refrain from fitting out their warships for the term of fourteen weeks, during which period they also agreed to supply the British fleet with provisions. In a letter written several weeks later to the prime minister, Henry Addington, Nelson was at pains both to justify the terms of this settlement and to summarize his Baltic strategy.

> Our destruction would have been Copenhagen and her Fleet; then we had done our worst, and not much nearer being friends. By the Armistice we tied the arms of Denmark for four months from assisting our Enemy and her Allies, whilst we had every part of Denmark and its provinces open to give us everything we wanted. Great Britain was left the power of taking Danish Possessions and Ships in all parts of the world, whilst we had locked up the Danish Navy, and put the key in our pocket; time was afforded the two Countries to arrange matters on an amicable footing;

[1] Nieburh, *Life and Letters* (1852), I, pp. 176–7.
[2] A. A. Feldborg, *A Tour in Zealand* (1805).

besides, to say the truth, I look upon the Northern League to be like a tree, of which Paul was the trunk, and Sweden and Denmark the branches. If I can get at the trunk, and hew it down, the branches fall of course; but I may lop the branches, and yet not be able to fell the tree, and my power must be weaker when its greatest strength is required.[1]

In accordance with this policy, Nelson was all anxiety to get up to Reval before the frost broke up at Kronstadt, 'that the twelve sail-of-the-line might be destroyed'. Hyde Parker's fleet, having been recently reinforced from home, now totalled eighteen of the line. At Reval the British would occupy an interior and commanding position between the hostile squadrons at Reval, Kronstadt, and Karlskrona, and in strength superior to any one of them. 'I am trying to get over the grounds,'[2] wrote Nelson on 10 April, 'but Sir Hyde is slow, and I am afraid the Reval fleet will slip through our fingers. Why we are not long since at Reval is past my comprehension.'

The armistice having been duly signed and ratified, the fleet on 18 April entered the Baltic. To Nelson's disgust, however, instead of sailing immediately to Reval with a fair wind, Parker, after an unsuccessful excursion to intercept a Swedish squadron which escaped under the batteries of Karlskrona, anchored in Kioge Bay, which lay more than four hundred miles from Reval, there to await further instructions from England. While the Commander-in-Chief remained thus inactive, Nelson, as Fremantle declared, was 'the life and soul of the Squadron': so burdened that he had not a moment's respite by day and was unable to sleep at night; the combined effects of fatigue, frustration, worry, and the rigours of the bleak northern climate had in fact gravely affected his health, and it was doubtful whether he would be able to remain in the Baltic. At last, on 5 May, dispatches arrived relieving Parker of his command and appointing Nelson to succeed him.

The new Commander-in-Chief's first signal was to hoist in all boats and to prepare to weigh. On the 7th the squadron left Kioge Bay and anchored off Bornholm Island. There Nelson left the greater part of his vessels to watch the Swedes, who while their ultimate intentions remained uncertain, had at all costs to be prevented from joining the

[1] *Nelson's Dispatches*, IV, p. 361.
[2] These Grounds were the shoals in the narrow channel between the islands of Saltholm and Amager.

Russians; from whom an assurance was presently obtained that British commerce in the Kattegat and Baltic would not be molested: and then, with his ten best sailing 74s and a few cruisers ('as fine Ships, and in as good order, as any in Europe') he sailed for Reval, to test the dispositions of the Russians. Leaving astern the granite hills of Bornholm, the squadron passed Ösel and Dagö and finally stood to the eastward along the rocky, pine-clad, deeply indented shores of the Gulf of Finland. A fair wind brought him in four days to Reval roads, only to discover that the early melting of the ice that year had enabled the twelve sail of the line, scarcely three days before, to re-join the rest of the Russian fleet at Kronstadt. For four days the squadron lay in the outer bay in view of the massive grey walls, high-pitched red gabled roofs, and hoary castle rock of Reval. A careful inspection of the harbour and wooden mole confirmed his belief that but for Parker's inactivity throughout the campaign the destruction of the Russian squadron would have been assured. 'Nothing,' he con-cluded, 'if it had been right to make the attack, would have saved one Ship of them in two hours after our entering the Bay.'[1] Such were the consequences of the procrastinating and lethargic strategy pursued by the late Commander-in-Chief.

When Nelson went ashore he was cordially received by the Governor and acclaimed by the citizens as 'the young Suvuroff'.[2] Next day the Governor returned the visit, and was shown all over the *St. George*. Nelson was satisfied from what he saw and heard that 'the Baltic people will never fight me if it is to be avoided'.

'I hope you will approve of our coming here,' he wrote to St. Vincent; 'we now know the navigation, should circumstances call us here again.' With the same end in view Colonel Stewart during this time made a chart of the Bay of Reval which Nelson forwarded to the Admiralty.

On 17 May the squadron left Reval to return to the anchorage in Kioge Bay; and on their way down the Baltic they received news of the release, at the instance of the new Tsar, of the British vessels arrested by Paul.

In the event the ill-effects of Parker's *idleness* (as Nelson termed it) had but little influence on the issue of the negotiations. The truth was,

[1] *Nelson's Dispatches*, IV, p. 371.
[2] Marshal Suvuroff was Russia's leading general, and a national hero.

the resounding defeat of the Danes at Copenhagen—followed as this soon was by the news of Tsar Paul's assassination—had shattereed the Armed Neutrality; and off Rostock, on 26 May, a Russian lugger brought a placatory letter from the Tsar.

> The Lugger, on leaving our Fleet with Lord Nelson's answer to this gracious letter, fired a salute, which implies much more in the Russian service than in many others. Lord Nelson observed to his Secretary, on his return from the shore, 'Did you hear that little fellow salute? Well, now, there is peace with Russia, depend on it: our jaunt to Reval was not so bad, after all'.[1]

The new Tsar, Alexander I, quickly reversed his father's policy. The commercial interests of the Russian Empire demanded that Hanover and Hamburg, which had been occupied by the Prussians and Danes, should be cleared of foreign troops. He therefore called on the King of Prussia to withdraw his forces from Hanover and the north of the Elbe; and shortly after the Danes were induced to evacuate Hamburg. During the months which followed the various problems arising out of the Armed Neutrality were gradually resolved, and our relations with the Northern Crowns steadily improved. The free navigation of the Ems, Weser, and Elbe was restored. A convention was signed on 17 June with Russia and some months later with Denmark and Sweden. Great Britain obtained an explicit acknowledgement of the Rule of 1756, prohibiting direct traffic between hostile Powers and their colonies by neutral intermediaries, and the renunciation, on Russia's part, of the doctrine that the neutral flag covered the enemy's goods; whilst renouncing, on our side, the claim to seize naval stores as contraband of war. In future the vital rights of search and seizure of enemy goods in neutral shipping were no longer contested by the Baltic Powers.

Nelson (who meanwhile had been keeping a watchful eye on the motions of the Swedish fleet) remained in the Baltic until he was fully satisfied of the friendly intentions of Tsar Alexander's government. Throughout these months he kept the squadron in admirable order and well supplied with fresh water and provisions, to which may in large measure be ascribed the uniform good health and discipline which prevailed among his ships' companies; during all this time we had, as Nelson avowed, 'twenty-two Sail of the Line, and

[1] *Ibid.*, IV, p. 393.

forty-six Frigates, Bombs, Fire-ships, and Gun-Vessels, and in the Fleet not one man in the Hospital Ship'; and it is noteworthy that the consumption of stores was as economical here in the Baltic as it was in the squadron afterwards under his command in the Mediterranean.[1]

On 19 June, in response to his urgent appeals to the Admiralty, Nelson, whose health had been giving cause for anxiety, was relieved by Admiral Sir Charles Morice Pole and returned to England. The latter remained on the station until the end of July, when, there being no longer any need of a large squadron in the Baltic, he was ordered home.

[1] *Ibid.*, IV, p. 376.

VIII

Land Power and Sea Power

I

On the conclusion of the Peace of Lunéville in February 1801 the war had come to an end all over the Continent; the military supremacy of France was unchallenged throughout Europe; only Great Britain stood out against her. The man who had sworn to expunge the word *impossible* from the French vocabulary was now virtually dictator of France. He proposed to extort favourable terms of peace from the enemy by a timely show of force.

In spite of the failure of so many of their previous attempts at invasion, the French still entertained hopes of a successful descent upon the British Isles. In the spring of 1801 Bonaparte issued orders for a huge assembly of flotilla craft to be organized in twelve divisions and distributed among the ports between the Morbihan in Brittany and Flushing on the Flanders shore; the idea being to land a force of 30,000 troops on the English coast, presumably for a swift and devastating raid on London. The flotilla was put under the command of one of Bonaparte's leading admirals, La Touche-Tréville.

The French preparations were actively pursued and occasioned the usual alarm on this side of the Channel. By June there were more than 100,000 regular troops under arms, besides nearly double that number of yeomanry, militia, and volunteers. In numerous towns and villages in the southern and eastern counties meetings were held to discuss defensive measures. On 25 July the Horse Guards suspended all leave; on the 22nd the volunteers paraded in Hyde Park; towards the end of the month a number of French gun-boats carrying troops were clearly distinguished off the enemy's coast from Fairlight and the surrounding hills, and the Hastings volunteers turned out. 'The French', wrote Collingwood from his post off Brest that summer, 'are making such preparation of their fleet and army on the whole extent of their coast that I do not expect we shall return to port until the Autumnal gales drive us in.'[1]

Within a few weeks of his return from the Baltic, Nelson was given the command of 'a squadron on particular service'. This was a miscellaneous force of frigates and lesser craft distributed along the coast between Orfordness and Beachy Head. After carefully studying all the available intelligence relating to the threatened invasion, Nelson, on 25 July, submitted a memorandum on the defence of the Thames estuary; two days later he hoisted his flag in the *Unité* frigate at Sheerness, and on the 29th journeyed to Deal by post-chaise, intent on getting the Sea-Fencibles afloat. This turned out to be impossible, for the men had their livings to consider and were in any case suspicious of the Admiralty—Nelson observed 'they were always afraid of some trick'.

'These men say,' he reported to St. Vincent on 7 August, 'our employment will not allow us to go from our homes beyond a day or two, and for actual service: but they profess their readiness to fly on board, or any other duty ordered, when the Enemy are announced as actually coming on the sea. This, my dear Lord, we must take for granted is the situation of all other Sea-Fencibles: when we cannot do all we wish, we must do as well as we can.'[2]

About this time Nelson shifted his flag to the *Medusa*, the frigate in which he was to spend most of his time during the ensuing months. After looking into Boulogne, he prepared, on 5 August, to sail for Flushing; then changing his mind when the wind came easterly, next day was back at Margate, doing his 'utmost to get the Fencibles afloat'. A few days later the *Medusa* was anchored off Harwich, and Nelson was remembering the far-off days of his youth when his uncle, Captain Maurice Suckling, had placed him in command of the *Triumph*'s long-boat—'I have', recalled the Admiral, 'been a tolerable Pilot for the mouth of the Thames in my younger days'; on 10 August 'Mr. Spence, the Maritime surveyor of this Coast' piloted his frigate at high water across the Naze Flat to the Nore, by a channel, according to Nelson, 'which was never yet navigated by a Ship of War of this size'. On the same day he epitomized the audacious blockading policy inaugurated by Sir Edward Hawke during the Seven Years' War and

[1] Hughes, *op. cit.*, p. 128.
[2] *Nelson's Dispatches*, IV, p. 446.

lately revived by Lord St. Vincent—'*Our first defence is close to the Enemy's Ports.*'[1]

On 15 August a daring attempt was made on the hostile flotilla at Boulogne; the attack was repulsed with heavy losses, but the experience served to emphasize the insuperable difficulties likely to be encountered by flat-bottoms endeavouring to get across the Channel through the strength of the tidal streams and the uncertainty of the weather. Nelson, for one, was convinced of its impossibility. 'The craft which I have seen,' he observed, 'I do not think it possible to *row* to England; and sail they cannot.'

Discounting the danger from Boulogne, Nelson supposed that the most likely attempt would be made from Flushing and the other Flanders ports. 'This boat business', he remarked, 'may be part of a great plan of invasion, but it can never be the only one.' He was apparently still hopeful of an encounter with the enemy at sea. 'Great preparations at Ostend: Augereau commands that part of the Army,' he noted. 'I hope to let him feel the bottom of the Goodwin Sands.'[2]

As yet Nelson had not visited the approaches to Flushing: and he now felt it necessary to satisfy himself on that point. On the 24th, accompanied by a number of pilots, he accordingly stood over to the Flanders coast with a force comprising thirty sail. The wind was northerly and light, with fine weather. He found himself confronted by a situation calling for all his youthful experience of coastal navigation. Several leagues distant across the edge of the shoals, beyond a congeries of banks and sands and the perilous confusion of sluicing tides, with the long, low Netherlands coastline in the background, lay the enemy flotilla: manifestly not to be approached except at the greatest hazard. The officer in command of the blockading force off Flushing was confident that something might be done. Nelson, however, after inspecting the ground, took a different view. 'I cannot but admire Captain Owen's zeal in his anxious desire to get at the enemy,' observed the Admiral, 'but I am afraid it has made him overleap sandbanks and tides, and laid him aboard the enemy.' Rather was Nelson inclined to put his trust in the mature judgment of one Yawkins, master of the hired cutter *King George*, who had been with him at the blockade of Cadiz in 1797, and whom he described as 'a knowing

[1] *Ibid.*, IV, p. 452.
[2] *Ibid.*, IV, p. 450.

one'; and he was confirmed in his opinion two days later following an expedition up the Wielingen Channel with old Yawkins, when 'the tide running strong up, and the wind falling,' it was necessary to get out again; his pilots, too, declared it impossible, without buoys or beacons, 'for our ships to get up to Flushing, nor could they return without a fair wind and flowing water.'[1]

Early in September he became concerned for the safety of the blockading force off Dunkirk should the wind come north-westerly; since the tides, he remarked, 'both flood and ebb, for half the tides set on the shore. Therefore, if it comes to blow to close-reefed topsails, none of our Square-rigged Vessels can beat off the shore, and have only to trust to their anchors and cables, and I much fear we should lose our Gun-brigs and the Sloops of War.' At the same time he proposed that the squadron under Captain Owen should be allowed to withdraw into Margate Roads on the appearance of blowing weather, leaving a cutter or two to keep watch on the motions of the enemy—and further, observing that Calais, Boulogne, and Dieppe likewise lay in bights and with the wind right in 'hardly any Ship can beat out', recommended that, except in fine weather, the squadron should retire to the Downs, leaving cutters on the station to serve as look-outs.[2]

It was in vain that Nelson, fretful, weary, and seasick in his small frigate tossing in the Downs, had earnestly desired to be relieved of his command and to go ashore. The First Lord was deaf to his re-monstrances. 'The public mind is so much tranquillized by your being at your post,' St. Vincent declared, 'it is extremely desirable that you should continue there . . . and give up, at least for the pre-sent, your intention of returning to town, which would have the worst possible effect at this critical juncture.' Nelson firmly believed that the First Lord and Troubridge were plotting to keep him from Lady Hamilton. 'The threat of Invasion is still kept up,' he noted on 2 September, 'and the French are trying to make their grand collection of Boats at Boulogne; but I find it difficult to believe that they can ever get half-way over.' Lying there in an open roadstead with heavy surf pounding on the beach for days on end, under sullen autumn skies, sometimes unable even to land, the Admiral lived only for the

---

[1] *Ibid.*, IV, pp. 478–9; Adm. 51/4019, 26 August 1801.
[2] *Ibid.*, IV, pp. 483–4.

hour of his release. Already peace negotiations had been opened with France. The great invasion project—or show of it—was plainly at an end; and within a couple of years Bonaparte's assemblage of flat-bottoms lay rotting at their moorings.

It would be easy, perhaps, to exaggerate the effect of this menacing parade of preparation upon the ordinary Englishman. The alarm, such as it was, was for the most part confined to the southern and eastern counties. Throughout the war there had been these recurrent apprehensions of a sudden descent upon our shores. Parson Wood-forde duly noted them in his diary, along with other items of local and national importance, and continued, as before, immersed in personal and parochial affairs: the supervision of his farm and garden, fishponds, dairy, and still-room; the ailments of his own and neigh-bouring households; his annual tithe audit 'frolics'; presents given and received; games of cribbage and back-gammon; his distribution of pennies, on St. Valentine's Day, to all the youngsters of the place; the perambulation of the local club round the village at Whitsun 'with pipe and drum and colours flying', and other parish occasions. Day by day the old parson placidly recorded the passage of the seasons. Across the Channel the warring columns might march and counter-march, but on our side of those protecting waters the islanders pursued the even tenor of their way as they had done long ago in the days of Philip II, of the Grand Monarch, and, more recently, of Saxe, of Choiseul, and of d'Orvilliers. The familiar rhythm of country life continued unchanged. The patient ox-teams drew their heavy ploughs across the plains; on the southern hills great flocks of sheep grazed as usual around their shepherds; in the fine summer weather the corn was ripening, and presently the bands of stalwart labourers came and wrought mightily with their sickles. The annual feast that marked the completion of the harvest signified very much more in the eyes of the countrymen than any campaign on the distant Continent.

In the North and midlands the industrial revolution that was swiftly transforming the face of the countryside continued unchecked by the wars and turmoils which had cast so many States of the Continent into the melting-pot. Each succeeding year the gaunt grey mills were spreading deeper and deeper into the damp Pennine valleys. The cotton manufactures of Lancashire now rivalled the woollen trade of Yorkshire. The abounding prosperity of Manchester, the capital of the whole area, was already a portent of the shape of things to come. The broadcloth of Leeds, cutlery of Sheffield, and earthenware of the Potteries were famous throughout Europe. Among the coal- and iron-fields of the Black Country the whir and clatter of machinery grew ever louder and the tall factory chimneys and forges belched out continually increasing quantities of smoke. In the vicinity of Birmingham, James Watt was turning out steam-engines which were the marvel of the age. The turn of the century saw the network of new turnpikes and canals for the carriage of coal extended widely throughout the industrial areas.

The utter security of this island, ever since the overthrow and destruction of the Spanish Armada, made the prospect of actual invasion seem incredibly remote to the bulk of its inhabitants. Though the *Moniteur* was filled daily with diatribes against England, faith in our wooden walls never faltered. Underneath all the superficial alarm lay large reserves of robust self-confidence. A song entitled 'The Snug Little Island', from a patriotic piece by Thomas Dibdin, *The British Raft*, which enjoyed an amazing vogue in the latter part of the year, admirably reflects this mood.

> Since Freedom and Neptune have hitherto kept time,
> In each saying "this shall be my land";
> Should the army of *England*, or all they could bring land
> We'd show 'em some play for the island.
>   We'll fight for our right to the island,
>   We'll give them enough of the island,
>   Invaders should just, bite at the dust,
>   But not a bit more of the island!

2

After a siege of two years the famished garrison of Valetta had surrendered to the small British force under Colonel Sir Thomas Graham on 5 September 1800. Bonaparte had given imperative orders to revictual the fortress, but in vain. During the whole period of the siege no more than five vessels had managed to run the blockade and during the last twelve months not even one—so close had been the Navy's watch. Gradually their stocks of food, water, and fuel were exhausted; and towards the end men were dying by the hundred daily.

Captain Alexander Ball, who had been in command of the blockading squadron, was rewarded with a baronetcy and the governorship of Malta, which he held for the remainder of his life. By his single-minded devotion to their interests he came to occupy a place in the affections of the native Maltese never held by any other Englishman before or since. His governorship of the islands firmly cemented the British hold on Malta.

The same cause that determined the fall of Malta also held the French Army of Egypt completely blocked in, unable either to escape or to receive effective reinforcements. The utmost exertions used by Bonaparte would not avail to relieve his forces in Egypt or even to secure authentic intelligence of the situation there. Already the Egyptian expedition had cost France a fleet; it seemed likely to cost her an army. Vessel after vessel had been sent out to Egypt with men, stores, and dispatches. The capture of nearly every one of these ships attested the complete and unchallenged control of the Mediterranean by Great Britain.

Desirous of using the British army to support the Allied cause in southern Europe, the government presently dispatched these troops against one objective after another, hesitating and vacillating for so long that nothing whatever was accomplished. During the summer of 1800 the great convoy of transports wandered vainly up and down the Mediterranean—from Minorca to Leghorn, from Leghorn to Malta, from Malta back to Minorca, and from Minorca to Gibraltar. Still endeavouring to exploit its unique power of amphibious attack, the government meditated an attempt, first, on Ferrol, and then on Cadiz. In the event both had to be abandoned. The instructions sent to Abercromby by the Cabinet during these months mark, perhaps, the lowest ebb of British military strategy in the war.

In the autumn, however, a three-fold plan of campaign was devised against the French in Egypt. First, a substantial British force based on Malta was to invade Egypt from the sea; second, a Turkish army was to work round against Egypt from Asia Minor; and third, an Anglo-Indian force led by Major-General David Baird, under escort of a small squadron commanded by Sir Home Popham, was to be brought round from Calcutta and to advance up the Red Sea to cooperate in the enterprise, in conjunction with a force sent out from England by way of the Cape of Good Hope. Trusting to the protection of the

Navy against the French invasionary force preparing across the Channel, our government proceeded to drain the kingdom of troops to strengthen the Egyptian expedition. The command of the army in the Mediterranean was entrusted to Sir Ralph Abercromby, and the convoy was escorted by a strong squadron under Keith. Before the troops reached their destination, however, the success of the expedition was jeopardized by the escape in January 1801 of a small force commanded by Ganteaume from Brest. In the words of St. Vincent, 'had the French squadron on entering the Mediterranean proceeded directly to Alexandria, according to its orders, Lord Keith would have been beaten in detail, the French army effectually supplied with men and means, and our own efforts completely baffled.' But Ganteaume's vessels were battered by storm and so short of naval stores that the squadron retired to Toulon. By the time he put to sea again the British were ready to block his next move. Later in the same year Ganteaume made two other attempts to reach Egypt, which were similarly unsuccessful.

Towards the end of November 1800 Keith's squadron and its convoy reached Malta; and a month later sailed for the advanced base in Marmorice Bay on the southern coast of Asia Minor, where they were to take in supplies and make their final preparations for the descent. In this deep and spacious anchorage, which was completely land-locked, Abercromby's men were exercised in embarking and disembarking with order and rapidity. The general himself now realized that they would have to depend on their own efforts and resources only. Little reliance was to be placed on the cooperation of their Turkish allies—nor, as the event proved, was there much chance of the forces converging on the Red Sea arriving at their destination on time (when Abercromby came in sight of Alexandria, Baird, in fact, had scarcely reached Bombay on the long journey to Egypt).

After a protracted delay, due largely to the non-arrival of part of the Turkish contingent, the huge convoy of supply ships and troop-transports, with about 16,000 men on board, under the escort of Keith's flagship, the *Foudroyant*, 80, and the *Kent*, *Ajax*, *Minotaur*, *Northumberland*, *Tigre*, and *Swiftsure*, all 74s, about a dozen cruisers, and a large division of warships armed *en flûte*, together with a few Turkish vessels, at last sailed majestically out of the entrance to Marmorice Bay. The whole armada then stood southward across the

Mediterranean; during the passage a westerly gale arose; on 1 March they came in sight of the Pharos of Alexandria and the low, flat, sandy coast of the Nile delta; and on the following day Keith's squadron, with the *Minotaur* and *Swiftsure* leading, bore up for their anchorage in Aboukir Bay, steering through the sunken wrecks which still bore witness to Nelson's great victory of 1798.

They had arrived at the anchorage too late in the day to be able to land the troops; and on the 3rd it was blowing hard from the northward with a heavy swell. For nearly a week the sea ran so high that a landing was out of the question; but on the 7th the northerly winds finally moderated, and very early the next morning at the appointed signal—a rocket soaring aloft from Keith's flagship—the work of disembarkation began. The whole operation was under the direction of Captain Alexander Cochrane of the *Ajax*;[1] it had been carefully planned and the landing-orders left nothing to chance. Shortly after dawn most of the boats were at the rendezvous—two gun-boats anchored close to the shore. But such was the extent of the anchorage occupied by so large a fleet, and so great the distance of many of the boats from the rendezvous, that all were not assembled in proper order until nine o'clock, when 'the whole line immediately began to move, with great celerity, towards the beach between the Castle of Aboukir, and the entrance of the Sed'.[2]

The sun blazed down on the long line of boats, each of them crammed with troops and their accoutrements, led by Captain Cochrane in his barge, advancing steadily towards the shore. The landing-place was a narrow strip of beach on the Aboukir peninsula, backed by a great sandhill; to the south was a range of lower sandhills, rising in tiers one behind the other, interspersed with patches of scrub; to the north lay Aboukir Island and the castle, with its guns enfilading the shore as far as the great central sandhill. The heights commanding the beaches were lined with troops and bristling with cannon. At the back of the sand-dunes lay a tract of sandy desert dotted with groves of date-palms. As soon as the flotilla came within range of the enemy's guns, a murderous cross-fire opened up on the advancing lines of boats. Grape and canister ploughed up the waters; several of the boats were sunk and many lives were lost; but the seamen rowed

---

[1] Adm. 1/140, 8 March 1801.
[2] *Ibid.*, 10 March 1810.

coolly on. As the first division of boats touched the strand a tremendous cheer arose; next moment the troops had scrambled ashore, and, quickly forming in the order so often rehearsed during their sojourn in Marmorice Bay, charged, with fixed bayonets, up the steep slope of the sandhill. 'I saw the British commanding officer, Sir John Moore, in front,' an eye-witness records, 'waving his men onward with his hat. Up the sandhills they rushed, appearing to me like a heavy wave rolling up a sandy beach.' On either side of the flotilla a force of gunboats and armed launches supported the landing with their covering fire, and a battalion of 1,000 seamen, under Captain Sir William Sydney Smith of the *Tigre*, cooperated with the troops; Sydney Smith also had charge of the launches with the field artillery accompanying the troops.

The storming of the great sandhill was the decisive moment of the day, followed as it was by the speedy retirement of the defenders. To the south our troops had similarly formed under heavy fire, and then first repulsed a cavalry charge, and later driven the infantry back from the sand-dunes, capturing several guns. All the enemy's attempts to break through to the beachhead were repelled, and the British remained in firm possession of the shore. 'The boats returned without delay for the second division,' declared Keith in his dispatch; 'and before the evening, the whole army, with few exceptions, was landed, with such articles of provisions and stores, as required the most immediate attention.'[1]

For several days Keith's fleet was engaged in landing guns, stores, and water for the troops, who advanced slowly on Alexandria. Aboukir Castle was taken on the 18th; three days later General Menou—who had recently succeeded to the command of the French army following Kléber's death—attacked the invaders, but was heavily defeated at the battle of Alexandria, in which Abercromby fell mortally wounded. The French army was in consequence cut in two—one part withdrawing to Cairo, while the other was shut up in Alexandria. Following on the arrival of a Turkish army, Alexandria was occupied on 19 April. The ensuing weeks saw the slow but systematic conquest of Egypt by Abercromby's successor, Major-General Hely-Hutchinson, who, drawing his supplies from the fleet, left nothing to chance and achieved his end with remarkably few casualties. Cairo fell at the end of June,

[1] *Ibid.*

and 13,000 French troops surrendered with their artillery. In the meantime Baird and his Sepoy army had landed on the Red Sea coast and painfully traversed the desert into Upper Egypt, but arrived too late on the scene of action to be of much service.

The landing of Abercromby's army in Aboukir Bay is one of the classic instances of a well-planned, well-conducted, and completely successful conjoint operation. 'I have always said, and I do think,' Nelson declared, 'that the landing of the British army was the very finest act that even a British army could achieve.' This verdict has been endorsed by one of the most eminent authorities of our own time. 'As an example of a particular class of military operation it stands on a pinnacle of its own in the warfare of modern times. Landings in defiance of a formidable enemy in position have rarely been attempted on so great a scale. There is scarcely a precedent for an enterprise so hazardous and so difficult, leading to startling tactical results within the space, it may almost be said, of a few minutes, and of a disembarkation in face of the enemy virtually deciding the issue of an important campaign almost before it had begun.'[1] It is noteworthy that the most cordial harmony and cooperation had prevailed between the sister Services. Though the difficulties of the enterprise had proved far greater than had originally been anticipated they had been effectively overcome; and the successful disembarkation of our expeditionary force had been the brilliant prelude to a long series of skilful operations—in which the Navy continued to play its part—culminating in the eviction of the enemy from Egypt. After the capture of Alexandria, Hely-Hutchinson wrote, 'The labour of the Navy has been continued and excessive; it has not been of one day or one week, but months together in the Bay of Aboukir, in the new inundation, and on the Nile for 160 miles. They have been employed without intermission and have submitted to many privations with a cheerfulness and patience highly creditable to them and advantageous to the public service.'

3

In the summer of 1801, with peace negotiations already impending, it became imperative for Bonaparte to restore the situation in Egypt. To this end three ships of the line under Rear-Admiral Linois were

[1] Q. Callwell, *Military Operations and Maritime Preparations*, p. 358.

sent from Toulon to join the Spanish division in Cadiz, to make yet another attempt to revictual and reinforce the French army shut up in Egypt. On 4 July Linois arrived safely in the Straits of Gibraltar, but, on learning that a British force of greatly superior strength was cruising off Cadiz, put into the Bay of Gibraltar and anchored off Algeciras. Early in the morning of the 6th Saumarez's squadron, led by the *Venerable*, with the *Caesar*, *Pompée*, *Spencer*, *Hannibal*, and *Audacious* following, were seen coming round Cabrita Point from the westward. 'It certainly was a sight', declared an eye-witness, 'to see those magnificent ships with their white sails shining in the sun and following each other at intervals.' The squadron rounded the point and stood to the northward.

It was a beautiful summer's day with a light westerly breeze. Linois's three battleships—the *Formidable*, *Dessaix*, and *Indomptable*—were moored close in with the town, in shoal water, protected by the batteries on the cliffs above. In the action which followed the determining factor was the light and failing wind. The British lost steerage way, and drifted rather than sailed towards the enemy line. 'In opening Cabrita Point', declared Saumerez in his dispatch, 'I found the ships lay at a considerable distance from the enemy's batteries; and having a leading wind up to them, every reasonable hope of success in the attack was afforded.'[1] At first all went well; and, after an hour's fighting, the enemy's ships appeared badly damaged. Then, at the crisis of the action, through a flaw of wind, the *Pompée*'s head fell off, and her guns could not be brought to bear on her opponent: instead of continuing to rake the *Formidable*, she was now raked in her turn: eventually she had to be towed out of her dangerous situation by the boats of the squadron. At this point Saumarez, observing that the enemy were warping closer inshore, signalled to his ships to follow them; soon after, the *Hannibal*, in endeavouring to get between the *Formidable* and the land, ran aground under the plunging fire of the shore batteries and exposed to the raking broadsides of Linois's flagship. In the meantime the four remaining ships of the squadron were attempting to work up to the enemy. But the wind again failing, Saumarez was obliged to abandon the *Hannibal* to her fate, and retired with his force to Gibraltar. After a gallant resistance, Captain Ferris struck his colours and the *Hannibal* was made a prize.

[1] Adm. 1/140, 6 July 1801.

Linois shortly after sent to Cadiz for a squadron to escort his battered force and their prize there. On the afternoon of the 9th the *Superb*, Captain Richard Keats, which with the *Thames* frigate had continued on watch off Cadiz, was seen standing through the Straits of Gibraltar under a heavy press of sail, with the signal for an enemy flying: scarcely had the two ships doubled Cabrita Point, when the hostile squadron, comprising six of the line and three frigates, under the command of Don Juan de Moreno, was seen in pursuit of them; the Spaniards thereupon anchored off Algeciras with Linois's squadron.

Meanwhile on the other side of the bay the unremitting exertions of the ships' companies had succeeded in getting most of Saumarez's crippled ships ready to fight again. The *Pompée* was too badly damaged to leave any hopes that she could be repaired in time; and at first all idea of refitting the *Caesar* was also on the point of being abandoned. Whereupon, relates his flag-captain, he entreated Saumarez to permit him to keep the crew in the flagship so long as any chance remained of getting her into a state to receive his flag again.

> On communicating to the people what had passed, there was a universal cry, 'All hands all night and day until the ship is ready!' so earnest were they to carry the flag of their beloved Admiral again into battle, and so sanguine in the expectation of victory, notwithstanding the disparity of force,—nearly *two to one*! This I could not consent to, as they would have been worn out and incapable of further exertion; but I directed that all hands should be employed during the day, and that they should work *watch and watch* during the night. They immediately commenced their various duties, with all the energy and zeal that could be expected from men under such powerful causes of excitement. The new mainmast was got in forthwith, and extraordinary efforts made to refit the rigging.[1]

Though these preparations required a good many men to be sent ashore for gunpowder and other stores, there was not a single complaint of drunkenness or absence from duty. Within the short space of five days Saumerez's half-disabled ships were ready for action again— and in the nick of time. For at daybreak on the 12th the enemy were seen to be preparing to sail; in the course of the morning they got under way and began to work out of the bay. An hour or so after noon their leading ships had cleared Cabrita Point, where they brought-to, to wait for the others to come up.

[1] Sir John Ross, *Memoirs . . . of Admiral Lord de Saumarez* (1838), I, p. 394.

It was a fine, clear afternoon with a freshening easterly breeze. At half-past two, with the signal for general chase flying and the band of Saumarez's flagship playing 'Heart of Oak'—to which a military band drawn up on the mole-head responded with 'Britons, Strike Home'—the *Caesar* hauled out of the mole: at the same moment the Admiral's flag was re-hoisted on board the *Caesar*, and, sail being made upon her, she weighed amidst the deafening acclamation of the garrison and an immense concourse of spectators assembled on the ramparts and batteries of Gibraltar.[1]

> Heart of oak are our ships, heart of oak are our men;
> We always are ready, steady boys, steady,
> We'll fight, and we'll conquer again and again. . . .

Off Europe Point, Saumarez signalled to his small force to close on the flagship and to prepare for battle. Meanwhile the enemy were forming their line off Cabrita Point, about five miles to leeward; at sunset they bore up through the Straits, sailing in two divisions in line abreast, with the Spanish ships in the rear. Saumarez presently ordered Keats in the *Superb* to go ahead and 'bring the enemy's rear to action, and keep between them and the Spanish shore'; whereupon the *Superb* set her courses and topgallant-sails, and, making between 11 and 12 knots, stood on past the *Caesar* and the *Venerable* and disappeared into the gathering darkness. About 11 p.m. the sternmost vessels of the enemy were brought to action. Keats got within three hundred yards of a Spanish first-rate, the *Real Carlos*, 112, without being seen, then shortened sail and opened fire and poured in several rapid broadsides; after which the *Real Carlos* caught fire, and Keats broke off the action, pressing on in pursuit of the *St. Antoine*. Following the *Superb*'s surprise attack, the crew of the *Real Carlos* immediately began firing wildly in all directions. Several of the shots struck one of their own ships, the *Hermenegildo*, another first-rate, which, mistaking her for an enemy, first engaged and presently collided with her. Both vessels were soon ablaze.[2] Again to quote Saumarez's flag-captain:

> I was at this time standing on the poop ladder, near the Admiral, when he seized me by the shoulder, and, pointing to the flames bursting out, exclaimed, 'My God, sir, look there! the day is ours!' A more magnificent

[1] *Ibid.*, I, p. 403.
[2] Adm. 1/140, 13 July 1801.

scene never presented itself, as may be easily imagined, than two ships of such immense magnitude as the Spanish first-rates, on board of each other in flames, with a fresh gale, the sea running high, and their sails in the utmost confusion. The flames, ascending the rigging with the rapidity of lightning, soon communicated to the canvas, which instantly became one sheet of fire.[1]

Shortly after midnight the flames reached the magazines, and both ships blew up with a tremendous explosion and the loss of nearly 2,000 lives. Meanwhile the *St. Antoine* had been overhauled and brought to action by the *Superb* and after an hour's fighting obliged to surrender. Together with the *Venerable* and *Spencer*, Saumarez's flagship bore up after the enemy, who were carrying a press of sail, standing out of the Straits. Throughout the night the pursuit continued. At dawn the *Venerable* came up with Linois's flagship, the *Formidable*, which had fallen astern of her consorts; but, after engaging her for about an hour and a half, the *Venerable* ran aground on a shoal, losing her foremast and mizenmast. For a while the latter's destruction appeared certain: for the breeze failing them, the *Caesar* and *Spencer* lay at some distance off becalmed, and five of the enemy's vessels were sighted in the N.W., coming down with a westerly wind: then a breeze sprang up which enabled the *Thames* frigate to tow the *Venerable* clear of the shoal.

The *Formidable* and her consorts, most of which had been badly mauled in the action, made the best of their way to Cadiz, where they were later blockaded by the victors, while Saumarez returned in triumph to Gibraltar. 'Sir James Saumarez's action', observed St. Vincent complacently, 'has put us upon velvet.'

When the news of Algeciras reached England it took the City by storm. The London mail drove down to Plymouth flying the Royal Standard and the Union Jack and emblazoned with the words *Saumarez and Victory*. Saumarez's name was lauded to the skies; he was made a K.B. and received the thanks of both Houses of Parliament; he was now, as his sister-in-law declared, 'the theme of every conversation, the toast of every table, the hero of every woman, the boast of every Englishman'. Nelson, who for long had nursed resentment at a tactless criticism on Saumarez's part of the tactics of the Nile, forgot his dislike of a commander so totally different to himself in

[1] Ross, *op. cit.*, I, p. 407.

temperament and demeanour and expressed whole-hearted admiration at a gallant feat of arms. 'Again and again I rejoice with you at Sir James Saumarez,' he wrote to St. Vincent. '. . . The promptness with which he refitted, the spirit with which he attacked a superior force after his recent disaster, and the masterly conduct of the action, I do not think were ever surpassed.' Saumarez was a proud and sensitive man whose fate it was to feel that he was not appreciated. After Algeciras his fame was secure.

4

The tidings of Algeciras came as a joyful climax to the triumphs of 1801. First, Abercromby's landing and Menon's defeat in Aboukir Bay; next, the destruction of the Danish fleet at Copenhagen; and now, following hard on the heels of the earlier reverse off Algeciras, the report of Saumarez's resounding stroke against the Franco-Spanish squadron under Linois. While the battle squadrons of France were virtually laid up in port, British cruisers and privateers had swept the enemy's shipping from the seas and subjected the trade of the maritime neutrals with the Republic to the severest limitations of international law. One after another nearly all her colonies had passed under the British flag. In short, for France the struggle at sea had been as disastrous and disheartening as that on land had been glorious and triumphant. Not only her own fleets, but also those of her allies, Spain, Holland, and Denmark, had been successively overthrown.

The whole matter was on a colossal scale. It was the clash of two titanic forces. For the British battle fleets, like the armies of revolutionary France, represented a degree of martial power unparalleled in history. At the outset of hostilities Great Britain had possessed 135 of the line and 133 frigates; in the final year of the Revolutionary War she had 202 of the line and 277 frigates, in addition to considerable numbers of battleships and frigates building. In 1792 the total personnel of the Service amounted to only 16,000 men; by 1802 it had attained the unprecedented figure of 135,000. The bases and stations from which our squadrons and detached divisions operated extended all over the globe. At this time the Royal Navy was superior to the combined navies of all Europe. There was no power on earth that could challenge its control of the oceans and seas.

Under the protection of the Navy the total exports of Great Britain had more than doubled and her imports had increased by over 60 per cent. Whereas on the Continent industrial progress had been brought almost to a standstill through the ravages of war and revolution, in this country there had been no such retardation.

> We can most incontrovertibly prove, that under the pressure of new burdens, and during the continuance of the eventful contest in which we are engaged, the revenue, the manufactures, and the commerce of the country, have flourished beyond the example of all former times. The war, which has crushed the industry, and annihilated the trade and shipping of her rival, has given energy and extent to those of Great Britain.[1]

Despite the commercial and industrial crisis of 1797, the national economy remained sound. All this led to a vast increase in the industrial activity of Great Britain, which was fast becoming the workshop, as well as the warehouse, of the world. The increasing use of machinery, and the consequent lowering of prices, multiplied sales. Although wide areas of the Continent were forbidden territory, British goods continued to find their way in large quantities, by devious routes, into the interdicted markets. A considerable part of our export trade was at this time diverted from the Mediterranean to the countries of northern and central Europe. The lucrative trade with Russia and Prussia continued to expand; while British exports to Bremen and Hamburg multiplied no less than six-fold. The demand for Manchester goods steadily increased. 'Mercator,' writing to the *Manchester Mercury* in 1801, remarked that 'during a war which hath continued nine years, our trade hath suffered less, perhaps, than any other manufacture in the Empire, and is even far more extensive than it was at the commencement of that period.' The export of British manufactures, and the re-export of tropical produce, were the two main sources of this astonishing prosperity. Through the conquest of the hostile colonies—French, Spanish, Portuguese, Dutch, Danish, and Swedish—in the East and West Indies, the customs receipts had risen by at least one-half. 'If we compare this year of war', declared Pitt, 'with former years of peace, we shall in the produce of our revenue and in the extent of our commerce behold a spectacle at once

[1] George Rose, *A Brief Examination into the Increase of the Revenue, Commerce, and Manufactures of Great Britain from 1792 to 1799* (1799).

paradoxical, inexplicable and astonishing.' It was this soaring commercial prosperity which alone made possible the lavish financial aid that Great Britain extended to her allies during the Revolutionary War.

Nevertheless, after eight years of war, high prices, and unprecedented taxation, the whole population yearned passionately for peace. 'I wish all these victories', Betsey Fremantle declared after Copenhagen, 'may lead to peace.' 'An unmanly impatience for peace', Coleridge observed, 'became almost universal.' All this time the cost of living was increasing. 'Bread now very high,' wrote Woodforde in January 1801—'a formerly 6 Penny Loaf is now sold at the high Price of seventeenpence.' The dearness of bread in the period 1800–1 was due largely to the failure of the harvest of 1800 as the result of a series of disastrous rainstorms and to the closure of the Baltic by the Northern Powers from December 1800 to April 1801. The price of meat, butter, and sugar had doubled. 'All sorts of nourriture or clothing', observed Madame d'Arblay, 'seem to rise in the same proportion.' Added to this, the British population was rapidly rising. The census of 1801 showed an increase of eleven per cent. in ten years. The sufferings of the poorer classes became severe; a large number had actually been brought to the verge of starvation. 'Visited all the poor in the village,' wrote Betsey Fremantle in the spring of 1801; 'some are truly starving and look the picture of death.' 'The misery endured by the poor', Fox told his brother, 'and indeed by those a little above the poor and who are not able to give charity when they are in a position rather to ask it themselves has for the last twelve months been dreadful.' There was rioting in London and other places and the volunteers had to be called out to quell the disturbances. Since 1795 the Habeas Corpus Act had been continually suspended. Pitt began his administration with the hope of extinguishing the national debt; since 1793 that debt had more than doubled. The necessity of meeting the heavy expenses of the war and the subsidies to our Allies led to ever-increasing taxes. 'The new threefold assessment of taxes has terrified us rather seriously,' Madame d'Arblay had written in December 1797. '. . . We have, this very morning, decided upon parting with four of our new windows.' The prevailing war weariness was reflected in the correspondence of the Fleet. 'This fleet is in a wretched way for ships and men,' observed Keith in June

1801, off Alexandria—'all short, and scarcely half British.' 'Would to God that this war were happily concluded,' wrote Collingwood from the stormy post off Brest; 'nothing good can ever happen to us short of peace.' 'I am almost done up,' declared Nelson in October 1801, 'but I hope there will be but little more occasion for war.' The task of stemming the progress of the revolution on the Continent was manifestly beyond our powers. The hegemony of France was an accomplished fact. It was with the full support of popular opinion, therefore, that Addington's ministry pressed forward the negotiations with the republican government.

5

With the turn of the century France entered upon one of the most brilliant periods in her history. The triumph of Marengo had firmly implanted the Napoleonic legend in the national consciousness and secured the hold of the First Consul on the army and the nation. The greatest military genius that the world has ever known was now fairly launched forth upon his dazzling career; all the enemies of France, save only one, had been overthrown; and *la grande nation* was once more mistress of Europe. With the incorporation of Belgium, the Rhineland, Savoy, and Piedmont the boundaries of the French republic were extended to the limits of ancient Gaul. The Batavian, Helvetic, Cisalpine, and Ligurian republics acknowledged her protectorate. Italy was controlled by France. Holland and Sweden were dominated by French influence. Spain was submissive to her policy. Great Britain, notwithstanding her all-conquering Navy, was manifestly impotent on the Continent.

Firmly ensconced in the seat of power by virtue of his victorious arms and strong and able administration, Napoleon, with the aid of the highly efficient Civil Service which he had called into being, established, during the next five years, the laws and institutions of modern France. With extraordinary dispatch and dexterity he repaired the ravages wrought by the Revolution and restored order and authority. After ten years of ferment and convulsion there ensued a period of intensive practical activity. Everywhere chaos was succeeded by order, and licence by discipline. Proceeding with almost superhuman energy, organizing genius, and capacity for sustained labour, he overhauled every department of administration, central and local, and permanently secured for the mass of Frenchmen the material benefits of the Revolution. The Consulate marked the final transition from the old France to the new. French life is today based in large measure on his highly centralized system of local government, of justice, and of education. By his Concordat with the Vatican he restored religion in the half-infidel society which was the legacy of the Revolution. Possibly the most enduring achievement of the era of the Consulate was Napoleon's codification of French law. His great Code was destined to exercise a profound influence, not only upon France, but also upon the neighbouring States. Napoleon also inaugurated a system of education which was to endure for generations. He endowed France with an extensive network of admirable highways and canals; he deepened and extended her ports, improved her bridges, and adorned Paris and her other principal cities with magnificent public buildings.

Despite the triumph of his arms and diplomacy on the Continent, however, Napoleon was still confronted by Great Britain's mastery of the sea. It was through the overwhelming naval preponderance of her enemy that France had lost both her commerce and her colonies. The Directory was constrained to declare, in January 1799, that there was not a single merchantman trading under French colours—almost all the mercantile shipping of France had in fact been swept from the sea, raw materials cut off from her manufactories, and her commerce practically ruined. With the exception of Guadeloupe and Mauritius the whole of her colonial empire was now in British hands. The shipping of Spain and Holland had likewise disappeared from the sea. The Spaniards had lost nearly all their West Indian islands to Great Britain, and the Dutch the greater part of their rich colonial empire. Both Denmark and Sweden had been deprived of their possessions in the West Indies. Almost all the Portuguese colonies in the East Indies had been captured by the British, who had also occupied Madeira. No further maritime combination against Great Britain was even remotely possible, for no other fleets in a condition to fight us remained anywhere in Europe. Since the outbreak of the war the enemy had lost no less than 81 sail of the line, 187 frigates, and 248 sloops. Owing to the British blockade, and the consequent dearth of naval stores, it was moreover impossible for them to build and equip new squadrons.

Peace with the great Sea Power was clearly essential to the revival of the French Navy and the restoration of the French colonial empire. Napoleon's secret projects at this juncture extended far beyond the limits of Europe. He dreamed of vast French territories along the Mississippi. Still closer to his heart was Egypt, with a canal stretching across the Sinai isthmus to the gulf of Suez; and of a great French empire arising in the Indian Ocean.

The strategical stalemate between Land Power and Sea Power was complete. The French Army could no more overcome the British Navy than the British Navy could overcome the French Army. Eager to bring the long and exhausting struggle to a close the British government allowed themselves to be outmanœuvred at the peace negotiations; and in the spring of 1802 signed a treaty with Napoleon whereby this country agreed to the restitution of all the conquests made against France, Spain, and Holland with the exception of Trinidad and Ceylon. Egypt was to be given up to the Sultan of Turkey, and a number of leading questions, including the future of Malta, were still left undecided.

IX

Napoleon and Great Britain

I

Napoleon reached the summit of his popularity in France when, after difficult and protracted negotiations, the definitive treaty was signed with Great Britain on 27 March 1802. The Peace of Amiens confirmed the French hegemony of Europe, and, by restoring to the Republic all its lost colonies, had apparently rendered possible the realization of Napoleon's dreams of maritime expansion and overseas empire. The enthusiasm of the French people at the brilliant prospects opening out before them was unbounded. Already, under the leadership of the new Caesar, they had seen their enemies brought low in Italy and Germany, the territory of the Republic extended to the limits of the Alps and the Rhine, and the pre-eminence of France in the councils of Europe freely acknowledged. The most stubborn and irreconcilable of all their antagonists had finally abandoned the struggle and made peace. A plebiscite held in August made Napoleon First Consul for life with greater powers than any Bourbon had ever possessed.

With the restoration of peace Paris was once more the centre of Europe. 'A most magnificent place,' was the admiring tribute of a Scottish traveller of this era. The central parts of the city were now in process of rebuilding in the neo-classical style recalling the glories of ancient Rome. British visitors in their thousands flocked across the Channel to take the road to the capital; there to saunter in the beautiful walks of the Champs Elysées and the gardens of the Tuileries, to admire all the fine shops in the new and splendid thoroughfares, to feast their eyes on the incomparable treasures of the Louvre, and to behold, from the windows of the Tuileries, perhaps the most impressive spectacle of all—the young conqueror himself, clad simply in the plain blue uniform of the Chasseur Guards, with generals and

Mameluke orderlies in his train, reviewing his troops on the Place du Carrousel.

In the Mediterranean, friendly relations with Turkey were restored and the French consulates re-established in the Levant. A powerful fleet and a large army were dispatched to San Domingo, to suppress a negro revolt which had broken out on the island during the late war. On the American mainland, it was Napoleon's aim to develop the immense territories of Louisiana which had been returned to France under the provisions of the Franco-Spanish treaty of 1800; and an expedition was then fitting out to take possession of the colony. Early in March 1803 a squadron under the command of Rear-Admiral Linois sailed from Brest for the east; on board the flagship was General Decaen, whose mission was to work for the expulsion of the British from India and the recovery of the former French possession there. A French geographical and scientific expedition to Van Diemen's Land, or Tasmania, was alarming the British authorities both in London and in Sydney. A mission was sent to Egypt to revive French influence in the country, and another to Muscat to woo the favour of its ruler.

At the same time Napoleon was determined to restore and reorganize the French Navy. Throughout the era of the Consulate and Empire his Minister of the Marine was Vice-Admiral Decrès—an able administrator if a somewhat over-cautious and uninspiring chief. The prefects placed in charge of the principal naval ports were also highly capable men. Discipline and morale markedly improved. Reserves of naval stores were built up, the harbour of Cherbourg much improved, and great arsenals projected at Antwerp and Spezzia. But though there was a genuine naval revival the service lacked first-class leaders; and, in any case, the work of reconstruction was not given enough time to get very far before the war-clouds again began to gather on the horizon.

The Treaty of Amiens was followed by thirteen months of uneasy peace, during which time Napoleon pursued a policy of aggrandizement on the Continent, and his agents were active in Asia and Africa. On the day following the signature of the treaty Switzerland had been occupied by an army under General Ney. The French garrison still remained in Holland. The tale of annexations continued. Before the close of 1802 the expansionist tendency of France under the Consulate was made manifest to all the world.

At the same time British commerce had been rigorously excluded from all territories within the French orbit; the total tonnage of foreign-going ships which cleared from the ports of Great Britain during 1802 actually showed a decrease from the last twelve months of the war. The sea-route to India was imperilled by the restitution to Holland of the Cape of Good Hope; and Napoleon was beginning to embark upon far-reaching schemes of overseas expansion of ominous significance to the statesmen responsible for the safety of the British Empire. Above all, the presence in the Rhine delta of the greatest naval and military Power of the Continent constituted a standing threat to our national security. A cardinal principle of British policy was deeply involved. To quote the late Sir Herbert Richmond, 'It was Napoleon's refusal to evacuate Holland that brought matters to a head, for the Britain of Addington could no more tolerate the presence of a powerful naval and military Power at Antwerp and in the Schelde than the England of Elizabeth.'[1]

Relations between Great Britain and France became increasingly strained. Napoleon angrily demanded the expulsion of the Bourbon princes and certain other *émigrés* from this country and the suppression of British newspapers which had attacked him. He still refused to withdraw his troops from Holland. The resolution of the British government and people progressively stiffened in the face of the dictator's threats and encroachments. Our press continued to say what they thought of Napoleon and all his works, and across the Channel the *Moniteur* was only too anxious to repay these courtesies. In the end the quarrel centred on the ownership of Malta. Here, on the face of it, Napoleon had a strong case. Though the British had bound themselves, under the provisions of the Treaty of Amiens, to relinquish the island, they were showing no inclination to do so. Alexandria was, indeed, evacuated by our forces; but its garrison remained on Malta, which was further defended by a capital squadron.

The British government—now thoroughly alive to the high importance of Malta—continued, notwithstanding strong Russian opposition, to hold the island. Of all the Mediterranean bases formerly in our possession, only Malta now remained. The retention of this island, as Lord Mulgrave was afterwards to declare, was actually in the interests of friendly Powers as well as those of Great Britain.

[1] H. W. Richmond, *Statesmen and Sea Power* (1946), p. 216.

'There is no quarter', he observed, 'in which the naval power of Great Britain is more necessary to check the further progress of French ambition on the Continent during the war, or counter-act the sudden revival of its activity during peace, than the Mediterranean. The particular possession in these seas by which the means of naval exertion in the Common Cause can be most securely provided is Malta.' Not all the arts of Napoleon and Talleyrand would induce British ministers to loose their hold on the island; and the protracted and extremely complicated negotiations ended in complete deadlock. A popular cartoon of the day summed up the matter succinctly—'I axe pardon, Master Boney, but as we say: "Hands off, Pompey, we keep this little spot to ourselves." '[1]

On 13 March 1803 an angry scene in the presence of the entire diplomatic corps at a reception in the Tuileries brought these differences to a head. In his dispatch to Lord Hawkesbury, the Foreign Secretary, the British Ambassador related how the First Consul had suddenly addressed him, Lord Whitworth, 'in a voice like a coachman's'.

He began by asking me if I had any news from England. I told him that I have received letters from your Lordship two days ago. He immediately said, 'So you are determined to go to war!'—'No, Premier Consul,' I replied, 'we are too sensible of the advantage of peace.'—'We have already', he said, 'made war for fifteen years.' As he seemed to wait for an answer, I observed only, 'That is already too long.'—'But,' said he, 'you want another fifteen years. You are forcing me to it [*vous m'y forcez*]'.

Napoleon then went his round of the room, and was observed by all those to whom he addressed himself to be under the stress of great agitation. In a few minutes he came back to Whitworth and, to the latter's intense annoyance, began the quarrel anew.

'Why these armaments? Whom are these precautions directed against? I have not a single vessel of war in the ports of France; but if you want to arm, I shall arm too; if you want to fight, I shall fight too. Perhaps you may destroy France, but you will never intimidate her.'—'Neither the one nor the other', I said, 'would be desirable. We should like to live on terms of good understanding with her.'—'Then respect must be paid to treaties,' replied he. 'Woe to those who do not respect treaties! They shall be made answerable to all Europe!'[2]

[1] Q. Bryant, *Years of Victory* (1944), p. 16.
[2] Q. Frischauer, *England's Years of Danger* (1938), pp. 128–9.

The First Consul was by then in such a state of wrath and excitement that Whitworth considered it imprudent to prolong the conversation. He accordingly made no reply, and Napoleon took himself off to his own apartment repeating angrily, '*Ils en seront résponsables à tout l'Europe*'. It is to be remarked, concluded the Ambassador drily, that all this passed loud enough to be overheard by the two hundred persons who were present.

So ended Napoleon's final attempt to browbeat the British people. He began at this stage to plan the invasion of England; while, on our side, Addington's government was hurriedly preparing for war. Whitworth received instructions to present an ultimatum, requiring not merely the permanent retention in our hands of Malta but also the withdrawal of the French forces from Holland and Switzerland. Failing the acceptance of these terms, the British Ambassador was directed to leave France.

As the war-clouds drew nearer, Napoleon resolved to abandon his oceanic ambitions and to concentrate his forces in Europe. Even *la grande nation*, he realized, had not resources enough for both European and overseas expansion. Determined to free his hands to deal with the enemy across the Channel, he parted with the vast territories comprising Louisiana to the United States and attempted to play for time until his scattered warships could reach safety.

Meanwhile, obdurate to all the dictator's wiles and blandishments, Whitworth proceeded inexorably with his preparations for departure. Talleyrand's solicitations were in vain. Whitworth was not to be moved from his purpose. On his way to the coast he was followed by surreptitious messages, hints, and reproaches, all to no effect. During these last few weeks the British government declined in any way to abate its demands; with which Napoleon had no intention of complying. Finally Great Britain, on 18 May, declared war on France.

The Admiralty immediately prepared to resume its blockade of the enemy's ports. Thanks to St. Vincent, we had a Navy far superior to that with which, ten years earlier, we had entered the war against republican France. In the early months of the year there were thirty-two of the line in commission; by 1 May there were twenty more, and a month later another eight, besides a large number of cruisers. An increase of 10,000 seamen and marines for the Navy was voted by Parliament unanimously.

'Every movement from the Admiralty, the great source of our naval activity, to our dockyard and military ports, "gives note of dreadful preparations",' declared *The Times* on 11 March. '. . . Ten additional sail of the line are ordered to be immediately commissioned.' And on the 12th: 'In every department of Government the utmost alacrity continued to manifest itself. . . . Six line of battleships, in addition to those we mentioned in yesterday's Paper, have been ordered into commission. . . . The Admiralty telegraph was at work the whole of yesterday.' At Portsmouth the *Dreadnought, Royal Sovereign, Britannia,* and other ships had been put into commission; and 'in such a hurry were they to get all these ships ready,' recorded the *Naval Chronicle*, 'that the master carpenters of the ships in ordinary were ordered to the dockyard to assist as working hands.' In the next month the *Victory* was again commissioned at Portsmouth. During the two previous years she had undergone an extensive refit and had been largely rebuilt. Her open galleries had been removed and her stern made 'flat'; her elaborate figurehead, too, had been replaced by one far less ornate. At Plymouth, according to the *Naval Chronicle*, the *Tonnant* had been refitted early in the year, 'the artificers even working their dinner hours to complete her for commission'. In March: 'The activity which pervades every department of the dock-yard . . . is astonishing'; and in April: 'Cawsand Bay and Plymouth look as gay as in the height of war, there being in the former nine men-of-war, and in the latter two men-of-war and six East Indiamen'.

In early spring the press was operating in Portsmouth, Plymouth, and other parts of the coast with unexampled speed, secrecy, and efficiency, and large numbers of prime seamen were impressed for the coming war. Once again the streets and alleys of our coastal towns echoed to the ominous tramp of the press-gang. So hot was the press at Portsmouth that all the colliers then in port were swept clean of men and unable to put to sea. 'It is with the utmost difficulty that people living on the Point can get a boat to take them to Gosport,' recorded the *Naval Chronicle* in March, 'the terror of a press gang having made such an impression on the minds of the watermen that ply the passage.' At Plymouth several detachments of Royal Marines marched through the town on the evening of 9 March, raided the quays and gin-shops, and boarded ships in the Catwater and the Pool. 'A great number of prime seamen were taken out, and sent on board the Admiral's ship. They also pressed landmen of all descriptions; and the town looked as if in a state of siege. . . . One gang entered the Dock theatre, and cleared the whole gallery except the women.' In the Thames close on a thousand seamen were taken in a single night. Once again frigates and smaller cruisers scoured the Channel, boarding merchantmen and fishing-vessels and pressing part of their crews. Again to quote the *Naval Chronicle:* 'Last night [30 March] the *Boadicea*, of 44 guns, Captain Maitland, boarded, by her boats, the whole flotilla, of trawl-boats then fishing off the Eddystone light-house, and took two seamen out of each trawl-boat, about forty in number, and sent them on board the flagship in Cawsand Bay'. 'While the six East Indiamen were lying to off the Eddystone, for the easterly wind, on Monday last [10 April], the English cruisers in the Channel, manned and armed, boarded them all, and made a fair sweep of nearly 300 prime seamen for the service of the fleets; the crews of the Indiamen, till boarded, had not the most distant idea of an approaching rupture with France'.

The Impress Service was also busy in the north-east ports, which swarmed with likely recruits for the Navy. At Newcastle and the neighbouring towns the keelmen who manned the sailing barges which brought the coal to the colliers lying in the harbours at the rivermouths were a tempting quarry for the press-gang. At the same time it was understood that any injudicious move in that direction might well bring the entire coal trade to a standstill. After protracted negotiations a compromise agreement was finally arrived at whereby in return for general protection for the keelmen and other watermen, they undertook to provide a substantial quota of recruits for the Navy.

The press continued very active for several weeks. As a result of these preparations, Cornwallis sailed on 17 May from Torbay with five of the line; and two days afterwards, was back with his frigates at his old post off Brest. On the day that war was declared Nelson joined the *Victory* at Portsmouth and on the 20th sailed for the Mediterranean. He was accompanied by the last and most famous of all his flag-captains, Thomas Masterman Hardy. On the 19th Keith hoisted his flag as Commander-in-Chief on the North Sea station. On the West Indian station, a squadron consisting of nine of the line and sixteen frigates cooperated with the Negro forces in San Domingo. Expeditions were also sent out to capture St. Lucia and Tobago from the French, and Demerara, Essequibo, Berbice, and Surinam from the Dutch. The British declaration of war caught France unprepared. Her dockyards, drained of essential stores during the blockade, were only partially replenished. Half of her ships in commission were away in the West Indies, engaged in putting down the Negro revolt in Haiti. One of these was captured by the British and the remainder, hurriedly recalled, took refuge in Ferrol, where they were at once blockaded by Sir Edward Pellew. The French arsenals were once more closely invested, and French trade was swept off the seas. Napoleon's reorganization of the French marine had scarcely got under way when it was rudely interrupted by the renewal of the war. To the end France remained weak in one of the essential elements of sea power. 'If she had resources that would not bend under her weight, where will she find seamen? neither money, enterprise, nor genius will suddenly make seamen,' the *Hampshire Telegraph* declared, 'nothing but commerce and time will make them. France may build ships, she has wood and money, but where will she get seamen?' The naval power of France had been dealt, at the outset of the war, a crippling blow from which it was destined never to recover.

2

On the outbreak of hostilities Napoleon had embarked upon preparations for an invasion of the British Isles on a scale far more formidable than that of anything previously attempted. Three army corps, under the leadership of Davout, Soult, and Ney—the veterans of Marengo and Hohenlinden—were encamped by the French Channel ports in readiness to embark. As two years earlier, Boulogne was the chief rendezvous of the army of invasion. The flotilla was placed under the command of Admiral Bruix. Napoleon's plan was to ferry an army of more than 100,000 picked troops across the narrow part of the Channel in flat-bottomed barges armed with cannon, which were to be assembled in the shallow tidal harbours at and around Boulogne: at a favourable moment the whole flotilla was put to sea, and, evading the British blockade, slip across the Straits under cover of mist or darkness. To build up the huge armada of flat-bottoms the dockyards of France were stripped clean of workmen and materials to the detriment of the battle fleet. Even so, there were protracted delays while the barges were building and moving up and down the coast to the point of assembly. The harbour was widened and deepened, and the neighbouring anchorages had similarly to be improved; forts were constructed for the effectual protection of the outer roadsteads; the 'Army of England', encamped on the hills above Boulogne and along the low-lying stretches of shore from Étaples to Vimereux, was assiduously practised in the critical evolutions of embarking and getting under way.

Throughout France the war spirit rose to the highest pitch. Every shipyard and river port in the northern provinces now resounded with the hammering of the artificers, and the foundries were roaring at Douai, Liège, and Strasbourg. But the passage of the army presented insuperable difficulties: it was found impossible to get the whole flotilla to sea in a single tide; two tides at least were needed, and while the second half of the flotilla was getting out to sea the first would be obliged to wait outside for some hours, protected by the shore batteries; it was found, too, that these light, keel-less invasion craft were unmanageable in the shifting winds and tides of the Channel, and, in any case, could not possibly be kept together in darkness or fog. By the spring of 1804 Napoleon had abandoned the idea of making the descent by flat-bottoms alone. His next plan was to ensure a temporary command of the Channel in order to cover the passage of the transports. 'Let us', he wrote in July, 'be masters of the Straits for six hours and we shall be masters of the world.'[1] Napoleon himself came down to the coast to supervise the invasion preparations, taking with him the Bayeux tapestry which depicted the triumphant descent of 1066. In fine summer weather he carried out a tour of the principal ports, which were decked with flags and laurels in his honour. There were endless parades and inspections. At Calais they drank to the review of the Grand Army in St. James's Park. Later in the year, as he gazed on the white cliffs of Kent through his telescope, he declared the Channel was only a ditch that could be leaped by the bold. He continued to press on the preparations and to instruct his admirals. In anticipation of his expected triumph, Napoleon caused a victory medal to be struck inscribed with the legend: *Descente en Angleterre, Frappé à Londres en 1804.*[2]

[1] *Correspondance de Napoléon*, X, p. 406.

[2] Wheeler and Broadley, *Napoleon and the Invasion of England*, II, 238–9.

His aim was now to lure our squadrons away from the entrance to the Channel.[1] It was proposed that the Toulon fleet under La Touche-Tréville should slip out through the Straits of Gibraltar, and then, releasing the squadrons locked up in Ferrol and Rochefort, make a wide circuit around Cornwallis's force before Brest, and either sail straight up the Channel or proceed north-about, dispersing the British flotilla and covering the passage of his army. To weaken the British defence, further operations were planned against Ireland and the West Indies. But his efforts were in vain. The French squadrons still remained divided and impotent; and not all Napoleon's scheming and striving served to shift Cornwallis's battleships from their appointed station, where they secured the approaches to the Channel.

The enemy's preparations were nevertheless taken very seriously by the Ministry and the great majority of the British public. Such an alarm had not been experienced in our island since the time of the Armada. 'Thinking men', Cockburn declared, recalling the days of his youth, 'were in a great and genuine fright, which increased in proportion as they thought. The apparent magic of Napoleon's Continental success confounded them.'[2] Throughout the fine summer and autumn of 1803 the tension steadily heightened. Intelligence from abroad told of the march of endless columns of troops towards the French invasion ports. On this side of the Channel the quiet country towns and villages along our south-cast coast suddenly swarmed with soldiery. Large numbers of troops were hurriedly quartered or encamped throughout Essex, Kent, and Sussex. In August and September martial enthusiasm rose to its height with volunteers enrolling by the thousand. The peace of the English summer was rudely broken by the bawling of serjeants and the clamour of drums and bugles. In town squares and on village greens the new intake drilled assiduously. At various strategic points new barracks and redoubts were rapidly constructed.

Anxiety centred on certain vulnerable beaches on the Kent and Sussex coasts, which lay in dangerous proximity to the enemy's ports.

[1] More than a generation before, the French had prepared a wide range of plans designed to break down the British system of defence. The object of most of them was to disperse the British squadrons and thereby attain a decisive French superiority in the Channel. See Castex, *Les Idées Militaires de la Marine du XVIIIiéme siècle*, Chapter VII.

[2] H. Cockburn, *Memorials of His Time* (1856), p. 196.

In July Major Landmann was directed to carry out a systematic examination of 'every spot where a debarkation might be accomplished, even such as required very favourable circumstances, of wind, weather, etc.' Captain Frederick Austen, R.N., engaged in a similar investigation between the North Foreland and Sandown, reported that in moderate weather a landing might be accomplished on many parts of this coast, especially in Pegwell Bay—'any time of tide would be equally favourable for the debarkation of troops on this shore.' Presently a chain of strongly built martello towers began to arise along the lonely levels of Romney Marsh and Pevensey Bay.[1] Seaford Bay and Newhaven were guarded by a strong body of troops stationed in Blatchington barracks to the west of Seaford; Brighton, by this time a gay and fashionable watering-place, was also strongly garrisoned; even such a remote and secluded strand as Cuckmere Haven, to the eastward of the Seven Sisters cliffs, where, in times past, so many cargoes had been run by local smugglers, was protected by a barracks, supported by a quite substantial military establishment in the neighbouring town of Alfriston.[2]

It was proposed that Major-General Sir John Moore's Light Brigade, encamped at Shorncliffe in Kent, should first fight a delaying action on the coast, and then fall back in good order on the main body at Chatham under Sir David Dundas. Two separate defensive systems were organized to guard the capital, the one on the north side of the Thames estuary, at Chelmsford, and the other on the south, at Chatham. Defensive works were to be prepared on the main roads leading to London, and there were also plans to establish a continuous line of entrenchment and batteries along the Middlesex and Surrey hills. A major action with the French was to be avoided; but the regular troops were to attack their flanks and rear while the volunteers continually harassed their communications.

In the circumstances no other strategy was perhaps possible. 'It would have been madness in the British to have risked a general battle in the field,' declared General Bunbury, 'even in such tempting positions as the chalk hills offer. Our troops were not then of a quality

[1] The martello towers, together with the Sea Fencibles, the signal stations on the coast, and liason with the military authorities, came under Keith's command.
[2] *Sussex Weekly Advertiser*, 1803–4 *passim*.

to meet and frustrate the manœuvres of such an army as that which Napoleon would have led to the attack.'[1] Arrangements were made for driving off all the cattle, sheep, and horses to appointed places of refuge, and for firing all the corn and haystacks. Pickford's and other leading firms offered their wagons for transport. Chains of beacons had been erected up and down the country to give warning of the enemy's approach.[2] These beacons were constructed of cord-wood, furze or faggots, and three or four barrels of tar; there was also provided a considerable quantity of straw, 'both wetted and in readiness to be wet', to make a smoke by day. Each of the signal posts was manned by three or four men under a serjeant; one of whom, equipped with a telescope, was always on look-out, day and night.[3]

In circumstances of national peril which called for a Chatham or a Churchill, Great Britain found herself under the uninspiring leadership of an amiable mediocrity whose only idea of making war seemed to be to get as many young men—trained or untrained, armed or unarmed (only about one-half of the volunteers, in fact, possessed muskets)—into uniform, and between Downing Street and the threatened south-east coast, as he possibly could. Addington tamely surrendered the initiative to the enemy and remained consistently on the defensive. The government's naïve proposal to protect the Thames

---

[1] H. Bunbury, *Narrative of Certain Passages in the Great War with France* (1852), pp. 177–8.

[2] The following is the official list of the beacons in Kent—Shorncliffe, Canterbury, Barham, Shollenden, Lynne-Heights, Isle of Thanet, Postling Down, Charlmagna, Egerton, Tenterden, Coxheath, Highgate near Hawkhurst, Bexley Hill, Goudhurst, Chatham Lines, Wrotham Hill; in Sussex—Fairlight Down, near Hastings, Brightling Hill, Crowborough Down, Jevington Windmill, Firle Hill, Mount Harry, Hollingbury Castle, near Brighton, Wolstonbury Hill, Chanctonbury Ring, Duncton Hill, Rook's Hill, Upperton Common, near Petworth, Near Stone Lodge, in St. Leonard's Forest, Siddlesfield Common, near West Hoathly.

[3] Cf. Lord Dorchester's letter to Henry Bankes of Kingston Lacy, Dorset, dated 12 October 1803: 'I beg of you that you will give directions for an assemblage of faggots, furze, and other fuel, also of straw to be stacked and piled on the summit of Badbury Rings so as the whole may take fire instantly and the fire may be maintained for two hours. It is to be fired whenever the beacon of St. Catherine's is fired to the eastward, or whenever the Lytchett or Woodbury Hill beacons are fired to the westward' (*Q.* Geo. Bankes, *The Story of Corfe Castle*, p. 278).

estuary with blockhouses evoked one of Canning's characteristically caustic verses.

> If blocks can a nation deliver,
> Two places are safe from the French:
> The one is the mouth of the river,
> The other the Treasury Bench!

While the threat of invasion hung over the country, no pains were spared to exacerbate popular feeling against the French. Clerics thundered from their pulpits, actors ranted from their boards. Broadsheets and handbills poured from the presses, bearing such suggestive titles as, *Ring the alarum bell! Britons, to arms! Bob Rousem's Epistle to Bonaparte, Death or Victory, John Bull all a-gog! An address to the British Navy, Bonaparte's true character, Countrymen, beware! Horror upon horrors!* Very much in vogue, too, were sham playbills like the following: 'In Rehearsal, *Theatre Royal of the United Kingdoms.* Some dark, foggy night, about November next, will be *attempted*, by a strolling Company of French Vagrants, an Old Pantomimic Farce, called *Harlequin's Invasion*, or the *Disappointed Banditti*,'[1] An old air of Purcell's, 'Britons, strike home', sprang into sudden popularity later in the year and was presently heard all over the kingdom. About Napoleon himself, of course, there was hardly anything too bad to be said. He was denounced as a pervert, an ogre, a brigand, a murderer, and a demon caitiff; he was accused of seducing his own sisters; as time went on they even found that he was the authentic, original, and veritable *Beast* of the Apocalypse, whose number was 'six hundred and sixty-six'. 'There had suddenly', General Bunbury observed, 'blazed up in the breasts of millions a fierce, unenquiring, unappeasable detestation of the individual.' 'The most savage Devil', declared Lord Paget, 'that ever disgraced human nature.' In the cartoons of Gillray and others, it has been truly said, the public were shown not a man, but a monster. Even to the little ones the Corsican Ogre had become a figure of terror.

> Baby, baby, naughty baby,
> Hush, you squalling thing, I say;
> Hush your squalling, or it may be
> Bonaparte may pass this way.

[1] Wheeler and Broadley, *Napoleon and the Invasion of England*, II, pp. 276–8.

Baby, baby, he's a giant,
Tall and black as Rouen steeple;
And he dines and sups, rely on 't,
Every day on naughty people.

Baby, baby, he will hear you,
As he passes by the house,
And he limb from limb will tear you,
Just as pussy does a mouse.[1]

Eastbourne, that August, was almost deserted; and there was a rumour, subsequently proved false, of a French landing on Pevensey Levels. At Hastings horses and wagons were held in constant readiness to evacuate the women and children. At Dover no officer was permitted to sleep out of camp. Towards the end of September the volunteers were under orders to march at an hour's notice. In autumn, with the advent of spring tides and easterly winds, the invaders were expected almost daily. 'This is the day of the spring tides,' recorded Betsey Fremantle on 15 October, 'and on which the French are expected to land.' 'The approaching invasion', wrote Francis Horner, 'has driven away every other topic from conversation.' By November more than 340,000 volunteers had been enrolled. 'Still', observed General Bunbury, 'our preparations were only in their infancy; and if Napoleon could have crossed the Channel in the war of 1803–4, as he first designed, our means to meet his veteran troops would have been found utterly unfit for battle.'[2] There were at this stage of the war only about 28,000 regular troops to protect the whole island; 20,000 more were tied down in a still sullen and rebellious Ireland: the British government therefore ordered home from Malta the 3,000 men who had been stationed in that island after their withdrawal from Alexandria. Towards the end of the year there were fresh alarms. 'I think', wrote Keith to Markham in November, 'the plot begins to thicken on the other side, and something will soon be tried.' It was known that in the Atlantic ports of France intense activity prevailed; on 26 December Captain Owen, cruising off Boulogne, reported that the encampment on the neighbouring downs was vaster than ever; and when, on the 30th, the Channel fleet was driven from its station

---

[1] Q. Broadley and Bartelott, *Nelson's Hardy*, p. 148.
[2] Bunbury, *op. cit.*, p. 174.

by violent gales, reports reached the Ministry that the French were on the move.

The true extent of the alarm of 1803–5 is not easily gauged. 'All are convinced that the French will make great attempts to invade us,' noted Joseph Farington in his diary, 'but there does not seem to be any apprehension.' 'Some people say they will never attempt it,' Pitt's niece, Hester Stanhope, observed in the autumn; 'I differ from them. I have seen the almost impassable mountains they have marched armies across.' 'Bonaparte is so pledged to make an attack upon this country,' opined the Secretary for War a few months later, 'that I do not well see how he can avoid it.' To be sure, the menace of the flat-bottoms across the Channel exercised much the same mesmeritic influence upon certain fearful elements over here as it had half a century earlier in the Seven Years' War. Also the enormous number of invasion pamphlets, caricatures, etc., gave significant testimony of the widespread apprehension aroused in this country by the enemy's preparations. But, as first weeks and then months went by, and still the French did not come, a note of scepticism began to appear. A popular song that year, sung to the air of 'The Bluebells of Scotland', was:

> When, and O when, does this little Boney come?
> Perhaps he'll come in August, perhaps he'll stay at home.[1]

'What! he begins to find excuses,' wrote Nelson from the Gulf of Lyons; 'I thought he would invade England in the face of the sun! Now he wants a three days' fog that never yet happened.' With invasion apparently imminent towards the close of the year, the volunteers redoubled their exertions. But nothing came of the alarm; and during 1804 the scepticism of the islanders increased.

> When rich men find their wealth a curse,
> And freely fill the poor man's purse,
> Then little Boney, he'll come down
> And march his men on London town.

---

[1] Wheeler and Broadley, *op. cit.*, II, p. 116. Cf. *Bob Rousem's Epistle to Bonypart:* 'This comes hoping you are well, as I am at this present; but I say, Bony, what a damn'd Lubber you must be to think of getting *soundings* among us English. I tell ye as how your Anchor will never hold; it isn't made of good Stuff, so luff up, Bony, or you'll be *fast aground* before you know where you are. We don't mind your Palaver and Nonsense; for tho' 'tis all Wind, it would hardly fill the Stun' sails of an English Man of War' (*Ibid.*, II, p. 277).

The Admiralty, indeed, had never shared these apprehensions. 'As to the possibility', said Pellew in the House of Commons, 'of the enemy being able in a narrow sea to pass through our blockading and protecting squadron with all the secrecy and dexterity and by those hidden means that some worthy people expect, I really, from anything I have seen in the course of my professional experience, am not much disposed to concur in it.' St. Vincent in the upper chamber was no less explicit. 'I do not say, my Lords,' he observed grimly, 'that the French will not come. I only say they will not come by sea.' He refused to be stampeded by popular clamour into constructing a multitude of small craft—contemptuously described by Pellew as a 'mosquito fleet'—at the expense of the battle fleet on which the safety of the kingdom really depended.

The truth was that Napoleon's invasion project was considered by the Admiralty to be quite impracticable. Their present strategy was soundly based on defensive preparations made during earlier invasion alarms, dating back to Vernon's dispositions in 1745. As in previous wars, the navigational conditions in the Channel proved a decisive factor. East of Brest there was no good natural harbour; and since the French had no heavy ships in their northern ports it was plainly impossible for the transports to cross until their battle fleet had come up into those waters and cleared the way for the passage of the army. The hostile transports assembling between Texel and Havre were watched day and night by a superior flotilla of sloops and gun-boats, supported by a division of frigates, while Lord Keith lay in the Downs, with a squadron of six of the line and thirty-two frigates, and another ship of the line lay at St. Helens. In mid-Channel and along the French coast Keith's cruisers were continually on watch, ready to fall on any of the enemy's craft which ventured outside the sands and batteries by which they were protected. Until the blockading flotilla was destroyed or dispersed the French transports could not move; and the flotilla itself was unassailable so long as the enemy's battleships were immobilized in port. The British capital squadrons lying off Brest, Rochefort, and Toulon barred the way, therefore, against the Army of Invasion.

British naval dispositions in European waters were briefly as follows.

In the extreme north, off the Texel, was a force under Keith's command which by April 1805 comprised eleven of the line to blockade the Texel and to hold the Straits of Dover. Under the same command were the frigates and smaller craft watching the French invasion flotilla along the North Sea and Channel coasts, with orders that, in the event of an attempted landing, the enemy's transports were to be regarded as the 'principal object' of attack. Early in the summer, when Napoleon's troops invaded Hanover, the Elba and Weser were blockaded, thus closing the ports of Hamburg and Bremen.

Blocking in the enemy's principal fleet at Brest was the Western Squadron, or Channel fleet—then, as always, the pivot of the British defensive system—whose main and ultimate function was to hold the approaches to the Channel, and to prevent a hostile concentration at Brest. The strength of this force off Brest varied from ten to twelve of the line in winter to twenty-four in spring and summer. A margin of about 40 per cent. had to be provided to allow for sending ships into port to revictual and repair. The main body of the squadron (including the three-deckers) cruised, as usual, off Ushant. The inshore squadron of two-deckers with frigates, brigs, and cutters, was stationed close in with the port itself; both the Passage du Four and the Passage du Raz being closely watched and guarded. In heavy westerly gales, when the larger vessels were compelled to bear up for Torbay, the inshore squadron would endeavour to gain the shelter of Douarnenez Bay. There was little risk of the enemy's escaping on such occasions, since the same wind which forced the blockaders off their station likewise prevented the French from leaving port. Detachments of varying strength were stationed off the lesser arsenals of Rochefort and L'Orient. At the same time a network of cruisers kept up communications with Cornwallis off Ushant, protecting British merchantmen and intercepting the enemy coasters upon which the blockaded French fleet depended for its stores. 'The English are constantly off our coasts,' reported the naval prefect at Brest in January 1803; 'some vessels to windward of Ushant, four or five anchor in day-time by the Black Rocks, a frigate and a corvette lie in Douarnenez Bay under sail, a corvette and a cutter come right up to the entrance of the

Goulet and cruise there continually.'[1] The close investment of Brest, between May 1803 and November 1805, constitutes one of the most impressive achievements of British seamanship.

Owing to the scarcity of ships occasioned by St. Vincent's untimely reforms, the force which could be spared for these blockading duties was barely sufficient for the purpose; and, though the best of the vessels available were assigned to the vital post off Ushant, several of them were badly in need of repair. 'We have been sailing for the last six months', Collingwood wrote that winter, 'with only a sheet of copper between us and eternity.' 'Our ships', observed the Second Secretary of the Admiralty, 'are so worn down that they are like post-horses during a general election.'

The year closed with a succession of strong westerly gales. Two of them occurred in November; and the December of 1803 was, perhaps, the stormiest in living memory. At midday on the 24th the wind, which had backed to S.W., increased to gale force, with a great swell coming in from the westward. On the 25th the wind, still backing, blew with redoubled fury. It was cloudy, squally weather, with heavy rain. With reeling masts and flooded waists and the dismal clank of pumps perpetually at work, Cornwallis's ships, under storm-canvas, were driven to the eastward. The *Impétueux*, laid on her beam-ends, nearly foundered, and the *Atalanta* became almost a wreck.[2] At noon

[1] Q. Leyland, *The Blockade of Brest*, I, p. 81.
[2] From the log of the *Impétueux*, 25 December 1803: A.M. Strong gales and squally weather. At 2 furled the fore and mizen topsails. . . . At half-past 6, strong gales with heavy squalls, carried away the starboard main brace and larboard main topsail sheet; sail blew to pieces. Set a storm mizen and fore-stay sail. Lost sight of the Admiral. At half-past seven the storm mizen and forestay sail blew to pieces, and mainsail blew from the yard. At eight obliged to scuttle the lower deck: ship labouring very much and gained six inches on the pumps. At quarter-past eight the carpenter reported the head of the mizen mast was sprung, in consequence of the vangs of the gaff giving way. At half-past eight was struck with a sea on the larboard quarter, stove in eleven of the main-deck ports, half-filled the main-deck full of water, and carried away all the wardroom bulkheads. At 11 hard gales with violent squalls. Carried away the chain-plate of the foremast main shroud. Bore up under a reefed foresail. Noon: Lizard N.E., distance 18 leagues. P.M. Hard gales and squally weather. Under a reefed foresail. At 3 saw the Lizard bearing N.E. b. N., distance 3 or 4 leagues. At half-past 4 the Lizard NW½W, distance 10 miles. D° *Atalanta*: A.M. Increasing gales; took in fore and main topsail. At 5 bore up. At 9 hard gales: hove 12 guns overboard. Bore up; shipped a great quantity of water. At noon clear weather. P.M. Hard

most of the squadron were strung out across the middle of the Channel; and, as the short dark winter day drew to its close, a few of them sighted the Lizard. On the 26th the *Foudroyant*, which at the height of the storm had been so far to leeward that 'great fears had been entertained for her safety',[1] finally rounded the Rame Head, followed on the 27th by the *Thunderer*, *Impétueux*, and *Royal Sovereign*, and on the 31st by the *Culloden*. One after another the storm-battered ships arrived in the anchorage.

'There are now in Cawsand Bay ten sail of the line,' observed the *Naval Chronicle* on 28 December, 'several of which need much re-fitting. . . . The wind is S.S.W. and at present there is no chance of its shifting to the eastward, there need not therefore be any apprehension entertained of the enemy's fleet and transports getting out of Brest, while the wind remains in this quarter.'

The *Plantagenet* had sought shelter to the westward, in Gwavas Lake off Newlyn; but she sailed again, when the weather moderated on the 28th, to resume her vigil off Brest, where she was presently found by the other ships as they returned, 'alone on her station, as if the look-out ship of the inshore squadron'.

Meanwhile Cornwallis in the *Ville de Paris* had likewise been forced off his station by the strong sou'-westerlies; and on the morning of the 30th—the wind still blowing from that quarter, with every

---

gales and clear; shipped several heavy seas. At 2 more moderate; saw the Bolt Head—Set the foresail and topsails. At 8 came to in Tor Bay with the best bower (Adm. 52/3632, 52/3554).

[1] D° *Foudroyant*, 25 December 1803: A.M. Strong gales and squally. Up mainsail. ½ past 1 furled fore and mizen topsails. At 3 up foresail. Strong gales. Set fore, main, and mizen storm staysails. At 4 hard gales: lost sight of squadron. ½ past 4 the gale increasing. At 5 in taking in the main topsail split it and blew away part of it from the yard. Hauled down fore storm staysail. Gave way mizen staysail stay and the sail blew all rags. Chock'd lower deck guns: hard gales: carried away a cutter from the starboard quarter. At 10 saw a sail on the lee bow. The courses split to pieces, likewise the mizen foresail. Made signal to the *Impétueux* which it did not answer. Noon: wore ship. Three sail in sight. Ending a heavy gale: carried away the starboard gangway rail. Parted company from the *Impétueux*. Fresh gales and cloudy. Employed unbending the courses and mizen foresail and bending new ones. At 4 ditto weather. Set mizen topsail. Squadron not in company. Bent the main topsail: close reeft and furled it, likewise the foresail. At 11.30 sounded in 55 fathoms. Midnight: fresh gales and hazy, squadron not in sight (Adm. 52/3614).

appearance of continuing so to do—accompanied by the *San Josef* and *Dreadnought*, he bore up for Torbay, where the *Atalanta* and a few other vessels had already taken refuge. As soon as the ships had anchored, all boats were hoisted and dispatched to the shore for water; and a number of fishing-boats were hired to assist them. Down by the strand butchers were hard at work slaughtering cattle to supply the squadron with fresh beef. Lighters were on their way round from Plymouth with beer. Some of the sick were dispatched to hospital. Hour after hour hands were busy about the ships, repairing the damaged rigging, hoisting in and stowing water, heaving out empty casks, and taking in beef and other stores. The south-westerly weather continued throughout the day. But on the morning of the 31st the Blue Peter flew at the mast-head of the flagship and all boats had been hoisted in; the wind had come north-easterly and Cornwallis was informing the Admiralty in his dispatch, 'the weather having moderated this morning, I am proceeding off Brest'.[1] The squadron weighed and made sail; and by midday all the ships had cleared the bay.

In the latter half of January there were more heavy gales. On the 17th, in thick and blowing weather, with a great swell from the westward and rain, the wind backed from W.N.W. to S.W., and on the 19th increased to gale force, with violent squalls and hail showers. The sou'-westerly weather continued; and most of the squadron was driven off its station. The captain of the *Plantagenet*, one of the few ships remaining off Brest, reported from Cawsand Bay on the 22nd that 'the loss of a main topmast and main yard, with almost all the principal sails of the ship, reduced me on the 19th to the extremity of bearing away to this anchorage'. On the night of the 28th it blew hard again from the S.W.; and Cornwallis, then off the Start, fearing that he would be driven to the eastward, bore up for Torbay. Once again the fleet was back in the familiar anchorage under Berry Head, looking out on the sullen grey expanse of the bay and the lonely shore with its broad shelving sands and low reddish cliffs and the square sandstone tower of Paignton showing above the tree-tops, with the Mewstone and Hope's Nose away in the misty distance. 'I have just received your letter,' wrote Lord Cornwallis to his sailor brother, 'and shall be glad that the wind may continue for some time

[1] Adm. 1/124, 1 January 1804.

longer in the South-West, that you may enjoy a little quiet, and re-
fresh your seamen, who must have had a most fatiguing service.' 'In
the middle of last month,' said Collingwood in February, 'we put
into Torbay, where we were a week; but the being in Torbay is no
great relief, for no person or boat goes on shore.

Towards the close of December 1803, the blockading force off Brest
had actually been reduced to only four ships; and during the fortnight or so following there were seldom more than six. 'Several of our
ships have gone in from accidents,' Cornwallis informed the Admiralty. 'They remain a long time in port, probably from not being
able, on account of the bad weather at this season, to get their supplies,
or defects made good.' The Admiralty thereupon directed Sir Charles
Cotton to hurry all the ships under Cornwallis's orders to join him
off Ushant without a moment's delay.

'A severe gale,' remarked Keith in February 1804—'God preserve
all our ships! Billy[1] will be blown to the westward, in despite of all his
endeavours, and they have been not a little during this vile weather.'
'I wonder,' wrote Cornwallis a few months later on receiving the thanks
of the City of London, 'if they [the Corporation] truly appreciate the
hardships all have suffered in the winter that is past.'

In the autumn of 1804 Cornwallis was thrice driven back into Torbay.
During the winter several of the vessels were reporting serious
damages. In the afternoon of 19 December the wind, which had
shifted from easterly to south-westerly, freshened to a heavy gale,
with hard squalls and a great sea. The *Ville de Paris* had worked out
to a position nearly fifty miles to the westward of Ushant. There, in
the open Atlantic, labouring in the mountainous seas, she and her
consorts rode out gale after gale, sustaining many injuries, until the
winds moderated. 'The gales have continued with a few hours' intervals for a fortnight,' wrote Cornwallis on 6 January 1805, 'and as
we were seldom able to carry any sail, and a very great sea, I was with
the squadron driven far to the westward, and the ships have laboured
very much. Four of them have shifted topmasts, and the *Prince George*
reported to be leaky.... Both the *Ville de Paris*'s tillers have given
way, and Captain Guion, of the *Prince*, has reported the same. Upon
endeavouring to make Ushant since the wind came round, the 1st. inst.,
to enable us to make easting, it has inclined to the southward with

[1] Cornwallis.

thick weather.' 'Since the easterly wind ceased,' he added two days later, 'it has generally blown either from the southward or northward, and it has been so unsettled as to oblige me to keep the sea.' On 8 March he reported that 'the stern frame of the *Ville de Paris* was much shaken, with other defects occasioned by the very severe gales and remarkably heavy sea in December, which did so much damage to all the three-deckers that they all have to be docked a considerable time in port.'[1] 'The blockade of Brest, by the gallant Admiral Cornwallis, for a period of such unprecedented length,' observed the *Naval Chronicle*, 'at this season of the year, is beyond all panegyric.' To his vigorous investment of the enemy's principal naval arsenal was due the ultimate failure of Napoleon's great strategic plan.

'I have hardly known what a night of rest is these two months,' declared Collingwood; 'this incessant cruising seems to me beyond the powers of human nature.' It was without question a searching test of courage, morale, and physique, as well as of professional competence. In this arduous duty the unceasing strain, monotony, and discomfort were diversified only by recurrent nerve-shaking crises when the lives of all on board hung by a hair (the *Impétueux*, which had taken such a battering in the gale of Christmas 1803, was, when separated from the rest of the squadron, nearly wrecked in a fog off Ushant the following summer, and there were several other cases of vessels going aground on the Black Rocks). Nevertheless, it was the exigencies of the stern blockading service that made the British Navy what the French could never hope to be.

It was one of the compensations of these great blockades that they raised the standard of seamanship and endurance throughout the British fleets to the highest possible level. The lonely watches, the sustained vigilance, the remoteness from all companionship, the long wrestle with the forces of the sea, the constant watching for battle, which for English seamen marked these blockades, profoundly affected the character of English seamanship. When, indeed, has the world seen such seamen as those of the years preceding Trafalgar?—hardy, resolute, careless alike of tempest or of battle; of frames as enduring as the oaken decks they trod, and courage as iron as the guns they worked; and as familiar with sea-life and all its chances as though they had been web-footed.[2]

[1] Adm. 1/126, 6 and 8 January, 8 March 1805.
[2] W. H. Fitchett, *How England Saved Europe*, II, pp. 174-5.

In misty weather when the flood stream set towards the chain of islands and rocks to the south-east of Ushant: in westerly gales when the Parquette and the Black Rocks were a welter of foam and broken water: in the long dark nights when the need for vigilance and cool nerve was redoubled—in winter and summer alike the inshore squadron clung to its post off that perilous lee shore, contending continually with 'tides and rocks, which', as Collingwood observed, 'have more of danger in them than battle once a week.' Yet such was the courage and skill of the crews that few of their vessels were lost.[1] 'It was a station of great anxiety,' declared Collingwood, when in command of the inshore squadron, 'and required so constant a care and look out, that I have been often a week without having my clothes off, and was sometimes upon deck the whole night.'

'We have had nothing now for the last month,' declared the eleven-year-old Bernard Coleridge, one of the midshipmen of the *Impétueux*, in July 1804, 'but salt beef, biscuit, stinking water, and brandy.' The boy's thoughts turned with longing to the well-stocked garden of his Devonshire home, with its abundance of 'sallads, green peas, and strawberries.' The following October, when the *Impétueux* anchored for a while in Torbay, he thankfully lay in a store of '100 apples, 4 cakes of gingerbread, 3 pounds of cheese, and one pound of butter and a loaf—most magnificent!' Yet in the midst of all these privations Bernard remained content and happy, and, ensconced securely at the masthead, would gaze with rapt attention at the distant vista of masts and yards in Brest harbour. 'Indeed I do like this life very much,' he wrote to his parents; observing that 'all the midshipmen are good fellows, but they swear rather.' He read Virgil with their chaplain, played marbles on the poop with the other 'young gentlemen', and was occasionally invited to dine in the wardroom. Notwithstanding its manifold hardships, it was a life that a good many English youngsters of Bernard Coleridge's age and caste would have heartily envied.[2]

[1] The principal losses were those of the *Magnificent*, 74, which on 25 March 1804 ran on a sunken and uncharted reef near the Black Rocks; the *Venerable*, 74, which the following November went aground in Torbay; and the *Doris*, 36, which on 12 January 1805 ran on a sunken rock at the entrance to *Quiberon Bay* and had to be abandoned.

[2] Lord Coleridge, *The Story of a Devonshire House* (1905), *passim*. Cf. George Elliot in his *Memoir*: 'I never slept on shore as a midshipman except

Meanwhile off Ferrol, five hundred miles from Plymouth, his nearest base, Sir Edward Pellew, with a squadron of seven of the line, watched the six French ships which had taken refuge there. His force suffered severely during the heavy gales of the winter of 1803-4. In mid-December the south-westerly wind freshened and veered to N.W., then shifted back again to the old quarter. For several days it blew hard with heavy squalls and rain, and most of his ships had their sails split; on the 21st there came a lull, but on the 24th it came on to blow hard again from S.W. Pellew's flagship, the *Tonnant*, which had successively lost her main-topsail, fore-topsail, and main and mizen staysails, lay under storm canvas off Cape Ortegal, 'in a great hollow sea, with a heavy swell rolling in from the westward and none of the other ships in sight'.[1] During the night of the 27th the *Ardent* lost her main-yard. A few days later the wind veered to N.W., and at the end of the month the gale blew itself out. On 4 January the ships of the squadron reassembled. 'We have none of us a second topsail fit to bend,' he reported, on the 7th, to Cornwallis.

As a result of this experience Pellew determined to find shelter. To maintain his squadron so far from home on that broken, rugged coast, he presently established his anchorage in the neighbouring Betanzos Bay. Though sufficiently sheltered, the bay bore an ill reputation (the Spaniards believed there was no holding ground there), and during the ensuing weeks the French waited hopefully for a gale severe enough to cause the British squadron to drag its anchors. 'The south-west winds having set in to blow hard on the 4th,' Pellew informed

---

when paying off the *Goliath* and commissioning the *Elephant* early in 1800; and I had probably been in port, on average, a fortnight in the year, unless attacking or defending some place. . . . I can safely say, that out of the five years I actually served as a midshipman, I had not one unhappy day, and no power could have persuaded me to quit the service.'

[1] From the log of the *Tonnant*, 24 December 1803: a.m. Strong gales with a great sea from the westward; handed the mizen topsail. . . . 8 p.m. Hard gales and squally; storm main and mizen staysails set; a great sea running; none of the squadron in sight. 25th a.m. The ship rolling very much; hard gales with a very heavy sea; carried away the main runners. . . . 26th a.m. Fresh gales and cloudy; at 9 fresh winds with a swell from the westward; . . . split the jib, unbent it and bent another; . . . at 11 a loud squall; up courses; handed the topsails at 12. Squally with thunder, lightning, and hail. . . . 27th a.m. At 5 hard gales with a heavy sea. . . . p.m. at half-past 2 the mizen staysail blew to pieces: . . . at 5 set main topsail; at half-past 5 it split . . . (Adm. 52/3707).

Cornwallis on 9th February, 'I ran for the anchorage. . . . I am happy to say the bay equals our fullest expectations, having never started an anchor during the violent gales we have had, and from which, had we continued at sea, we should in all probability have been completely crippled.' Here Pellew proceeded to refit his battered squadron and replace the lost sails. Betanzos Bay afforded an excellent view of the entrance to Ferrol, which remained firmly blockaded.

By his tactful and diplomatic approach Pellew succeeded in establishing a good understanding with the local authorities and in obtaining a regular supply of fresh provisions; notwithstanding, he declared, 'the loud complaints of the French commodore, Gourdon, who is excessively irritated at our taking this position'. Betanzos Bay remained the customary anchorage of the squadron during the rest of the year.

> We are upon the most friendly terms with the Dons, who visit me all day long from Ferrol. Monsieur Gourdon comes frequently to the Beach to see us (he says) driven on shore, and most excessively angry he is. We are not permitted to go so near their ships, but our look-out Lieuts. meet at a Wind-Mill on a hill between the two Ports—out of one Window my Lieut. spies them, and out of the opposite one looks their officer upon us. The Squadrons only three mile apart. Buller proposes a Pic-nic there with Monsieur Gourdon, as we find they dine there frequently.[1]

In March Pellew was hurriedly recalled to England, his support being urgently needed by the government against Pitt's attacks in the House of Commons on St. Vincent's policy. In one of the keenest debates in our parliamentary annals he delivered a vigorous and effective speech and was warmly applauded. Pellew then returned to Plymouth and the *Tonnant*, and soon afterwards resumed the close blockade of Ferrol. The government presently showed its appreciation of his assistance by appointing him to the command of the East India station—one of the richest prizes of the Service, which enabled Pellew to make his fortune. Towards the close of April he was consequently again recalled to England and on 9 May sailed for India. He was succeeded on his station by Rear-Admiral Alexander Cochrane, who carried on the investment of Ferrol with the same zeal, though scarcely the same degree of tact—where the Spaniards were concerned—as his predecessor.

[1] Q. Cornwallis-West, *op. cit.*, p. 409.

At the southern extremity of the long chain of blockading squadrons which girdled the coasts of Europe from the Texel to Toulon, Nelson, with a force which in July 1803 consisted of nine of the line and three frigates, watched the enemy fleet in Toulon and prevented it from assisting in any move against Sicily and other regions to the eastward. On this station, though many of his ships were desperately in need of repair and adequate stores were frequently lacking, he kept the sea in all weathers, and maintained his crews in a state of health and morale that has no precedent in naval history. He did this by keeping his squadron constantly on the move; by paying careful attention to the men's clothing; by keeping his ships dry and warm between decks; by obtaining regular supplies of fresh vegetables and fruit, especially onions and lemons, as a preventive against scurvy; and by encouraging 'music, dancing, and theatrical amusements' for the diversion of his men.

Towards the end of the year, Nelson took his squadron under Cape San Sebastian on the neighbouring Spanish coast, leaving a division of frigates to watch the enemy fleet in Toulon. The Gulf of Lyons was notorious for its bad weather, particularly in the winter and early spring. In north-westerly weather the wind might be expected to rise rapidly and, in a very short time, freshen to a severe gale, with a very heavy sea. These north-westerly gales would sometimes prevail in the Gulf for days on end.

The state of his ships was a constant anxiety to Nelson; for, as a result of St. Vincent's economies, the dockyards at Gibraltar and Malta were almost empty of stores, and reinforcements were slow in arriving. 'I bear up for every gale,' he had written on 16 September. 'I must not, in our present state, quarrel with the North-Westers.' 'Such a place as all the Gulf of Lyons, for gales of wind from the N.W. to N.E., I never saw,' he observed on 7 December; 'but by always going away large, we generally lose much of their force and the heavy sea of the gulf. However, by the great care and attention of every Captain, we have suffered much less than could have been expected.' 'My crazy Fleet are getting in a very indifferent state,' he went on several days later, 'and others will soon follow. . . . I do not believe that Lord St. Vincent would have kept the sea with such ships.' 'Every bit of twice-laid stuff belonging to the *Canopus* is condemned,' he wrote on 21st December, 'and all the running-rigging in the Fleet, except the *Victory*'s. We have fitted the *Excellent* with new main and mizen-rigging; it was shameful for the Dock-yard to send a Ship to sea with such rigging.'[1]

Leaving a frigate or some smaller cruiser at the appointed rendez-vous, with intelligence as to where the flagship was to be found at any time, and dispersing his cruisers at various strategic points to keep watch for the enemy, Nelson sailed to and fro across a wide stretch of sea—between Toulon and the Balearics, Spain and the islands of Corsica and Sardinia—through which the Toulon fleet, wherever bound, would be obliged to pass. 'It is easier for an Officer to keep men healthy,' he wrote on 11 March 1804, 'than for a Physician to cure them. Situated as this Fleet has been, without a friendly Port, where we could get all the things so necessary for us, yet I have, by changing the cruizing ground, not allowed the sameness of prospect to satiate the mind—sometimes by looking at Toulon, Ville Franche, Barcelona, and Rosas; then running round Minorca, Majorca, Sardinia, and Corsica; and two or three times anchoring for a few days, and sending a Ship to the last place for *onions*, which I find the best thing that can be given to Seamen; having always good mutton for the sick, cattle when we can get them, and plenty of fresh water. In the winter it is the best plan to give half the allowance of grog, instead of all wine. These things are for the Commander-in-Chief to look to; but shut very nearly out from Spain, and only getting refreshments by stealth from other places, my Command has been an arduous one.' 'Our men's minds', he added, 'are always kept up with the daily hopes of meeting the enemy.' After eighteen months at sea, in December 1804, he was able to inform the Admiralty: 'The Fleet is in perfect good health and good humour, unequalled by anything which has ever come within my knowledge, and equal to the most active service which the times may call for, or the Country expect of them.'[2]

It is always to be understood that, so far from attempting to keep the enemy locked up in port, Nelson's one great object was to lure him out to fight. 'Day by day, my dear friend,' he wrote to his agent in England, 'I am expecting the French to put to sea—every day, hour and moment; and you may rely that, if it is within the power of men

---

[1] *Nelson's Dispatches*, V, pp. 203, 302, 306. 319.
[2] *Ibid.*, V, p. 438, VI, p. 300.

to get at them, it shall be done; and I am sure that all my brethren look forward to that day as the finish of our laborious cruize.' 'I beg to inform your Lordship', Nelson observed to the Lord Mayor of London, 'that the Port of Toulon has never been blockaded by me: quite the reverse—every opportunity has been offered to the Enemy to put to sea.' To this end he had for long based his squadron on Agincourt Sound,[1] on the north coast of Sardinia. The anchorage was well sheltered and within striking distance of whatever route the enemy might follow; moreover, it was possible to get away, by either the eastern or western exit, in any wind. From Sardinia, too, he could replenish his fleet with fresh supplies and water. St. Vincent, who wanted the Mediterranean fleet based on Malta, was strongly opposed to these dispositions. The disagreement between the two was seriously aggravated by a long-standing grievance of Nelson's concerning prize-money.

On the renewal of hostilities in 1803 French influence had closed the ports of Naples and Sicily, on which our Mediterranean squadron had been based in the late war, to Nelson's ships. He had no regular base nearer than Gibraltar and Malta, situated respectively nine hundred and seven hundred miles from his station off Toulon. Gibraltar was inadequate as a fleet base, and in any case it was too distant. Nelson's opinion of Malta, as a base for watching the hostile force in Toulon, is well known: experience had convinced him that the sailing distance between these two points was too great. 'Malta is at such an immense distance', he declared on 13 October 1803, 'that I can send nothing there that I may want under six or seven weeks.'[2] Again: 'Malta and Toulon are entirely different services.' But Malta remained the key to the control of the central and eastern Mediterranean; and on it were based all naval forces watching the enemy's base in Apulia and the mouth of the Adriatic, and protecting British commerce in the Levant.

Nelson's great anxiety centred on his ignorance of the Toulon fleet's intended objective. 'I have', he wrote on 15 October 1803, 'as

[1] The value of Agincourt Sound as a fleet anchorage was first discovered by Captain Ryves of the *Agincourt*, 64, after which ship it was named. The entrance to the Sound was protected by the Maddalena Islands, which formed an excellent breakwater.

[2] *Nelson's Dispatches*, V, p. 244.

many destinations sent me as there are Countries.' When our army, evacuated from Egypt to Malta, had to be ordered home to protect the British Isles against invasion, Nelson expressed his regret at the loss of these troops, which might have furnished a much-needed strategic reserve, and declared that 'not less than 10,000 men should be kept for the service of the Mediterranean.' St. Cyr's forces in southern Italy threatened simultaneously Sicily, Greece, Turkey, and the routes to India; and Nelson's fleet was all we had to counter them. He was above all concerned for the safety of Sicily, 'which,' he declared, 'if they [the French] were once to get a footing in, it would be totally lost for ever'. Moreover, Malta's value as a naval base would be seriously impaired should Sicily ever fall under enemy control. The danger lay in the navigational conditions obtaining in the Straits of Messina. 'A few Boats', Nelson had observed in the previous June, 'would very soon bring over from Reggio some thousands of Troops; nor could all the Navy of Europe prevent the passage, the current running seven miles an hour.' To oppose any attempt on the enemy's part to invade Sicily, he therefore dispatched a frigate and a sloop to cruise off Tarento, with orders, 'if the French move coastways in Vessels, to take, sink, or destroy them'.[1]

The French threat to Greece was to some extent met by the Russian occupation of Cattaro and the Ionian Islands. Russian military forces were needed to garrison these regions, but the support of the British Navy was essential both to transport and to maintain them there. Reinforcements of both ships and men continued to reach Corfu from the Baltic and the Black Sea; and by the first weeks of 1805 the Russian squadron comprised four sail of the line, four frigates, and a corvette, under the command of Commodore Grieg.

Our first defence, as Nelson had observed in 1801, 'was close to the Enemy's Ports'. It was the close and unremitting grip of the blockade which effectually prevented a great combination such as Napoleon continually, but ever in vain, strove to achieve. Though it was quite impossible, as our sailors well knew, to make absolutely sure of 'hermetically sealing' any one port, it was within their power— enjoying as they did the advantage of interior positions and lines— to prevent a concentration from all the ports. In accordance with the strategical tradition born of centuries' experience of sea warfare,

[1] *Ibid.*, V, pp. 83, 97, 104, 257.

adequate forces were stationed off the minor French bases, and, in the event of any of the enemy's detachments breaking out of port, orders were given for the outlying British squadrons to fall back on their strategic centre off Brest, so as to follow the French either to Ireland or up the Channel. In the latter contingency the enemy would also have to reckon with Lord Keith in the Downs and with the North Sea squadron; in short—and this is the crux of the whole matter—however they might for a time evade the vigilance of the blockading squadrons, a powerful British force would be ready to bring them to action as they approached the vital point.

The truth was that Napoleon—who for all his supreme strategic genius could never comprehend the realities of naval warfare—had entirely failed to grasp the all-important fact that the command of the sea was not to be had without fighting for it, and that, until this command had been secured by a decisive victory, the Grand Army could not pass. It was once more the delusion of ulterior objects. For months he contrived ingenious but impracticable plans to disperse the British concentration; but without getting any nearer his goal. To the last the problem of invasion over an uncommanded sea defied every attempt at solution. Napoleon might delude himself into supposing that such a thing were possible. But his admirals knew better. As Mahan has declared in a pregnant passage, 'They were dull, weary eventless months, those months of watching and waiting of the big ships before the French arsenals. Purposeless they surely seemed to many, but they saved England. The world has never seen a more impressive demonstration of the influence of sea power upon its history. Those far distant, storm-beaten ships, upon which the Grand Army never looked, stood between it and the dominion of the world.'[1]

[1] Mahan, *The Influence of Sea Power upon the French Revolution and Empire*, II, p. 118.

X

The Campaign of Trafalgar

I

In December 1804, following upon the seizure of her treasure ships by four British frigates, Spain entered the war on the side of France, and her fleet, the second largest on the Continent, went to swell the naval strength of our enemy. The new situation materially increased the burden laid on the Navy. Extra ships had to be detached from Cornwallis's fleet off Ushant to watch Ferrol, while a force under Sir John Orde invested Cadiz.

At the same time the scarcity of timber for shipbuilding threatened to become a crippling handicap. At the turn of the century the Admiralty had been confronted with a crisis of the first magnitude in the long-pending and long-expected exhaustion of our oak groves, on this occasion far more complete than ever before. A survey of oaks in the royal forests showed that this particular source of supply was by now almost negligible; generations of mismanagement and neglect had done their work—during the past half-century the royal forests had furnished the fleet with barely the equivalent of four years' consumption. As for the private woodlands, which had for long provided the bulk of the supply, they were on the verge of extinction. The fine oak-woods of the Kent and Sussex Weald were but a shadow of their former selves. 'If the country gentlemen', Collingwood observed, 'do not make it a point to plant oaks wherever they will grow, the time will not be very distant when to keep our Navy, we must depend entirely on captures from the enemy.' The agricultural revolution was transforming the face of the countryside; all over the kingdom corn was rapidly supplanting oak; and following the wholesale destruction of hedgerows it had become virtually impossible to secure the great and compass timbers which were required for the construction of a ship of the line. As a result of the increasing drain on our reserves during the war with revolutionary France, the timber piles at Portsmouth and Plymouth had fallen to a periliously low level; and this scarcity was intensified at the peace by St. Vincent's well-intentioned but inopportune reforms, and the consequent alienation of the timber contractors.

It was with the object of introducing these reforms that St. Vincent, who had long been of opinion that the Civil Branch of the Navy was 'rotten to the very core', had looked forward to the termination of hostilities. 'Nothing short of a radical sweep in the dockyards can cure the enormous evils and corruptions in them,' he had told Spencer in January 1801; 'and this cannot be attempted till we have peace.'[1] In the face of strong opposition he insisted on a Parliamentary Commission to inquire into conditions in the dockyards, and virtually forced it on the Cabinet. 'We find abuses to such an extent as would require many months to go thoroughly into,' he told Addington, 'and the absolute necessity of a Commission of Enquiry to expose them appears to the Admiralty Board here in a much stronger light than ever.' Plymouth, Portsmouth, Chatham and other dockyards were all visited in turn, and in each of them grave abuses were disinterred.

It was not only that timber for shipbuilding was desperately scarce, but that some of the most valuable pieces were actually being wasted. According to one report: 'In the yards we see the noblest oak of the forest, worthy to have formed the ribs of the proudest three-decker of Great Britain, sawed and hacked and chipped to make the floor of a sloop'; and it was alleged that 'the shipwrights would deliberately build and repair small vessels with timber of the highest classes'.[2] The Commission revealed the significant fact that the dockyard officials were actually receiving more pay from the contractors than from the government. (Troubridge was of opinion that 'all the master shipwrights ought to be *hanged*, every one of them, without exception'.) St. Vincent appointed a new set of timber inspectors and ordered the strict scrutiny of 'all oak delivered on contract'. Yards were closed down, and the purchase of timber and various stores was largely suspended.

It was speedily apparent that by these measures St. Vincent had stirred up a hornet's nest; for the all-powerful timber contractors,

---

[1] Tucker, *Memoirs of the Earl of St. Vincent*, II, p. 123.
[2] Q. E. Berckman, *Nelson's Dear Lord* (1962), p. 73.

who enjoyed what was practically a monopoly of the available supply of home-grown oak, were now on the war-path. The 'Timber Trust' were still further alienated when presently the authorities advertised publicly for timber in the local newspapers. The appeal was in vain and the price of oak went on rising, while the 'Timber Trust' retaliated by withholding all oak supplies from the dockyards.

There can be no question that St. Vincent's insistence on retrenchment and reform at this critical moment seriously weakened the Navy. 'The rigid measures that were passed at this time,' Barham was later to observe, 'would have produced much good to the service if they had been delayed till the peace was established; and I am persuaded that Lord St. Vincent must have thought it secure when he attempted this measure of reformation. On any other ground it was madness and imbecility in the extreme.'[1] When the short peace ended the dockyards lacked the necessary materials for repairing vessels worn out by long years of service. Inevitably the blockading squadrons began to lose their numerical superiority over their opponents. In the crucial spring months of 1805 Great Britain had no more than eighty-three sail of the line in commission against the combined fleets of France, Spain, and Holland; moreover, a good many of these were in urgent need of repair.

On Pitt's return to office in May 1804 he chose Melville as his First Lord. The latter immediately reversed St. Vincent's policy, restoring the old system and appeasing the contractors. By drawing his timber supplies from all available sources Melville obtained sufficient oak to patch up, in the next eighteen months or so, thirty-nine sail of the line, or about one-third of the total British battle fleet. But St. Vincent continued stoutly to defend his policy, and in February 1805, the Commission of Naval Enquiry issued its Tenth Report, showing that 'gross irregularities' had occurred while Melville was Treasurer during Pitt's previous premiership. Amid the storm of execration that followed upon this exposure Melville was hounded out of office and replaced in April by Admiral Sir Charles Middleton, who took the title of Lord Barham. The new First Lord, a strategist and administrator of the first rank, set to work to get as many of the ships laid up in the dockyards to sea as possible; the result being that in the nick of time the fleet was reinforced. No less than twenty-two of

[1] *Barham Papers*, III, p. 69.

the line and five frigates were patched up for temporary service early in the campaign of 1805, and three of them were fitted out and sent to Nelson within a month of Trafalgar.

In January 1805 Missiessy with a minor squadron escaped from Rochefort in a snow-storm, with orders to sail for the West Indies, where the Toulon fleet was to join him. (The frigate *Doris*, hastening under a heavy press of sail to warn Sir Thomas Graves—who had taken his squadron to water in Quiberon Bay—of Missiessy's impending departure, ran on a rock near the entrance to the Bay and was lost.) A week later Villeneuve with eleven of the line and nine cruisers sailed from Toulon.

The situation in the Mediterranean was all this time becoming increasingly difficult and dangerous. Since the Spanish declaration of war in the previous December, Nelson had had to reckon with a second hostile squadron outside his own at Cartagena, where the Spaniards were rapidly preparing for sea; while his own squadron was now outnumbered by the enemy's force in Toulon. The enemy's destination was still uncertain. Apart from Nelson's fleet, Sardinia, Sicily, and Egypt were virtually defenceless. 'From Sardinia', Nelson informed the foreign secretary, Lord Hawkesbury, 'we get water and fresh provisions.' If that island should be lost, he did not think that his fleet could remain off Toulon. But the government, he was told, could spare no reinforcements for the Mediterranean.

Nelson's squadron was revictualling at the anchorage in the Maddalena Islands when at 3 p.m. on the 19th his frigates brought the news of Villeneuve's escape. He made the signal to weigh; his squadron ran through the perilous Biche passage, and four hours later gained the open sea. He stood to the southward and off Messina on the 31st sent six of his cruisers in search of the enemy; on the same day his fleet beat through the Straits of Messina—'a thing unprecedented in nautical history,' as Nelson observed; 'but although the danger from the rapidity of the current was great, yet so was the object of my pursuit.'[1]

Hurrying from Messina to Morea, and from Morea to Alexandria, Nelson could find no trace of Villeneuve, and eventually returned to his station. What had actually happened was that the enemy, after encountering a heavy gale, had put back almost immediately into Toulon.

[1] *Nelson's Dispatches*, VI, p. 341.

During the next few weeks the Toulon fleet was hard at work refitting. 'These gentlemen are not accustomed to a Gulf of Lyons gale,' Nelson remarked on 9 March, 'while we have buffeted for twenty-one months, and not carried away a spar'; and a few days later he added: 'Buonaparte has often made his brags, that our Fleet would be worn out by keeping the sea—that his was kept in order, and increasing by staying in Port; but he now finds, I fancy, if *Emperors* hear truth, that his Fleet suffers more in one night, than ours in one year.'[1]

Meanwhile Pitt, during the winter of 1804–5, had been patiently laying the foundations of the Third Coalition and endeavouring, in the face of almost insurmountable obstacles, to satisfy the Russians' insistent demand for a British military expedition to cooperate with them in a combined offensive. What the Tsar had earlier suggested was an army of 15,000 men capable of striking effectively against the enemy's flank in Italy; but this was turned down by Mulgrave on the grounds that, the bulk of our forces being ear-marked for the defence of the British Isles, we could undertake no major military effort in the Mediterranean.

Early in 1805, however, it was found possible to release a number of newly raised battalions to relieve the force of seasoned British troops then engaged in garrisoning Malta: the latter would thereby become available to form a much-needed strategic reserve in the Mediterranean, for the protection of Egypt, Sardinia, and Sicily— especially the last. This reserve force, which eventually comprised some 7,000 men, was placed under the command of Lieut.-General Sir James Craig. The destination of the relieving force was kept a profound secret. On 27 March orders were dispatched to Cornwallis, Calder, Orde, and Nelson to cover the passage of Craig's transports past the enemy's ports. For some weeks the transports lay windbound at Spithead: then, on 17 April, the forty-five transports comprising the Secret Expedition, as it was called, weighed; and, escorted by Vice-Admiral Knight with two ships of the line, stood down the Channel on the first lap of its 2,000-mile journey to Malta. With northerly winds it made a good passage across the Bay of Biscay and sailed down the coast of Portugal. Craig's original orders had contained no mention of an Anglo-Russian offensive. By the time of its

[1] *Ibid.*, VI, p. 359.

arrival in Malta, however, the Third Coalition was an accomplished fact; at long last the Russian and British governments had reached agreement; and Craig was instructed to support the Russian forces in Italy.

Pitt's preparations for the offensive marked a new and highly important development in the struggle, and one that was destined to have momentous consequences. It was a bold and skilful attempt to wrest the initiative from Napoleon.[1] Hitherto the position of Great Britain had been one of perilous isolation, and her policy essentially defensive. Now she was about to counter-attack. In view of the slender military resources at her disposal, the cooperation of the Russian land forces was indispendable. The dispatch of Craig's expedition was in fact the crux of the bargain that had been struck between the two governments. The risks entailed in sending this great convoy past no less than five enemy squadrons were indeed very high; but they were risks that had to be run.

In the meantime Missiessy's mission in the West Indies had failed. Though he had captured most of Dominica the garrison still held out; and, without making any attempt on St. Lucia, he had raided and exacted ransoms from the smaller islands to the northward. On his return to rendezvous with Villeneuve in Martinique, he received intelligence that the latter had after all failed to break out of the Mediterranean and that the Rochefort squadron was to return home. Accordingly, after landing the last of his troops and supplies in San Domingo, Missiessy sailed for Europe.

It was at this stage that Napoleon embarked on his third and final design for the invasion of England.[2] Once more he strove to secure a temporary superiority in the Channel by means of a powerful combination with which to overwhelm the Western Squadron and the flotilla blockading Boulogne, and thus to enable the Grand Army to cross. This time, however, his plans included a concentration on the further side of the Atlantic. Ganteaume with the Brest squadron,

---

[1] For the crucial part played by Pitt in the campaign of 1805, see J. S. Corbett, *The Campaign of Trafalgar* (1905), pp. 32–4, 236–8, 272–4; J. Holland Rose, *Dispatches relating to the Third Coalition* (1904), pp. 155–8, also *William Pitt and the Great War* (1911), pp. 527–8, 531–2; Piers Mackesy, *The War in the Mediterranean, 1803–10* (1957), pp. 57–71.

[2] E. Desbrière, *Projets et tentatives de débarquement aux îles Britanniques* (1901), IV, pp. 359 *et seq.*

comprising twenty-one of the line, was to put to sea, raise the blockade of Ferrol, and then sail in company with the Spanish squadron to the West Indies, there to join forces with Missiessy. At the same time Villeneuve with the Toulon squadron was to evade Nelson and make for the same destination after releasing the Spanish fleet in Cadiz. 'I think', Napoleon declared, 'that the sailing of these twenty ships of the line will oblige the English to dispatch over thirty in pursuit. This will enormously weaken their strength in the Channel.' The Combined Fleet, under the command of Ganteaume, would then return to Europe and appear in overwhelming force at the mouth of the Channel to cover the passage of the army. Napoleon appears by now to have persuaded himself that his brilliant paper strategy had completely befooled and outmanœuvred the dull-witted islanders, and that he would soon have a vastly superior concentration at the entrance of the Channel.[1]

On 24 March, Ganteaume, reporting that the strength of the British force off Brest had fallen to only fifteen sail, requested permission to attack. But Napoleon would not hear of it. 'A naval victory now', was his reply, 'would lead to nothing. Have but one aim—to fulfil your mission. Sail without fighting.'[2] Thus an opportunity was let slip. A few weeks later the blockading force had been substantially strengthened, and the strongest French squadron was safely locked up. One half of Napoleon's project had broken down at the outset. The hurried dispersal of British naval forces on which he had been reckoning had not occurred. To the end he never really appreciated the strength of Cornwallis's interior position.[3] The tenacity of this Admiral and his captains was one of the decisive factors in the frustration of Napoleon's plans for securing a great French concentration at the entrance of the Channel.

Six days after Ganteaume had lost the opportunity of defeating Cornwallis's force off Brest, Villeneuve with eleven of the line slipped out of Toulon under cover of darkness and, shaking off the pursuing

[1] *Correspondance de Napoléon*, X, pp. 314–15, 321.

[2] *Ibid.*, X, pp. 261–2.

[3] 'In case Villeneuve approached, it was scarcely possible that the two hostile squadrons, dependent upon the wind, which if fair for one would be foul to the other, could unite before he had effectually crushed one of them' (Mahan, *The Influence of Sea Power upon the French Revolution and Empire*, II, p. 175).

British frigates during the night of 31 March, steered through the Straits of Gibraltar with a favouring wind.[1] Reaching Cadiz on 9 April and driving off the squadron under Orde (who reprehensibly made no attempt to dog their track and ascertain their course), they were joined by one French and six Spanish sail of the line. That night the whole force sailed for Martinique, where it arrived on 14 May.

2

It was not until 25 April that intelligence reached the Admiralty that the Toulon fleet had passed the Straits and that Orde, surprised by Villeneuve, had raised the blockade of Cadiz. With the French fleet at large on the sea routes and strong Spanish forces free to issue at any moment from both Cadiz and Cartagena, the Secret Expedition, escorted only by a 98 and a 74, was apparently sailing blindly to its doom. The news reached Pitt in the midst of the ministerial crisis occasioned by the fall of Melville. 'I think', he wrote urgently to Barham, 'we must not lose a moment in taking measures to set afloat every ship that by any means of extraordinary exertion we can find means to man.'

Now was the testing time for the new First Lord. The news of Barham's elevation had been received in informed circles with mixed feelings. 'A superannuated Methodist at the head of the Admiralty,' Creevey had jeered, 'in order to catch the votes of Wilberforce and Co.' A common view of the matter was that he was a mere stopgap. Barham, after all, was approaching eighty; he was nearly the oldest admiral in the Navy List; he had been a captain afloat while Nelson was still in his cradle. Pitt had insisted on his appointment in the face of strong opposition. Even those who recognized his distinguished services in the past and his exceptional qualities for the high office to which he had been suddenly called were filled with misgivings on the score of his great age. Despite his disappointment in not getting

---

[1] Two hours afterwards the *Fisgard* frigate, then at Gibraltar, sailed for Ushant to warn the Channel fleet. In the Bay of Biscay dispatches were put on board a Guernsey lugger, which was forthwith ordered into Plymouth. See Leyland, *Blockade of Brest*, II, p. 237; Adm. 51/1549, 10 April.

the Admiralty himself, Charles Yorke freely acknowledged Barham's ripe experience and outstanding ability with this reservation.

> I was not aware that at his advanced age his health and faculties were equal to such a post. If they are he is indisputably the fittest man that could be chosen to occupy it at the time. His abilities were always considered great, his experience is consummate, and he has few equals in application and method of business.[1]

He had succeeded Nelson's uncle, Sir Maurice Suckling, as Comptroller of the Navy in 1778, and in that office had done much to restore the efficiency of the service during and after the War of American Independence. The greatest naval administrator since Anson, he had now reached the plenitude of his powers. None knew more than Barham of all that appertained to the building and repairing of men-of-war. His grasp and understanding of the strategic problems then confronting the Admiralty were probably unequalled—as also was the promptitude with which he acted. 'If possible', he wrote to Pitt that spring, 'the whole machine should be made to move a little brisker, so as to afford us some prospect of success.' Under Barham's direction, the staff work of the Admiralty attained, perhaps, the highest level of efficiency that was reached in the whole course of the war. As soon as he became First Lord he proceeded to divest himself of routine responsibilities and other distracting calls upon his time and energies by delegating the various branches of administration to subordinates while reserving to himself the higher direction of the war at sea. At the same time the regulations were overhauled and brought up to date and serving officers were prohibited from absenting themselves from their ships in order to attend Parliament.[2]

By noon on the 30th the Admiralty messengers were spurring down the Exeter road with orders framed to cover every contingency. The Secret Expedition was, if possible, to be stopped and brought back to Cork or Falmouth; Calder's force cruising before Ferrol was to be reinforced, and every ship fit for sea was to be rushed out at once to strengthen the Western Squadron. At the same time orders were given, in case of necessity, for Orde and Calder to fall back on the

[1] Add. MSS. 35706, 26 April 1805.
[2] Adm. 3/256, 25 April 1805.

centre of our defensive system at the mouth of the Channel.[1] These dispatches were put on board the *Beagle* brig, which sailed at midday on 3 May from Plymouth Sound and, two days later, joined the Channel fleet off Ushant and delivered them to Cornwallis.[2]

Once again Nelson was beside himself with anxiety for news of the enemy fleet. On 4 April he had learned from his frigates that the French had escaped him; and he promptly took his station midway between Sardinia and the African coast, disposing his look-outs on either side, and covering the vital positions to the eastward. 'I am most unlucky', he complained to the British minister at Naples, 'that my Frigates should lose sight of them; but it is vain to be angry, or repine: therefore, I must do the best I can. . . . I shall neither go to the Eastward of Sicily, or to the Westward of Sardinia, until I know something positive.' He remained cruising within these limits till he had certain news that the enemy had gone to the westward. Then, in the teeth of a spell of strong westerly gales, he began to beat back to the west again. 'My good fortune seems to have flown away,' he lamented to Ball on 19 April. 'I cannot get a fair wind, or even a side wind. Dead foul!—dead foul!' A week later he wrote: 'I believe Easterly winds have left the Mediterranean.' Tacking or wearing every few hours, with his squadron very much dispersed, Nelson was a whole month in getting down the Mediterranean; a passage which the enemy had accomplished in nine days. Once again he experienced the long-drawn-out strain and anguish of spirit which had possessed him years before when in pursuit of Brueys and the Army of Egypt. 'O French fleet French fleet,' he exclaimed during this long beat down to the Straits, 'if I can but once get up with you, I'll make you pay dearly for all that you have made me suffer!' Not until 6 May did the squadron reach Gibraltar Bay, arriving on the 9th off Cape St. Vincent, where it was learned from reliable reports that Villeneuve had sailed for Martinique.[3]

In accordance with an old and well-established tradition the Commander-in-Chief on the Mediterranean station at once prepared to follow in pursuit. 'My lot is cast, my dear Ball, and I am going to the West Indies', Nelson wrote that day to Ball, 'where, although I

---

[1] Adm. 2/1363, 30 April; 3/153, 1 May 1805.
[2] Adm. 52/3735, 3–5 May 1805.
[3] *Nelson's Dispatches*, VI, pp. 430–2.

am late, yet chance may have given them a bad passage, and me a good one: I must hope for the best.'[1]

Apprised that Craig's expedition, under convoy of Rear-Admiral Knight, was approaching, Nelson filled in the time of waiting by preparing for a long chase. At four o'clock in the afternoon of 11 May the Secret Expedition arrived in Lagos Bay; to its escort of two of the line, Nelson now added a third—the *Royal Sovereign*: all three vessels being under the orders of Rear-Admiral Sir Richard Bickerton, whom Nelson left in command on the station. By nightfall the rest of the squadron, formed in two columns, was already twenty miles to the north-west of Cape St. Vincent—*Victory, Superb, Donegal, Spencer,* and *Tigre; Canopus, Leviathan, Belleisle, Conqueror,* and *Swiftsure;* together with three frigates, *Decade, Amphion,* and *Amazon* —under full sail for Barbados. The squadron stood to the southward and westward into the trade winds. The passage was uneventful. Fortune smiled on them; the north-east trades carried Nelson and his force across the Atlantic in little more than three weeks (Villeneuve took nearly five), 'at a rate of 135 miles a day,' wrote the Admiral, 'that is at about 5 or 6 knots, a speed of 9 knots being sometimes attained.' Nelson's crews were as usual healthy and in first-rate fighting trim (Villeneuve, on the other hand, had to disembark 1,000 sick as soon as he reached land). His plan of attack, based on the relative strength and efficiency of the rival forces, was carefully prepared and explained to all his captains.

The *Superb*, a fine 80-gun ship under the command of Captain Richard Keats, the hero of Algeciras, was badly in need of a refit and, consequently, a dull sailer. But Keats secured permission to carry his sail while the other ships communicated, also he lashed his studding-sail booms to the yard. By these expedients the *Superb* was always under full sail, and the Admiral hastened to reassure him. 'My dear Keats,' Nelson wrote, 'be assured I know and feel that the *Superb* does all which is possible for a ship to accomplish, and I desire that you will not fret upon the occasion.'[2]

The weather was fine and clear; day after day the steady trade-winds blew; day after day the tell-tale fair weather clouds lay over the western horizon at sunset; day after day the sun shone from a dark

[1] *Ibid.,* VI, p. 431.
[2] *Nelson's Dispatches,* VI, pp. 442–3; Adm. 52/3694, 12 May–4 June 1805.

blue sky on the gleaming, foam-flecked combers which were presently alive with bonitas and flying-fish. 'Our passage', recorded Nelson on 27 May, 'although not very quick has been far from a bad one.' In the early morning of 4 June the look-outs sighted Barbados about six leagues to the westward. At noon the squadron sailed past Needham Point into Carlisle Bay and anchored in the roadstead off Bridgetown.

Bickerton saw the Secret Expedition safely through the Straits and well to the eastward of Cartagena; then he detached three frigates to convoy Craig to his destination while he himself turned back with the three battleships to act as a covering squadron for the Secret Expedition by taking station off Cartagena. Thus in the face of five undefeated hostile squadrons straddling its line of passage the safety of Craig's force had been assured.

At the news that Villeneuve had gone to the West Indies something like a panic prevailed in the City. Consols dropped to 57. No news of Nelson's squadron had reached the Admiralty. 'The City people are crying out against Sir John Orde,' wrote Lord Radstock to his son, who until lately had been serving in the *Victory*, 'and, as usual, are equally absurd and unjust.' Towards the end of May the alarm was reflected in successive leaders in the daily press. 'Bonaparte', observed the *Morning Chronicle* on the 27th, 'has not for a single hour relaxed in any one effort calculated to inspire a wise fear of invasion.' And again: 'It is sufficiently alarming to the people of this country that even the track of the enemy is so long unknown.' There was a growing uneasiness, too, lest the Admiral should be following a false scent. 'His only eye', Yorke predicted to Lord Hardwicke, 'is directed eastward, and we shall find ourselves in a great scrape.'[1] As seven years earlier, feeling at the Board of Admiralty had hardened against Nelson. 'I feel', wrote Lord Radstock to his son, 'your gallant and worthy chief will have much injustice done him on this occasion, for the cry is stirring up fast against him, and the loss of Jamaica will at once sink all his past services into oblivion.' The arrival of the Combined Fleet in the West Indies nearly doubled the insurance rates on the return passage from the islands. Such was the crucial importance of the West Indian trade that, only the year before, Nelson himself had observed: 'If our islands should fall,

[1] Add. MSS. 35706, 30 April 1805.

England would be so clamorous for peace that we should humble ourselves.'

Actually the situation was not so critical as it appeared. The Navy still retained its advantage of interior lines, and its admirals were still guided by the historic tradition of British strategy: to fall back, in the hour of danger, on the vital position at the mouth of the Channel. Thus Bickerton stood to the northward with the three battleships which had guarded the Secret Expedition to join Calder off Ferrol; Collingwood with his Flying Squadron soon after hurried down to the Gut to protect Craig's transports lying in Gibraltar Bay, and later sent his two fastest 74s across the ocean to reinforce Nelson. When in July these two ships arrived in the West Indies, Rear-Admiral Cochrane, having in the meantime received intelligence of Villeneuve's departure for Europe, immediately sent them home again. 'Every line of battle ship that can be spared', he wrote to the Admiralty, who that very week were requiring the return of the two ships in question, 'from hence may be wanted in the Channel'—yet another example of the 'living tradition'. Meanwhile Collingwood, having learned of Nelson's departure for the West Indies, took his station with six of the line off Cadiz, where he effectually covered the entrance of the Mediterranean and thereby prevented the junction of the Cartagena squadron.

The orders which Villeneuve had received from Napoleon were to wait for reinforcements, and in the meantime to attack British possessions and trade in the West Indies; but Missiessy, who was to have joined him there, was already on his way back to Rochefort, nor was there any sign of Ganteaume (the latter, as we have seen, had never got to sea at all); during the next few weeks Villeneuve neither accomplished nor even attempted anything of importance, and on 9 June, having learned that Nelson was already off Barbados, he immediately abandoned all his projects against our West Indian islands and sailed for Ferrol.[1]

Five days earlier the pursuing British squadron had arrived at its destination. The Combined Fleet was, in fact, but a hundred miles away—and the wind was fair for Martinique. Misled, however, by a message from Brigadier-General Brereton in St. Lucia to the effect that the enemy had been sighted on the night of 28–29 May standing south

[1] Journal de Reille; A.M., BB4, 233.

for Trinidad, he followed in pursuit. 'But for that false information,' Nelson complained to the Duke of Clarence, 'I should have been off Port Royal, as they were putting to sea; and our Battle, most probably, would have been fought on the spot where the brave Rodney beat de Grasse.' (For weeks the memory of General Brereton and 'his damned intelligence' continued to rankle. 'The name of General Brereton,' he declared wrathfully on 23 July, 'will not soon be forgot'.) Nevertheless, Nelson could reflect with satisfaction that by his tenacious pursuit of the Combined Fleet he had driven the enemy out of the West Indies and thereby preserved our colonies 'and more than two hundred Sail of sugar-loaded ships'. On 13 June, after sending a sloop to England with dispatches and another vessel to warn Calder off Ferrol, the Admiral weighed and sailed for Gibraltar, arriving off the Spanish coast several days ahead of Villeneuve.

The news of Nelson's speedy return to Europe spread consternation in official circles in Paris. 'This unexpected union of forces undoubtedly renders every scheme of invasion impracticable for the present,' Talleyrand informed Napoleon on 2 August. It was at once apparent that the whole plan of campaign had collapsed.

'Either the distance between the different quarters of the globe are diminished,' wrote Hugh Elliot, the British minister at Naples, to Nelson, 'or you have extended the powers of human action. After an unremitting cruise of two long years in the stormy Gulf of Lyons, to have proceeded without going into port to Alexandria, from Alexandria to the West Indies; from the West Indies back again to Gibraltar; to have kept your ships afloat, your rigging standing; and your crews in health and spirits—is an effort such as never was realized in former times, nor, I doubt, will ever again be repeated by any other admiral.'[1]

3

Far away in the First Lord's room at the Admiralty the aged but indomitable Barham bent over his charts and minutes, dealing with each new situation as it arose with practised ease, and viewing these intricate strategical problems with the eye of a master. The sloop which Nelson had sent to England with his dispatches sighted and

[1] Q. Mahan, *Life of Nelson*, II, p. 310.

passed the Combined Fleet on its way[1]; crowding on sail, she arrived at Plymouth on 7 July, and her captain posted at once to London; in the early morning of the 9th Barham received the intelligence which enabled him, while Villeneuve was still in mid-ocean, so to dispose our forces that Napoleon's intended concentration was rendered impossible. Though it remained uncertain whether the enemy were actually making for Brest or Ferrol, Barham's dispositions provided for both contingencies. Cornwallis was directed to cruise to the southwest of Brest, to raise the blockade of Ferrol, and to send the five ships which had been stationed there to join Calder's force of ten off Ferrol; and Calder was ordered, with the fifteen now under his command, to cruise a hundred miles off Cape Finisterre in order to intercept Villeneuve and to forestall his junction with the squadron in Ferrol.[2] In either case the enemy would be brought to battle so far from the port that they were making for that the squadron in harbour would be unable to assist them.

Barham's prompt and decisive action consequently enabled the British squadrons to exploit the strategic advantage which the blockading force must necessarily possess over the blockaded. With Collingwood stationed before Cadiz (to which Nelson was at this moment returning) and Cornwallis cruising off Brest, the new disposition effectually checkmated the emperor's design. Barham's orders were issued and executed with such dispatch that Napoleon was completely baffled. By 9 a.m. on the 9th the Admiralty messenger was hurrying down the Exeter road with these orders in his wallet; in the afternoon of the 11th the *Niobe* frigate was standing out of Plymouth Sound and early on the 16th delivered the dispatches to the Admiral off Ushant[3]; Cornwallis, leaving half a dozen of his cruisers to watch Brest, stood to the south-westward with Barham's instructions, while Stirling off Rochefort and Calder off Ferrol duly received their orders;

---

[1] Adm. 51/1473, 20–21 June 1805.

[2] 'If we are not too late, I think there is a chance of our intercepting the Toulon fleet—Nelson follows them to Cadiz and, if you can immediately unite the Ferrol and Rochefort squadrons and order them to cruise from 30 to 40 leagues to the westward, and stretch out with your own fleet as far and continue 6 or 8 days on that service, and then return to your several posts, I think we have some chance of intercepting them' (*Barham Papers*, ed. J. K. Laughton, IV, p. 258).

[3] Adm. 52/3780, 11–16 July 1805.

with the result that by the 19th the latter had reached his appointed position with fifteen of the line.

After cruising on this station for only three days, Calder, on the morning of 22 July, encountered Villeneuve in a thick fog. All things considered, the odds were, perhaps, slightly in Calder's favour; but owing to the weather he could not engage until late in the afternoon, and towards the end the rival gunners, unable to view their targets, aimed at the flashes of the enemy's guns. A confused and indecisive action followed. It is possible that the part played by the weather has been somewhat exaggerated; for according to Captain Ekins:

> notwithstanding the thickness of the fog at intervals, when he could with difficulty see the ship a-head and a-stern of him, it was also, at times, so clear, that he could discover the movements of the van ships of the enemy, by which he himself was guided. When they tacked in succession, he performed the same manœuvre, which brought on an action of four hours, which he appears to have quitted without a sufficient reason; for merely to cover the two captured ships will not be admitted to be so.[1]

In short, by nightfall the British Admiral had taken two prizes and his squadron lay between the enemy and Ferrol. Though widely scattered, his ships had suffered but little damage. But Calder's preoccupation with the safety of his prizes and apprehension of what might happen if the Ferrol squadron should come out and join Villeneuve blinded him to the fact that it was his imperative duty to bring to action the largest and most formidable of the converging divisions of the enemy. Nelson had been prepared to risk the destruction of his squadron, provided only he could be certain of crippling that of the enemy;[2] not so Calder. On the evening of the 24th the wind was fair to carry him to the enemy: yet he parted from them. During the night it blew fresh and several of Villeneuve's vessels lost sails and sustained other injuries. But Calder's squadron was nowhere to be seen.[3]

---

[1] Ekins, *Naval Battles* (1824), p. 263.

[2] *Nelson's Dispatches*, VI, p. 489.

[3] The crux of Calder's defence at the ensuing court-martial was: 'I could not hope to succeed without receiving great damage; I had no friendly port to go to, and had the Ferrol and Rochefort squadrons come out, I must have fallen an easy prey. They might have gone to Ireland. Had I been defeated it is impossible to say what the consequences might have been.' Calder was found guilty of not having done his utmost to destroy every ship of the enemy's fleet, and he was sentenced to be severely reprimanded.— *Naval Chronicle*, Vol. 15, p. 167.

'Does not the thought of the possibilities remaining to Villeneuve', exclaimed Radstock, 'make your blood boil when you reflect on the never to be forgotten 22nd of July?' The usual outcry arose against the hapless Admiral. When all is said and done, a considerable risk had been run by Barham to place him in a position to cripple the Combined Fleet once and for all. But the projected counter-stroke had miscarried; Calder had bungled the business. 'Sir Robert Calder', observed the *Naval Chronicle* sternly, 'has not yet, even to the Admiralty, given the explanation of his conduct which his country expects and his character demands.'

Meanwhile, with a view to dispersing the British concentration at the entrance of the Channel by creating a diversion off the west of Ireland, Allemand had sailed out of Rochefort, on 16 July, with a strong squadron of five battleships, three frigates, and two sloops. The Irish project fell through; and, in accordance with his instructions, Allemand endeavoured to rendezvous with Villeneuve off Cape Finisterre. After remaining unseen on that rendezvous for several days without receiving intelligence of the Toulon fleet, he proceeded to a second rendezvous about 150 miles south-west of Ushant. Thence, on the approach of some of Cornwallis's cruisers, making a long stretch to the westward, he stood away on 10 August for Vigo, where he received Villeneuve's orders to rendezvous off the Penmarcks. He passed the first week of September cruising some fifteen leagues from that headland—once more without success—while Stirling, detached by Cornwallis to seek him out, actually passed inshore of the French without sighting them. On 7 September Allemand sailed southward for Cadiz in another attempt to join Villeneuve.[1]

Meanwhile the junction which it had been Calder's mission to prevent materialized. On 28 July Villeneuve entered Vigo Bay, and on 2 August joined hands with the Ferrol squadron. Twenty-nine French and Spanish ships were now concentrated at Ferrol. On the 3rd Barham wrote to Nelson directing him to return to England. But before these orders could reach him the latter on his own initiative was already standing to the northward. Presently Calder, having raised the blockade of Ferrol, was likewise hurrying northward. Once again our Admirals were instinctively closing on the centre of their defensive system. Squadron by squadron our forces were massing in the very

[1] Desbrière, *op. cit.*, IV, pp. 655 *sqq.*, 759 *sqq.*

track that Villeneuve was ordered by Napoleon to follow. On the 13th Stirling joined Cornwallis off Ushant with his squadron of six of the line; a few hours later they were joined by Calder with nine; and on the 15th Nelson, too, arrived from Gibraltar with his squadron, bringing the total strength of Cornwallis's force up to thirty-five. In short, Napoleon's grand design had ended, not in dispersing the British defence as he had intended, but in concentrating it in the vital area, in the approaches to the Channel.

With the approach of the spring tides, the Admiralty warned Cornwallis early in August that a hostile descent from the Dutch ports and Boulogne was apprehended. 'We shall make you up 20 for your own force as soon as we are able,' Barham declared, 'but the Downs must be kept strong during the height of the spring as the Dutch are in great force at the Texel and the flotilla too numerous to be dealt [with] without some heavy ships.' And later, on the 10th: 'I just write one line to apprise you that the Ministers look to an invasion soon, and have given directions to prepare all the military corps. I have done the same privately to the Admirals at all the ports, that they may be prepared to give every kind of assistance to our naval force in the Channel. . . . The Dutch can only get to sea at the height of the spring, and which is the time to guard against.' And on the 15th: 'The enemy to the eastward are active in appearance, but as many things must concur to bring such an armament to sea, they cannot attack us unobserved.'[1]

At this moment the problem of trade protection was exercising the Admiralty to a far greater degree than the threat of invasion.[2] For the presence of the Combined Fleet in Ferrol on the flank of our vital line of communications imperilled, not only an expeditionary force, under Sir David Baird, which had been sent out to recapture the Cape, as well as the fleet of transports which was about to sail for Odessa to carry a Russian army into the Mediterranean, but also the homecoming convoys, upon the safe arrival of which the City's credit largely depended. Furthermore, Allemand's raiding force was still at large on the trade-routes. It was of crucial importance to the nation that commerce should be kept flowing.

Shortly afterwards, to the profound relief of Lloyd's and the mer-

[1] Historical Manuscripts Commission: *Various Collections*, VI, pp. 410–11.
[2] See *infra*, p. 389. Cf. *Barham Papers*, III, pp. xxxii, 26.

chants of the City, news reached the capital of the arrival of the convoys. Early in August the great trading fleets at last came in sight of the western headlands and steered slowly up the Channel. On the 10th the telegraph stations flashed the news from hill-top to hill-top between Portsmouth and London as they passed by the Isle of Wight.[1]

Though the worst danger was now past, the threat to the trade still remained; for the bold and elusive Allemand was to cruise for several months longer. Well did his force earn from the French the name of the 'Invisible Squadron'. Finding that Villeneuve was securely locked up in Cadiz by the British blockade and beyond their reach, the Rochefort squadron stood out into the ocean for the great trade focal at the entrance of the Channel. There Allemand only just missed Popham with a rich convoy and Baird's transports. Popham had, in fact, been delayed by baffling winds, otherwise they must have met. Meanwhile Stirling, having failed to locate Allemand in the Bay, now proceeded to a position some fifty leagues W.S.W. of Scilly, eventually rejoining Cornwallis. Allemand remained for several days off the mouth of the Channel, refitting some of his vessels and taking a number of prizes.[2] Then, just before Cornwallis stood out with his squadron to destroy him, the Frenchman fled to the southward. Strachan also, early in October, failed to intercept him; while Allemand chased, first the *Agamemnon* on her way to join Nelson's fleet, and later the *Amiable* with the Portugal convoy. Later in the same month the Rochefort squadron ran for the Canaries, where they revictualled, and then in December returned to the coast of Portugal, where they learned of the destruction of the Combined Fleet at Trafalgar. Allemand's luck had held to the last. With the aid of thick weather and a favouring wind he managed to slip back into Rochefort, unobserved, on 24 December.[3]

4

Since the squadron cruising off Ushant constituted the pivot of our strategy, both defensive and offensive—or, as Barham expressed it,

[1] *Hampshire Telegraph*, 12 August 1805.
[2] Allemand's total 'bag' amounted to one sail of the line, three corvettes, and forty-two merchant vessels.
[3] Desbrière, *op. cit.*, IV, pp. 791 *sqq.*

'the main spring from which all offensive operations must proceed'—
it was the First Lord's constant care 'to keep it as strong and effective
as possible'.[1] Cornwallis was presently directed by the Admiralty to
detach part of this force to deal with the Combined Fleet. Cornwallis,
however, had already anticipated these orders. On 16 August he had
detached eighteen of the line under Calder and sent them to blockade
Villeneuve in Ferrol. With the force under his command now comprising no more than eighteen of the line—though these included ten
three-deckers—he held the entrance of the Channel and blockaded
Ganteaume in Brest. Meanwhile at home orders were given 'to get
everything to sea that would float'.

On Nelson's return to England, a few days later, the whole system
of cruiser control was carefully overhauled and reorganized by Barham
and Nelson with a view to securing more efficient communications and
protection of commerce. A line of frigates was directed to cruise
between Cape Clear and Finisterre, and between Finisterre and St.
Vincent, for the dual purpose of intelligence and trade protection. To
the same end the telegraph signal code which had recently been
devised by Sir Home Popham was issued to frigates as well as to
battleships.

The crisis of the campaign came in mid-August. With Austria
plainly threatening war, it was Napoleon's last opportunity of com-
passing the destruction of the island State before he was obliged to
march eastward to meet the new attack. At this culminating moment
the Emperor was with his men on the heights above Boulogne,
anxiously scanning the western horizon for the first glimpse of Villeneuve's topsails, confident that the stratagems he had set in motion for
dispersing the enemy's squadrons had succeeded and that the French
concentration was about to be achieved. He reckoned on the presence of
at least fifty sail of the line in the Channel to cover the passage of his
troops. It would appear that he had fallen into the very error against
which he often used to warn his generals: he had, in fact, 'made himself a picture'. On 22 August he received news that the Combined
Fleet had sailed from Ferrol; upon which he ordered Ganteaume to be
ready to leave Brest so that Villeneuve should not lose a single day,
while to the latter he wrote: 'I trust that you have reached Brest.
Get to sea, lose no time, not a moment, and enter the Channel with my

[1] H.M.C., *Various Collections*, VI, p. 411.

united squadrons. England is ours!'[1] Everything now turned on the plan devised to secure passage for the army of 132,000 of the finest troops in the world. Everything was calculated for the transportation of this army across the Channel, in two tides, within twenty-four hours. Not until the last days of August did Napoleon finally abandon his project for a decisive stroke against Great Britain.

Across the Channel the invasion scare suddenly revived. Once more the island was in the grip of anxiety and suspense; and in the Board Room of the Admiralty eyes were again turned to the wind-dial. The Combined Fleet was believed to be heading for the Channel. 'There is such an universal bustle and cry about invasion', Radstock declared, 'that no other subject will be listened to at present by those in power.' Already, through an accidental alarm, the beacons had been lit in the North. Anxious leaders appeared in the national press about the formidable preparations in progress in the Dutch and French in-vasion ports, and about the perturbing lack of intelligence from Nelson. 'Every day, every hour,' wrote Lady Elizabeth Foster on 5 August, 'they expect to hear from him, and the impatience and anxiety is beyond all expression.' It was known that Boulogne harbour was crowded with invasion craft; there were assembled in the port more than 1,000 gun-boats and flat-bottoms and the neighbouring coasts bristled with cannon. With the advent of the spring tides the danger increased: all leave was stopped, the volunteers were called out, patrols were dispatched to watch likely landing-places, and wagons were even assigned to carry off the treasure from the Bank of England. When on the 11th heavy firing was reported from the direc-tion of Boulogne, general alarm prevailed. The volunteers received warning that all furloughs for working during the harvest were sus-pended. Meanwhile the outward-bound East India fleet was detained at Plymouth. 'There has been the greatest alarm ever known in the City of London', Lord Minto observed, 'since the combined fleet sailed from Ferrol. If they had captured our homeward-bound convoys, it is

---

[1] Napoleon ordered Ganteaume by telegraph not to permit Villeneuve to anchor in Brest. 'Vous ne souffriez pas qu'il perde un seul jour, afin que, profitant de la supériorité que me donnent 50 vaisseaux de ligne, vous mettiez sur-le-champ en mer pour remplier votre destination et pour vous porter dans la Manche avec toutes vos forces' (*Correspondance de Napoléon I*, XI, p. 115).

said the India Company and half the city must have been bankrupt.'[1]

On 13 August, before Calder could get off Ferrol, Villeneuve at last put out with twenty-nine of the line and ten frigates. Before leaving port he had sent the *Didon* frigate to seek out Allemand at the secret rendezvous which had been arranged off Finisterre. But on her way to carry out her mission the *Didon* was intercepted by one of our frigates, the *Niobe*, which after a hard-fought action forced her to strike. Villeneuve attempted to make contact with Allemand's force, but failed to find him. After a half-hearted attempt to push northward into the Bay, in continual apprehension of being caught and over-whelmed, the former in despair ordered his fleet to bear up for Cadiz, where he was promptly blocked in by Collingwood and Calder. That was the end of Napoleon's plan for the invasion of England. On 29 August the vast camp at Boulogne was broken up, and the Grand Army was marching to the Danube. Barham's bold and sagacious dispositions had regained for our Navy the interior lines and positions and secured our control of the Channel and Mediterranean; save for Allemand's small division, every enemy squadron was safely bottled up, and our homecoming convoys were saved.

5

Meanwhile, on 18 August, still damning General Brereton, Nelson had arrived at Spithead in the *Victory*, accompanied by the *Superb*. As soon as his flag was sighted, the news went round Portsmouth and the populace flocked to the harbour. Long before the Admiral's barge had pulled to the shore the ramparts were lined with eager spectators, and he was received with loud and ceaseless cheering. All the way up the Portsmouth road to his home at Merton in Surrey there were similar scenes of enthusiasm. The long-drawn-out pursuit of Villeneuve across the Atlantic and back again had caught the imagination of his countrymen; and once more, as after the Nile, Nelson found himself the hero of the hour.

In London the welcome he received was as enthusiastic and sincere, observed the *Times*, 'as if he had returned crowned with a third great naval victory'. Letters of congratulations poured in at Merton from all over the kingdom. The newspapers chronicled his every movement,

[1] Q. *Life and Letters of Sir Gilbert Elliot*, ed. Countess of Minto, III, p. 368.

and he attracted a crowd every time he appeared in the street. 'The town is wild to see him,' wrote Lady Hamilton to Nelson's sister Catherine. 'What a day of rejoicing was yesterday at Merton!' On the 20th thousands gathered outside the Admiralty to catch a glimpse of him. He was 'mobbed and huzza'd in the City', and pursued down Piccadilly by admiring crowds. 'Lord Nelson arrived a few days ago,' said Lord Radstock. 'He was received in town almost as a conqueror, and was followed round by the people with huzzas.' Charles Lamb saw him walking one day in Pall Mall, 'looking', he declared, 'just as a Hero should look.'

Those last few weeks Nelson spent in England represented a kind of naval triumph. No seaman in history, indeed, had received a like ovation. In his own lifetime he had become a legend. '*There is but one Nelson*,' as St. Vincent had truly observed. 'Wherever he appears he electrifies the cold English character,' wrote the Duchess of Devonshire, who was herself one of Nelson's most devoted admirers, 'and rapture and applause follow all his steps. Sometimes a poor woman asks to touch his coat The very children learn to bless him as he passes, and doors and windows are crowded.'[1]

The ensuing weeks Nelson spent partly at Merton Place, and partly in town; for in the present crisis his views were eagerly sought by ministers, and he passed many hours, not only with Barham, but also with Pitt, Castlereagh, and others. In the last week of August the naval and political tension rose to its height. For, though the invasion peril was now at an end, the presence of the Combined Fleet in Cadiz was an abiding threat both to our convoys and to our projects in the Mediterranean, where Sicily was in imminent danger of attack. During this time Nelson held himself at the disposal of the government and awaited the summons which he was confident would come. 'I have refused for the present all invitations,' he told one of his friends on the 31st. 'Every Ship, even the *Victory*, is ordered out, for there is an entire ignorance whether the Ferrol Fleet is coming to the Northward, gone to the Mediterranean, or cruizing for our valuable homeward-bound [trading] fleet.' 'My time and movements must depend upon Buonaparte,' he wrote on another occasion. 'We are at present ignorant of his intentions.'

This uncertainty was soon to be dispelled. For the past week or so

[1] *Q*. D. M. Stuart, *Dearest Bess* (1955), p. 123.

the *Euryalus* had been standing, first to the northward, and then to the eastward, under a press of sail, from Cape St. Vincent with the news that the Combined Fleet had gone into Cadiz. With the wind northerly, she ran up the Channel on 1 September (with her studding-sails set between Portland and St. Albans); and in the evening, in uncertain squally weather, with baffling winds, brought-to off Lymington at the entrance to the Solent.[1] Here Captain Blackwood landed in haste and drove through the night in a post-chaise, arriving in Merton at five o'clock in the morning. He found the Admiral, always an early riser, already up and dressed. 'I am sure you bring me news of the French and Spanish fleets,' exclaimed Nelson, 'and I think I shall yet have to beat them.' A few minutes afterwards the captain continued on his way to the Admiralty, where Nelson presently followed him, saying—'Depend on it, Blackwood, I shall yet give Mr. Villeneuve a drubbing.'

'Thank God! Thank God!' wrote Radstock to Nelson the following day, 'a thousand thousand times that these Jack o' Lanterns are once more safely housed without having done that mischief which was justly dreaded. The papers tell us you will shortly be after them.' The decision was forthwith taken at the Admiralty that Calder should be recalled, and Nelson again appointed to the Mediterranean command. It was to be his mission to bring this great hostile combination to action and to destroy it.

Meanwhile events on the Continent were moving in our favour. Napoleon had annexed Genoa, and the Russian ambassador had been recalled to Paris; early in August Austria, too, had joined the alliance. Later in the month news arrived from St. Petersburg that the Tsar had ratified the treaty of alliance and that a Russian army was moving to the support of Austria. Vienna presently sent an ultimatum to Paris, which Napoleon rejected. Plans were already far advanced for an Anglo-Russian landing in southern Italy. Craig's expedition had at last completed its hazardous passage and arrived safely in Malta. Napoleon affected to despise this enterprise as one more example of the 'combinations de pygmées,' but all the same it was causing him gnawing anxiety.[2]

Nelson had hardly returned home before he was preparing to be off

[1] Adm. 52/3752, 23 August–2 September 1805.
[2] *Correspondance de Napoléon I*, X, p. 549.

again. (Afterwards he reckoned he was only twenty-five days, 'from dinner to dinner', absent from the *Victory*.) 'All my things', he declared on the 5th, 'are this day going off for Portsmouth.' Next day he wrote to his friend from the Admiralty—'My dear Coll., I shall be with you in a very few days, and I hope you will remain Second-in-Command.' On the 8th he passed some hours with his friend Lord Sidmouth and told his host how he intended to destroy the Combined Fleet, sketching a plan with his finger on a little study table. 'Rodney', he said, 'broke the line in one point; I will break it in two.' He also discussed his plan of attack with Captain Keats at Merton.

It was on the 12th, Nelson's last day in town, that there occurred the celebrated encounter with Sir Arthur Wellesley in the anteroom at the Colonial Office. Though the two had never met before, Wellesley, as he afterwards declared, immediately recognized the one-armed Admiral, who having entered into conversation with him, resorted to a boastful and histrionic style of address which made no very favourable impression upon the young victor of Assaye. Then—

> I suppose something that I happened to say may have made him guess that I was a *somebody*, for he went out of the room for a moment, I have no doubt to ask the office-keeper who I was, for when he came back he was altogether a different man, both in manner and matter. All that I had thought a charlatan style had vanished, and he talked of the state of this country and of the aspect and probabilities of affairs on the Continent with good sense, and a knowledge of subjects both at home and abroad, that surprised me equally and more agreeably than the first part of our interview had done; in fact he talked like an officer and a statesman. The Secretary of State kept us long waiting, and certainly, for the last half or three-quarters of an hour, I don't know that I ever had a conversation that interested me more.[1]

Another encounter, also on the 12th, this time with the future Sir John Barrow (then Second Secretary of the Admiralty) is not so well known: but it sheds a revealing light on Nelson's profound absorption in the coming campaign and his keen interest in communications. The 'code of signals' to which Barrow refers was the one actually used at Trafalgar.

> He had been with me at the Admiralty in the morning, anxiously inquiring and expressing his hopes about a code of signals just then improved and enlarged. I assured him they were all but ready; that he should not be

[1] *The Croker Papers*, ed. L. J. Jennings, II, p. 233.

disappointed, and that I would take care they should be at Portsmouth the following morning. On his way, in the evening, he looked in upon me at the Admiralty, where I was stopping to see them off. I pledged myself not to leave the office till a messenger was dispatched with the signals, should the post have departed, and that he might rely on their being at Portsmouth the following morning. On this he shook hands with me; I wished him all happiness and success, which I was sure he would command as he had always done; and he departed apparently more than usually cheerful.[1]

At a late hour on 13 September Nelson left his home for the last time and drove through the night over Hindhead and the Hampshire hills down to Portsmouth. He breakfasted at the George inn, where he spent the morning transacting business; and, early that afternoon, to avoid the crowds which had assembled in the street through which he was expected to pass, he was smuggled out through the narrow, stone-flagged back entrance of the George into Penny Street, and, accompanied by the port admiral, hurried down a by-lane to the beach where the bathing-machines were drawn up. An American visitor to this country who happened to be in Portsmouth that day saw him pass, 'elegantly dressed—his underdress white, with white silk hose, small clothes and shoes; coat blue and elegantly illuminated with stars and ribbons'. By the time he arrived on the beach some hundreds of people had collected in Nelson's train, 'pressing all around him, and pushing to get a little before him to obtain a sight of his face'.[2] Many were in tears; many knelt down before him, and blessed him as he passed. They struggled to touch him, to shake his hand. The concourse presently swelled to a great multitude, and at the water's edge the people broke through the line of sentinels and crowded cheering on the parapet to gaze their last on the slight, battle-scarred figure of the Admiral as he went down into the waiting barge.

As his barge pushed off from the shore, the people raised three cheers, which Nelson returned by waving his hat—at the same time he turned to Hardy sitting beside him with the words: 'I had their huzzas before—I have their hearts now!' Later that day Rose and Canning dined with him on board the flagship. At eight o'clock the following morning the *Victory* weighed, and, accompanied by the *Euryalus*, stood down the Channel.

[1] Sir John Barrow, *An Auto-biographical Memoir* (1847), pp. 280–1.
[2] Silliman, *A Journal of Travels* (1812), p. 115.

6

Nelson joined the fleet off Cadiz on the 28th. 'A sort of general joy', according to Codrington, 'was the consequence of his arrival'; for Collingwood and his system had not been popular among the captains of the fleet; and the same authority goes on to pay tribute to the 'superiority of Lord Nelson in all these social arrangements which bind his captains to their admiral'. On the two days following his arrival he entertained his flag-officers and captains to dinner and explained to them the brilliant and audacious plan which, with certain modifications, formed the basis of the British tactics at Trafalgar. Several days later the discussion of 29–30 September was embodied in the famous Memorandum of 9 October, described by Thursfield as 'the last tactical word of the greatest master of sea tactics the world has ever known, the final and flawless disposition of sailing-ships marshalled for combat'. It was Nelson's intention to bring such overwhelming force against a part of the enemy's line (*the rear and centre*) as to destroy it in time to deal with the remainder (*the van*) before nightfall. This was to be done by dividing the fleet into two squadrons, one of which was to surround and destroy the enemy's rear, while the other first contained the van and then overwhelmed the centre. The overriding importance of the time factor is seen in the emphasis laid on 'bringing the Enemy to Battle in such a manner as to make the business decisive', to which end it was laid down that 'the Order of Sailing is to be the Order of Battle'. 'Something must be left to chance,' wrote Nelson; 'nothing is sure in a Sea Fight beyond all others. Shot will carry away the masts and yards of friends as well as foes; but I look with confidence to a Victory before the Van of the Enemy could succour their *friends* [in the Rear]. . . . But, in case', he added, 'Signals can neither be seen or perfectly understood, no Captain can do very wrong if he places his Ship alongside that of an Enemy.'[1]

Such in essence was the 'Nelson touch', embodying as it did a daring and revolutionary method of attack based on a right assessment of the fighting value of the British ships compared with that of their

[1] Add. MSS. 37,953.

opponents. For, though few of the crews at present under his command had been with him in the Mediterranean, such was the compelling power of Nelson's leadership that, within the short space of three weeks, the whole fleet was wrought into a superb, perfectly tempered instrument of war.

'Such a fleet as Lord Nelson will have in another week,' exclaimed Blackwood, who, on his arrival off Cadiz on 29 September had been appointed to command the frigate squadron stationed inshore to watch the motions of the enemy, 'indeed as he has already, England never sent out before.' 'In our several stations, my dear Admiral,' observed Nelson to Knight on the following day, 'we must all put our shoulders to the wheel, and make the great machine of the Fleet entrusted to our charge go on smoothly.' Once again he was consciously aiming to revive the 'band of brothers' tradition handed down from the Nile. 'We can, my dear Coll., have no little jealousies,' he exhorted his second-in-command. 'We have only one great object in view, that of annihilating our Enemies, and getting a glorious Peace for our Country.'

In those mellow autumn days while the fleet lay off Cadiz admirals and captains crowded one after another into the great cabin of the *Victory* which, long years ago, had echoed to the joyous chatter and laughter of Betsey and Jenny Wynne. The three weeks which were all that now remained to Nelson after his forty-seventh birthday on 29 September were, perhaps, the happiest of his life. Around him were his old and trusted comrades of St. Vincent and the Nile: Collingwood, Louis, Fremantle, Hallowell, and, above all, Hardy—Hardy, the closest of all Nelson's friends, who for years had been a tower of strength to him, who had taken part in all his principal actions, and who was to remain with him to the end. It was very nearly the conclusion of that glorious era which had opened ten years earlier. Only the faithful Tom Allen was missing—Tom Allen, who was his link with far-off Burnham Thorpe, who had been the Admiral's *wally de cham*, and (as he was fond of relating) had followed his fortunes 'in fourteen skrimmages and fifteen reg'lar engagements'.[1]

Early in October most of the captains had their ships painted in the Mediterranean style—the hulls black, with a yellow band, or strake, along each tier of ports, but with black port-lids: so that when closed they produced a striking chequer-board effect. During the next

[1] *Nelsonian Reminiscences*, ed. W. H. Long (1905), p. 276.

fortnight or so nearly every ship in the fleet was decorated in this way. 'I have been employed this week past', observed Captain Duff of the *Mars*, 'to paint the ship *à la Nelson*, which most of the fleet are doing.' 'We are all busy', wrote Fremantle to his wife Betsey, 'scraping our ship's sides to new paint them in the way Lord Nelson paints the *Victory*.'

It was Nelson's aim to deprive the enemy of essential supplies by a close coastal blockade, and at the same time to conceal the full strength of his fleet by withdrawing the main body fifty miles out into the Atlantic, where he could command the entrance to the Straits. Meanwhile the *Euryalus* and the other frigates were to keep constant watch on the enemy in Cadiz.

In Captain the Hon. Henry Blackwood, who had so greatly distinguished himself while in the *Brilliant* in an engagement against the *Regenerée* off Santa Cruz in 1798 and while in the *Penelope*, two years later, in the pursuit of the huge *Guillaume Tell*, he had a heaven-sent frigate captain. 'Those who know more of Cadiz than either you or I do,' he urged Blackwood on 9 October, 'say, that after those Levanters, come several days of fine weather, sea-breezes Westerly, land wind at night; and that if the Enemy are bound into the Mediterranean they would come out at night, which they have always done, . . . and catch the sea-breezes at the Mouth of the Gut, and push through whilst we might have little wind in the offing. In short, watch all points, and all winds and weathers, for I shall depend upon you.' And on the following day—'Keep your five frigates, *Weazle* and *Pickle* and let me know every movement.'[1]

The reinforcement which had been promised him by the Admiralty was anxiously awaited during these critical weeks before Trafalgar. 'I am *very, very, very* anxious for its arrival', Nelson had written on 6 October, 'for the thing will be done if a few more days elapse; and I want for the sake of our Country that it should be done as effectually as to have done nothing to wish for . . . it is, as Mr. Pitt knows, annihilation that the Country wants, and not merely a splendid Victory of twenty-three to thirty-six,—honourable to the parties concerned, but absolutely useless in the extended scale to bring Buonaparte to his marrow-bones; numbers only can annihilate.'[2] Gradually his

[1] *Nelson's Dispatches*, VII, p. 96.
[2] *Ibid.*, VII, p. 80.

strength increased. On the 13th his old ship, the *Agamemnon*, was signalled. Her captain was Sir Edward Berry, who had accompanied Nelson in the boarding of the *San Nicolas* and the *San Josef* at St. Vincent and who had been his flag-captain at the Nile, and the captor of the *Guillaume Tell*. Berry was reputed to have assisted in more fleet actions than any other captain in the Navy. 'Here comes Berry,' exclaimed the Admiral, rubbing his 'fin' with glee; 'now we shall have a battle.'[1] There were now with Nelson twenty-seven of the line including seven three-deckers.

To forestall the Allied offensive in Italy, Napoleon ordered the Combined Fleet into the Mediterranean, there to join hands with the Spanish force in Cartagena and to transport troops to Naples. His intention was for the Combined Fleet to cooperate with St. Cyr's army in southern Italy to resist the expected Anglo-Russian invasion. At the same time he sent orders for Villeneuve to be succeeded by Admiral Rosily. The former, on hearing of his supersession, and learning that several of Nelson's ships were within the Straits, determined to sail with the first fair wind.

On the 19th the wind came light and southerly. Shortly after daybreak the signal was made by the *Sirius*, the frigate closest inshore: 'Enemy have their topsail yards hoisted.' An hour later the first of the enemy's ships were coming out of port. The news flashed from ship to ship. By 9.30 Nelson, then nearly fifty miles to the westward of Cadiz, had received the signal and ordered: 'General chase, south-east.' At noon the weather was clear and the sea calm.[2]

On the following morning the dawn revealed a threatening sky, thick rainy weather, and the British fleet sailing under close-reefed topsails, with the wind S.S.W. The enemy was nowhere to be seen: but Blackwood and the other frigate captains were certain of his general position behind the drifting veils of haze.

7

Owing to delay in getting out of harbour it was not until noon on the 20th that the whole of the Combined Fleet had cleared Cadiz, and that

[1] According to tradition, what Nelson actually said was, 'Here comes that d – d fool Berry'.
[2] Adm. 52/3699, 52/3711, 19 October 1805.

afternoon stood to the southward. Nelson steered for the Gut of Gibraltar to head them off from the Mediterranean; then, not finding them there, stood back to the north-west. During the morning of the 20th it was thick south-westerly weather with heavy rain. Shortly after noon, the weather clearing up a little, the *Euryalus* sighted the enemy to leeward under low sail on the larboard tack, and so close that she immediately went about and made all possible sail to look out for the British fleet in the S.S.W.[1]

Throughout the 20th and the night of the 20th–21st the rival battle-fleets did not come within sight of each other; and the British frigates dogging the enemy could see their own fleet only from the mast-head. In the late afternoon Blackwood reported: 'The enemy appears determined to push to the westward.' Nelson replied: 'I rely upon your keeping sight of the enemy.'

The Admiral was at this time walking on the poop; happening to observe a group of midshipmen assembled near him, he said to them with a smile, 'This day, or to-morrow, will be a fortunate one for you, young men.' Later at dinner he told some of these midshipmen, 'To-morrow I will do that which will give you younger gentlemen something to talk and think about for the rest of your lives.' A fleet action was now certain.

Just before nine o'clock that evening Nelson wore and stood to the south-west. During the hours of darkness the enemy held their course to the southward, watched by the pursuing frigates, while some nine or ten miles to windward the British fleet stood on under topsails and foresails, anxiously awaiting daylight. With the advantage of the wind, they could attack the Combined Fleet when they pleased. Throughout the night Blackwood, keeping two or three miles upon the enemy's weather beam, constantly informed the Admiral of their position by means of guns, blue lights, and rockets, as did also the other look-out frigates. At midnight the body of the enemy fleet lay about three miles to the south-east, and the British fleet '5 or 6 miles to the southward and eastward'. According to a young midshipman in the *Euryalus*:

For two days there was not a movement that we did not communicate, till I thought that Blackwood, who gave the orders, and Bruce, our signal

[1] Adm. 52/3752, 21 October 1805.

midshipman, and Soper, our signal man, who executed them, must have died of it; and when we had brought the two fleets fairly together we took our place between the lines of lights, as a cab might in Regent-street, the watch was called, and Blackwood turned in quietly to wait for the morning.[1]

Meanwhile Villeneuve, apprised of the rockets and signal-guns that had been seen and heard ahead, at about 7.30 p.m. ordered the Combined Fleet, which had been sailing in three columns, to form a single line of battle. In the ensuing confusion some of the duller sailors dropped astern and the various squadrons became mixed together.

The morning of 21 October was calm and clear. A long westerly swell was setting into the Bay of Cadiz, and the wind at W.N.W. was light and failing. During the last two days the fine autumnal weather had shown signs of breaking up; and the sullen swell rolling in from the west was the certain precursor of a gale—'the dog before his master', as the west country fishermen say. The sun rising behind Cape Trafalgar shone down upon a smooth sea and the freshly painted hulls of the long line of French and Spanish battleships stretching out along the entire eastern horizon. 'It was a beautiful sight when their line was completed,' related Midshipman Lovell of the *Neptune*: 'their broadsides turned towards us, showing their iron teeth.' Soon after six Nelson made the signal to form order of sailing in two columns—the weather and lee divisions, comprising twelve and fifteen of the line respectively. The latter, led by Collingwood in the *Royal Sovereign*, was to attack the last twelve ships of the enemy's line, while the former, led by Nelson in the *Victory*, was, first, to threaten their leading ships so as to prevent them from going to the assistance of the rear, and, second, to envelop and destroy their centre. At the same time Nelson altered course to cut the enemy off from Cadiz.

At 6.50 the *Victory* bore up to the eastward, shook the reefs out of her topsails, set studding-sails and royals, and cleared for quarters. One of the marine officers of the *Belleisle* has related how he was awakened that morning by the cheers of the seamen and their swarming up the hatchways to get a glimpse of the enemy fleet. He describes the scene on the gun-decks as the men stood at quarters: 'Some were

[1] Sir Hercules Robinson, *Sea Drift* (1858), p. 209.

stripped to the waist; some had bared their necks and arms; others had tied a handkerchief round their heads; and all seemed eagerly to await the order to engage.' Another marine officer, belonging to the *Ajax*, depicts a similar scene on board his own ship. 'The men were variously occupied; some were sharpening their cutlasses, others polishing the guns, as though an inspection were about to take place instead of a mortal combat, whilst three or four, as if in mere bravado, were dancing a hornpipe; but all seemed deeply anxious to come to close quarters with the enemy. Occasionally they would look out of the ports, and speculate as to the various ships of the enemy, many of which had been on former occasions engaged by our vessels.' On board the *Bellerophon* the ship's company had chalked on their guns the words: '*Bellerophon! Death or glory!*'[1] At eight o'clock the Combined Fleet wore together and stood northward towards Cadiz. But it was impossible for them now to avoid a general engagement. Indeed, they showed no sign of desiring to do so.

An hour later, accompanied by his four frigate captains, who had been summoned on board to receive final instructions, Nelson made the round of the different decks of the *Victory* and addressed the men at quarters. In the half-light of the gun-deck, by the long curving line of guns, each with their store of powder and shot and tackle laid out across the deck, the crews, stripped to the waist, watched their great leader, dressed as usual in his Admiral's weather-stained frock-coat bearing the stars of his four Orders on his left breast, go quickly by. 'So we cleared away our guns,' recounted one of the seamen of the *Victory*, 'whilst Lord Nelson went round the decks and said, "My noble lads, this will be a glorious day for England, whoever lives to see it". . . . So we piped to dinner and ate a bit of raw pork and half a pint of wine.'

Afterwards, walking on the poop with Blackwood, the Admiral showed great anxiety to close with the enemy and commented on the resolute bearing of the Combined Fleet: but added quickly, 'I'll give them such a dressing as they never had before'; regretting, at the same time, the vicinity of the land. Towards eleven Nelson left the poop and went below. Some time later the signal lieutenant, going down to the Admiral's cabin with a message, discovered him kneeling by his

[1] Joseph Allen, *Memoir of Sir William Hargood*, pp. 278–81; Edward Fraser, *Nelson's Sailors*, pp. 215–16.

desk as he entered these lines in his journal, the last that he ever wrote.

> At daylight saw the Enemy's Combined Fleet from East to E.S.E.; bore away; made the signal for Order of Sailing, and to Prepare for Battle; the Enemy with their heads to the Southward; at seven the Enemy wearing in succession.[1] May the Great God, whom I worship, grant to my Country, and for the benefit of Europe in general, a great and glorious Victory; and may no misconduct in anyone tarnish it; and may humanity after Victory be the predominant feature in the British Fleet. For myself, individually, I commit my life to Him who made me, and may his blessings light upon my endeavours for serving my Country faithfully. To him I resign myself and the just cause which is entrusted to me to defend.

The weather and lee divisions, sailing from to windward in two almost parallel lines, with all sail set stood slowly down for the enemy, who now, close-hauled on the port tack and standing to the northward, formed, as Collingwood noted, 'a crescent convexing to leeward'. Towards noon, owing to the lightness of the wind, the *Victory*, with royals and studding-sails on both sides, was making hardly more than a knot. The marine bands were playing on board the British ships as the two columns moved, ever more slowly, through the water. Owing to the supreme importance of the time factor, the oblique attack had to be abandoned for one made almost head-on[2]—thereby exposing the leading British vessels to a tremendous raking fire before they could come into action. It was for this reason that Nelson's column was headed by powerful three-deckers—the *Victory*, *Téméraire*, and *Neptune*—closely supported by four 74s, as Midshipman Lovell of the *Neptune* observed, 'their jib-booms nearly over the others' taffrails'. At 11.40 Nelson made the general signal, 'England expects that every man will do his duty'; and towards noon, as the *Fougueux* opened fire on the *Royal Sovereign*, he made his last signal, 'Engage the enemy more closely': this remained flying at the mizen topgallant mast-head of the *Victory* until shot away. About the same time the ships of both divisions similarly hoisted their colours; and every Spanish ship also

[1] But see Oliver Warner, *Portrait of Lord Nelson* (1957), p. 344.

[2] The risks of this head-on approach were greatly increased by the light and uncertain quality of the wind. However, the pronounced curve or sag in the enemy's line, as Professor Michael Lewis has pointed out, 'made Collingwood's approach much easier than it would otherwise have been, since, in advancing upon his prey, he was no longer sailing at right angles to them but at a fairly pronounced acute angle' (M. A. Lewis, *The Navy of Britain* (1948), p. 565).

hung at the end of her spanker-boom a large cross. As the *Victory* was about to enter the zone of fire, Blackwood took his leave to warn each captain to take whatever course he thought best to get quickly into action. 'God bless you, Blackwood!' exclaimed Nelson in farewell; 'I shall never speak to you again.'

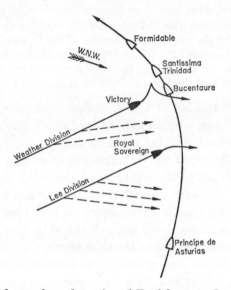

The British attack at the action of Trafalgar, 21 October 1805

Shortly before noon the *Royal Sovereign*, at a range of about 1,000 yards, came under fire of seven of the enemy's ships and suffered severe punishment until at 12.8 she broke the line between the *Santa Ana* and the *Fougueux* and discharged a double-shotted broadside into the stern of the *Santa Ana*, which disabled fourteen guns and killed or wounded nearly 400 of her men.[1] The *Royal Sovereign* ranged alongside the *Santa Ana* so close that their yard-arms locked together, thereafter coming under a murderous crossfire from the *Fougueux*,

[1] 'It was a glorious sight to see the *Royal Sovereign* commence the action,' observed Midshipman Roberts of the *Victory*. '. . . She fired a most tremendous broadside to begin with, but we did not see her but a very short time, she was soon involved in smoke, and the flash of the guns made it appear awfully grand; and at this time we could see nothing but the Royals above the clouds' (Broadley and Bartelot, *Nelson's Hardy* (1909), p. 264).

San Leandro, and others, which ceased as soon as these enemies realized that they were injuring themselves as well as the *Royal Sovereign*. Three minutes later the *Belleisle*, looming vast and spectral in the smoke, followed her leader through the gap; she fired her port broadside into the *Santa Ana* and her starboard broadside into the *Fougueux;* and then, running on board the latter, she remained closely engaged with her for upwards of an hour, assailed, like the *Royal Sovereign* before her, by a merciless cross-fire.

'The smoke was so thick in the action,' wrote a midshipman of the *Royal Sovereign*, 'we could hardly make out the French from the English.' 'They fought us pretty tightish for French and Spanish,' related one of the ship's company: '. . . to tell you the truth of it, when the game began, I wished myself at Warnborough with my plough again; but when they had given us one duster, and I find myself snug and tight, I bid fear kiss my bottom and set to in good earnest.'

Soon the enemy's line was also broken lower down. The *Algésiras* then tried to cross the stern of the *Tonnant*. 'She filled her Main Top sail,' observed Lieutenant Clement of the *Tonnant*, 'and shot up to rake us, but we put our helm up and tumbled on board of her and fought it out.' At 12.20 the *Tonnant* passed between the *Algésiras* and the *Monarca;* she fired her starboard broadside into the *Algésiras*, and her port broadside into the *Monarca*, and continued to engage these two ships for the next quarter of an hour. 'Our guns were all double-shotted,' wrote another of the *Tonnant*'s officers. 'The order was given to fire; being so close, every shot was poured into their hulls, and down came the Frenchman's mizenmast, and after our second broadside the Spaniard's fore and crossjack yards.' When shortly after one the *Monarca* hauled off and dropped astern, about half her people had been killed or wounded.

By about 12.30 the first eight ships of Collingwood's division were in close action with their opponents. For want of a breeze to carry it off, the murky powder-smoke from hundreds of guns rolled in an ever-thickening cloud over the rear of the Combined Fleet, increasing the confusion into which it had fallen. During the ensuing fighting the course made good by the enemy rear gradually became more easterly than northerly. The *Bellerophon*, passing through the line about this time, was shortly after caught between the *Bahama, Mon-*

tanes, *Aigle*, and *Swiftsure*. Forty minutes later her captain was killed, and her first lieutenant, William Pryce Cumby, assumed command. The *Bellerophon* at this time, observed Cumby, had suffered severely, and 'was totally unmanageable, the main and mizen-topmasts hanging over the side, the jib-boom, spanker-boom and gaff shot away, and not a trace or bowline serviceable.' At 12.40 the *Colossus*, looming up out of the smoke, opened fire on the *Argonaute* with her starboard, and on the French *Swiftsure* with her port, guns. Ten minutes later the *Argonaute* broke off the action and ran to leeward, having lost nearly half her ship's company. At 1.10 the *Fougueux* shot away the *Belleisle's* mizen mast and, drifting clear, poured her port broadside into the stern of the *Mars*, shattering her sails and rigging and killing her captain. 'In a few minutes', recorded Midshipman Robinson of the *Mars*, 'our poop was totally cleared, the quarter-deck nearly the same, and only the Boatswain and myself left alive.' The *Mars* paid off, thereby exposing her stern to a heavy raking broadside from the *Pluton*, which left her practically a wreck; she drifted helplessly away to the north-eastward.

By 1.20 the three rear ships of the Combined Fleet—the *Principe de Asturias* (flagship of the Spanish Commander-in-Chief, Admiral Don Frederico Gravina), *Berwick*, and *San Juan Nepomuceno*—had not yet been brought to close action; but the *Defiance* and the *Dreadnought* were closing in on them.

During the first phase of the action the weather division kept Dumanoir and his squadron in a state of uncertainty as to the direction of the British attack, and, favoured by the lightness of the wind, prevented them intervening until it was too late. Finally the *Victory*, after making a feint of falling upon the van, hauled to starboard and steered for the enemy's centre, raked, as she slowly advanced, by the fire of several hundred guns, to which she could make no reply. The carnage on board the flagship was terrific; before she fired a shot, a single ball slew eight of the marines drawn up on the poop; another, narrowly missing the Admiral, smashed his secretary, Scott, to mangled pulp; within a few moments she had fifty killed and wounded, had lost her mizen topmast, and had her wheel shot away (she was afterwards steered from the gun-room, the first lieutenant and the master 'relieving each other at this duty'). Still the *Victory*, enduring 'such a fire as had scarcely before been directed at a single ship', held on her course.[1] For a full half-hour her crew sustained this ordeal, reserving their fire, until, at 12.30, crossing the wake of the French flagship, they almost shattered the stern of the *Bucentaure* with a treble-shotted broadside at a range of thirty feet, and then, breaking the line, ran aboard the *Redoutable*.

As in the midst of that hail of fire Nelson and Hardy paced up and down the quarter-deck of the *Victory*, a shot, plunging into the fore brace bitts, flung up a shower of splinters, one of which struck and bruised Hardy's foot. The two friends looked at each other. Nelson smiled and said, 'This is too warm work, Hardy, to last'. At the same time he commended the coolness and resolution of the men at their guns.

Villeneuve had found an able second in the French *Neptune*, which, just as the *Victory*'s bows opened clear of the *Bucentaure*'s stern, poured into them a most destructive fire. The *Téméraire*, following her leader through a tempest of fire, was soon in much the same condition as the *Victory*. The *Redoutable* had brought down her mizen mast and the French *Neptune* her foreyard and maintopmast, and severely damaged her sails and rigging.

The *Victory* was by now wholly enshrouded in smoke, through which, at intervals, loomed the hulls and rigging of the enemy ships surrounding her. Down in her gloomy cockpit, beneath the swinging horn-lanterns, the scene of horror and suffering was such that it haunted her chaplain for years afterwards—'It was like a butcher's shambles'. At last, unable to bear it any longer, the chaplain rushed up the blood-stained companion-ladder and gained the upper deck, where, amid 'all noise, confusion, and smoke', he saw Nelson fall, on the same spot where his secretary, Scott, had been killed an hour earlier. 'They have done for me at last, Hardy,' the Admiral said to his friend bending over him. '. . . My back-bone is shot through.' As the men were carrying him below, Nelson covered his face and the decorations on his breast with a handkerchief, so that he might not be recognized. It was shortly after a quarter-past one.

About ten minutes later the *Redoutable* attempted without success to board the *Victory;* both ships then fell aboard the *Téméraire*,

[1] Never, declared Villeneuve after the action, had he seen anything like the irresistible line of the British ships; 'but that of the *Victory*, supported by the *Neptune* and *Téméraire*, was what he could not have formed any judgment of' (*Nelson's Dispatches*, VII, pp. 226–7).

whose broadside immediately cleared the *Redoutable*'s upper-deck, killing or wounding about 200 men. Following the *Téméraire*, the *Neptune*, *Leviathan*, *Conqueror*, *Britannia*, *Ajax*, and *Agamemnon* came successively into action. The *Orion*, however, hauled out to starboard and went to the support of Collingwood's division, moving in stern and disciplined silence into the heart of the battle—'the *Agamemnon* far astern of us', commented Codrington, 'blazing away and wasting her ammunition.'

The action was now at its height. The mile-long line of fighting ships was all but enveloped in a billowing cloud of smoke and flame out of which rolled the reverberating thunder of the broadsides, punctuated by the sudden splintering crash of falling spars. 'There never was such a Combat', Codrington wrote afterwards, 'since England had a Fleet.' The two great squadrons were locked together in a struggle to the death. Codrington, as he bore down on the enemy in the *Orion*, called all his lieutenants up on deck to behold a spectacle none of them would ever forget to the end of their lives. 'After passing *Santa Ana* dismasted', he related, 'and her opponent, the *Royal Sovereign*, little better, on our larboard side, besides three of our ships and some of those of the enemy all lumped together on our starboard bow, we passed close to the *Victory*, *L'Indomptable* (Fr.), *Téméraire*, and *Bucentaure* (Fr.), all abreast or aboard each other, each firing her broadside and boarding the other at the same time. . . . We were the only people who could have a distinct uninterrupted view of that grand and awful scene. The shot from both friends and foes were flying about us like hailstones, and yet did us hardly any damage whatever.'[1]

Several of the enemy's ships, especially the *Redoutable*, put up a magnificent fight. Out of a crew of less than 600, she had 491 killed and 81 wounded. The *Intrépide* had nearly as many casualties as the *Redoutable*. 'Her captain surrendered after one of the most gallant defences I ever witnessed,' wrote Lieutenant Senhouse of the *Conqueror*. '. . . The *Intrépide* was the last ship that struck her colours about half-past five.' For three hours the *Redoutable*, assisted by the French *Neptune*, engaged two first-rates, the *Victory* and the *Téméraire*, effectually checking their advance and preventing them from joining in the fighting ahead.

[1] Bourchier, *The Life of Sir Edward Codrington* (1873), I, p. 64.

But the resistance of the centre was speedily overwhelmed by the crushing superiority of the British fire at close range, with the result that soon after 2 o'clock the action in the centre was virtually over. Too late, Villeneuve at 1.30 had signalled the van to wear. At 1.40 the *Conqueror* brought down the *Bucentaure*'s main and mizen masts. Colliding with the *Trinidad*, the *Bucentaure* next carried away her bowspit, and soon after her foremast fell.

'The greater part of our guns were already dismasted,' observed Villeneuve, 'and others were disabled or masked by the fall of the masts and rigging. Now, for one moment, the smoke-fog cleared and I saw that all the centre and rear had given way. . . . All the fleet astern of the *Bucentaure* was, as I have said, broken up. Many ships were dismasted; others were still fighting, in retreat towards a body of ships to the east.'

At 1.45 the *Bucentaure*, now helpless, with all three masts and bowsprit shot away and half her ship's company killed or wounded, struck her colours. 'Our ship was so riddled,' her captain related, 'that she seemed to be no more than a mass of wreckage.' A few minutes later the *Fougueux*, emerging from the smoke to the southward, received, at a range of about 100 yards, the *Téméraire*'s starboard broadside—then, shattered and helpless, with most of her people killed or wounded, and all her guns dismounted, she drifted aboard the *Téméraire*, where she was immediately lashed by her fore rigging to the latter ship's spare anchor. Within ten minutes she was boarded and carried. At a quarter-past two the *Victory* broke away from the *Redoutable*. The *Redoutable, Téméraire*, and *Fougueux* now swung round to the southward, and almost at once the main and mizen masts of the *Redoutable* came crashing down, the mainmast falling on board the *Téméraire*'s poop. Five minutes later a boarding-party, headed by the second lieutenant of the *Téméraire*, swarming across on the fallen spar, took possession of the *Redoutable*, whose heroic resistance had enabled the van to escape and the French *Neptune* and two of the Spaniards to go to the assistance of the hard-pressed rear. When the *Bucentaure* struck, the *Santissima Trinidad* made sail to draw clear of the enemies encircling her; but soon after she was raked by the *Neptune*, losing her main and mizen masts; after which the *Neptune* luffed up alongside her, and the *Conqueror* opened a distant fire upon her to windward; finally, at 2.12, the *Santissima Trinidad*'s foremast fell. Soon after, the *Santissima Trinidad* ceased firing and lay an unmanageable wreck upon the water. The dismasting of the giant Spaniard was described in a letter from one of the officers on board the *Conqueror*.

> This tremendous fabric gave a deep roll, with a swell to leeward, then back to windward, and on her return every mast went by the board, leaving her an unmanageable hulk on the water. Her immense topsails had every reef out; her royals were sheeted home, but lowered; and the falling of this majestic mass of spars, sails and rigging, plunging into the water at the muzzles of our guns, was one of the most magnificent sights I ever beheld.[1]

By about two o'clock the resistance of the rear was nearly at an end. By cutting the line at the sixteenth, instead of the twelfth ship from the rear, Collingwood had of course sacrificed numerical superiority in order to gain time. But the British superiority in seamanship, gunnery, and discipline enabled him to carry out the task which had been allotted to him of overwhelming the enemy's rear. One after another the remainder of the lee division steered into the fight, and, engaging the enemy at close range, accounted altogether for twelve of them. Shortly before two o'clock, as the *San Juan Nepomuceno* was bearing down to rake the *Bellerophon*, the *Dreadnought* ranged up alongside her and, with a rapid succession of heavy broadsides, silenced her fire, dismounting most of her guns and bringing down her foremast and mizenmast: whereupon the *Dreadnought* sent a boat to take possession. Meanwhile the resistance of the *Santa Ana* and *Algésiras*, which had been closely engaged with the *Royal Sovereign* and *Tonnant* respectively for over an hour, was rapidly weakening. At about 2.10 the *Santa Ana*'s guns ceased firing. Close on 250 of her ship's company had been killed or wounded, and many of her guns dismounted. Her fore and mainmast fell over the side, and at 2.20 she struck her colours. The *Royal Sovereign*, though victorious, was also by this time almost a wreck. At 2.30 her mainmast fell, taking with it the mizenmast. Her foremast, too, was badly damaged. Collingwood ordered the *Euryalus* to come and tow him. At about the same time the *Algésiras*, which had likewise sustained severe injuries, and had lost more than 200 of her men, struck to the *Tonnant*. Meanwhile the *Orion*, approaching the enemy's line from to windward, was about

[1] Sir Hercules Robinson, *Sea Drift* (1858), p. 216.

to take the French *Swiftsure*, when the latter made sail and bore away, masking the guns with which one of her consorts, the *Bahama*, had hitherto been engaging the *Colossus*. The *Colossus* forthwith flung several heavy broadsides into the *Swiftsure;* and the latter fell astern. The *Colossus* thereupon engaged the *Bahama* and brought down her mainmast; and she struck. In the meantime the *Swiftsure* had attempted to wear under her enemy's stern; but the *Colossus* wore more quickly and gave the *Swiftsure* her full starboard broadside, bringing down her mizenmast; after which the *Orion*, coolly reserving her fire till running under the *Swiftsure's* stern, poured her first broadside into it. 'When the smoke cleared away,' observed the master of the *Orion* in his journal, '[we] perceived all his masts down, and his colours gone.' Hauling to the wind, the *Colossus* took possession of the *Swiftsure* and the *Bahama*, while the *Orion* stood on towards the van.

By about three o'clock the battle was declining. In the extreme rear Gravina was desperately resisting an ever-increasing concentration of Collingwood's ships. The *Belleisle*, which had been in the closest of action for nearly three hours and had lost all her masts and had her rigging and sails cut to pieces—and, with her colours still flying from the stump of her foremast, was stoutly engaging three of the enemy with every gun that could be brought to bear—was saved by the opportune arrival of the *Defiance*, *Swiftsure*, and *Polyphemus*. At 3.30 she took possession of the Spanish *Argonauta*. At about the same time the *Aigle* struck to the *Defiance*, the *San Ildefonso* to the *Defence*, and the *Berwick* to the *Achille*. At about this time, too, Gravina's flagship, the *Principe de Asturias*, which, alone of her squadron, still remained in the fight, was overhauled by the *Prince*: the latter, bearing down close under her stern, gave her two raking broadsides; and the *Principe's* guns ceased firing. At four, however, the *Prince*, with the *Dreadnought*, *Thunderer*, and *Revenge*, abandoning the pursuit of the *Principe*, beat up to the support of the ships to windward engaged with Dumanoir.

In conformity with Villeneuve's last signal, Dumanoir and the ten ships of the enemy's van had at last wore on the starboard tack; but they were split up into three groups and cut off from their centre and rear by the rear ships of Nelson's division. To cover the prizes in his rear Hardy, at about three o'clock, made the signal to form the line of battle on the port tack; whereupon the *Victory, Mars, Royal Sovereign,* and a few others successively opened fire on and eventually drove off the attackers, three of which—the *San Agustin, Intrépide,* and *Neptune* —were dismasted and forced to strike.

Down in the dimly lighted cockpit of the *Victory,* crowded with wounded and dying men, as fire was opened on Dumanoir's ships passing to windward and the *Victory*'s timbers shook to the explosion of the guns, the dying Nelson, apostophizing his ship, exclaimed, 'Oh, *Victory, Victory,* how you distract my poor brain!' and after a short pause he added, 'How dear life is to all men!' At intervals there came a burst of full-throated cheering from the decks above. 'Every ship that was seen to strike by our men they gave three cheers immediately,' observed Midshipman Roberts, 'which was re-echoed by some of the poor wounded then in the cockpit and it seemed to give new life to Lord Nelson.' To Hardy, come to congratulate him on a brilliant victory and the surrender of at least fourteen or fifteen enemy vessels, he replied, 'That is well, but I had bargained for twenty.' And then (mindful of the ominous groundswell rolling in from the Atlantic) he said urgently, in a stronger voice, '*Anchor,* Hardy, *anchor!*'

The final phase of the action consisted of a number of separate engagements fought by small groups of vessels under a blinding pall of smoke and ending in the retreat of fifteen of the enemy towards Cadiz and the south-west, the lightness of the wind much hampering the British pursuit. Eighteen of the thirty-three vessels of the Combined Fleet had been made prizes or destroyed. 'Partial firing continued until 4.30,' records the *Victory*'s log; 'when a Victory having been reported to the Right Hon. Lord Viscount Nelson, K.B., and Commander-in-Chief, he died of his wound.'[1]

Illumined by the rays of the sinking sun, the *Victory* and the crippled vessels around her, trailing their shattered sails and rigging, drifted slowly on the swell. To the southward lay the *Royal Sovereign* and a similar group of ships. In the background the remnant of the enemy fleet was making for Cadiz. 'The *Achille* had burnt to the water's edge,' says the marine officer quoted above, 'with the tricolour ensign still displayed, about a mile from us, and our tenders and boats were using every effort to save the poor fellows who had so gloriously defended her; but only two hundred and fifty were rescued, and she blew up with a tremendous explosion.' So the evening drew on—

[1] Adm. 52/3711, 21 October 1805.

with the scattered clusters of battered warships preparing as best they might to weather a night of which the angry sunset and the moaning of the wind gave an ill promise.[1]

On the day following the action it blew a southerly gale, with squalls and heavy rain. On the 23rd the gale increased and some of the prizes parted tow. On the 24th and 25th the gale continued to increase, and the British vessels, most of which were severely damaged and many dismasted, were dispersed in all directions, so that it was only by the most strenuous exertions that they could be saved; as it was no more than four of the prizes survived to reach Gibraltar. The ships which had anchored fared best in this ordeal. During this time the frigates did their full share both in preserving and destroying several of the prizes. Writing to his wife, Blackwood related:

> All yesterday and last night the majority of the British fleet have been in the most perilous state, our ships much crippled with dismasted prizes in tow, our crews tired out, and many thousands of prisoners to guard— all to be done with a gale of wind blowing us right on the shore. . . . The melancholy sights we experienced yesterday of ships driven on shore, others burning, and the rest that we have been forced to sink, after withdrawing as many men as we could for fear of their again falling into the hands of the enemy cannot be described.[2]

On 4 November, however, four of the enemy battleships which had escaped from Trafalgar were engaged by Captain Strachan near Cape Ortegal. After a long chase in thick and blowing weather, lasting until the morning of the 5th, two of Strachan's frigates hung on the quarters of the *Scipion*, the slowest of the enemy squadron, so that Dumanoir was obliged either to abandon his consort or to fight. He chose the latter course; and in the engagement which followed all the French ships were dismasted and taken. They were carried to Plymouth and eventually added to the Royal Navy. 'The subsequent action of Strachan', wrote Captain Charles Paget with satisfaction, '. . . makes the smash complete.' The remaining ten enemy ships that had survived Trafalgar never—except for a brief appearance outside Cadiz—put to sea again.

[1] J. Allen, *Memoir of Admiral Sir William Hargood* (1841), pp. 287–8; H. Robinson, *op. cit.*, p. 207.
[2] Q. *Blackwood's Magazine*, Vol. 34, p. 13.

8

'The most decisive and complete Victory that ever was gained over a powerful Enemy,' observed Collingwood, writing to the British minister at Naples a few days after the battle. '. . . The Combined Fleet is annihilated. I believe there are not more than four or five Ships in Cadiz which can be made ready for sea.' 'Yet,' he added in a later letter—'Yet this great event has been the cause of far more lamentation than joy. Never did any man's death cause so universal a sorrow as Lord Nelson's.' This note of mingled triumph and sorrow is reflected in almost all the letters which came pouring from the fleet in the aftermath of Trafalgar. Both officers and men felt, indeed, that they had suffered the most grievous personal loss in the death of Nelson. 'We have on the 21st Instant', declared Hardy, 'obtained a most Glorious Victory over the Combined Fleets, but it has cost the Country a Life that no money can replace, and one for whose Death I shall for ever mourn.' In his letters home after the battle Codrington announced, first, 'the greatest victory in our annals' and then, 'the irreparable loss of the greatest Admiral England ever knew'. 'He fell gloriously', observed a midshipman of the *Royal Sovereign*, writing home to his parents, 'just as a Briton ought to die— he has done his duty to his Country, and has gone to rest where neither war nor slaughter reach.' 'Our dear Admiral Nelson is killed!' lamented a seaman belonging to the same ship, 'so we have paid pretty sharply for licking 'em. I never set eyes on him, for which I am both sorry and glad; for, to be sure, I should like to have seen him—but then, all the men in our ship who have seen him are such soft toads, they have done nothing but blast their eyes and cry. Bless you!— chaps that fought like the devil sit down and cry like a wench.'

The *Pickle* schooner, Lieutenant Lapenotière, ordered home on 26 October with Collingwood's dispatches, was delayed for several days by baffling winds and heavy seas. On the 2nd, arriving in the chops of the Channel, she encountered calm weather and thick fog. In the small hours of the 3rd she sighted the Lizard light and in the morning brought-to off Pendennis Castle, near Falmouth,[1] where Lapenotière disembarked and set off for London in a post-chaise.

[1] Adm. 52/3669, 26 October–4 November 1805.

Approaching the city on the night of the 5th, he was further delayed by the thickest fog which London and its environs had experienced for many years. The fog extended for several miles outside the suburbs; traffic was brought almost to a standstill; the stage-coaches were hours late; the streets of the metropolis became a chaos of blinding, smothering darkness, bewildered horsemen, crawling and stationary vehicles, and flickering flames of flambeaux, from the midst of which came the 'holloing of drivers and the screams of people on foot'. It was nearly an hour after midnight, and Whitehall was well-nigh deserted, when Lapenotière's chaise at last drew up in the cobbled court of the Admiralty; and the Lieutenant, ascending the staircase below the dome which led up to the Board Room, was ushered into the presence of Charles Marsden, the Second Secretary, who that night was working late at his papers. Lapenotière's first words were: 'Sir, we have gained a great victory; but we have lost Lord Nelson!'

Old Barham and his staff were immediately roused from their beds; and the rumour of portentous tidings spread rapidly through the capital. At a very early hour the news was posted up at Lloyd's, and a *Gazette Extraordinary* appeared. Presently the Park and Tower guns began to thunder, and the church-bells to peal. The news of the victory came just at the crucial moment to raise the spirits of the people, which were depressed by the recent disastrous defeat of the Austrians at Ulm. 'The battle of Cadiz', the *Morning Post* exclaimed, 'cannot fail to impress on our enemies a deep and indelible sense of the invincible title by which we hold the sovereignty of the seas.'

Throughout the whole country there was the same intimate mingling of pride and poignant grief which the fleet had experienced a fortnight earlier. At Brighton Mrs. Codrington's servant burst suddenly into the room and told her 'there has been a great action and Lord Nelson was dead'. 'The Newspaper Offices were besieged in an unexampled manner,' recorded the *Hampshire Telegraph;* 'indeed, no detail can describe the general emotion excited by the two events, by the victory and the death, which was its too dear price. This does honor to the British people, honor to their character.' 'I never saw so little public joy,' said Lord Malmesbury. 'The illumination seemed dim, and as if it were half clouded by the desire of expressing the mixture of contending feelings; every common person in the streets speaking first of their sorrow for Nelson, and then of the victory.' 'This day,' the future Duchess of Devonshire declared, 'will be ever memorable for the greatest victory, and the greatest loss this country ever knew.' 'Poor Nelson!' observed Betsey Fremantle sorrowfully; 'had he survived, it would have been glorious indeed. Regret at his death is more severely felt than joy at the destruction of the Combined Fleets.'

During the evening of the 6th the mail-coaches, dressed in shining laurel, rolled out of Lombard Street to carry the tidings of the victory and the death of Nelson through the length and breadth of the kingdom. In country towns and villages there was ringing of churchbells and tapping of beer barrels.[1] For the next two nights London was brilliantly illuminated; but throughout all these rejoicings there was an air of sorrowful recollection. At Drury Lane the interlude of *The Victory and Death of Lord Nelson*—which, it was said, 'seemed to affect the audience exceedingly'—was put on; and at Covent Garden, after the opera, all the principals came forward and sang 'Rule, Britannia', with the whole audience joining in the chorus. The mourning for Nelson by all classes of the population was deep and sincere. 'Not a Peasant have I met since the disastrous Story has been told', a friend wrote to Nelson's nephew, George Matcham, 'that has not with a warmth which I scarce conceived them capable of, enquired the Truth of the disastrous Event & on receiving the painful Confirmation, the poor Fellows have hung their Heads and mourned the fallen Flower of English Manhood.'[2] 'The feelings of grief and regret for the loss of your incomparable Admiral,' Josiah Wedgwood observed to Captain Tyler, 'were so general and so strong as quite to check and abate the delight that the victory would otherwise have created in all our bosoms.'[3]

'His career of services had been long,' summed up the *Sheffield Mercury;* 'but it was only in the last war that he burst upon the eye

---

[1] In Captain Hardy's native Dorset young William Roberts wrote to his sailor brother on board the *Victory*: 'We had bell ringing and beer drinking the night that we received the list of the killed and wounded, and likewise when we received your letter. The colours were hoisted on the tower. Mother had hard work to keep the beer barrel a running. . . . All the Bridport Volunteers went to Church on Thanksgiving Day' (*Q.* Broadley and Bartelot, *Nelson's Hardy*, pp. 268–9).

[2] *Q.* J. Eyre-Matcham, *The Nelsons of Burnham Thorpe*, p. 239.

[3] *Q.* Wyndham-Quin, *Sir Charles Tyler* (1912).

of the public as a luminary of the first magnitude. At the battle of Aboukir, he rose like the sun in the east, and like the sun too, after a summer's day of cloudless glory, he set in the west, at the battle of Trafalgar, leaving the ocean in a blaze as he went down, and in darkness when he descended.'

On 9 December the Lord Mayor's procession of barges up-river to Westminster was followed by the customary banquet at the Guildhall. The day was fine and the streets were thronged. In Cheapside the horses were taken from Pitt's carriage, and he was drawn in triumph through cheering crowds to the Guildhall. That evening, to a brilliant assembly seated below inscriptions of *Nelson and Victory*, Pitt replied, when they toasted him as the deliverer of Europe, in the shortest speech of his career. 'England', he declared, 'was not to be saved by any single man. England has saved herself by her exertions and will, I trust, save Europe by her example.'

9

On 4 December the *Victory* arrived at St. Helens with Nelson's body. 'It is', wrote Hardy, 'a distressing sight to now see the Ships Flags and Pendants half Mast on the melancholly occasion.' The *Victory* was sent round to Sheerness, whence the body was carried up the river to Greenwich. For three days it lay in state in the Painted Hall, where thousands came to visit it. On the 8th the coffin was taken down to the waterside and placed on board the State Barge, which was followed, in single line, by many other barges carrying the Lord Mayor of London and other great men, besides Admiral Sir Peter Parker, the Chief Mourner, and other senior officers of Nelson's own Service.

Favoured by the flood, though opposed by the wind, the procession moved slowly up the river to London, with every flag at half-mast and the boats of the River Fencibles firing minute guns the whole way from Greenwich to Whitehall Stairs. Not a ship or a boat was allowed to disturb the solemn order of the procession. All the premises over-looking the waterway were densely crowded with spectators; a large number of these were in deep mourning, the black mantles, bonnets, and muffs of the women being particularly noticeable. In fact, not only the shore, but also the decks, yards, masts, and rigging of the numerous vessels in the river were pressed into service as grand-stands; and during the time the procession was passing, the streets of London were almost deserted. At half-past three the procession arrived at Whitehall Stairs. There also great crowds had assembled—in the streets, at the windows, and even on the roof-tops overlooking the route—to view 'the Arrival of the Body'. At about four o'clock the coffin was slowly carried into the Admiralty. The scene is graphically described by the future Duchess of Devonshire, who was present among the many thousands of onlookers.

> ... soon we heard distant music and distinguished the Dead March in Saul—all besides was profound silence—the music sounded louder and louder—at last a murmur was heard of 'Hats off!' 'Hats off!' was repeated on all sides—the procession entered the great gates—the trumpets drew up and continued playing—the attendants, the Admirals and officers bearing his flags, in solemn slow pace, scarcely heard on the sand which had been everywhere spread, advanced to the Admiralty doors through the great columns.[1]

The coffin lay during the night of the 8th–9th in the Captains' Room, attended by Nelson's favourite chaplain, Dr. Scott. An immense crowd waited outside the Admiralty during the evening, and until a late hour that night.

The following morning, as early as between three and four o'clock, large numbers of people were hurrying along the darkened streets, intent on securing places on the route of the procession. The preparations in the streets between the Admiralty and St. Paul's had gone on, almost without intermission, during the whole of the night. All wheeled traffic within the area was prohibited. A small army of men was employed in scattering sand. An hour before daybreak the drums of the volunteer corps stationed in the metropolis beat to arms; the summons was promptly obeyed; and shortly after, these troops lined the streets two-deep along the route of the procession. At half-past eight the great bell of St. Paul's began to toll. It was a fine frosty morning. The sun shone down from a pale blue January sky on a scene that was to have no parallel for close on a hundred years. Not until the death of Queen Victoria in 1901, in fact, was the metropolis again to behold anything comparable to the funeral of Lord Nelson.

The procession was headed by 10,000 regular troops led by General

[1] Q. D. M. Stuart, *Dearest Bess* (1955), p. 131.

Sir David Dundas. They were followed by several hundred mourning carriages in which rode the Princes of the Blood and many of the first men in the realm. More than thirty Admirals and a hundred Captains attended the greatest naval commander in history to his last resting-place. At Temple Bar they were joined by the Lord Mayor and his train, who took their place after the Prince of Wales. The procession was so long that the Scots Greys who marched at the head of it were entering the cathedral before the officers of the Navy and Army who brought up the rear had even left the Admiralty. To the sorrowful strains of the 'Dead March in Saul' played on the fifes and muffled drums, it moved forward at a slow and solemn pace. The entire procession took more than three and a half hours to pass.

The windows and balconies all along the route were black with spectators, and every inch of standing room on the pavements was filled. For days people had been flocking in from the country to witness Nelson's funeral. 'Town was never so full.' The behaviour of this vast concourse of onlookers of all ranks was surprisingly quiet and orderly. It was said that a greater degree of decorum was observed than was ever before noticed in so great a multitude.

The most interesting part of the cavalcade, however, and that which seemed to make the strongest impression on the crowd, was the company of four dozen seamen from the *Victory* who marched ahead of the carriages bearing the two shot-scarred Union Jacks and the St. George's ensign belonging to the flagship. The sight of these sturdy, weather-beaten tars in their well-loved uniform made a stronger appeal to the sympathies of the onlookers than all the pomp and pageantry of the procession.

It was not only the common people who thought this way. 'It was magnificent,' related Mrs. Codrington, who, as one of the 'wives of Trafalgar', was privileged to witness the funeral service in the cathedral; 'it was solemn and impressive to the last degree'; yet, as she had to admit, 'the part that spoke to my heart most powerfully (and that I must acknowledge did touch me deeply) was when the sailors of the *Victory* brought in Nelson's colours; and this I attribute to its being the only thing that was *Nelson*—the rest was so much the *Herald's Office.*'

The coffin was carried into the cathedral at two p.m., and the service lasted for nearly four hours. Dusk had deepened into darkness when the choir took up the concluding anthem: *His Body Is Buried in peace*, and the response soared triumphantly into the shadowy recesses under the vas tdome: *But His Name Liveth Evermore.* At half-past five the coffin was lowered into the grave, in which the flags of the *Victory*, furled up by the seamen, were also deposited. (But not, it is stated, before these 'brave fellows . . . desirous of retaining some memorials of their great and favourite Commander' had torn off a considerable part of the ensign, of which all managed to secure a small portion.) The long service came to an end shortly before six o'clock, though it was not until nine that the cathedral was completely cleared.

'Thus terminated', the *Naval Chronicle* declared, 'one of the most impressive and most splendid solemnities that ever took place in this Country, or perhaps in Europe.'

CHAPTER

XI

The Continental System

I

With the destruction of the Combined Fleet at Trafalgar ended, for all practical purposes, Napoleon's attempts to contest the control of the sea. The enemy fell back upon mere commerce raiding, which, although sufficiently destructive to British shipping, could never be a decisive factor in the struggle. The Admiralty decided that the close blockade of the French and Spanish ports could now be safely relaxed. 'It is to little purpose now', Barham declared, 'to wear out our ships in a fruitless blockade during the winter.' Frigates were accordingly disposed outside Brest and the Passage du Raz; Cornwallis's squadron abandoned the post off Ushant where they had cruised so long, and spent most of the ensuing months in Torbay or at Falmouth. The overwhelming preponderance of the British Fleet—there were at this time over a hundred sail of the line in commission—confined the victorious arms of France to Continental Europe. Within four years of Trafalgar our enemy was to lose a further twenty-three of the line and thirty frigates. Never before or since has the sea power of Great Britain attained to such a position of absolute and untrammelled supremacy as in the decade succeeding Trafalgar.

Early in the following year the French Navy sustained another severe blow. On 13 December 1805 about half the Brest fleet had got safely away to sea. Six of these ships under Rear-Admiral Willaumez shaped a course for the South Atlantic to attack British trade between St. Helena and the Cape. Five others under Rear-Admiral Leissègues sailed for the West Indies. Two British squadrons, commanded respectively by Sir John Borlase Warren and Sir Richard Strachan, were promptly sent out after them; but without success. Meanwhile Vice-Admiral Sir John Duckworth, blockading the remnants of the Combined Fleet in Cadiz, received news of a hostile squadron in the vicinity of Madeira. Imagining this to be Allemand's, he sailed in pursuit—but, sighting Willaumez's division on 26 December, unaccountably let them get away. He next sailed for the Leeward Islands, where he was joined by Rear-Admiral Alexander Cochrane (then in command on that station) and soon after received news of a French squadron lying off San Domingo. At daybreak on 6 February Duckworth came in sight of the enemy anchored in Occa Bay, at the eastern end of the island, where Leissègues was engaged in landing troops and stores for the relief of the French garrison. The French immediately slipped their cables and retired to the westward. Duckworth's squadron, formed in two lines, steered to cut the course of the three leading French ships—Leissègues's flagship and his two seconds.

Shortly after 10 a.m. the *Superb*, which was Duckworth's flagship, closely supported by the *Northumberland* and the *Agamemnon*, closed upon the bow of the *Alexandre*, the leading French ship, and commenced the action; but after three broadsides she sheered off. Leissègues's flagship, the *Impérial*, which had already badly mauled the *Northumberland*, was then engaged by the *Superb;* and the British superiority in gunnery and seamanship left the issue in little doubt.

'By this time', wrote Duckworth in his dispatch, 'the movements of the *Alexandre* had thrown her among the lee division, which Rear-Admiral Louis happily availed himself of, and the action became general, and continued with great severity till half-past eleven, when the French admiral, much shattered and completely beaten, hauled direct for the land, and, not being a mile off, at twenty minutes before noon ran on shore, his foremast then only standing, which fell directly on her striking; at which time the *Superb*, being only in 7 fathoms water, was forced to haul off to avoid the same evil; but, not long after, the *Diomède* . . . pushed inshore near his admiral, when all his masts went.'[1]

Two of the enemy's ships (one of them, the *Impérial*, the finest first-rate in the French Navy) were thus driven ashore and later burnt by their captors, and the remaining three were captured; only the frigates escaped.

The division under Willaumez, after achieving some minor successes, was dispersed: its component ships were either lost, or interned in American ports, or else returned singly to Europe.

[1] *London Dispatch*, 24 March 1806.

In the Mediterranean, Collingwood's immediate concern was to keep watch on the enemy's squadrons shut up in Cadiz and Cartagena. Though he had few ships, and those few were in bad repair, he refused to withdraw from his post. 'The blockade of Cadiz has never been remitted for one moment,' declared the Admiral, writing on board the *Queen*, off Cartagena, on 4 December: 'for, considering how precarious an anchorage Gibraltar Bay is at this season, I kept the sea after the action with the least injured ships, until many of the crippled ones had sailed for England. . . . When the Bay was cleared of ten of them, I proceeded to Gibraltar, to forward the departure of the rest.' Collingwood added, that he had another object in keeping the sea at this time, which was 'to show the enemy that it was not a battle nor a storm which could remove a British squadron from the station which they were directed to hold'. For the next two and a half years the bulk of British strength in the Mediterranean was engaged in blockading Cadiz. For a period there was no capital squadron within the Straits: to watch the enemy's vessels lying in Cartagena and Toulon, Collingwood had to rely on the vigilance of his cruisers. The squadron off Cadiz, numbering sixteen of the line on 23 February 1806, was constantly being diminished as ships were drawn away by other services. Numerically his force was often inferior to that of the enemy. 'I have ten ships in all employed here', wrote Collingwood on board the *Ocean*, off Cadiz, on 18 October, 'and cannot keep them up at this season without two being absent for victualling, so that I have eight left to keep at bay twelve of the enemy.' 'A battle is really nothing to the fatigue and anxiety of such a life as we lead,' he continued on 9 December. 'It is now nearly thirteen months since I let go an anchor, and for what I can see, it may be as much longer. They are increasing their navy daily, while ours is wearing out.' But the enemy's morale had been shattered by Trafalgar; and their crews, compared with the British, were unskilled and inexperienced.

'My ships', declared Collingwood, early in 1807, 'are complete in everything; they never go into port more than one at a time: as for myself, . . . on the first day of the year [I] had not a sick man in the ship.'[1]

In certain respects Collingwood's work was complementary to that of St. Vincent and Nelson. For though he was destined never again

[1] *Correspondance of Vice-Admiral Lord Collingwood*, ed. G. L. Newnham Collingwood (1828), p. 239.

to assist in a fleet action, by far the most important part of his career still lay ahead. It has been justly said that there was no ambassador on whom a weightier responsibility was imposed than the Commander-in-Chief on the Mediterranean station. The vital diplomatic work which henceforth devolved on Collingwood involved him in endless political correspondence with princes, ministers, consuls, and merchants all around the Mediterranean. 'It is a justice which I owe to you and to the Country,' wrote Lord Mulgrave, then First Lord, 'to tell you candidly, that I know not how I should be able to supply all that would be lost to the service of the Country, and to the general interests of Europe, by your absence from the Mediterranean.'

Although Napoleon's plans of invasion had failed, on land he was everywhere triumphant. The Coalition had aimed to envelop him on all sides: in addition to the main assault, by the Austrians and Russians, on the Danube, an Anglo-Russian offensive, as we have seen, was to be launched against St. Cyr in the south of Italy; and a formidable Russo-Swedish expedition, strengthened by an Anglo-Hanoverian contingent, was set in train against Hanover. Napoleon ignored these diversionary operations. His armies struck swiftly, secretly, and in overwhelming strength at the decisive point, viz., the enemy's forces in central Europe. Before the Austrians and Russians could concentrate their forces against him, the Grand Army, hurrying eastward by forced marches, was on the Danube. Against a long scattered line of hostile troops Napoleon brought greatly superior forces. On the eve of Trafalgar—20 October 1805—the Austrian van, under General Mack, outnumbered and out-manœuvred, capitulated at Ulm. On 2 December the combined armies of Russia and Austria, under the Archduke Charles, were defeated by Napoleon at Austerlitz with heavy loss; whereupon what was left of the Allied forces fell back in hopeless confusion to the eastward. The British army which Pitt had dispatched to the north German coast had to be recalled at the news of this disaster; and the Coalition which he had with such infinite pains and toil raised up against Napoleon was no more. In the past few months the great minister's health had been seriously declining; his end was hastened by the tidings of Austerlitz; and, early in the morning of 23 January 1806, Pitt breathed his last.

The Anglo-Russian offensive in southern Italy was short-lived.

The issue of the struggle was in fact decided on the battlefields of central Europe. Though St. Cyr's corps had evacuated Apulia to reinforce Masséna in the north, the collapse of the Third Coalition left the Italian peninsula at the mercy of the French. The Allies had landed at Naples on 26 November 1805; by January 1806 35,000 French troops were marching on Naples; it was time for Craig to revert to his original instructions and to secure Sicily. 'We must not', Nelson had observed, 'risk Sicily too far in trying to save Naples.' At the news of Austerlitz, Craig at once prepared to evacuate his force. On 14 January the British began to embark; the Russians, two days later. On the 22nd 7,000 British troops disembarked at Messina in Sicily, which from this time onward became the British headquarters in the central Mediterranean; the Russians retired to Corfu.

The campaign of Ulm and Austerlitz illustrates in a striking degree the limitations of amphibious power operating against a great continental empire.[1] Craig's small force, even with the support of a vastly superior fleet, was quite incapable of achieving a decisive stroke against the vast hosts at Napoleon's command. Though in the campaign of 1805–6 St. Cyr had elected to abandon Apulia, it had no effect on the outcome of the struggle. Ulm and Austerlitz in fact restored French domination in southern Italy as well as in Lombardy. In June 1805 Napoleon had crowned himself with the iron crown of the Lombard kings in Milan cathedral. He proceeded to incorporate Venetia in his Italian kingdom and dispatched Masséna to drive the Allies out of Naples.

In the Mediterranean, it was Collingwood's main task to prevent the French breaking out of their present frontiers and advancing eastwards against the Ottoman Empire and India; at the same time harrying their seaborne commerce and covering the flow of trade between Great Britain and the Levant. Writing to his wife in March 1808 Collingwood declared that 'to stand a barrier between the ambition of France and the independence of England is the first wish of my life.' On this task were concentrated all his energies during the few years that remained to him.

[1] See Piers Mackesy, *The War in the Mediterranean, 1803–10* (1957)—a masterly study of naval, military, and diplomatic affairs in this theatre: a work which goes far to refute 'the historical myth of amphibious power—the myth that an army with control of the sea could strike tellingly and often at a vastly superior continental enemy.'

To exercise effective control of the Mediterranean, it was above all necessary to secure Sicily. The French under General Reynier had invaded the Kingdom of Naples on 9 February 1806, and, occupying the capital, arrived on 25 March at the Straits of Messina. Craig's army and its flotilla secured the Straits against an immediate attack. To strengthen the British garrison of Sicily, reinforcements were presently dispatched from Malta and Gibraltar. Captain Sotheron of the *Excellent*, 74, supported by the *Intrepid*, 64, having escorted the Sicilian royal family safely to Palermo, then took steps to counter the enemy's plans for a full-scale invasion of the island. His cruisers proceeded to attack the vessels laden with Reynier's guns and stores as they moved down the Calabrian coast; and, further to strengthen the island's defences, Collingwood later detached another two of the line to lie off Sicily. For the rest of the war, however, the vulnerability of Sicily continued seriously to embarrass our naval and military forces in the Mediterranean.

For geographical and strategical reasons, the British government had set their faces against any full-scale offensive in the Mediterranean theatre. They were in fact unable to spare either the troops or to keep them supplied for such an offensive. Gibraltar, Malta, and Sicily were secured against surprise by large garrisons which consequently were not available to assist our continental Allies. Nevertheless, the defensive strategy that had been determined on for the Mediterranean was vigorously pursued. The Russian offensive in the Adriatic soon slackened and British relations with Russia gradually worsened; the advance of the French forces in Dalmatia threatened the frontiers of European Turkey; but Collingwood's squadron served largely to fill the gap, and became the prime buttress of the Ottoman Empire against invasion. Through the control of the Mediterranean, the British government was able to maintain contact with Vienna by way of Malta and Trieste. Under the protection of the battle squadrons stationed off Cadiz and Sicily, a busy traffic continued to pass through the Straits of Gibraltar; and, as an ever-widening area of the Continent was barred to British trade, the value of these commercial outlets in the Mediterranean steadily increased. At the same time British cruisers carried on active war against the enemy's merchantmen, harrying the trade-routes to such effect that French commerce was almost driven off the sea. In July 1806 Collingwood sent Captain

Patrick Campbell of the *Unité*, 40, in command of a division of frigates, to blockade Venice and later Fiume and Ragusa. In the narrow waters of the upper Adriatic Campbell's five frigates speedily gathered in a rich harvest of enemy ships. When Turkey presently became our enemy, the trade war was extended to the coasts of the Ottoman Empire. The range and complexity of these various services strained the resources of Collingwood's command to the limit. 'I am', he complained on 6 March 1806, 'very much pinched for force to spread over the extensive seas which I have to range.' By the year 1808 the fleet under his command had increased to eighty vessels, of which about one-third were sail of the line.

After Austerlitz, Napoleon was firmly resolved to conquer Sicily. The French under Reynier advanced into Calabria, and began to make extensive preparations for crossing the Straits. To ward off the impending blow, Sydney Smith was detached by Collingwood and given command of a squadron of four of the line, several frigates, and some smaller vessels, to operate off the coast of Naples. Sydney Smith proceeded to Gaeta, which was still in Allied hands, and threw in supplies of ammunition and guns; after which he seized the island of Capri. In May, having garrisoned the island, Sydney Smith returned to Palermo and assisted a British force of 5,000, under Sir John Stuart,[1] to cross over into Calabria, where, three days later, it decisively defeated an army of 7,000, under Reynier, at Maida. After these initial successes the campaign languished. Masséna was advancing southward with large forces; and he presently captured Gaeta. Stuart and his men finally returned to Sicily. Nevertheless, as a result of this well-planned conjunct operation, a numerically superior French army had been soundly beaten and had sustained heavy losses; the arms and stores assembled for the projected invasion had fallen into the victors' hands: in short, Maida had completely destroyed the French hope of carrying Sicily by a *coup de main*. In the ensuing years, with the repair of forts, the multiplication of batteries, and a gradual trade revival, the island's defences were progressively strengthened; though for the rest of the war the internal affairs of Sicily continued an abiding anxiety to the British Commander-in-Chief.

With a view to assisting the Russians, Collingwood received in-

---

[1] On account of ill-health, Craig had been succeeded in March by Major-General Sir John Stuart.

structions in December to detach a squadron for the purpose of forcing the Dardanelles and bringing pressure to bear on the Sultan. Whatever chances of success the project may have had were, however, doomed by a succession of delays, the last of which occurred while the passage of the Straits was closed by contrary winds and the Turks were effectively strengthening their defences. The squadron, under Sir John Duckworth, finally passed through the Straits on 19 February, and, after the rear division under Sydney Smith had destroyed a weak Turkish force *en route*, anchored within eight miles of Constantinople; after which, having no military force to support it, and the enemy's strength increasing day by day, it was obliged to retire again, not without casualties, into the Mediterranean. The repulse of Duckworth's squadron only served to increase French influence with the Sultan. About the same time an expedition was sent to Egypt, but, being too small for the purpose, was similarly unsuccessful. This double failure provided yet another example of the improvident dissipation of our military resources which characterized British policy during the greater part of the Revolutionary and Napoleonic Wars.

2

Despite the bitter quarrel which had hopelessly estranged the Earl of St. Vincent from the prime minister, the government proposed to appoint the veteran Admiral to the command of the Channel squadron in succession to Cornwallis. Their offer was instantly and indignantly rejected. But on Pitt's death in January 1806, and the accession of Grenville to office,[1] the offer was made again, and this time accepted. St. Vincent's second term in command of the Channel squadron marks the final phase of his professional career.

On 12 March he sailed from St. Helens in the *Hibernia*, 110, with Sir Charles Cotton as his second-in-command, Rear-Admiral Edward Osborne as captain of the fleet, and Captain Thomas Western as his flag-captain, having under his command forty-two sail of the line, fifteen

[1] In the Ministry of All-the-Talents (1806–7) Lord Grenville was prime minister, Fox his foreign secretary, and Lord Howick First Lord of the Admiralty. On Fox's death in September 1806 Howick became Secretary of State for Foreign Affairs, while Thomas Grenville (brother of the prime minister) succeeded him as First Lord.

frigates, and a number of smaller vessels; after encountering off the Isle of Wight, in a north-easterly gale, 'the heaviest snowstorm I ever saw on this side of the Atlantic', and lying for some days in Falmouth Harbour, he resumed his former station off Ushant. Presently he detached Rear-Admiral Sir Richard Strachan in the *Caesar* with six of the line to watch Ferrol, Captain Sir Joseph Yorke in the *Barfleur* with four of the line to cruise some fifty leagues to the westward of Belleisle, and appointed Rear-Admiral Eliab Harvey in the *Tonnant* with five of the line to the station off Cape Finisterre. He himself cruised with the main body of the fleet in the Brest approaches.

Once more St. Vincent paced his quarter-deck off the enemy's principal naval arsenal. He was older by six years now—somewhat stooping, beetle-browed and white-haired, quizzical and saturnine, much resembling the figure familiar to us in Hoppner's portrait. With advancing years, his demeanour had somewhat mellowed. 'I have,' St. Vincent declared, 'guarded against the natural quickness of my temper and by that means avoided everything querulous.' At the same time he would still refer to his flag captain as 'this blister'.

'We are between Ushant and the Black Rock,' he informed Rear-Admiral Markham at the Admiralty on 29 March, 'in the day—and stand off at night and in at four in the morning. The *Mars* anchored off the Black Rocks; *Diamond*, *l'Agile*, and small craft, off the Parquette, and the *Crescent* looks out to the northward of Ushant. I cannot approve the rendezvous of my predecessor "seven leagues SW of Ushant", and intend to change it for "well in with Ushant during an easterly wind." '[1] St. Vincent's policy was still the close blockade, and he would brook no excuses. 'Without a squadron of good two-deck ships,' he observed, 'constantly kept off the Black Rocks, under an able officer, the French may go in and out of Brest with impunity.'[2] 'The Commander-in-Chief was astonished to see a ship of the Inshore Squadron without Ushant this morning, after a clear night and fine weather and the wind at E.N.E.,' he observed severely on 8 April, 'a circumstance which could only be justified by stress of weather and the wind blowing directly into the Iroise Channel.' As of old, he showed himself ever ready to face odds. 'This squadron,' he told the Admiralty, 'should be ten, for although I have felt very much at my

[1] Brenton, *Life and Correspondence of . . . St. Vincent*, II, p. 248.
[2] *Correspondence of Admiral Markham*, ed. C. Markham (1904), p. 38.

ease, I doubt whether other sea officers, with the exception of Cornwallis, would have slept quietly with six to ten.'

'We have performed a good day's work,' he remarked, on 17 April, when close in with Ushant, 'in completing the provisions, of all species (of the *Prince George* and *Formidable*, out of the *San Josef*, and filling up the water of this ship, eighty tons, out of that ship), between half after eight in the morning and four o'clock in the evening. The weather was most propitious, water smooth; and by furling all the sails, the ships drifted alike, and I do not believe the most trifling accident has happened, not even the jamming of a finger.'[1]

St. Vincent was mindful, as ever, of the propensity of his commanders to linger in port longer than was strictly necessary for them to complete the business which took them there. Both to Torbay and the vicinity of the other fleet anchorages the wives of these captains, accompanied perhaps by some of the younger children, appear to have resorted periodically in the hope of being reunited with the husbands they so rarely saw: to the detriment of their husbands' official duties.

'Torbay is become a bugbear,' St. Vincent told his secretary, Benjamin Tucker, 'and Falmouth Harbour preferred because of its repose and difficulty of getting out of it; our wives have found their way to Flushing, and ply on board the ships of their husbands the moment they appear, and inhabit the cabins, and even contrive to get into quarantine, to go a cruise.'[2] The Admiral, as was his custom, made the punishment fit the crime. 'The *Penelope*', he ordered on 10 April, assigning that frigate to the highly unpopular inshore station by the Black Rocks, 'is destined to relieve Captain Rathbourne; for those who loiter in port must have Siberia.'[3]

Once again the port of Brest was blockaded with the same vigilance, rigour, and efficiency as six years earlier; the Admiral appointed the same rendezvous for the main body of the fleet, assigned to his detached divisions the same stations, decreed the same order of sailing, the same tack or wear—all officers being ordered to be present on deck at night—and required the same punctual refit from the individual vessels ('six clear days exclusively of the date of arrival and that of sailing, which is considered ample for these purposes'), as in

[1] Brenton, *op. cit.*, II, p. 274.
[2] Tucker, *Memoirs of the Earl of St. Vincent*, II, p. 271.
[3] The advanced station near the Black Rocks.

the years 1800–1. Despite his age, he soon showed that he had lost none of the ruthless determination that had made 'the discipline of the Mediterranean' a byword in the Service. He revealed the same watchful concern for the health and well-being of his ships' companies; peremptorily put a term to slack station-keeping; demanded a proper economy in the consumption of supplies; and on all occasions exacted the highest standards of discipline and seamanship.

'I think the system is now established on such principles,' he declared on 17 May, 'it cannot be departed from; the more especially as Sir Charles Cotton has been witness to the certainty of keeping hold of Ushant in any wind or weather, by taking shelter under that island in an easterly gale, and profiting of the tides (which are as advantageous as about Scilly) in other circumstances.' 'We have just finished filling up the squadron here, with five months' provisions, and as much water as the ships can stow,' he informed Rear-Admiral Markham a couple of months later: 'the people are in high health, and both they, the captains and officers improve in all things.' 'We have not split a sail,' he recorded in August, 'or met with the most trifling accident, although we have been close in with Ushant, every day.'

As in his earlier cruise on the same station, he was not easily satisfied and showed himself sharply critical of his subordinates. 'Admiral Young must not interfere with the ships under my orders,' he protested to Markham. 'He is a Jesuit of the first order, and, as I observed to you before, composed of paper and packthread, stay tape and buckram.' 'For God's sake,' he exclaimed to the same correspondent, 'put Lord Howick upon his guard against the artful and presumptuous proceedings of Tom Wolley, who thinks he sees his way to the top of the navy office, or some other important situation. He is the meanest thief in the whole profession, abounding as it still does with Cape Bar[1] men.' 'The *Egyptienne* carried out four topmasts to Admiral Harvey's squadron the other day,' he wrote severely about the same time, 'and if we continue to throw away topmasts at this rate, the forests of the north will not furnish an adequate supply. There is great lack of seamanship in the service, and the young people now coming up are for the most part frippery and gimcrack.' Though always critical, he could still be fair. 'It does not appear to me,' he

[1] Cape Bar, or Cap-a-bar, was a current catch-phrase for the misappropriation of government stores.

observed to Markham later in the year, 'that Admiral Young is aware of the hazard too great a number of ships in Cawsand Bay put the whole to. He has been too long a theorist to retain much practical sea knowledge—if he ever possessed it, which I very much doubt; but he is by far the best port admiral I ever saw,'[1]

During the ensuing months St. Vincent continued to cruise off the Brittany coast. His station, as has already been said, was close in with Ushant; and occasionally his squadron anchored well within the Iroise, in sight of the ruined monastery (now a signal-post) upon St. Mathieu Point, with the narrow opening of the Goulet to the eastward, and the tall cliffs of Toulinguet Point and the Bec du Raz and the Saints showing, in clear weather, far away across the water. So rigorous was the blockade that, throughout the whole year, no ship of the line succeeded in getting out of the beleaguered port. From March to August, except for two brief visits, in the summer, to Spithead, the Admiral remained before Brest; and then was ordered, at an alarm that the French were preparing to invade Portugal, to Lisbon.

Leaving Sir Charles Cotton in command of the main body of the fleet off Ushant, St. Vincent sailed with a squadron of six of the line for the Rock of Lisbon: with instructions that, if the worst came to the worst, they were to carry off the Portuguese fleet before the enemy could seize it, and also to assist the Portuguese royal family to escape to Brazil.

The arrival of the British squadron and its formidable Admiral in the Tagus immediately put new heart into the House of Braganza. The authority and prestige of the Earl of St. Vincent were immense. Though both his officers and crews were strictly forbidden to set foot ashore, the Commander-in-Chief presently threw open all his vessels to the inhabitants of Lisbon, who, day by day, crowded on board (says Brenton) to admire 'their beauty, their resistless force, and the perfect discipline of their crews'. For two months St. Vincent remained in the Tagus, sustaining the Portuguese court and people by his presence; and then, the danger for the time being averted, he returned to the Bay of Biscay. 'I have every reason to believe', he observed to his brother on 10 October, on resuming for a brief period his former post off Brest, 'that we had the blessings of the whole country from the Prince Regent down to the meanest peasant.'

[1] Markham, *op. cit.*, pp. 48, 51, 53, 54; Brenton, *op. cit.*, II, p. 330.

He remained on this station until late in October when, detaching a squadron to watch the enemy in Brest, he brought the main body of the fleet into Cawsand Bay for the winter, exercising the command from a residence ashore. St. Vincent was at this time in a poor state of health ('one gale of wind would have done me up for the winter, probably rendered me *hors de combat*'); and he retained the command only in deference to the urgent promptings of the Grenvilles. That it would be difficult, if not, indeed, impossible to replace him was a view of the matter in which the Admiral fully concurred. 'I am sorry to say', he informed Howick, 'there are few flags at the main or the fore I have any respect for.' 'I do not know', he wrote several weeks later to the Admiralty, from Rame House near Cawsand Bay, where he had established his headquarters, 'one Flag-Officer upon half-pay, senior to Sir Charles Cotton, whom, if I filled the station you do, I could confide in to guard the Port of Brest—There is such a de-ficiency of nerves under responsibility, that I see officers of the greatest promise and acquired character sink beneath its weight.'[1]

In the autumn he was concerned with one of the most important responsibilities of his station—the duty of trade protection. 'Admiral Almand [Allemand],' he wrote to the First Lord, 'appears to me to be the ablest sea officer in the French Navy, and will do us incredible mischief, if he gets into the ocean.' And again: 'The season is now fast approaching for the privateers from St. Malo's pushing out to intercept our homeward bound ships on the outer edge of Soundings and off Cape Clear; and if frigates employed for the protection of trade in those parts are not kept within proper limits, you must expect to hear of great injury being done to our commerce, particularly to that of Liverpool, Bristol, and the ports of Ireland; short days and long nights being very favourable to the enterprise of the Malouins.'[2]

In the early spring of 1807, requesting on a change of ministry to be relieved of his command, St. Vincent hauled down his flag for the last time. 'I have great encouragement to believe that no ships have got out of Brest,' he observed on 23 March to Grenville, '. . . so that I hope to leave all the ships of the enemy fast in their ports to those who take the watch from, Sir, etc.—*St. Vincent.*' For a few more

[1] Brenton, *op. cit.*, II, pp. 327–8.
[2] J. S. Tucker, *Memoirs of the Earl of St. Vincent*, II, p. 309. See *supra*, pp. 104–5.

years he put in an occasional appearance in the House of Lords to speak on naval questions before he finally withdrew to the peace and tranquillity of Rochetts, his Essex home—retiring, as Sheridan declared, with 'his triple laurel, over the enemy, the mutineer, and the corrupt'. The memorable lines that Livy wrote of Cato in his indomitable old age might well have been applied to this great Admiral: *In parsimonia, in patentia laboris periculque ferrei prope corporis animique, quem ne senectus quidem quae solvit omnia fregerit.*[1] St. Vincent died, full of years and honours, in March 1823.

3

After Austerlitz, Napoleon had induced Prussia, with the bribe of George III's electorate of Hanover, to close her ports to British commerce. Great Britain retaliated by seizing three hundred Prussian merchantmen at sea. Prussia then executed a sudden volte-face: demanding the immediate evacuation of Germany by the French, she ordered the mobilization of her forces, and finally declared war. The Tsar had previously promised his aid: but once again Napoleon struck first—with lightning speed and vastly superior force. Unsupported in the event by either Russia, Austria, or Great Britain, the Prussians were hopelessly outmatched and outwitted when, on 14 October 1806, the decisive encounter took place in the Thuringian highlands. As so often before, Napoleon's favourite strategy of surprise, speed, and an overpowering concentration was employed with complete and crushing success. In a single day the Prussians were heavily defeated at Jena and Auerstadt by Napoleon and Davout respectively; and the invaders swept unopposed across Saxony and Brandenburg. Cities and fortresses surrendered in rapid succession; the remnants of Hohenlohe's and Blücher's corps laid down their arms; and on 27 October—within thirteen days of Jena—Napoleon entered Berlin in triumph. The proud military monarchy, which the genius of Frederick the Great had exalted to the rank of a Great Power, was stripped of its eastern and western provinces and bereft of half its population. Berlin and other leading cities and towns were held for the next seven years by French garrisons and the Prussians were saddled with crushing indemnities.

The Talents ministry, headed by Fox, which had succeeded Pitt's

[1] *Historia*, xxxix, c. 40.

last administration, was ill-fitted to conduct such a struggle as this. Their attempts to make peace with Napoleon failed, and they were soon in difficulties with the King over the Catholic relief question; when they went out the following spring they were never again to hold office under George III. The autumn of 1806 marked the peak of Napoleon's military career. Great Britain soon found herself without a single fighting ally on the Continent; her national economy was about to be threatened by the enemy's new measures against her trade, and her rulers were in the toils of partisan strife: again and again had arrived news of a fresh disaster. After Austerlitz and Jena there was a feeling in the air that we were grappling with titanic forces of which even yet we had not taken the full measure and entering on the darkest phase of a struggle of which no man could tell the outcome. This feeling was reflected in a sonnet published by Wordsworth early in 1807.

> Another year!—another deadly blow!
> Another mighty Empire overthrown!
> And we are left, or shall be left, alone;
> The last that dare to struggle with the Foe.
> 'Tis well! from this day forward we shall know
> That in ourselves our safety must be sought;
> That by our own right hands it must be wrought.

After these swift and brilliant campaigns of 1805–6, in which the great Germanic monarchies had been crushingly overthrown, Napoleon determined to destroy Great Britain, since he could not hope to invade her, through the ruin of her commerce. By a series of Decrees, the first of which was signed at Berlin on 21 November 1806, he endeavoured to work the downfall of his enemy by closing the ports of the Continent to British trade. British goods were to be excluded from France and from all her dependencies, and they were to be declared forfeit wherever found. To achieve this end he ordered the occupation of the Baltic and North Sea littoral and dispatched some of his best troops to enforce the blockade. Allies and neutrals as well as subjects were forced to submit to the Decrees. Portugal was informed that she had to choose between war with France, and war with Great Britain. A similar ultimatum was addressed to Denmark. It was Napoleon's avowed aim to 'conquer the sea by the land'; he claimed that there was not a port, nor an estuary, that was not within reach of his sword; and throughout the remainder of the war the Continental Blockade, and the portentous issues it brought in its train, became the crux of the whole struggle.

The British government replied with a series of Orders in Council proclaiming a blockade of all ports that adhered to the Continental System. British ships were henceforth forbidden to trade with France or with any of her dependencies. Further, if Great Britain was to be cut off from the carrying trade of Europe, she intended to deny that trade to neutrals also. For these ports there was to be 'no trade except through Great Britain'. And, owing to the overwhelming numerical superiority of the British Navy in the period following Trafalgar, she was in a position to make that prohibition effective.

Chief among these neutral carriers were the Americans, most of them New Englanders. Since 1800 American re-exports had been steadily rising. The produce of the enemy's colonies was being carried in American bottoms to American ports, and thence re-shipped to Europe in the guise of produce of the United States. The Rule of the War of 1756 had been virtually abrogated. James Stephen's famous pamphlet entitled *War in Disguise, or The Frauds of the Neutral Flags*, which appeared in the year of Trafalgar, called for the more vigorous enforcement of our maritime rights. 'The fabrics and commodities of France, Spain, and Holland', Stephen declared, 'have been brought under American colours to ports in the United States; and from thence re-exported, under the same flag, for the supply of the hostile colonies. Again, the produce of those colonies has been brought, in a like manner, to the American ports, and from thence re-shipped to Europe.'[1] In the spring of 1805 the *Essex* decision to enforce the doctrine of the continuous voyage struck hard at the American carrying trade. During the whole of the previous and the opening years of the present war Great Britain had interfered very little with American commerce. But from 1805 onward the attitude of the government stiffened, and British attacks on the neutral carrying trade became both more frequent and more aggressive.

On the renewal of the war with Napoleon in 1803 Great Britain had lost many of her important continental markets. The trade boom which accompanied the short-lived peace of Amiens had been followed

[1] James Stephen, *War in Disguise, or The Frauds of the Neutral Flags* (ed. 1917), p. 38.

by a period of pronounced recession. Trade was now recovering; but this was mainly owing to the fact that the steady expansion of our export trade to America as a whole more than made up for the decline of certain branches of our European commerce. The Continental Blockade after all only affected the European markets. The all-important trade with the United States and other parts of the New World, as well as with the world-wide territories of the British Empire, was altogether outside the reach of the Continental System. In 1805–6 the value of our exports to America as a whole rose by one-third: so that, despite the closure of so many European markets, 1806 was actually a year of expansion for British trade. Moreover, the full pressure of the Continental Blockade was not applied until well on in 1807. British merchants and their factors abroad had readily adapted themselves to the changed conditions; vast quantities of our manufactured goods were pouring into Europe through the Danish port of Tonningen; and our traffic with Holland, through the connivance of the French and Dutch officials, was actually increasing. For some time after the promulgation of the Berlin Decrees, therefore, Great Britain continued to prosper notwithstanding the loss of much of her former trade with Europe.

Towards the end of 1806 the Russians crossed the frontier and invaded Prussian Poland—too late, however, to be of service to their western allies. Shortly after, the opposing armies went into winter quarters. On the resumption of operations in the following year, a bloody but inconclusive engagement took place at Eylau, which resulted in the temporary exhaustion of both combatants. During the brief respite which followed, Napoleon rushed up reinforcements from every part of his empire; on 14 June—the anniversary of Marengo—the Russian army was overthrown at Friedland; and its remnants were driven back to the Niemen.

Following on the Polish campaign of 1806–7, the Tsar on 25 June met Napoleon at Tilsit and there, in return for large accessions of territory, bound himself by secret clauses, not only to support Napoleon's Continental System himself, but also to oblige Austria, Sweden, Denmark, and Portugal to support it. It was further agreed between them that if Great Britain remained obdurately at war the navies of the aforesaid Powers were to be used against her. In this way a large fleet would be once more at the enemy's disposal, and the Baltic would become a French lake. The enemy also secured naval bases in the eastern Mediterranean at Cattaro and in the Ionian Islands. After Tilsit Napoleon stood at the summit of his power. Three of his brothers sat upon thrones. The Emperors of Austria and Russia were his obedient allies. National sentiment, that later was to undermine his vast cosmopolitan empire, as yet lay dormant. In Continental Europe, Sweden alone fought on, surrounded by foes. Great Britain's commerce with Europe was progressively declining under the stranglehold of the Continental Blockade; for the pact of Tilsit had entailed an immense extension of the enemy's coastline. British exports, which had stood at £40.8 millions in 1806, dropped to less than £35.2 millions in 1808. Tilsit marked one of the great crises of the war. Napoleon, in fact, had regained the initiative; the Continental Blockade was rigorously enforced, and Great Britain was forced back on the defensive.

As six years before, Denmark was the key to the situation in the Baltic. She now found herself faced by a double peril. Her territories on the mainland were all too vulnerable to French attack. Her maritime and colonial interests were at the mercy of the British Navy. A strong French army of 70,000 men, commanded by Marshal Bernadotte, was encamped by the Danish frontier, ready to coerce Denmark if she hesitated. In the event of a French ultimatum to Denmark, which was expected almost hourly in London, it was believed that the Danes would not resist. Were the French to occupy the Danish island of Zealand, Sweden would be threatened with invasion. There was also the probability of the Danish fleet of eighteen sail of the line falling into the enemy's hands and the closing of the Sound to British shipping. The dangers of the situation were suddenly brought to a head by the news of Tilsit. Canning, as Foreign Secretary, was forced to take a swift decision. He accordingly resolved to forestall Napoleon. Before winter could bind the Baltic with its icy grip Admiral Gambier was sent out to Copenhagen with a great fleet of twenty-five of the line and a large army, with instructions to coerce Denmark and to demand the instant surrender of her fleet. The unfortunate Danes were to be confronted with what Canning called 'a balance of opposite dangers'.[1]

[1] For a lucid and comprehensive survey of the causes of the British expedition against Copenhagen, see A. N. Ryan in *English Historical Review*, Vol. 68 (1953).

Nelson's strategy of six years before was not to be repeated in 1807. The harbour of Copenhagen was now powerfully defended against a naval attack and a direct bombardment of the dockyards from the King's Deep was no longer possible. The city would have to be attacked from the land by a military force and compelled to surrender. While the main body of the British fleet lay off Elsinore, a squadron of four of the line and three frigates under Commodore Keats was sent through the Great Belt to hold the entrance to the Baltic. The result was that no considerable reinforcement could now be brought from the mainland to Zealand, the island on which Copenhagen is situated. Through the speed and secrecy of the British preparations the Danes had been taken unawares. The isolation of Zealand was really the decisive factor in the campaign which followed. For the bulk of the Danish army was then in Holstein and the garrison of Zealand was altogether outmatched by the British troops in point of numbers, organization, and discipline.

On the rejection of the British terms our army under Lord Cathcart was disembarked under the guns of the fleet, and the Danish capital was besieged both by land and sea. After enduring a three days' bombardment the Danes surrendered; and most of their fleet passed into British keeping for the duration of the war. This coup of 1807 constitued an effective blow against Napoleon's Continental System. It was followed soon after by the seizure of Heligoland, which henceforth became an important centre for smuggling British produce into Central Europe.[1]

At the other end of Europe Portugal was being similarly threatened by Napoleon. Portugal, traditionally our friend and ally, refused to sever relations with Great Britain at the Imperial bidding; and Napoleon sent Junot with an army against her, to occupy her capital and to seize her fleet. The latter, however, was forestalled in the nick of time by a squadron under Sydney Smith which sailed off to Brazil with the Prince Regent and the Portuguese fleet.[2] The result was that

[1] 'With a small expense this island may be made a little Gibraltar and a safe haven for small craft even in winter,' wrote Vice-Admiral Russell to the Secretary of the Admiralty on 6 September 1807. 'It is a key to the rivers Ems, Weser, Jade, and Eyder.'

[2] Towards the end of 1807 the Madeira Islands, with Portuguese consent, were occupied by British troops, thereby securing an important base on the route to the Cape of Good Hope and India.

though the ports of Denmark and Portugal were henceforth closed
to British trade, their navies, comprising altogether twenty-five of the
line, were saved from falling into the enemy's hands.

4

The desertion of Russia after Tilsit considerably increased the difficulties of Collingwood's command. The Russians abandoned the
Mediterranean and surrendered their bases in Dalmatia and the
Ionian Islands to the French. The enemy was now established along
the Turkish frontier. His occupation of the Ionian Islands intensified
the threat to Sicily. On the renewal of hostilities in 1803, the French
had controlled only a comparatively limited stretch of the Mediterranean littoral. In the intervening years the progressive expansion of
Napoleon's power in southern Europe had given him the seaboard of
the Italian peninsula, Venice, Dalmatia, then, finally, the Ionian
Islands.

Collingwood's capital squadrons were dispersed over an immense
area between the Aegean and the south-west coast of Spain. Six of the
line lay with the Commander-in-Chief off the Dardanelles. There
were two more with Hallowell off Alexandria; five with Thornbrough
guarding Sicily, and ten with Purvis blocking up Cadiz. His cruisers
in the Adriatic barred the sea-routes to the Ottoman Empire.

Following upon the pacification of the Continent, Napoleon's hopes
had revived of weakening the British hold on the central Mediterranean
by evicting Stuart's force from its base at Messina. The island of
Sicily was one of the vital strategic points of the Mediterranean. It
was essential to the British control of those waters; it was further of
the greatest importance as the granary of Malta, whose inhabitants
were unable to feed themselves. Napoleon had long desired to seize
the island. A favourable opportunity appeared to present itself at the
close of 1807, when the news reached the Emperor that the British
garrison at Messina had been substantially reduced. He ordered the
squadrons lying in his Atlantic ports to sail for the Mediterranean,
and dispatched detailed instructions to his brother Joseph at Naples
for the invasion of Sicily. In February 1808 the French carried Sicily's
outer line of defence by capturing Reggio and Scylla. No more than
two miles of water lay between the threatened island and 9,000 enemy

troops assembled, with their flotilla, on the further shore; at Naples another 10,000 awaited the squadron from Toulon. In accordance with Napoleon's orders, Joseph completed his preparations for the projected descent. But in Messina harbour lay four British cruisers supported by the *Montagu*, 74; and Joseph could not hope to get his troops across the Straits without the support of a battle squadron from France.

In the event only the resourceful and elusive Allemand managed to get away with the Rochefort squadron, comprising five of the line and two smaller vessels, on 17 January 1808. He sailed southward with Sir Richard Strachan in hot pursuit, and, early in February, arrived off Toulon, where he was joined by Ganteaume and his squadron. But Napoleon had changed his plans. He had in fact become increasingly anxious for the safety of Corfu, which he proposed to use as his base in the event of a French move against Turkey. An offensive was now replaced by a defensive project. Ganteaume was ordered to relieve Corfu, which was being blockaded by a British division under Captain Harvey. Off Toulon, on the night of 10 February, Ganteaume's force had been dispersed by a north-westerly gale. With the main body of the fleet he arrived safely in the Ionian Islands; and then, leaving his flagship, the *Commerce de Paris*, which had been dismasted in the gale, at Corfu to refit, he cruised from 25 February to 13 March in the mouth of the Adriatic in search of his missing ships.[1] The latter eventually arrived at the island on the day before Ganteaume's return; and the fleet was at last united. On the 16th, having received intelligence of a British concentration off Sicily, Ganteaume sailed with his whole force from Corfu, and, skirting the coasts of Africa, Sicily, and Sardinia,[2] well to the eastward and south-

[1] From 24 February to 13 March Ganteaume's fleet was pursued by the *Active*, 38, and the *Porcupine*, 22. The latter warned Harvey of the enemy's approach when off the Ionian Islands; and Harvey sailed immediately for Sicily. He missed Collingwood, off Syracuse, by the narrowest of margins. See Adm. 52/4023, 52/3851, 52/3796, 24 February–13 March 1808.

[2] The *Spartan*, 38, Captain Jahleel Brenton, had been ordered by Rear-Admiral Martin to cruise between Cape Bon and Sardinia, 'where', records Brenton, 'on 1st April she discovered the French fleet carrying a press of sail to get to the westward.' Ganteaume was pursued for three days with admirable skill and tenacity by Brenton, who also sent off a launch with dispatches to warn Martin at Palermo and Ball at Valetta. Ball dispatched every available vessel in search of the Commander-in-Chief; but without success.

ward of Collingwood's fleet, anchored once more in Toulon on 10 April.

When on 22 February 1808 Collingwood learned that the Rochefort squadron had entered the Mediterranean, he concentrated his forces off the Maretimo, where, on 2 March, Thornbrough brought him news that the Toulon squadron was also at sea.[1] What Collingwood, however, did not know was that the enemy forces had united and had already passed the Sicilian narrows. Leaving part of his force at Palermo, he sailed with the rest to search the Bay of Naples. 'Sicily', he declared on 13 March, 'is the point to which their force seems now to be directed, and every report which might remove my force to a distance from it is likely to be circulated. I am endeavouring now to get intelligence where the Toulon ships are, and whether they have been joined by those from Rochefort, or any others.' He sent away all his available cruisers in search of information; there was indeed no other means of securing it—for, as he had complained a week earlier, 'there is not a ship on the sea from which any information of the enemy can be collected'; and until he had certain knowledge of Ganteaume's whereabouts he did not propose to move from the vicinity of Sicily, the enemy's most probable objective. Such items of intelligence as reached him proved both dubious and conflicting. At last, on 21 March, Collingwood learned at Syracuse from Harvey that the hostile forces lay to the eastward;[2] and he sailed for the Adriatic. On the 23rd, expecting almost hourly to meet the French, he issued his fighting instructions.[3] Several days later he drew near the mouth of the Gulf of Taranto, where, according to his latest information, he imagined Ganteaume to be lying. The *Apollo* frigate, with a sloop, was sent on to reconnoitre. On the 30th, however, the frigate returned with the news that the hostile fleet was nowhere to be seen; and on the following day a report reached the Commander-in-Chief of an impending enemy concentration near Tunis. Collingwood at once hurried back to the Maretimo, where, on 6 April, the *Weazle* sloop brought him news that four days earlier the French fleet had been sighted off the south coast of Sardinia on a westerly course.[4] 'Sir Richard Strachan, having pursued them to this station, makes the

[1] *Private Correspondence of Admiral Lord Collingwood*, ed. E. A. Hughes (1957), pp. 350–1.

[2] Adm. 52/3796, 21 March 1808.

[3] Hughes, *op. cit.*, pp. 359–62.

[4] Adm. 51/1892, 2, 6 April 1808.

fleet strong enough for any thing,' observed Collingwood on the same day; 'but Sicily itself is as weak as weak can be.' 'One strong impression on my mind is that Sicily is the object they have in view', he declared some days later, 'and all this capering about it for the purpose of deception and to draw our force from that quarter; with this impression I shall be very careful how I suffer myself to be drawn too far from it.' Persuaded that Port Mahon was the enemy rendezvous and that an invasion of Sicily was imminent, he again concentrated his forces off the Maretimo and threw out a chain of cruisers to watch the approaches to the enemy's proposed objective. It was not in fact until 25 April that Hoste in the *Amphion* frigate arrived with certain intelligence that the French fleet was in Toulon.[1] Hoste at once returned to watch the enemy with a division of cruisers; and early in May the main body of the British fleet, under the Commander-in-Chief, was off Toulon.

Collingwood's failure to intercept Ganteaume must be ascribed partly to the paramount necessity of securing Sicily against invasion, partly to a series of regrettable mischances, and partly to his own perpetual preoccupation with political and administrative matters—to the detriment of his duties as a fighting admiral—and the inadequacy of his methods of obtaining intelligence. Impossible to imagine Nelson below in his cabin, huddled for endless hours over his desk, while the French were at sea! Nor does Collingwood's correspondence during the greater part of the time when Ganteaume was ranging the Mediterranean suggest anything like Nelson's fierce and feverish anxiety to seek out and destroy the enemy. When every possible allowance has been made for the difficulties confronting the Commander-in-Chief, the fact remains that Ganteaume was permitted to continue at large in the relatively narrow waters of the Mediterranean for no less than eight weeks.

By the spring of 1808 the combined effect of the Continental Blockade and the operations of enemy privateers had been gravely to depress British commerce and industry. The north of Italy, Holland, Naples, northern Germany, Prussia, Russia, Portugal, Spain, Denmark, central Italy, and Austria had, in turn, been compelled to submit to Napoleon's decrees; and at last only Sweden and Turkey stood outside the Continental System. The blockade against British

[1] Adm. 51/1909, 25 April 1808.

commerce was intensified by the Milan Decrees of 23 November and 17 December, 1807, outlawing all neutral vessels which submitted to British search or entered a port in Great Britain or any of her colonies. Such vessels were to be deemed lawful prizes for French privateers. Since 1806 Great Britain had been availing herself to an increasing degree of the services of neutral shipping, particularly those of Holland and northern Germany, in order to get her merchandise past the blockade. As a result of Napoleon's new measures, the insurance rates of neutral shipping bound to continental ports rose steeply. In 1806 more than 11,000 ships had passed through the Sound, entering or leaving; but in 1807, scarcely 6,000—and British vessels were excluded from all the Baltic ports, save those of Sweden.

Gradually but surely the pressure of the continental blockade increased; one after another the accustomed markets for our exports were being lost.[1] With the notable exception of Archangel, the British trade with Russia was far below the level of normal years until well on in 1808. (Archangel being outside the effective surveillance of the Tsar's government, from 200 to 300 ships arrived there during these months, most of them laden with colonial produce.) Tonningen had been closed to British trade since the rupture with Denmark in 1807. The commerce with Holland was virtually destroyed a few months later. By the close of 1807 the passage of Jefferson's Embargo Act threatened to deprive British merchants and manufacturers of the American trade which had become one of the pillars of our national economy. The American market, indeed, was not completely closed; but there was certainly a serious recession, and the spring shipment of 1808 was insignificant. Moreover, our hopes of capturing a valuable South American market were destroyed by the overthrow of Whitelock's force in Buenos Aires. There was in fact only one branch of our commerce which might be said to be prospering and of which great expectations were entertained. That was the trade to Brazil.

In short, it was the closure of most of our continental markets, combined with the almost complete stoppage of trade with the United

[1] For a detailed and authoritative account of the operation of the Continental Blockade in those sectors which were of the greatest consequence to British exporters—viz. the coasts of the Baltic and North Sea—and also of the measures taken to foster and protect our trade in those regions, see François Crouzet, *L'Économie britannique et la blocus continental*, I, pp. 285–99, II, pp. 422–48, 589–604, 650–69.

States, that occasioned the severe depression of 1807–8. It was not only the export trade that was involved. An important aspect of the present crisis was that in certain cases the supply of raw materials was being cut; viz. cotton from the United States. The warehouses were packed with manufactures that could find no market; the stocks of sugar and coffee that were lying unsold had reached an unexampled level, and the prices of these commodities were steadily falling. With mills and factories closing down, unemployment was rife among the work-people of Birmingham and Sheffield, also in Yorkshire and the West Country, and, above all, in the Lancashire cotton industry. In the last-named region there had even been serious rioting.

That the distress occasioned in this country by the continental blockade was not far worse was mainly owing to the inadequacy of the measures taken to enforce it. The truth is that as the year advanced Napoleon was too much occupied with more pressing matters to be able to give more than partial attention to the enforcement of his decrees. Starved of colonial produce by the operation of the Orders in Council, the Continent clamoured for British re-exports at almost any price. When normal trade was declared illegal, a flourishing contraband traffic naturally took its place. Along the shallow, sandy coast between the mouths of the Ems, Weser, and Elbe, with its fringe of outlying islands, where the navigational conditions so greatly favoured the smuggler, a large proportion of the populace was engaged in this lucrative traffic. The inhabitants of Hamburg and its environs in particular displayed an extraordinary degree of resource and ingenuity in their various stratagems for evading the vigilance of the customs officials.[1] Even in the later stages of the war, when the blockade was far more vigorously enforced, smuggling in Holland was widespread. The whole coastal population was more or less involved; and not only contraband, but political propaganda also, poured in from across the North Sea.

[1] 'Barges and women, dogs and hearses, were pressed into service against Napoleon. The last-named device was for a time tried with much success near Hamburg, until the French authorities, wondering at the strange increase of funerals in a river-side suburb, peered into the hearses, and found them stuffed full with bales of British merchandise. This gruesome plan failing, others were tried. Large quantities of sand were brought from the seashore, until, unfortunately for the housewives, some inquisitive official found that it hailed from the West Indies' (J. Holland Rose, *Life of Napoleon I*, II, p. 218).

In the latter half of 1808 the clouds began to lift. While Napoleon's attention was diverted to Spain and Austria, in various parts of both northern and southern Europe trade was at last recovering. In the Baltic our commerce was noticeably increasing. Over 700 vessels entered Russian ports during these months. The expansion of our trade with North Germany was even more impressive. A good deal of this commerce now went through Heligoland, which became the great entrepôt of the contraband traffic with central Europe. No less than 200 British merchants and agents were settled on the island in 1808, and a Chamber of Commerce had been established there. About 120 vessels arrived at Heligoland in the summer and autumn.[1] The contraband traffic was carried on with the aid of small fishing-vessels known as 'schuyts', which used to land their cargoes on the off-shore islands. A small division of cruisers (comprising a frigate, three sloops, a brig, and four gun-boats) was stationed off Heligoland to prevent the enemy from interfering with these operations; and, since it was found that the gun-boats drew too much water to run in with the schuyts, it was proposed to purchase a number of these craft to serve as escorts for the trading-schuyts.[2]

In the latter part of 1808 the continental blockade was also relaxed in the Mediterranean. Following the Spanish uprising in June, large orders reached England from the Peninsula which served as a powerful stimulus to an export trade and enabled our industrialists to dispose of immense stocks of manufactures; at the same time successive ship-loads of wines, fruits, and wool arrived in our ports from Spain. British exports poured into Austria through Trieste. In the eastern Mediterranean Malta had become the entrepôt of an extensive contra-band traffic similar to that of Heligoland in the North Sea; and, as in the latter case, carried on under the protection of the cruisers of the Royal Navy. The warehouses on the island were crammed to over-flowing with all kinds of goods; and there was not enough shipping to handle this rapidly expanding trade. Great quantities of British cottons and other manufactures reached the contiguous countries through the island entrepôt, which probably enjoyed its greatest

---

[1] An important advantage of Heligoland from the navigational standpoint was that in the thick weather which so often prevailed in the Bight the sound-ings afforded a dependable guide for making the island.

[2] Adm. 2/1366, pp. 48, 372, 397.

prosperity towards the end of 1808. 'Malta is one of the gayest places in the world,' declared Collingwood early in that year: 'the merchants having now the entire trade of the Mediterranean are become very rich and are dashing away in a great style.'

Despite all Napoleon's endeavours to seal up the coasts of Europe against British trade, the demand for British produce, both manufactured and colonial, was too strong to be resisted. 'So cheap were the machine-made manufactures of England,' writes Bryant, 'so indispensable to starved palates her colonial wares that whole divisions of douniers could not keep them out. The very depreciation of her currency, partly due to the drain of foreign war and the embargo on her exports, only assisted the process by lowering the costs of smuggling.'[1] Through the omnipresence of her Navy, Great Britain was in a position to enforce her policy, as Mahan has said, 'of forcing neutrals to make England the storehouse and toll-gate of the world's commerce.' The result was that, at the zenith of Napoleon's power, British goods continued to penetrate the Continental Blockade.

The recovery of our export trade was by no means confined to Europe. The fear that war was imminent between Great Britain and the United States, which had for long paralysed business on both sides of the Atlantic, gradually passed away. The result of these improved relations was large sheaves of orders for the fall shipment, which showed a distinct improvement on the spring shipment. In the same way our trade with South America continued, despite numerous obstacles, to make headway. It was the expansion in 1808 of our exports to South America and British North America which afforded some measure of compensation for the decline of the United States trade.

An immense expansion of the contraband traffic based on Heligoland was one of the crucial developments of 1809. Our exports to Holland were also up on those of 1808. British goods poured into Prussia and Russia mainly by way of Gothenberg and other Swedish ports; so that, towards the end of the year, additional convoys had to be run. The trade with Archangel was as busy as during the previous year. In August alone, 100 ships left that port with cargoes for Great Britain. The exports of cottons had more than doubled. This prosperity was carried on into the early months of 1810. The tendency for British exports to the Continent to decline had, in fact, completely

[1] Arthur Bryant, *Years of Victory* (1944), p. 347.

reversed; and this was the essential cause of the boom of 1809–10. The history of these years well illustrates one of the most telling points made by Crouzet in treating of the commercial struggle: 'La situation économique de la Grande Bretagne devait donc être déterminée plus que jamais après les Ordres en Conseil par les vicissitudes de la situation politique et militaire: paix en Europe, crise en Angleterre; guerre en Europe, *boom* en Angleterre'.[1] The efficacy of Napoleon's commercial measures depended, after all, upon the preservation of peace on the Continent. It was only under such conditions that his land blockade could be maintained. But the peace established by the pact of Tilsit had already broken down. In the significant words of a witness at the Parliamentary inquiry of 1812: 'In 1809 the trade through Heligoland was most extensive; Bonaparte had his hands full with the Empire of Germany and with the Spaniards, and had no time to attend to the coast. . . . The trade to the Mediterranean increased very much; the quantity of goods taken out that year greatly exceeded any previous year, for reasons that at that time we could not account for.'[2]

The year 1809 also saw a welcome revival of our trade with the United States. On the abandonment of the embargo in March an apparently endless flow of shipping sailed from American ports, laden with cotton, timber, and tobacco. By October 500 vessels had arrived in Liverpool alone. Later when Non-Intercourse was suspended the British export trade likewise revived and there was a heavy fall shipment to the United States. In the last few months of the year some 300 vessels laden with British manufactures arrived in New York. On the abolition of all restrictions in the spring of 1810 the traffic between Great Britain and the United States swelled to a boom. The manufactories of Manchester, Leeds, and Birmingham drove a roaring trade executing large American orders. The fall shipment of 1810 was immense. When towards the middle of that year the Continent was once more closed to British commerce the American trade was still booming, which helped to tide the manufactories over the early part of the next great industrial crisis. From the early weeks of 1809 a heavy spate of orders from the expanding South American market had also occasioned an intense activity in the northern and midland manufactories.

[1] Crouzet, *op. cit.*, I, p. 283.
[2] *Parliamentary Papers*, 1812, III, p. 522.

The whole period from the spring of 1809 to that of 1810 was marked in fact by a feverish and sustained industrial activity, when both the production and export of British manufactured goods reached a level never before approached. Most prosperous of all was the cotton industry, which during these months broke all records; but even the lesser industries, such as the potteries and brickworks, shared in the general prosperity.

5

In consequence of Tilsit the Baltic became a crucial theatre of the struggle. Russia declared war on Great Britain. Prussia was compelled by force of circumstances to acquiesce in the new situation created by the treaty between Napoleon and the Tsar. Tilsit enabled the Russians to make their bid for the possession of Finland, which had been so long the object of their ambition. Denmark had also hoped to expand at Sweden's expense. In February 1808 the Russian army invaded Finland, and in the ensuing months the Danes prepared to launch an invasion across the Sound into southern Sweden.

The Danish invasion was effectually prevented, first, by the arrival off Zealand of a detachment of the North Sea fleet under Captain George Parker, and, some months later, by the insurrection of 9,000 Spanish troops stationed in Denmark who were to have formed a large part of the invasion forces. The Spaniards and their commander, the Marquis de la Romana, were taken off by the British warships cruising in the Great Belt, and presently sent home to assist in the national uprising against Napoleon. In response to Sweden's appeal for assistance, the British government dispatched a squadron of sixteen of the line, under Vice-Admiral Sir James Saumarez, to the Baltic, which henceforth became one of the most important stations held by the Navy.

In Finland, the struggle went badly for Sweden. Navigational conditions on the Finnish coast made it impossible for their British allies to assist them effectually in this area. The Russian army soon overran the duchy, assisted on the coast by the Russian flotilla. The Swedes suffered a series of heavy defeats, the most serious of which was the loss of the great fortress of Sveaborg, near Helsinki. With Sveaborg were lost a hundred gun-boats of the *skärgårdsflottan*, the only type of warship able to operate in the coastal passages within the chain of islets and rocks which fringed the Finnish coast. The loss of Sveaborg and its flotilla was a severe blow to Sweden; it not only sealed the fate of southern Finland, but also laid the coast of Sweden open to invasion across the Gulf of Bothnia.

The most difficult problem confronting Saumarez was how to assist the Swedes effectively against the Russians and Danes. In the summer a small British force joined the Swedish fleet off Hangö Udd at the entrance to the Gulf of Finland to intercept the enemy's coastal traffic. At the same time a detachment was stationed in the Sound and in the Great Belt, and another off the enemy's ports on the south side of the Baltic, to counter any attempt to invade Scania. The only kind of fleet action fought in this war was a skirmish between the Russian fleet and the Anglo-Swedish force off Hangö Udd, in August, which resulted in the destruction of a Russian sail of the line; the poor sailing qualities of the Swedish vessels preventing their coming up with the enemy and bringing on a general engagement which might well have ended in the capture of most of the Russian fleet. A British expedition of 10,000 troops under the command of Sir John Moore, which arrived off Gothenburg in May, was unable to accomplish anything owing to the Swedish king's intransigence and subsequently had to be withdrawn. With Finland lost beyond redemption, the year ended disastrously for Sweden.

In 1809 a division under Saumarez again cruised off Hangö Udd and in the Gulf of Finland.

There was a further duty incumbent upon Saumarez's squadron which, at this juncture, was of crucial importance to Great Britain; namely, the defence of the Baltic trade.

During the earlier part of the Napoleonic War British exports to the Baltic had increased by leaps and bounds. Though all the ports of the Continent which were under French control had been closed to British commerce, down to the post-Tilsit era those of the Baltic still remained open to our shipping, and they continued to attract a major share of the traffic which had been diverted from its normal channels. Again, throughout all these years the supply of Baltic timber to this country was virtually uninterrupted. But after Tilsit timber imports sharply declined, and the price of timber in Great Britain correspondingly increased.

With the intensification of Napoleon's commercial blockade, the national economy of Great Britain was threatened with imminent disaster if the Baltic was not kept open to her trade.[1] Every country in the region, except Sweden, was pledged to close its ports to British shipping. Though, through the seizure of her fleet, Denmark no longer had the means of closing the Sound and the Belts, both the Danes and Norwegians were hard at work fitting out large numbers of gun-boats and privateers with which to assail our trade. They were based on ports situated up and down the coasts of the Skagerrak and Kattegat, along the Sound and the Great Belt, and on the islands of Bornholm and Ertholmene.[2] In addition to these there were French privateers working out of Danzig and other ports along the southern coast of the Baltic. The crucial test of the Continental System may therefore be said to have occurred in this region, which during these years became the scene of a protracted and hard-fought *guerre de course*.

In the ensuing campaigns the vital point was the entrance to the Baltic. There the enemy were at their strongest and might well succeed, if not prevented, in barring the passage of the British convoys. So formidable, indeed, did these attacks become that the convoys had in the following year to be re-routed through the Belt instead of through the Sound. Towards the end of July 1808 Saumarez was ordered to detach a squadron under Rear-Admiral Keats to cruise in the Belt for the protection of our trade entering or leaving the Baltic. The admirable system of convoys established in the latter half of this year was in large measure due to Keats and was continued by his successor, Rear-Admiral Manley Dixon.[3] So successful was the new system that the passage through the Sound was largely discontinued. In the summer and autumn of 1809 well over 2,000 merchantmen were shepherded safely through the Baltic.

Despite every obstacle British commerce with northern Europe

[1] Within two months of Tilsit Canning sent Sir Stephen Shairp as consul-general to St Petersburg with instructions to take such measures 'for insuring the speedy departure of all British vessels which may still be loading in the Russian ports, but more especially to expedite the sailing of such as may be laden with hemp, iron, or other articles required for naval purposes' (F.O. 65/71, 13 August 1807).

[2] The group known collectively as Ertholmene (*anglice*, 'the Eartholms') were a cluster of rocky islets which formed a fine natural harbour situated to the north-east of Bornholm.

[3] See *infra*, p. 393.

still made headway; and in the King's speech at the opening of Parliament on 19 January 1809 it could be claimed that 'the public revenue, notwithstanding we are shut out from almost all the continent of Europe and entirely from the United States, has increased to a degree never expected, even by those persons who were most sanguine.'

A highly important measure for the protection of commerce was the occupation, in the spring of 1809, of Anholt. This was a small sandy island with a lighthouse; there being a long dangerous reef extending for nearly two miles from it. The object of this capture was not only to wipe out a troublesome nest of privateers but also to secure a rendezvous for convoys and a plentiful supply of water. There was a further and, perhaps, even more pressing reason. 'Of the importance of Anholt', wrote Byam Martin to Saumarez several years later, 'for the benefit and safety of the trade there can be no doubt, for the navigation of the Kattegat (at all times dangerous) would be most perilous in the fall of the year without the light to guard against the dangers wherewith the island is surrounded.' Two years later the Danes endeavoured, without success, to retake the island.

The same year, as has already been said, was marked by a major trade boom, due to a number of causes. In the first place, during the greater part of 1809 Napoleon was busy in Austria, and in his absence the North Sea traffic returned to something like its normal proportions. Secondly, the Tsar designedly turned a blind eye to British commerce carried on in Russian ports by neutral ships provided with British licences. Large fleets of these licensed vessels sailed to the Baltic in 1809 laden with British manufactures and colonial products, and returned with the grain, timber, and naval stores of the North. Between 1808 and 1809 the imports to the United Kingdom of naval stores, chiefly from the Baltic, more than doubled.

In 1810, when imports through the North Sea ports had practically ceased, the diversion of commerce to the Baltic was almost complete. The Baltic, in fact, became the main channel of British commerce with North and Central Europe. West Germany, Austria, and even France were drawing supplies through Königsberg and the other towns on the south coast of the Baltic which had taken over the traffic of the Dutch and Hanse ports. Gothenburg, too, became a great entrepôt for the distribution of the colonial produce which the Continent so badly needed; the imports to Gothenburg increased and multiplied between the years 1807 and 1813.[1] With the cooperation of the Swedish government, Hanö Bay, about 20 miles south of Karlshamn, was used both as an anchorage for Saumarez's squadron and as a clearing-house for colonial goods and British manufactures. When eventually Sweden, weakened and impoverished by internal strife, made peace with Russia, Denmark, and France, she was compelled, in the latter part of 1809, to exclude British shipping from her ports. Even so, however, she made no attempt to interfere with the assembly of our convoys in Hanö Bay.

How effectively Napoleon's measures to destroy British commerce with the Continent were countered in the vital Baltic theatre is shown by the fact that, in 1806, the value of our trade with northern Europe had been £7½ million; and on its stoppage, in 1808, dropped to £2 million. But it recovered thereafter and in 1810 rose to £7,700,000. Despite, on occasion, very heavy losses, casualties were kept down to a tolerable percentage and the flow of traffic between Great Britain and the Baltic was maintained. To circumvent the Continental system a large number of American and other neutral merchant vessels were employed for the carriage of cargoes to and from the Baltic (all of which, of course had to conform to the British regulations and to sail in convoy through the Belt): an arrangement which also made it easier to disguise the real origin and ownership of the cargoes concerned by false papers and other devices. During the years which followed freight rates for the Baltic voyage continued to rise.

During all these diverse operations in the Baltic the losses in action sustained by Saumarez's squadron were comparatively light; but a grievous toll continued to be levied by the dangers of the sea which—as in almost every war we ever fought—cost us a great deal more in ships and lives than the utmost that enemy action was able to exact. In some years the toll was heavier than in others; the worst by far being in 1811.

In that year the last homeward convoy from Hanö Bay did not sail with its escorts until as late as 9 November, only to be overtaken by a strong south-westerly gale, with a heavy swell, in the course of which the convoy was dispersed and a number of ships either ran aground

---

[1] It is on record that in September 1810 there were nineteen British men-of-war and more than 1,100 merchantmen anchored in the roadstead off Gothenberg. See Eli Hekscher, *The Continental System* (1922), pp. 236–7.

or foundered.[1] In the same gale the *St. George*, 98, flagship of Rear-Admiral Robert Reynolds, lost both her rudder and all her three masts. She was refitted as well as circumstances would permit, with jury masts and rigging, and taken in tow by the *Cressy*. The escorts and the remnant of the convoy arrived on 1 December in Vingå Sound near Gothenburg, where Saumarez was lying with the *Victory* and the rest of his squadron. Despite the latter's misgivings, Rear-Admiral Reynolds and the captain of the *St. George* were still determined to make the passage to England. On 17 December, in fine weather and with a favouring wind, the whole fleet weighed anchor and stood out of Vingå Sound. Two days later, the wind backing to the N.N.E., the merchant vessels with their escorts were obliged to put back to the anchorage. Saumarez's squadron, however, continued their voyage; the *Victory* and most of the other ships arriving, after a rough passage, safely off the Suffolk coast.

On the night of 19–20 December the *St. George* and a few other ships had parted company with the squadron. They first bore up for Vingå Sound, and then, the wind coming round to the north-east, shaped a course for England. They stood down the Skagerrack and some time later, off the west coast of Jutland, the *St. George* was observed to be in difficulties with her makeshift rudder. The north-westerly wind freshened and there was a current setting strongly to the south-east; to leeward lay the dangerous shoals off Jutland. The *St. George* under close-reefed courses and topsails then stood to the north-west, so as to clear the land to starboard and to keep the Skagerrack open. Disabled as she was, she was unable to make this course good and continually fell away to leeward. 'Jury masts,' observed Captain Boteler many years afterwards, 'were very well in fine weather, but they were not of sufficient weight in a gale.' In the late evening of the 23rd the *Cressy* wore and stood out to sea; but the *Defence* followed the flagship into the land. The wind had increased to gale force, with furious squalls of wind and rain, and the flagship, under storm-mizen staysail and trysail, laboured heavily in a tremendous sea. The captain of the *St. George*, taking the opportunity of a lull, had attempted to club-haul his ship and get her round on the other tack; but in vain. In the early hours of the 24th the *St. George* and the *Defence* drove

[1] The convoy on the 12th had imprudently anchored off Nysted, near the southern entrance of the Great Belt—a most perilous spot in a sou'-wester.

on the shoals and a few hours later went to pieces in the mountainous seas; there were only eighteen survivors.

Meanwhile, on 18 December, the merchantmen and their escorts had sailed from Vingå Sound. That part of the trade bound for London and Portsmouth sailed under convoy of the *Hero* and a brig. The captain of the *Hero* was badly out in his reckoning, believing himself to be on the Great Silver Pits when he was actually eighty miles to the east of them. (This was due to the easterly set in that area occasioned by the recent spell of strong north-easterly winds.) In the small hours of the 24th the *Hero* ran upon the Haak Sand, off the Texel, and was lost with all her ship's company.[1]

There had been no such catastrophe in our naval annals since the loss of Sir Clowdisley Shovel's flagship, with several other ships of the squadron, on their return from the Mediterranean in 1707. The disasters of 1811 cost the service three fine ships and the lives of 2,000 officers and men, which represented a far heavier loss than that sustained in any of the major actions of the Revolutionary and Napoleonic Wars. It was followed by severe and by no means unjustified criticism in the press.

'A more disastrous close of the season in the Baltic has seldom been experienced,' said the *Edinburgh Weekly Chronicle*; 'and it ought to serve as a useful lesson, that the homeward bound fleet should sail for England at least a month earlier in the season.' 'The melancholy fate of the Baltic ships', declared the *Newcastle Chronicle*, 'must call upon Parliament to inquire by what imperious necessity the squadron was detained in that sea to so late a period in the boisterous season.'

Admittedly the hazards of a late return from the Baltic were a risk which had to be run in the interests of trade protection. But it is scarcely possible to acquit the captains and the other officers concerned of extreme imprudence. The fact is that the *St. George* was in no condition to make such a voyage at such an advanced season. In her disabled condition she was only fit to sail in fine weather, which was not to be expected so late in the year.

If the loss of this ship (involving also that of the *Defence*) was due to bad seamanship, the loss of the *Hero* was apparently due to faulty navigation. Despite all these return passages from the Baltic each

---

[1] See the admirable account of the disaster by A. N. Ryan in *Mariner's Mirror*, Vol. 50, pp. 123–34, and also W. E. May in the same journal, p. 282.

autumn, it appears that the Navy had singularly failed to profit from experience. Only a few weeks before, the *Dictator*, on the same passage, had completely lost her reckoning in the middle of the North Sea; and actually rode at anchor for three days until a fishing craft arrived and gave the captain his bearings, after which he was able to proceed to the Swin. Moreover, the previous year another 74, the *Minotaur*, had similarly fetched up on the Haak and was lost with all hands. It is worth noticing that the merchantmen which had left Vingå Sound in company with the *Hero* had steered a safe course; but the captain of the *Hero*, failing to take the easterly set into account, had found himself, like the *Minotaur*, on the wrong side of the North Sea.

XII

The Peninsular War

I

In the meantime the struggle had taken a new turn. Napoleon's attempt to place his brother Joseph Bonaparte on the throne of Spain encountered, for the first time since the beginning of the war, a truly national resistance. In the spring of 1808 the Spaniards rose suddenly and spontaneously against the invaders; at Badajos, Cartagena, and Cadiz the pro-French governors were murdered by the mob; the revolutionary Junta at Seville appealed to the British governor of Gibraltar for arms and funds; caught between our blockading force and the now hostile batteries ashore, Rosily at Cadiz was presently forced to surrender with his squadron; and at Baylen, on 22 July, an entire French army laid down its arms. By August the revolt had spread to Portugal.

Considering, in view of the fact that the enemy's forces in southern Italy were much reduced and the Toulon fleet was not prepared for sea, that Sicily was in no immediate danger, Collingwood, on 29 May, announced his intention of leaving Vice-Admiral Thornbrough with a division to watch Toulon, while he proceeded with the rest of the fleet to the south of Spain to assist the insurgents. The Spanish revolt had put an end to the danger of an enemy concentration at Cadiz; the squadron which Collingwood had sent to blockade that port could now be withdrawn; moreover, his fleet had secured the use of Port Mahon, which presently became his base for the blockade of Toulon. The insurgents were speedily assisted by the British with arms, ammunition, and money; when our officers went on shore in Cadiz they were loudly cheered, and when the Commander-in-Chief visited that city on the Feast of the Assumption, 15 August, the Spanish cavalry had to clear a way for his party through an immense crowd of 40,000 people, while the streets and squares resounded with the cry of 'Viva King George! Viva Collingwood!' Baylen marked the beginning of the nationalist uprisings against Napoleon's power. It was the opportunity for which the British Cabinet had long been waiting. In response to Spanish appeals it was resolved at once to send out an army to support the insurgents. This force, under the command of Sir Arthur Wellesley, landed at the mouth of the Mondego on the Portuguese coast, and began to advance on Lisbon. On 19 August Junot, rashly attacking with the French Army of Portugal in the broken, wooded country between Vedras and Vimiero, was heavily defeated; and under the terms of the Convention of Cintra the French evacuated Portugal.

The Spanish uprising was not only important from the military and political standpoint, but also as a turning-point in the commercial war. In the first place it opened a yawning breach in the south-western section of the Continental Blockade, and in the second it materially reduced its efficacy elsewhere. Important new markets were opened up to our merchants alike in the Peninsula and in Spanish America, enabling them rapidly to dispose of immense stocks of manufactures and also of colonial produce. Scarcely less important was the psychological effect of these developments on the entire commercial community. Almost at once business began to revive. Even those professed pessimists, the leaders of the Parliamentary opposition, quickly came to realize that the Spanish uprising might well prove the salvation of British trade and industry. What might conceivably have happened if the peace of Europe had remained unbroken and the Continental System intact can never be known. The all-important fact is that peace in Europe was essential to the success of the Continental Blockade, and that, at this crucial moment, that peace was shattered. Napoleon and the Grand Army were drawn away across the Pyrenees, and a busy contraband traffic at once sprang up in many parts of northern Europe and along the shores of the Mediterranean.

In the autumn of 1808 Sir John Moore was appointed to command an expeditionary force of some 40,000 troops with instructions to support the Spanish armies in their attempt to encircle the French; but before he could concentrate his forces at the intended rendezvous —Valladollid in central Spain—the military situation in the Peninsula had been transformed by the sudden arrival of Napoleon with a splendid army of 200,000 men. During November every Spanish

Spain and Portugal

army was successively overthrown; resistance in northern and central Spain collapsed and Valladollid itself was in enemy hands; Moore's communications with Portugal were cut, and his army in danger of encirclement. To draw Napoleon off from the still unconquered regions of the Peninsula, Moore thrust eastward to threaten his life-line to France. The news of this stratagem reached the Emperor on 19 December, by which time the British were already half-way across his lines of communication. Napoleon acted with characteristic promptitude. Crossing the passes of the Guadarrama on foot at the head of his men, in a blinding blizzard, he pursued Moore with an overwhelmingly superior army across the plains of León. On New Year's Day, 1809, he learned that his quarry had reached the Galician mountains, and that the last hope of a decisive success had passed. At the same time intelligence reached Napoleon from Paris that Austria was arming for war; whereupon, handing over the command to Soult, he instantly resolved to quit Spain. Moore's stratagem had proved completely successful; it had gained for the Spanish insurgents several vital months of respite; Napoleon's plans for the subjugation of the Peninsula had had to be abandoned, and Portugal and southern Spain were safe for the winter.

But the price had been a heavy one. The campaign, indeed, very nearly cost Great Britain the entire army—the only one that she had left. In those hard-pressed columns, racing desperately in the closing days of 1808 for the Esla and the Galician defiles before they should be cut off by the encircling enemy force, discipline and morale cracked under the strain. On 31 December the Commander-in-Chief dispatched the Light Brigade under Major-General Crawford towards Vigo in order to cover his southern flank. The demoralization of Moore's army increased apace on the long mountain road to Corunna, where his line of retreat was marked by an ever-lengthening trail of dying soldiers, camp-followers of both sexes, horses, and mules. The country through which they passed was almost desert; and, the commissariat failing, the troops were nearly starving. For the best part of 150 miles, in appalling weather, they struggled on; until, at a cost of 5,000 casualties, they came out at last on the coastal plain and on 10 January reached Corunna.

Moore at once began to embark his sick and wounded in the hospital and supply ships which lay in the bay. But the transports and their escorts (including the *Victory*, *Ville de Paris*, *Zealous*, and *Audacious*), which had been ordered round from Vigo, failing to weather Cape Finisterre, did not arrive until the evening of the 14th, when the harbour was crowded with something like 250 sail, with the men-of-war lying out in the offing. The position was hazardous in the extreme. A sudden change in the wind might put the whole fleet in jeopardy. Early on the 16th the last of the stores and baggage were taken on board the transports; but by that time Soult's forces had occupied the surrounding heights and were about to attack; and, in the afternoon, to cover the embarkation of the army, Moore fought and won the famous rearguard action in which he lost his life. The French showing no disposition to renew the fight, the embarkation was carried out in good order under the supervision of Commissioner James

334

Bowen.[1] Leaving only pickets along their front, regiment after regiment marched down to the quays and beaches. Hour after hour the boats of the fleet (some of whose crews had no food or sleep for nearly two days) were employed in ferrying the troops to the waiting transports. Throughout the night of the 16th and the day following, the embarkation continued. On the 17th the wind suddenly freshened. 'The weather is now tempestuous and the difficulties of embarkation are great,' remarked Rear-Admiral de Courcy. 'All except the rearguard are embarked.'[2] The French presently occupied a position from which they could cannonade the shipping that still lay in the harbour 'as thick as a wood', despite the orders the masters had received to proceed to sea immediately they had got their quota of troops or stores on board. The masters now hurriedly cut or slip, and a number of the transports 'through fright or mismanagement' ran on shore. 'The dangers of the situation were great,' wrote de Courcy—'had the wind been otherwise than southerly the whole would probably have been lost.'[3] On the 18th most of the ships lay in the offing, while a single brigade which had remained to cover the retirement of the rest embarked safely from a position behind the citadel. The crowded transports with their escorts ran before a heavy south-westerly gale, and in a few days reached English ports.

News of further Spanish disasters followed the return of Moore's army from Corunna. Soult and Ney overran Galicia, and Corunna and Ferrol capitulated to the French. Joseph was crowned in Madrid. St. Cyr routed the Spaniards at Valls and occupied most of Catalonia, and Saragossa surrendered. The north and centre of Spain were held down by strong enemy forces. But though the Spaniards had suffered grievous reverses, their spirit was unbroken and they continued grimly to resist, supported and supplied in the coastal areas by the ships and squadrons of the Royal Navy.

Surrounded on three sides by the sea, the Peninsula was an ideal

---

[1] James Bowen, formerly master of Howe's flagship, the *Queen Charlotte*, was probably the only officer who, after greatly distinguishing himself in what St. Vincent termed 'that most useful and important branch of the service', rose to the top of his profession. He was promoted to post rank in 1795; was appointed Commissioner of the Transport Board in 1803, and retired, in 1825, with the rank of rear-admiral.

[2] Adm. 1/140, 17 January 1809.

[3] *Ibid.*, 23 January 1809.

theatre for amphibious warfare. The British forces could be supplied from home with comparative ease, while the French, dispersed throughout a wasted wilderness, were dependent upon bad roads which were also, at some points, open to attack from the sea. (The vital line of communication between France and eastern Spain, which followed the coast all the way from Perpignan to Barcelona, was a case in point.) The exploits of Captain Cochrane in the *Impérieuse*—a 38-gun frigate, the fastest of that class in the Navy—had shown what was possible to a single ship's crew when well led. The daring and resource displayed by Cochrane on this cruise were beyond all praise. It has been truly said, 'No officer ever attempted or succeeded in more arduous enterprises with so little loss'. Cruising off the Catalan coast in 1808–9, Cochrane blew up roads and bridges, attacked batteries and signal-posts, interrupted supplies and harassed enemy columns on the march, and, cooperating with the Spanish guerrilla bands, encouraged the people to rise against their oppressors. The log of the *Imperiéuse* from the early part of March 1808 to the end of January 1809 reads something like the précis of a boy's adventure story.[1] Many years afterwards Captain Frederick Marryat, then a famous novelist, recalling these stirring times, declared:

The cruises of the *Impérieuse* were periods of continual excitement, from the hour in which she hove up her anchor till she dropped it again in port; the day that passed without a shot being fired in anger, was to us a blank day: the boats were hardly secured on the booms than they were cast loose and out again; the yard and stay tackles were for ever hoisting up and lowering down. The expedition with which parties were formed for service; the rapidity of the frigate's movements night and day; the hasty sleep snatched at all hours; the waking up at the report of the guns, which seemed the only keynote to the hearts of those on board, the beautiful precision of our fire, obtained by constant practice; the coolness and courage of our captain, inoculating the whole of the ship's company; the suddenness of our attacks, the gathering after the combat, the killed lamented, the wounded almost envied; the powder so burnt into our faces that years could not remove it; the proved character of every man and officer on board, the implicit trust and adoration we felt for our commander; the ludicrous situations which would occur in the extremest danger and create mirth when death was staring you in the face, the hair-breadth escapes, and the indifference to life shown by all—when memory

[1] Adm. 51/2462, 6 March 1808–31 January 1809.

sweeps along these years of excitement even now, my pulse beats more quickly with the reminiscence.[1]

Other frigates which were harassing the enemy's communications on the coast at this time were the *Spartan* and *Cambrian*. Another important service rendered by the Navy in the early years of the Peninsular War was the repatriation of most of the 15,000 Spanish auxiliaries, who had been serving Napoleon in the Baltic theatre, to stiffen the insurgent forces in northern Spain.

Notwithstanding the disappointment of the hopes that had been entertained by very many in Great Britain of the speedy overthrow of Napoleon's power in the Peninsula, the Cabinet, urged on by Castlereagh, was still determined to persevere in this theatre. Other signs were not lacking of an approaching revolt against the French hegemony. Despite the heavy defeats that she had sustained in the campaigns of 1805–6, Austria was still a great military Power. She had lately reorganized her army, and, in the autumn of 1808, began secret negotiations with London with a view to renewing the struggle. Though there was no formal treaty between the two States, it was well known to the British government that the Austrians hoped much from the diversions made by our forces in the Peninsula and North Germany. Moreover, the Austrian appeal for a British expedition to the Dutch or north German coast was reinforced by a warning from the Admiralty that Napoleon was planning an invasion of the British Isles from Antwerp. In the early months of 1809, however, there were not sufficient troops available for anything more than a raid; and in the end the government decided to prepare for a full-scale expedition to the Scheldt later in the year.

A further complication then arose. In the spring of 1809 the Brest squadron, comprising ten of the line, got away to sea and took refuge in the Aix roads off Rochefort, where it was followed, and once again blocked in, by the Channel fleet under Admiral Lord Gambier. The presence of this strong force in the Bay of Biscay endangered the British communications with Portugal and constituted a threat to our possessions and trade in the West Indies. The government yielded to the urgent representations of the City merchants; and Captain Cochrane—then at the height of his fame—was requested by the

[1] Q. *Life and Letters of Captain Marryat*, ed. Florence Marryat (1872).

Admiralty to expel the French battleships from the anchorage with explosion vessels and fireships.

After careful preparation the attack was launched on the dark and windy night of 11 April. 'A more daring plan was never made,' said Marryat, who himself took part in the action. With a favouring wind and tide Cochrane launched his explosion vessels against the huge triangular boom which protected the anchorage, and then sent in his fireships. As the explosion vessels erupted in flame and thunder and the fireships bore down on the enemy's line, the French cut their cables in panic haste and drifted away from the protection of the shore batteries; all but two of their vessels took the ground. Gambier had only to act with promptitude and their destruction was assured.

But the Commander-in-Chief, who disliked both Cochrane and his method of attack, continued to ignore the latter's signals, and remained with his force in the offing. At 5.48 a.m. Cochrane made the signal, 'Half the fleet can destroy the enemy. Seven on shore'. Then at 6.40, 'Eleven on shore'; an hour later, 'Only two afloat'; and at 9.30 a.m., 'Enemy preparing to heave off'. The young flood was making, and the enemy were preparing to float their ships off the banks. Eventually in desperation Cochrane, without orders, stood in alone in the *Impérieuse*, and attacked and destroyed one of the stranded battleships; and then, with the deliberate intention of forcing his superior's hand, he threw out in succession the following signals. At 10.30 a.m.: 'The enemy's ships are getting under sail'. At 1.40 p.m.: 'The enemy is superior to the chasing ship'. At 1.45 p.m.: 'The ship is in distress, and requires to be assisted immediately'.[1] This finally shamed the Admiral into sending in the *Indefatigable*, supported by a few frigates and smaller vessels, and half an hour later two further battleships, which accounted for four more of the enemy.[2]

On 22 April 1809 Wellesley returned to Portugal as Commander-

---

[1] Adm. 52/4149, 11–13 April 1809.

[2] On his return to England in the *Impérieuse* Cochrane was created a K.B. Then, despite the strong remonstrances of Lord Mulgrave, the First Lord, he proceeded to oppose the Parliamentary Vote of Thanks to Gambier. That was the end of Cochrane's brilliant career in the Service. He was slighted in every possible way and never employed again. Some years later he was 'framed' and convicted in connection with a stock exchange fraud, expelled from Parliament and the Navy, and thrown into prison. On his release Cochrane left England to take part in the South American wars of liberation.

in-Chief. This was largely owing to Castlereagh's firm support of the Peninsular campaign and of Wellesley in the Cabinet. The reinforcements lately dispatched to Lisbon brought the British forces stationed in Portugal up to a total strength of 20,000 men, added to which were about 16,000 Portuguese. Opposing them were Marshal Soult in the north with 23,000 men, Marshal Victor with 25,000 more to the eastward, and a force of about 6,000 near Ciudad Rodrigo. About 200,000 other French troops were stationed in various parts of the Peninsula. Large enemy forces had, however, been recalled to France as a result of the Austrian crisis; and another favouring factor was the departure from the Peninsula of Napoleon himself, whose presence in the field, according to Wellesley, 'made a difference of 40,000 men'.

Wellesley presently marched against Soult in the north and took him by surprise at Oporto before he could fall back on his reserves. By crossing the river in his rear, he forced the Marshal to retire precipitately across the frontier into Spain, with the loss of all his guns and stores. Shortly after, Wellesley, advancing deep into Spain, defeated the French, on 28 July, at Talavera. But the Spanish authorities having failed to make good their promises as to supplies, he was soon obliged to retire. Henceforth Wellesley refused to cooperate with the Spanish armies, or to rely upon these feckless Allies for food and stores. By so doing in the campaign of Talavera he had lost a third of his army. For the next six months or so his troops were in cantonments in northern Portugal, while the frontier was defended by the Light Division under Major-General Robert Craufurd and his Portuguese auxiliaries.

For their part the French could spare only limited forces for an advance across the barren Portuguese highlands; for in the face of the savage guerrilla warfare the bulk of their armies were tied down in garrison and convoy duties throughout Spain. Many of the garrisons were at times completely isolated. The three-hundred-mile lifeline from Bayonne to Madrid came under almost continual attack. None but the strongest convoy could expect to pass safely through a tract occupied by a powerful guerrilla band. In short, they could only bring sufficient force against Portugal by jeopardizing the whole position in Spain. 'If we can maintain ourselves in Portugal,' Wellesley predicted, 'the war will not cease in the Peninsula, and, if the war lasts in the Peninsula, Europe will be saved.'

Napoleon's hope of a decisive victory in Spain, as has been said, had been frustrated by the action of Sir John Moore. The Emperor's absence in the Peninsula had given Austria, revengeful and resurgent, the opportunity for which she had been waiting. It was the prospect of imminent war which drew Napoleon, driving furiously, to Paris. Austria was the centre of widespread movements of revolt, in the Tyrol and elsewhere. Nevertheless, the Austrian war failed to develop into a general nationalist uprising. Before the struggle could spread Napoleon had struck with lightning speed at the spine of resistance in central Europe. The opening phase of his campaign against the Archduke Charles on the middle Danube ranks among the master-pieces of the art of war. The Five Days' Battle—18 to 23 April—was, in fact, the victory of swift and supple manœuvre over hesitancy, caution, and delay. On 13 May Napoleon entered Vienna. All this happened while the British were still in the preparatory stages of their intended expedition to relieve the pressure upon Austria. It was in vain that one of the Austrian envoys warned Canning that 'the promptitude of the enemy had always been the key to his success.' The Archduke's army, however, proved a far more formidable oppo-nent than it had been three years before. At the action of Aspern-Essling, on 21–22 May, the French sustained severe losses, following which Napoleon established himself in the island of Lobau in the Danube, emerging seven weeks later to gain a Pyrrhic victory over the Archduke at Wagram on 6 July. For the second time Napoleon entered Vienna in triumph at the head of his troops and dictated peace in the palace of Schönbrunn. Austria lost one-fifth of her population and territory to the conqueror, and the Hapsburg emperor gave him his daughter's hand in marriage. The Tyrolese and other Austro-German uprisings were stamped out by French, Bavarian, and Italian forces.

Three weeks after Wagram the largest expedition which had ever left the shores of Great Britain was sent out to capture Antwerp and to destroy the enemy's battleships lying in the Scheldt; nearly 40,000 troops and thirty-two sail of the line, besides 200 lesser craft, took part in it.

It is to be remembered that Antwerp was not merely a naval base, but also a shipbuilding centre of the first importance in time of war; since timber from the forests of northern France and Germany could be brought down to the shipyards by way of the Meuse and

Rhine when the sea route to Brest through the North Sea was barred by the British blockade. The orders of the Admiralty were 'to sink, burn, and destroy the whole of the enemy's ships of war afloat in the Scheldt, or building at Antwerp, Terneuse, or Flushing; and, if possible, to render the Scheldt no longer navigable for ships of war'. It was hoped by this stroke to remove a potential threat to our national security and also, by inducing the Prussians to throw in their lot with the Allies, to create a diversion to relieve the hard-pressed Austrians.

But the expedition was badly planned, and—at least so far as the army was concerned—worse led; the naval commander, Sir Richard Strachan, did not agree with the military commander, Lord Chatham; there was none of the speed and urgency which had marked the expedition against Copenhagen; the result was a series of disastrous delays. The situation was well summed up in a contemporary epigram:

> Lord Chatham, with his sword undrawn,
> Stood waiting for Sir Richard Strachan;
> Sir Richard, longing to be at 'em,
> Stood waiting for the Earl of Chatham.

The result was that our Austrian Allies had been beaten out of the war before the expedition even started. For a few weeks the fate of Antwerp hung in the balance. The British forces were disembarked with great skill by the Navy, on 30 July, on the island of Walcheren; but owing to a south-westerly gale the landing had to be made, not on the south-west coast near Flushing, but at the far end of the island.[1] Before the first British troops could reach Flushing reinforcements had been ferried across to the port from the mainland; and Flushing, with its batteries facing the Wielingen Channel up which the transports must presently advance to gain the West Scheldt, held out until 18 August—by which time 'polder fever' had broken out among our troops on the island, and Marshal Bernadotte, galvanizing his subordinates into violent activity, had flooded the levels to the north of Antwerp, mounted naval guns on the surrounding forts, and gathered some 26,000 troops for the city's defences. Meanwhile another force of 8,000 British troops had landed on South Beveland and overrun most of that island, arriving by 2 August within sight of

[1] Adm. 1/561, 4 August 1809.

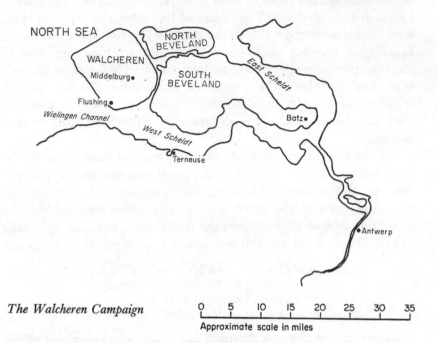

NORTH SEA

NORTH BEVELAND

WALCHEREN

Middelburg•

SOUTH BEVELAND

East Scheldt

Flushing•

Wielingen Channel

Batz•

West Scheldt

Terneuse

•Antwerp

The Walcheren Campaign

0   5   10   15   20   25   30   35

Approximate scale in miles

the towers and spires of Antwerp, from which they were separated only by the narrowest stretch of the East Scheldt. But the barges and gun-boats which were to ferry them across were still fifty miles away on the wrong side of the Wielingen Channel. By the time the transports began to advance up the river it was too late; it was clearly out of the question to launch an attack in the face of such forces as were now collected before Antwerp. Already one-fifth of the British army was down with fever, and many more were sickening. The attempt was in consequence called off; and first South Beveland, and later Walcheren, were evacuated. The port and arsenal of Flushing had, indeed, been destroyed; but the real objectives of the expedition— namely, the seizure of Antwerp and the destruction of the enemy's ships—had not been achieved.[1]

[1] 'It is hardly too much to say that the primary cause of the failure at Walcheren lay in the obliviousness of all concerned, from minister to military commander, to the importance of Time. It was lost in preparation and squandered in execution' (H. W. Richmond, *Statesmen and Sea Power* (1946)).

2

As a result of the Spanish insurrection in the previous year, the strategical situation in the Mediterranean had become a good deal easier. The division of the battle fleet into two powerful squadrons was no longer necessary; and a few days after the battle of Vimiero Collingwood, leaving Purvis with a 74 and five frigates to lie off Cadiz and protect the trade, sailed for Toulon.[1] Next year, however, through the collapse of Austria and the rapid advance of Napoleon's power down the eastern shore of the Adriatic, the threat to Turkey was once again renewed. To forestall a possible attack on the Ottoman Empire, it was decided by the Cabinet to seize certain of the Ionian Islands. The occupation was effected in the latter part of 1808 by a force of 1,900 troops escorted by the *Warrior*, 74, and the *Philomel* sloop. But the development of the Peninsular uprising indefinitely postponed the partition of Turkey. This was, in fact, much to the advantage of Great Britain. For, had Napoleon been able to carry into effect his designs of eastward expansion, our forces could not seriously have impeded the enemy's advance, on account of the vast distances involved.

The tide of war now flowed westward: after the failure of Murat's attempt to invade Sicily, in 1810[2], operations in the Mediterranean languished. Marmont left Dalmatia to face Wellington in Spain. At the same time the Cabinet moved troops out of Sicily to reinforce our army in the Peninsula. To block the enemy's communications with the east coast, the port of Toulon was closely invested.

It was the war in Catalonia which brought about the only notable engagement of Collingwood's command. In the autumn of 1809 a small French division left Toulon, escorting a convoy of some twenty

---

[1] The blockade of Toulon presented peculiar difficulties: in clear weather the blockading squadron could be sighted fifteen leagues at sea; and when its position was known to the French they could slip past it under cover of night.

[2] The enemy had assembled nearly 30,000 troops on this side of the Straits of Messina, and 500 transports were held in readiness for the descent. In the summer the French heavily bombarded the British positions across the Straits: but when on 17 September they attempted to cross they were repulsed with heavy losses.

vessels for the relief of Barcelona. A few weeks earlier Collingwood had retired before a gale to Minorca, where, in view of the enemy's preparations in Toulon, he concentrated his forces, stationing three frigates and a sloop to windward to look out for the French. On the morning of 23 October one of his scouting frigates made the signal for a fleet to the eastward. The French warships—three of the line and several frigates—hauled their wind on sighting the British cruisers and separated from their convoy. With eight of Collingwood's fastest ships, Rear-Admiral George Martin then chased the enemy into the hazardous shoal waters off the coast of Languedoc, where on the 25th all the Frenchmen ran ashore, the 80-gun flagship *Robuste* and the *Lion* being burned by their own crews; after which Martin's vessels— some of which had got within the five-fathom line—hauled their wind and stood off. Shortly after Collingwood sent in a cutting-out expedition, under Captain Hallowell, which captured or burnt most of the convoy in Rosas Bay.

After Wagram, and the subsequent submission of Austria to Napoleon, the Fourth Coalition fell to pieces. But Collingwood's powerful fleet continued to exert an invisible but potent influence on all the Mediterranean coastline—contesting Napoleon's Berlin Decrees, supporting the British garrison in Sicily, inducing Turkey to reopen her ports to British trade, labouring to compose the differences of the Juntas, and encouraging the insurgents of Catalonia and Valencia with British arms and supplies.

Year after year in his flagship, the *Ocean*, the ageing and ailing Collingwood remained doggedly at his post, combining the offices of admiral and diplomatist. Moving between the coast of Spain, Sicily, Port Mahon, and the approaches to Toulon, he continually resisted the French attempts to expand to the southward and eastward. The defensive strategy ordained by the Cabinet for this theatre proved wholly successful. Only in the Ionian Islands had Napoleon succeeded in breaking out of his continental bounds—and even there his forces were held in the grip of the British blockade. In the spring of 1809 Collingwood shifted his flag from the *Ocean*, which had been badly damaged in a gale, to the *Ville de Paris*. The change, indeed, made little difference to the Commander-in-Chief; for, as he himself confessed, he very seldom left his cabin. Throughout these years he carefully looked after the health and well-being of his men, inquiring after their diet and amusements, insisting on clothes and hammocks being regularly aired on the booms, and giving orders for the decks to be kept dry and well ventilated. Above all, he stressed the need for economy in supplies and stores of all kinds. 'In the course of your short voyage', he remarked to one offending captain, 'there has been more masts, sails and rigging lost than in all the squadron besides, and far beyond proportionate to the service you had to perform.' Of another he observed acidly, 'That officer should never sail without a store-ship in company. He knows as much seamanship as the King's Attorney General.' But this passion for economy was carried to excessive lengths in his later years; and his meticulous attention to detail became an obsession. 'He seems to do everything himself', Codrington had declared, 'with great attention to the minutiae.' To this absorption of Collingwood's in *paperasserie* was almost certainly due, in part at least, his failure to intercept Ganteaume. 'I have been in this ship four or five days,' he declared, on shifting to the *Ville de Paris*, 'and like her very much; but all ships that sail well and are strong are alike to me; I see little of them, seldom moving from my desk.' 'I am ceaselessly writing', he observed on another occasion, 'and the day is not long enough for me to get through my business.' Collingwood's thoughts and energies were in fact centred too much on the papers on his desk, and too little on the ships and sea around him. 'The conduct of a fleet consisting of thirty sail of the line and upwards of forty smaller vessels involved a great deal of clerical work, exclusive of political correspondence,' Laughton has declared, 'but a commander-in-chief who seldom moves from his desk can scarcely be absolved of neglecting other most necessary parts of his duty. It is to this, in a measure, that the uneventful nature of Collingwood's command must be ascribed.'[1]

Collingwood's deficiencies in the field of action were to some extent repaired by the resource and initiative of certain of the captains under his command. 'We are carrying on our operations in the Adriatic and on the coast of Italy with great éclat,' he wrote on 30 June 1809. 'All our frigate Captains are great Generals, and some in the brigs are good Brigadiers. . . . The activity and zeal in those gallant

---

[1] See J. K. Laughton's article on Collingwood in the *Dictionary of National Biography*. The majority of naval historians in the past have for the most part concurred in Laughton's strictures on Collingwood: for a contrary view, see Piers Mackesy, *The War in the Mediterranean, 1803–1810*, pp. 230–58.

young men keep up my spirits, and make me equal to bear the dis-
agreeables that happen from the contentions of some other ships. . . .
Those who do all the service give no trouble; those who give the
trouble are good for nothing.' Foremost among these subordinate
commanders were Lord Thomas Cochrane, Patrick Campbell,
Thomas Harvey, William Hoste, and Jahleel Brenton. Cochrane's
activities on the east coast of Spain, during the years 1808–9, have
already been mentioned. Collingwood's cruiser squadrons in the
Adriatic played a major role in the protection of Turkey—harassing
the enemy's communications with his two forward bases, Ragusa and
Corfu, from which he threatened the Ottoman Empire. Campbell, in
the *Unité* frigate—'the smartest ship in the sea,' as her captain proudly
claimed—who until Tilsit had been engaged in blocking the sea passage
between Venice and northern Dalmatia, was in September 1808
ordered to watch Corfu. Harvey, in the *Standard*, 64, was also, earlier
in 1808, stationed in the lower Adriatic, where he intercepted reinforcements and supplies from southern Italy to Ragusa and the Ionian
Islands. Later Harvey and the *Standard* returned to England; and
Captain Eyre in the *Magnificent*, 74, was appointed to command the
Adriatic squadron. In January 1809 Campbell returned to his old
hunting-grounds in the upper Adriatic, where he was later supported
(and ultimately superseded) by Hoste. The latter, a Norfolk man who
had formerly been under the particular care of Nelson in the *Agamemnon*, distinguished himself during the years 1808–10 by a brisk and
successful series of attacks on the enemy's coast and shipping in the
Adriatic. During the latter half of 1808 in his frigate, the *Amphion*,
Hoste captured or destroyed no less than 218 of the enemy's ships and
virtually stopped his coastal trade. In the following year, assisted by a
single sloop, he kept blocked up in Venice, Ancona, and Trieste
greatly superior French, Venetian, and Russian forces. 'The truth is',
Hoste observed, 'they are afraid of the weather, and are very badly
manned; we are all well manned, and do not care a fig about the
weather.' Off Lissa, on 13 March 1811, in command of a squadron of
four frigates, he outmanœuvred and decisively defeated a hostile
force of almost double his strength. Returning to the scene of his
former triumphs in the *Bacchante*, 38, in 1812, Hoste achieved a
number of further successes against the enemy's convoys and flotillas
and in 1813 played a leading part in the reduction of Cattaro. Apart

from his audacious pursuit in the frigate *Spartan* of Ganteaume's fleet in 1808, Brenton's principal services in the Mediterranean were his share in the reduction of several of the Ionian Islands in 1809 and his victory over a small squadron off Naples in 1810.

Under the strain of the arduous blockading routine and the difficulties and dangers of the constantly changing military and political situation, worn out before his time by long years of heavy and incessant mental toil, Collingwood's erstwhile strong constitution was progressively undermined. Weighed down by the grievous burden of his responsibilities, and sick with longing for family and home, he nevertheless obliged himself to endure the unnatural life he led.[1] At last in March, 1810, his health broke down altogether, and the doctors ordered him home to England. But it was then too late; he died on the first day of the homeward passage. He was succeeded on the station by Admiral Sir Charles Cotton.

3

Following the débâcle of the British expedition to the Scheldt, the Cabinet decided to concentrate its main military resources on the Peninsular campaign. It did so in the face of marked public disapprobation of the Peninsular War in general and of Wellesley (lately raised to the peerage as Viscount Wellington) in particular. It was widely felt that blood and treasure had been sacrified in this region in vain. The Cabinet, however, still retained its faith in its chosen commander. To enable him to hold Portugal against the French, reinforcements were presently ordered to the Tagus both from home and from garrisons overseas; and not before it was time. Already Masséna, the ablest of Napoleon's marshals, was massing his forces on the Portuguese frontier preparatory to the great offensive which should roll the British into the sea. Three times in the last three years a French army had attempted to gain Lisbon. This time Masséna was determined there should be no mistake. As the French completed their formidable preparations,

---

[1] 'I hardly ever see the face of an officer except when they dine with me,' Collingwood observed on 14 June, 1807, 'and am seldom on deck above an hour in the day, when I go in the twilight to breathe the fresh air' (*Q. D. F.* Stephenson, *Admiral Collingwood* (1948), p. 12).

public opinion in England inclined to the belief that the evacuation of Wellington's army was inevitable.[1]

The Anglo-Portuguese army fell back before the hostile advance, snatching a hasty victory at Bussaco before retiring in good order, through a region swept bare of supplies, to Torres Vedras on the Lisbon peninsula. In this broad, rugged chain of hills between the Atlantic and the Tagus estuary, Wellington, during the previous twelve months, had had three great lines of defence constructed. Here, drawing his supplies from the sea, he could hold out indefinitely. The position was one of immense natural strength; and no pains had been spared to enhance the difficulties confronting the assailant by every device of military science. Trenches had been dug along the flanks of the hills; forts and redoubts established at strategic points; roads torn up; bridges mined; ravines barricaded with tree-trunks and rock walls; the crest of the hills scarped for miles; rivers dammed up, turning entire valleys into quagmires. To bind the whole system together, a chain of signal-stations, manned by sailors, reached from end to end of the lines. As the French came within range, the British gunboats in the Tagus opened fire. The enemy advance was abruptly stayed. Masséna was unable to force even the first of the lines. For six weeks the French remained before these impregnable defences, unable to advance and unwilling to retire, while hunger and disease did their work. The campaign ended with a general retirement towards Santarem, thirty miles to the northward, where, half-famished, they passed the winter.

The whole campaign was a masterpiece of defensive strategy; for Wellington's object, for the best of reasons, was not to lose men in battle, but to wear down his adversary by starvation and sickness. 'I could lick these fellows any day,' he declared, 'but it would cost me 10,000 men, and, as this is the last army England has, we must take care of it.'

The following April Masséna's army retreated across the frontier,

---

[1] It is worth noticing that Moore had always been of opinion that Portugal could not be held. 'Its frontier,' he informed Castlereagh in November 1808, 'is not defensible against a superior force. It is an open frontier, all equally rugged, but all equally to be penetrated. If the French succeed in Spain, it will be vain to attempt to resist them in Portugal. The British must in that event immediately take steps to evacuate the country' (Q. Oman, *History of the Peninsular War*, I, p. 599).

exhausted and utterly demoralized, with a loss of about 35,000 of their number and nearly all their baggage, leaving Portugal still unsubdued. The repercussions of Torres Vedras were considerable. It put new heart into the Spanish irregulars; the murmurings of the opposition in the British Parliament were temporarily stilled; the tone of the Russian notes to Napoleon hardened; and though 370,000 enemy troops still occupied the Peninsula, they were unable to hold Wellington in check, or beat down the insurgent forces, supported from the sea by British cruisers, which held out in the mountains of Navarre, Asturia, and Galicia, in the Sierra Nevada and Murcia. Never again did the French venture to enter Portugal. 'We have', Wellington wrote to Liverpool late that year, 'certainly altered the course of the war in Spain; it has become to a certain degree offensive on our part.'

At the same time another French army, under Marshal Victor, was checked before Cadiz—a city which, like Lisbon, had become a great arsenal regularly supplied from the sea. Early in March 1811 the French besiegers were attacked and defeated, at Barrosa, by Sir Thomas Graham.

Throughout the war Wellington's strategy never failed to turn to good account the immense advantages conferred by the British command of the sea. The small British army could operate in this region with an effectiveness out of all proportion to its numbers. Again and again the strategy of the war pivoted on the simple fact that the French armies could not maintain themselves in a desert, and were consequently compelled to disperse, while the British were securely supplied from the sea. Convoy after convoy laden with provisions and military stores sailed from England to the Peninsular ports in Allied hands. The quays of Lisbon were piled high with supplies, which were presently transported in slow, creaking ox-wagons in the wake of Wellington's army.

The geography of the Peninsula, and, still more, the psychology of the Spanish people (who, after the defeat of their regular troops, revealed an unexpected genius for guerrilla warfare) were factors which had a decisive influence upon the course of the war. The regular Spanish armies had failed; but the guerrilleros—some of them under very able commanders—were succeeding. They rendered the communications of the enemy at all times difficult and dangerous.

Continual raids were made on convoys of provisions and stores passing along the great Bayonne-Madrid trunk-road—the main highway and artery of Napoleon's army of occupation—on their way to his forces in the Peninsula. A roving band of Catalans had even crossed the Pyrenees and carried the war into France itself. Naval support materially extended and intensified the constant guerrilla pressure on the enemy. In the summer of 1811 the Spanish commander Ballasteros, aided by the Navy, by his successive descents and re-embarkations along the Andalusian coast kept a number of Soult's divisions pinned down in the south. In February 1812, with the help of guns landed from Collier's squadron, the guerrilla chieftain Mina captured Tafalla. Throughout this period Codrington commanded a detached division on the east coast of Spain, cooperating with the Spaniards and waging an amphibious, harassing war against the French army of occupation. 'The courage they show in the guerrilla warfare is quite astonishing,' he said of his Allies, whom he assisted and sustained by every means in his power. In 1812 Hallowell, now promoted to flag rank, also arrived to support Ballasteros's troops. In the following spring he convoyed an Anglo-Sicilian force to the siege of Tarragona; but, largely owing to the bad relations between the naval and military commanders, and the incompetence of the latter, the attempt on Tarragona failed.

During the years 1809–11 Wellington's army had alternately advanced and retired on its Portuguese base. Masséna's bid 'to drive the leopards into the sea' had disastrously failed. In the latter part of 1811 Wellington, now ready to take the offensive, made secret preparations for a winter assault on Ciudad Rodrigo, the key-fortress to northern Spain. So opened the crucial year 1812.

The factors which had always militated against the success of the enemy's operations in the Peninsula proved decisive in the course of the next two years. The mutual jealousies of the marshals and their failure to support King Joseph prevented the timely concentration of force which alone might have stemmed the British onset. Napoleon's invasion of Russia, and the withdrawal of many of his veteran battallions from Spain, gave Wellington the chance for which he had been waiting. In January and April 1812 the British forces had stormed the frontier fortresses of Ciudad Rodrigo and Badajos. In June Wellington advanced once more into Spain.

About the same time that Wellington began his offensive, Commodore Sir Home Popham arrived from England in the *Venerable*, 74, to succeed Captain Sir George Collier in command of the squadron stationed on the north coast of Spain.

Soon after his arrival he joined Don Gaspar, the leader of the local guerrillas, in an attack on Lequitio town and fort. One of the *Venerable*'s guns was with difficulty brought to shore through a heavy breaking sea, and dragged by oxen, aided by guerrillas and seamen, to a neighbouring hill overlooking the fort; before sunset the wall had been breached and the fort stormed by the guerrillas. Next day the garrison of Lequitio surrendered.[1]

In the ensuing months Popham cooperated to good effect with Mendizabal, Longa, Don Gaspar and other guerrilla chieftains, supplying them with arms, ammunition, and stores (the Spaniards even borrowed guns from his cruisers), destroying coastal batteries and capturing various small ports, and harassing the main French supply route where it skirted the shore at San Sebastian. The guerrillas in the Basque provinces had by this time become so formidable that even with the small force at his disposal Popham was able to achieve a great deal. 'The peasantry are arising everywhere', he reported to Keith, 'and I have hourly solicitations for arms. The enemy is so considerably harassed by our sudden movements that I am inclined to think he will divide his force for two points, Guetaria and Santona.'[2]

The Cantabrian sierras, with their steep, rugged mountain chains stretching roughly parallel to the Bay of Biscay, the slopes densely forested for most of their height and the summits serrated ridges of naked rock, offered incomparable opportunities for guerrilla war. In conjunction with the roving bands of partisans, who knew every smugglers' track and goat-path of their native hills, readily furnishing the supplies without which they could never have carried on their struggle against the French, Popham effectively exploited all the advantages of amphibious warfare.

The result of Popham's activities more than fulfilled Wellington's expectations. He and the Basque guerrillas achieved a prime strategic objective with a remarkable economy of force; for by these conjoint operations on the Biscayan coast he and his allies had prevented about

[1] *Keith Papers*, III, pp. 269–70; *Naval Chronicle*, Vol. 28, p. 74.
[2] *Keith Papers*, III, p. 274.

35,000 men under Caffarelli from reinforcing Marmont, and thereby contributed materially to Wellington's victory at Salamanca on 22 July. In the same week that Salamanca was fought Popham's squadron assisted the guerrillas to take Santander.[1]

The British army entered Madrid in triumph, while Joseph fled to Toledo. But Joseph, Soult, and Souchat were hurriedly uniting their forces against him; the Spanish generals had once again defaulted, and Wellington's position was becoming hazardous. After an abortive assault on Burgos—the northern fortress which commanded the enemy's line of communications with the Pyrenees—the British forces fell back, disheartened and demoralized, on Ciudad Rodrigo. So ended the campaign.

Nevertheless, the moral effect of Salamanca was tremendous: the French power in Spain had received a blow from which it never recovered. Some 20,000 prisoners had been taken, with a very large number of guns. The whole of southern Spain had been liberated from the invader. The guerrillas had been enabled by the French concentration to extend their control over an immense area of the country. In the north these guerrillas were more formidable than ever during the winter of 1812–13. In Navarre, the redoubtable Mina dominated the whole countryside, and occasionally came over to the Basque provinces to assist the insurgents there. On the Cantabrian coast, Longa was besieging Santona, and Don Gaspar was operating in Biscay.

With our army's retirement into Portugal in the autumn, relations between the two services deteriorated. Wellington urged Popham to remain on the coast, but so late in the year as it was the position of his squadron was becoming untenable. Not the least of Popham's difficulties throughout the campaign was Wellington's total inability to comprehend the exigencies of naval warfare. He was now obliged to inform the Field Marshal that the large ships could not safely remain on the coast and that Mendizabal had proved an undependable ally. To the end of 1812 Wellington's criticisms of the Navy continued; though both Melville,[2] the First Lord, and Keith, the Commander-

---

[1] Oman, *op. cit.*, V. p. vi, VI, p. 55; *Wellington's dispatches*, IX, p. 333.

[2] Lord Melville, the son of James Dundas, the first Lord Melville, was appointed First Lord in 1812 and continued during the next fifteen years to hold that office, in which he displayed remarkable administrative abilities.

in-Chief of the Channel fleet, strongly supported Popham. As Keith was at pains to declare, writing from his flagship off the Brittany coast in October:

> I consider it right to observe that it is extremely important that the naval forces under your orders should remain on the north coast of Spain so long as it can be of the least use to the operations of Lord Wellington, but you are never to forget that if his Lordship's army retires, or suddenly withdraws to any more distant service the enemy will rapidly advance and that if the wind should be westerly or northerly the ships in the harbour of Santander would be *en prise*; and in order, while you continue to use that harbour, that you may be protected from such a calamity, you are to solicit his Lordship to give you the most speedy notice of any movements of the nature above mentioned.[1]

On the approach of the north-westerly gales of winter, the *Venerable* lay in the harbour of Santander; while in the offing the *Surveillante* and some of the other cruisers, under storm canvas, pitched and rolled for days in a heavy, breaking sea. The month of November ushered in a succession of heavy gales. The whole region in north-westerly weather became a dead lee shore. It was no place for ships of the line. Towards the end of December Popham, who had previously requested to be recalled, sailed for England, leaving Captain Duncombe Bouverie with the *Surveillante* and a few small cruisers at Santander. During the remainder of the winter this small force continued to convoy the Army's supply ships and to assist the Spanish guerrilleros.

4

As a result of Wellington's far-sighted strategy in the campaign of 1813, the French were unable to concentrate their forces to meet the impending attack. Souchet was tied down to the Mediterranean region by Murray's expedition against Tarragona. In Biscaya, Foy could not move on account of the scale and intensity of the guerrilla warfare which had blazed up in the mountainous coastlands. In Navarre, Clausel, Caffarelli's successor, was sent to hunt down the great guerrillo Mina. In consequence of these demands, King Joseph had parted with half his available effectives. With the remainder of his force he occupied the central valley of the Douro and covered the

[1] *The Keith Papers*, III, p. 287.

great highway leading from Madrid to Burgos, through the Pyrenees to Bayonne. His line of defence on the Douro appeared to be almost impregnable, while his right was covered by the wild and trackless highland region stretching from the Tras-os-Montes to the upper Ebro, and assumed by the French to be impassable to the passage of an army with baggage and artillery.

Wellington's aim in the ensuing campaign was to turn the enemy's defences on the Douro by a swift and secret flanking march around their right wing while Joseph was preparing to meet a frontal attack similar to that of the previous year. With the intention of presently drawing his supplies through Santander, he requested the Admiralty for a strong squadron in the Bay and a vigilant watch on the whole coast between Bayonne and Corunna; and with the same object in view he started to assemble supply-ships, artillery, and ammunition at Corunna. In the middle of May 1813 Lieut.-General Sir Thomas Graham, with the main body of Wellington's army, totalling about 50,000 men, having crossed the Douro well inside the Portuguese frontier, set out on his 200-mile outflanking march through the wilds of the Tras-os-Montes.

Week after week Graham's men pushed on towards their goal: sometimes plodding through deep defiles and tangled forests; sometimes struggling through swirling mountain torrents; hauling their heavy baggage (including the cumbersome bridge-building materials) up and down rocky slopes; manhandling their guns past crags and screes, and lowering them down precipices with ropes. By 28 May the entire force had crossed the frontier and was heading for the Esla. The following day they reached the river; and, finding it in flood, crossed it by the help of pontoons. Nowhere did they encounter any serious resistance, for the French, with their whole attention upon the advent of the British right wing upon the Douro, were taken by surprise.

Meanwhile, to distract the enemy's attention, Wellington and Hill with the rest of the army, numbering 30,000 men, had advanced on the 22nd to Salamanca. All the French in the vicinity retired at once towards the Douro, where Joseph expected the British attack to be launched. Wellington and Hill, however, made no attempt to get across the river, but halted for a week behind a screen of cavalry while away to the north Graham's force completed their great turning march round the enemy's right. Joseph's strong position on the Douro was instantly turned. The French army had no option but to retreat or be cut off; they hurriedly fell back towards Burgos.

During all these weeks Collier's squadron, cooperating actively with the guerrillas along the Biscayan coast, acted as an effective covering force to the rapid flanking marches which decided the campaign[1]. As the spring advanced Clausel was pressing Mina hard; but the guerrillas, though dispersed, were by no means defeated; and presently Joseph, being in desperate need of reinforcements for the main army at Burgos, ordered him to break off these operations; whereupon the guerrillas swarmed back into their accustomed strongholds. Except for San Sebastian and a few other towns and ports, the entire Cantabrian coast was now in Allied hands.

On 1 June Wellington rode swiftly and secretly to join the main body of his army, leaving Hill in command of the rest; three days later the whole of the Allied forces, numbering 81,000 strong, was safely across the Douro. Fearing for his communications, Joseph retired behind the upper Ebro. Preceded by their cavalry, the British army marched steadily on through the rolling cornfields of the fertile plain of León, the 'Tierra de Campos'. Day after day the sun shone down brilliantly from a cloudless sky on the scarlet columns and swirling clouds of dust. The peasantry came out singing and dancing from the neighbouring villages to welcome their deliverers.

Stationing a cavalry screen near the Burgos-Bayonne highway to deceive the enemy, Wellington turned north over the mountains to outflank Joseph in the Ebro valley. His plan was, first, to cross the head waters of the Ebro, and then to march eastward, so as to take the French in rear at Vittoria, when the French must either fight or withdraw from Spain altogether. Moreover, by this strategy he would be able to join hands with the guerrillas on the Cantabrian coast, and also to open his new line of communications through Santander. Such an advance would have been impossible in such country except in high summer and without the use of well-organized mule trains. Heading northward on parallel routes, Wellington's columns after a series of very hard marches finally entered the beautiful Ebro valley. Once again the French were taken by surprise; and Marshal Jourdan, commanding King Joseph's army, ordered a general retreat.

[1] Oman, *op. cit.*, VI, pp. 253–6.

Encumbered with the spoils of every province in Spain, their rearguard fighting desperately to hold off the Allied assault, Joseph's army was thrust back and back towards the Spanish frontier. Finally, on 21 June, his forces, penned in the shallow valley of Vittoria, were overwhelmingly defeated, with the loss of nearly all their artillery and stores. Such was the triumphant termination of the first completely successful offensive launched by the British army since the beginning of the war.

Vittoria marked the last and decisive phase of the Peninsular War. Hitherto the tide of battle had ebbed and flowed in each succeeding campaign, while the final issue hung still uncertain. During these years the British and their Portuguese Allies had alternately advanced and retreated. But after Vittoria there was to be no more ebb, no more retrogression; but an exultant, irresistible advance.

The Allied forces rapidly overran the whole north coast of Spain. Too late Napoleon ordered Marshal Soult, who, at the prompting of his brother Joseph, had been recalled after Salamanca, back to Spain. The sieges of the frontier fortresses, Pampeluna and San Sebastian, temporarily held up the British advance; and Soult took advantage of this breathing-space to rally and reorganize his scattered forces, afterwards fighting a series of desperate rearguard actions in the passes of the Pyrenees; but for all his skill and resource, he could not stave off defeat, as the British pressed on relentlessly towards France.

5

All this time provisions and stores for Wellington's troops were pouring in through Santander and the neighbouring ports. Transports and victuallers were being hurried out from Plymouth. Convoys arrived, too, from Lisbon and other Portuguese ports. As the summer advanced convoys reached Pasajes almost daily. On 20 September nearly fifty transports and victuallers were counted in the narrow roadstead there; and the anchorage was in danger of becoming choked with shipping.

In the later stages of the campaign Collier's squadron was blockading Santona and cooperating with the guerrillas in the siege of San Sebastian. Several weeks earlier, blockading Castro Urdiales with his cruisers, he had forced the starving garrison to surrender.

All this had been accomplished in the face of the most formidable difficulties. The fact was that Collier was rendering supremely important services to the Allied cause with very slender resources. Though his squadron had been strengthened that summer, there were altogether only four frigates, four sloops, and six lesser vessels on the coast. These were all that could be spared him. The resources of the Navy had been stretched to the limit by the outbreak of war with the United States. As Keith had occasion to observe, the number of small cruisers at the disposal of the Commander-in-Chief of the Western Squadron was limited.[1] There was a chronic dearth of such small vessels, including cutters for urgent dispatches. To assure the safety of all convoys engaged in supplying the manifold needs of our Army in the Peninsula was a task which taxed his resources to the utmost. It would be hard to assess too highly the value of Keith's services in the grand strategy of the war at this juncture; he was not in the line of the great fighting admirals, but he was one of the ablest administrators that our Navy ever had.

These amphibious operations on the north coast of Spain, especially in the latter part of the campaign, presented peculiar difficulties. The bight of the Bay of Biscay, from late September to late May, was a mariner's nightmare. On the whole Biscayan coast there was no safe harbour except Pasajes, and in the frequent north-westerly gales of winter it was all a dead lee shore, with strong easterly currents setting towards the head of the Bay. The smaller vessels were also exposed to the danger of foundering in a high breaking sea. Even in the summer that coast was subject to gales of wind and a heavy swell. For a ship of the line it was almost suicidal to anchor there, and hazardous even for the larger cruisers. With a gale blowing directly on a part of the shore where there was no anchorage but a port still in the enemy's possession, the safety of the ship would depend on her gaining an offing in time. Even so, strong winds would force the crew to take in sail, and heavy seas set them inexorably to leeward.[2] As early as 8 September,

---

[1] It is worth noticing that at this time there were no less than six of the line, sixteen frigates, and a large number of smaller vessels unable to sail for want of seamen to man them.

[2] A square-rigged vessel cannot sail so close to the wind in a heavy sea as she can in smooth water. Moreover, to wear ship in heavy weather requires several miles' offing: when obliged to shorten sail she makes increased leeway in proportion to the reduction in sail area; and even when hove-to she loses ground at the rate of something like four miles an hour.

Collier wrote to Keith when off San Sebastian, the whole squadron was forced to sea, with the exception of the *Surveillante* and *President*. Off Cape Ortegal, on 2 March 1814, two fine sloops, the *Rover* and the *Derwent*, only saved themselves from foundering in a terrific nor'-wester by heaving more than half their guns overboard.[1] Nowhere in Europe, perhaps, was there a coast so hazardous for naval operations as that between Bayonne and Pasajes. It was perilous in the extreme for square-rigged vessels to venture close inshore, and often imprudent even for cutters and schooners.

In the later stages of the campaign Collier experienced the same sort of difficulties with our Army headquarters that Popham had done. Wellington complained that line-of-battleships were not made available on the north coast; that supplies from Lisbon and Corunna were delayed for want of convoy; that the blockade of Santona was ineffective, and the siege of San Sebastian hindered through lack of proper naval cooperation; and he criticized the lack of naval assistance generally—viz., that the squadron was so weak as to be unable to assist in the offensive, that soldiers were obliged to load and unload transports, and that the coasting trade between Gironde and Bayonne was not being intercepted.[2]

The Admiralty, as might have been expected, reacted strongly to these suggestions, observing that it was hazardous to dispose line-of-battleships on a coast where there was no shelter from most prevailing winds, and where, if a ship parted her cable, there would be scarcely any possibility of saving her; that the *Surveillante* had already lost two anchors, and when at Wellington's desire a ship of the line had anchored there, her cable had been badly frayed.'[3] 'I will take your opinion in preference to any other person's as to the most effectual mode of beating a French army,' the First Lord wrote warmly, 'but I have no confidence in your seamanship or nautical skill.'

Melville therefore warned Wellington not to expect any assistance in the siege of San Sabastian from ships of the line, seeing that from the situation of the place, and the nature of the coast, they could not anchor there without extreme risk and would be exposed to almost

[1] *Keith Papers*, III, pp. 30819; Adm. 51/2844, 1 March 1814.
[2] *Wellington's Dispatches*, VIII, pp. 223–7.
[3] *Letters and Papers of ... Sir Thomas Byam Martin*, ed. Admiral Sir Richard Hamilton, II, pp. 359–71.

certain destruction in a gale of wind, 'since from the direction in which it blew they could neither haul off nor run for shelter into any port'.

'Our military officers on the frontiers of Spain do their duty on shore most admirably,' he had observed to Keith some days before; 'but they seem to consider a large ship within a few hundred yards of the shore off San Sabastian as safe in its position and as immovable by the winds and waves as one of the Pyrenean mountains.'[1]

Wellington showed himself as impatient of the restrictions of the convoy system as any of our merchants or shipowners. He apparently expected protection to be provided for each individual ship, or else that she should be able to sail safely without any protection. For their part the Admiralty refused to be responsible for ships sailing 'singly or without convoy between Great Britain and Spain or Portugal, or for any considerable distance along the coasts of those countries'; observing that no amount of cruisers on those stations could secure such vessels from occasional capture, that an adequate force of cruisers had been made available for escort duties, and that cases of capture were negligible.

Writing to Keith about this time, Melville succinctly summed up the situation from the seaman's angle: 'Neither Lord Wellington nor those who are employed on the coast appear to have the least conception of what is physically practicable by ships and boats and seamen, and to be strongly impressed with the usual and complimentary notion that they can do anything'.[2]

In September Rear-Admiral Thomas Byam Martin was dispatched by the Admiralty on a mission to the Army headquarters in the Peninsula, to explain to Wellington what was and what was not practicable by the Navy on that coast, so late in the year; and to learn from him the extent of his wants and expectations as to naval cooperation. Popham's mission satisfactorily resolved the misunderstanding between the two services. Wellington was forced to admit that no ship of the line was really needed; and it was agreed that Collier's primary object should be the protection of supply-ships.

The Peninsular War furnishes one of the most striking examples in history of the influence of sea power upon military strategy. From first to last all the main offensive and defensive operations undertaken

[1] *Keith Papers*, III, p. 300.
[2] *Ibid.*, p. 263.

by the British Army in Portugal and Spain had hinged upon our command of the sea. It was sea power which gave the Army strategical mobility. It was sea power which constantly assured its communications and support. For more than four years, though vastly outnumbered by the enemy, it had with the assistance of the Navy been able to launch campaign after campaign in a theatre where it effectually undermined the fabric of Napoleon's power. Finally, the Navy continued to nourish and support the Army on its seaward flank after the fall of the frontier fortresses and the victorious advance into southern France.

XIII

The War on Trade, 1803–15

I

Though there were no more fleet actions after Trafalgar and the enemy no longer attempted to dispute the command of the seas, the *guerre de course* was progressively extended and intensified. The French government held firmly to the belief that a war directed against the commerce of Great Britain was a sure and certain means of destroying her. The French privateersmen showed themselves worthy successors of Jean Bart and Du Guay Trouin. During these years they continued to keep the sea when the hostile warships were for the most part blocked up in port. As the French hegemony spread southward and northward across Europe, the raiders operated further afield. Some of them, based on Naples and Ancona, cruised up and down the Italian peninsula. Others ventured northward and worked out of Amsterdam, Hamburg, Cuxhaven, Elsinore, Copenhagen, Stralsund, Rostock, Lübeck, and, above all, Danzig.[1] By the middle of the war the attack on British trade had attained unexampled proportions and, added to the cumulative effect of the Continental Blockade, represented a grave threat to our national economy.

In home waters, the proximity of the enemy's North Sea, Channel, and Atlantic ports to the great focal areas of British commerce enabled him to levy an ever-increasing toll on our shipping. The geography of, and the navigational conditions on, these coasts constantly played into the hands of the privateer. In particular, the bights and headlands of our Channel coast offered unparalleled opportunities to the marauder familiar with the ground. The home-coming merchantman, on the last lap of his voyage, was forced to run the gauntlet of a score of possible ambushes, and every promontory might conceal a lurking foe. The immense numerical superiority of the Navy was of small avail

[1] H. Malo, *Les dernières corsaires* (1925), p. 235.

in the face of these destructive, mosquito-like tactics. In the spring of 1809 numerous reports in the press drew attention to the vulnerability of our shipping and the mounting success of the privateers. 'Shipping', observed the *Naval Chronicle*, 'under the British flag, with the coasting trade, forming *an endless train of transit* on our coast, these attacks cannot fail of success greatly disproportioned to the pecuniary risk of their adventure.'

How closely observant was the French privateersman of the motions of our cruisers can be gauged from the advice tendered to Napoleon by one of them, Jacques Broquet of Boulogne, when the Emperor was preparing plans for the invasion of England. 'Sire,' Broquet declared, 'it happens about ten times a year, and particularly in winter, that the wind blows from the south at the beginning of a bad spell—as the weather becomes worse, the wind shifts to the south-west. In those circumstances the English division cannot keep its station but runs for shelter to the Downs, which are funnel-shaped, and behind which it is at ease because it is not afraid of an invasion during rough weather. There you will find every armed vessel for miles around.'[1]

Bad weather was always the privateersman's opportunity, and he was usually prompt to take it. A westerly gale would force the British cruisers to run for the nearest roadstead. It was then that the raider would swoop down on his prey. Gardner in his *Recollections* relates how, when the wind blew strong from the westward, and our cruisers were compelled to take refuge under Dungeness, the enemy privateers were certain to slip over and pick up the struggling merchantmen before the men-of-war could work back to their station off Beachy Head.[2] During the winters of 1809–10 and of 1810–11 there were many accounts of such depredations in the narrow part of the Channel between Fairlight and South Foreland.

'In these long dark nights,' commented the *Naval Chronicle*, 'when the wind blows fresh on the French coast, they incur very little danger of capture, for the Pilots of the King's vessels do not then feel themselves warranted to make too free of the French shore, and the privateers, aware of this, are careful to time their departure from the English side, so as to enable them to reach their own coast before

[1] *Q.* W. B. Johnson, *Wolves of the Channel* (1931), p. 295.
[2] *Recollections of James Anthony Gardner*, ed. Hamilton and Laughton (1906), p. 253.

day-break. If they succeed in making a capture during the night, which they frequently do, the run across that part of the Channel is so short, that three or four hours carries them either into their harbours or under their batteries, and of course out of reach of capture.'[1]

The severe winter weather of 1810–11 greatly assisted the French. In mid-November a heavy gale at S.S.E. to S.W. scattered our convoys and drove our cruisers into the Downs. Some weeks later the North Sea was scourged by a strong northerly wind with snow. Early in the New Year there were severe gales from the east in the Channel; as a result of which the coasts of Devon and Cornwall were strewn with wreckage for weeks and the lightship over the Goodwin Sands was torn from her moorings. In the first half of February there was a series of heavy westerly gales; and the Channel squadron took refuge in Torbay.

Hazy weather likewise favoured the privateer, whether it was the blinding summer mists so often associated with calm seas, or the thick sou'-westerly weather experienced at all seasons in the Channel. Such conditions enabled him both to surprise and to secure his prize, and afterwards to get back safely to port. Over and over again reference is made in contemporary reports to one of these privateers having made good his escape in mist or fog.

Not only were the commanders of the privateers to be numbered among some of the finest seamen in France, but they were also possessed of a personal and particular knowledge of our coasts and of the routes followed by the trade, both coastal and foreign; of the tactics of the British cruisers stationed in these waters, and of the times of arrival and departure of convoys. As in the last war, a good many of these commanders were fishermen, with all the fisherman's inbred skill and resource for ascertaining his position—even without the aid of soundings—in darkness or thick weather; relying on the observation of certain birds, seals, or fish, and, above all, on the colour and run of the seas. Their forefathers had known these waters before them—the inshore rocks and shoals, the peculiarities of the local tides,[2] the rips and eddies, the sudden gusts that would sweep down the river valleys or out of the combes of a range of cliffs like so many

---

[1] *Naval Chronicle*, XXV, p. 45.
[2] In the days of sail this intimate knowledge of the tides was, of course, of crucial importance in coastal navigation.

funnels, the anchorages and sheltered places up and down the coast, and the signs of the weather. Such local knowledge would give the raider a substantial advantage over his opponent, whether the captain of a cruiser or master of a merchantman, and might very well make all the difference between success and failure. The vessels the privateersmen commanded were fast and handy, most of them not very large but crowded with men to the limit of their capacity—for large numbers were always needed both to capture the prizes and afterwards to man them.

Once again, the privateers' chosen hunting grounds were off the major headlands along our southern and eastern coasts. Though during the stormy winter season there might be a sufficiency of cruisers lying up in harbours or sheltered roadsteads in the vicinity, they were not, as a rule, to be found where they were most badly needed, in the open sea off these promontories. When convoys were standing up and down the coast, it happened not infrequently that the leading vessels of the convoy would have weathered a point, while the privateer, slipping in unperceived, had captured and carried off several of the heavy and slower vessels sailing to leeward and out of sight of the escorts.[1] Sometimes a sudden dying away of the wind would give one of the smaller privateers, crammed with men and propelled by oars, a heaven-sent opportunity of pulling alongside some unlucky merchantman, immobilized by calm and with a weak crew, and swiftly overpowering her while any other ships in the vicinity were powerless to interfere. A convoy would often be dispersed when obliged to work to windward, and this, again, was the raider's opportunity. An ingenious stratagem often practised by the privateersmen, when they had by some means surprised and taken a vessel sailing in convoy, was to proceed with the convoy, under easy sail, for several days to avoid detection; and then at last to make their escape by night, steering for one of their own ports. On one occasion, according to the *Naval Chronicle*, a single privateer operating off the east coast of England took no less than thirty prizes out of a fleet of coasters—that is, as many as she could spare hands to man them; the same privateer was known to lie for a fortnight off our coast, until the long-awaited opportunity presented itself.[2] It was when the convoy was just leaving

[1] *The Naval Chronicle*, Vol. 27, p. 102.
[2] *Ibid.*, Vol. 25, p. 291.

or approaching the land that the danger was greatest. As the trade approached its destination, the individual masters were under strong temptation to press on so as to be first at the market, and so fell an easy prey to the privateers. It often happened that the crew of a merchantman kept so bad a look-out that a burst of musketry was the first intimation of an enemy being in the midst of them. And so it went on. 'A few guns, and a crew of ragged rascals', remarked the *Naval Chronicle*, 'are put on board a miserable privateer, she sallies out from one of their ports, she takes perhaps half a dozen of valuable prizes, and escapes back to her own harbours.'[1]

It was operating against the teeming coastwise traffic that the enemy's smaller privateers—light, swift-sailing, easily manœuvreable craft— reaped their richest harvest. Like the trade to Ireland, this local traffic was exempt from the provisions of the Convoy Act; for the highly individualist conditions that obtained in the coasting trade rendered it impracticable to impose upon it the same rigid discipline and regulation as was enforced upon the overseas, long-distance traffic by the Convoy Act. In the coasting trade there were cargoes that had to be delivered within very narrow time limits; markets that must be lost if a vessel sailed in convoy whose speed was necessarily that of the dullest sailer. Moreover, the gradual assembly of a coastal convoy would not infrequently mean losing a fair wind—and, though the delay of a week or two was not especially important in the long-distance trades, it was a very different matter in the short hauls of the coastal traffic. The bulk of the coastwise shipping, therefore, sailed without convoy, and suffered severely at the hands of the privateers.

The scale and severity of the attack on trade in the Channel has never, perhaps, been fully appreciated. British merchantmen were continually being taken close inshore, to the consternation of the inhabitants, who viewed 'the national colours of our enemy floating, with gasconading insolence, along our shores'—a spectacle (as the *Naval Chronicle* declared) humiliating in the extreme to an Englishman, 'accustomed as he is, to behold the vanquished streamers of the foe, waving in submission beneath the tricolour'. 'The French privateers,' commented a Canadian visitor about this time, 'now dash by dozens into every fleet, and make prizes in sight of the farmers of England.'[2]

---

[1] *Ibid.*, p. 492.
[2] *Ten Years in Upper Canada*, ed. M. Edgar (1891), p. 70.

This deplorable state of things evoked not only strong representations from the Committee of Lloyd's, but a series of well-informed articles and reports in the *Naval Chronicle* and a general outburst in the press. As early as February 1809 Lloyd's had urged the necessity of checking 'the depredations of the numerous privateers, with which the Channel has been for some time past and is now infested', and later in the same year forwarded to the Admiralty a letter from Dover which declared that 'the depredations committed by the enemy's privateers on this coast during the last few months, are truly lamentable, and call loudly for some effectual system being adopted, to prevent a continuance of what is so injurious to trade, and so disgraceful to the nation.'[1]

In the course of 1810 the attack on British commerce was intensified. Certainly a good many of the privateers were taken this year; but these captures bore a very unequal proportion to the swarms of the marauders still at sea and to our own much more serious losses in merchantmen. The coasting trade was hardest hit of all; and at Dover, in September, the warning signals were out almost every day, announcing the approach of hostile privateers. It is significant that increasing use was made of the roads and inland waterways; and even new canals began to be planned, in the south of England, as an alternative to the vulnerable coastal navigation.[2] The Channel was infested with these enemies to such a degree that the force of small cruisers stationed along the coast, like the *Alphaea* and her consorts, appeared impotent.[3]

'We have more than once referred to this very surprising fact,' observed the *Naval Chronicle* about this time—'that, with a fleet surpassing the navy of the whole world, and by which we are enabled to set so large a portion of it at defiance, we cannot guard our coasts from insult.'

Once again the privateers—sometimes as many as three or four at a time—lay in wait in the vicinity of Beachy Head, in the fairway of the busy traffic passing up and down the Channel. Considerable stretches of that lonely coastline were practically undefended, as the Frenchmen well knew. They accordingly sailed close in under the

[1] Adm. 1/3993 *passim.*
[2] P. A. L. Vine, *London's Lost Route to the Sea* (1965), pp. 9, 32.
[3] *Naval Chronicle*, Vol. 24, pp. 327, 490; *Sussex Weekly Advertiser, Exeter Flying Post, passim.* See also *infra*, p. 384.

cliffs to the west of Newhaven; off Seaford Head sloping down to Hope Gap and the spacious saltings beside Cuckmere Haven; along by the Seven Sisters, Birling Gap, and the new lighthouse above on Bel Tout; and under the chalk crags of the great headland itself, beyond which lay the broad expanse of Pevensey Levels and the bold curve of the martello towers flanking the bay, with Fairlight Point in the distance.

The skilful tactics of the privateersmen, their intimate knowledge of this part of the Channel, and the manifest deficiencies of our patrol system are convincingly revealed in a couple of letters, forwarded by the Committee of Lloyd's from their correspondents at Seaford and Newhaven respectively, to the Admiralty. The occurrences referred to in these letters took place on 30 November 1810.

Six or seven privateers came out from the opposite ports in France, as usual upon the subsidence of strong westerly gales: no British cruizer then to be seen. These privateers were discovered from the signal station at Seaford (where an admirable look-out is kept) about noon, standing in for Seaford Bay; the usual alarm signal, of a flag and two balls, was immediately hoisted: it was never noticed at the Beachy Head station, though the day was remarkably fine and clear: about 3 o'clock the enemy took a coasting vessel within a short distance of the shore in Seaford Bay; not a gun being mounted either at Seaford or Blatchington Batteries, both being under repair. About 4 o'clock they followed a ship, pouring musketry into her, close in under the gun lately mounted at the signal station at Seaford, by which she was saved from capture. Another coasting vessel within the ship chaced sought a shelter at the mouth of Cuckmere Haven, from whence she might have been taken, and also the ship (after she had run to the eastward of the gun on the heights) if the enemy had pursued, as no guns have yet been placed at the barracks at Cuckmere; four guns destined for that place have been for some time lying at Blatchington barracks: it is of importance during the defenceless state of Seaford Bay, that they should be got forward to their destination immediately. The signal station at Beachy Head is much neglected; no signal has been hoisted there for some time: the reason given is, that the yard used for suspending signals is broken, that a new one is to come from Portsmouth; in the meantime surely a substitute might be resorted to without difficulty: the fact is, that at present nothing is done there upon the greatest emergency; and except some representation is made, such may continue to be the case for some time.

Six lugger privateers were off this port [Newhaven] yesterday afternoon: one of which chaced a brig that was bound up Channel, and got so near to her off Seaford, as to fire at her with small arms, and continued so to do, until the brig had sailed past the signal house to the eastward of Seaford town, when shots were fired from a gun at the signal house, and thrown so near the lugger, that she tacked, and for a short time stood to the westward; soon after she hauled down her sails, and laid to, with another lugger, that had stood in from the S.E.: the gun from the hill threw shots over the lugger when her sails were down, but I was sorry to see the firing so very slow: I made enquiry why the firing was not more brisk, when I was informed the officer at the signal station had no ammunition, and was obliged to send to Seaford for a supply: had not this been the case, I am convinced that the lugger might have been disabled: however the brig that was chaced was saved, and proceeded up Channel. Four other luggers were close in under the land to the westward of Newhaven harbour, where the battery guns could not be brought to bear upon them: they drove the sloops *Dove* and *Swallow* of Weymouth laden with Portland stone on shore at Bearshide Gap, where they were however got off the next tide: they afterwards took a small Customs hoy; several vessels were at this time coming up Channel, and I much fear many of them fell into the hands of the enemy, as not a single British cruizer was to be seen in the Channel . . . at present there is not one gun between Newhaven and Brighton, and the luggers knowing this will come close under the west land without any fear of interruption.[1]

During the ensuing weeks the depredations of enemy privateers, and the complaints of shipowners and shipmasters about the lack of protection, continued. On 19 December the *Robert* was 'bagged' from an outward-bound Jamaica convoy, about twenty miles south of Beachy Head, by a lugger privateer called the *Petit Loup*. Early that morning they were all becalmed; but the crew of the privateer got their sweeps out and, in spite of their opponents' dogged resistance, captured the Jamaicaman and carried her off to Dieppe. 'They did not get us in here until next day at 5 o'clock in the evening,' complained the master of the *Robert* indignantly; '26 hours of as fine weather as ever was, and not a single British cruiser in sight.'[2]

The early weeks of the new year saw no perceptible slackening in the attack on commerce in the English Channel. 'To such an extent is the privateering system now carried on,' *The Times* declared, 'that unless some vigorous measures are taken immediately, the naval trade of the country will be at a stand.' At about the same time the *General Evening Post* expressed itself in even stronger language.

[1] Adm. 1/3993, 4 December 1810.
[2] *Ibid.*, 23 December 1810.

The depredations daily committed upon our Commerce by the Enemy's Privateers in the Channel, imperiously demand the attention of the Admiralty Board. Within the last fortnight, about twenty vessels are ascertained to have been captured, close upon our shores, and, during that time, only a single Privateer has been taken, though the Channel has swarmed with them. They seem to calculate upon a periodical intermission of vigilance on the part of the Admiralty; and of these occasional lapses of attention, they avail themselves with uncommon activity. . . . Is it not a disgrace to a country which prides itself in its Naval superiority, that insurances cannot be effected upon vessels bound up Channel, but at the most exorbitant premiums? We are assured by the master of a West Indiaman lately arrived, that from the time he came into Soundings, until he brought up in the Downs, he did not fall in with a single man of War!!![1]

With its long coastlines, its abundance of convenient harbours, anchorages, and hiding-places on the mainland and in the islands, and its narrow focal areas through which a considerable volume of traffic must always pass, the Mediterranean presented peculiarly favourable opportunities to the privateer. The raiders exacted a heavy and continuous toll at a time when our trade with the Mediterranean was prospering. Large numbers of these privateers were fitted out in the ports of southern France and up and down the Italian peninsula. Many of them operated far outside their own territory in allegedly neutral harbours. Early in the war there were raiders based on Sicilian ports; row-boats assembled at Tariffa and Ceuta which cut out the stragglers from convoys almost in the shadow of the Rock; corsairs which swarmed in the deep recesses of the Adriatic Sea, among the Ionian Islands, and along the Barbary coast. British commerce suffered severely and a stream of protests reached the Admiralty. 'The protection afforded the Enemy's Privateers and Row-boats', complained Nelson in the summer of 1804, 'in the different Neutral Ports in these seas, so contrary to every known law of Neutrality, is extremely destructive to our Commerce, and will certainly prove so in spite of all the force which can be brought against these Pirates.'[2] As the war continued, the privateers increased and multiplied. The teeming commerce of Malta suffered severely from their depredations. So heavy and so persistent, indeed, became the attack on trade in the Mediterranean that Collingwood and his successors were hard put to

[1] *General Evening Post*, 24 January 1811.
[2] *Nelson's Dispatches*, VI, p. 267.

it to provide sufficient escorts from their overtaxed cruiser forces.

Even the far-off, stormy track to Archangel was by no means immune from the depredations of the privateers. In the lower part of the North Sea corsairs from Dunkirk were active, and marauders from Boulogne periodically hovered off the Orkneys; off the coasts of Norway and of Russian Lapland merchant vessels were exposed to sudden attack by Danish and Norwegian privateers. The Admiralty was accustomed to send one of the smaller men-of-war to cruise in the vicinity of the North Cape; but for various reasons it was not always on its station. Thus, during the summer of 1809, when there were a hundred and more merchantmen loading for English ports at Archangel, a Danish privateer captured several of these vessels on their homeward passage; and the Admiralty, in response to an urgent appeal from Lloyd's, hastened to provide stronger protection for the remainder.[1] When the United States declared war in 1812 there was danger from another quarter. During the summer of 1813 at least twenty British merchantmen were taken by three American ships cruising off the North Cape. Over and above the chance of enemy attack there were, as ever, 'the dangers of the sea'. Across the North Sea a wide berth had to be given to the outlying dangers of the Lofoten Islands. Under the lowering grey Arctic skies observations might be impossible for days on end, with consequent uncertainty as to the ship's position. When sailing off the Murman coast the utmost vigilance and caution were necessary on account of the strong indraught which invariably sets on shore, the prevalence of fog, and the unreliability of the compass in this area. At the same time ships were obliged to approach this dangerous coast in order that they might sight Cape Sviatoi Nos (*anglice* 'Cape Sweet Nose'), an important landfall.

As year by year Napoleon's power grew and the Continental System spread farther and farther across Europe in the wake of his conquering armies, Great Britain found herself threatened with exclusion from the vital Baltic markets. The main danger in this region came from Denmark. The Danes were naturally incensed against the British. Their battle fleet had been seized and carried off by the latter in 1807; but there was no lack of skilled and experienced seamen in the small kingdom to man their gun-boats, which were being constructed by dozens and scores, and which, under certain conditions, were a

[1] Adm. 1/3993, 6 September 1809.

formidable threat even to sail of the line. These gun-boats were vessels of light draught usually propelled by oars and also fitted with masts and sails. In a calm, they had much superiority over a ship. By means of their oars, they could pull round a ship in any direction; and, being small, they were exceedingly difficult to hit. But their range of operations was limited; they could not leave port when the wind was strong and the sea rough; and even in fine weather they were restricted to coastal waters.

The Baltic Sea and the North

As a result of the increasing difficulties of the Baltic trade, the premiums for that voyage, which in the year of Trafalgar had varied between 3 and 5 per cent. (that is, a figure lower than for any other foreign voyage), rose rapidly to from 20 to 40 per cent., which was approximately three times the average premium on other foreign voyages. The high premiums henceforth paid for the Baltic are to be accounted for by the combined dangers of the sea and of enemy attack, in addition to the ever-present risk of confiscation of ship and cargo in port.[1]

When in the spring of 1808 convoys had begun to sail to the Baltic, they were at first sent through the Sound, on account of the navigational hazards of the passage through the Belt, with its winding channels and strong currents—convoys could not hope to make this passage in less than four days, usually it would take even longer; the frequent calms favoured the hostile gun-boats and fettered the British cruisers; moreover, when the convoys were obliged to anchor for the night it must be within easy striking distance of the enemy's bases.

But the grave disadvantages of the Sound passage were soon made manifest. A large flotilla of gun-boats was stationed off Elsinore in constant readiness to attack any of our convoys attempting to pass Kronborg. Further, at the other end of the Sound the greatest difficulty was experienced in passing the convoys through the narrow and intricate Malmö channel close in with the Swedish shore; the enemy having at this time a force of about thirty gun-boats based on Copenhagen, besides numerous privateers. Surrounded by extensive and dangerous shoals the merchantmen were an easy prey for Danish gun-boats sallying out from Zealand. Our losses were so heavy that Saumarez, therefore, sought and secured permission to dispatch the convoys through the Belt.

The numerous rocks, shoals, and narrow, winding channels at the southern end of the Baltic, combined with the proximity of the hostile bases, greatly favoured this kind of attack. While the British cruisers lay becalmed, the Danish gun-boats, being propelled by oars, would manœuvre into a position just out of carronade range and open fire with their long 24s. Where so much would depend on the weather, chance was necessarily a major factor in the situation. A striking example of this occurred in June 1808. In the early afternoon of the 9th, with 'a commanding breeze with every appearance of its continuance', a convoy of seventy-six sail was standing to the northward

[1] Wright and Fayle, *A History of Lloyd's* (1928), pp. 187 *sqq.* and A. N. Ryan in *English Historical Review*, Vol. LXXIV (1959), p. 461.

up the Zealand coast towards the entrance of the Sound, their rear brought up by two bomb-vessels, the *Turbulent* and *Thunder*. They were almost abreast of the south end of Saltholm when the wind began to slacken and indicate appearances 'all too favourable for the enemy'. The captain of the *Thunder* observes:

The body of the convoy by this time was so far advanced, as to make returning impossible—the enemy's sailing boats were out, and about 5 p.m. their gun boats—25 in number—including mortar boats—began the attack on our rear. The *Turbulent* returned their fire, and we their shells—but as they fast approached within the range of mortars, we commenced with our guns—the Ship had now little better than steerage way when I observed an unfortunate shot had carried away the *Turbulent*'s topmast—she made what resistance she could, but the contest was too unequal. Her fate was inevitable. The enemy passed close alongside and I had the mortification of seeing her fall, without a possibility of affording the smallest aid. I had made the signal for the brigs to assist—but they were too distant—and what wind there was was unfavourable. Immediately after the surrender of the *Turbulent* at 6 p.m. the enemy formed on both our quarters and astern, pulling up with confidence. . . . The fire now until nearly 10 p.m., was incessant and many were the efforts made by the enemy to close on all sides—but as our case became desperate, so in proportion did the officers and people display energy and spirit. Had we fallen, nothing could have saved the convoy. . . . I believe the Enemy took 12 sail, 4 of which they burnt, and I consider myself fortunate in having pass'd 64 sail clear. What damage the Enemy received I know not, but have every reason to believe it considerable, as they never would have left us, it being a dead calm, the whole night.[1]

'Those now in the ship, who were in Lord Nelson's last action at Trafalgar', declared one of her officers, 'say, this surpassed it for hard fighting. . . . If the daylight had continued two hours longer, and the enemy persevered with a little more judgment, they had killed two-thirds of us, or sunk the ship.'

During the second half of 1808 our convoys experienced serious and sustained opposition from the enemy's flotilla. One of the smaller British sail of the line, the *Africa*, 64, while on convoy duty and lying becalmed off Malmö Island, was fiercely attacked, on 20 October, by a swarm of hostile gun-boats from Copenhagen. The latter, stationing themselves on her bows and quarters, where her guns would not bear, poured in a devastating fire. Only nightfall and the retreat of

[1] Adm. 1/6, 9 June 1808.

the gun-boats saved the *Africa*, whose masts and yards were so badly damaged, and her running rigging so cut up, that she was obliged to retire, first to Karlskrona, and presently to England, for repairs.[1] In December another convoy suffered severe losses.

In the same month 'the dangers of the sea' exacted a heavy toll. On the 22nd the last convoy of the year left Karlskrona for Great Britain. Steering for the Sound by way of the Malmö passage, it was presently lost when caught in the newly formed ice, while three of the escorting brigs-of-war were wrecked.

There were further heavy losses in 1810. In July a convoy bound for Long Hope Sound in the Orkneys was attacked and some forty-two ships taken, and in August another forty-seven captured from a home-ward-bound convoy off the Naze.[2]

In the late summer of 1810 a new and formidable type of gun-boat appeared in the Belt. It was equipped with a greatly improved sail-plan and rigging. The new craft soon proved their worth. In September a strong force of raiders, descending suddenly upon the convoy on a dark and stormy night, managed to cut out and bear off a number of the merchantmen. In 1811 the enemy again had recourse to these tactics. 'We had the usual employment of taking large convoys through the Belt', observed John Boteler, then serving in the *Dictator*, 'when, night after night, there were the same alarms from different parts of the convoy—blue lights, rockets, tar barrels, &c.—and, of course, on our part of "all boats away." ' On 20 May Manley Dixon sailed from Vingå Sound with a convoy and three weeks later reported to Saumarez:

I beg to acquaint you that the enemy in the Belt has increased very considerably his means of annoyance this year to the trade, in large Row howitzer boats 34 feet in length, and a variety of privateer craft which had absolutely swarmed about the convoy the first ten days, but our success in taking three of them and killing and wounding several of their Men in the Boats has made them more cautious of late, but I am given to understand, that at Nyborg and Korso there are assembled forty of their heavy gun boats and a great number of other craft, waiting our passing that passage.

It is not only my own opinion but likewise that of every captain of this squadron that if I had not had the force of four sail of the line and the

[1] Adm. 1/7, 29 October 1808.
[2] Adm. 1/3845, 26 July and 17 August 1810.

two brigs, it would hitherto have been impracticable to guard and protect the trade entrusted to my care with any success, and I believe our losses from this convoy would have been considerable, as it is in the strongest breezes when our guard boats can with the utmost difficulty maintain their stations, that these pests drop in the night time alongside the merchant vessels and take their most favourable moment for cutting them adrift.[1]

In November 1811 there came another damaging attack. But already the war on trade in the Baltic was languishing, and the privateers working from Danish and Norwegian bases were less active. More-over, the Danes had failed in their attempt to retake Anholt.

On the renewal of the war in 1803 the Caribbean once more swarmed with corsairs which preyed unceasingly on the rich traffic plying between Europe and the West Indies, and among the various islands. Most of the damage, indeed, was suffered by the busy inter-island trade, where—as in the parallel case of our own coasting trade—a certain measure of elasticity and independence was essential to effici-ency, and the shipping could not be forced into the rigid framework of the convoy system. 'This favoured the depredations of the light, swift, and handy cruisers', observes Mahan, 'that alone are capable of profiting by such an opportunity, through their power to evade the numerous, but necessarily scattered, ships of war, which under those circumstances must patrol the sea, like a watchman on beat, as the best substitute for the more formal and regularized convoy protec-tion, when that ceases to apply.'[2]

Though the individual vessels engaged in the inter-island trade were quite small, the aggregate tonnage involved was very consider-able, and presented a tempting target to the privateer. Throughout the archipelago there existed a multitude of sheltered, secure, well-situated bases where the raiders might take refuge with their captures. Here they could refit and revictual and dispose of their prizes. The Caribbean was one of the most lucrative hunting grounds in the world for the privateer. Owing to the fine weather which generally prevailed in these waters the smallest vessels could be put to profitable use. Here again an intimate knowledge of the local navigational conditions was a factor of crucial importance. The constant trades, the land

[1] Adm. 1/12, 9 June 1811.
[2] Mahan, *Sea Power in its Relations to the War of 1812*, II, p. 220.

breezes, the local flaws of wind, the regions of calm, the tides, and the currents were often controlling elements in the situation.

As in the previous war, privateers from Martinique and Guadeloupe cruised to the windward of Barbados in the track of the outward-bound traffic from Europe, while the waters around Cuba and Haiti were infested with smaller vessels based on those islands. So long as these secure refuges remained in the enemy's possession, the defensive measures undertaken by the Navy could be no more than a palliative; and, year in, year out, a heavy toll continued to be levied on the trade.[1] This was the more serious, towards the middle of the war, in view of the gradual closing of continental markets to British trade, and our increased dependence, in consequence, upon the traffic to the East and West Indies.

Charles Decaen, who had been appointed governor of the French possessions in the East Indies by Napoleon in 1802, had arrived at Pondicherry with Vice-Admiral Linois[2] shortly before the renewal of the war; but, finding the preparations carrying on under the British governor-general, Marquis Wellesley, so formidable that effective resistance was seen to be out of the question, he determined to withdraw with all his forces to Mauritius, where, during the next eight years, he endeavoured to concert plans of common action with the Mahratta courts and to harass British commerce. In the first of these he failed; but in the second he achieved a substantial measure of success. A man of outstanding administrative ability, Decaen effectually overhauled the defences of Mauritius and the neighbouring Bourbon Island, and, drawing the bulk of his supplies from Madagascar, made this insular stronghold one of the principal centres of the war on trade. A new generation of French naval commanders was just then coming to the fore; leaders such as Bergeret, Epron, Hamelin, Duperré, and Bouvet (the son of Rear-Admiral Bouvet) were greatly to distinguish themselves in the final phase of the war in the Indian Ocean; while the daring exploits of the French corsairs—above all, of Surcouf, Lemême, Dutertre, Perroud, and Courson—constitute one of the most brilliant and dramatic pages in the annals of the *guerre de course*.

On the outbreak of the war the British Commander-in-Chief on the East India station was Vice-Admiral Peter Rainier. Rainier, whose duty

[1] Adm. 1/327, 328, 329, 330 *passim*.
[2] The victor of the first action off Algeciras in 1801.

it was to protect the British possessions and commerce in the east from attack, had served under Hughes in the memorable campaign against the Bailli de Suffren, and had passed many years on this station. The opening phase of the war witnessed a series of destructive raids on our shipping in the Bay of Bengal and the successive cruises of the *Marengo*, 84, Linois's flagship. Despite Rainier's unrivalled experience of the Indian Ocean, Linois contrived continually to elude him. Meanwhile considerable damage was done to our trade; for Rainier, apprehensive both of a French invasion of India and of the Dutch squadron at Batavia, was reluctant to weaken his squadron by detaching ships for convoys. It was not, indeed, until a later stage of the war that he realized that there was no possible chance either of a French landing in India or of their receiving effective aid from the Dutch.

Early in 1804 Linois missed his only chance of inflicting a really disastrous blow on British commerce, and made himself the laughing stock of Europe and the target of Napoleon's angry scorn. His squadron, comprising the *Marengo* and three powerful frigates, was then cruising off the Straits of Malacca in the hope of intercepting the homeward-bound China convoy from Canton. On 14 February the tea fleet, under Captain Nathaniel Dance, came in sight—sixteen Indiamen and eleven country ships. This being rather more than Linois's intelligence had led him to expect, he was apprehensive of discovering men-of-war among them. The bold front put on by Dance confirmed him in his error. Dance, with his fleet formed in line of battle, stood on under easy sail, lay-to during the night, and next morning as before stood on under easy sail. When Linois manœuvred to cut off some of the rearmost ships, Dance gave the order to tack in succession and engage the enemy. 'This manœuvre was correctly performed', Dance wrote in his report, 'and we stood towards him under a press of sail.' The leading part in the engagement which ensued was taken by the crack ship of the Honourable Company, the *Royal George*. Linois, now quite convinced that there were warships sailing with the convoy, hauled his wind and retired. With that the action, if it can really be called an action—for there were only a few hasty broadsides exchanged between the two forces—came to an end. Dance then made the signal for a general chase, and for the next two hours was seen the amazing spectacle of merchantmen pursuing warships. 'At two p.m. I made the signal for a general chace, and we pursued them till four p.m. when, fearing a longer pursuit would carry us too far from the mouth of the Streights, and considering the immense property at stake, I made the signal to tack, and at eight p.m. we anchored in a situation to proceed for the entrance of the Streights in the morning.'[1] A fortnight later the tea fleet was met by two 74s, which accompanied them to St. Helena, where they were joined by escorts for the final lap of the voyage. Captain Dance and his principal officers were on their return to England enthusiastically received and lavishly rewarded. From the standpoint of French prestige this encounter between Linois's squadron and the British tea fleet was about as bad as it could be. 'The essence of Linois's offence was not a violation of his country's honour, whatever Napoleon might say. If that had been all he would have been forgiven more readily. He had done worse than that—he had provided the English with a joke.'[2]

Year after year the corsairs sallied forth from the French islands on the trade-routes. Towards the close of 1803, François Lemême had reappeared in the Bay of Bengal in the *Fortune* privateer, of twelve guns, manned by a crew of 160. On this cruise his success was phenomenal. Within a very brief period he had captured fifteen prizes. It was said by the French that when the British merchants in the ports of India, on receiving news of each fresh disaster, inquired as to the identity of the marauder, the stereotyped reply was invariably, '*Toujours Lemême*'. Eventually, however, he was hunted down by the *Concorde*, 48—a faster sailer as well as a much more powerful ship than the *Fortune*; in the ensuing engagement the privateer was pounded almost to wreckage by the frigate and forced to strike. Once again a prisoner of war, Lemême expired on the passage to England. About the same time Dutertre had also returned to his old cruising ground in the Bay of Bengal. He soon had a long list of captures to his credit, and during his cruise of 1804–5 became once more, with his comrade Courson, the terror of the eastern seas.

During the years which followed the corsairs continued to increase and prosper. The division of the command, in the summer of 1805, between Pellew and Troubridge undoubtedly militated against the efficient organization of trade protection in the Indian Ocean. The rival Admirals were soon at loggerheads. 'I wish to God I was out

[1] Q. Charles Hardy, *A Register of Ships* (1811).
[2] C. N. Parkinson, *Sir Edward Pellew, Viscount Exmouth* (1934), p. 338.

of it,' complained Pellew in June 1806. 'I would rather command a Frigate with her Bowsprit over the rocks of Ushant all my life, than command here on such terms.'[1] Eventually the Admiralty recalled Troubridge and appointed him to the command of the Cape of Good Hope station. Troubridge sailed from Madras on 12 January in the *Blenheim*—a forty-five-year-old ship which was actually unfit for sea and leaking badly as she lay in the roads off Madras: but on his way to the Cape he was caught by a heavy gale off the coast of Madagascar; and the *Blenheim*, with the *Java* frigate, foundered with all hands.

At the end of June 1805 Linois achieved his most notable success in the *guerre de course* in the capture of the Honourable Company's ship, the *Brunswick*, off the coast of Ceylon. Pellew hurriedly sent ships to intercept him, but in vain. Shortly after, not wishing to be based any longer on Mauritius on account of a quarrel with Decaen, Linois steered with the *Belle Poule* frigate for the Cape of Good Hope. But the Cape passed into British keeping early in January 1806; and Linois thereupon resolved to return to France. On 13 March, however, he encountered a greatly superior British squadron under Sir John Borlase Warren. The *Marengo* and *Belle Poule* fought stubbornly against overwhelming odds, but were finally obliged to strike.

Relatively speaking, Linois had accomplished little. But the presence of the 84-gun *Marengo* in the Indian Ocean was an anxiety that had weighed heavily on Pellew. With the departure from the station of Linois and his flagship, there was no longer much risk of any of our cruisers being taken. Now that the *Marengo* was safely out of the way and the East India station once again under one command the strain was greatly eased.

For the future Decaen was in effective command of what was left of the French squadron based on Mauritius. In the summer of 1806 this small force was materially strengthened by the arrival of two fine frigates from home, the *Piémontaise* and the *Cannonière*, both 40s. During the same year our merchants in Calcutta had once more to lament their losses when one of the most famous of the enemy's privateers, the *Bellone*, Jacques Perroud, fell upon our shipping in the Bay of Bengal, despite the many British cruisers patrolling the station. Eventually the *Bellone* was run down and captured off the coast of Ceylon by the *Powerful*, 74, and the *Rattlesnake* sloop, to

[1] Q. C. N. Parkinson, *War in the Eastern Seas* (1954), p. 284.

379

the no small satisfaction of the Commander-in-Chief. 'I reflect with much pleasure on the capture of *La Bellone* in particular,' wrote Pellew in his dispatch, 'as well from her superior sailing, as her uncommon success in the present and preceding war against the British commerce, in the Indian and European seas.' In spite of the British blockade of Mauritius, which was gradually being drawn tighter, both frigates and privateers continued to enter and leave port. Though four of the enemy's best privateers had been taken during 1805–6, there was still a strong force of these formidable raiders operating in the Indian Ocean.

The year 1807 saw the return to his former hunting-ground of the greatest corsair of them all. Robert Surcouf sailed from St. Malo in March in the 18-gun *Revenant*, which had been especially designed for privateering and was one of the fastest vessels afloat. Sighting Bourbon Island at the end of May, Surcouf slipped through the blockading squadron and entered Port Louis on 10 June. To add to the dwindling food reserves of Mauritius, Decaen suggested that he should try to intercept some of the rice-ships plying between Bengal and Madras. Surcouf accordingly sailed for the Bay of Bengal and harassed the trade to such effect that the government presently set a price on his head and imposed an embargo on all the shipping in the Hooghli. The frigate *Piémontaise* was on the same station at this time and for months on end the two ships virtually blockaded the port of Calcutta. Then, having made the Sandheads too hot to hold him, Surcouf vacated the station and cruised off the Pegn coast for a while, eventually returning to his post off the Hooghli. In vain did the merchants of Calcutta petition Sir Edward Pellew for more effective protection, alleging the utter inadequacy of the cruiser force stationed in the Bay of Bengal, and observing that no other 'extensive branch of British commerce, either European or colonial, ever suffered such a series of single captures, in so short a period, as has been made by the *Revenant* privateer, on the coast of Coromandel'.[1]

What actually preserved Surcouf during this cruise was not the absence of British cruisers—for he was chased repeatedly while in the Bay of Bengal—but the superior sailing qualities of his vessel, the *Revenant*. It was a striking example of the inability of the patrol system to deal with one fast-sailing privateer even when that privateer's

[1] *Q.* J. K. Laughton, *Studies in Naval History* (1887), pp. 449–50.

cruising ground was approximately known, and there was a greatly superior naval force stationed in the vicinity. After the *Revenant*'s departure the *Piémontaise* continued to harass British shipping in the Bay of Bengal. On his return to Europe, in 1809, Surcouf settled ashore for good in his native St. Malo as the owner of a large fleet of privateers.

In the early years of his command there had not been sufficient ships available for Pellew to maintain a constant blockade of the French islands from India. But with the capture of the Cape in 1806 and the restoration of that station as a separate command the situation had changed. Troubridge was succeeded by Rear-Admiral Stirling, and Stirling by Rear-Admiral Bertie. Mauritius and Bourbon Island were blockaded by a squadron commanded by Captain Josias Rowley and based on the Cape. As the year 1808 drew to its close the blockade became increasingly effective, and the enemy's supplies were cut off.

By this time there was hardly any squadron worthy of the name left at Port Louis. Faced with the threat of famine, Decaen appealed to the Emperor for aid. This was eventually forthcoming. With the arrival in 1808–9 of a strong force of frigates, comprising the *Manche*, *Caroline*, *Bellone*, and *Vénus*, under the command of Commodore Jacques Hamelin, the war in Indian waters entered on a new phase.

There were now five frigates, two corvettes, and a number of privateers based on Mauritus. The effective blockade of the French islands had become impossible. Though commerce might be cut off, the privateers could still get in and out. Hamelin's division was vigorously commanded. A new generation of French naval officers was now coming to the fore. Under the leadership of such commanders as Hamelin himself, Pierre Bouvet of the *Minerve* and Victor Duperré of the *Bellone*, this squadron added one last brilliant chapter to the history of the *guerre de course*. Early in 1809 the *Caroline*, cruising off the Sandheads, captured two East Indiamen, while Hamelin with the *Vénus* and the *Manche* accounted for three more. All of these were homeward bound from Bengal, and several of them richly laden. In past years most of the damage had been done among the country shipping. The Honourable Company's ships had little to fear from the privateers. The losses suffered in 1809 were without precedent. In the same period five more East Indiamen foundered at sea, and three more were cast ashore. In this one year the Company had sustained almost as much damage as the sum total of all the losses suffered in the last war.

The success achieved by Hamelin's division was due partly to surprise and partly to the faulty disposition of our forces in the Indian Ocean. The arrival of the French frigates was quite unexpected. In his anxiety to appease the merchants in Calcutta Pellew had assigned most of his force to the Bay of Bengal. On his departure, in February 1809, his successor, Vice-Admiral William O'Brien Drury, who cared little either for commerce protection or for the protests of the merchants, hastened to reverse his dispositions.

It was the havoc wrought by Hamelin's squadron in 1809 which finally forced the hand of the British government and led directly to the expedition, in 1810, against the French islands which resulted in their capture.

The year 1811 witnessed the crisis of the hard-fought economic war between Napoleon and the British government. It was by far the worst year of the whole struggle for the national economy, which was now showing ominous signs of sagging beneath the strain. The export of British manufactures and colonial produce had fallen by very nearly one-third, compared with that of 1810. Entire areas of the industrial North and midlands were heavily hit. To the intensification of the Continental Blockade had lately been added the slump in the South America market and the growing alienation of the United States resulting in the Non-Intercourse Act. One thing was certain, Great Britain must export or perish: yet her export trade, it was all too clear, was calamitously declining.

On top of all this had come the intensification of the *guerre de course*. Year by year, with but one exception, British shipping losses were increasing. A total of 222 captures in 1803 had risen in 1804 to 387; in 1805 to 507; in 1806 to 519; in 1807 to 559. Though in the following year there was a substantial reduction to 469, in 1809 the significant upward trend was again renewed, the total rising to 571, and in 1810 to 619—the highest figure of the war.[1] Moreover, a high proportion of these losses were foreign-going ships. By the middle years of the Napoleonic War the attack on British trade in home waters had become, in fact, more daring and destructive than ever before. At the same time our losses were constantly mounting up in the Mediterran-

[1] C. B. Norman, *Corsairs of France* (1883), p. 453.

ean, and across the ocean, both in the Caribbean and in the Indian Ocean. And so long as the enemy held the all-important bases in Martinique, Guadeloupe, San Domingo, Cuba, and elsewhere in the West Indies, and on the other side of the globe in Mauritius and Bourbon Island, it was certain that these losses would continue.

Another alarming item on the debit side of the account was the fact that for years mercantile construction had been drastically curtailed. Between 1793 and 1803 the mercantile tonnage throughout the British Empire had increased by approximately one-third. But from 1803 onward the rate of new construction slackened, and did not regain the level that it had held in the year following the Peace of Amiens until after the war.

2

As in the French Revolutionary War, measures were set in train to seize the overseas bases from which the raiders operated. A few of the hostile bases had been captured in the first year of the war. Once again the islands of St. Pierre and Miquelon, off the coast of Newfoundland, had been taken. The Cape of Good Hope was again occupied early in 1806, Curaçao off the Venezuelan coast in 1807, and Anholt in the Kattegat in 1809. In the middle years of the war a number of expeditions were sent out which captured French Guiana, Martinique, Guadeloupe, and San Domingo, on one side of the globe, and Bourbon Island, Mauritius,[1] Amboyna, and Java,[2] on the other.

The system of patrolling focal areas, notably the English Channel, proved, at any rate, for long periods, remarkably ineffective. Notwithstanding that large numbers of our smaller cruisers were employed on this duty, the privateers appear for weeks and even months on end to have come and gone very much as they pleased. The cruisers themselves were frequently poor sailers, and their commanders all too often not the most zealous of their kind. Success, indeed, was so poorly rewarded that these officers had small inducement to exert themselves. Consequently they were seldom to be found at sea in bad weather and on exposed stations (e.g. off Beachy Head or the Lizard)

[1] See infra, pp. 399-400.
[2] See infra, p. 401.

where the raiders were most likely to be encountered; and the gales which drove our cruisers from off the headlands into sheltered anchorages were usually the signal for the enemy's privateersmen to put to sea. According to the Committee of Lloyd's, those few of the British cruisers which were fast sailers preferred lying in the track of smugglers (whom they generally succeeded in intercepting) to that infested by privateers, 'leaving the trade almost unprotected'.[1]

The *Alphaea* and the other small cruisers patrolling the Channel coast did little to hold these marauders in check. Much of their time, indeed, was passed, not at sea, but in sheltered roadsteads. '8 a.m.: weighed and made sail,' runs a typical entry in the *Alphaea*'s log, 'but finding it blowing strong bore up again and anchored.' The enemy was well aware of these deficiencies and naturally took advantage of them.

Last Friday afternoon, a large ship, supposed to be a homeward-bound West Indiaman, was boarded and captured not a league and a half from the shore, off Beachy-head, by a French privateer, when a telegraphic communication was, in consequence, made from the Signal-house at Seaford, but not attended to until it had been occasionally repeated for four hours, when the *Alphaea* schooner made sail in pursuit, but with what success we have not been able to learn.[2]

The explanation given in the *Alphaea*'s log was that the signals from the Seaford station were 'not clearly understood', with the result that the privateer and her prize made good their escape to France.[3] It is to be observed that lately there had been a long spell of hazy weather—always a favourable circumstance for the privateer.

The dispatch of several additional cruisers in the summer of 1809 to the station off Beachy Head brought about an immediate, if short-lived, improvement. 'The French privateer', declared the *Sussex Weekly Advertiser* in August, 'which a few days since made her

---

[1] Throughout the Napoleonic War paragraphs continued to appear in the local press concerning landings of contraband goods at Crowlink Gap and other favoured strands along the south-east coast, and the seizure of boats 'laden with spirits' in Cawsand Bay and elsewhere in the west. These smugglers, of course, had resource to the same stratagems and devices and relied upon much the same knowledge and experience as did the privateersmen. See *Sussex Weekly Advertiser* and *Exeter Flying Post*, *passim*.

[2] *Sussex Weekly Advertiser*, 28 July 1809.

[3] Adm. 52/4411, 28 July 1809.

appearance, in company with another, off Beachy-head, has been taken by the *Osprey* sloop.'[1] And in September: 'We are happy to state that we have heard of no interruption to our Channel Trade, since Government ordered an additional number of cruizers near and about Beachy-head. Of these we believe the *Iris* frigate is the principal.'

There were numerous complaints about the slackness of certain of the cruisers stationed along the south coast, of which the following is a fair example.

We had the mortification of seeing *two* colliers captured the other evening, close under the North Foreland, when not a single cruiser was in sight, except *one in Margate Roads*. See if there is not a Lieutenant Leach commanding the *Cracker* gun-brig, and if that gun-brig is not on the Foreland station. This gentleman, I understand, has a house at Birchington where he usually sleeps, and for this purpose Margate Roads is a very convenient place for his vessel to lie in. The Admiral must be remarkably good-natured to grant him this indulgence, so advantageous to the enemy's privateers.[2]

A number of these cruisers, however, gave a remarkably good account of themselves and rid the seas of some notable scourges. Such a case occurred in the autumn of 1804 when the *Cruizer*, sloop-of-war, after an epic chase finally ran down the redoubtable Jean Blanckmann in his newly built *Contre Amiral Magon* and compelled him to strike. Blanckmann had arrived from Dunkirk on his cruising-ground off Flamborough Head and was lying, out of sight of land, in wait for the Baltic trade. The chase which ensued continued for nearly nine hours, throughout the whole night of 17 November, in thick and blowing weather. The easterly wind freshened considerably during the hours of darkness, and the *Cruizer* lost most of her studdingsail-booms, her maintopgallant-mast and foretopsail-yards, and had at one time four feet of water in her hold. At four o'clock the following morning, according to her log, the *Cruizer* 'observed the chase to have anchored, shortened sail and hailed her, proved her to be the *Contre Amiral Magon* commanded by the noted Blanckmann'.

[1] The *Osprey* sloop-of-war, which had the reputation of being a smart cruiser, had seen a great deal of Channel service during the war, especially in this area (Adm. 52/3284 *passim*).

[2] Sir John Barrow to Croker; *Croker Papers*, i, p. 33.

A few hours later, when the sea had somewhat gone down, the *Cruizer* at last boarded and took her in tow, and made sail for Yarmouth. The capture of this famous privateersman, observed the *Naval Chronicle*, preserved the trade from disastrous losses during the following winter. 'It is a circumstance also, in which we have much to rejoice, that he fell in with the *Cruizer*, which is, perhaps, the only vessel in that sea that could have come up with him.'[1]

Another outstanding example of a smart cruiser, employed effectively in this patrolling service, was the *Scorpion*. 'Upon our arrival at Plymouth, after a refit,' declared her first lieutenant, 'we were kept on that station; and became the scourge of the Channel. Many French privateers, recaptures, etc., fell into our hands; such were the effects of a good look-out, good sailing, and *deception*. The officers were able to pay their mess, and never returned to Plymouth without a prize.'[2]

In this connection it is interesting to note that what in our own day was to become known as the 'Q-ship' stratagem (but was then called 'disguise' or 'deception') was often resorted to by both sides in the Napoleonic War. Thus the *Scorpion* was sometimes rigged as a bark—on other occasions with the foretopgallant-mast on deck. It is said that one of her prizes, the ketch-rigged *Glaneuse* privateer, was so fast that she would not have been captured had she not mistaken the *Scorpion* for a merchantman.

Later on Symonds became first of the *Pique*, whose sailing qualities he greatly improved and whose people he so trained that she was celebrated for her smartness and good order. Stationed in the Straits of Dover and off Beachy Head in 1811–12, the *Pique* did much to hold the corsairs in check. Then, within twelve months of the outbreak of the American War, she captured nearly two dozen American vessels in the West Indies.[3]

It is interesting to notice that in the final stages of the Napoleonic War the enemy raiders fell, in rapidly increasing numbers, a prey to the British cruisers. A most probable explanation would be that by this time most of the smarter privateers had been captured.

[1] Foncart and Finot, *Défence nationale*, II, pp. 750–75; *Naval Chronicle*, Vol. 12, pp. 454–6; Adm. 52/3585.

[2] J. A. Sharp, *Memoirs of Vice-Admiral Sir William Symonds*, p. 33; Adm. 51/1735, 51/1916.

[3] Adm. 51/2696, *passim*; Sharp, *op. cit.*, p. 38.

An important ancillary measure undertaken by the Admiralty for the protection of trade in the seas around the British Isles was the provision of signal stations, situated on our principal headlands and islands, to give warning of an enemy's approach. As early as 1795 a chain of signal stations had been erected along the south coast of England. The system was later extended to all the coasts of the United Kingdom. By this means the approach of the enemy's cruisers or privateers was immediately made known, and our convoys apprised of any danger. The signal stations were furnished with comfortable quarters for a lieutenant, a midshipman, and two seamen; their signals were made by means of balls and flags, or pendants displayed on a mast or yard, rigged for the purpose. Commander James Anthony Gardner, whose *Recollections* forms one of the most interesting and important sources of information for the social history of the Old Navy, was in charge of one of these signal stations during the years 1806 to 1814. He relates how, just before the outbreak of the Revolutionary War, he was conversing with the first lieutenant of the *Barfleur*, while they were standing down Channel—

'In passing Fairlight, near Hastings, on our way from the Downs to Spithead, Chantrell, pointing out to me the cliff near the church on Fairlight Down, said, "Jemmy, how would you like to be perched up there in the winter?" Little did he imagine,' observes Gardner, 'that in some years after, when the war broke out and signal stations were erected along the coast, he should be the first officer appointed to this very spot, and I, the last.'

Gardner goes on to say that when a friend of his applied to the Admiralty for a signal station, stating that he was unfit for active service in consequence of a stroke which had affected his arm and one of his eyes, the then First Lord, the Earl of St. Vincent, wrote in reply, 'That an officer of a signal station ought to have two eyes, and damned good eyes they ought to be.' However, the Admiralty complied with his request.[1]

In 1805 the Committee of Lloyd's proposed to the Admiralty that copies of coastal signals should be distributed to merchant shipping which had hitherto been unable to take in the warning. This was done; and some years afterwards, in consequence of a communication

[1] *Above and under hatches* (*Recollections of James Anthony Gardner*), ed. C. C. Lloyd, p. 82.

from the Admiralty, the Committee made strong representations to shipowners 'particularly and strictly' to enjoin the masters 'to keep near the English coast in proceeding up Channel, otherwise the Lieutenants at the Signal Posts cannot make known to Merchant Vessels the approach of any Enemy's cruizers.'[1]

Immediately on the resumption of hostilities with France in 1803, on the basis of the last ten years' experience the Compulsory Convoy Act was brought in introducing a comprehensive and highly organized convoy system and imposing severe penalties upon ships which were guilty of indiscipline or broke convoy; to which was added the deterrent that ships which broke convoy and were subsequently lost to the enemy forfeited their insurance. At the same time an embargo was placed on all shipping movements until escort forces could be assembled for the various trades.

As in the previous war, large rather than small convoys were the rule; and, notwithstanding the large numbers of the convoy, the merchantmen were sufficiently safe under normal conditions—it was only when they were dispersed by a gale or a prolonged calm that the raiders got their chance and wrought havoc in the convoy. Later on convoys of as many as 300, 400, and even 500 ships were sometimes to be seen entering or leaving the great trade focals like the mouth of the Channel or the entrance to the Baltic.

During the spring of 1805 the First Lord of the Admiralty, Lord Barham, set out a list of the qualities which were required of the officer put in charge of cruisers, convoys, etc.

> He should be a perfect master of arrangement. Without this, he must be in continued perplexity, misemploy and lose the force which is put under his direction. He should be deeply skilled in practical professional knowledge, so as to know, from a sloop to a first-rate, what each is capable of performing, the time it will take to take to fit her, the services she is capable of performing and what time is necessary to perform it in. In preparing convoys for general services, he should have his ships in such readiness as to be at the rendezvous by a given day, so as to prevent the merchant ships or store ships being kept in demurrage.[2]

Later in the same year Barham framed a series of detailed and specific orders relating to convoy. It was therein laid down that a printed copy

[1] Adm. 1/3993, 7 November 1805.
[2] *Barham Papers*, III, pp. 37–8.

of instructions was to be presented to each master in the convoy, and that these instructions were to be kept secret; that no officer should be permitted to receive anything in the nature of a fee from any master or owner; that the officer in command of the convoy was to regard the protection of his convoy as his most important duty; that he was to take all possible precautions against surprise, and that none of the escorts were to chase 'so far from the Fleet as to run any risk of being separated from it'; and was moreover to take care to keep the convoy together, to render assistance to any vessel in distress, and to 'proceed with all possible expedition'—though he must not carry more sail than would allow the dullest sailer in the convoy to keep station. When convoys bound to different ports sailed in company for better protection, the merchant vessels were to keep station within their own convoys and the escorts were to fly their own distinguishing pendants, so that eventually the different divisions of the convoy would be able to part company without confusion. These regulations, which were the product of centuries of experience of commerce protection, continued in force down to the end of the war.

The imperative importance of commerce protection, even in the great naval crisis of 1805, is strikingly apparent in Barham's orders to Cornwallis. Napoleon's stratagems to achieve a diversion in preparation for his projected invasion of England seemed partially to have succeeded. Yet it is clear that the most pressing anxiety which the escape of the Toulon fleet and Allemand's division had caused the Admiralty was for the safety of the troop-transports and the great trading fleets. The concentration of the French and Spanish squadrons at Ferrol placed them in imminent jeopardy; and British apprehensions were naturally increased by Villeneuve's hurried departure shortly afterwards. At the very height of the invasion alarm, in response to an appeal from the Chairman of the East India Company,[1] Barham took steps to protect the trade.

> I have for the time determined to have as many heavy frigates as we can spare ... for the express purpose of cruising to the westward, not only

[1] 'The value which will be at stake in the fleet being so immense, and the enemy having now so large a naval force at Ferrol, to which our ships will be exposed, I earnestly hope your lordship notwithstanding the numerous calls upon you, may be able to afford the India fleet an effectual protection when it approaches the shores of Europe' (*Ibid.*, p. 276).

for the annoyance of the enemy's cruisers, but for the protection of the homeward and outward bound convoys and also of the western coast when necessary. By these means much strength will be added to the convoys where they stand in need of them.[1]

A week later Barham wrote again:

I wish you may be able to contrive it so as to spare four ships and a frigate to cruise in the chops of the Channel for about ten days, for the preservation of these convoys. I trust Sir Robert [Calder] will take care to keep between them and the French squadron. The safety of these fleets must be our first object, and as soon as they have got within the Channel we shall be able to make you strong in all quarters.

In the event neither support force nor hostile raiding squadron met the immensely wealthy trading fleet, under convoy of Admiral Rainier in the *Trident*, which, steering a secret route that took them two hundred miles west of the Azores, entered the Channel in the first week of September and on the 8th came in sight of the Start. Slowly, in fine summer weather, with a westerly breeze, the convoy passed up the Channel. That night they were off Portland Bill and next morning at daybreak sighted Dunnose in the Isle of Wight. In the evening they passed Beachy Head and on the 10th rounded the South Foreland, and, after saluting 'the flag of Admiral Lord Keith with 13 guns which was returned with 13 guns', at noon shortened sail and came to anchor in the Downs.[2] The news of Rainier's arrival was at once reported by telegraph to the Admiralty.

Within five years of Trafalgar, when the attack on trade had assumed unprecedented proportions, the complex and extensive system of convoy organized by the British Admiralty attained, perhaps, its fullest development, unsurpassed, and possibly unequalled even, by the hurriedly improvised ramifications of convoy in the unrestricted U-boat campaign of 1917–18. The world-wide range and scope of the system then in operation can be readily appreciated from the following table.[3]

[1] *Ibid.*, p. 206.
[2] Adm. 52/3709.
[3] D. W. Waters, *Notes on the Convoy System of Naval Warfare*. Admiralty MS.

CONVOY	FREQUENCY
U.K.: Coastal Convoys	
U.K.: North Sea Convoys	Frequent—Once a week or more often.
U.K.: Ireland Convoys	
U.K.: Channel Island Convoys	
U.K.: Baltic Convoys	Every 14 or 21 days.
U.K.: Greenland and Davis Strait Fisheries	Occasionally.
U.K.: North America—Newfoundland— Quebec Convoys	Monthly, between March and September.
U.K.: West Indies and Guiana Convoys	Monthly, and occasional extra convoys.
U.K.: South America Convoys	Monthly, and occasional extra convoys.
U.K.: East Indies—China— Cape of Good Hope—St. Helena— South Seas Convoys	Monthly.
U.K.: Portugal and Spain Convoys	Monthly, and occasional extra convoys.
U.K.: Military Store Convoys, for Portugal and Spain	As necessary.

On the Mediterranean station, so serious were the depredations of the hostile privateers and so insistent was the demand for convoys, that in previous years Nelson had found his resources taxed to the limit to provide the necessary escorts and to keep the whole complicated machinery of convoy in smooth and punctual running order. His correspondence during this period clearly reflects the vital role filled by the convoy system in the protection of our seaborne trade and at the same time sheds a revealing light on the day-to-day operation of that system.

'As I feel the protection of our Commerce a very essential and important part of my duty,' he informed the Admiralty in November 1803, 'their Lordships may be assured that everything which remains with me shall be done, to prevent any of the Trade of his Majesty's Subjects from falling into the hands of the Enemy.' The merchant vessels were accordingly collected from the recesses of the Levant and the neighbouring seas, and, assembled at last in one large convoy, conducted to Gibraltar under escort of a frigate or ship of the line in addition to one or two small cruisers. Meanwhile at Gibraltar small bodies of merchant shipping had similarly been assembling from along the shores of the western Mediterranean; and, following on the arrival of the Malta convoy, would all sail together for England under a strong escort. It is apparent, as Nelson pointed out, that the utmost precision and punctuality were necessary in ordering these arrangements.

> The going on in a routine of a station, if interrupted, is like stopping a watch—the whole machine gets wrong. If the *Maidstone* takes the convoy, and, when *Agincourt* arrives, there is none for her or *Thisbe*, it puzzles me to know what orders to give them. If they chace the convoy to Gibraltar, the *Maidstone* may have gone on with it to England, and in that case two ships, unless I give a new arrangement, will either go home without convoy or they must return [to Malta] in contradiction to the Admiralty orders to send them home.[1]

In the latter years of the war numerous convoys were organized for the traffic to Archangel. These convoys would assemble in Long Hope Sound in the Orkney Islands. From twelve to twenty merchantmen, after receiving their instructions, would be shepherded across the North Sea by a couple of small cruisers. In fog or thick weather the escorts fired signal-guns to keep the convoy together. The escorts would sometimes part company with their convoys off the North Cape, and sometimes accompany them all the way to Archangel. From time to time they would sight the land—the distant mountain peaks of Norway, the North Cape, some outlying island or group of rocks, the barren, black cliffs of the Murman coast, or 'Cape Sweet Nose'; whence, with a fair wind, it was no more than a few days' sailing to Archangel. In these high northern waters, even in the summer months, sleet, snow, and severe gales, with heavy breaking seas, were frequently encountered. In certain winds it might be necessary even to steer as far north as the latitude of Bear Island. A convoy might be scattered before a gale or in a calm. Sometimes a cruiser would take one of the dull sailers in tow, or go down to the assistance of a vessel that was in difficulties.

For the commerce with the Baltic the Admiralty relied as usual on the two-fold system of trade protection. The trade from the British ports would be accompanied by escorts, and the principal focal areas patrolled by adequate cruiser forces. On passage up the east coast a number of small convoys would 'snowball' into large fleets and rendezvous at the Nore, the Humber, Leith, or Long Hope Sound

[1] *Nelson's Dispatches*, VI, pp. 51–2.

in the Orkneys. Usually the trade was shepherded across the North Sea by one or two small cruisers, accompanied on occasion by a sail of the line on its way to join the Baltic squadron. Except in the case of the northernmost rendezvous, convoys were provided at fortnightly intervals between spring and autumn. Beyond the Naze cover was provided by the Baltic fleet. The Skagerrak was patrolled by a strong force of brigs and sloops which intercepted the enemy's cruisers and privateers and prevented the raiders based on Norwegian ports from pursuing an active offensive. The rendezvous appointed for these convoys was in Vingå Sound, near Gothenburg. In this anchorage they assembled in large fleets in preparation for the most dangerous lap of the voyage, the passage of the Great Belt.

In accordance with the system established in 1808 by Rear-Admiral Keats, a ship of the line was stationed at either end of the Belt to take charge of the convoys as they arrived from the Kattegat or the Baltic, and to escort them through the passage. Four more of the line were stationed approximately midway through the Belt, as a support force against gunboats and privateers from the neighbouring Danish bases. Writing to Saumarez on 27 November, Keats emphasized the necessity of a strong force stationed in the Belt. 'Convoys', he declared, 'passing thro' Belt, besides the escort requisite for the Kattegat and Baltic Sea, should be strongly guarded; for if the wind fails them, especially in the navigation between Sproë and the south end of Langeland, which may be considered the centre of their flotilla force, they must expect to be attacked by a formidable number of gunboats.'[1]

After leaving the Belt, the convoys continued on their passage up the Baltic under the protection of the escorts which had joined them in Vingå Sound. That part of the trade which was bound for Swedish ports proceeded there under escort, while the remainder also sailed under escort until about fifty leagues east of Bornholm, after which the convoys broke up and the ships proceeded to their various destinations.

After parting company with the outward-bound convoys the escorts made the best of their way to the rendezvous of the trade bound for England. At Karlskrona or Hanö Island convoys were provided at fortnightly intervals, 'as far as wind and weather allowed', between the months of April and November. The master of one of the American

[1] Adm. 1/6, 27 November 1808.

merchantmen engaged in the Baltic trade, George Coggeshall, describes the roadstead between Hanö Island and the Swedish mainland
as a 'good, safe anchorage' and a 'great rendezvous for British warships.'

> Here they lie until a sufficient number of merchant ships have collected,
> when the admiral sends a frigate or two to convoy them through the Belt
> and Kattegat to Gothenburg. When I arrived, I found about 20 sail
> waiting convoy, and after lying here eight days, the number had aug-
> mented to about 50; and on the 9th of June we left Hano, under the
> protection of a frigate and two sloops-of-war, and soon got into the
> Great Belt, where we saw lying at anchor the *Vigo*, 74, Admiral Dixon,
> and several frigates and sloops-of-war. At this season of the year, men-
> of-war can anchor with perfect safety in almost any part of this passage.[1]

The homecoming convoys, like those outward bound, were escorted
through the Belt by the squadron stationed there; and as a rule they
were accompanied by a ship of the line from that squadron as far
north as Anholt Island. In Vingå Sound the large convoys which had
been conducted through the Belt were divided into smaller ones for
the return passage across the North Sea, under escort of the cruisers
which had accompanied the outgoing trade; and they would sail for
home with the first fair wind.

Sometimes these Baltic convoys were very large indeed. Thus in
October 1809, before the admiring eyes of Marshal Bernadotte, who
called it 'the most beautiful and most wonderful sight that he had ever
beheld', a vast convoy of 1,000 merchantmen, together with their
escorts, lay in the spacious anchorage of Vingå Sound. 'The day was
very fine; the fleet was anchored in a close compact body, with the
Victory in the centre, bearing the Admiral's red flag at the fore,
surrounded by six ships of the line, and six frigates and sloops disposed
for the complete protection of the convoy.'[2]

Though convoys normally sailed through the Belt, an interesting
case occurred in the early winter of 1811 when, the wind being con-

---

[1] Geo. Coggeshall, *Second Series of Voyages* (1852), p. 104. Coggeshall
thus describes the usual order of sailing: 'A line of battle ship ahead to lead
the van, one or two frigates astern, and a sloop of war, and a brig or two to
protect the flanks or outside ships, those nearest the land on both sides of the
passage, and notwithstanding all these precautions, the Danish boats would
now and then intercept a straggler'.

[2] Ross, *Memoirs of Admiral Lord de Saumarez* (1838), II, p. 215.

trary for that route and favourable for the Malmö channel, of a large convoy being safely led through the intricate and hazardous navigation of the latter passage by Captain Acklom in the *Ranger*. A few days later, when they were all safely anchored near Kronborg, the wind flew up to N.N.W. and blew a heavy gale, which would have entailed the destruction of a good many of them had they been caught in an open anchorage in the Belt. For this service Acklom was promoted to the rank of post-captain.[1]

Convoys left England for the West Indies from about the middle of autumn until May. On the outward passage the fleet would sail down to the latitude of Madeira, and then shape a course across the Atlantic for Barbados with the trade wind; from Barbados the ships, under convoy, proceeded to their various destinations. The trade went home in two separate divisions, from Jamaica and from the Windward Islands. Since the routes commonly followed by the trade were exposed to the depredations of the hostile privateers which infested the archipelago, vessels were shepherded to the appointed rendezvous by escorts. For the homeward passage escorts were provided by the two squadrons in the Caribbean, on the Jamaica and Leeward Islands stations. Additional escorts were usually furnished for convoys until they were clear of the danger zone, after which the former would return to their own stations. The protection of these large West India trading fleets was frequently provided by the periodical reliefs, both proceeding to, and returning from, the Jamaica and Leeward Islands stations.

Shipping from London would usually assemble at Spithead; but in the later years of the war the convoys were accustomed to wait off Falmouth for any vessels from the north which desired to join them. Ships from the east coast of England and Scotland bound westward, and also those from the Baltic on the same course, would assemble in Long Hope Sound; similarly ships from the west bound for our east coast ports or the Baltic would call at Long Hope Sound to obtain their escorts for the last lap of the voyage. Before the convoys sailed, the masters of the merchantmen were well briefed as to the day and night signals.

One of the most serious disadvantages of the system for the West

[1] Adm. 1/14, 24 December; 52/3858, 20-23 December 1811; Ross, *op.cit.*, II, p. 267.

Indies traffic was the fact that, in practice, convoys sailed at most irregular intervals. For this and other reasons, many of the vessels bound for the West Indies (particularly for the outlying islands) sailed without convoy. Shipping from Bristol and the ports in the north would save much time by sailing independently. To be a successful runner, however, a ship had to be specially designed for the purpose. She must be large enough to cross the Atlantic with a good-sized cargo, and well-armed; and, further, she must be fast enough to elude the privateers which swarmed in the Channel and Caribbean. As high a proportion as one-quarter of the ships engaged in the West Indies trade sailed without convoy.

As in other branches of our overseas trade, Lloyd's continually collaborated with the Admiralty to improve the organization of the convoy system. Thus on New Year's Day, 1810, the Committee of Lloyd's advanced the following suggestion.

> The convoy now collecting at Portsmouth bound to the West Indies, consist of above 150 sail. As the fatal effects of so large a fleet in one body experiencing a gale of wind in the Channel, or Bay of Biscay, was so seriously felt in the year 1796, under the late Admiral Christian, the Committee beg leave to suggest to their Lordships the advantage that would arise from dividing the convoy by the ships bound to Jamaica (about 70 sail) being sent under a separate protection (not less than two ships of war) direct to Jamaica, without calling at Barbadoes or any other island, which would lessen the risk, shorten the voyage at least ten days, and benefit the island by the more speedy arrival out of the plantation stores; which would be much wanted on account of the fleet having been detained for six weeks by contrary winds.[1]

In the Napoleonic War the trade between British North America and our islands in the West Indies began to suffer as severely as in the late war, and large numbers of frigates and smaller cruisers were consequently needed to protect the shipping on this and other trade-routes in North American waters. Owing to the increasing demand for frigates in other theatres of the war, recourse was had to brigs, sloops, and smaller vessels for escort duties in the Newfoundland trade. Then, following a disastrous reverse in 1804, as the result of entrusting the entire Newfoundland convoy to the protection of a single escort vessel, the 13-gun sloop *Wolverine*, Lloyd's protested indignantly against

[1] Adm. 1/3993, 1 January 1810.

what was becoming quite a usual practice, that of allowing convoys comprising 50 to 70 merchantmen to sail with only one small cruiser as escort; and shortly afterwards escorts were substantially strengthened. Though there was little actual fighting until the outbreak of the American War in 1812, the arduous convoy-and-patrol work up and down the Western Ocean demanded the highest standards of seamanship and vigilance; for the sporadic incursions of the enemy were seldom as formidable as the dangers of the sea, which claimed a grievous and continuous toll. The Newfoundland in company with the Halifax and North American trades would leave England in early spring: smaller convoys would follow in the summer and autumn. Largely in consequence of the Convoy Acts, the traffic was carried on with remarkable regularity.

The East India Company's shipping lent itself readily to the exigencies of the convoy system; for the trade to India and China for various reasons was largely seasonal in character and the ships were under no temptation to compete with each other. Though the Honourable Company's ships were exempt from the provisions of the convoy acts they very seldom sailed without naval escorts. Frequently a man-of-war would accompany a convoy through the entire passage; for the East Indies squadron was constantly sending ships home for refitting, and receiving others fresh from England; and these invariably sailed with a convoy. After the conquest of the Cape early in 1806 the East Indies trade was usually escorted by warships as far southward as St. Helena, at which point the warships would return to England, and the East Indiamen would come under the protection of escorts provided by the squadron stationed at the Cape. These escorts would then shepherd the merchantmen across the Indian Ocean to their destination. Indiamen bound to China by the direct route would be escorted by a warship through the whole passage to Canton and home again. It was customary to sail from England in the summer, and from India in the autumn; while the China fleet usually sailed in the summer and returned in the autumn.

The command of one of these outgoing- or homeward-bound convoys was by no means a sinecure. In the first place, a convoy would have to run the gauntlet of the numerous hostile privateers in entering or leaving the Channel and its approaches. Again, in the course of the voyage a convoy would often be dispersed, not only by bad weather, but also by a calm, which would leave vessels sailing many miles apart from each other. A convoy was also apt to be dispersed when obliged to work to windward. When this occurred the normal procedure was for the convoy to reassemble at the next rendezvous. Further, relations between the senior officers of the Royal Navy and those of the Honourable Company were not always of the best. The escort commanders occasionally expressed strong criticism of the masters under their charge. 'I am sure', complained Troubridge in the summer of 1805, 'to take India Ships under Convoy is the worst Service that can fall to the Lot of a Zealous officer, for he can never gain Credit by his care and attention, but will always be kept on the fret, by the gross ignorance and unseamanlike Conduct of the greater part of the Captains.'[1]

During the early half of the Napoleonic War, as a result of the British merchants' obstinate refusal to submit to the restrictions of convoy, the trade of Calcutta suffered very heavy losses—on one occasion nineteen ships were lost in two months. Following the capture in the summer of 1805 of the Honourable Company's ship, the *Brunswick*, by the *Marengo*, and the loss of another ship which was run ashore by her crew on the coast of Ceylon, Pellew protested to the Admiralty:

> It should be observed that the Sailing of these Ships without protection was totally in contradiction of my purposes, and had their Commanders thought proper to avail themselves of the Convoy appointed to sail from Bombay early in the approaching Month with the regular Ships, this loss would have been effectually prevented, and it is still less excusable when it is known to result from considerations of Individual profit arising from an early market.[2]

On the other hand, one of the most important and vulnerable trade-routes in eastern seas—namely, that between Bombay and Canton—was so well protected by Pellew's dispositions that losses by capture were actually less than those by the dangers of the sea, and the premium if sailing with convoy was only five per cent.; that is, fifty per cent. lower than at any former period. Even in the threatened focal area in the vicinity of the Straits of Malacca, Pellew's protective measures—adequate convoy escorts, coupled with an occasional cruiser stationed in the Straits—appear to have been effective.

[1] Q. C. N. Parkinson, *Trade in the Eastern Seas* (1937), p. 314.
[2] Adm. 1/176, 22 July 1805.

It had surprised Napoleon to learn that Mauritius was still in French hands in 1808. What he was unable to comprehend was why the British had not captured the place long ago. There were others who shared his astonishment. 'It is difficult,' Captain Beaver observed a few months before the final attempt on Mauritius, 'to assign a reason why this measure has not been resorted to before, for this island has for many years nourished a vile nest of buccaneers against our Oriental commerce.' The truth of the matter seems to have been that the Isle of France was saved owing partly to the division of the East Indies station during the period 1805–7, and partly to the Honourable Company's decided *penchant* for economy. As has been said, it was the disastrous losses sustained in 1809 that caused the authorities at long last to set in train the expedition against the French stronghold in the Indian Ocean.

Drury had been in favour of an attack on both Mauritius and Bourbon Island with a somewhat larger force than that which had been assembled; but he was overruled by Minto. It was decided to make the attempt on Bourbon Island first. While this operation was in progress, in July 1810, the blockade of Mauritius was abandoned, as all the available warships were required to cover the landing. As soon as this had been successfully achieved, the blockade of Mauritius was resumed.

The first attempt on the great French stronghold proved abortive. A slightly superior British force under Captain Samuel Pym stood in on 23 August to Grand Port to attack a French squadron under Duperré before Hamelin's division of three powerful frigates should arrive from Port Louis. But Duperré had taken up a strong defensive position in the recesses of Grand Port, his ships being flanked by heavy batteries on shore manned by seamen and further covered by shoals and sunken rocks. The *Magicienne* (Br.) struck one of these rocks and went aground. Duperré then signalled to his ships to cut their cables. As his own ship, the *Bellone*, stood slowly towards the land, the *Sirius* pursued her, but, not knowing the ground, soon after ran on a coral reef which held her fast and helpless; the *Néréide* (Br.) following her, also went aground. The *Magicienne* was so badly damaged that next morning she was abandoned and set on fire; the *Sirius* was likewise abandoned and blown up; the *Néréide* was forced to strike her colours; and on the 27th the *Iphigenia* surrendered to

Hamelin's squadron, which had appeared off the entrance to the harbour. On 18 September Hamelin also captured the *Ceylon*, 32, carrying Major-General Abercromby and his staff.

But Rowley quickly recovered the initiative. Within a few hours he had arrived with the *Boadicea* and two sloops, and shortly afterwards retook the *Ceylon*, and also captured the flagship *Vénus* with Abercromby aboard. The odds were not so heavily against him as at first sight appeared, for several of Hamelin's squadron had been so severely damaged in the action of Grand Port that they were laid up for months to come.

The capture of the French flagship was the turning-point in the campaign. By the end of September Rowley's effective force had been augmented by the arrival of several more frigates and he was able to institute a close and rigorous blockade of Port Louis; meanwhile his damaged vessels were hastily refitting. He had also carefully explored the rock-fringed shores of Mauritius and discovered a safe landing-place. In October the *Nisus*, 38, Captain Philip Beaver—a specialist in combined operations—brought Rear-Admiral Bertie from the Cape. There was a further delay while the various naval and military forces gradually assembled; and the fleet lay out of sight of Mauritius until the weather came favourable. The landing of the troops, which took place on 29 November under the direction of Captain Beaver, was, like the disembarkation ten years earlier in Aboukir Bay, ably planned and skilfully conducted.[1] Decaen found himself confronted by overwhelmingly superior forces, and on 3 December he capitulated. There fell into the hands of the conquerors seven frigates, three Indiamen, a large number of country ships, and an immense quantity of booty.

Mauritius had fallen; but Holland at this stage was firmly under French control, and Java had been saddled with a French governor. It was possible that Batavia, the capital of the island, would become a first-class naval base still more favourably placed for harassing our commerce than Mauritius and Bourbon. In spite of navigational hazards which were then believed to be more formidable than they actually were, Minto was determined to press on to the conquest of Java. 'I have still one object more,' he declared, '. . . which will fill

[1] Jas. Prior, *Voyages in the Indian Seas*, pp. 227–30; Adm. 1/63, 6 December 1810.

up the whole scheme of my warlike purposes, and which will purge the Eastern side of the globe of every hostile or rival European establishment.'

A force of over 80 sail was collected at Malacca and, in the middle of June 1811, sailed for Java in small divisions, each under the charge of a frigate, and accompanied also by smaller cruisers. The approach of this squadron to Java down the west coast of Borneo, in the face of contrary winds—but making use of occasional flaws, northerly squalls, and the land and sea breezes along that shore, as suggested by Lord Minto's son, Captain the Hon. George Elliot—was one of the most remarkable feats of navigation in the war.[1] Once again a British conjoint enterprise was swift and successful. Early in the morning of 4 August the disembarkation of the army took place under the experienced direction of Captain Cole of the *Caroline*, who hurried the first boatloads of troops ashore before the Dutch could arrive at the landing-place.[2] Before nightfall the whole army was safely disembarked, and a few days afterwards Batavia surrendered. A couple of frigates from Nantes which had brought out the new French governor to Java just got away in time and eventually returned to France.

The conquest of Java brought the war in the eastern seas to an end. Napoleon no longer possessed a base anywhere near India, and the Honourable Company's territories and commerce were secure. Throughout the rest of the war there was peace in the Indian Ocean. Our East Indies squadron was considerably reduced in strength—in 1815 it comprised only four 74s and eighteen frigates or sloops.

As has already been said, one of the main factors in the protection of our seaborne trade during the French Revolutionary and Napoleonic Wars was the immense influence exerted by Lloyd's. On the eve of hostilities in 1793, Lloyd's Coffee House, now located in the Royal Exchange, was far and away the greatest centre of marine insurance in the world. Under the leadership of such magnates as John Julius Angerstein, Sir Francis Baring, and 'Dicky' Thornton, it successfully stood the strain of the war years. (The risks covered at Lloyd's during 1809 amounted to something approaching £100 millions.) It is worth noticing that the Coffee House had become so well patronized by

[1] See Rear-Admiral A. H. Taylor in *Mariner's Mirror*, Vol. 35, pp. 326–7.
[2] Adm. 1/184, 19 August 1811.

shipmasters that it was already beginning to be referred to as 'The Captains' Room'. Lloyd's, to a far greater degree than the Society of Shipowners, represented the shipping industry in its dealings with the Admiralty and the government.

In the course of the eighteenth century Lloyd's had built up a unique and unrivalled system of shipping intelligence which was further extended, during the present struggle, by John Bennett the younger, who in 1804 had been appointed Secretary to the Committee. Intelligence of arrivals and departures, both at home and overseas, together with other news of naval and military importance, from Lloyd's agents, was sent on immediately to the Admiralty; and the Admiralty in turn forwarded convoy lists and other useful information to Lloyd's.[1]

The authority and prestige of Lloyd's were such that its recommendations in every branch of trade protection—especially with regard to the convoy system—received the most careful consideration from both Admiralty and government. The Convoy Acts of 1793, 1798, and 1803 had been largely due to the influence of Lloyd's; for the experience of successive generations of underwriters had shown that convoy afforded by far the most efficacious means of trade protection, and throughout the war Lloyd's cooperated with the Admiralty in enforcing these Acts.[2] The Committee of Lloyd's considered complaints forwarded by the Admiralty from commanders of escorts concerning masters who broke convoy or disobeyed instructions; and Lloyd's would not infrequently prosecute such masters. The Committee likewise received complaints from masters regarding com-

---

[1] 'As the war went on it became more and more an established practice for the Admiralty (and occasionally for Commanders-in-Chief on Foreign Stations) to consult the Committee on such questions as convoy regulations, ports of assembly and sailing dates, and for the Committee to volunteer suggestions on matters of trade defence.... Both the Minute Books at Lloyd's and the Admiralty preserved at the Public Record Office bear evidence of a close and continuous cooperation which was of incalculable value in the defence of British trade. Had some of its results been studied in time, they might have proved of as great value in 1914–18' (C. E. Fayle in *The Trade Winds*, ed. C. N. Parkinson, p. 45).

[2] In an admirable study of convoy statistics based on the Convoy Books preserved at the Admiralty, Lieut.-Commander D. W. Waters has observed that the 'Marine insurance premiums afford a quantitive estimate of the value of convoy as a system of shipping defence in a long series of wars' (*Notes on the Convoy System of Naval Warfare*, Admiralty MS.).

manders of escorts. It protested against the folly of ships sailing up Channel 'as they frequently do with the wind westwardly, single and unprotected'; also against the issue of licenses to sail without convoy to ships 'by no means sufficiently armed and manned, to make any defence against privateers'.

In March 1809, in response to a strongly worded complaint from the Committee of Lloyd's concerning the severe losses suffered in the Channel during the previous six months, the Admiralty enunciated a detailed defence of its measures for trade-protection, observing that:

> many of these ships were taken in consequence of having quitted their convoys, in direct opposition to their orders, and frequently after every possible effort had been made by the commanders of convoys, to prevent them from parting convoy. Several of these captures were also made after the convoys, to which the vessels belonged, had been dispersed by stress of weather; and it has frequently happened during the last winter, that the cruizers in the Channel have been blown from their several positions, and that the enemy's privateers have thereby been afforded an opportunity of putting to sea, and committing depredations on that part of the coast which they could fetch, before it was possible for the cruizers to get back to their stations.

The Admiralty argued that the proportion of ships lost to the enemy was, in fact, remarkably low when compared with the total number of voyages made to foreign ports.

> In order to make a just estimate upon this subject, it is necessary to observe, that in the six months during which it is stated in the lists that 48 vessels have been carried into enemy ports in the Channel, there sailed from the ports of Great Britain and Ireland, under convoy for foreign ports, according to official returns now at the Admiralty one thousand five hundred and nineteen merchant ships and vessels. Within the same period, one thousand two hundred and twenty-one sail of merchantmen, homeward bound, received convoy instructions from His Majesty's Ships, as appears by their lists transmitted to the Admiralty; and there were also, during the same space of time, nine hundred and seventy-two licences for ships to sail without a convoy taken out at the Admiralty— making altogether a total of 3,762 sail of ships!—without including the coasting and Irish trades, which it is well known amount to a very great proportion of the general commerce of the country.

The Admiralty proceeded to turn the tables on the complainants by drawing attention to the following very pertinent facts:

The Convoy Act does not compel any vessel to take convoy between any two ports of the United Kingdom, and ships may freely sail without convoy from port to port, within the United Kingdom, without taking out a licence from the Admiralty.... The owners may direct their merchantmen never to quit one port in the United Kingdom for another without convoy: an obedience to this order cannot be enforced by the Admiralty, but every facility is uniformly given for the encouragement of such precautions, and it must be well known to those concerned in the trade of the country, that all applications made for coasting convoys are favourably received by the Admiralty, and invariably granted as a matter of course.

These proposals were equally applicable to the Irish trade:

convoys are granted for the protection of the Irish trade whenever they are demanded;—the Admiral at Cork has particular instructions on this head—and indeed either from Cork, or from any other Irish or British port, there is not an instance, within the recollection of the present Board of Admiralty, of a coasting convoy being refused.

The Admiralty ended by defending the system of licences to ships to sail without convoy, observing that:

That the discretion exercised in granting licences has been beneficial to the public there is strong reason to presume, from the very small comparative number of licensed vessels that have been captured by the enemy.[1]

The year 1810, as has already been said, marked a turning-point in the war on trade. In that year British losses had reached a total of 619 ships. But in 1811 they dropped abruptly to 470; in 1813, to 371; in 1814 to only 145. There had also been a steady decline in the number of privateers fitted out. In 1810 there were at least 200 of them at sea; but in 1812 no more than 93. At the same time there was increasing difficulty in securing crews for these ventures, so great was the throng of privateersmen now languishing in British prison hulks.

To sum up: in consequence of all these measures of commerce protection, but more especially by virtue of the world-wide organization of the convoy system, British losses, though severe, were kept within tolerable limits;[2] and the constant flow of trade was sustained. The elaboration of the convoy system, set in train at the crisis of the

[1] Adm. 1/3993, 8 March 1809.
[2] The estimates vary, but it was probably something between 2½ and 3 per cent. of the total tonnage.

struggle, represented in fact a powerful and effective counter-stroke at Napoleon's maritime and commercial strategy. Convoy, supplemented by cruiser patrols in the focal areas, proved, during the wars of 1793-1815, the most effectual means of protecting the vital long-distance trades upon which the prosperity of Great Britain—and consequently the lavish financial contributions she was able to make to the Allied war effort—always depended. It is not too much to say that the sustained expansion of British commerce throughout the war years was rendered possible by the progressive reorganization of the convoy system, coupled with the rapid extension of the marine insurance market centred in London.

XIV

The Crisis of the Commercial War

I

In the latter part of 1809 Napoleon concentrated his chief energies on the stricter enforcement of the Continental Blockade. With his hands freed by the defeat of Austria, he sent large numbers of French troops to occupy the ports and coasts. Market after market was closed to British trade. Contraband goods were seized and burnt. His brother Louis having relinquished the throne of Holland, this kingdom was promptly incorporated in France. Frederick VI of Denmark rigorously enforced the Continental System throughout his realm. Sweden was obliged to cede Finland and later to close her ports to British shipping. By the end of 1810 the Continental System had been further strengthened by the annexation of Oldenburg, the northern part of Berg, Westphalia, Hanover, Bremen, Hamburg, and Lübeck. The estuaries of the Ems, Weser, and Elbe were brought under French control; the contiguous coasts were fortified so that the small British cruisers stationed off those rivers were obliged to withdraw; and Marshal Davout, in Hamburg, was entrusted with the supervision of the entire brigades that lined the shore. The coastal provinces of Spain were similarly governed by French generals.

'England', Napoleon had earlier observed, 'sees her merchandise repelled by all Europe, and her ships, loaded with useless wealth, seek in vain, from the Sound to the Hellespont, a port open to receive them.'[1]

During 1810 the duel between France and Great Britain was rapidly approaching a climax. In the ensuing twelve months it seemed as if the latter must finally succumb to the pressure of Napoleon's land blockade. With a large proportion of her steadily increasing population dependent upon manufacture and commerce the over-

[1] *Correspondance de Napoléon*, XV, p. 659.

sea trade was vital to her existence. Without exports she could not live. Though she enjoyed something like a monopoly of trans-oceanic trade, the new lands were for the most part undeveloped and could not possibly make up for the loss of her European markets.

In June the situation in the North took a bad turn. Napoleon's forces overran the south-west coasts of the Baltic. At Rostock, Danzig, and other ports large stocks of colonial produce were impounded at Napoleon's orders, and a number of ships arrested. But the worst was yet to come. Despite the disquieting rumours that had been arriving from Prussia and Russia, British merchants, as in the previous year, determined to dispatch vast quantities of exports to the Baltic. By ill chance our convoys were delayed for more than two months at Gothenburg by contrary winds, so that when at last they were able to sail it was already autumn and the trap was about to be sprung. On 21 October a heavy gale, in which 150 vessels are said to have been lost, dispersed the convoy. Under pressure from Napoleon hundreds of merchantmen were presently seized up and down the Baltic and a large proportion of that year's exports to the North were confiscated. By the close of 1810 the coasts of the Baltic were rigorously barred against British commerce.

That a great many of the vessels arrested were neutral, American as well as German, naturally made no difference in Napoleon's eyes; for all effective purposes they made part of the British merchant fleet and of the Baltic trading system. The blow was one of the heaviest that the underwriters had sustained during the war—they stood to lose a total of nearly £1 million on the shipping seized in Swedish ports alone—and occasioned a crisis of the first order at Lloyd's; a formal vote of censure being passed by subscribers and members on their Committee.

In the autumn of 1810 Sweden was finally constrained by French pressure, not merely to close her ports to British commerce, but even to declare war against us. In the following spring she proceeded to arrest a large number of merchantmen which had taken refuge in her southern ports. Saumarez thereupon threatened the Swedes with reprisals; but in a private interview on board the *Victory* with Count Rosen, the governor of Gothenburg, the matter was amicably settled, the Swedish government agreeing to pay fair compensation for the

The Coasts

FINLAND

Kronstadt
St. Petersburg

Reval

SWEDEN
Stockholm

GOTLAND

Gothenburg

Riga

Karlskrona
Karlshamm

Moscow
Borodino

Copenhagen

BALTIC SEA

RUSSIAN EMPIRE

Vilna

Stralsund
Königsberg
Danzig   Tilsit

PRUSSIA
Berlin

GRAND DUCHY
OF WARSAW

Leipzig

Wagram

Vienna

AUSTRIAN EMPIRE

Trieste

BLACK SEA

ADRIATIC SEA

Naples
KM. OF
NAPLES

OTTOMAN Constantinople

EMPIRE

KM. OF SICILY

AEGEAN SEA

Smyrna

MALTA

CRETE

rope in 1810

cargoes they had seized; and Saumarez having declared that he 'would not fire the first gun', things went on as usual.[1]

All these losses imposed a heavy strain on the British economy, already disorganized by the increasing rigour of the Continental Blockade. But, thanks to the firm but conciliatory policy pursued by Saumarez, no attempt was made to retaliate against Swedish commerce; and the formal war never developed into actual hostilities. In the end the presence of Saumarez's strong squadron in the Baltic played an important part in encouraging both Sweden and Russia to stand firm against Napoleon's demands. When, following the Swedish declaration of war, the British minister had to leave Stockholm, the political as well as the naval direction of affairs in this region devolved upon Saumarez, whose flagship became the centre of the growing resistance to France in the North, and the skilful diplomacy and personal popularity of the Admiral were a major contributory factor in the development of the alliance against Napoleon in 1812. Saumarez, indeed, may be said to have played much the same role in the Baltic that Collingwood played in the Mediterranean.

Though the main channel of traffic with Russia had been effectively broken, the trade to her White Sea ports still continued. Even at the worst crisis of the commercial war 141 vessels sailed from Archangel, two-thirds of them for British ports. The principal exports were iron, timber, hemp, cordage, linen, pitch, tallow, and corn. The imports were no less important. Long trains of sledges in winter and wagons in summer, loaded with the colonial produce for which Europe craved, were drawn by horses through the pine forests of the North southward to Moscow and thence to Kiev and Vienna. The soaring price of coffee and sugar in Austria made this traffic profitable despite the great distances involved. The value of the rouble steadily recovered.

Meanwhile on the other side of the globe British relations with the United States had become strained to breaking-point. In the spring of 1811, under the Non-Importation Act, the vital American market was almost lost to us. British vessels were henceforth forbidden to enter American ports; and, while American vessels could still carry their cargoes to England, they could bring back neither British manufactures nor colonial produce. British imports from the United States

---

[1] Ross, *Memoirs of Admiral Lord de Saumarez*, II, p. 247; *Saumarez Papers*, p. 185.

had declined by only one-tenth; but our exports to that country dropped by more than four-fifths.

For England, as has already been said, 1811 was the worst year of the Napoleonic War. The economic crisis resulting from the shrinkage of trade was exacerbated by the heavy shipping losses of the previous year, which had reached the highest figure of the whole war, and by the wholesale expropriation of ships and cargoes in the Baltic at Napoleon's orders. Sweden had been forced into the French orbit, and British exports to northern Europe had fallen to but one-fifth of their former level. The contraband traffic between Heligoland and the neighbouring coasts was practically paralysed; for months the warehouses on the island were packed with nearly £4 millions' worth of goods for which there was no sale. The trade between Holland and Great Britain had reached its lowest level in 1811, only slightly recovering in 1812.

The blockade of the coasts of Europe against British commerce, which was effectually achieved in the latter half of 1810, remained practically unbroken throughout 1811 and the first half of 1812. The flood of British exports to the United States, which had sustained our manufactories during the summer of 1810, was by now almost dried up. The trade and shipping of Liverpool suffered grievously during 1812. It was the combination of the Continental Blockade and the Non-Importation Act which nearly overthrew the British economy. There was little to counter-balance this enormous loss of trade. The lavish dumping of large accumulations of goods which could no longer be exported to the Continent had ended by hopelessly glutting the new South American market. Moreover, the erection of huge warehouses at the London docks had resulted in excessive storing of products from all parts of the world and subsequent speculation by middlemen. In comparison with the major European and American markets, the Peninsula, southern Europe, the West Indies, British North America, and our other colonies could absorb only a relatively small proportion of our manufactures. The strain on our tottering economy was intensified by the fact that all this came on top of a great trade boom. The total British exports had risen in 1810 to nearly £61 millions: in the following year they dropped suddenly to £43 millions. The cumulative effect of all these developments engendered the financial crisis of 1810–11.

In the great ports of the kingdom the warehouses were crammed with manufactured goods and colonial produce which could find no sale. 60,000 tons of coffee lay for months in the warehouses of London, unsaleable at sixpence a pound; while the price of the same commodity on the Continent had risen to between four and seven shillings.

'There is a general stagnation of commerce,' wrote a young Canadian then living in England, 'all entrance into Europe being completely shut up. . . . Merchants have either become bankrupt, or retired, while they could, from business. Their clerks are all discharged, and gone into the army, or country. Those merchants who formerly kept ten or fifteen clerks, now have but two or three. There are now many thousands half-starved, discharged clerks, skulking about London; in every street you see, "A counting-house to let". The foreign trade is almost destroyed, the Custom House duties are reduced upwards of one half. . . . The East India Company have their great warehouses filled with the most valuable goods, spoiling and wasting, as England is the only part of Europe that consumes of them. . . . As for the West India Company . . . besides their own immense warehouses they have hired additional ones to the cost of £42,000, which are all filled with their overplus produce. The Royal Exchange is miserably attended; no foreigners, but about a dozen Hamburgers, very few Americans. . . . Such a time as this was never known in England.'[1]

The financial and commercial crisis was followed in the second half of 1810 by a severe and intractable industrial crisis which became steadily more serious throughout the following year and continued until well on in 1812. One after the other the basic industries of the country were more or less gravely affected. Vast stocks of manufactures were piling up in the northern and midland industrial regions which could now find no outlet. The winter of 1810–11 found this country plunged in the gravest industrial depression of the war.

All this was a direct result of the Continental System and Non-Intercourse—of which, it is to be remembered, the latter was by far the more injurious. The manufactories of Manchester, Birmingham, and Sheffield were deeply involved in the loss of the American market, as were also the potteries. Hardest hit of them all was the cotton industry. In Glasgow and its environs the depression was even worse

[1] *Ten Years in Upper Canada*, ed. M. Edgar (1891), pp. 52, 58.

than in Lancashire. It is estimated that production was down by something like a quarter. Throughout the industrial regions, in fact, there was a general loss of confidence. The wheels of industry were noticeably slowing down. Even so, the situation would have been a good deal worse had not the manufacturers carried on business as usual in the hope that the Orders in Council would soon be revoked and matters would improve.

There had been labour troubles and rioting in Lancashire in the earlier depression of 1807–8. Things were a great deal worse in 1811. Mills and factories were having to close down, the cost of bread had risen almost to famine point, and, with large numbers of hands unemployed and wages down to starvation level, riots and machine-breakings broke out in the industrial areas. These disorders were only suppressed with great difficulty and by the use of substantial bodies of troops. Machine-breaking was made a capital offence. Mills were burned down, and in 1812 40,000 cotton weavers came out on strike. Petitions to Parliament flowed in from the depressed industrial regions. In the end the pressure of the commercial community obliged the government to withdraw the Orders in Council; but it was too late to avert a war with America, which aggravated the distress of the manufacturers. In London, Manchester, and other cities bankruptcies doubled in number. 'These failures throughout the kingdom', the *Monthly Magazine* had recorded as early as December 1810, 'have wonderfully affected the manufacture of every description of goods, and a general want of confidence exists between the manufacturer and the export merchant.' Taxation was soaring—it was to reach its peak in 1815, when the national debt stood at £860 millions—and the purchasing power of money steadily declined. To add to the general distress, there had lately occurred a run of bad harvests, which inevitably drove up the price of bread.

Notwithstanding every prohibition, however, British goods continued to find their way to the markets of the Continent. Some measure of compensation for the loss of our trade with northern Europe was found in that with the Peninsula and other southern regions. After the final evacuation of Portugal by the French in the spring of 1810, British exports increased rapidly; and Wellington's victories in Spain opened more markets to British merchants and industrialists.

Moreover, an elaborate and extensive system of licences issued by both Great Britain and France enabled the traffic to be carried on. Once again Napoleon had failed to maintain the Continental Blockade at its utmost rigour for a sufficient length of time to produce decisive results. Coffee was once more allowed into France and her wines were exchanged for British sugar. In consequence trade revived rapidly in 1812; for under cover of this authorized trade a large-scale traffic in smuggled goods was going on. The Grand Army itself was shod with British boots which had been smuggled into the Continent by way of Heligoland, and it could be fairly claimed that 'not only the accoutrements but the ornaments of Marshal Soult and his army are made in Birmingham'. According to Napoleon's secretary, Lucien Bourrienne:

> The Emperor gave me so many orders for army clothing that all that could be supplied by the cities of Hamburg, Bremen, and Lübeck would have been insufficient for executing the commissions. I entered into a treaty with a house in Hamburg, which I authorized, in spite of the decree of Berlin, to bring cloth and leather from England. Thus I procured these articles in a sure and cheap way. Our troops might have perished of cold, had the Continental System, and the absurd mass of impracticable decrees relative to English merchandise been observed.[1]

The relaxation of the Continental Blockade had come, indeed, not a moment too soon for Great Britain, lying as she did under the shadow of the gravest economic crisis of the war. What with the simultaneous glutting of the South American market, the mounting hostility of the United States, the ominous decline of our Baltic commerce, and soaring inflation, our national economy was becoming dangerously overstrained. In the commercial war of attrition the question was which of the two combatants would be able to hold out the longer. In the event it was France that had cracked first—inasmuch as, by thus reversing his former policy, Napoleon may have let slip his best if not his only opportunity of accomplishing his purpose.

2

It was in large measure through the wealth drawn from her immense seaborne trade that Great Britain was enabled to sustain the onerous burden of war-time taxation. Year by year her output continued to

[1] Bourrienne, *Memoirs of Napoleon* (1893), III, p. 109.

increase. While her imports rose from £19 millions at the beginning of the war to £32 millions at the end of it, her exports soared from £27 millions to £58 millions. A prime factor in this resilient commerce was her as yet unrivalled industrial system. Through the increasing application of machinery and steam power in her factories, she could turn out manufactured goods on a scale such as the world had never known before, which commanded a ready sale on the Continent and overseas. As early as 1781 Boulton had written to Watt: 'The people in London and Manchester are all *steam-mill* mad.' In the last two decades of the eighteenth century the steam-engine had been establishing itself as the main source of motive power. Pumping engines were set up in the mining districts of Cornwall; flour-mills, paper-mills, silk-mills, and cotton-mills were fitted with steam-engines; steam-engines were ordered for the great new iron-works which were springing up in the North and midlands; steam-engines were installed in the American saw-mills and West Indian sugar-mills. Machinery became increasingly complex, and was applied to one industry after another. The textile trades were revolutionized by the new inventions. Every year the huge sprawling manufacturing towns, with their gaunt, barrack-like factories, tall chimneys, and crowded, insanitary streets and alleys, canopied by a perpetual smoke-cloud, spread their tentacles over an ever-widening area. The coalfields on which all these new activities were based yielded an ever-increasing toll of the vital fuel. The many-storeyed warehouses lining the quays of London, Liverpool, and Bristol; the teeming traffic about the docks; the intricate network of canals, roads, and rail-tracks linking together towns, works, factories, mines, and sea-ports; the 'dark Satanic mills' of the Lancashire cotton towns; the busy midland ironfields, smoking like a slag-heap by day and illuminated with the lurid glare of innumerable furnace-fires by night—were all part of the same story.

After several years of the Continental Blockade the wheels still went on turning; our iron-works, cotton-mills, and potteries had never been more actively employed; and when port after port of the Continent had been closed against our commerce, our industry and trade continued to expand. It was the new steam factories that financed the successive coalitions which Pitt raised up against Napoleon; and it was the new iron-works that produced the armaments which eventually overthrew him. British manufactures, which were desired for their cheapness as well as for their excellence,[1] were conveyed to their destination by remote and round-about routes; British cottons were landed in Salonika and transported on pack-horses across the Balkans to Vienna, and thence distributed throughout the Germanies; and, as has already been said, Napoleon himself was constrained to waive his own restrictions to admit British clothing and boots for his forces.

Moreover, the loss of most of the European markets was partially offset by the expansion of our ocean trade. Rather less than half our total exports, after all, went to the Continent; two-thirds of our imports were drawn from countries outside Europe. All this lucrative commerce lay outside the limits of Napoleon's Continental System; for the sea was England's. In the years following Trafalgar small British squadrons and military expeditions gathered in the spoils of her unchallenged sea power. On 3 January 1806 Baird's troops disembarked at the Cape of Good Hope under cover of the guns of Sir Home Popham's squadron; a week later the whole colony was in British hands, and the sea-route to India secured. By the end of 1810 all the French, Dutch, and Danish possessions in the West Indies had passed into British keeping. In 1811 Cayenne, Senegal, the Seychelles, Amboyna, and Banda Neira all surrendered to local British forces; and the following year saw the conquest of Java. The duties from 'the Con'd Colonies' went to increase the national revenue.

On the ruins of the old mercantile empire which had perished in the American Revolutionary War was arising the world-wide maritime and commercial polity envisaged by Shelburne. It was along these lines that British expansion began again during the ten years' peace following the Treaty of Versailles, and was markedly accelerated during the long-drawn-out struggle with the French Revolution and Empire. 'There is an end of the old world,' wrote Earl Fitzwilliam, on learning that the fragments of the Prussian army were in full flight after Jena; 'we must look to the new.'[2] The emphasis was now on

[1] 'The French have always, in ridicule, called us a Nation of shopkeepers —so, I hope, we shall always remain, and, like other shopkeepers,' Nelson had shrewdly observed in the previous war, 'if our goods are better than those of any other Country, and we can afford to sell them cheaper, we must depend on our shop being well resorted to' (*Nelson's Dispatches*, IV, p. 350).

[2] Q. A. N. Ryan in *Transactions of the Royal Historical Society*, 5th Series, Vol. 12 (1962), p. 125.

trade, rather than on territory. Through the closing of so many European markets to her commerce Great Britain was driven to developing the resources of transoceanic trade to the utmost. During the whole of this period the national urge continued unabated for acquiring naval bases, ports of call, tropical plantations, and trading stations which were needed to provide markets for British exports and raw materials for British industries. Through our alliance with the Peninsular Powers their vast overseas possessions had been thrown open to our trade. Traffic in colonial produce became virtually a British monopoly.

The Napoleonic War saw the last era of West Indian prosperity. The immense fleets of West Indiamen continued to carry home larger and larger cargoes of sugar each year; the production of coffee and cotton also reached record levels. The importance of the West Indian islands to the national economy and finances can scarcely be set too high. They supplied what was necessary at home and provided a lucrative market for British manufacturers,[1] bringing wealth to the national coffers and, incidentally, breeding large numbers of prime seamen for the Navy. The West Indies were largely responsible for maintaining a favourable balance of trade. 'The sugar islands', Sir Charles Middleton had observed a generation before, 'are the best and surest markets for our staple commodities, and the most productive of all our colonies. They are the easiest source of our revenues.'[2] The boom in sugar was slackening; but it was still possible for the fortunate proprietors to make huge fortunes out of their planatations. The islands were no less important to us as the outlet for great quantities of British manufactures. 'Not a button or a shoe, a pocket handerchief or a hat are obtained elsewhere than in Great Britain,' stated a contemporary pamphlet. 'London, Birmingham, Bristol and Carron supply alike the mill-work, the nails, the hoes, the tools, the utensils of domestic life, and the implements of husbandry: the ash-coppices fall to bind the casks, and six millions of hoops are annually split in

---

[1] 'The cargoes carried back and forth between the West Indies and Great Britain comprised a large proportion of the total trade of the Mother Country. On the official books of the Customs the West Indian trade was estimated at about one-seventh of the total exports of Great Britain. But the imports were worth even more; in 1808 they were £9.5 against £27.8 millions official value' (L. F. Horsfall in *The Trade Winds*, ed. C. N. Parkinson [1948], p. 163).

[2] *Barham Papers*, II, p. 270.

the service of the planter.'[1] The aggregate tonnage of the British shipping to the West Indies greatly exceeded that of any other trade outside Europe. The political influence of the West Indian interest in the City had increased and was still increasing.

Despite the severance of political ties, the products which the British and Americans bought from each other continued practically unchanged; and the trade with the United States ranked second only to trade with the British Empire. The bulk of American imported manufactures came from these islands, and nearly one-half of their exports went to Great Britain and her possessions. The former were the products of the British industrial revolution—textiles, pottery, hardware, cutlery, sheet glass, guns, spades, saws, nails, paint, and coal; the latter were chiefly timber, tobacco, grain, flax seed, potash, tar, and turpentine. After the outbreak of hostilities in 1793 by far the greater part of Anglo-American trade was conducted in American bottoms. Down to the close of 1805 the course of this trade ran fairly smooth (in that year the American market absorbed more than a quarter of all British exported manufactures). Through the operation of the Embargo in 1807-9 British exports were halved: but this loss was partially offset by the expansion of our exports to British North America and South America, while during 1810 there was a short-lived trade boom; in that year it has been estimated that North and South America together took more than half of British exports.

With the arrival of a continuous stream of settlers into the valley of the St. Lawrence the population of the Canadas steadily increased. Montreal, the metropolis of the two provinces, boasted, by 1801, a population of 22,000. Early in the new century lumber had become a staple industry in the Canadas as well as in the Maritime Provinces. Through the threatened interruption of the Baltic traffic, the Canadian timber trade developed rapidly. Later, as extensive areas of the interior were gradually cleared of timber, large quantities of wheat and flour were regularly exported to Great Britain. The economy of Nova Scotia was largely based on fishing and shipbuilding. Numerous fleets of schooners sailed regularly to the Grand Banks, while the inshore fisheries were developed by small boats. Newfoundland was and remained essentially a fishing colony, with most of its population distributed along the coast. The war brought great prosperity to the

[1] Bosanquet, *Thoughts on the value ... of the Colonial Trade* (1807), p. 40.

Maritime Provinces, especially to Halifax. The main centre of the fur trade in the northern regions was the historic Hudson's Bay Company, whose scattered posts were visited annually by the Company's ships, with the newly formed North West Company, of Montreal, as an increasingly formidable rival.

Some measure of compensation for the closure of the main European and United States markets in the crisis of 1807–8 was found in the trade with South America. The flight of the Portuguese royal family to Brazil, Sir Home Popham's daring attack on Buenos Aires, the seizure of Montevideo, and, above all, the Spanish uprising of 1808 opened new and immensely profitable markets to our merchandise. In April of that year no less than fourteen convoys, totalling 288 vessels, sailed from Spithead for Brazil.[1] Rio was soon glutted with fine English cloth, cottons, cutlery, 'Brummagen goods', pottery, and glassware. During 1808 at least £1 million's worth of British goods had been sent to Brazil. With them went out British merchants and factors. It is recorded that there were about 100 British business men settled in Rio alone. The wharfage in that port proved, indeed, quite inadequate for the flood of trade; and most of the cargoes had to be discharged into barges. In the ensuing years, however, the British commercial colony gradually got matters improved. For the growing traffic with South America the shipping formerly employed in the slave trade (which had been abolished in 1807) was used. In the summer of 1809 Vice-Admiral de Courcy, in command on the South American station, asked that his squadron should be substantially strengthened in view of the continual demands for convoys, 'as the trade betwixt England and this country continues progressively to increase and as the British merchants at Rio are likely to apply often for escorts for their homeward-bound commerce'.[2] By 1811 our trade with Brazil was large enough to require a special convoy. The traffic with the neighbouring Spanish colonies was also substantial. In 1810 the conclusion of a highly favourable commercial treaty materially assisted the development of British trade with Buenos Aires and the rest of La Plata province. Towards the end of the Napoleonic War Great Britain enjoyed a virtual monopoly of South

[1] Adm. 7/64, April 1808.
[2] *The Navy and South America, 1807–1827*, ed. G. S. Graham and R. A. Humphreys (1962), p. 42.

American commerce. British interests in this important new field were further advanced by the remarkable diplomatic ability exhibited by many of our commanders on the South American station.

Since the outbreak of the French Revolutionary War all the anti-British elements in India had been eagerly awaiting their opportunity and a large number of French officers had entered the service of native princes. The pacific policy favoured in recent years by the British government was thereupon reversed; and the Marquess Wellesley was dispatched to India with a free hand. The destruction of Brueys's fleet in Aboukir Bay, together with the defeat and death of Tippoo Sahib in the following year, put an end to any serious threat to the British raj. The Revolutionary and Napoleonic Wars quickened the pace of British expansion: before Wellesley's recall, in 1805, more than a third of India had been brought effectively under British rule or influence.

As we have already seen, the national economy was becoming increasingly dependent on the Asian traffic. The conquest of Bengal, with the immensely fertile valley of the Ganges, and Calcutta, one of the finest cities in Asia, had secured for the East India Company an enormous store of silver which was used for our trade in the East, especially with China, without the necessity of drawing on our reserves at home, which could therefore be devoted to fostering the industrial revolution.[1] Another factor was working powerfully in the same direction. The Honourable Company's trade to the East was accompanied by a significant increase in the value of British goods exported. In earlier years there had been a heavy drain of bullion annually. Henceforth, in proportion as the export in goods increased, that of bullion diminished. From 1766 to 1792 the value of goods exported exceeded bullion in the proportion of three to one; from 1793 to 1810, in the proportion of nearly four to one. In 1806 no silver at all was exported, and in 1807 only very little. None in 1808, 1809, and 1810; but more than £1 million in woollen goods in those years, for the most part to China.

The extension of the British commercial system over the East

---

[1] The possession of the province also gave this country the monopoly of good Bengal saltpetre; there can be no doubt that one of the advantages which accounted for Great Britain's superiority in sea warfare in this era was the excellent quality of the powder used.

Indian archipelago, hitherto monopolized by the Dutch, was largely due to Sir Stanford Raffles. Though nearly all the Dutch possessions were restored to them at the end of the war, Great Britain retained Bencoolen, which lay, like Penang, on the route to China; until a few years later Raffles, authorized to seek out a port not in Dutch keeping, founded the great British entrepôt of Singapore. Among the advantages he justly claimed for Singapore was that the port 'afforded facilities for hereafter establishing another factory still further East whenever it may be deemed expedient to do'.

In the Far East, the headquarters of our lucrative trade with the Chinese Empire was at Canton. The British hongs, or factories, extended for a considerable distance along the banks of the river fronting the city. They consisted of large and handsome buildings with broad verandas reaching down nearly to the water's edge and each having a flagstaff erected before it.

To guard the British communications with India and the Far East became one of the principal duties laid upon the Navy. The Mediterranean was henceforth of increasing importance as an artery not only for its trade, but as a highway to the East. The century that followed saw the expansion and exploitation of all these great possessions.

The year before the Paris mob stormed the Bastille, Captain Arthur Phillip, R.N., the newly appointed governor of New South Wales, had arrived in Botany Bay with his fleet of convict ships. Phillip founded his settlement on the shores of Port Jackson, a fine natural harbour which he truly described as 'the finest in the world, in which a thousand sail of the line may rest in perfect security', and named the new settlement Sydney, after Lord Sydney, the Secretary for the Colonies. In 1803 another convict settlement was founded in Van Diemen's Land, later known as Tasmania. The war years saw the development, first, of the whaling industry, and, later, of sheep-breeding and the export of merino wool. In 1813 the stock-breeders began to move westward to the rich savannah beyond the Blue Mountains, and the first inland settlement, Bathurst, was founded. Thus Australia was becoming a large-scale producer of wool at the very time that the expansion of the factory system in Great Britain vastly increased the demand for this raw material of the textile industry.

The period under review also witnessed the early stages of traffic with New Zealand. In the first decade of the nineteenth century British, French, and American whalers regularly visited the waters around the two islands, and gangs of sealers worked the coasts to such effect that the formerly vast herds of seals were almost wiped out. Ships called at the northern bays for cargoes of Kauri pines, 'such masts', as Captain Cook had declared, 'as no country in Europe can produce.' About the same time schooners based on Sydney trafficked with the South Sea islands in quest of the sandalwood and edible bird's-nests required for the China trade.

Just as Great Britain was constrained to expand her transoceanic commerce in order to make good some of the grievous loss occasioned by the Continental Blockade, so also was the Admiralty, cut off from its normal supplies of Baltic timber and spars, forced to look to our overseas possessions for its naval stores. By far the most urgent problem was the supply of timber. First-rate masts, and in adequate quantities, were forthcoming from British North America.[1] But in the matter of the great and compass timbers no satisfactory substitute for 'good, sound Sussex oak' was readily available. Some idea of the immensity of the Navy's requirements may be gauged from the fact that close on 1,000 ships of all classes were maintained in commission during the decade succeeding Trafalgar. Within a short time, however, oak timber from Canada and the Maritime Provinces helped to fill part of the gap. Lesser sources of supply were India, West Africa, and New Zealand. Before the end of the Napoleonic War, rather less than one-quarter of the timber used in the construction of warships was drawn from our own forests.

From all parts of the world came the ships bringing Great Britain her vast stores of colonial produce both for home consumption and for the re-export trade, the food-stuffs for her rapidly growing population which her own soil could no longer supply in full, and the raw materials for her busy manufactories. There were the fabulously wealthy convoys of East Indiamen carrying tea, spices, pepper, silks, muslims, nankeens, cottons, calicoes, saltpetre, and drugs; fleets of

[1] From about 1795 on nearly all the masts used by the Royal Navy came from New Brunswick, until in 1804 the centre of the industry shifted to the St. Lawrence valley. About the same time masts of the New Zealand kauri pine were fetched home in transports which would otherwise have made the return passage in empty ballast.

West Indiamen with sugar, rum, coffee, cocoa, ginger, and tobacco; Yankee packets with tobacco, rice, raw cotton, and corn; immense convoys of brigs and snows from the Baltic with grain, timber, naval stores, iron, linen, and hemp; topsail schooners with citrons and other fruits from Smyrna and the ports of Greece; deep-laden whalers from the Arctic and South Seas with their rich cargoes of train-oil; wineships from the Peninsula, Madeira, and the Canaries; sturdily built vessels of the Hudson's Bay Company with furs and skins. There were wines, drugs, and dye-stuffs from the Mediterranean; ivory, gold, gums, and palm-oil from North and West Africa; mahogany, sarsaparilla, jalap, cocoa, ginger, vanilla, indigo, cochineal, and quicksilver from Central and South America. The outgoing ships were laden with manufactured textiles, linens, laces, and silks; books, stationery, musical instruments, paint, and candles; Birmingham hardware, Sheffield cutlery, pottery, leather goods, rock salt, and refined sugar.

In the last years of the Napoleonic War British mercantile shipping was approaching $2\frac{1}{2}$ million tons, and the number of vessels employed in foreign trade had increased to something between 4,500 and 5,000. Though much of the continental trade that still remained to us was necessarily carried on in neutral bottoms, the tonnage of British shipping engaged in the long-distance trades had substantially risen. At the turn of the century an enormous mass of shipping had choked the River Thames almost without a break from Greenwich to the Pool of London. Between 1802 and 1815, however, an extensive system of docks, comprising the West and East India, London, Commercial, and Surrey Docks, had been built, enabling the shipping to leave the river, and dispensing with the need for numerous fleets of barges and lighters. The separation of the shipping and lighter traffic greatly relieved the congestion in the Thames.

The year 1802 saw the completion in the Isle of Dogs of a spacious new dock system for the rich West India trade. The work was facilitated by the gravelly subsoil of the area, which provided a firm foundation for the walls. The West India Docks were planned on the greatest scale and sufficed for the accommodation of 600 vessels of from 300 to 500 tons. The line of warehouses which had been erected for the safe custody of large quantities of valuable goods extended nearly three-quarters of a mile. They were for the most part five-storeyed buildings, far in advance of anything other ports at this time could show. Vessels were moved by gangs of workers hauling on ropes or taken in tow by large rowing boats. In the same way cargoes were unloaded by gangs of men operating cranes and winches. The new docks were surrounded by a high wall, with a guardhouse at the gate.

Another important system of docks, the London Dock at Wapping, was brought to completion, towards the close of 1805, 'for the greater accommodation and security of shipping, commerce, and revenue within the Port of London'. Here also was erected a range of vast warehouses for the safe storage of costly imports like wine, brandy, and tobacco. The construction of these edifices enabled a system of bonded warehouses to be inaugurated and import duties to be paid when the goods were sold and not when they were landed.

The following year, 1806, witnessed the completion of the East India Docks. Since the Honourable Company had its own warehouses in the city, none had to be erected in the docks; the goods being carried to London in closed and locked wagons. The enormous stores of tea, drugs, indigo, and piece-goods which poured into the Company's warehouses were periodically disposed of by auction in the Sale Room of the East India House in Leadenhall Street.

South of the river, in the vicinity of Southwark, the Commercial Dock Company, formed in 1807, was busy extending the old Greenland Dock, mainly for the accommodation of vessels laden with timber and grain.

The Thames was patrolled by constables, and the docks were guarded by sentries. (A Marine Police Force had been established, in 1798, with headquarters at Wapping New Stairs.) As a result of all these measures the depredations of the water-thieves, which had previously been on the greatest scale, were for the most part put a stop to. The era of the Night Plunderers, Light Horsemen, Mudlarks, and Scuffle-Hunters was finally closed. The new system of docks proved adequate to the needs of London throughout the following half-century.

Meanwhile, behind the shield of the Fleet went on the ordinary day-to-day life of that peaceful England which Constable and Gainsborough painted and Jane Austen faithfully portrayed in her novels. Nothing, indeed, could be further removed from battle and bloodshed than those dreaming landscapes and decorous conversation pieces.

And it was a true enough picture. Although on occasion a laurel-decked mailcoach might dash through the cheering streets of country town or village as it carried the tidings of yet another glorious British victory across the broad shires, the daily round continued for the most part unaltered in the quiet countryside in which old Parson Woodforde lived out his last years and little Miss Mary Russell Mitford grew to womanhood. The squire fished, shot, rode to hounds, looked after his estate, and administered justice in quarter and petty sessions; his wife and daughters employed themselves at home in leisurely household tasks, paid calls, gossiped, sat at the pianoforte, strolled in their gardens, and looked forward to the next card-party or assize ball. The ancient mummers' play of St. George and the Dragon was performed on New Year's Day; May Day was observed, as usual, with singing and morris dancing; bonfires blazed on northern and western hills on midsummer night; in early autumn the farmer and his men celebrated the consummation of the farming year with a bounteous harvest home; Guy Fawkes Day, or 'Gunpowder Plot', was honoured with bonfires and fireworks all over the kingdom; and, as Christmas drew near, parties of men and boys would go round the parish 'wassailing', or carol-singing, in the larger houses. On Sundays, smock-frocked yokels trooped to parish church: the cattle and sheep lay out each market day in square or open street of rural towns: summer by summer the golden harvest was gathered in, and the price of wheat continued to rise.

'The poor suffered by the war,' Trevelyan observes. 'But at no period had the landed gentry been wealthier or happier, or more engrossed in the life of their pleasant country houses. The war was in the newspapers, but it scarcely entered the lives of the enjoying classes. No young lady of Miss Austen's acquaintance, waiting eagerly for the appearance of Scott's or Byron's next volume of verse, seems ever to have asked what Mr. Thorpe or Mr. Tom Bertram were doing to serve their country in time of danger.... While Napoleon was ramping over Europe, the extravagance and eccentricity of our dandies reached their highest point in the days of Beau Brummell, and English poetry and landscape painting enjoyed their great age.'[1]

[1] G. M. Trevelyan, *English Social History* (1944), p. 466.

XV

The Uprising of the Nations

I

After Trafalgar, as has already been said, Napoleon had recourse to the time-honoured strategy of a fleet in being. He would allow his enemy no chance of winning any more resounding triumphs at sea, and at the same time he would keep the hostile battle squadrons permanently tethered in European waters while he sent out his cruisers and privateers to prey on British commerce all over the globe. Though the Combined Fleet had been practically wiped out, he had other squadrons which were still undamaged and undefeated. Moreover, in the possession of the Texel and the Scheldt—as well as of Venice, Genoa, and other Mediterranean naval ports—he still possessed the means of replacing his lost force. Throughout these years he continued to spend immense sums on his navy, and to build and build. Admiral Decrès, his Minister of Marine, put all his trust in 'a fleet in being'. It was hoped that in consequence of this huge shipbuilding programme the naval superiority of Great Britain would be gradually reduced. 'Louis XIV had only Brest; I have all the coasts of Europe. In four years I shall have a Navy,' Napoleon boasted in 1811. '. . . I can build 25 sail of the line a year.' In point of fact no fewer than eighty-three of the line and sixty-five frigates were completed during these years; and before the restoration of peace the French Navy totalled 103 of the line and 157 frigates. A large hostile fleet, therefore, had to be reckoned with to the end of the war, necessitating a heavy drain on our resources in the way of blockade and convoy duties.

The French squadrons were only very rarely sent to sea, and their crews were for the most part raw and untrained. But they represented a permanent threat to British sea-communications. Despite all the vigilance of the blockading squadrons, it was impossible wholly to prevent privateers, cruisers, and even an occasional small squadron from getting away to sea. In 1805 Allemand's elusive squadron had been at large on the trade-routes for more than 160 days; and he was to get away to sea again in the spring in 1812. At the zenith of Napoleon's power, the length of the hostile coast-line to be watched was so vast that the resources of the Navy were stretched to the limit. A high percentage of our fighting ships, both sail of the line and frigates, had to be permanently assigned to these arduous blockading duties.

'It is not fighting, my dear William,' Codrington had informed his brother shortly after Trafalgar, 'which is the severest part of *our* life, it is the having to contend with the sudden changes of season, the war of elements, the dangers of a lee shore, and so forth, which produce *no food for honour or glory* beyond the internal satisfaction of doing a duty *we* know to be most important, although passed by others unknown and unnoticed.'[1]

Year in, year out, the blockading forces played their part faithfully and well. Though Europe was held fast in the grip of the Grand Army and its coasts closed to British commerce by the Continental Blockade, Napoleon's power stopped short at the water's edge. Formidable as the enemy's squadrons might appear on paper, they lacked the training and experience which could only be acquired by long cruises. Though in 1811 the Emperor had in commission nearly sixty of the line, not one of these vessels ever ventured out of sight of the land. The *Annual Register* summed up the position in the following year:

It seems, in the present year, to have been a leading object in the policy of the French emperor to establish a marine force capable in time of contending with the Navy of Great Britain, which he feels to be the principal remaining obstacle to his gigantic plans of aggrandizement. For this purpose, he has endeavoured to provide a large body of sailors by a maritime conscription; and has annexed to his empire all the sea-ports which lay within his grasp, and employed every resource for obtaining supplies of naval stores by inland communications. He has thus been enabled to fit out a fleet which in number and equipment makes a formidable show, but which has not hitherto exhibited any of that confidence and courage which is required for the arduous task of contending with the masters of the ocean. In no year of the war has the French navy been less adventurous, or, in the few actions that have occurred, has proved less a match for its antagonist.

[1] Bourchier, *The Life of Sir Edward Codrington* (1873), I, p. 73.

The British ships on their blockading stations seldom afforded any great spectacular display such as that presented by the Grand Army on the march, with its glittering squadrons of cuirassiers, lancers, chasseurs, and dragoons, its serried ranks of bearskins and plumes, its clanking train of cannon, moving forward to the harsh rattle of drums and the surging chorus of *Sambre et Meuse*. Usually all that could be seen of England's unchallengeable sea power was no more than a few weather-stained topsails just lifting above the horizon—yet, to the seeing eye, there was something deeply impressive about the pertinacity with which those ships, in summer and in winter, in fair weather and in foul, clung to their stations.

In the latter part of 1812 the strain on the Navy began to be eased. In March, Russia had declared war on France. But the ships brought home from the Baltic could not be employed on other stations until the following year, on account of the necessity of refitting. And there still remained the powerful enemy forces in European waters, totalling from sixty to seventy sail of the line and a large number of cruisers. Ships were needed also on overseas stations to deal with any sudden emergency, to provide reliefs and to strengthen escort forces. War with the United States had recently broken out. It was presumably in apprehension of a French squadron reaching some American port where it could receive a crew of first-rate seamen that ten of the line were presently sent out to reinforce the British forces on the North American station. In 1812 Great Britain had at sea no less than 125 of the line and 145 frigates, besides 421 smaller cruisers.[1] Large as was our Navy, however, its numbers were by no means excessive for all the services it was called upon to perform.

In the far North, Saumarez's strong squadron controlled the Baltic and prevented Napoleon's Continental System from imposing a total veto on British commerce in a region which was now essential to the survival of our national economy.

Throughout these years Admiral Sir William Young blockaded the ports of the Netherlands, wherein there still lay a considerable enemy force. With his flag in the *Impregnable*, 98, and eleven of the line under his orders, he kept his station by the maze of banks and channels fringing the mouth of the Scheldt in the bitterest weather. In the far distance the squadron would occasionally sight the high

[1] *Naval Chronicle*, Vol. 28, p. 248.

sand-dunes protecting the western shores of the islands of Zeeland, and sometimes a steeple or windmill. Usually, however, they saw only the leaden, misty horizon under the grey North Sea sky. William Symonds, who spent seven months with the squadron off Walcheren during 1811, declared:

> This was a very extraordinary and monotonous service; so many sail of the line lying in an open sea; Middlebourg steeple just in sight, but the land rarely visible. We were always at single anchor. When it blew hard, we veered out, sometimes three cables. The only variety experienced, was sighting the anchor, or now and then trying rate of sailing. Occasionally the Yarmouth and Deal boats brought us out fruit and vegetables.[1]

John Boteler, then a midshipman in the *Sceptre*, has shed some interesting light on the victualling arrangements of the squadron. 'Every fortnight', he related, 'four ships of the line were sent away to Hosely Bay, on the Norfolk coast, to complete water and get about twenty bullocks for the fleet, then to go off the Texel, to be in sight of the large Dutch and French fleets at anchor in the Zuyder Zee, and there remained four or five days. Spring tides were the only time those ships could get out. We generally counted from twenty-three to thirty large ships. While backing and filling off the Texel, we would have our large trawl net over the side.'[2]

Within the Scheldt lay Vice-Admiral Missiessy with fifteen of the line and a number of smaller ships; at Antwerp there were three of the line refitting, and up the Texel seven more ready for sea. Next year these numbers were increased, and in the autumn new ships were ordered to be laid down at Amsterdam and other ports. The hostile fleet in the Scheldt, together with the dockyards of Flushing and the arsenal of Antwerp, remained a constant anxiety to the British government. But throughout all these years not one of the enemy ever ventured out to challenge the smaller British blockading squadron.

On the death of Sir Charles Cotton, Lord Keith was appointed in February 1812 to the command of the Channel squadron. Though his principal duty was the close blockade of Brest, the extensive area under his command extended from Portsmouth to the north coast of Spain. Keith was now in his later sixties and in poor health; on that

[1] J. A. Sharp, *Memoirs of Vice-Admiral Sir William Symonds* (1858), pp. 36–7.
[2] *Captain Boteler's Recollections*, ed. Bonner-Smith (1942), p. 30.

account he spent much of his time ashore, while the command of the blockading force off Brest was usually exercised by Rear-Admiral Sir Harry Neale. In the closing year of the war the squadron was broken up into a number of small detachments, operating for the most part off the coasts of France and the Peninsula; for numerous other places had to be watched in addition to Brest, L'Orient, and Rochefort: in this capacity it continued to play a vital, though too often overlooked, role in the struggle against Napoleon. During these years only one squadron got away to sea, when, in the night of 8 March 1812, Allemand slipped out of Rochefort with four 74s and two corvettes and slipped through his pursuers in a fog. He remained at sea for several weeks, taking a few prizes, and anchored in Brest roads on the 29th. The squadron in Brest were thereby reinforced by four of the line. Neale's division was ordered to watch the enemy as long as they could keep the sea; 'taking special care', Keith directed, 'to resume your station off Brest, as soon as the weather moderates, or becomes favourable to the enemy.'[1] When in heavy westerly gales the ships of the line were forced to take refuge in Cawsand Bay or in Torbay, the frigates and smaller cruisers were ordered to watch the French. To quote John Boteler, midshipman of the *Sceptre*, again:

> We went into Cawsand Bay and after a little delay hoisted the flag of Sir H. B. Neale, and together with the *Dreadnought* 98 and two 74's, sailed to watch the enemy fleet in Brest Harbour. We kept the sea, having a frigate inshore to observe the Frenchman's movements. We had a hard gale from the south-west with a very heavy sea on from the poop at times, although as clear as possible, every now and then we could not see the masthead vanes of either of the squadrons—the sea as it came foaming above seemed as if it must break right over us, instead of which all at once it rolled beneath us.[2]

In 1812, when there were some ten of the line and twelve frigates in the Atlantic ports of France, the strength of the Channel fleet was fifteen of the line, fourteen frigates, and ten smaller cruisers. Later the demands made upon Keith's force materially increased. In the summer of 1813 the harbour of Cherbourg was improved to such an extent as to become an important naval port; and shipbuilding on a large scale was carried on there. At the same time swarms of American

[1] Adm. 1/149, 5 May 1812.
[2] Bonner-Smith, *op. cit.*, p. 28.

privateers based on French ports were endangering the supply lines to Wellington's army in the Peninsula. In the final year of the war the strength of the Channel squadron was increased to twenty of the line, seventeen frigates, and 110 lesser vessels. By this time the facilities in Torbay had been greatly improved. A stone quay had been erected at Brixham; a large hospital for seamen was built at Goodrington, and another for officers near Berry Head.

Sir Edward Pellew succeeded Sir Charles Cotton in command of the Mediterranean fleet—then comprising sixteen of the line—off Toulon in July 1811; his flagship was the *Caledonia*, 120, a fast sailer and usually reckoned one of the finest ships in the Navy. Pellew and the main body of the fleet lay, as a rule, off Hyères, with a small advanced squadron of one sail of the line and a few frigates on the blockading station off Cape Sicié. During the ensuing years subsidiary squadrons were stationed at Malta, Gibraltar, in the Gulf of Genoa, and off the south coast of Spain. A number of cruisers on detached service harassed the shores of France and Italy, and supported the guerrilla bands operating in the southern and eastern coastlands of the Peninsula.

Sometimes a large division of what our ships' companies were pleased to call 'the Toolong fleet'[1] would weigh and manœuvre outside the roads—but only on such occasions as there was a leading wind to ensure their speedy return. The enemy fleet continued to increase in numbers if not in fighting strength. In 1813 it numbered twenty-one of the line and ten large frigates, while three more of the line were on the stocks. Despite this increase the blockading force had actually been reduced to thirteen of the line; for the enemy squadron was seriously undermanned, large numbers of seamen-gunners having been taken from it in 1812 to reinforce the Grand Army, and as a fighting force it was not rated high.

During the last few years of the war the duties of the British squadron were far less onerous than they had been; and the Mediterranean must have been one of the pleasantest stations in the Service. 'My ship [the *Ville de Paris*] is in good order and I am almost full manned,' wrote Vice-Admiral Fremantle, in the summer of 1812,

[1] 'The Toolong fleet,' explained Lieut. O'Brien in Marryat's *Peter Simple*, 'so called, I thought, because they remained too long in harbour, bad luck to them.'

to his wife Betsey, 'my captains and officers suit me, my menage is very tolerable, and my band are excellent; in short all I want is your society and that of my children.'[1]

These, then, were the principal blockading stations of the British Navy in the latter part of the Napoleonic War; but off every minor naval port, arsenal, or shipyard on the hostile coasts from the Baltic to the Aegean was stationed either a small division, or even a single vessel, detached from the main body of the squadron. In the course of the blockade the Navy occupied the islands of Saint-Marcouf, Clausey, Molène, Glénans, Houat, Haëdic, and Hyères, and frequently refitted in Douarnenez and Quiberon Bays, also in the Gulf of Fos.

A commonly unnoticed factor in the growth of British sea power in the latter half of the eighteenth and the early decades of the nineteenth centuries was the progress of hygiene and logistics. The history of many a campaign during this period illustrates, with telling effect, the intimate connection between hygiene and supply, and strategy and tactics. There is much truth in Dr. James Lind's observation, in his preface to *An Essay on the most effectual means of Preserving the Health of Seamen*, that 'the number of seamen who died by shipwreck, capture, fire, famine or sword are but inconsiderable in respect of such as are destroyed by the ship diseases and by the maladies of intemperate climates'.[2] Indeed, it could be fairly claimed that it was the advance of naval medicine, both curative and preventive, together with the system of efficient victualling which had been introduced by Hawke in the campaign of 1759 and re-established by Jervis, Duncan, Nelson, Keith, and others, that enabled the large squadrons of the Revolutionary and Napoleonic Wars to remain on their stations throughout the long years of the blockade.

A leading part in these developments was played by the physician referred to above, Dr. James Lind, whose *Treatise on the Scurvy* did much to draw attention to the importance of vegetables, fresh fruit, and lemon juice as anti-scorbutics; by Dr. Gilbert Blane (author of *Observations on the Diseases incident to Seamen*—a medical classic), whose innovations while serving under Rodney marked a new era in the hygiene and living conditions of the service; by Dr. Thomas

[1] *The Wynne Diaries*, ed. A. Fremantle, III, p. 360.
[2] *Q.* C. C. Lloyd in his preface to *The Health of Seamen* (1965), p. vii.

Trotter, who rose from surgeon's mate to be Physician of the Channel fleet, and by Dr. Andrew Baird, who was responsible for many of the improvements introduced in the same squadron under St. Vincent.

In a word, the standards of hygiene on shipboard were immeasurably improved; there was a more adequate and regular supply of medicines (though it was not till 1804 that all drugs were issued free); and the pay and status of the naval surgeon were materially raised. With the regular issue of lemon juice, scurvy, which from time immemorial had been the scourge of seamen, was virtually eradicated from the service. As a result of the salutary reforms introduced by St. Vincent, Trotter could truly say of our Mediterranean ships that, 'disciplined as they now are, they are capable of preserving themselves from pestilential contagion on those very shores that are said to give it birth. This could not have been the case in former times.' During the Napoleonic War the improvement was even more marked. On the first day of 1807 it was reported that there was not a single case of sickness in the flagship of the Mediterranean squadron. 'The doctors,' wrote Collingwood, 'are the only people who are in danger of scurvy, if want of employment be a cause of it.'[1] According to Sir Gilbert Blane, in the five years between 1806 and 1811 there were only a quarter of the numbers on the sick list, compared with the period 1793–98. 'It is', declared the same authority, 'highly satisfactory to contemplate the many proofs of substantial benefit that have accrued to the sea service in the last forty years, both in war and commerce, in all quarters of the world, from the zeal, humanity and good judgment displayed in promoting the health of seamen. It has been proved that it has added at least one third to the national force, and therefore subtracted in the same proportion from the national expenditure.'[2]

The evils of drink still remained. The lavish issue of rum in the service led directly to drunkenness, accidents, and harsh punishments. This was not infrequently deplored, but no remedy could be suggested —at any rate so long as the war continued. 'It is', Keith wrote, 'at all times a delicate point to interfere with what is called an allowance or right, and the present may not be the moment for reforming so

[1] *Correspondence of Vice-Admiral Lord Collingwood*, ed. G. L. Newnham Collingwood (1823), p. 239.
[2] Q. Lloyd and Coulter, *Medicine and the Navy, 1714–1815*, p. 184.

great an evil; but in the event of peace I am satisfied that not a more essential service could be rendered to the nation than to reduce the quantity of spirits now used in the Navy.'[1]

Much of the sickness which had formerly ravaged the service was to be attributed to the inferior quality of the provisions supplied to the seamen, through the incompetence, neglect, and, at times, corruption of those responsible for victualling the Navy. It was largely due to the representations of Dr. Trotter that the victualling of the Channel squadron had so far improved that, in August 1799, he could declare that 'liberal supplies of cabbages, onions, turnips and carrots are now sent to sea'. Towards the end of the war canned meat was issued to the sick in the same squadron with very beneficial results.[2] About the same time tea was commonly supplied for breakfast. It appears that Dr. Trotter would have liked to see cocoa, too, issued to the Channel squadron. 'In a cold country it could be singularly beneficial: what a comfortable meal would a cup of warm cocoa or chocolate be to a sailor in a winter cruise in the Channel or North Sea, or coming from a wet deck in a rainy morning watch!'[3]

Apart from all these improvements in victualling, mention must also be made of ships' bands and amateur theatrical performances, encouraged by some of the captains, which had done much to relieve the tedium of life on shipboard and to raise the morale of the ships' companies. 'We have an exceedingly good company of comedians,' Collingwood told his wife, 'some dancers that might exhibit at an opera, and probably have done so at Sadler's Wells, and a band consisting of twelve very fine performers. Every Thursday is a play night, and they act as well as your Newcastle company.' During these years such dramas as *The Triumph of Friendship*, *The Siege of Colchester*, *The Tragedy of Pizaro*, and *Catherine and Petrucio* were put on, some of them quite elaborate productions.

---

[1] *Keith Papers*, III, p. 20.

[2] 'Had canned meat been invented a generation earlier the lot of the blockading squadron would have been immeasurably improved, and they would have been able to keep the sea for longer at a time. As it was, the importance now attached to a supply of fresh vegetables, the invention of portable soup and the introduction of sauerkraut were events which should figure more largely in naval history than, for example, the frigate actions on which our ancestors loved to dwell' (Lloyd and Coulter, *op. cit.*, p. 93).

[3] *Ibid.*, p. 90.

2

The paramount importance of seamanship as a factor in naval operations can be gauged from the fact that, throughout the war, by far the greater part of the losses sustained by the British Navy were due, not to enemy action, but to the 'dangers of the sea.'[1] During these last years of the Long Blockade the principal hazard was still the 'dangers of the sea'.

The squadrons and small divisions blocked up in the hostile ports might present no very serious threat to the blockading forces; the enemy were seldom in a state even to put to sea: but the exigencies of the hard blockading service meant exposing our ships, for months on end, to every hazard of rocks, tides, waves, and weather. There was danger not only in the iron-bound coast of Brittany but also in the outlying islands, reefs, and rocks flanking the entrance of the Channel, as well as off the headlands along the south coast of England. In the Seven Years' War Hawke's former flagship, the *Ramillies*, had been lost with nearly her entire crew in a cove near the Bolt Tail. In the present war the old *Venerable* was lost, one dark and foggy night, on Paignton Ledge in Torbay. Each year witnessed its toll of disasters. It is on record that more than 300 British warships—including several 3-deckers and a good many 74s—were lost through 'the dangers of the sea'.

The seamanship of the service does not seem to have suffered any such general deterioration as its gunnery had. The reason for this is not far to seek. For, while the enemies it had to face were not sufficiently formidable to keep the crews on their toes, the 'dangers of the sea' were always with them. Again and again vessels were forced off their post by gales, or obliged to work to sea to avoid being driven on shore—it is significant that references to 'club-hauling'[2] begin to

---

[1] See Fairbrother, *List of Ships Lost*, Public Record Office MS.

[2] '*To club-haul*. A method of tacking a ship by letting go the lee-anchor as soon as the wind is out of the sails, which brings her head to wind, and as soon as she pays off, the cable is cut and the sails trimmed; this is never had recourse to but in perilous situations, and when it is expected that the ship would otherwise miss stays' (Admiral William Smyth, *A Sailor's Word-Book*). Reference is made to club-hauling in the treatises of W. Hutchinson, Falconer, J. J. Moore, Darcy Lever, and others from 1781 onwards. It was, however, so seldom attempted that, according to Boteler, the evolution might be 'the luck of one sailor's lifetime to witness'; and Boteler goes on to relate how

appear in nautical manuals about this time. Though there were plenty of exceptions to the rule (for instance, the loss in 1807 of the two small cruisers *Atalanta* and *Pigmy* appears to have been due simply to bad seamanship), the general standard of seamanship was usually high; and the masterly handling of ships and squadrons in the investment of the enemy's coasts and ports represents one of the greatest achievements of British nautical skill.

The year 1812 witnessed two outstanding examples of fine seamanship.

In May of that year Captain Henry Hotham of the *Northumberland*, 74, in company with the *Growler* brig, intercepted three French cruisers, on their return from a destructive raid against our trade, off L'Orient. The enemy force was sighted about ten miles south of the Ile Groix, crowding all possible sail before a light westerly wind for L'Orient.

Hauling to the wind close to leeward of Groix, Hotham fetched to windward of the harbour entrance before the enemy force could reach it. Favoured by the freshening wind, which had veered to W.N.W., the Frenchmen made a bold and determined attempt to run between their adversary and the shore, under cover of the numerous batteries both on the mainland and on Groix. To prevent the chase from hauling outside a rock called Le Graul, Hotham steered as close to it as he dared without running on it himself.

It was a superb feat of seamanship. For all this time the *Northumberland* was under heavy fire, and the master could scarcely see the rock at all, through the dense cloud of powder-smoke rolling ahead of them. Fearing lest before nightfall they should be overtaken if they hauled to the wind, the enemy in desperation endeavoured to pass *inside* of the rock, where there was not sufficient water for them to pass— with the result that all three vessels presently went aground, under full sail, on the rocks between Le Graul and the mainland.

Captain Williams successfully club-hauled his ship, the *Dictator*, 74, in February 1811, when caught on a lee shore near Inchkeith. (See *Captain Boteler's Recollections*, ed. D. Bonner-Smith, p. 14, and Adm 51/2293, 27 February 1811.) The late Commander H. W. Noakes, R.N.R., once explained to the writer how he club-hauled his ship off the Lizard in 1899; and a still later instance of club-hauling—off Cape Horn in 1912—has been recorded by Captain Jewell.

It being only one-quarter ebb, the Frenchmen could safely be left to the operation of the falling tide while the *Northumberland* drew off to repair her badly damaged sails and rigging, working to windward during that time under what sail could be set, to prevent her falling to leeward; after which she anchored, with her broadside bearing on the enemy vessels, at point-blank range. All three vessels had rolled over on their beam ends as the tide receded, exposing their copper to the British fire. For over an hour the *Northumberland* kept up 'a deliberate and careful fire', while all the time she herself was under fire from the shore batteries. At nightfall, when the enemy vessels were seen to be on fire, the *Northumberland* shifted her berth to be out of range of the batteries. At midnight she weighed, and, with the *Growler* in company, 'profiting by the brightness of the moon', stood out to sea. The wind was northerly and very light, and progress was slow. Before they lost sight of the land, however, they had the satisfaction of seeing all three French vessels blow up.[1]

'When', wrote Keith in his dispatch to the Admiralty, 'the gallantry of the action with such a force, under numerous galling batteries, and the intricacy of the navigation amidst dangerous rocks, in the very entrance of the enemy's harbour, are taken into consideration, the performance of so important a service, while it reflects the highest honour upon the courage, skill, and extraordinary management of all concerned, adds fresh lustre to the naval annals of the country. The selection of Captain Hotham for the station off L'Orient, does great credit to the judgment of Rear-Admiral Sir Harry Neale, for no officer but one who possessed great local knowledge, could, under such difficult circumstances, have ventured to undertake the service that Captain Hotham has so bravely and so effectually performed.'[2]

The second example was the club-hauling of the *Magnificent*, 74, by Captain John Hayes, which, as Laughton justly observes, 'even in that age of brilliant seamanship, was considered remarkable, and won for him the title of "Magnificent Hayes".'[3]

On the evening of 16 December the *Magnificent* lay in the entrance

---

[1] Brenton, *Naval History of Great Britain*, V, pp. 18–22; *Naval Chronicle*, Vol. 27, pp. 508–11; Adm. 51/2333, 52/4551, 22 May 1812.

[2] Adm. 1/149, 30 May 1812.

[3] See J. K. Laughton's article on Hayes in the *Dictionary of National Biography*.

to Basque Roads. The wind was westerly, and freshening, with every sign of worse to come. The topgallant yards and masts were got down, but at nine the ship was found to be driving. On the smaller bower being let go, it brought her up in ten fathoms. The lower yards and topmasts were then struck. Though the moon was invisible it was not a dark night, but gave just enough light to reveal the sea breaking heavily on the neighbouring reef, about a quarter of a mile astern; it was now blowing a gale, the wind at W.S.W., with small rain, and a heavy sea.

Since the ship lay in the midst of rocks, the cables were liable at any moment to be cut. To make matters worse, there was a lee tide and the heavy sea was setting right on the reef, about one cable's distance, on which, if she drove, the vessel must infallibly go to pieces. One of the officers on board related that it was impossible to cast her clear of the reef and to make sail, especially as the yards and topmasts were down.

The captain, however, gave orders to sway the fore-yard two-thirds up; and, while that was doing, to get a hawser for a spring to cast the ship by from the starboard quarter to the spare cable; while this was doing, the spare cable parted, and we had only the sheet anchor at the bows; but, as she did not drive, that was not let go. The main yard was now swayed outside the topmast, two-thirds up the same: as the fore-yard and spring brought on the small bower cable, people were sent on the yards to stop each yard-arm of the top-sails and courses with four or five spun-yarn stops, tied in a single bow, and to cast off and make up all the gaskets: the people were then called down, except one man to each stop, who received very particular orders to be quick in obeying the commands given them, and to be extremely cautious not to let a sail fall, unless that sail was particularly named: if particular attention were not paid to this order, the ship would be lost. The yards were all braced sharp up for casting from the reef, and making sail on the starboard tack. The tacks and sheets, top-sail sheets, and main and mizen-stay-sail hallyards were manned, and the spring brought to the capstan and hove in.

The captain now told the people, that they were going to work for life or death; if they were attentive to his orders, and executed them properly, the ship would be saved; if not, the whole of them would be drowned in five minutes. Things being in this state of preparation, a little more of the spring was hove in; the quarter-masters at the wheel and bow received their instructions. The cables were ordered to be cut, which was instantly done; but the heavy sea on the larboard bow would not let her cast that way. The probability of this had happily been foreseen. The spring broke, and her head paid round in towards the reef. The oldest seaman in the ship at that moment thought all lost. The captain, however, gave his orders very distinctly, to put the helm hard a-starboard, to sheet home the fore-top-sail, and haul on board the foretrack, and aft fore sheet, keep all the other sails fast, square the main and mizen topsail yards, and cross-jack-yard, keep the main-yard as it was. The moment the wind came abaft the beam, he ordered the mizen-top-sail to be sheeted home, and then the helm to be put hard a-port—when the wind came nearly aft—haul on board the main-tack aft, main sheet, sheet home the main-top-sail, and brace the cross-jack-yard sharp up. When this was done (the whole of which took only two minutes to perform), the ship absolutely flew round from the reef, like a thing scared at the frightful spectacle. The quarter-master was ordered to keep her south, and the captain declared aloud, 'The ship is safe.' The gaff was down, to prevent its holding wind, and the try-sail was bent ready for hoisting, had it been wanted. The main and mizen-stay-sails were also ready, but were not wanted. The fore-top-mast stay-sail was hoisted before the cables were cut: thus was the ship got round in less than her own length; but, in that short distance, she altered the soundings five fathoms. And now, for the first time, I believe, was seen a ship at sea under reefed courses, and close-reefed top-sails, with yards and top-masts struck. The sails all stood remarkably well; and, by this novel method, was saved a beautiful ship of the line, and five hundred and fifty souls.[1]

The Long Blockade progressively lowered the morale and diminished the efficiency of the hostile fleet while it increased the sea-keeping qualities and fighting strength of our own. 'A sailing fleet cooped up in port not only rapidly lost its spirit', Corbett has written, 'but, being barred from sea-training, could not be kept in a condition of efficiency, whereas the blockading fleet was quickly raised to the highest temper by the stress of vigilance and danger that was its incessant portion.'[2] Strategically, the significance of the blockading squadrons is that they formed the essential covering screen for the multitudinous activities of our warships and merchantmen all over the world. It was the blockades which secured the small divisions and single ships guarding the far-flung territories of the British Empire. Without these covering squadrons the operation of the convoy system would have been impossible. So, too, would have been the numerous conjunct expeditions against the French colonies, and the continual

[1] *Naval Chronicle*, Vol. 29, pp. 19–21; Adm. 51/2546, 16–18 December 1812.

[2] J. S. Corbett, *Maritime Strategy*, p. 204.

flow of supply-ships which nourished the British Army in the Peninsula.

In short, the blockades did the work that was expected of them. Gradually but surely, Napoleon was urged on to his destruction. The abiding and determining factor in the chapter of events between Nelson's last and greatest victory and the crucial Russian campaign of 1812 was the maritime supremacy of Great Britain and the unremitting blockade of the enemy's ports.

3

Napoleon's efforts to overthrow the British economy by his Continental System had come within measurable distance of success. There is no knowing indeed what might have happened if the stranglehold on our commerce had not been relaxed at the eleventh hour. But the Continental System was a double-edged weapon: its ill effects were by no means confined to England.

In 1811 France was herself visited by an acute commercial crisis. This was in large measure due to the lack of cotton and other raw materials which forced the manufacturers to reduce production. The lucrative luxury trades which had enriched her in the past could now find no outlet. Her merchants were failing, her manufactories closing down, and her workmen unemployed and starving. Costly products like Lyons silks and velvets, Lille, Amiens, and Roulaix linens, and Valenciennes laces could no longer be sold overseas; and even the European markets had fallen off appreciably. The impoverishment of the once wealthy classes in Europe was reflected in the disastrous decline in the market of French luxury goods and wines. In the capital financial houses were failing. Lyons and other industrial towns were falling into decay; and not only the manufacturing cities of France, but also the wine-producing regions of Rheims, Burgundy, and Bordeaux were in the toils of the crisis. The markets for brandy and corn, too, were glutted. In the winter of 1811–12 Napoleon found it necessary to assist both manufacturers and workmen out of the public funds.

The lot of the vassal States, whose interests were ruthlessly sacrificed to those of France, was necessarily far worse. The rigid restrictions of the Continental System could only be enforced by the harshest measures. A whole army of custom-house officials kept watch on the coast, and the ports swarmed with spies. (The Apostolic Nuncio to Brazil, entertained at a public dinner at Plymouth, observed that the whole Continent was become a prison.) From time to time immense quantities of the forbidden products would be seized by the authorities and publicly burnt, to the accompaniment of martial music and in the presence of local magnates. These *autos-da-fé* were regularly reported in the *Moniteur*. Conflagrations blazed throughout the Napoleonic empire and its appanages—with the single exception of Denmark—during the winter of 1810–11. In Holland and many parts of Germany the population watched with ever-increasing resentment the destruction of large stocks of British cloths and cottons, and sugar, coffee, cocoa, spices, and other colonial produce, by the Emperor's orders. The cost of living was forced up in country after country, and bankruptcies occurred all over the Continent. In the end the deprivations endured by the peoples of Europe as a result of the long-drawn-out struggle, intensified by the operation of the blockade and counterblockade, were a determining factor in the general uprising of the nations which led to Napoleon's overthrow. According to Bourrienne:

> The ill-advised Berlin decree could not but produce a reaction fatal to the Emperor's fortune by making whole nations his enemies. The hurling of twenty kings from their thrones would have excited less hatred than this contempt for the wants of people. . . . It is necessary to have witnessed as I did the countless vexations and miseries occasioned by this deplorable system, to form a due conception of the mischief its authors did in Europe, and how greatly the hatred and revenge which it produced contributed to Napoleon's fall.[1]

The truth was that the climatic range of the French empire—vast though it was—was utterly inadequate to satisfy the needs of civilized man. Its inhabitants were in consequence forced back upon unacceptable substitutes, such as acorn coffee and cabbage tobacco. Attempts to grow cotton in southern France and Italy failed miserably. (The successful production of soda from sea salt was a notable exception.) From 1810 to 1812 the economy of the whole Continent was forced back on itself and cut off the lifegiving flow of commerce by the remorseless, inexorable pressure of the land and sea blockade.

It was the economic struggle, too, which was fundamentally

[1] Bourrienne, *Memoirs of Napoleon* (1893), III, p. 87.

responsible for the 'Spanish ulcer', which steadily undermined the strength of the Napoleonic empire. The Emperor was under no illusions as to the danger of the situation now arising, facing, as he did, a possible war on two fronts. According to Bourrienne, the Emperor had more than once shown regret at being engaged in the Spanish war; but since he had the English to fight there, no consideration could have induced him to abandon it, the more so as all that he was then doing was to defend the honour of the Continental System.

Napoleon was determined to maintain his hold on both the Peninsula and northern Europe. The leak in the Continental System through northern Europe was, however, of far greater consequence than through the Peninsula; and he who had once insisted on the paramount necessity of concentrated effort was now prepared to divide his forces. He accordingly turned over the command of the French army in Spain to Masséna, while he devoted the chief of his own energies to the northern blockade.

These regions which, either by commerce or by industry, were directly connected with overseas trade were of necessity severely affected by the economic war. The great North Sea ports of Hamburg, Bremen, Amsterdam, Rotterdam, and Antwerp were particularly hard hit. The quays of Hamburg were almost deserted; more than 300 ships were laid up in harbour, and only one out of several hundred sugar refineries was still in operation. The trade of Bremen was virtually destroyed. The year 1811 was similarly a time of crisis in Holland. Since her incorporation in the French empire in 1810, her maritime trade had been rigorously restricted by the vigilance of the French customs officials. She had been deprived of both her colonies and her historic carrying trade, while her fisheries had decayed through lack of salt. Added to this, the Dutch had suffered the customary evils of the Napoleonic regime—conscription, police surveillance, and heavy taxation. There was unemployment and increasing discontent on all sides.

Such highly industralized areas of the Continent as Berg, Switzerland, and Silesia were also seriously involved in the crisis of 1811.

As with Holland and the Hanse towns, Sweden's commercial interests were closely bound up with those of England. In vain had Sweden desired to be allowed to remain neutral in the war. 'There are no longer any neutrals,' had been Napoleon's brusque rejoinder;

'you may choose between war and friendship.' Swedish pride had been severely wounded by the manner in which the Continental System was enforced, and by the seizure of Finland by the Russians, with the support of France, in 1809. Early in 1812 Napoleon ordered Marshal Davout to march into Swedish Pomerania.

In Russia, too, matters were rapidly approaching a climax. The Court aristocracy were growing restive under the Napoleonic yoke. The Tsar considered war inevitable. Hardly any country had suffered more from the restrictions of the Continental System than Russia. The rouble had sunk to a third of its former value. The vast stocks of Russian timber could no longer find a market. Confronted both with the ruin of her export trade to Great Britain (on which the revenue of her noble families chiefly depended) and with the loss of the colonial imports, such as sugar and coffee, that were almost indispensable to civilized life, Russia finally relinquished her former policy of friendship with France, and, in the course of 1811, withdrew, together with Sweden, from the Continental System.

The opening of the Baltic ports came in the nick of time for Great Britain. It not only breathed new life into our overstrained economy, but it also enabled us to import large quantities of grain from Russia just as the supply of Canadian corn was threatened by American privateers. All this meant certain war between France and Russia. For it was not to be expected that Napoleon would endure secession on so vast a scale from the combination which he had set up to destroy Great Britain. In order to make the commercial blockade effective, it was imperative that all countries should strictly enforce the ban. The Russian defection undermined the whole structure of the Continental System. Already immense quantities of British merchandise were pouring into the markets of central Europe. Throughout the year relations between France and Russia further deteriorated; and both emperors prepared for war.

So long as the British government held out, the struggle would never end; and Great Britain was invulnerable save through Russia. The causal chain between Trafalgar and the fateful decision of 1812 was now complete.[1] The crucial and conclusive factor in the struggle on land—the almost illimitable resources in territory and man-power

---

[1] On the French side, the causal chain is lucidly and logically set out in Nicolas's *La puissance navale dans l'histoire* (1958), pp. 349–66.

of the enormous Russian empire—was about to be brought into play. From first to last the Napoleonic strategy had been baulked by British sea power. Only a decisive victory over Great Britain would relieve the beleaguered fortress of Europe. Penned in to the west, north, and south by the blockading squadrons of his implacable enemy, Napoleon resolved to strike eastward across the plains of Muscovy. On 24 June the Grand Army, numbering at least 420,000 men, crossed the Niemen and entered Russia.

Led by Murat and his cavalry, the whole vast host advanced towards Vilna, where the enemy was believed to be concentrating. Heavily outnumbered, the two widely separated Russian armies, under Barclay and Bagration, which lay close to the frontier, immediately retired. After a long delay at Vilna, owing to the breakdown of its supply system, the Grand Army pressed on in the sweltering summer heat across the broad Lithuanian plains; the ochre dust rose in choking clouds around the advancing columns; water was scarce, and the troops were tormented by swarms of flies; disease and the merciless heat took a heavy toll of their number. All this time the Russians continued to retreat, setting fire to stores and habitations for miles to northward and to southward of the French line of advance.

On his entry into Vitebsk on 28 July, Napoleon learned that Barclay had again slipped away and was hurrying towards Smolensk to join forces with Bagration. Once more the Emperor's hopes of a speedy decision had been disappointed. The Russians eluded him again at Smolensk. On reaching the suburbs of that city, Napoleon learned that the two Russian armies had united. His first attack on Smolensk was heavily repulsed; and Davout's attempt to outflank the Russians, and to cut off their retreat, failed. Napoleon was beset by gloom and indecision. The campaign was not going as he had expected.

In the middle of August Count Kutuzov was appointed to command the Russian army. Kutuzov showed himself even more reluctant than Barclay to seek a general action. His intention was to force Napoleon to extend his line of communications still further and to intensify the 'scorched earth' strategy. To that end villages and hamlets, hay- and straw-ricks, supplies and stores of every description were systematically burned by the retreating Russians. On the 24th Napoleon resumed his advance through the charred and devasted wilderness fringing the

Moscow road. For another fortnight or so his army marched on through the choking, blinding dust. Kutuzov continued to fall back to the eastward.

A general action was, however, inevitable for political reasons. The fact was that Kutuzov dared not yield Moscow without a fight. Suddenly the Russian army slowed down its retreat, halted, and faced round on its pursuer. On 6 September, to the accompaniment of a terrific artillery duel, the opposing armies struggled desperately from dawn till dusk for the Russian positions encircling the village of Borodino. The Semenovsky ravine was won and lost several times. It was the most sanguinary encounter of the era. At the close of the battle, with nearly 57,000 men dead or dying on the field (among them the renowned Russian commander, Bagration, and about forty French generals), Kutuzov's forces retired in good order; and a few days later Napoleon entered Moscow.

When Kutuzov learned that night that half his army had been destroyed, he resolved to save the other half and to surrender Moscow without another fight. The last of his troops were marching out of the city on 16 September just as Murat and his cavalry were riding in. When the news reached St. Petersburg, the Tsar and his court were in despair. But Kutuzov bided his time; already he had begun the brilliant flanking manœuvre towards Ryazan, then southward to the old Kaluga road, and along that road to positions in and around Tarutino. For several days the Cossacks contrived to deceive Murat and his corps, then in pursuit, leading them off on a false trail; until at last Kutuzov's great flanking movement was completed.

No sooner had Moscow been occupied by the Grand Army than reports reached Napoleon of fires breaking out in various parts of the city. Next day these fires spread; during the night of 14–15 September, fanned by a fierce wind, they reached the centre of Moscow, and the Emperor and his suite were forced to quit the Kremlin. The conflagration raged for two days more, and then, towards the evening of the 18th, the fires gradually died down; by which time the central parts of the city had been reduced to a charred and smoking ruin.

The autumn was mild and sunny. For five weeks Napoleon lingered in the gutted and deserted city; and throughout that time the position of the Grand Army became more and more precarious. Not a word had come from the Tsar at St. Petersburg. Strong Russian forces were massing against him. Cossacks and partisans harassed his long-drawn-out line of communications by sudden raids on his baggage trains, stores, and couriers. Convinced at last that not even the occupation of the ancient capital would compel the Russians to treat for peace, Napoleon embarked on that retreat which was destined to become one of the most appalling tragedies in the annals of war. Forestalled by Kutuzov's stratagem from making a detour to Smolensk through a region which as yet had escaped the devastation of war, the Grand Army was forced to retire over its own wasted line of advance. For his part Kutuzov, determined not to incur unnecessary losses, pressed on in pursuit by flanking, parallel marches several miles to the southward.

The winter of 1812 set in at an abnormally early date and proved to be exceptionally severe. Before they reached Smolensk an impenetrable fog closed down on the discomfited army. Presently snow began to fall and a furious wind moaned through the woods. The snowdrifts and the bitter frosts intensified the progressive dissolution of Napoleon's forces. Many of the wagons and heavy guns had to be abandoned, through the lack of horses. There were not enough supplies left in Smolensk to feed what remained of the Grand Army and what little there was was largely wasted; after a few days' rest they were obliged to continue their retreat. The situation became desperate. The Russian armies were fast closing in upon them. At any moment they might be surrounded and forced to surrender. A mild spell had lately thawed the river ice. It was imperative to get across the Berezina before the Russians cut off their retreat.

By a skilful manoeuvre, Napoleon deceived the enemy as to the location of his intended crossing. Two pontoon bridges were swiftly erected by sappers toiling waist-deep in the icy water—one for the troops and the other for the artillery; by these the whole army crossed in safety. The bridges were afterwards burnt by Napoleon's orders to delay the enemy's pursuit, at the sacrifice of a great number of stragglers and sick on the further bank.

After the passage of the Berezina, heavy frosts set in. Exhausted by hunger and fatigue, stumbling through deep snow-drifts, the men perished by thousands. By this time order and discipline had vanished. The remnants of the Grand Army were strung out in one ragged column stretching for miles. The line of their retreat was marked by an ever-lengthening trail of frozen corpses, derelict wagons and carts, miscellaneous baggage, and abandoned guns. Towards the end of November the cold became so intense that the wounded and exhausted were left behind to freeze to death. The retreat had degenerated into a headlong flight. The army that straggled into Vilna on 9 November was an emaciated, undisciplined, demoralized rabble. Of about 80,000 who were left after the crossing of the Berezina, about a half were lost on the road to Vilna, and many more before they reached the frontier. With the Cossacks still in pursuit, the wretched survivors arrived at last before the frozen Niemen. Of the 420,000 men who had advanced into Russia the previous June, only 20,000 or so— exhausted, famished, and diseased—struggled back into Prussia in mid-December.

The superb military machine by which Napoleon had imposed his will upon the Continent for so many years, the most formidable host which the world had known since the fall of the Roman Empire, had been swept off the board. That was the primal fact with which the chancelleries of Europe were confronted in the ensuing months. *The Grand Army was no more.*

4

During the winter of 1812–13 the wreckage of Napoleon's army fell back slowly from the Niemen to the Vistula, from the Vistula to the Oder, and from the Oder to the Elbe. Resentment against the Continental System was reinforced by the surging tide of national feeling. Insurrections broke out at Hamburg and in the Grand Duchy of Berg. The risings were ruthlessly suppressed; but the spirit of resentment which had inspired them was far from being extinguished.

The decisive hour had struck. Headed by Prussia, the nations of northern and central Europe rose against Napoleon, several of whose armies were still locked up in Spain, far from the crucial theatre. By almost superhuman efforts the Emperor, in the course of the winter, had been able to gather a well-equipped army of over 200,000 men, with an approximately equal number of reserves in training; but most of these new levies were raw and unseasoned, and almost all the French cavalry had been lost in Russia. A series of important engagements was fought in the following May in Saxony and Silesia, as a result of which Napoleon materially improved his position: at Weissenfels, Lutzen, and Bautzen the Russians and Prussians were heavily repulsed. By consenting to an armistice, however, the victor forfeited many of the advantages he had secured. Austria went over to the coalition. On the renewal of hostilities Napoleon made the fatal error of underestimating both the numbers and the skill of his opponents. Three Allied armies, under Bernadotte, Wittgenstein, and Schwarzenberg, advanced from the north, east, and south respectively. Though on 27 August Napoleon gained a brilliant victory over the Allied main army under Schwarzenberg near Dresden, in the terrible three-days struggle around Leipzig known as the 'Battle of the Nations' (16–19 October) he was decisively defeated; his power in central Europe was shattered, and the remnants of his army retired to the Rhine. By the middle of November he was back in Paris.

When in the early winter of 1812 the news of the débâcle of the Grand Army reached England the mood of gloom and pessimism engendered by the long trade depression vanished as if by magic. It was confidently expected that the North would soon be re-opened to British commerce, and that the entire structure of the Continental System was on the verge of dissolution. The government therefore refused to grant any more licences for trade with France. Confidence, and with it commercial and industrial activity, speedily revived. 'Since our last report,' the *Tradesmen* stated in the following January, 'an unusual degree of vigour has been felt in the mercantile world, arising from the late astonishing events in Russia, and which has extended itself through most, if not all the channels of our chief commerce.' During the spring of 1813 these expectations were in large measure fulfilled. Hull and Leith were crowded with shipping preparing for sea. Conditions were reported more favourable in the Baltic than at any time since Tilsit. In May alone more than 120 vessels arrived from this country at Memel, laden with colonial produce; later 170 more entered Riga, and 340 St. Petersburg. Immense quantities of British manufactures, as well as coffee and sugar, poured into northern Europe. That Michaelmas there was a great display of British goods on view at Leipzig Fair. The numbers of our convoys bound to the Baltic reached an unprecedented total.

The barriers to direct commerce with Germany were also breaking down. With the Russians moving westward, the Hanse towns, including the great international commercial and financial centre of Hamburg, rose in revolt. The cordon of douaniers was swept away. Heligoland regained its lost prosperity. Later the French successfully counter-attacked, and Davout recaptured Hamburg. But Germany was already flooded with British manufactures and re-exports; and, notwithstanding certain temporary setbacks and reverses, our trade continued to expand. Vittoria, and the liberation of almost the entire Peninsula, served as a further stimulus to this boom. The Austrian ports were freed at last, and the barriers of the Continental Blockade abolished in the kingdom of Naples. Across the Atlantic, also, the situation was improving. True, we were still at war with the United States; but our trade with South America was fast recovering. Leipzig marked another milestone in the commercial war. Napoleon's defeat at the 'Battle of the Nations' was as much a death-blow to his Continental System as it was to the French hegemony of central Europe. The news of the great allied victory had an electrifying effect on the markets generally, and trade was brisk in Manchester and Birmingham. Finally, towards the end of the year, our blockade of the Elbe, Weser, and Ems was discontinued; and the north German ports were again open to direct trade with this country.

Leipzig, and Castlereagh's success in holding together the Fifth Coalition, sealed the fate of the Napoleonic empire. In the campaign of 1813 Napoleon had been fighting for the hegemony of Europe: in that of 1814 he was fighting for France. Within a few months of Leipzig all his allies had abandoned him; all these allies, save only Denmark, were soon to fight against him. Even Bernadotte, the Crown Prince of Sweden, who had formerly been one of his Marshals, led a Swedish army into the fray. The Prussian General von Bülow invaded Holland, and Amsterdam rose in revolt. Presently the nation declared for the House of Orange. Towards the end of 1813 Commodore Owen, in command of the inshore squadron off the mouth of the Scheldt, landed with a force of seamen and marines to assist the Dutch. In Italy, Murat was about to change sides. Despite these heavy odds Napoleon refused to make any serious effort to treat for peace, and continued to put his trust in a final crowning victory which would miraculously restore his failing fortunes and destroy his enemies once and for all. These hopes were vain. The lost ground could never be regained. No recovery was possible from the disastrous Peninsula

P

War, from the retreat from Moscow, or from the holocaust of Leipzig. Once again, in the ensuing campaigns, the armies of the coalition were sustained by lavish subsidies from the British government, who at the same time poured troops and supplies into the Peninsula.

Meanwhile, in the Mediterranean Pellew's squadron continued to confine the French within the limits of continental Europe and finally to join in the general Allied offensive which ended the war. Like Collingwood before him, Pellew was statesman as well as admiral. As the hour of liberation drew near, he strove unceasingly to undermine Napoleon's position in southern Europe and to encourage the subject peoples to rise against him. By the end of February 1814 every enemy stronghold in the Adriatic had surrendered; and in the following month, as the Austrian army advanced across northern Italy, an expedition under Lord William Bentinck sailed from Palermo, and, supported by a squadron under Commodore Rowley, landed on the Ligurian coast: on the arrival of Pellew, in the middle of April, with a number of line-of-battle ships, Genoa capitulated to the Allies, while a force under the command of Colonel Montresor was detached to seize Corsica.

In January 1814 the Allies crossed the Rhine. The speed of their advance took Napoleon by surprise, for he had not expected that they would move against him until the spring. France was invaded from the north and east by the Russians, Prussians, Austrians, and Swedes; while in the south the British army under Wellington, having crossed the Pyrenees in December, was advancing northward. By the first week of February the Allies had overrun more than a third of France with two great armies, commanded by Schwarzenberg and Blücher, while in the north-east a third army under Bernadotte was moving down from Flanders. Cossack patrols had penetrated to the very heart of France. Bülow and Graham overran Holland. Brussels was taken and Antwerp besieged. Early in the new year Murat had deserted to the Allies, followed soon afterwards by the King of Denmark. Though his empire lay in ruins around him and his Marshals had abandoned all hope, the Emperor, in the face of overwhelming odds, fought on with the genius and resilience of his youth. For nine anxious weeks the struggle swayed to and fro between the frontier and Paris. The last actions which Napoleon, with vastly inferior forces, fought against Blücher and Schwarzenberg in the valleys of the Seine and the Marne are reckoned among his masterpieces. By the skilful use of interior lines, he was able to defeat his opponents piece-meal. Again and again the Allied armies, for all their superior numbers, were forced back. At the last moment Napoleon had saved his capital. In March, however, the tide turned. Three times Blücher had found himself outmanœuvred and repulsed; then at last he broke through the enemy's front at Laon and Crayonne and marched on Paris. As he drew near the city he joined hands with the Austrians and stormed the heights of Montmartre. Napoleon, hastening westward in pursuit, just failed to save the capital, which, on 30 March, capitulated to the Tsar. On the following day the Tsar and the King of Prussia entered Paris at the head of the Russian and Prussian guards. On 11 April Napoleon abdicated and was exiled to the island of Elba.

XVI

'Mr. Madison's War'

I

On the outbreak of hostilities between France and Russia, the British government had at once revoked the Orders in Council as applied to the United States. It was too late. Only five days before, on 18 June, the American Republic had declared war.

This decision followed as the culmination of various long-standing American grievances arising out of the British conduct of the maritime war against France, the chief of which centred on the Orders in Council and the claim to search American shipping for British seamen. As has already been seen, relations between the two countries had become increasingly strained; such concessions as Great Britain had seen fit to make had been insufficient to appease the Americans; to vindicate their national rights they had resorted to such economic measures as the Embargo Act and the Non-Intercourse Act; these having failed to accomplish their purpose, Madison recommended Congress to declare war.

The United States mercantile marine, which was profiting immensely by the long-drawn-out struggle in Europe and was capturing much of the colonial carrying trade, had become a formidable rival to the British. Its tonnage had practically doubled. There had been a corresponding increase in the number of seamen employed in American merchantmen, of whom by all accounts more than one-half were British. Between 1795 and 1806 the seaborne trade of the United States had actually doubled. The seafaring population of the eastern seaboard was in a fair way to becoming what the Dutch had formerly been, 'the wagoners of all the seas'. It was this very lucrative carrying trade which was threatened by the British action. 'These Orders in Council', observed Senator Giles of Virginia, 'were the besom which was intended to sweep, and would have swept, our commerce from the ocean.'

In the end Madison allowed himself to be humbugged by Napoleon's announcement that his decrees against neutral shipping would be revoked; whereupon the President declared that, France having given this undertaking, non-intercourse would be revived against Great Britain if within three months the Orders in Council were not repealed. Despite the fact that French interference with American shipping still continued, Madison was blind to the realities of the situation. In March 1811 non-intercourse was put into effect and the United States virtually brought into the Continental System.

The controversy which had arisen between the two countries over neutral rights was exacerbated by the British refusal to relinquish the practice of impressing seamen claimed as British from American merchantmen on the high seas—among whom, it was not to be denied, were a considerable number of deserters from the Royal Navy. 'The only compensation which the squadron have received for the continued desertion to the United States,' wrote the acting Commander-in-Chief on the North American station to Robert Liston, the British minister at Washington, 'is the power they have exercised in taking British seamen out of American vessels.'[1] To have abandoned the right of search would have made it impossible to recapture deserters. Nevertheless, Great Britain's claim to impress her native-born subjects was stoutly resisted by the United States; and intense indignation had been aroused by the high-handed British methods of search and impressment (in 1807 the seizure of a number of alleged British deserters from the American frigate *Chesapeake* had all but led to war).

Finally, an underlying and perhaps decisive cause of the War of 1812 was the uncontrollable land-hunger of the American frontiersmen and the desire of a strong party in the House of Representatives to see Canada annexed to the United States. It was the pressure of this group, the Anglophobe 'War Hawks', as they were called, headed by Henry Clay and John Calhoun (and *not* the representatives of the New Englanders, who, in fact, voted overwhelmingly against the declaration of war), which forced America into the conflict; and eventually hostilities were begun by the United States with the slogan, 'Free Trade and Sailors' Rights!'

The American declaration of war came at a time when Napoleon was still supreme on the Continent and the demands made upon our Navy

[1] Adm. 1/495, 22 July 1800.

were at their heaviest. Great Britain at this juncture was unable either to reinforce her garrisons in Canada or to spare adequate naval forces for the North American theatre. The consequence was that the Americans were free to invade Canada and to embark on extensive depredations against our trade.

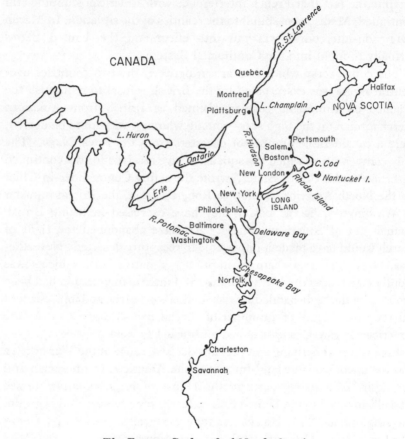

The Eastern Seaboard of North America

The United States possessed about ten times the population of British North America and an even greater superiority in material resources. The geographical advantage was also with the United States. From New York and its environs there was an almost unbroken line of water communication to the Canadian border. Moreover, the naval superiority on Lake Champlain, throughout the first year of the war,

454

was with the Americans. The belief was widely held in the United States that the Canadian campaign would be literally a 'walk-over'. Thomas Jefferson had confidently predicted that the conquest of Canada would be 'a mere matter of marching', while Henry Clay had boasted that they would be able to conquer that territory with the Kentucky militia alone.

In the event the American offensive was a complete fiasco. In 1812 the Americans attempted to invade Canada at three points: at each of these points they were decisively repulsed. Under the leadership of the able and experienced General Isaac Brock, governor of Ontario, the American advance into Canada was not only halted, but the British were able to wrest from the enemy two key-points, Mackinac and Detroit, controlling the vital line of water communications. Every attempt to invade Canada during the ensuing years was foiled; and our forces there held out successfully until the defeat of Napoleon and the restoration of peace in Europe permitted the dispatch of large numbers of regular troops to the American theatre.

From first to last New England remained bitterly opposed to the war. Madison incurred considerable unpopularity as disaster followed disaster. The Federalists of Massachusetts clamoured for his resignation, and even appeared to be moving towards secession. The alienation of the wealthiest and most populous region of the country severely handicapped the American army in its successive campaigns against Canada. The New Englanders for the most part openly held aloof from 'Mr. Madison's War' and continued to trade with the provinces across the frontier and even to lend money to the British government.

At sea, however, things went badly for Great Britain, who, owing to the exigencies of the war in Europe, had by no means enough ships for the increasing demands of the North American station. On the outbreak of war the total strength of the forces on that station had been brought up to three sail of the line, twenty one frigates, and thirty-seven smaller cruisers. Sir John Borlase Warren, who had lately been appointed Commander-in-Chief of the Halifax, Jamaica, and Leeward Islands stations was presently convinced (as he informed the Admiralty) by the great numbers of hostile privateers infesting the trade-route between the St. Lawrence and the West Indies 'of the impossibility of our trade navigating these seas unless a very extensive squadron is employed to scour the vicinity'.

Effectively to blockade the 1,000-mile eastern seaboard with such forces as were available was out of the question. Furthermore, the United States Navy, though small—it comprised, at this time, no more than ten frigates and eight smaller cruisers—was remarkably well trained and highly efficient. Most of the American captains were experienced commanders who had already distinguished themselves in the Barbary War. John Rodgers, who had been first second-in-command and later Commander-in-Chief of the American squadron in the Mediterranean, had finally brought both Tripoli and Tunis to terms. Stephen Decatur had also distinguished himself in the Barbary War. Among the other leading commanders of the United States Navy were William Bainbridge, Isaac Hull, James Lawrence, David Porter, Isaac Chauncey, Charles Stewart, Thomas Macdonough, and Oliver Perry. Unlike Uncle Sam's aged and incompetent generals, these naval commanders were all of them young men or else in the prime of life. The American gunnery and seamanship were superlatively good. In the War of 1812 American shooting proved to be as accurate as it was rapid, even in bad weather. Their fine seamanship was another prime cause of their success. Their crews were composed of picked men. Their ships were fast sailers and manœuvred with admirable skill and precision.

In 1812 the three American 44s—the *Constitution*, *President*, and *United States*—exerted an influence upon the course of the war out of all proportion to their numbers. The most powerful frigates afloat, and the keenest sailers, they could outgun any British cruiser and outsail any British ship of the line. It was these three strong cruisers which effectually prevented the British from covering each port with a frigate to lie in waiting for all the homecoming American trade during the critical summer of 1812. In particular, it was the powerful squadron commanded by Commodore John Rodgers[1] which compelled the British enemy to concentrate a considerable portion of his most active force and thus prevented him from instituting an effective blockade of the eastern seaboard. The British force dared not disperse in view of the superior fighting power of the American frigates. 'We have been so completely occupied in looking out for Commodore Rodger's squad-

[1] This squadron comprised three frigates, the *President* and *United States*, each rated of 44 guns, and the *Congress*, 38, besides the sloop *Hornet*, 18, and the brig *Argus*, 16.

ron,' observed an officer of the *Guerrière*, 'that we have taken very few prizes.' There was another disturbing consequence of the operations of the powerful American frigates. 'The necessity,' wrote the Secretary of the Admiralty to Warren, 'for sending heavy convoys arises from the facility and safety with which the American navy has hitherto found it possible to put to sea.' These conditions prevailed down to the spring of 1813.

At the outset of the maritime war the *Constitution* showed her mettle, when chased for three days by a squadron of five British frigates, by evading her pursuers by means of every trick and device known to seamanship—starting her water, damping her sails, towing, and kedging—until, the wind presently freshening, she began to go through the water and to gain on her pursuers, a sudden rain-squall enabling her to increase her lead by another mile: and finally she disappeared triumphantly over the horizon. Her commander, Captain Isaac Hull, handled his vessel with consummate skill and resource. A few weeks later he and his men were to prove that they could do as well with the guns as they had with the sails.

In the latter half of 1812 the *Constitution* and *United States* were the victors in three famous frigate duels.

In the first of these engagements, fought between the *Constitution* and *Guerrière* off Nova Scotia on 19 August, the *Constitution*, with her superior fire-power and more highly trained crew, succeeded in shooting away the mizen-mast of the *Guerrière* within ten minutes of the opening shot being fired. Not only was the *Constitution* more skilfully manœuvred, but the fire of her gunners was more accurately synchronized with the scend of the seas; and the well-aimed broadsides shattered the *Guerriere*'s rigging and crashed into her hull between wind and water. 'Being alongside within half-pistol shot,' reported her commander, 'we commenced a heavy fire from all our guns, double shotted with round and grape and so well directed were they, and so warmly kept up, that in fifteen minutes his mizen-mast went by the board, and his main-yard in the slings, and the hull, rigging, and sails, very much torn to pieces.' The *Constitution* took prompt and effective advantage of her opponent's crippled state to take up a commanding position on the *Guerrière*'s bow from which she flung in a couple of raking broadsides. The *Guerrière*'s bowsprit becoming entangled with the *Constitution*'s mizen-rigging, the crews of both ships prepared to repel boarders. But the fore and main-mast of the *Guerrière* collapsed together, 'taking with them every spar, except the bowsprit'; and soon after she struck her colours.[1] The *Guerrière* was so badly damaged that she had to be set on fire and abandoned; whereupon, after taking his prisoners into his own ship, the American commander, Isaac Hull, sailed for Boston.

On 25 October, shortly after daybreak, Captain Stephen Decatur in the *United States* sighted the *Macedonian* off the Madeira Islands. The American was the slower ship of the two but greatly superior in gun-power. Decatur manœuvred with such skill and caution that the *Macedonian* was kept for a considerable period at the distance and bearing most favourable to her long 24s; and when the *Macedonian* made her final approach she was already more than half-beaten, with many of her men killed or wounded, spars and rigging severely damaged, and her carronade battery disabled. Before she could get alongside her antagonist, the *United States* had succeeded in shooting away all three of her topmasts. 'The enemy, comparatively in good order,' related the captain of the *Macedonian*, '. . . now shot ahead, and was about to place himself in a raking position, without our being enabled to return the fire, being a perfect wreck and unmanageable log.'[2] Shortly after, the *Macedonian* surrendered.

In the last of these engagements, fought between the *Constitution* and the *Java* off Bahia on the South American coast on 29 December, the *Constitution* had recourse to a succession of skilful manœuvres in which every resource of seamanship was brought into play by her new commander, Captain William Bainbridge. In the face of heavy odds—the *Constitution* was much the more powerful ship of the two and her crew were better trained—the British frigate put up a far stiffer resistance to the *Constitution* than had the *Guerrière* four months before. Against the superior fire-power and gunnery of the *Constitution*, however, the *Java* had little chance. Such was the injury to her spars and rigging (her bowsprit was shot away, and her fore and main-masts were badly damaged) that her captain could see no hope unless he could board his enemy. But, before he could do so, the *Java*'s foremast had gone overboard, and her maintopmast also collapsed. In this hopelessly crippled condition the *Java* fought on, and her flag was kept flying,

[1] *Captain's Letters*, 30 August 1812.
[2] *Naval Chronicle*, Vol. 29, p. 77.

though her captain fell, mortally wounded. Finally her mizen-mast, too, went by the board, and about an hour afterwards the British frigate hauled down her colours. The *Java* was too badly injured to be worth taking home as a prize; and she was later set on fire by the victors.

All this came as a very painful shock to the pride and confidence of our Navy and people. As Canning had lately declared in the House of Commons, 'It cannot be too deeply felt that the sacred spell of the invincibility of the British Navy was broken by these unfortunate captures'. In the decade of almost continuous warfare against the French Republic and Empire, which had opened with Nelson's engagement with the *Ça Ira* and culminated in the victory of Trafalgar, Great Britain had arrived at the highest pinnacle of her naval glory. To the world-famed fleet actions of Howe, Jervis, Duncan, and Nelson was to be added the triumphant outcome of hundreds of minor and single-ship engagements. The result was that British sea-officers in general had tended to become complacent and over-confident, and the skill of their gun-crews had markedly declined.

This weakness was said by the historian William James to have extended to two-thirds of the British Navy. It was exemplified in the actions fought by the American sloops-of-war as in those fought by the American frigates. On 13 October the *Wasp* sloop, Captain Jacob Jones, had left the Delaware on a cruise. Between four and five hundred miles to the eastward she sighted a British convoy under escort of a small cruiser, the *Frolic*. To enable her convoy to escape, the *Frolic* dropped astern and presently engaged the hostile sloop. After a stubbornly fought, close-range artillery duel, lasting about three-quarters of an hour, on converging courses, in a heavy sea, the *Wasp* finally grappled her opponent and poured in a raking broadside; the *Frolic* being unable to bring a gun to bear. This ended the action: for when a boarding-party from the *Wasp* tumbled on board the *Frolic* it met with no resistance. The enemy's superiority in gunnery was even more pronounced in the action between the American *Hornet* and the British *Peacock*, on 24 February 1813, off the Brazilian coast. After her victory over the *Java*, when the *Constitution* had sailed for home, Bainbridge had left the *Hornet*, Captain James Lawrence, to blockade Bahia, until the appearance of a British 74 presently obliged the *Hornet* to proceed northward to Demerara, where she encountered the *Peacock*. The two vessels were of much the same size; but the *Peacock* was decidedly inferior in fire-power, and, further, her poor shooting contributed materially to her defeat. 'She was well handled,' declared Roosevelt, 'and bravely fought; but her men showed a marvellous ignorance of gunnery. It appears that she had long been known as "the yacht"; the breechings of the carronades were lined with white canvas, and nothing could exceed in brilliancy the polish upon the traversing bars and elevating screws.'[1]

Now, for the first time for many years, Great Britain found herself confronted by a foe of at least equal nautical calibre. Her Navy had made the disastrous error of underrating its adversary. 'Never before in the history of the world,' *The Times* declared, following on the news of the *Guerrière*'s surrender to the *Constitution*, 'did an English frigate strike to an American . . . Good God!' *The Times* went on, 'that a few short months should have so altered the tone of British sentiment! Is it true, or is it not, that our Navy was accustomed to hold the American in utter contempt? Is it true, or is it not, that the *Guerrière* sailed up and down the American coast with her name painted in large characters on her sails, in boyish defiance of Commodore Rodgers?'

More was at stake than merely British prestige. An important part of our commerce throughout the world was only too vulnerable to attack by American raiders. Within a week of the declaration of war the *Statesman* had published the urgent warning:

America cannot certainly pretend to wage a maritime war with us. She has no navy to do it with. But America has nearly 100,000 as good seamen as any in the world, all of whom would be actively employed against our trade on every part of the ocean in their fast-sailing ships-of-war, many of whom will be able to cope with our smaller cruizers; and they will be found to be sweeping in the West Indian seas, and even carrying desolation into the chops of the Channel. Every one must recollect what they did in the latter part of the American war. The books at Lloyd's will recount it; and the rate of assurances at that time will clearly prove what their diminutive strength was able to effect in the face of our navy, and that, when nearly one hundred pendants were flying on their coast. Were we then able to prevent their going in and out, or stop them from taking our trade and our storeships, even in sight of our garrisons? Besides, were they not in the English and Irish channels, picking up our homeward trade, sending their prizes into French and Spanish ports, to the great terror and annoyance of our merchants and shipowners? . . . The Americans will be found to be a different sort of enemy by sea than the

[1] Theodore Roosevelt, *The Naval War of 1812*, p. 169.

French. They possess nautical knowledge, with equal enterprise to ourselves. They will be found attempting deeds which a Frenchman would never think of; and they will have all the ports of our enemy open, in which they can make good their retreat with their booty.

Despite the lessons of the earlier war, the scale and intensity of the American *guerre de course* took the Admiralty by surprise. On the verge of hostilities the majority of American merchantmen had gone overseas to escape the embargo; and many of the vessels now fitted out for privateering—to which service they were admirably adapted— were pilot schooners. They carried a large spread of canvas, particularly for use in light airs. With their larger blocks and thinner ropes they did not present so smart an appearance as the British, but undoubtedly they were easier to work. They were faster and more skilfully manœuvred than any other vessels of their class. They could generally overhaul any merchantman and elude any man-of-war. With their light construction and immense spread of canvas they could wear or tack and dart away under a frigate's guns long before their heavy opponent could come about. They were well adapted to attack either merchantmen or 'running ship'. By night they could run right into the midst of a convoy and cut out some unlucky merchantman; by day they could pounce on laggards and stragglers. The privateers were commonly equipped with one long-range gun and also with a small carronade or a few swivels. They carried a large crew and an ample store of small arms, relying for the most part on their 'Long Toms' and boarding. Though they could fight well enough when they had to, the privateer's proper business was to run and not to fight. As the war advanced the number of these raiders at large on the trade-routes greatly increased, both through the conversion of old vessels and the fitting out of new ones. In 1813, twenty-six privateers were built in New York alone.

The war saw the heyday of the 'Baltimore clipper'. These were fast-sailing schooners and brigs especially designed to carry a heavy press of sail under most conditions of weather and sea—long, lightly built, raking craft with a low freeboard, high bulwarks, and wide, clear decks. The shipwrights of Baltimore had succeeded in turning out a vessel which was capable of outsailing, on nearly every point, any other craft afloat. The captain of a British frigate, after capturing one of these vessels, paid this tribute to her commander:

'In England we cannot build such vessels as your Baltimore clippers; we have no such models, and even if we had them, they would be of no service to us, for we could never sail them as you do.' Even though from time to time one of these vessels fell into the hands of the British, added the captain, it brought the captors small profit; for it was not only the craft, but also the knowledge and experience how to handle them, that was needed. 'We are afraid of their long masts and heavy spars, and soon cut down and reduce them to our standard. We strengthen them, put up bulkheads, etc., after which they lose their sailing qualities, and are of no further service as cruising vessels.'[1]

There was no lack of prime seamen to man the privateers. From Boston, Gloucester, Salem, Portland, and other sea-ports in New England, from New York, Philadelphia, and elsewhere in the middle states, and from Baltimore, Savannah, and Charleston in the South, came forth tough old salts in hundreds and thousands. Not only the large mercantile marine of the United States, but also the fishing and whaling fleets served to supply the privateer crews.

Soon after the outbreak of the war a damaging attack was made on the trade and fisheries of British North America. The Newfoundland trade had already paid a heavy toll to French privateers. The War of 1812 occasioned still greater losses. The insurance rate rose gradually from 3 to 10 per cent., and at times even higher. The premium for the Newfoundland–West Indies passage was between 15 and 25 per cent. Yankee privateers swarmed in the Bay of Fundy and haunted the criss-cross of trade-routes off Halifax. Two of the most successful of these early ventures were those of the *Rossie* of Baltimore, which cruised off the Grand Banks of Newfoundland, and the *America* of Salem, which operated in the Western Approaches. When later the Admiralty strengthened our naval forces on the western side of the Atlantic, more and more of the privateers sought their quarry further afield. Soon the gleam of their white cotton canvas became an all too familiar danger-signal in every sea. As early as November 1812 it was reported to Keith from the Bay of Biscay that 'the Americans are running in and out like rabbits'. The West Indian archipelago also swarmed with shipping among which the privateers wrought great havoc. Even the seas around the British Isles, as was exemplified by the cruise of the brig *Argus* in the summer of 1813, proved a most profitable hunting-

[1] G. Coggeshall, *Second Series of Voyages*, p. 263.

ground; for there much of the traffic was unprotected. 'The navy of America roams the seas', declared the *Tradesman*, 'committing depredations on our shipping, and in spite of our blockade of their ports, returns in safety with the spoils captured from the British.' Not the least disturbing factor in the situation was the threat to British communications with the Peninsula and the vital supplies required for Wellington's army.

2

In the spring of 1813 the struggle entered upon its second phase. The British forces in North American waters were strengthened to ten of the line and nearly a hundred cruisers. The reinforcements enabled the blockade to be extended to New York, Charleston, Savannah, and the estuary of the Mississippi. In June Warren passed the Capes of the Chesapeake with a strong squadron of eight of the line, twelve frigates, and a large number of small cruisers; a smaller British squadron lay in the Delaware River; another division, under the command of Captain Thomas Hardy, blockaded the enemy frigates in New London, and other divisions cruised off Boston and New York. The object of this strategy was to prevent American warships from slipping out into the Atlantic by posting substantial forces off every port of consequence between Maine and Georgia, while frigates and sloops patrolled the coast. At the same time small divisions of ships of the line were stationed in the Madeira Islands and the Azores to protect our commerce against the enemy's frigates.

The blockade of the United States ports, both naval and commercial, was the principal task assigned to the North American squadron in 1813. It was a service with which both officers and men had long been thoroughly familiar. Once again they cruised off a hostile coast, or lay in sheltered roadsteads, watching the enemy's shipping by day and by night, maintaining a ceaseless vigil in summer and winter alike, and seizing every opportunity to stop his coastal trade and to run down his national economy. Engaged in the continual blockade of the American ports were some of the finest seamen in the Service—Captains Henry Hotham, Thomas Hardy, Philip Vere Broke, the 'Magnificent Hayes', and many others.

Some of the stations presented no particular difficulty: our squadrons lay in secure anchorages in the entrances of the Delaware and Chesapeake estuaries, which could be almost hermatically sealed. On certain other parts of the coast, however, the navigational conditions made the close blockade of the enemy's ports difficult, if not actually impossible: for the same northerly gales which drove the blockading squadron off its station also enabled the blockaded force to get away to sea; and even

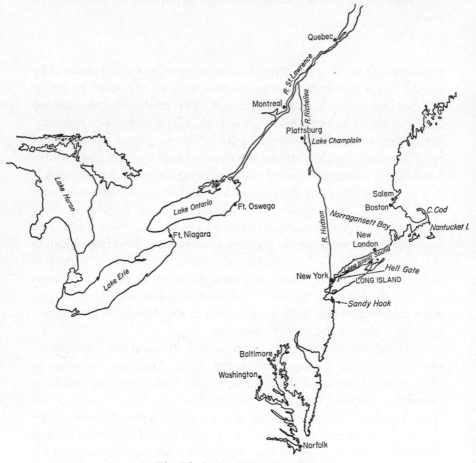

The Blockade of American Ports

in the most rigorous phase of the blockade a blizzard would sometimes permit the blockaded force to slip out. The conditions obtaining on the eastern seaboard of the United States were very different to those obtaining on the Brittany coast. During the winter months Boston could not be closely blockaded; nor could Narragansett; and there was always the danger of a frigate or a sloop getting out 'in one of the dark blowing nights'. Again, the currents which were encountered near the land, especially off the New England coast, depending as they usually did on the winds that had been blowing, were for the most part un-known quantities. Fogs were experienced—sometimes for days on end—off the bleak New England coast in the spring and early summer. Fog commonly occurred with easterly and southerly winds; westerly and north-westerly winds tended to disperse it. These fogs were especially prevalent in the entrances to Long Island Sound and Narragansett Bay—indeed, to the west of the latter the vicinity of Port Judith had become known as 'the fog-hole'.

The effects of the blockade were soon made manifest. The *Constellation*, Captain Charles Stewart, was early in February 1813 forced to take refuge in Norfolk, Virginia, by a squadron of three ships of the line, three frigates, and two smaller cruisers, and was there shut up for the rest of the war. The *United States*, accompanied by her prize, the *Macedonian*, had reached New York in December 1812. Before the two ships could be refitted, the approaches to that port had been effectively sealed. 'Both outlets,' wrote Jacob Jones, captain of the *Macedonian*, in April 1813, 'are at present strongly blocked, but I believe at dark of the moon we shall be able to pass without much risk.' Next month, however, found the two frigates still in New York. Decatur in the *United States* hoped to slip out to sea during stormy weather by way of Sandy Hook; but a strong British force remained continually off the bar. 'The last gale,' he observed, in May, 'which promised the fairest opportunity for us to get out, ended in light southerly winds, which continued till the blockading ships had regained their stations.' After lying for several days at Sandy Hook and finding no chance of escape that way, he resolved to push round the back of Long Island, through the intricate and hazardous passage of Hell Gate, and get to sea down Long Island Sound. But the blockading ships were already lying in wait off the entrance when, on 1 June, the American cruisers were seen 'coming down with studding-sails set'. Both forces hauled to the wind under all the sail they could carry.[1] Decatur stood up the Sound again and took refuge off New London, Connecticut, where he was closely blockaded. Neither the *United States* nor the *Macedonian* got to sea again during the war.

[1] Adm. 1/503, 13 June 1813.

Meanwhile the enemy squadron in Boston Harbour was watched by Captain Thomas Capel in *La Hogue*, 74, with several cruisers, including the *Shannon* and *Tenedos*. These two frigates, according to Captain Capel, were 'invariably as close off the Port of Boston as the circumstance of the weather would permit, but the long continued fogs that prevail on this part of the coast at this season of the year give the enemy great advantage'.[1] It was in foggy weather and aided by a sudden favouring shift of wind that on 1 May Captain John Rodgers in the *President*, accompanied by the *Congress*, weighed and slipped out past the blockading force. The two ships got safely away and made a wide sweep of the Atlantic, but to little profit.[2] (The convoy system, now strictly enforced by the Admiralty, had cleared the seas of British shipping, except where the marshalled trading fleets sailed to and fro on their lawful occasions with their escorting warships.) On Rodgers's return in the early autumn he was able to get in, but throughout the whole of 1814 he remained in New York, closely watched by the blockading division in the approaches. For many months Stewart (who had lately been transferred from the *Constellation* shut up at Norfolk to the *Constitution* refitting at Boston), fine seaman though he was, was unable to leave port. The smaller American cruisers and privateers, on account of their lesser draught, could still slip away to sea; but none of them was strong enough to constitute a threat to either our convoys or dispersed cruisers. By the end of 1813 the American war effort was seriously handicapped by the effects of the blockade.

The extensive shores and inlets of the Chesapeake proved all too vulnerable to amphibious attack. To Rear-Admiral Sir George Cockburn, Warren's second-in-command, was entrusted the congenial task of harassing the surrounding countryside. With a force composed of some of the lighter vessels of the squadron he carried destruction far and wide. Cockburn had been one of the young captains of Jervis's fleet who, long ago, had paid court to Betsey and Jenny Wynne. The two damsels had found him pleasant enough. He now appeared in a quite different light. 'Where there was looting and destruction, there was Sir George. Where the war assumed its harshest aspects it was a good guess that Sir George was around. So thoroughly did he go about the business of harassing and terrifying the civilian population that within a few

[1] *Ibid.*, 11 May 1813.
[2] *Captain's Letters*, 27 September 1813.

months his name was the most feared and fated of all His Majesty's officers on service in America.'[1] Cockburn's division pushed higher and higher up the Bay. The militia of Virginia and Maryland put up the feeblest show of resistance. Both here and in the Delaware hostile operations were methodically set in train over an immense area, with a general burning and pillaging of farms, hamlets, and towns, and the whole country in a perpetual state of alarm.

After the winter of 1812–13 American commerce, both coasting and foreign, rapidly declined; for at the end of May 1813 the commercial blockade was gradually extended along much of the eastern seaboard, including the principal ports of the southern states (Narragansett Bay and all the coast to the northward, however, remained exempt from the restrictions of the economic blockade). The pressure of the blockade was increasingly felt. The price of sugar, tea, and coffee rose to unprecedented heights. At the close of 1813 exports, except from Georgia and New England, virtually ceased. On the federal revenue the blockade operated with similar effect.

With nearly twenty years' blockading experience on the Atlantic and Mediterranean coasts of Europe behind them, the officers of the Royal Navy progressively tightened their grip upon the American seaboard. The English, as Napoleon had once observed, were good at blockading. They harassed the enemy's trade off capes and promontories where his coasters had to sail farthest from any place of refuge and where our cruisers could come close in with least risk to themselves. The concentration of British cruisers off the principal blockaded ports effectually cut communications between the different parts of the coast. The flow of shipping was in consequence soon reduced to a mere trickle, and later, for long periods, practically dried up altogether.

Philadelphia and Baltimore were severed from the sea for the rest of the war. By the end of the summer about 250 vessels were laid up in Boston; and New York and certain other ports were likewise crowded with idle shipping. The once vigorous coastwise traffic of the United States, upon which the national economy depended, was practically annihilated; and for the exchange of commodities the northern and southern states were forced to resort to wagon transport, which was of necessity expensive, inadequate, and slow. Under the heading 'New Carrying Trade' a Boston paper on 28 April reported the arrival of 'a

[1] P. F. Beirne, *The War of 1812*, p. 170.

large number of teams from New Bedford with West India produce, and four Pennsylvania wagons, seventeen days from Philadelphia'. 'Four wagons loaded with dry goods', announced *Niles' Register* at about this time, 'passed to-day through Georgetown, South Carolina, for Charleston, *forty-six days* from Philadelphia.'[1] The inhabitants of Nantucket Island were almost starving. A contemporary journal, the *Columbian Centinel*, thus portrayed the plight of the Republic: 'Our coasts unnavigable to ourselves, though free to the enemy and the money-making neutral; our harbors blockaded; our shipping destroyed or rotting at the docks; silence and stillness in our cities; the grass growing upon the public wharves.'[2]

That the commercial blockade was not applied at the outset with all possible rigour was due to the fact that a certain amount of American trade was still permitted to our West Indian possessions, the British forces in Canada and Spain, and even the British Isles. But in the autumn of 1813 Wellington's army entered France, and no longer required American supplies. Warren thereupon extended the commercial blockade as far up the coast as New York.

It was largely because of the long succession of reverses at sea that had marked the opening phase of the War of 1812 that the news of the success achieved by the British 38-gun frigate *Shannon*, Captain Philip Vere Broke, in the summer of 1813, was received with such enthusiasm in this country.

The *Shannon* had formed part of the division dispatched in 1806 to protect British whalers in the Arctic. From 1808 to 1811 she had cruised off the Brittany coast, mainly off Ushant and the Black Rocks. When she arrived at Halifax a year before the outbreak of the American War, she could boast one of the finest ship's companies in the Service. The *Shannon* was for some months engaged in watching the newly commissioned American frigate *Chesapeake*, Captain James Lawrence, in the port of Boston. The *Chesapeake* was the larger vessel, and her crew was numerically the stronger. But in every other respect, as a fighting unit, she was inferior to the *Shannon*, as the *Guerrière* had been to the *Constitution*. The *Chesapeake*'s people had had no chance to shake down together, and there had been no time for gunnery exercise, while Broke, during the seven years in which he had had the *Shannon*, had,

[1] Q. Mahan, *Sea Power in its Relations to the War of 1812*, II, p. 194.
[2] *Ibid.*, pp. 17–18.

by the assiduous training of his guns' crews, brought his command up to the highest pitch of efficiency; so that when, on 1 June, the *Chesapeake* stood out of harbour to engage her rival, she was decisively outmatched.

The action took place between Cape Ann and Cape Cod. The *Shannon* hove-to to await her opponent's attack. At the *Shannon*'s first broadside, fired at point-blank range, a hundred of the *Chesapeake*'s people were killed or wounded. A second deadly broadside completed the destruction wrought by the first. The back of the enemy's resistance was now broken: the captain, first lieutenant, master, marine officer, and boatswain of the *Chesapeake* had all fallen mortally wounded. The *Chesapeake* thereupon fell aboard the *Shannon*, 'her mizen channels locking in with our fore-rigging'. It was in vain that the dying Lawrence delivered his final order which became part of his country's naval tradition—'Don't give up the ship'. His guns' crews had quitted their posts; and, led by Captain Broke, a boarding-party from the *Shannon* forthwith swarmed down on the quarter-deck of the *Chesapeake* and drove the crew forward. 'The enemy made a desperate but disorderly resistance,' concluded Broke in his dispatch; observing that 'the whole of this service was achieved in fifteen minutes from the commencement of the action.'[1]

Meanwhile an interesting and important series of naval operations was in progress on the great inland waters which separated the United States from Canada. The military situation on the long land frontier of the United States depended primarily upon the control of the Great Lakes. Since the frontier ran through an immense wooded wilderness which was virtually impassable to an army, no large-scale offensive operations were possible without the command of one or other of these lakes. Accordingly both British and Americans set to work on their respective shores to construct miniature fleets with which to contest the control of the vital water communications.

In these inland waters the overwhelming numerical superiority of the British Navy counted for little. Both sides started practically from scratch. The command of the American naval forces on Lakes Ontario and Erie was presently entrusted to Captain Isaac Chauncey, one of the ablest and most energetic officers in the United States Navy. To Commander Oliver Perry was assigned the command on Lake Erie.

[1] Adm. 1/503, 6 June 1813.

On the British side Captain Sir James Yeo was appointed Commander-in-Chief on the Lakes, with Captain Barclay in command on Lake Erie.

On Lake Ontario, where the largest and most powerful squadrons were assembled, there was little fighting, but much construction. 'Towards the end,' Theodore Roosevelt observed, 'the contrast became almost farcical, for it was one of shipbuilding merely, and the minute either completed a new ship the other promptly retired into the harbour until able in turn to complete a larger one.'[1]

The shipbuilding race on Lake Erie was followed on 10 September 1813 by a hard-fought action in the course of which the American superiority in armament (especially in carronades) played a decisive part. Perry, finding the British long-range gunnery more formidable than he had expected, unhesitatingly accepted the risk of closing his opponent, though exposed to a murderous fire to which for long he could make no reply; and thus brought his squadron within carronade range of Barclay's force, which was heavily defeated. This decided the issue of the campaign in the North-West.

As a result of the destruction of Barclay's force the British military positions in the vicinity of Lake Erie were rendered untenable; and Detroit, Michigan, and the surrounding territory were again in American hands. In effect, the struggle for the control of the Great Lakes may be cited as a perfect example in miniature of the influence of sea power upon history. Unlike the successes achieved by the American frigates, brilliant though they were, victory in this region did have a decisive influence upon the result of the war.

In 1814 the size of many of the American privateers had substantially increased; they were now large, heavily sparred, well-armed brigs and schooners of about the same tonnage as the smaller sloops-of-war of the Royal Navy. The experience of the last few years had brought about a notable improvement in design. The qualities principally aimed at were still speed and weatherliness. These would sometimes be carried to extremes. Over sparring was a common enough fault—there were numerous instances of privateers being driven under while chasing an enemy, or being pursued; though they were usually safe in the hands of an experienced commander. Such vessels were able to operate far

[1] Theodore Roosevelt, *Naval Operations of the War between Great Britain and the United States*, 1812–1815, p. 189.

from port and to inflict immense damage on the enemy's shipping without any capital squadron to support them. Though the majority of these craft hailed from New England and the middle states, a large number of them belonged to the South—especially to Baltimore, the renowned privateering base.[1]

The skill and experience of the commanders had likewise increased. In hundreds of encounters all over the oceans and seas their seamanship, initiative, and resource had been continually tested. They had more than justified the apprehensions entertained by the more perspicacious of their enemies at the outset of the struggle. They had finally forced their adversary to overhaul and reorganize his convoy system; and, even then, British shipping was not safe: for, as *The Times* complained, 'The American cruisers daily enter in among our convoys, seize prizes in sight of those that should afford protection, and if pursued "put on their sea wings" and laugh at the clumsy British pursuers. It must indeed be encouraging to Mr. Madison to read the logs of his cruisers. If they fight, they are sure to conquer; if they fly, they are sure to escape.'[2]

Coggeshall has related how the American privateers would lie in ambush for the homeward-bound convoys from the West Indies. These vessels were commonly laden with sugar, coffee, and other costly produce, and, consequently, objects of great temptation to the marauders. They would be dogged and watched from the time of their departure from the ports of the West Indies until their arrival at their own home ports. Two privateers in company, Coggeshall explained, stood a much better chance than one alone; for, while a man-of-war was sent away in pursuit of one of them, the other was ready to pounce instantly upon one of the merchantmen. As soon as any prizes were taken, the prize-crews were ordered to run to leeward of the fleet, and afterwards to separate and steer in different directions. While the war-

---

[1] Despite the blockade, which effectively prevented the passage of large vessels down the deep-water channel, only about 2½ miles wide at the entrance, the privateers could still get out of the Chesapeake. 'Nor', Warren had reported to the Admiralty in December 1813, 'can anything stop these vessels escaping to sea in dark nights and strong winds.' He observed that it was impossible to station the blockading ships so as to watch the motions of the American frigates, and at the same time to prevent the escape of the enemy's fast-sailing schooners (Adm. 1/506, 20 December 1813).

[2] *The Times*, 11 February 1815.

ship was chasing the privateer, the prizes had a chance to make good their escape. Sometimes the raiders would dog a convoy for days, and even weeks, on end in fine weather, with no opportunity of taking any prizes; but should a gale or thick weather disperse the convoy, then was the privateer's chance of making a rich haul—of which chance he took instant advantage.

Wherever on the ocean the British merchantmen sailed, thither the American privateers followed. Their keels furrowed the waters of the Indian Ocean and the China Seas; and they made prizes of vessels that sailed from Bombay, Madras, and Hong Kong. They swarmed in the West Indies, where they landed and burnt small towns, leaving behind them proclamations that thus they had avenged the burning of Washington. They haunted the coasts of the British colonies in Africa; they lay off the harbor of Halifax, and plundered the outgoing and incoming vessels, laughing at the ships of the line and frigates that strove to drive them off. Above all they grew ever fonder of sailing to and fro in the narrow seas over which England had for centuries claimed an unquestioned sovereignty. They cruised in the Bristol Channel, where they captured, not only merchantmen, but also small regularly armed vessels. The Irish Sea and the Irish Channel were among their favourite cruising grounds; they circled Scotland and Ireland; one of them ransomed a Scottish town. The *Chasseur* of Baltimore, commanded by Thomas Boyle, cruised for three months off the coast of England, taking prize after prize, and in derision sent in, to be posted at Lloyd's, a proclamation of blockage of the sea-coast of the United Kingdom.[1]

This Thomas Boyle had become an almost legendary figure on the seas. In his successive cruises in the *Chasseur* he covered wide areas of the North and South Atlantic, the English Channel and the Irish Sea, leaving a trail of destruction in his wake. Among other notable privateers in the later stages of the war were the *Scourge* and *Rattlesnake*, which attacked our Archangel traffic (the *Rattlesnake* alone sent into Norwegian ports prizes to the value of £1 million); the *Comet*, which was the terror of merchants and masters in the Caribbean; the *Governor Tompkins*, which burned fourteen vessels one after the other in the English Channel; the *Harpy*, which operated off our south coast and in the Bay of Biscay; and the *Neufchatel*—an excellent example of a fast American schooner—which during the spring and summer of 1814 wrought havoc in the Channel and in the Irish Sea and, chased by no

[1] Theodore Roosevelt, *The Naval Operations of the War between Great Britain and the United States*, 1812–1815, pp. 247–8.

less than seventeen British men-of-war, succeeded in giving them all the slip.

Two large American sloops-of-war were prominent in this attack on British trade. The newly built *Wasp* left Portsmouth, New Hampshire, on 1 May 1814 with a strong crew of New Englanders. Slipping through the ring of blockading cruisers she arrived safely on her station in the approaches to the English Channel, where she remained for several weeks, burning and scuttling many vessels. Her final exploit was the engagement on 28 June which ended in the capture and destruction of the British brig-of-war, the *Reindeer*. Like the *Wasp*, the *Peacock* was newly built and strongly manned. She had sailed out of New York early in March. While cruising in West Indian waters she captured a small British cruiser, the *Epervier*, after which she made a wide sweep of the Atlantic, penetrating as far south as the Azores and as far north as the Faeroe Islands, and accounting for about fourteen prizes.

Insurance rates rocketed. They were at least double what they had been during the Napoleonic War. The ravages of the privateers increased every month. Even though this country had a Navy of close on 1,000 ships, the *Annual Register* complained bitterly, 'it was not safe for a vessel to sail without convoy from one part of the English and Irish Channels to another'. Lloyd's published a list of well over 800 British vessels that had been captured by the Americans. (Before the end of the war several hundreds more were to be added to the list.) At a crowded meeting of merchants, manufacturers, shipowners, and underwriters assembled in Glasgow on 7 September 1814 it was,

> Unanimously resolved, that the number of American privateers with which our channels have been infested, the audacity with which they have approached our coasts, and the success with which their enterprise has been attended, have proved injurious to our commerce, humbling to our pride, and discreditable to the directors of the naval power of the British nation, whose flag, till of late, waved over every sea, and triumphed over every rival. There is reason to believe, that in the short space of less than twenty-four months, above 800 vessels have been captured by that power, whose maritime strength we have hitherto impolitically held in contempt. That, at a time when we were at peace with all the rest of the world, when the maintenance of our marine costs so large a sum to the country, when the mercantile and shipping interest pay a tax for protection, under the form of convoy duty, and when, in the plenitude of our power, we have

declared the whole American coast under blockade, it is equally distressing and mortifying that our ships cannot, with safety, traverse our own channels; that insurance cannot be effected but at an excessive premium; and that a horde of American cruisers should be allowed, unheeded, unresisted and unmolested, to take, burn or sink, our own vessels, in our own inlets, and almost in sight of our own harbours.[1]

3

The downfall of Napoleon in the spring of 1814, which liberated the British blockading squadrons, ushered in the third and concluding phase of the American War. The North American, Jamaica, and Leeward Islands stations again became separate and independent commands; and Warren was succeeded by Vice-Admiral Sir Alexander Cochrane, whose flagship, the *Tonnant*, together with the main body of the fleet, continued for the most part to lie in the Chesapeake. The blockade was maintained with ever-increasing rigour and gradually extended over the whole littoral of the United States. The ports of New England were no longer permitted to carry on their trade. 'All America blockaded,' Lieutenant Napier of the *Nymphe* grimly recorded in his journal on 22 May. 'I have it much at heart', wrote Cochrane, a few months after his appointment, to the Secretary for War, 'to give them a complete drubbing before peace is made.' The tightening up of the blockade was due in part to the change in the Commander-in-Chief —Cochrane showed himself to be a very different type of man to Warren, and the campaign of 1814 took on a new vigour and purpose.

The American frigate *Essex*, which had been engaged in attacking the British whale-fishery in the Pacific, was finally brought to action off the coast of South America, in March 1814, by the frigate *Phoebe* and the sloop *Cherub*. The American vessel, being armed with carronades only on her gun-deck, stood no chance at all in a long-range action; and the captain of the *Phoebe*, who was well aware of the inferiority of the *Essex*'s armament, first skilfully destroyed his enemy's rigging and sails, then kept his distance and battered the *Essex* into wreckage with his long 18s. The American sloop *Frolic*, which had sailed from Boston on 18 February, was taken by the *Orpheus* off Cuba on 20 April. In May Decatur and his ship's company from the *United States* shut up in New London were transferred to the *President* fitting out in New York.

[1] Q. Coggeshall, *American Privateers* (1856), pp. 301–2.

Meanwhile Captain Charles Stewart in the *Constitution* had long been penned in in Boston. The difficulties of the station for the blockading squadron have already been mentioned. Seizing his opportunity in a northerly gale, Stewart on 31 December 1813 got away to sea unperceived. 'It appears,' wrote Hayes in his report, 'she sailed in a N.W. gale some days back; in fact for the last fortnight we have had such repeated gales with frost and snow, it would have been extraordinary if she had not made her escape.'[1] After a cruise in the Caribbean which brought him but few prizes (he narrowly missed taking the *Pique* frigate in the Mona Passage through the worn-out state of his sails), Stewart decided to return home. In the vicinity of Cape Cod the *Constitution* had a lucky escape. She was sighted, early in the morning of 3 April, 'standing to the westward with all sail set', by the *Junon* and *Tenedos*. The wind was northerly, and it was fine, clear weather. Steering for Marblehead, and hurriedly jettisoning a quantity of provisions and spare spars in order to lighten ship, the *Constitution* succeeded in getting safely into port. From Marblehead Stewart was able to slip into Salem on the flood, and thence into Boston. There he was to remain for more than eight months.

A few months after Napoleon's abdication, a powerful expeditionary force of Peninsular veterans, under General Robert Ross, sailed for America. The object of the expedition was to create a diversion in the Chesapeake Bay area to relieve American pressure upon Canada. On 19 August the British squadron sailed up the Patuxent and disembarked the troops while the veteran warrior Commodore Joshua Barney, in command of a large American flotilla in the Chesapeake, after falling back before a force of armed boats and tenders under Cockburn, destroyed his boats and retired with his men. The landing was unopposed and for five days the British army marched in the fierce summer heat on the capital without a shot fired on either side. Cockburn, who had suggested and planned the expedition, accompanied the troops. On the 24th they discovered an American army of 7,000, under General Winder, barring the road to Washington at a village called Bladensburg. The bridge over the river, a tributary of the Potomac, across which the British would have to pass, was covered by artillery. The head of the column was mown down by the American fire; but the experienced troops pushed on and forced their way across.

[1] Adm. 1/505, 8 January 1814.

The American army made little attempt to resist. Their first line, which was composed almost entirely of militiamen, indifferently armed and undisciplined, bolted at the outset of the fight; before the second line could be properly engaged, Winder ordered a general retirement. 'The rapid flight of the enemy,' reported Ross, 'and his knowledge of the country, precluded the possibility of many prisoners being taken.' Barney and his 400 seamen put up a gallant resistance, but they were too few to affect the issue; they were quickly surrounded and forced to surrender, and the same evening Ross was in Washington. In reprisals for the burning of Toronto in 1813 the British proceeded to fire the White House, the Capitol, the Treasury, the War Department, and the office of the *National Intelligencer*. Looting and the destruction of private property were not allowed: an act of clemency which did not, however, meet with the approval of Cochrane, who complained to Ross, 'I am sorry you left a house standing in Washington—depend upon it, it is mistaken mercy'. Meanwhile a small force of cruisers under Commodore Gordon had advanced up the Potomac to within two miles of Washington and carried off a number of vessels laden with merchandise.

Shortly after the attack on Washington the British forces re-embarked in their transports and proceeded to their next objective, Baltimore.

This city, the third largest in the Republic, was situated on the banks of the Patapsco River, some twelve miles above Chesapeake Bay, with Fort McHenry, flanked by other defensive works, covering the water-approach. The London newspapers had long urged the Admiralty to extirpate this nest of privateers. The British expected to batter the place into submission. The Patapsco was too shallow for ships of the line. On 12 September the frigates, sloops, and bomb-vessels of Cochrane's squadron sailed up to the attack, while troops and seamen moved against the city by road.

Shortly before the bombardment, a local lawyer, Francis Scott Key, visited Cochrane in his flagship in an attempt to secure the release of a friend, Dr. Beanes, who had lately been captured by the British. Key was courteously treated, and his request was granted; but he was informed that his friend and he would have to remain with the squadron until the fighting was over. It thus happened that the two were eye-witnesses of the attack on Fort McHenry.

Away beyond the forest of masts and yards which covered the

Patapsco River were the low walls of the beleaguered fort, surmounted by a flag-staff from which floated a great flag. With their gaze fixed anxiously on the Stars and Stripes, Key and his friend awaited the outcome of the assault. At nightfall the flag itself, of course, was invisible; but the continuance of the bombardment was sufficient proof that the defenders still held out. Towards morning the uproar momentarily ceased; there was an ominous silence, and in the grip of suspense the two waited until, shortly before daybreak, the bombardment blazed up anew. At last it was seen that the city's defences were intact; the assault had failed; the range was too great, and the bombardment of Baltimore had failed in its object of turning the defenders' flank. The British were falling back to their ships; and in the first light of day the two Americans saw the great flag still floating defiantly over Fort McHenry. It was then, with swelling heart, that Key wrote down on the back of an old letter the famous lines with which his name will always be associated.

> O! say can you see by the dawn's early light,
> What so proudly we hailed at the twilight's last gleaming,
> Whose broad stripes and bright stars through the perilous fight,
> O'er the ramparts we watch'd, were so gallantly streaming?

Key's thoughts went back to those anxious hours of darkness when, though the flag itself was hidden from their view, '. . . the Rockets' red glare, the Bombs bursting in air, Gave proof through the night that our Flag was still there'; and he recalled the surge of sudden relief with which, in the half-light, they had beheld the Stars and Stripes waving over the ramparts across the water.

> Now it catches the gleam of the morning's first beam,
> In full glory reflected new shines in the stream:
> 'Tis the Star-spangled Banner, O! long may it wave
> O'er the land of the free and the home of the brave!

Though it was unknown to Key and his contemporaries, the war which was welding the people of the United States into a nation had also given them a national anthem. One thing, however, was certain: Baltimore was saved. General Ross had been killed and the British were in full retreat. The attempt on the great commercial centre and privateering base was abandoned. During the ensuing months Cockburn continued his operations in the Chesapeake, while Cochrane, with the main body of the fleet and the army, moved round to the mouth of the Mississippi.

Throughout the summer of 1814 the British forces had also harassed the coasts of New England and occupied part of the District of Maine. Later Cockburn led a division southward to assail the coast of the Carolinas and early in 1815 extended these operations to Georgia. Nor was an element of *schrecklichkeit*, or 'frightfulness', by any means absent from the British calculations. Apparently the whole idea was to bring the war home to the consciousness of the American people. 'I am fully convinced', Captain Codrington declared, 'that this is the true way to end this Yankee war, whatever may be said in Parliament against it.' By this time, indeed, the whole eastern seaboard of the United States was more or less in a constant state of alarm; as a result of which the national economy suffered incalculably more indirect loss than even the direct injury sustained. 'The Government has declared war against the most powerful maritime nation,' summed up the Governor of Massachusetts, 'and we are disappointed in our expectations of national defence.'

During the autumn of 1814 the *United States, Macedonian*, and *President* were blockaded at Bristol, Rhode Island, by no less than three 74s, four frigates, and three sloops.

Meanwhile for several months past Hayes in the *Majestic*, a *razée* 74, together with a few cruisers, had been blockading Boston, where the *Constitution* was now ready for sea. In December came a succession of northerly gales with squally weather and occasional snow. On the 17th one of these gales gave Stewart his opportunity. The blockading force had lately quitted the coast, leaving the roads virtually unwatched. Acclaimed by the crowds assembled on the quay, the *Constitution* stood down Boston harbour with a fresh north-westerly breeze. It was cold and overcast, and presently it began to snow. 'At 4.30 passed the lighthouse in safety,' recorded Stewart, '. . . and made sail for sea; no ships or cruisers in sight.' Once again the *Constitution* got away to sea and fought her last successful action a few weeks afterwards when she successively captured the *Cyane*, a small frigate, and the *Levant* sloop off the Madeira Islands.

Shortly after, Hayes was appointed to command the division stationed off New York to prevent the escape of Decatur and his squadron. Repeatedly blown off the coast by winter gales, it was his invariable practice, as soon as the weather moderated, to place his force on that point of bearing from the Hook he judged likely, in the existing circumstances, would be the enemy's track. On New Year's Eve, 1814, the *President* was still in New York Bay, awaiting a chance to sail. On the evening of 13 January Hayes's ships were blown off the shore in a severe snow-storm. On the next day the weather moderated; but, with the wind blowing fresh from the W.N.W., his squadron could not get in with the Hook. Hayes, therefore, as before, steered to intercept the enemy on the track he expected them to take. Just before daylight Decatur's force, comprising the *President* and a merchant brig which was to act as a supply ship, was seen standing down the coast of Long Island. Headed by the *Endymion* frigate, Hayes's force chased the enemy throughout the day, each side employing every resource of seamanship to outsail the other. From time to time the *Endymion* yawed and flung a broadside into the *President*; which, for fear of being overhauled, dared not delay long enough to turn her broadside towards her assailant. By the late afternoon the *Endymion* had crept up on the starboard quarter of the *President*, within point-blank range. Then, as the two ships stood to the southward on parallel courses, the *President*'s fire stripped the *Endymion*'s sails from her yards. Decatur's one hope was to beat the *Endymion* out of the fight before the other British vessels could get up, and then to escape under cover of darkness. The battered *Endymion* was finally obliged to fall astern; but some hours afterwards the *Pomone* and *Tenedos*, overhauling the *President*, forced her to strike.[1] The merchant brig, through her superior sailing, managed to escape.

A week after Decatur's abortive attempt to run the blockade out of New York harbour, the sloops *Peacock* and *Hornet* made the same attempt, with better fortune. On 20 January the strong north-east winds freshened to a gale, with snow. The two sloops immediately put to sea and passed the bar by daylight under storm-canvas—'at which time,' Hotham reported to Cochrane, 'His Majesty's ships stationed off Sandy Hook were unable to keep in with the land.'[2] A few days afterwards the two vessels parted company, intending to rendezvous at the remote island of Tristan da Cunha in the South Atlantic.

The *Hornet*, arriving first on the rendezvous, almost immediately

[1] Adm. 1/508, 17 January 1815; 51/2543, 13–15 January 1815.
[2] Adm. 1/508, 12 February 1815.

encountered the British sloop *Penguin*. The two vessels hauled to the wind on parallel courses; and after a brisk running fight, which lasted little more than fifteen minutes and in the course of which the *Hornet*'s gunnery showed itself markedly superior, the *Penguin* endeavoured to board, her bowsprit becoming entangled in her opponent's rigging: but, failing in the attempt, dragged herself clear with the loss of her foremast and bowsprit. Thus hopelessly crippled, with heavy casualties, the *Penguin* surrendered, and was later scuttled by her captor. It was the last naval combat of the war.

With the arrival of strong reinforcements from Europe it was the turn of the British to assume the offensive on the Canadian frontier. In view of the existing American preponderance on Lakes Erie and Ontario it was decided to stage an attack to the eastward on Lake Champlain, which now became the crucial theatre of the war on the northern frontier. Since the naval control of these waters would enable the invaders to draw their supplies from the St. Lawrence, it was essential to the success of the whole enterprise. The respective commanders of the British and American squadrons on Lake Champlain were Captain Downie and Captain Thomas Macdonough.

As on the other lakes, a feverish shipbuilding race ensued. On the American side the strongest ship was the 26-gun *Saratoga*, whose possession for the time being gave the United States commander the uncontested control of Lake Champlain. From the British standpoint everything depended on the completion of the 37-gun ship *Confiance*, which was launched on 25 August 1814 and went into action, barely finished, less than three weeks later.

On 31 August a British army of 11,000 men, under the command of Sir George Prevost, who was also Governor of Canada, began its advance down the west bank of the lake. At Plattsburg the line of march was blocked by a small American force entrenched behind the River Saranac overlooking Plattsburg Bay, where Macdonough's squadron was lying within long gunshot of the shore batteries awaiting the British attack.

The American squadron could not have remained there if Prevost's army had stormed the works and captured the batteries. Had this been done, Macdonough would have been driven from his anchorage to the open lake, where the long-range guns of the *Confiance* could have been used to full advantage. As the British Commander-in-Chief on the

Lakes Station, Sir James Yeo, later declared: 'There was not the least necessity for our squadron giving the enemy such decided advantages by going into their bay to engage them. . . . Had our troops taken their batteries first, it would have obliged the enemy's squadron to quit the bay and given ours a fair chance.'

As it was, imbued with much the same ignorance of the realities of naval warfare that Wellington had lately revealed in the Peninsula, Prevost on 11 September goaded Downie into a hazardous attack on an enemy moored in a strong defensive position where the superior fire-power of the *Confiance* would necessarily be sacrificed. These circumstances, combined with a sudden shift of the wind and the inspired and skilful leadership of the American commander, more than neutralized the material superiority of the British force. Once again the deadly American carronade fire decided the issue. Downie fell, mortally wounded, at the outset of the fight. In the bloody and destructive action that followed the British squadron was heavily defeated. With her rigging shattered, her sails torn to ribbons, her hull riddled with shot, her hold fast filling with water, and three-quarters of her people killed or wounded, the sole surviving lieutenant in the *Confiance* hauled down his colours; whereupon the British resistance collapsed. As a result of this defeat, the greatly superior army of Peninsular veterans led by Prevost immediately abandoned their attempt to invade the United States and retired into Canada.

The action of Plattsburg proved decisive in the war. The American squadrons were now in complete control of the Great Lakes, and a British invasion of the United States from Canada was clearly impossible.

The attempt on New Orleans was the last major effort undertaken by the British in the war. The expeditionary force, which was based on Jamaica, was strengthened by fresh drafts from home, totalling eventually about 10,000 regular troops, under the command of Major-General Sir Edward Pakenham, brother-in-law of the Duke of Wellington. To defend New Orleans the American general, Andrew Jackson, had only 5,000 men, of whom three-quarters were militia. These troops established themselves in entrenchments about five miles south of the city, between the river and a great morass.

The struggle for New Orleans comprised four separate engagements spread over a period of seventeen days. The first action took place on

23 December, when Jackson stopped a surprise march on the city with cannon and musketry. Five days later the British renewed the attack: but they were caught between the frontal fire from the American entrenchments and the oblique fire from the armed schooner *Louisiana* moored in the river and obliged to retire, while a force which was successfully flanking the American left was recalled by Pakenham following the repulse of the main frontal assault. After the action of the 28th, Jackson extended his left flank, which rested on a swamp, by an outwork of improvised rafts manned by tough Tennesseans. For their part the British threw up entrenchments and brought up siege guns. In a fierce artillery duel fought on 1 January 1815 the British were once more worsted and retired with the loss of several of their heavy guns.

The final and decisive engagement took place on the 8th. Early in the morning Pakenham imprudently launched a direct frontal assault of 5,300 troops in close column formation against Jackson's 3,500 protected by a canal and high mud breastworks strengthened by sugar barrels. Having neither ladders nor fascines, the British hurled themselves against the enemy's entrenchments in vain. They were mown down first by his artillery and later at point-blank range by the Americans firing from behind their defences. Meanwhile a flank attack by a smaller British force on the west side of the river had come within an ace of success. The American right flank was pushed back and their artillery captured. But the attack was not made in sufficient strength or in time. The result was that, on the failure of the main assault on the east side of the river, a general retirement was ordered; and the flanking operation was called off before its success could be exploited. Pakenham and two of his subordinate generals had been killed in the fighting; altogether the British sustained 2,600 casualties —killed, wounded, or captured: the Americans had only eight men killed and thirteen wounded.

In the course of 1814 American commerce, with certain important exceptions already mentioned, had practically ceased to exist. American exports, which in the last year of unrestricted trade had amounted to $108 millions, declined, in 1814, to barely $7 millions. Shipbuilding was at a standstill. The once flourishing mercantile and maritime interests of the United States were faced with imminent ruin. In one part of the country there was an absolute dearth of produce which in another part was just a drug on the market. The price of flour was nearly three times as much in Boston as in Richmond, and rice was four times as much in Philadelphia as in Charleston. The distress was widespread throughout the land. The merchant had lost all his trade, and could no longer employ his former work-people. The farmer raised crops which he could not sell. In not a few parts of the country shipowners, shipbuilders, merchants, and agents, together with those engaged in ancillary occupations, had been reduced to penury.

Peace negotiations had long been in progress, and the war was nearing its close. It had in fact become very unpopular in Great Britain—not least because of the heavy taxation it entailed (Castlereagh himself had referred to the financial situation of this country as 'perfectly without precedent in our financial history'). British seaborne trade continued to suffer severely from the depredations of the American privateers, and British merchants and industrialists did not cease to lament the loss of the lucrative American market. Moreover, both government and nation had been disappointed in their expectation of an easy victory in 1814. 'We are convinced', observed the *Tradesman* severely, 'that with the naval force which we now possess on the American station, the puny Navy of the Americans ought by this time to have been annihilated.' Though the defenders of Washington had bolted at the first encounter and their capital had been set on fire the news was quickly followed by that of the British repulse before Baltimore and of Macdonough's fine achievement on Lake Champlain necessitating Prevost's retreat across the border.

In their reluctance to end the war without securing a strategic frontier for Canada, the British government had thoughts of sending out Wellington to restore the situation; and they presently sounded him as to the prospects of a successful offensive. The Duke's reply was characteristically prompt and uncompromising: 'That what apears to me to be wanting in America is not a general . . . but a naval superiority on the lakes'.[1] This, it appeared, they could not hope to achieve; and a settlement on the basis of the *status quo ante bellum*, which had been sustained all along by the American commissioners, was at last reluctantly accepted by the British. In the event the lack of a strategic frontier was to prove of little consequence; for the threat to Canada never recurred. It is worth noticing that the original causes of the war,

[1] *Wellington's Dispatches*, XII, p. 224; *Supplementary Dispatches*, I, p. 426, IX, p. 438.

namely, neutral rights and the impressment issue, were not even mentioned in the treaty signed at Ghent on 24 December 1814. It was weeks, and even months, before the restoration of peace could become known in the various theatres of the war. The final repulse of the British before New Orleans took place a fortnight after the conclusion of the peace treaty. Fighting was still going on in the more distant seas for a much longer period.

CHAPTER

XVII

The Hundred Days

I

The wave of prosperity which had characterized most of 1813 was carried over into the following year. Such was the huge demand for both British manufactures and colonial produce that, despite the prevailing high level of prices, the flood of foreign orders showed no sign of abating. 'Never did a year close with more brilliant successes than the *last*', the *Manchester Mercury* recorded in January, 'or a year open with brighter prospects than the *present.—*England is about to reap the proud and glorious harvest of her unexampled toils.' 'The trade of Manchester in all its branches', declared the *Tradesman* about the same time, 'has attained a briskness which rivals the best days in good old times.' In London, Thames Street and various other riverside thoroughfares were almost choked with the endless trains of carts and wagons laden with goods destined for shipment to the Dutch ports. At Liverpool, there were almost daily arrivals of shipping from the United States. The warehouses which during the worst times of the Continental Blockade had been filled to overflowing with goods for which there was no outlet were now rapidly emptying. There was full employment and rising wages in most of the manufacturing areas.

With the cessation of hostilities in Europe there was a substantial reduction in the strength of the Navy. During the ensuing months ship after ship returned home and was duly paid off (many of these vessels being either sold or broken up, while others were laid up in the Tamar and other backwaters). One after another the Admirals struck their flags and came ashore. Throughout that summer large numbers of seamen and marines were given their discharge, beginning with those who were already in the Service prior to the outbreak of war in 1803. Money flowed freely in Portsmouth and the other great naval ports in those days. July witnessed what must have been the most successful Free

Mart Fair on record. Elsewhere the rejoicings at the peace, though quieter and more decorous, were no less heartfelt. Families were reunited after long years of separation. While such scenes were yet fresh in her memory, Jane Austen in *Persuasion* wrote a lively account of Captain Harville comfortably settled with his family at Lyme, and of some officers on a visit to Bath forming 'a little knot of the Navy' whenever a few of them chanced to meet in the streets.

Meanwhile, throughout the country a winter which had witnessed heavy snowfalls and frosts unprecedented in living memory (in January the Thames was frozen over, and a great 'Frost Fair' was staged between Blackfriars and Westminster, with booths, swings, skittles, and dancing on the ice) was succeeded by a glorious spring.

The rejoicings and illuminations which had followed upon the news of Napoleon's abdication were renewed a few weeks later. From the first week of May, a continuous stream of distinguished visitors from all parts of Europe began to arrive in London; and the tempo of life quickened. The weather was unusually fine, and almost every day there was free entertainment for all in the streets and public places. The Tsar's sister, the Grand Duchess of Oldenburg, had been over here for some time, and was being made much of by the populace. Parties of foreign officers were loudly cheered whenever they appeared—foreigners, in fact, had seldom been so popular in the metropolis. The London season was one of exceptional brilliance. Vauxhall was thronged, Almack's at the height of its glory. In the afternoon the Park was crowded with men, women, and children of all classes to see, usually between three and four o'clock, the grand cavalcade of carriages, curricles, phaetons, and four-in-hands, accompanied by large numbers of gentlemen on horseback, that had become such a feature of the season. By night the drawing-rooms of the great houses resounded to the strains of gay country dances and the new lilting waltz measure. There were concerts, card-parties, levées, assemblies, *conversazioni*, suppers, and balloon ascents, even, in apparently endless succession.

Next month the Tsar and the King of Prussia were to visit England. 'Never, indeed,' observed the *Hampshire Telegraph*, 'did the whole face of the country present a more impressive representation of national joy than at the present moment. The arrival of the Emperor and the King will form an era in our history.'

The Allied Sovereigns crossed from Buologne in the *Impregnable* on

6 June and next day arrived in London. For several nights the metropolis was illuminated with fairy lamps and transparencies. The multitudes thronging the streets proffered a boisterous but good-humoured welcome to the 'illustrious visitants'. The singing and cheering continued far into the night. There followed three weeks of continuous junketings and festivities. The Allied Sovereigns drove down to the Ascot races, attended the Opera, rode in Hyde Park, danced at Almack's, visited Oxford (where they received honorary degrees), banquetted at the Guildhall, and inspected the Bank, the British Museum, the Docks, Westminster Abbey, and St. Paul's. On 21 June a sumptuous fête was given in their honour by White's Club at Burlington House. Among the crowd of 'fashionables' who graced the occasion was the irrepressible Betsey Fremantle, who, with her husband and daughters, had come up from the country to view the illuminations, and wrote the following account of the fête.

> We went early and got in without the smallest difficulty, the courtyard of Burlington House was most splendidly illuminated and had a beautiful effect. The rooms were brilliant, and looked like a Fairy Palace. Great numbers of people were there when we came in, all the men in full dress Uniforms and the Ladies in plumes, and most rich dresses. The Emperor of Russia with the Duchess of Oldenburg, King of Prussia and all arrived at ten o'clock, I was close to them when they first walked round the Ball room and saw them very plain, they afterwards mix'd in the Crowd and Alexander danc'd the whole evening and flirted with his partners. . . . I stayed till seven o'clock in the morng. and met almost every body I know in London, Fremantle got tired and went home an hour before us. Old Blücher is a delight![1]

The tough old Prussian was the idol of the citizenry. On his arrival in the capital, a wildly excited mob seized the shafts of his carriage and hauled it bodily into Carlton House. On his visit to the Admiralty (where he showed particular interest in the working of the manual telegraph), the courtyard was so thronged with spectators that when he came out again, attended by the First Lord, it was some time before a way could be cleared for his coach. When he appeared at the Opera there was such an ovation that the performance had to be suspended.

Towards the end of their stay in this country the Allied Sovereigns expressed a desire to visit Portsmouth. Their wish was gladly granted. 'It was natural to expect', *The Times* observed, 'that before they left this

[1] *The Wynne Diaries*, ed. A. Fremantle, III, p. 372.

land they would come down to Portsmouth, and see something of that great national arsenal and harbour, where, in a main degree, have been formed, and whence have issued those tremendous armaments which have swept from the face, or sunk to the bottom of the ocean, the hostile fleets of contending nations, and consecrated to Britain the domination of the seas.'

The Prince Regent and the entire Board of Admiralty thereupon repaired to Portsmouth, which was crowded as never before in its history. Visitors flocked into the town, not only from the metropolis, but also from the western counties, so that it held, it was stated, more than treble its normal population. The streets were gaily decorated with flags and other patriotic emblems and resounded with the pealing of bells. For two days little or no business was done in the town; the principal shops were all shut (outside one of them was exhibited the inscription, *Not dead, but gone to Spithead*); on both nights Portsmouth and Gosport were brilliantly illuminated, with transparencies and other decorations; lodgings were only to be had at astronomical prices; many folk travelled miles for a bed, and hundreds slept on the ground; the crowds in the High Street and on the Parade were tremendous.

The first day of the review, the 23rd, was a radiant June day. Cruising in the Solent were innumerable vessels and boats crowded with holiday-makers. The sea was smooth and sparkling in the sunshine. The long lines of warships, comprising more than fifty sail, stood out against the background of green hills and woodlands of the Isle of Wight. Among the fifteen line-of-battle ships were many first-rates and with them proud trophies of the late war, like the *Tigre, San Domingo*, and *Norge*. The ramparts where the inhabitants of Portsmouth were accustomed to take their ease on a fine summer evening were thronged with spectators. Southsea Common and all the beaches from Fort Monckton as far as Blockhouse Point were covered with immense crowds of men, women, and children. 'All seemed to exult with just satisfaction and patriotic joy at a view not more magnificent as a picture', *The Times* remarked, 'than honour and glory to the great nation which alone could present it.'

The proceedings opened with a grand procession of barges, headed by the Royal Barge bearing the standard of the Prince Regent, followed on either quarter by the barges of the Russian Emperor and the King of Prussia, flying their national colours, and rowed by George III's watermen. As the barges moved down the lines the yards were manned and each vessel fired a royal salute of twenty-one guns. It was a lively and inspiriting scene, with the hearty cheering of the ships' companies and the spectators in the surrounding boats mingling with the recurrent roar of the cannon. The barges proceeded all along the line and then turned back again and came alongside the flagship *Impregnable*, where the Duke of Clarence was waiting to receive them. The Tsar and his sister presently sampled the grog, and the ship's company were granted a double tot. The distinguished visitors proceeded to explore the ship, each as he or she pleased; and later there was a banquet at which the honours were done by Rear-Admiral Sir Henry Blackwood as Captain of the Fleet. 'The dinner party', the *Naval Chronicle* recorded, 'consisted of some of the most gallant defenders of their country by sea and land, and every delicacy of the season was on the table.'

Next morning, the 24th, the Allied Sovereigns visited the dockyard, and afterwards went on board the Royal yacht to view the manœuvres. After receiving their Majesties with a general salute, the whole squadron slipped their cables and stood out to sea with a fresh north-easterly wind; off St. Helens the Prince Regent and the King of Prussia repaired on board the *Impregnable* again. Out in the Channel the squadron, now under full sail, performed a series of evolutions by signal 'with amazing accuracy'. At 4 o'clock, when about five leagues from the anchorage, the squadron tacked and worked back again to Spithead, where it arrived three hours or so later.

From Portsmouth the Allied Sovereigns, escorted by a troop of cavalry, made a leisurely journey to Dover, after a brief sojourn at Hastings where there was much hand-shaking with the local peasantry and largesse of cakes and sweets to their children. On the 27th they crossed the Channel.

The climax of the national rejoicings was the jubilee celebration on 1 August to mark the centenary of the Hanoverian succession. The Royal Parks were thrown open to the public for the occasion. The crowds strolled about the lawns and patronized the beer booths. In the Green Park there was a lively representation of the siege of Badajos, and another on the Serpentine of the battle of the Nile. Sadler, the celebrated aeronaut, sailed away in his balloon into the empyrean to the rousing strains of 'The White Cockade'. 'For many hours', observed the *Morning Post*, 'all the streets leading to the Parks presented but one unbroken crowd.' The Green Park was ablaze with Roman candles, catherine-wheels, flower-pots, serpents, and rockets, while away in Kensington Gardens there was a yet more imposing display. 'Never', ended the *Morning Post* in retrospect, 'was any entertainment announced which raised public expectation so high, and never was expectation raised so high to be consummately gratified.'

Meanwhile, all over the country there were bands, processions, concerts, balls, bonfires, fireworks, cricket matches, entertainments for the poor, market towns bedecked with flags and foliage, ringing of church-bells, Maypoles, and dancing on the green. Not since the Year of Victories, 'the Great Fifty-nine', had there been such widespread revelry and rejoicing.

2

In September the centre of interest shifted to Vienna, where the delegates had begun to assemble for the Congress. Already the press was devoting long and anxious columns to the momentous proceedings which were to fix the frontiers of the nations for generations to come.

Alone among the Powers, Great Britain had secured her vital interests in advance of the general settlement. In November 1813, following the expulsion of the French from Holland, Castlereagh had sent 6,000 men under Sir Thomas Graham to the Scheldt. But for the firmness of the British Cabinet in general and of Castlereagh in particular France would certainly have secured her 'natural frontiers' at the peace. On this vital issue there could be no giving way. During the Christmas of 1813 the Cabinet met no less than three times (one of them on Christmas Day itself) to consider the instructions which were to guide the British plenipotentiary. 'The absolute exclusion of France from any Naval establishment on the Scheldt, and especially at Antwerp', and 'the restoration to Holland of her territory of 1792' were laid down as the indispensable conditions of their restitution to their former owners of colonial territories taken by Great Britain during the war. Ministers were agreed that Antwerp in the hands of France would be an abiding threat to England. Of all the ports of the Netherlands, it presented the most likely possibilities for sudden and swift attack. 'I must particularly entreat you', Castlereagh urged Aberdeen on 23 November 1813, 'to keep your attention upon Antwerp. The destruction of that arsenal is essential to our safety. To leave it in the hands of France is little short of imposing upon Great Britain the charge of a perpetual war establishment. After all we have done for the Continent in this war, they owe it to us and to themselves to extinguish this fruitful source of damage to us both.'[1] Wellington was similarly of opinion that Napoleon should not be left in possession of a great naval arsenal on the Scheldt.

The British Government had displayed similar firmness as regards maritime rights. Throughout the war the claims advanced by various neutrals had threatened to sap the foundations of British naval power and had been strongly and successfully resisted. At the peace negotiations the government no less effectively withstood any encroachment on our belligerent rights at sea. 'Great Britain may be driven out of a Congress', Castlereagh declared, 'but not out of her maritime rights; and if the Continental Powers know their business, they will not hazard this.' Later Lord Aberdeen assured the French plenipotentiary that 'no possible consideration could induce Great Britain to abandon a particle of what she felt to belong to the maritime Code, from which in no case would she ever recede.'[2] Finally Castlereagh got this vital issue expressly excluded from the matters to be discussed at the Congress.

That autumn Vienna was thronged with sovereigns and delegates from every State in Europe. Besides the Emperor Francis 1 and his chancellor, Prince Metternich, there were the Tsar and the King of Prussia, the Kings of Denmark, Bavaria, and Würtemberg, Castlereagh, Wellington, and Talleyrand, and an enormous multitude of courtiers, secretaries, couriers, and ladies of all degrees.

Day after day the Prater was filled with a brilliant throng driving, riding, and sauntering in the genial autumn sunshine. Along the principal avenue, which ran between double rows of horse-chestnuts, there was an unbroken line of carriages extending for a mile or more. The infinite variety of uniforms and ladies' gowns presented a dazzling kaleidoscope of colour and movement. In the Imperial palace and in the great houses of the Austrian aristocracy there was almost continual

[1] *Memoirs and Correspondence of Viscount Castlereagh*, IX, p. 73. 'Antwerp and Flushing out of the hands of France are worth twenty Martiniques in our own hands'—Harrowby to Bathurst, 19 January 1814 (H.M.C., *Bathurst Papers*, p. 260).

[2] *Memoirs ... of Viscount Castlereagh*, pp. 30, 34.

music and dancing. The crystal and gold plate gleamed and glittered in the light of thousands of candles. The ballrooms and galleries were transformed by countless bowls and baskets of flowers into gardens of enchantment. Fête succeeded fête. Every day brought its round of pleasures—balls, banquets, masques, and receptions. After the long winter of their discontent the aristocracies of Europe made joyous holiday. Even Metternich, it is said, occasionally subordinated business to pleasure. 'Le Congres ne marche pas,' the Prince de Ligne commented cynically, 'mais il danse.'

Nevertheless, behind the scenes a great deal of hard work was being done. The negotiators soon ran into difficulties. All this outward appearance of gaiety and splendour concealed a maelstrom of conflicting interests. The range as well as the complexity of the issues to be resolved for long defied solution. There was incessant quarrelling and manœuvring for position between the rival groups. The fate of France lay mainly in the hands of the four Powers—Great Britain, Russia, Prussia, and Austria—which had overthrown her. The Tsar wanted all Poland. The King of Prussia demanded the whole of Saxony. Neither got all they wanted. The visit of the Russian and Prussian sovereigns to this country failed to break the deadlock over the points at issue. Relations between the principal Powers steadily deteriorated. In the autumn the reverses to our arms in America had an adverse effect on British prestige at the Congress. A secret compact was formed between Great Britain, Austria, and France to resist the demands of the eastern Powers. Towards the end of 1814 there was even danger of war.

The festivities continued, with little interruption, until the early days of March. While the fate of Poland and Saxony was hanging in the balance, the sleighs glided merrily through the snow-bound streets of Vienna, bound for some ball or masque. The snows at last dispersed; the days grew warmer, and once more the lines of carriages rolled slowly down the grand avenue of the Prater. Then came the bombshell.

The news of Napoleon's landing at Cannes arrived in the middle of a great ball given by Metternich. The effect was electrifying. Though the orchestra continued playing, the waltz was abruptly broken off; hurriedly the dancers began to leave, and the alarm spread like wildfire throughout Vienna.

'Congress is dissolved!' Napoleon is reported to have declared, on setting foot once more on the soil of France.

3

During all this time Napoleon had been well aware of the dissensions prevailing at the Congress and also of the growing unrest in France. His escape from Elba through the cordon of Allied cruisers was marked by the same audacity which had characterized his expedition to Egypt. He found on landing that he had not mistaken the temper of the French people. He was accompanied on his way by cheering peasant throngs; the gates of cities were flung open at his approach, and entire regiments came over to his side. So great was the magic of his name that in nineteen days he marched from the Mediterranean to Paris without a shot fired.

Once back in Paris, Napoleon prepared to fight for his throne. There was no lack of soldiers in France—veterans lately returned in their thousands from German fortresses and from foreign prisons. But there was a serious scarcity of *matériel*, and the problem of competent subordinate commanders was never really solved; in the ensuing campaign the ardour and devotion of the rank and file did not make up for a defective staff.

At the news that their arch-enemy was heading for Paris, the quarrels of the allies in Vienna were composed as if by magic; they closed their ranks and made common cause against Napoleon, whom they pronounced an outlaw. Wellington recommended the immediate dispatch of an army to the Netherlands; a heterogeneous force was assembled, composed of large numbers of Germans, Dutch, and Belgians in addition to the British contingent; and, within a few weeks of Napoleon's return to France, the Duke established his headquarters in Brussels.

Napoleon's most pressing problem, therefore, was the impending Anglo-Prussian offensive. If he was to save his throne he must strike hard and immediately at the enemies assembling on his north-east frontier within a few days' march of Paris. He determined to seize the initiative, enter Belgium and destroy in turn the British and Prussians before they could unite their forces. He had under his command a well-armed and fully equipped army of 125,000 men—a larger force than either the British or the Prussians singly, but much inferior to them if they were able to combine. So suddenly and rapidly did the French army advance into Belgium that Wellington was taken by surprise. Before nightfall on the first day of the campaign Napoleon drove his army like a wedge between the Anglo-Dutch and Prussian forces.

He had divided his army into two wings: the right under Grouchy, and the left under Ney; while the Guard, which formed the reserve, he kept under his immediate control. On the 16th, sending Ney to contain the British at Quatre Bras, he flung the main body of his army on the Prussians at Ligny. His aim was to annihilate two-thirds of Blücher's army and to force the other third to retire upon Liège and away from Wellington. But Ney failed him, with the result that though Blücher was defeated he was not destroyed, nor was he cut off from his reserves; and the action at Quatre Bras ended in a draw. Napoleon sent Grouchy with 33,000 men to pursue Blücher; but on the 17th Grouchy permitted the Prussians to retire unmolested, so that they were able to reorganize their forces and to take the field once again; and on the next day he similarly failed to prevent Blücher from coming to Wellington's assistance.

In the early morning of the 17th, Wellington with most of his army was still at Quatre Bras. On hearing of Blücher's defeat and withdrawal, Wellington decided that he must retire also. Though ordered to attack the enemy, Ney remained inactive. Later in the morning, covered by a screen of cavalry, Wellington's troops began to retire. Too late Napoleon, arriving on the scene with the Guard, drove his forces forward in headlong pursuit. Ney's inactivity and a sudden violent thunderstorm saved the situation for Wellington, who was able to take up a strong position on the plateau south of Waterloo behind a low ridge fronted by a château named Hougomont and La Haye Sainte farm, where he meant to hold Napoleon until Blücher should arrive to his assistance.

Napoleon's plan on the 18th was first to breach the enemy's centre, and then to follow up the penetration. He seems to have been possessed of the *idée fixe* that at Ligny the Prussians had been knocked out once and for all and that it would now be possible to finish off Wellington at a single stroke. Yet, before action had been fairly joined, dark masses of troops could be descried in the distance, emerging from the woods to the eastward. It was the advance guard of the Prussian army.

Shortly after 1 p.m. Ney's two army corps advanced up the grassy slopes against Wellington's centre. The Duke's troops formed squares and beat them off; the attack failed, and the two corps were forced back by two British cavalry brigades. Later in the afternoon the attack was renewed, approximately forty squadrons of heavy cavalry being launched against Wellington's centre; an hour or so later another forty squadrons were thrown into the assault, and the whole plateau was flooded with cavalry. Had these great cavalry charges only been supported by artillery and infantry, success would have been assured to him. As it was, Ney's assault wholly failed to break the British squares.

At 6 p.m., ordered by Napoleon to take La Haye Sainte *coute qui coute*, Ney captured the farm and the neighbouring sand-hill with the remnants of d'Erlon's corps. He immediately followed up this success by bringing up a battery and next ordering forward his cavalry. This was the supreme crisis of the action. Wellington's position was almost desperate. His entire centre was in danger of cracking, his troops were exhausted, and his reserves inadequate. Finding his strength insufficient, Ney sent to Napoleon for reinforcements. The growing pressure of Blücher's army, however, prevented the Emperor from throwing in his reserve: he had already dispatched most of the Guard to secure his rear against the Prussian attack. The decisive moment passed and the French were forced back off the plateau.

Just before sunset, the French advanced to the attack all along the line. It was a last desperate throw. This time the Guard were launched against the Duke's centre. The British line held, and the assault was repulsed. Then, as the Guard recoiled, the whole French front gave way; and Wellington made the signal for a general advance. Headed by the hussars and dragoons, 40,000 troops moved purposefully down the slope. With Napoleon in their midst, the Guard slowly fell back, fighting with superb discipline, cleaving a way through the serried ranks of their foes. Elsewhere the French troops broke and fled in all directions. The Prussians pursued the fugitives throughout the night. A few days after Waterloo Napoleon abdicated—the Hundred Days was at an end.

For a while he lingered at Malmaison. Then, on the 28th, he left for Brittany, with the intention of sailing to America in one of the two frigates, placed at his disposal by the Minister of the Marine, then lying off La Rochelle. With increasing urgency the provisional government in Paris warned him to depart: but the wind hung westerly and foul, and every channel off the mouth of the Charente was watched by a British warship. From the Bourbons he could expect no mercy, and Blücher would have had him shot. In the end Napoleon made up his mind to surrender to the British, 'the most formidable, the most constant, and the most generous of my foes'.

4

Immediately after Napoleon's escape from Elba, Keith had been ordered to resume command of the Channel squadron. His subordinate admirals were Sir John Duckworth, Sir Benjamin Hallowell, and Sir Henry Hotham—the last of whom had so distinguished himself, when in command of the *Northumberland*, off Aix, in the spring of 1812. By the first week of July, at least thirty men-of-war were on their station between Ushant and Cape Finisterre. Once again their crews were gazing on the shores familiar to generations of British tars. These dispositions in the spring and summer of 1815 marked the final phase of that patient vigil off the enemy's ports which the Channel fleet had sustained for so many years.

'I am sending out all I have to look for Bonny if he takes to the sea,' Keith informed his wife. It was no easy task to prevent a swift vessel from secretly slipping away to sea; and it was mainly due to Hotham's intimate knowledge of the Brittany coast that Napoleon's plan of escape was effectively foiled. He now ordered Captain Frederick Maitland of the *Bellerophon* to keep a vigilant watch on the two frigates at Aix which were observed to be preparing for sea. Convinced by this time that escape was impossible, Napoleon on 14 July got into touch with Maitland, who presently dispatched his first lieutenant to fetch him in his barge.

On board the *Bellerophon*, the final preparations had been made and the atmosphere was tense with excitement. A general's guard of honour was ordered aft on the quarter-deck. The boatswain stood, whistle in hand, ready to do the honours of the side; the lieutenants were grouped on the quarter-deck, with the midshipmen behind them. Presently the barge approached and ranged alongside the *Bellerophon*; and the captain, who all this time had been on tenterhooks lest at the

496

last his prize should escape him, anxiously inquired of the first lieutenant as he came up the side:

'Have you got him?'

'Yes', was the curt response.

Preceded by General Bertrand, the Emperor thereupon came up the ship's side and stood there, 'a remarkably strong, well-built man', in his familiar olive-coloured great coat, cocked hat, and plain green uniform of the Chasseur Guards, before the assembled British officers; then, pulling off his hat, he said firmly to Maitland, 'I am come to throw myself on the protection of your Prince and your laws.'[1]

It must surely have been one of the most dramatic moments in history when the greatest military genius of all time came face to face with the men who had beaten him. The old *Billy Ruffian* had been in the thick of the fighting on the Glorious First, in Aboukir Bay, and at Trafalgar. Later, she had been employed in the arduous blockading service which finally set bounds to the hegemony of France. It was a far cry, indeed, from Nelson's victory in 1805 to Napoleon's surrender to that Fleet, to which—more than to any other single factor—he owed the final frustration of his vast designs; but the chain of causation runs clear and continuous from the cannonade of Trafalgar to this early morning arrival on board the *Bellerophon*.

Presently, with a slight bow to the officers, Napoleon accompanied Captain Maitland to his cabin. Afterwards the daily round continued as usual; and the ship's log recorded laconically—'At 7 received on board Napoleon Bonaparte, late Emperor of France, and his suite'.

The officers were then sent for, at Napoleon's request, and introduced to him. Shortly after, though warned by the captain that at this early hour he would find the men still scouring and furbishing, he expressed a desire to go round the ship. He accordingly went over all her decks, putting question after question to the captain, examining the sights of the guns (in which he seemed particularly interested), and inquiring about the weight of metal on the different decks. What struck him most, Maitland recorded, was the clean and neat appearance of the seamen. Next day, when the *Bellerophon* weighed anchor and made sail, he remained all the time by the break of the poop. The disciplined silence of a British man-of-war came as a revelation to Napoleon, who recollected all the chatter and excitement on board a

[1] Frederick Maitland, *The Surrender of Napoleon* (2nd ed., 1904), pp. 247-18.

French ship, where 'every one calls and gives orders, and they gabble like so many geese'.[1]

In accordance with his instructions, Maitland at once sailed for Torbay. The *Bellerophon* beat out of the Pertius d'Antioche and stood out to sea. A few days later, on Sunday, the 23rd, she passed close to Ushant. It was a fine clear day with a northerly wind—the *Bellerophon* was under royals; and Napoleon remained for hours on the poop. It was then that there occurred the incident that inspired Orchardson's famous painting, 'Napoleon on board the *Bellerophon*'; an incident which was to be recorded, many years later, by Midshipman Home.

> I shall never forget that morning we made Ushant. I had come on deck at four in the morning to take the morning watch, and the washing of decks had just begun, when, to my astonishment, I saw the Emperor come out of the cabin at that early hour, and make for the poop ladder. ... From the wetness of the decks, he was in danger of falling at every step, and I immediately stepped up to him, hat in hand, and tendered him my arm, which he laid hold of at once, smiling, and pointing to the poop, saying in broken English, 'the poop, the poop'; he ascended the poop-ladder leaning on my arm; and having gained the deck, he quitted his hold and mounted upon a gun-slide, nodding and smiling thanks, for my attention, and pointing to the land he said, 'Ushant, Cape Ushant'. I replied, 'Yes, sire', and withdrew. He then took out a pocket-glass and applied it to his eye, looking eagerly at the land. In this position he remained from five in the morning to nearly midday, without paying any attention to what was passing around him, or speaking to one of his suite, who had been standing behind him for several hours.[2]

Before they made the English coast, however, Napoleon had quite recovered his spirits; and, on opening Torbay, he showed himself much struck with the beauty of the shore, and exclaimed: 'What a beautiful bay! it very much resembles the bay of Porto Ferrajo, in Elba.'

The *Bellerophon* anchored off Brixham, and a boat was at once sent ashore with dispatches. The first lieutenant set out in a post-chaise to Keith at Plymouth, while the midshipman of the boat was carried off to tea at a neighbouring house by a party of young girls, who presently plied him with eager questions about the illustrious prisoner—'Were his hands and clothes all over blood when he came on board? Was his

[1] *Ibid.*, p. 95.
[2] *Ibid.*, pp. 249–50.

voice like thunder? Could I possibly get them a sight of the monster? etc. etc.'. No sooner had Napoleon's arrival become known in the neighbourhood than the ship was surrounded by a crowd of boats, and presents of fruit were sent on board. Maitland was presently confronted by applications from the local gentry for admittance into the ship; but his strict orders would by no means permit of these requests being granted—not even his own wife, it seemed, was to be allowed on board the *Bellerophon*. Early on the 28th the *Bellerophon* was ordered to leave Torbay for Plymouth, where Napoleon's presence instantly created a furore and gravely embarrassed the authorities. On Sunday, the 30th, it was estimated that about 1,000 boats were crowding around the *Bellerophon* and some 10,000 people were struggling to get a view of the almost legendary figure before whom the whole of Europe had trembled for nearly twenty years. When he showed himself on deck, the great man was enthusiastically cheered by his late enemies. The potent and indescribable charm by which Napoleon won the hearts of men immediately captivated the dour and taciturn Keith as it had already captivated the officers and men of the *Bellerophon*. 'D – n the fellow,' exclaimed the Admiral after their meeting, 'if he had obtained an interview with his Royal Highness [the Prince Regent], in half an hour they would have been the best friends in Europe.' When, on 7 August, Napoleon was transferred to the *Northumberland*, which was to carry him to his place of exile, there was scarcely a man on board the *Bellerophon* whose sympathies were not with the fallen Emperor.

5

In the definitive peace settlements of 1815, in accordance with Castlereagh's wise and generous policy of 'Security not revenge', the beaten foe was treated with magnanimity. The British government did not desire the destruction or dismemberment of France, but only a return to her former frontiers. This policy was favoured by Austria, who was apprehensive of the growing power of Russia and Prussia. Moreover, most of the colonies and ports of call taken by Great Britain during the war were restored to their former owners. Those which she retained at the peace were for the most part of strategic importance: they included Malta, which, during the last twelve years of the war, had proved an invaluable base for the Mediterranean squadron; the Cape, as essential for the sea-route to India; Mauritius, which as Castlereagh explained, was retained 'because in time of war it was a great maritime nuisance, highly detrimental to our commerce'; and also Trincomali, the finest natural harbour in the Indian Ocean. These bases served not only as naval depots but also, in the years to come, as important entrepôts for the rapidly expanding British commerce.

The restorations made by Great Britain were partly to avoid the reproach of monopolizing these desirable overseas territories to ourselves, but principally to secure a lasting peace. 'It is not our business to collect trophies,' Castlereagh observed, 'but to bring the world back to peaceful habits.' In his years of exile Napoleon expressed astonishment at the moderation of the British terms. 'Probably for a thousand years such another opportunity of aggrandizing England will not occur,' he declared. 'In the position of affairs nothing could have been refused to you.'

Throughout the brief remainder of his life Castlereagh concentrated all his energies on developing the Concert of Europe. After nearly twenty-five years of war, Europe was in desperate need of peace. Castlereagh knew that the restoration of the balance of power was essential to the security of the Continent, and consequently to the security of Great Britain. The efficacy of these measures is seen from the fact that for close on a century the general peace was not broken.

At the heart of the new order was a strong central Europe. Russia got most of Poland, but substantial parts of that ancient kingdom went to Austria and Prussia. In the face of the strong stand taken by Castlereagh, Metternich, and Talleyrand, Prussia abated her claims on Saxony and received in compensation extensive concessions on the left bank of the Rhine. Austria and Prussia were left strong enough to safeguard the settlements of 1814–15, and to serve as a check on Russia as well as on France. After Saxony had been disposed of, the solution of the remaining territorial problems was comparatively easy. Austria received Lombardy and Venice, and also recovered most of the Tyrol. Denmark lost Norway to Sweden. Naples was restored to the Sicilian Bourbons. Swedish Pomerania was ceded to Prussia. The Pope recovered the Papal States. Last but not least, the establishment between the Germanies and France of a kingdom uniting the northern and southern Netherlands, and buttressed by the expansion of Prussia in the Rhineland, marked the consummation of Great

Britain's historic policy in this vital region and the decisive defeat of that of France.

The gains made by Great Britain in the war and retained by her at the peace were almost entirely extra-European. At the conclusion of the long struggle her empire was vastly increased in area and its population more than trebled. The threat which had overhung her territories in the East and in the Americas was at last removed. The final settlement left Great Britain supreme in the eastern seas, and in unchallenged possession of India; the power of the Mahrattas was effectively broken, and the danger from France had disappeared. The United States' abortive attempt to conquer Canada during the war of 1812–15 was followed by a lasting peace between the two countries; and the long land frontier from the Great Lakes to the Pacific coast, as yet undefined, was left for the future undefended. Australia and New Zealand, both of which had been virtually unaffected by the Napoleonic War, were, together with Canada, destined to receive, in the second quarter of the nineteenth century, an immense accession of new emigrant strength from the mother country. With the vantage-points of Gibraltar, Malta, and Corfu in her hands, she was left in complete and exclusive possession of the Mediterranean.

Though this was far, indeed, from being his object, the aggrandizement of the British Empire was largely due to Napoleon and his aspirations for world supremacy. 'Great Britain has no greater obligations to any mortal on earth than to this ruffian,' Blücher's Chief of Staff, General von Gneisenau, had commented. 'For through the events which he has brought about, England's greatness, prosperity, and wealth have risen high. She is the mistress of the sea and neither in this dominion nor in world-trade has she now a single rival to fear.'[1]

Thus was Shelburne's vision of a new and more enduring British Empire, which was to succeed the old one lost at the peace negotations of 1783, finally realized. Through all the vicissitudes of the last few decades our country had retained its pre-eminence as a seafaring and trading power. Despite the trammels of the Continental System, the ever-spreading forests of masts and yards in the Thames, Tyne, Clyde, and Mersey gave testimony of the rapid and sustained expansion of British trade. Under the protection of her Fleet, Great Britain had been able to exploit to the full the opportunities offered by the new

[1] Q. Frischauer, *England's Year of Danger* (1938), pp. 316–17.

mechanical inventions and to profit by the convulsions which had disorganized the industry of the Continent: until, at the end of the war, she attained to her unique position as the great warehouse and manufactory of the world, without rival or second. By far the largest share of extra-European commerce was now in British hands. The bulk of the world's trade was carried in British bottoms: the ocean-going shipping on the British register probably exceeded that of all the other European countries combined; with the Navigation Acts once again in operation after the restoration of peace, the crews were composed of British seamen. Centred in the smaller as well as the larger ports of the British Isles, there was a vigorous and expanding shipbuilding industry which turned out craft of extraordinary durability—some of these were still afloat more than a century afterwards. London, whose population had by this time topped the million mark, was the centre of a world-wide industrial and commercial empire incomparably stronger and richer than the Hanseatic, Venetian, Spanish, Portuguese, Dutch, or any other trading system which had preceded it. Great Britain had become by far the greatest creditor nation in the world. For two generations and more she was to enjoy virtually a monopoly of oceanic trade and empire.

Great Britain emerged from this, the last of a long series of wars waged against France and her allies, with her sea power supreme in all its elements. In point of *matériel* and personnel the British Navy was superior to all the other fleets of the world combined: in the matter of bases and mercantile tonnage no other State could come anywhere near Great Britain; who had likewise abated not one jot or tittle of her cherished maritime rights.

6

No government in Europe was particularly anxious to assume the responsibility of acting as Napoleon's gaoler. After a long and earnest debate it was resolved that that office should devolve upon Great Britain, and St. Helena was decreed to be the place of his banishment. Thither the *Northumberland* sailed with her illustrious prisoner and his suite, arriving on 20 October—exactly three months after Napoleon's surrender to Maitland. Until the following April Rear-Admiral Sir George Cockburn doubled the offices of Governor of the island and Commander-in-Chief of the station.

St. Helena was a mountainous, craggy island remote from civilization; it lay in the desolate wastes of the South Atlantic almost equidistant from Africa and South America. It was eminently suited to serve as a State prison, and one from which escape should be impossible. There was only one anchorage. No vessel could come within sixty miles of the place without being instantly observed by the look-outs on the heights. The only accessible landing-places were commanded by batteries. Parliament passed a special Act which isolated St. Helena from the outside world 'for the better detaining in custody of Napoleon Bonaparte'. Four British warships were permanently stationed there (one of them was always kept cruising to the windward of the island); no vessels, except those of the East India Company, were permitted to call there unless through stress of weather, or when in need of water; and, to make assurance doubly sure, the two nearest islands, Ascension and Tristan da Cunha, which lay about 700 miles distant from St. Helena, were occupied by British garrisons.

When Cockburn sent a ship to claim Ascension Island for Great Britain, he was careful to inform the Admiralty that he did so 'to prevent America or any other nation from planting themselves there . . . for the purpose of favouring sooner or later the escape of General Bonaparte'. Though such a project might appear at first sight phantasmagoric, there can be no question that there were schemes afoot to rescue Napoleon; and his gaolers were taking no chances.

It had been agreed between the Great Powers to regard Napoleon as their common prisoner; and though Great Britain was alone to be responsible for his custody the governments of Austria, Russia, Prussia, and France were to appoint Commissioners to reside on St. Helena 'to assure themselves of his presence'. Prussia declined to avail herself of the privilege; but the other three Commissioners presently repaired to Napoleon's place of exile, where they continued to embarrass the Governor, Sir Hudson Lowe, and to engage in fruitless negotiations for a sight of the Emperor.

On this lonely rock Napoleon lived for nearly five years. He died, shortly after sunset, on the evening of 5 May 1821.[1] 'At 6 p.m.', wrote Captain Frederick Marryat of the *Beaver* sloop, which had lately been

---

[1] The *Beaver*'s log disproves the myth that Napoleon breathed his last in the midst of a violent gale. The wind that evening was from the S.E., 'moderate breezes and fine weather' (Adm. 52/4424, 5–6 May 1821).

cruising to the windward of the island, 'departed this life General Bonaparte.' A few days later it is recorded that the ships on guard duty at St. Helena 'fired 25 minute guns for General Bonaparte's funeral'; and Marryat was presently sent home with the dispatches announcing the Emperor's death.

Bibliography

GENERAL

The period under survey is covered by the works of two contemporary historians: *The Naval History of Great Britain* by Edward Brenton (1823) and *The Naval History of Great Britain, 1793–1820* by William James (1837). The French Revolutionary and Napoleonic Wars are treated in Vols. IV, V, and VI of Sir William Laird Clowes's *The Royal Navy*. This work has for long been the standard authority on British naval history, and is accessible in most of the larger libraries both here and overseas: but the latest of the volumes was published nearly seventy years ago, and the whole work is now largely out of date. Another general naval history which may be consulted is David Hannay's *Short History of the British Navy*, 2 vols. (1909). The most recent large-scale study of this particular era is *The Influence of Sea Power upon the French Revolution and Empire* by A. T. Mahan, 2 vols. (1892). Mahan's work is still of great interest and value, notwithstanding that, judged by modern standards, there are a number of rather serious deficiencies, and, save in brief outline form, it virtually finishes with the action of Trafalgar. A useful source of information concerning naval administration is F. C. F. Dupin's *Voyages dans la Grande Bretagne* (1820; E. trans. 1822), Vols. III and IV. A recent work of considerable value and interest is C. C. Lloyd's *Mr. Barrow of the Admiralty* (1970). An authoritative modern work which covers this era in outline is H. W. Richmond's *Statesmen and Sea Power* (1946).

For strategy and tactics, see *Some Principles of Maritime Strategy* by J. S. Corbett (1911), *Fighting Instructions, 1530–1816* (1905) and *Signals and Instructions* (1908), both ed. J. S. Corbett, *Théories stratégiques* by R. V. Castex, 5 vols. (1935), *A History of Naval Tactics from 1530 to 1930* by S. and M. Robinson (1942), and *Naval Warfare* by John Creswell (2nd ed. 1942).

For gunnery, see H. Douglas's *A Treatise on Naval Gunnery* (1820), F. L. Robertson's *Evolution of Naval Armament* (1921), Dudley Pope's *Guns* (1965), and Peter Padfield's *Broke of the 'Shannon'* (1966).

The following are useful authorities for ship-design and rigging: G. S. Laird Clowes's *Sailing Ships, their History and Development* (1936), G. Blake's *British Ships and Shipbuilders* (1946), Nepean Longridge's *The Anatomy of Nelson's Ships* (1955), and Sir Alan Moore's *Rig in the North* (1956).

For a clear and accurate explanation of terms and phrases in vogue during this era Admiral William Smyth's *A Sailor's Word-book* (1878) should be consulted.

For the social history of the Navy during this period, an admirable modern authority is M. A. Lewis's *The Social History of the Royal Navy, 1793–1815* (1960). Other authorities which should be consulted are *Adventurers of John Nicol, Mariner* by John Nicol (1822), *Memoirs* by the Hon. Sir George Elliot (1863), *Personal Narrative of Events from 1799 to 1815* by W. S. Lovell (1879), *A Sailor of King George* by F. Hoffman (1901), *Jane Austen's Sailor Brothers* by J. H. and H. C. Hubback (1906), *Sea Life in Nelson's Time* by John Masefield (1905), *Old Times Afloat* by C. Field (1932), *The Wynne Diaries*, ed. A. Fremantle (1940), *John Boteler's Recollections*, ed. D. Bonner-Smith (1942), *Naval Heritage* by David Mathew (1944), *Above and under hatches (Recollections of James Anthony Gardner)*, ed. C. C. Lloyd. (1957), *A Naval History of England, I. The Formative Centuries* by G. J. Marcus (1961), and *The British Seaman* by C. C. Lloyd (1968).

For the mercantile marine, seaborne trade, and colonial expansion, see *Short History of the World's Shipping Industry* by C. E. Fayle (1933), *History of the Merchant Navy* by Moyse-Bartlett (1937), *Founding of the Second British Empire, 1763–1793* by J. T. Harlow (1951), *Empire of the North Atlantic* by G. S. Graham (ed. 1958), *Short History of British Expansion*, II, by J. A. Williamson (ed. 1967).

The *Naval Chronicle*, founded in 1799 and published in twice-yearly volumes throughout the next two decades, is an invaluable source of important information concerning the Navy. The files of the *English Historical Review*, *Mariner's Mirror*, *Naval Review*, and *Royal United Service Institution Journal* should also be consulted.

For navigational conditions in the various theatres of the war at sea, reference may be made to the relevant *Pilots* and Charts, published by the Hydrographic Department of the Admiralty, which are cited below. It is to be emphasized that the earlier editions of these *Pilots*, or sailing directions, are generally to be preferred to the later; belonging, as the former do, to the last era of sail.

CHAPTER I   The French Revolution

For the political, economic, and social background to the French Revolutionary War, see J. Holland Rose's *Pitt and the Great War* (1911) and his *Life of Napoleon I* (ed. 1934), Fay's *Great Britain from Adam Smith to the Present Day* (1928), R. W. Seton-Watson's *Britain in Europe, 1789–1914* (1937), G. M. Trevelyan's *British History in the Nineteenth Century and After* (1937) and his *English Social History* (1944), Sir Arthur Bryant's *Years of Endurance* (1942), J. M. Thompson's *The French Revolution* (1943), T. S. Ashton's *An Economic History of England: the Eighteenth Century*

(1955), Steven Watson's *Reign of George III* (1960), and Paul Mantoux's *The Industrial Revolution in the Eighteenth Century* (ed. 1961).

The opening phase of the war at sea is covered by Brenton, James, Laird Clowes, and Hannay as above. A recent and most interesting account of the first fleet action of the war is *The Glorious First of June* by Oliver Warner (1961). In the absence of a modern authoritative biography of Howe, there is Sir John Barrow's *Life of Earl Howe* (1883), and this may be supplemented by *Memoir of Admiral Sir Edward Codrington* by Lady Bourchier (1873), which contains a good deal of information about Howe.

For the various problems involved in the close and distant blockade of Brest in earlier wars, see *Letters and Papers of Charles, Lord Barham*, ed. J. K. Laughton (N. R. S. 1910), G. J. Marcus's *Quiberon Bay* (1960), A. Temple Patterson's *The Other Armada* (1961), and Piers Mackesy's *The War for America* (1964). For the blockade of Brest in the French Revolutionary War, see Mahan's *Influence of Sea Power upon the French Revolution and Empire* (1892), Corbett's *Some Principles of Maritime Strategy* (1911), and also *The Spencer Papers*, I and II (1913), ed. Corbett.

For the political and social background in Ireland, see *A History of Ireland in the Eighteenth Century* by W. E. H. Lecky, III (ed. 1913), *A History of Ireland* by E. Curtis (1936), *Wolfe Tone* by Frank MacDermott (1939), and *Great Britain and Ireland* by E. M. Johnston (1963). An excellent account of the French expedition to Bantry Bay, written from the point of view of a professional seaman, is E. H. Stuart Jones's *An Invasion that Failed* (1950). Two other studies of this enterprise are Brendan Bradley's *Bantry Bay* (1931) and Richard Hayes's *The Last Invasion of Ireland* (1937). A contemporary record of considerable interest is the *Autobiography of Theobald Wolfe Tone*, ed. W. B. O'Brien (1893). For the part played by Pellew in these events, see Mahan's *Types of Naval Officers* (1902) and C. N. Parkinson's *Edward Pellew, Viscount Exmouth* (1937).

On the French side see *Batailles navales de la France*, I, by O. Troude (1868), *Histoire de la marine française sous la première république* by E. Chevalier (1886), *Projets et tentatives de débarquement aux îles Britanniques* by E. Desbrière (1902), *Hoche l'enfant de la Victoire* by M. A. Fabre (1947), *La puissance navale dans l'histoire*, I, by L. Nicolas (1958), and *La marine de l'an II* by N. Hampson (1959).

On the Dutch side see *Geschiodonis van het Nederlandsche zeewezen*, V, by Johannes Cornelis de Jonge.

For navigational conditions in the English Channel and in the approaches to Brest, see *Channel Pilot*, Parts I and II, and Charts 1598 and 2643; for the French descent on Bantry Bay, see *Irish Coast Pilot* and Chart 2424.

CHAPTER II   The Mediterranean

For the political background to the war in the Mediterranean, see *England*

and France in the Mediterranean, 1660–1830 by W. F. Lord (1901), *Pitt and the Great War* (1911) and *Life of Napoleon I* (ed. 1934), both by J. Holland Rose, and *Statesmen and Sea Power* by H. W. Richmond (1946).

For operations at sea, see Brenton, James, Laird Clowes, and Hannay as above; see also Mahan's *Influence of Sea Power upon the French Revolution and Empire* (1892) and his *Life of Nelson* (1897).

There is no adequate modern biography of Sir John Jervis (afterwards the Earl of St. Vincent); but the following works should be consulted: *Life and Correspondence of the Earl of St. Vincent* by E. Brenton (1838), *Memoirs of the Earl of St. Vincent* by J. S. Tucker (1844), *A Life of Lord St. Vincent* by O. A. Sherrard (1933), and *Old Oak. The Life of John Jervis, Earl of St. Vincent* by Sir W. M. James (1950).

The only full-scale, authoritative biography of Nelson, written from the point of view of a professional seaman, is Mahan's *Life of Nelson* already referred to. Russell Grenfell's *Nelson the Sailor* is a fine seamanlike study of Nelson's professional career; and Oliver Warner's *A Portrait of Nelson* is an excellent short biography with an admirably chosen title. Carola Oman's *Nelson* (1947) is to be accounted the best and fullest account of Nelson's private life, relatives, and friends which has ever appeared. Other works which should be consulted are J. R. Thursfield's *Nelson and other Naval Studies* (1909), Clennell Wilkinson's *Nelson* (1931), Mark Kerr's *The Sailor's Nelson* (1932), and S. W. Roskill's *Art of Leadership* (1964). An important collection which supplements *Dispatches and Letters of Lord Nelson*, ed. Nicolas (1844) is *Nelson's Letters to his Wife*, ed. G. P. B. Naish (1958).

A good deal of light is cast on the officers of Jervis's fleet in *Memoirs and Correspondence of Admiral Lord de Saumarez* by Sir John Ross (1838), *The Life and Services of Admiral Sir T. Foley* by J. B. Herbert (1884), *Nelson and his Captains* by W. H. Fitchett (1902), *Nelson's Hardy* by Broadley and Bartelot (1909), *The Wynne Diaries*, ed. A. Fremantle (1940), and *Nelson's Band of Brothers* by L. Kennedy (1951).

An important contemporary authority for the action of St. Valentine's Day, 1797, is Colonel John Drinkwater's *A Narrative of the Battle of St. Vincent* (1840). See also Mahan's *Influence of Sea Power upon the French Revolution and Empire* and his *Life of Nelson*. There is a very good modern account of the action by C. C. Lloyd in his *Battles of St. Vincent and Camperdown* (1963).

On the French side see Troude's *Batailles navales de la France* II (1868), Jurien de la Gravière's *Guerres maritimes*, II (1883), E. Chevalier's *Histoire de la marine française sous la première république* (1886), Tramond's *Manuel de l'histoire maritime de la France des origines à 1815* (ed. 1947), and L. Nicolas's *La puissance navale dans l'histoire*, I (1958).

On the Spanish side see *Armada espanola*, VIII, by C. F. Duro (1902).

For navigational conditions in the Western Mediterranean and in the approaches to Toulon, see *Mediterranean Pilot*, II, and Charts 449 and 2607.

CHAPTER III   The Naval Mutinies

For the political and social background to the Naval Mutinies, see Traill and Mann's *Social England*, V (1904), J. Holland Rose's *Pitt and the Great War* (1911), Sir Arthur Bryant's *Years of Endurance* (1943), and G. M. Trevelyan's *English Social History* (1944).

Two important authorities on the subject are *The Naval Mutinies of 1797* by Conrad Gill (1913) and *The Floating Republic* by G. Manwaring and B. Dobrée (1935). A more recent work is *The Great Mutiny* by James Dugan (1966). A valuable source of contemporary evidence is *The Spencer Papers*, I and II, ed. J. S. Corbett (1913). For the part played by Howe and St. Vincent in the crisis, see Sir John Barrow's *Life of Lord Howe* (1838), E. P. Brenton's *Life and Correspondence of the Earl of St. Vincent*, 2 vols. (1838), J. S. Tucker's *Memoirs of the Earl of St. Vincent* (1844), and Brian Tunstall's *Flights of Naval Genius* (1930).

For the Dutch War, see Brenton, James, Laird Clowes, and Hannay as above; and also the Earl of Camperdown's *Admiral Duncan* (1898) and C. C. Lloyd's *The Battles of St. Vincent and Camperdown* (1963).

On the Dutch side see Jonge's *Geschiedenis van het Nederlandsche zeewezen*, V.

For navigational conditions off the coast of Holland, see *North Sea Pilot*, IV, and Charts 2182 and 2322.

CHAPTER IV   The War on Trade, 1793-1802

The Naval Histories of Brenton and James contain many references to the *guerre de course*. Among the more important modern works on this subject are *Some Principles of Maritime Strategy* by J. S. Corbett (1911), *Trade Winds*, ed. C. N. Parkinson (1949) and *War in the Eastern Seas* by the same author (1954), and *Empire of the North Atlantic* (1958) and *Great Britain in the Indian Ocean* (1968), both by G. S. Graham.

For *la petite course* in home waters, see C. B. Norman's *Corsairs of France* (1883), E. P. Statham's *Privateers and Privateering* (1910), and W. B. Johnson's *Wolves of the Channel* (1931). For a clear and comprehensive survey of the enemy privateers engaged in *la grande course*, especially in the East Indies, see *War in the Eastern Seas* cited above; this may be supplemented by R. Surcouf's *Un capitaine corsaire, Robert Surcouf* (1925) and L. Nicolas's *La puissance navale dans l'histoire*, I (1958).

On the French side generally see *Les corsaires français sous la république et l'empire* by N. Gallois, 2 vols. (1847), *La Course à Nantes aux XVIIe et XVIIIe siècles* by A. Péju (1900), *Histoire d'un port normand* by Georges Lebas (1912), *Les derniers corsaires malouins sous la révolution et l'empire* by Robidou (1919), *Les derniers corsaires, 1715-1815* by H.   alo (1925), and *Corsaires basques et bayonnais du XVe au XIXe siècle* by Pierre Rectoran (1946).

For the protection of trade, see Mahan's *The Influence of Sea Power upon the French Revolution and Empire* (1892), which shows an appreciation of the crucial importance of convoy which was lacking in the same author's earlier work, *The Influence of Sea Power upon History* (1890). See also John Creswell's *Naval Warfare* (1942) and Owen Rutter's *Red Ensign, A History of Convoy* (1947). A very interesting and informative Admiralty Ms which should be consulted is D. W. Waters' *Notes on the Convoy System of Naval Warfare* (1947).

There is unfortunately at present no full-scale, authoritative history of Lloyd's: such a work would throw much light on the various methods of trade protection during the period under review. Useful and stimulating works on the subject are *The History of Lloyd's* by F. Martin (1876), *Our Next War* by J. T. Danson (1893), *A History of Lloyd's* by Wright and Fayle (1928), and *Lloyd's of London* by D. E. W. Gibb (1957).

For American trade and shipping, see Osgood and Batchelder's *Historical Sketch of Salem* (1879), R. D. Paine's *Ships and Sailors of Old Salem* (1908), K. S. Latourette's *History of Early Relations between the United States and China* (1917), S. E. Morison's *Maritime History of Massachusetts* (ed. 1941)—a modern classic. On the diplomatic side see *Jay's Treaty* by S. F. Bemis (ed. 1962).

For *la petite course* in the English Channel, see *Channel Pilot*, I, II, and III, and Chart 1598. For *la grande course* in the eastern seas, see *Bay of Bengal Pilot* and Charts 70 and 1355. For navigational conditions in the West Indies, see *West Indies Pilot*, II and III, and Chart 3273.

CHAPTER V   The Campaign of the Nile

For the military and political background to the war in the Mediterranean, see *Pitt and the Great War* (1911) and *Life of Napoleon I* (1934), both by J. Holland Rose, *The Spencer Papers*, III and IV, ed. Sir H. W. Richmond (1924), *Bonaparte's Adventurers in Egypt* by P. G. Elgood (1936), *Years of Endurance* by Sir Arthur Bryant (1942), and *The Reign of George III* by Steven Watson (1960). An important modern survey of this stage of the war, more especially from the strategic aspect, is A. B. Rodger's *The War of the Second Coalition* (1964), which is, however, fuller and stronger on the military, than on the naval, side. To these must be added John Creswell's *Naval Warfare* (1942).

For operations at sea, see Brenton, James, and Hannay as above, also *Dispatches and Letters of Lord Nelson* (1847).

For the battle of the Nile, see Sir Edward Berry's *An Authentic Narrative of the Nile* (1798), *Dispatches and Letters of Lord Nelson*, Nicol's *Adventures of John Nicol, Mariner*, Ross's *Memoirs and Correspondence of Admiral*

Lord de Saumarez (1838), and the Hon. Sir George Elliot's *Memoirs* (1863).
There are good modern accounts of the action in *Nelson* by Clennell Wilkinson (1931), *Years of Endurance* by Sir Arthur Bryant (1942), and *The Battle of the Nile* by Oliver Warner (1960).

On the French side see O. Troude's *Batailles navales de la France*, III (1868), Jurien de la Gravière's *Guerres maritimes de la France sous la république et l'empire*, I (1883), E. Chevalier's *Histoire de de la marine française sous la première république* (1886), La Jonquière's *L'expédition d'Egypt*, 5 vols. (1907), C. V. Castex's *Théories stratégiques*, II (1935), G. Lefebvre's *Le Directoire* (1946) and also his *Napoléon* (1953), A. A. Thomazi's *Napoléon et ses marins* (1950), and Vendriez's *De la probabilité en histoire* (1952).

Bruix's cruise of 1799 may be studied in the admirable account, *La campagne de Bruix en Méditerranèe*, Mars-Aout, 1799, by G. Douin (1923) and *The Keith Papers*, II, ed. C. C. Lloyd (1950).

For navigational conditions in the Mediterranean, see *Mediterranean Pilot*, II, IV, and V, and Charts 449, 2607, and 2630.

CHAPTER VI   In the Channel and Atlantic

For operations in home waters during the later years of the French Revolutionary War, see Brenton, James, Laird Clowes, and Hannay as above.

The close investment of Brest by St. Vincent and Cornwallis is covered by A. T. Mahan in *The Influence of Sea Power upon the French Revolution and Empire* (1892). See also Sir John Ross's *Memoirs and Correspondence of Admiral Lord de Saumarez* (1838), E. P. Brenton's *Life and Correspondence of the Earl of St. Vincent*, 2 vols. (1838), J. S. Tucker's *Memoirs of the Earl of St. Vincent* (1844), J. Markham's *A Naval Career during the Old War* (1883), Sir J. S. Corbett's *Some Principles of Maritime Strategy* (1911), *The Spencer Papers*, III and IV, ed. Sir H. W. Richmond (1924), O. A. Sherrard's *A Life of Lord St. Vincent* (1931), C. N. Parkinson's *Edward Pellew, Viscount Exmouth* (1937), and Oliver Warner's *The Life and Letters of Admiral Lord Collingwood* (1965).

For hygiene and supply, see R. S. Allison's *Sea Diseases* (1943), Lloyd and Coulter's *Medicine and the Navy, 1714–1815* (1961), and Thomas Trotter's *The Health of Seamen*, ed. C. C. Lloyd (1965).

The monthly Plymouth and Portsmouth Reports published in the *Naval Chronicle* should be consulted with regard to the weather, refitting of ships, supply, and other governing factors involved in the blockade.

On the French side see *Histoire de la marine français sous le consulat et l'empire* by E. Chevalier (1886) and *La puissance navale dans l'histoire*, I, by L. Nicolas (1958).

For navigational conditions in the approaches to Brest and in Cawsand Bay and Torbay, see *Channel Pilot*, I and II, and Charts 1598, 1613, and 2643.

CHAPTER VII   'Of Nelson and the North'

For the political and commercial background, see J. Holland Rose's *Life of Napoleon I* (1934), Sir Arthur Bryant's *Years of Endurance* (1942), and Steven Watson's *The Reign of George III* (1960).

The crucial issue of maritime rights is treated lucidly and comprehensively in *The Documentary History of the Armed Neutralities* by Piggott and Omond (1919) and in *Neutrality*, II, *The Napoleonic Period* by W. A. Phillips and A. H. Reade (1936). An important contemporary work on the subject is James Stephen's *War in Disguise, or the Frauds of the Neutral Flags* (1805).

For the Baltic campaign of 1801, see Brenton, James, Laird Clowes, and Hannay as above. The battle of Copenhagen and its sequel are treated at length in both Mahan's *Influence of Sea Power upon the French Revolution and Empire* (1892) and his *Life of Nelson* (1897). A good modern account of the Baltic campaign may be found in *Nelson's Battles* by Oliver Warner (1965). See also *Dispatches and Letters of Lord Nelson* (1847), *The Wynne Diaries*, ed. Anne Fremantle (1940), and *Nelson's Band of Brothers* by L. Kennedy (1951).

On the Danish side see *Tour in Zealand* by A. A. Feldborg (1805), *Mindeskrift om Slaget paa Reden København* by P. C. Bundesen (1901), *Denmark in History* by J. H. S. Birch (1938), *Danmarks Historie*, X, by Jens Vibæk (1964), and *Nøytralitet og Krig* by Olav Bergersen (1966).

For the Baltic campaign of 1801, see *Baltic Pilot*, I, and Charts 259 and 2115.

CHAPTER VIII   Land Power and Sea Power

For the political, economic, and social background, see J. Holland Rose's *Pitt and the Great War* (1911) and *Life of Napoleon I* (ed. 1934), C. R. Fay's *Great Britain from Adam Smith to the Present Day* (1928), *The Wynne Diaries*, ed. Anne Fremantle (1940), Sir Arthur Bryant's *Years of Endurance* (1942), Steven Watson's *Reign of George III* (1960), and Paul Mantoux's *The Industrial Revolution in the Eighteenth Century* (1961).

The invasion alarm of 1801-2 is covered by the following works: *Napoleon and the Invasion of England*, 2 vols, (1908), by Wheeler and Broadley, and *England's Years of Danger* by P. Frischauer (1938). For the naval countermeasures, see *Dispatches and Letters of Lord Nelson*, ed. N. H. Nicolas (1847), Mahan's *Influence of Sea Power upon the French Revolution and Empire* (1892), Corbett's *Some Principles of Maritime Strategy* (1911), and Sir H. W. Richmond's *Invasion of Britain* (1941).

For the British expedition to Egypt, see *Diary of Sir John Moore*, ed. F. Maurice (1904), *History of the British Army* by Sir John Fortescue, IV, ii (1906), *Years of Endurance* by Sir Arthur Bryant, and *The Keith Papers*, II, ed. C. C. Lloyd (1950); also A. Allardyce's *Memoir of Viscount Keith* which, although rather poor stuff, is the only biography of that admiral which has ever appeared.

For the two actions off Algeciras, see Brenton, James, Laird Clowes, and Hannay as above. There is a lively account of these engagements in Ross's *Memoirs and Correspondence of Admiral Lord de Saumarez*, 2 vols. (1838) and in R. G. Keat's *Narrative of the night of 12 July 1801*, ed. J. S. Tucker (1838).

On the French side see Guérin's *Histoire maritime de France* (1863), Tronde's *Batailles navales de la France* (1868), E. Chevalier's *Histoire de la marine française sous le consulat et l'empire* (1886), E. Desbrière's *Projets et tentatives de débarquement dans les îles Britanniques* (1902), Tramond's *Manuel d'histoire maritime de la France des origines à 1815* (ed. 1947), and G. Lefebvre's *Napoléon* (ed. 1953).

An important Spanish authority for this period is C. F. Duro's *Armada Espanola*, VIII (1902).

CHAPTER IX   Napoleon and Great Britain

For the general background, see J. Holland Rose's *Pitt and the Great War* (1911) and his *Life of Napoleon I* (ed. 1934), Sir H. W. Richmond's *Statesmen and Sea Power* (1947), H. A. L. Fisher's *History of Europe* (ed. 1952), and Steven Watson's *Reign of George III* (1960).

The great invasion scare of 1803–5 is treated from various viewpoints in *Narrative of Certain Passages in the Great War with France* by Sir Henry Bunbury (1852), *Memorials of his Time* by H. Cockburn (1856), *Napoleon and England* by Coquelle (1904), *England and Napoleon in 1803* by Oscar Browning (1907), *Napoleon and the Invasion of England* by Wheeler and Broadley (1908), *England's Years of Danger* by P. Frischauer (1938), *Invasion of Britain* by Sir H. W. Richmond (1941), and *Years of Victory* (1944) by Sir Arthur Bryant.

For British naval strategy, see *Dispatches and Letters of Lord Nelson*, ed. Sir N. H. Nicolas (1847), Mahan's *Influence of Sea Power upon the French Revolution and Empire* (1892) and his *Life of Nelson* (1897), *Papers relating to the Blockade of Brest*, ed. J. Leyland (N. R. S. 1901), *Life and Letters of Admiral Cornwallis*, ed. F. M. Cornwallis-West (1927), C. N. Parkinson's *Edward Pellew, Viscount Exmouth* (1937), and *Keith Papers*, III, ed. C. C. Lloyd (1955).

On the French side see E. Chevalier's *Histoire de la marine française sous le consulat et l'empire* (1886), E. Desbrière's *Projets et tentatives de débarquement aux îles Britanniques* (1902), C. V. Castex's *Théories stratégiques*, V (1935), and J. Godechot's *La grande nation* (1956). There is an excellent outline account of Napoleon's various invasion plans in Nicolas's *Puissance navale dans l'histoire*, I (1958).

For navigational conditions on the enemy's coasts, see *North Sea Pilot*, IV, and Chart 2182; *Channel Pilot*, I, II, and III, and Charts 1598 and 2643; *Bay of Biscay Pilot* and Chart 2648; *West Coasts of Spain and Portugal Pilot* and Chart 1755; and *Mediterranean Pilot*, I and II, and Charts 449 and 2607.

CHAPTER X   The campaign of Trafalgar

For the grand strategy of the Third Coalition, see J. S. Corbett's *Campaign of Trafalgar* (1910), *Letters and Papers of Charles, Lord Barham*, ed. J. K. Laughton (N. R. S. 1911), J. Holland Rose's *Pitt and the Great War* (1911), and Piers Mackesy's *The War in the Mediterranean, 1803–1810* (1957).

The main authority for the grave timber crisis of 1803–5 is R. G. Albion's *Forests and Sea Power* (1926). Other works which should be consulted are *Letters of Admiral the Earl of St. Vincent*, ed. D. Bonner-Smith (N. R. S., 1927), *Englands Versorgung mit Schiffsbaumaterialen aus englischen und amerikenischen Quellen* by Adler (1937), *Nelson's Dear Lord* by E. Berckman (1962), and *Navy Board Contracts, 1660–1832* by B. Pool (1966).

For the battle of Trafalgar, see Brenton, James, Laird Clowes, and Hannay as above; and also *Naval Battles* by Charles Ekins (1824), *Memoir of Admiral Sir William Hargood*, ed. Joseph Allen (1841), *Dispatches and Letters of Lord Nelson*, ed. N. H. Nicolas (1847), *Sea Drift* by Sir Hercules Robinson (1853), *Memoir of Sir Edward Codrington*, ed. Lady Bourchier (1873), *Personal Narrative of Events from 1799 to 1815* by W. S. Lovell (1879), *Life of Nelson* by A. T. Mahan (1897), *Naval Yarns*, ed. W. H. Long (1899), *A Sailor of King George* by F. Hoffman (1901), *Nelson and other Naval Studies* by J. R. Thursfield (1909), *Nelson's Hardy* by A. M. Broadley and R. G. Bartlot (1909), *Campaign of Trafalgar* by J. S. Corbett (1910), *Report of a Committee Appointed by the Admiralty: Cd. 7120* (1913), *Naval Warfare* by John Creswell (1942), *Trafalgar* by René Maine (1955), and *Nelson's Battles* by Oliver Warner (1965).

On the French side see Jurien de la Gravière's *Guerres maritimes de la France sous la république et l'empire*, II (1883), E. Chevalier's *Histoire de la marine française sous le consulat et l'empire* (1886), Edward Fraser's *The Enemy at Trafalgar* (1906), E. Desbrière's *La Campagne maritime de 1805* (1907), Eng. trans. *The Trafalgar Campaign* by C. Eastwick (1933), A. A. Thomazi's *Trafalgar* (1932), R. V. Castex's *Théories stratégiques*, II (1935), L. Nicolas's *La puissance navale dans l'histoire*, I (1958), and J. Thoey's *Ulm, Trafalgar, Austerlitz* (1962).

On the Spanish side see C. F. Duro's *Armada Espanola*, VIII (1902) and Conte's *En los Dias de Trafalgar* (1937).

CHAPTER XI   The Continental System

For the general background, see J. Holland Rose's *Dispatches relating to the Third Coalition* (1904), *Pitt and the Great War* (1911), and *Life of Napoleon I* (ed. 1934), Sir Arthur Bryant's *Years of Victory* (1944), and C. J. Bartlett's *Castlereagh* (1966).

The commercial struggle between Great Britain and Napoleon is comprehensively and accurately surveyed in François Crouzet's *L'Économie britannique et le blocus continental* (1958); a work which, it is to be noted, makes frequent and effective use of the Admiralty Papers. See also Mahan's *Influence of Sea Power upon the French Revolution and Empire* (1892) and E. F. Heckscher's *Continental System* (1922).

For St. Vincent's cruise of 1806–7, see Brenton, James, and Hannay as above. Much information is to be found in Brenton's *Life and Correspondence of the Earl of St. Vincent* (1838) and Tucker's *Memoirs of the Earl of St. Vincent* (1844). See also *The Correspondence of Admiral Markham*, ed. C. Markham (N. R. S., 1904) and O. A. Sherrard's *A Life of Lord St. Vincent* (1933).

For the Mediterranean theatre, see Brenton, James, and Hannay as above. See also *Public and Private Correspondence of Vice-Admiral Lord Collingwood*, ed. G. L. Newnham Collingwood (1829), *Life of Admiral Collingwood* by G. Murray (1936), *Admiral Collingwood* by D. F. Stephenson (1948), *Private Correspondence of Admiral Lord Collingwood*, ed. E. A. Hughes (1957), *The War in the Mediterranean, 1803–10* by Piers Mackesy (1957), and *Life and Letters of Vice-Admiral Lord Collingwood* by Oliver Warner (1965).

On the French side see O. Troude's *Batailles navales de la France*, IV (1868), E. Chevalier's *Historie de la marine française sous le consulat et l'empire* (1886), R. V. Castex's *Théories stratégiques*, V (1935), Tramond's *Manuel d'histoire maritime de la France des origines à 1815* (ed. 1947), G. Lefebvre's *Napoléon* (ed. 1953), and P. Masson and J. Muracciole's *Napoléon et la Marine* (1968).

For the war in the Baltic, there is Sir John Ross's *Memoirs and Correspondence of Admiral Lord de Saumarez* (1838), *Letters and Papers of Thomas Byam Martin*, ed. J. K. Laughton (1901), and *Captain Boteler's Recollections*, ed. D. Bonner-Smith (1942). No modern biography of Saumarez exists; but the hiatus is being gradually filled by A. N. Ryan in his introduction to *The Saumarez Papers, 1808–1812* (1968) and in various articles by the same author.

On the Scandinavian side see *Seemacht in der Ostsee* by H. Kirchhoff, 2 vols. (1907), *Danmarks Kapervaesen* by K. Larsen (1915), *Søkrigen i de danske-norske Farvende, 1807–1814* by C. F. Wandel (1915), *Sjömaktens Inflytande pa Sveriges Historia*, II, by C. L. A. Munthe (1922), *Svenska Flottans Historia*, II, ed. O. Lybeck (1943), *Viceamiral Carl Olof Cronstadt* (1954) and *Sveaborgs gåta* (1958), by W. Odelberg, *Kaperfart og Skipsfart* by J. N. Tønnessen (1955), *La Finlande* by P. Tommila (1962), and Jens Vibæk's *Danmarks Historie*, X, ed. Danstrup og Koch (1964).

For navigational conditions in the Mediterranean, see *Mediterranean*

Pilot, I, II, and III, and Chart 449; in the Baltic Sea, *Baltic Pilot*, I, II, and III, and Charts 259 and 2115.

CHAPTER XII   The Peninsular War

For the political and commercial background, see J. Holland Rose's *Pitt and the Great War* (1911) and his *Life of Napoleon I* (1934), E. F. Heckscher's *Continental System* (1922), F. Crouzet's *L'Économie britannique et le blocus continental* (1958), Lefebvre's *Napoléon* (1958), Steven Watson's *Reign of George III* (1960), and Bartlett's *Castlereagh* (1966).

For military operations in the Peninsula, see *Supplementary Dispatches and Memoranda of the Duke of Wellington* (1872), *Narrative of the Peninsular War* by A. Leith Hay (1879), *A History of the British Army* by Sir John Fortescue (1930), *A History of the Peninsular War* by Sir Charles Oman (1930), *Years of Victory* (1944) and *Age of Elegance* (1950), both by Sir Arthur Bryant, *Wellington in the Peninsula* by Jac Weller (1962), and *Sir John Moore* by Carola Oman (1963).

The vital role played by the Navy in this theatre of the war has been much neglected, but the following works should be consulted: *Life and Letters of Captain Marryat*, ed. Florence Marryat (1872), *Memoir of Admiral Sir Edward Codrington* by Lady Bourchier (1872), *How England Saved Europe*, III, by W. H. Fitchett (1900), *Letters and Papers of Sir Thomas Byam Martin*, ed. Sir R. V. Hamilton (1901), *Captain Marryat and the Old Navy* by C. C. Lloyd (1939), and *The Keith Papers*, III, ed. by the same author.

For the French side see J. Tramond's *Manuel d'histoire maritime de la France des origines à 1815* (ed. 1947).

For the Walcheren expedition, see Brenton, James, Laird Clowes, and Hannay as above; and also Fortescue's *History of the British Army*, VII (1912), A. Fischer's *Napoléon et Anvers* (1933), and Bryant's *Years of Victory* (1944).

For operations on the coasts of Spain and Portugal, see *Bay of Biscay Pilot*, *West Coasts of Spain and Portugal Pilot*, and *Mediterranean Pilot*, I, and Charts 1104, 1187, 1755, 2665, 2717, 2925; for the abortive attempt on Antwerp, see *North Sea Pilot*, IV, and Chart 1406.

CHAPTER XIII   The War on Trade, 1803–1815

For the war on trade generally, see Brenton and James as above; and also A. T. Mahan's *Influence of Sea Power upon the French Revolution and Empire*, II (1892), which contains a highly important chapter on the *guerre de course* over the years 1803 to 1815, and Sir J. S. Corbett's *Some Principles of Maritime Strategy* (1911).

The following authorities are useful for the depredations of the privateers in home waters, *la petite course*: C. B. Norman's *Corsairs of France* (1883),

E. P. Statham's *Privateers and Privateering* (1910), and W. B. Johnson's *Wolves of the Channel* (1931). These may be supplemented by a careful search through the relevant files of the *Naval Chronicle*.

For the Baltic, a vital theatre at this stage of the war, see *Memoirs and Correspondence of Admiral Lord de Saumarez*, ed. Sir John Ross (1838), *Danmarks Kapervaesen* by K. Larsen (1915), *Søkrigen i de danske-norske Farvende, 1807–1814* by C. F. Wandel (1915), *Captain Boteler's Recollections*, ed. D. Bonner-Smith (1942), *Kaperfart og Skipsfart* by J. N. Tønnessen (1955), *America, Russia, Hemp, and Napoleon* by A. W. Crosby (1965), and *The Saumarez Papers, 1808–12*, ed. A. N. Ryan (1968).

For the more distant operations of *la grande course*, see *War in the Eastern Seas* by C. N. Parkinson (1954), and *Empire of the North Atlantic* (1958) and *Great Britain in the Indian Ocean* (1969), both by G. S. Graham.

On the French side see *Les corsaires français sous la république et l'empire* by N. Gallois, 2 vols. (1947), *L'Île de France sous Decaen, 1803–1810* by Henri Prentout (1901), *Histoire de Surcouf* by C. Cunat (1917), *Les derniers corsaires malouins, 1793–1815* by F. Robidou (1919), *Un capitaine corsaire, Robert Surcouf* by R. Surcouf (ed. 1925), *La Méditerranée de 1803 à 1807* by G. Douin (1917), *Théories stratégiques*, V, by C. V. Castex (1935), and *Corsaires basques et bayonnaise du XVᵉ au XIXᵉ siècle* by Pierre Rectoran (1946). There is an excellent summary of both *la petite course* and *la grande course* during the Napoleonic War in L. Nicolas's *La puissance navale dans l'histoire* (1958).

The various methods of trade protection are fairly well covered by the following works: *Remarks Relative the Danger of Convoys* by A. Gower (1811), *Memoirs of Vice-Admiral Sir William Symonds* by J. A. Sharp (1858), *Some Principles of Maritime Strategy* by J. S. Corbett (1911), *Trade Winds*, ed. C. N. Parkinson (1949), *Above and Under Hatches (Recollections of James Anthony Gardner)*, ed. C. C. Lloyd (1957), and *Empire of the North Atlantic* by G. S. Graham (ed. 1958). Reference should also be made to the Admiralty Ms cited above, *Notes on the Convoy System of Naval Warfare* by D. W. Waters (1947).

For navigational conditions in the various theatres of the *guerre de course*, see *Channel Pilot*, I, II, and III, and Chart 1598; *North Sea Pilot*, IV, and Chart 2182; *Baltic Pilot*, I, II, and III, and Charts 259 and 2115; *Norway Pilot*, III, and *Arctic Pilot*, I, and Chart 2282; *West Indies Pilot*, II and III, and Chart 3273; *Bay of Bengal Pilot* and *Malacca Strait Pilot*, and Charts 70 and 1355.

CHAPTER XIV   The Crisis of the Commercial War

For the political, economic, and social background, see *Social England*, ed. Traill and Mann, V (1904), *Great Britain from Adam Smith to the Present Day* by C. R. Fay (1928), *Life of Napoleon I* by J. Holland Rose (ed. 1934),

English Social History by G. M. Trevelyan (1944), *The Industrial Revolution, 1760 to 1830* by T. S. Ashton (1948), and *Reign of George III* by Steven Watson (1960).

For the commercial duel between Great Britain and Napoleon, see Heckscher and Crouzet as above, and also *Napoléon et l'économie dirigée; le blocus continental* by de Jouvenel and *Napoléon et l'industrie française* by O. Viennet (1947).

For the Baltic theatre, see *Memoirs and Correspondence of Admiral Lord de Saumarez* by Sir John Ross (1838) and *The Saumarez Papers*, ed. A. N. Ryan (1968). On the Scandinavian side see *Seemacht in der Ostsee*, 2 vols., by H. Kirchoff (1907), *Søkrigen i de danske-norske Farvende, 1807–14* by C. F. Wandel (1915), and *Kaperfart og Skipsfart* by J. N. Tønnessen (1955), and *America, Russia, Hemp and Napoleon* by A. W. Crosby (1965).

Political and commercial relations with the United States are treated in A. L. Burt's *The United States, Great Britain, and British North America from the Revolution to the Establishment of Peace after the War of 1812* (1940).

For the overseas expansion of the British people during the period under survey, see *Thoughts on the Value to Great Britain of the Colonial Trade* by C. Bosanquet (1807). *A Treatise on the Wealth, Power and Resources of the British Empire* by F. Colquhoun (1815), *A History of Newfoundland* by D. N. Prowse (1895), *Development of the British West Indies* by F. W. Pitman (1917), *Development of the Organisation of Anglo-American Trade, 1800–1850* by N. S. Buck (1925), *John Company* by Sir William Foster (1926), *India under Wellesley* by P. E. Roberts (1929), *The Exploration of the Pacific* by J. C. Beaglehole (1934), *An Economic History of Canada* by M. Q. Innis (1935), *Trade in the Eastern Seas, 1793–1815* by C. N. Parkinson (1937), *Economic History of the American People* by E. L. Bogart (1942), *The British Overseas* by C. E. Carrington (1950), *Short History of the British Commonwealth*, II, by J. Ramsay Muir (ed. 1954), *English Overseas Trade Statistics, 1697–1808* by E. B. Schumpeter (1960), *The Navy and South America, 1807–1827*, ed. G. S. Graham and R. A. Humphreys (1962), *Short History of British Expansion* by J. A. Williamson (ed. 1967), and *Great Britain and the Indian Ocean* by G. S. Graham (1967).

For navigational conditions in the Heligoland Bight, see *North Sea Pilot*, IV, and Charts 1875 and 2181.

CHAPTER XV   The Uprising of the Nations

For the political and commercial background, see J. Holland Rose's *Life of Napoleon I* (1934), G. M. Trevelyan's *British History in the Nineteenth Century and After* (1937), E. V. Tarlé's *Napoleon's Invasion of Russia* (1942), Sir Arthur Bryant's *Age of Elegance* (1950), H. A. L. Fisher's *History of Europe* (ed. 1952), F. Crouzet's *L'Économie britannique et le blocus continental* (1958), Denis Gray's *Spencer Perceval* (1963), and C. J. Bartlett's *Castlereagh* (1966).

BIBLIOGRAPHY

For the 'long blockade' of the enemy's ports, see Brenton, James, Laird Clowes, and Hannay as above; and also *Memoirs and Correspondence of Admiral Lord de Saumarez* by Sir John Ross, (1838), *Memoirs of the Life and Services* of Sir William Symonds, ed. J. A. Sharp (1858), *The Mastery of the Mediterranean* by Sir Thomas Maitland (1897), *Edward Pellew, Viscount Exmouth* by C. N. Parkinson (1937), *Captain Boteler's Recollections*, ed. D. Bonner-Smith (1942), *The Keith Papers*, III, ed. C. C. Lloyd (1955), and *The Saumarez Papers*, ed. A. N. Ryan (1968). The highly important factor of hygiene and supply is treated comprehensively in *Medicine and the Navy, 1714-1815*, by Lloyd and Coulter (1961).

As regards the part played by the British Navy in the Baltic during Napoleon's invasion of Russia in 1812, *The Saumarez Papers*, ed. A. N. Ryan (1968) serves as a useful corrective to the exaggerated claims advanced by Admiral Sir Richard Vesey Hamilton in his introduction to *Letters and Papers of Sir Thomas Byam Martin* (N. R. S., 1900).

On the French side see O. Troude's *Batailles navales de la France*, IV (1868), E. Chevalier's *La marine française sous le consulat et l'empire* (1886), Thomazi's *Napoléon et ses marins* (1950), and Nicolas's *La puissance navale dans l'histoire* (1958).

For navigational conditions on the coasts which witnessed the interception of the three French frigates by the *Northumberland* and the club-hauling of the *Magnificent*, see *Bay of Biscay Pilot* and Charts 2352 and 2648.

CHAPTER XVI   'Mr. Madison's War'

For the general background to the War of 1812, see Henry Adams's *History of the United States 1801-17* (1891), A. L. Burt's *The United States, Great Britain, and British North America from the Revolution to the Establishment of Peace after the War of 1812* (1940), B. Perkin's *Prologue to the War between England and the United States, 1805-12* (1961), and Ulane Bonnel's *La France, les États et la guerre de course, 1797-1816* (1962)

The war on land is treated in *The Canadian War of 1812* by C. P. Lucas (1906), *The War of 1812* by F. F. Beirne (1949), *Growth of the American Republic* by S. E. Morison and H. S. Commager (ed. 1950), and *Short History of the British Commonwealth*, II, by J. Ramsay Muir (ed. 1954).

For operations at sea, see A. T. Mahan's *Sea Power in its Relations to the War of 1812*, 2 vols. (1905), Theodore Roosevelt's *The Naval War of 1812* (1882) and his *Naval Operations of the War between Great Britain and the United States, 1812-1815* (1910), Ira Hollis's *The Frigate 'Constitution'* (1931), D. W. Knox's *A History of the United States Navy* (1936), H. and M. Sprout's *Rise of American Naval Power, 1776-1918* (1939), R. G. Albion and J. B. Pope's *Sea Lanes in War Time* (1943), C. S. Forester's *The Naval War of 1812* (1957), G. S. Graham's *Empire of the North Atlantic* (1958), T. P. Hougan's *Old Ironsides* (1963), and L. F. Gutbridge and T. D. Smith's *The Commodores* (1969).

For the American war on trade, see Mahan and Roosevelt as above. Particular studies in this field are *A History of American Privateering* by George Coggeshall (1856), who himself commanded a privateer during the war, and *A History of the American Privateers* by E. S. Maclay (1900).

For navigational conditions on the eastern seaboard of the United States, see *East Coast of the United States Pilot*, I and II, and Charts 2480 and 2482.

CHAPTER XVII   The Hundred Days

For the general background to the Hundred Days and the Peace Settlements of 1814–15, see Sir Spencer Walpole's *History of England from the Conclusion of the War in 1815*, I (1890), H. A. L. Fisher's *History of Europe* (ed. 1950), C. E. Carrington's *The British Overseas* (1950), Sir Arthur Bryant's *The Age of Elegance* (1950), Steven Watson's *Reign of George III* (1960), and J. A. Williamson's *Short History of British Expansion*, II (ed. 1967).

Two of Jane Austen's novels, *Mansfield Park* (1814) and *Persuasion* (1818), present lively and attractive scenes of naval officers ashore with their families and friends.

The Congress of Vienna is covered by the following works: G. J. Renier's *Great Britain and the Establishment of the Netherlands, 1813–18* (1930), C. K. Webster's *Foreign Policy of Castlereagh, 1812–1815* (1931) and his *Congress of Vienna* (ed. 1934), A. Fischer's *Napoléon et Anvers* (1933), S. T. Bindoff's *The Scheldt to 1839* (1945), H. Nicolson's *Congress of Vienna* (1946), and C. J. Bartlett's *Castlereagh* (1966).

For Napoleon's surrender and exile, see *Napoleon; The Last Phase* by Lord Rosebery (1900), *The Surrender of Napoleon* by Frederick Maitland (ed. 1904), *The Keith Papers*, III, ed. C. C. Lloyd (1955), and *The First 'Bellerophon'* by C. A. Pengelly (1966).

Index

Am.   American
Br.   British
D.   Dutch
Dan. Danish
Fr.   French
Sp.   Spanish

Abercromby, General Sir Ralph, 53, 151, 199–203
Aberdeen, Lord, 491
Acklom, Captain, 395
Aboukir Bay, 128–9, 131–41, 150, 199–203
Acre, 143
Addington, Dr., 172–3, 188, 216, 218
Administration, 21–3, 82–3, 218–9, 229, 244–6, 251–2, 261–3, 302, 357 and n., 358–9, 426–7, 496. See also Dockyards, Manning of the Fleet, Victualling
Admiralty, 1, 18, 83, 89, 99, 140, 158, 218–9, 229, 251–2, 255, 257–8, 260–1, 267–9, 292–3, 295, 358–9, 366–7, 370, 388–90, 401–4, 487–8, 503
Adriatic Sea, 369
Agincourt Sound, 241 and n.
Aix roads, 337
Alexander I, Tsar, 191, 311–2
Alexandria, 128–9, 130–2, 138, 146, 150, 200–3, 210, 247
Algeciras, 204–8
Allemand, Vice-Admiral, 102, 260–2, 264–5, 315, 389, 430
Allen, Tom, 81, 181, 271
Alps, 151, 214
Amboyna, 57, 416
Amiens, Treaty of, 213–5
Amsterdam, 55, 361, 442, 449
Ancona, 361
Angerstein, John Julius, 401
Anholt, 175, 326, 375, 394
Antwerp, 215–6, 340–2, 429, 442. See also Scheldt
Archangel, 121, 318, 321, 370, 392, 410, 472

Armed Neutrality, 170–2, 191
Ascension I., 503
Audierne Bay, 47–8
Austen, Jane, 424, 486
Austerlitz, 298–9, 308
Australia, 421
Austria, 54, 61, 267, 298, 334, 340, 344

Badajos, 348, 353
Bainbridge, Captain William, 458–9
Baird, Sir Andrew, 156, 433
Baird, General Sir David, 199, 203, 261–2, 416
Ball, Captain Sir Alexander, 137, 146, 198–9
Ballasteros, 350
Baltic Sea, 172, 320, 324–6, 371, 407, 428
Baltimore, 462, 476–7
  clipper, 461–2
Bantry Bay, 44–9
Barbados, 254–5, 395
Barcelona, 344
Barfleur, Cape, 26
Barham, Lord, 21–2, 41–2, 83, 246–7, 251–3, 257–8, 260–2, 265
Baring, Sir Francis, 401
Barlow, Captain Robert, 15
Barney, Commodore Josiah, 475–6
Barrow, Sir John, 30, 268–9
Bart, Jean, 113, 361
Bastria, 59
Batavia, 400–1
Batavian Republic, 55
Bayonne, 358
Beachy Head, 75, 105, 114, 366–8
Beaver, Captain Philip, 400

R*

Bencoolen, 421
Bengal, Bay of, 113-5
Bennett, John, 402
Bere Island, 46-7
Berehaven, 46
Berkeley, Admiral Sir George, 154, 165
Berlin, 308
Berlin Decrees, 309, 441
Bernadotte, Marshal, 312, 341, 448-9
Berry, Captain Sir Edward, 65, 79, 131-2, 136, 139, 146, 273
Berry Head, 29 n., 160
Bertheaume Bay, 50
Bertie, Rear-Admiral Albemarle, 381
Betanzos Bay, 237-8
Bickerton, Rear-Admiral Sir Richard, 254-5
Birmingham, 198, 449
Biscay, Bay of, 357, 462
Biscaya, 353
Black Country, 198
Black Rocks, 162-7, 230, 235-6, 303-4
Blackwood, Rear-Admiral Sir Henry, 148, 267, 272-6, 278, 287, 489
Bladensburg, 475-6
Blankmann, Jean, 107-8, 385-6
Blockade: Alexandria, 138, 143, 150; Boston (Mass.), 463-4, 466, 475, 478; Boulogne, 196, 227, 229; Brest, 29, 31, 40, 42, 48-51, 145-6, 155-69, 220, 223, 230-6, 243, 250, 253, 258, 261-3, 295, 303-7, 429-32, 496; Bristol (Rhode I.), 478; Cadiz, 72, 80, 98, 100, 124-5, 142-5, 251, 258, 265, 297; Chesapeake, 463-4, 467, 471, 474; Delaware, 463-4; Ferrol, 221, 258, 260, 263; Flushing, 195-6; Leghorn, 71; Malta, 146-8; New London (Conn.), 463, 465-6, 474; New York, 463, 465, 474, 478-9; Norfolk (Va.), 465-6; Rochefort, 247, 258, 337-8; Texel, 40, 55-6, 92-5, 230, 261, 428-9; Toulon, 61, 65-9, 229, 239-42, 247-8, 250, 317, 331, 343 and n., 344, 431-2; Venice, 346. See also Strategy
Blücher, Field Marshal, 308, 450-1
Bombay, 114, 200, 398
Bompart, Rear-Admiral, 51-2
Bonaparte, Joseph, 315, 331, 335, 350, 353-6
   Louis, 406
   Napoleon. See Napoleon I
Bornholm I., 189-90, 325, 393
Borodino, 445

Boston, 121, 462, 464, 466-8, 474, 478
Botany Bay, 179 n., 421
Bothnia, Gulf of, 324
Boulogne, 103, 106, 194-6, 221-2, 227, 265, 370
Bourbon I., 381, 399
Bouverie, Captain Duncombe, 353
Bouvet, Captain Pierre, 376, 381; Rear-Admiral François, 44-7
Bowen, Rear-Admiral James, 28 and n., 335 and n.
Brazil, 318, 419
Bremen, 442
Brenton, Captain Edward, 39, 110; Jahleel, 346-7
Brest, 15, 21, 40, 42, 159, 243, 429-30. See also Navigational conditions: Brest approaches, and Blockade
Bridport, Admiral Lord, 30, 40, 42-3, 49, 83-5, 144, 153, 159
'Britons, Strike Home', 206
Brixham, 155, 158, 431, 498
Brock, General Isaac, 455
Broke, Captain Philip Vere, 463, 468-9
Broquet, Jean, 362
Brueys, Admiral, 126-7, 132, 135, 141
Bruix, Rear-Admiral, 44, 143-6, 221
Buckner, Vice-Admiral, 89
Buenos Aires, 318, 419
'Buggins's turn', 10, 49
Burgos, 354-5

Cabrita Point, 204-6
Cadiz, 72, 75, 80, 98, 100, 124, 126, 142, 144-5, 199, 204-5, 244, 250-1, 258, 262, 266, 271, 273, 286, 288, 300, 314, 331, 349. See also Blockade: Cadiz
Caffarelli, General, 351-3
Cairo, 128, 138, 202
Calais, 103
Calcutta, 113-4, 420
Calder, Rear-Admiral Sir Robert, 69, 75-6, 257-60, 265, 267
Calvia, 59
Camden, Lord, 43, 50
Campbell, Captain Patrick, 300-1, 346
Camperdown, 95-7
Canada, 418-9, 453-5, 469-70, 480-1, 483
Canals, 366
Cannes, 492
Canning, George, 226, 269, 312, 459
Canton, 121, 377, 421
Cape of Good Hope, 56-8, 116, 216, 381, 416, 499-500

Cape Town, 56
Capel, Captain Thomas, 466
Caribbean Sea, 102, 109–10, 115–6, 375, 462, 472
Carronade, 36, 97, 458, 470, 481. *See also* Guns and gunnery
Carrying trade, 120–3, 170–2, 327, 407, 502
Cartagena, 75, 255, 273, 297
Castlereagh, Lord, 266, 337, 339, 449, 490–1, 499–500
Catalonia, 350
Cattaro, 242, 312, 314
Cawsand Bay, 154, 157, 160, 219–20, 232, 307, 384 n.
Ceuta, 369
Ceylon, 116, 213
Champlain, Lake. *See* Great Lakes
Channel fleet, 145, 153–69, 230–6, 249, 252–3, 237, 262–3, 387
Charleston, 462, 468
Chatham, Lord, 18, 39, 341–2
Chauncey, Captain Isaac, 469
Cherbourg, 26, 430
Chesapeake, 463–4, 466–7, 475–7
China, 121, 125, 397, 421
Civita Vecchia, 124
Clausel, General, 353, 355
Clear, Cape, 114, 307
Club-hauling, 328, 435–6 and n.
Cochrane, Vice-Admiral Alexander, 201, 238, 256, 296, 474, 476–7, 479
Captain Thomas, 336–8
Cockburn, Rear-Admiral Sir George, 69, 466–7, 475, 478, 502–3
Cod, Cape, 469
Codrington, Rear-Admiral Sir Edward, 28, 282, 288, 350
Coggeshall, George, 394, 471–2
Cole, Captain, 401
Collier, Captain Sir John, 348, 350–1, 355–9
Collingwood, Admiral Lord, 17, 19, 64–66, 78, 154–5, 166, 211, 231, 234–6; second-in-command, Mediterranean fleet, 268, 270–1, 275, 277, 279, 284–5, 288; Commander-in-Chief, 297–301, 316–7, 331–2, 343–7
Colonial goods, 209, 318–9, 331, 382, 410, 412, 417, 422–4, 441–3, 448, 485
Colpoys, Admiral John, 42, 44, 49–50, 85–6
Combined Fleet, 255–7, 259, 262–3, 266–7, 273, 275
Commerce, Defence and prevention of,

23–5, 73, 102–4, 114–5, 119–20, 123, 212, 361–2, 382–3, 389–90, 404–5. *See also* Convoy, Lloyd's, Maritime rights, Privateers, Reduction of hostile bases, Signal stations, Strategy
Compulsory Convoy Act (1798), 120, 365
Conjunct operations: *British*, 42, 53–4, 56, 59, 65, 115–6, 141–2, 146–8, 151–2, 168, 198–203, 248–9, 251–3, 256, 299 and n., 301–2, 312–4, 326, 334–6, 341–2, 349–53, 357–60, 383, 399–401, 416, 449–50, 475–8; *Dutch*, 58; *French*, 43–7, 51–2, 61, 124–8, 143–6, 203–7, 247, 249, 273, 295–6, 343–4
Consulate, 214–5, 217–8
Continental System, 309–13, 317–22, 332, 361, 382, 406–17, 440–3, 447–9, 453, 485, 501
Convoy, 23–5, 31–3, 37–8, 102, 107–8, 111, 114–20, 248, 251, 255, 261–2, 320–1, 325, 349–50, 356–9, 363–5, 368–70, 372–5, 377–8, 388–98, 402–5, 407, 419, 439, 457, 466, 471–2; Act (1793), 116
Cook, Captain James, 422
Copenhagen, 140, 173–88, 312, 361
Corfu, 143, 242, 299, 315, 334–6, 346
Cork, 48
Corniche, 64 and n.
Cornwallis, Admiral William, 22, 40–2, 169, 220, 230–8, 250, 253, 258, 260–3, 295, 302
Corsica, 59, 61, 71
Corunna, 354, 358
Cosby, Vice-Admiral Philips, 27, 118–9
Cotton, Admiral Sir Charles, 303, 305, 307, 347, 429
Courcy, Rear-Admiral de, 335
Craig, General Sir James, 56, 248–9, 254–7, 267, 299–301
Cuba, 110, 376
Cuckmere Haven, 224, 367
Curtis, Rear-Admiral Sir Roger, 87–8, 126
Cuxhaven, 361

Dance, Nathaniel, 377–8
'Dangers of the sea', 38–9, 47–8, 57 n., 73–4, 97, 125, 159–60, 162–3, 165–7, 231–9, 247–8, 287, 315, 326–30, 353, 357–9, 370, 374, 379, 397–8, 407, 427, 435–6, 463–4

Danton, 18
Danzig, 325, 361
Dardanelles, 302
Davout, Marshal, 308, 406, 443–4
Decaen, Charles, 376, 379, 380–1
Decatur, Commodore Stephen, 456, 458, 465, 478–9
Decrès, Vice-Admiral, 126, 215
Delaware R., 463–4
Denmark, 170–89, 191, 311–8, 323–7, 370–5, 393–5, 406, 449, 500
Deserters, 453
Dibdin, Thomas, 139
Dieppe, 369
Directory, 126, 143, 150, 212
Discipline, 21, 31, 42, 64–7, 84, 89–90, 98–101, 130–2, 146–7, 153–8, 163–5, 173–4, 179, 205, 239–40, 259–60, 271, 281, 304–6, 313, 334, 336, 438–9. *See also* Mutiny
Dixon, Rear-Admiral Manley, 325, 394
Docks, 423–4
Dockyards, 22, 142, 168, 219, 245–7, 488–9
Douarnenez Bay, 166–7
Douro, R., 353–5
Dover, Straits of, 221
Downie, Captain, 480–1
Downs, The, 196, 362, 369
Drury, Vice-Admiral William O'Brien, 382, 399
Duckworth, Rear-Admiral Sir John, 118, 141, 145, 295–6, 302, 496
Dumouriez, General, 30
Duncan, Admiral Adam, 40, 55, 89–90, 92–7, 139
Dungeness, 105, 114, 362
Dunkirk, 103, 107–8, 370
Duperré, Victor, 376, 399
Dursey I., 45, 48
Dutertre, 113–4, 376

East India Company, 111–3, 139, 397, 399, 401, 412, 420; Station, 27, 57–8, 111–6, 376–83, 397–401
Ebro, R., 355
Eddistone Rock, 106
Egypt, 126–8, 138, 143, 145, 199, 213
Elba, 71, 73–5, 451
Elbe, R., 191, 319, 406, 447, 449
Elliot, Admiral the Hon. Sir George, 236 n., 401
Hugh, 149, 257
Elsinore, 175–7, 313, 361, 372

Embargo Act, 318, 322, 418, 452
Ems, R., 191, 319, 406, 449
Épron, 376
Erie, Lake. *See* Great Lakes
Ertholmene, 325 and n.
Esla, R., 354

Fairlight Point, 362, 367
Falmouth, 160, 288, 295, 304
Fearney, William, 79
Ferdinand, King, 146–7
Ferrol, 199, 258 and n., 259 and n., 260–1, 263, 265. *See also* Blockade: Ferrol
Finisterre, Cape, 334
Finland, 323, 443
Gulf of, 324
Fischer, Olfert, 184–5
Fitzgerald, Lord Edward, 51
Flushing, 195, 341
Fog. *See* Haze
Foley, Vice-Admiral Sir Thomas, 65, 70, 126, 134 and n., 177, 180–1, 185
Fox, Charles James, 308–9
France, 16–9, 150, 193, 211–3, 406–7, 443–4, 449, 492, 499, 502
Frederick VI, King, 406
Free ships, free goods, 121
Fréjus, 150
Fremantle, Betsey, 68–9, 139, 210
Vice-Admiral Sir Thomas, 65, 68, 70–1, 75, 174–5, 177, 180, 271–2, 431–2, 487
French Revolution, 16–20, 43, 212
Friedland, 311
Fundy, Bay of, 462

Gales, as factor in naval warfare, 28–30, 38–9, 46–8, 73, 94–5, 97, 125, 144–5, 159–60, 162–3, 166–7, 174, 200, 231–9, 247–8, 253, 287, 303, 315, 327–9, 335, 341, 353, 357–9, 362–4, 379, 388, 395, 430, 435–6, 438–9, 464, 475, 478–9
Gambier, Admiral Lord, 312, 337–8
Ganteaume, Vice-Admiral, 102, 126, 200, 249–51, 263–4, 315–7
Gardner, Admiral Alan, 27, 84–6, 118
Commander James Anthony, 61, 118–9, 262
Gaspar, Don, 351–2
Gell, Rear-Admiral John, 27
Genoa, 63; Gulf of, 61
Ghent, Treaty of, 484

Gibraltar, 65, 72–4, 99, 124–6, 142–5, 199, 204–7, 239, 241, 252, 257, 261, 274–5, 287, 297, 300, 331, 391
Straits of, 144–5, 206, 251, 300
Gillray, 17, 226
' Glorious First ', 34–8
Goodwin Sands, 195, 363
Gothenburg, 324, 326–7, 407
Graham, Lieut.-General Sir Thomas, 198, 349, 354, 490
Grand Army, 221–2, 243, 249, 263–5, 298, 332, 414, 428, 444–8
Grand Port, 399–400
Graves, Rear-Admiral Thomas, 175, 184, 187
Great Belt, 175–6
Great Lakes, 454–5, 469–70, 480–1, 501
Grenville, Lord, 170, 172, 302, 307
Grey, Lieut.-General Sir Charles, 53
Groix, I. de, 42, 436
Grouchy, Marshal, 46, 494
Guadeloupe, 53, 109, 383
Guerrillas, 335–6, 339, 348–53, 355–6
Guns and gunnery, 34–7, 41, 61–3, 77–9, 96–7, 130, 132–7, 143, 148, 151, 182–5, 201–2, 206–7, 259, 278–87, 296, 350–1, 367–8, 373–4, 456–60, 468–70, 474, 479–81

Haak Sand, 329–30
Haïti, 53, 110, 376
Halifax, 111, 397, 419, 462
Hallowall, Rear-Admiral Sir Benjamin, 65, 68–9, 76, 126, 137, 271, 314, 344, 350, 496
Hamburg, 191, 209, 230, 319 and n., 406, 442
Hamelin, Commodore Jacques, 381–2, 399–400
Hamilton, Emma, Lady, 142–9, 196, 266
Sir William, 140, 147, 149
Hampton Roads, 31
Hangö Udd, 324
Hanikoff, Vice-Admiral Peter, 55
Hano Bay, 327
Hardy, Captain Sir Thomas Masterman, 65, 129, 146–7, 180–1, 269, 271, 281, 286, 291, 463
Harvey, Captain Thomas, 346
Hawkesbury, Lord, 172–3, 217
Hayes, Captain John, 437–9, 463, 475, 478–9
Haze, as factor in naval warfare, 28–9, 33, 75, 104–5, 129, 162, 228, 235–6,

259, 273–4, 320 n., 363, 370, 384, 392, 430, 435, 465–6, 472
' Heart of Oak ', 206
Helder, 151
Heligoland, 313 and n., 320–2, 411, 414, 449
Helsingborg, 175
Hely - Hutchinson, Major - General, 202–3
Hoche, General Lazare, 44, 46, 94
Hohenlinden, 151
Holland, 54–5, 97, 111, 211, 406, 449
Holländer Deep, 176, 178–80
Hood, Vice-Admiral Lord, 57, 59; Captain Samuel, 126, 128
Hooghli, 113, 121
Hoste, Captain William, 317, 346
Hotham, Rear-Admiral Henry, 436–7, 463, 496
Vice-Admiral Sir William, 27, 59–64
Howe, Admiral Lord, 19 n., 27–39, 83–4, 87–8, 159
Hudson's Bay Company, 419, 423
Hull, 448
Hull, Commodore Isaac, 456–7
Humbert, General, 51
Hyères Is., 63, 431
Hygiene, 155–7, 432–3

Ice, as factor in naval warfare, 180, 190, 374
Impress Service. See Manning of the Fleet
India, 57, 111–3, 121, 125–6, 128–9, 139, 141, 216, 299, 316–7, 397, 401, 420, 501
Industrial Revolution, 197–8
Inshore squadron: Brest, 164–7, 232, 303–4; Cadiz, 98, 272; Texel, 55–6, 95; Toulon, 431. See also Blockade
Intelligence, as factor in naval warfare, 129–30, 143, 167–8, 263, 316–7, 402 and n.
Invasion alarms, 82, 92, 124, 193–8, 200, 221–9, 255, 261, 264
plans, 193–4, 221–3 and n.
Ionian Is., 242, 314, 343–4, 347, 367
Ireland, 42–52, 72, 75, 124, 144
Iroise Channel. See Navigational conditions; Brest approaches

Jackson, General Andrew, 481–2
Jamaica station, 110, 455, 481

Java, 400–1
Jay's Treaty, 122
Jefferson, Thomas, 318, 455
Jemaffes, 20
Jena, 308–9
Jervis, Sir John. *See* St. Vincent
Joaquim, 142
Jones, Captain Jacob, 459
Jourdan, Marshal, 355
Junot, General, 127, 313
Jutland, 328

Karlshamn, 327
Karlskrona, 189, 374, 393
Kattegat, 108, 174, 394
Keats, Vice-Admiral Sir Richard, 205–6,
    254, 268, 313, 325, 393
Keith, Admiral Lord: seizure of the
    Cape, 56; mutiny at the Nore, 92;
    Mediterranean fleet, 147, 168; North
    Sea fleet, 227, 229, 234, 243; Channel
    fleet, 352–3, 357–9, 429–30, 437, 496,
    498–9
Keppel, Admiral Lord, 19 n., 166, 170
Key, Francis Scott, 476–7
Killala Bay, 51
King's Deep, 176, 179, 181–2
Kioge Bay, 189–90
Kléber, Marshal, 127, 202
Kronborg, 175, 177, 372, 395
Kronstadt, 176, 189–90
Kutuzov, Field Marshal, 444–6

Lancashire, 197, 319, 413
Lands End, 114
Langara, Admiral, 27
Langney Point, 105
Lapenotière, Lieutenant, 288–9
Lawrence, Captain James, 456, 459–60,
    468–9
Leeward Is. station, 110, 455
Leghorn, 61, 64, 68, 71, 146, 149, 199
Leipzig, 448–50
Leissègues, Rear-Admiral, 295–6
Leith, 448
Lemême, François, 111, 376, 378
Lemon juice, 432
Leroi, Pierre, 115
Levant, 102, 125, 299
Leveille, Louis, 108
Lind, Dr. James, 432
Linois, Vice-Admiral, 203–5, 215, 376–8
Lisbon, 74, 101, 306, 332, 247–9, 358
Lissa, 346

Liverpool, 322, 411, 415, 485
' Living tradition ', 47, 256
Lizard, 106, 114, 231 n.
Lloyd's, 120, 261–2, 370, 387–8, 396–7,
    401–5 407
List, 114
Lodi, Bridge of, 67
Lofoten Is., 370
London, Port of, 17, 91, 103
Long Hope Sound, 374, 392–3, 395
Long Island Sound, 465
Longa, 351–2
Louis XVII, King, 59
Louis, Rear-Admiral Sir Thomas, 126,
    128, 147, 271, 296
Louisiana, 215, 218
Lowe, Sir Hudson, 503
Lübeck, 361
Lunéville, Treaty of, 152
Lyon, Gulf of, 125, 239–40
Lyons, 440

McBride, Admiral John, 22, 55–6
Macdonough, Captain Thomas, 456,
    480–1
Madeira Is., 313 n., 463
Madison, President James, 452–3, 455,
    471
Madrid, 339, 352, 354
Maida, 302
Maitland, Captain Frederick, 220,
    496–9
Malacca, Straits of, 111, 377–8, 398
Mallerousse, 114
Malmö, 372–4, 395
Malta, 127, 129–30, 137, 142–8, 198–
    200, 213, 216–8, 227, 239, 241–2,
    248–9, 267, 300, 314–5, 320–1, 369,
    392, 499
Man, Rear-Admiral Robert, 63, 72–3
Manchester, 209, 449
Manning of the Fleet, 23 and n., 208,
    219–20, 357 n., 453, 485–6
Mantua, 71
Manufactures, 197–8, 209, 311, 322–3,
    410–9, 448, 485, 502
Marengo, 151, 211
Maretimo, 316–7
Margate roads, 196
Marines, 99
Maritime rights, 122–3, 170–3, 191,
    310, 452–3, 484, 491, 502
Markham, Rear-Admiral John, 155,
    303, 305–6
Marmont, Marspal, 126–7, 343, 352

Marmorice Bay, 200–1
Marryat, Captain Frederick, 336–7, 431 n., 503–4
Martin, Rear-Admiral George, 344
Rear-Admiral Thomas Byam, 326, 359
Martinique, 53, 249, 383
Masséna, Marshal, 299, 301, 347–50, 442
Mauritius, 111–4, 376, 379–82, 399–400
Mediterranean Sea, 73, 82, 124–5, 141–2, 145, 297, 299–300, 320, 343, 433; fleet, 65–7, 80, 98, 101, 126, 137, 153–4, 239–40, 254, 270–1, 297–8, 314, 344, 431–2
Melville, James Dundas, the first Lord, 246
the second Lord, 352 and n., 358–9
Mendizabal, 351–2
Merchant shipping, 17, 103, 114–5, 382–3, 389–90, 422–3, 501–2
Messina, 299, 314–5; Straits of, 129, 242, 247, 300–1
Metternich, Prince, 491–2
Middleton, Admiral Sir Charles. See Barham
Milan Decrees, 318
Miller, Captain Ralph, 65, 70, 79 n., 126
Mina, 350, 353, 355
Minorca, 141–2
Minto, Lord, 399–401
Miquelon, 116
Missiessy, Vice-Admiral, 247, 249–50, 429
Mississippi, R., 213, 463
Mitchell, Admiral Sir Andrew, 151
Mizen Head, 45, 48
Molène I., 432
Mona Passage, 475
Montagu, Rear-Admiral George, 32, 38
Moore, General Sir John, 202, 224, 332–5, 438
Morard de Galles, Admiral, 21 n., 44
Moreno, Don Juande, 205
Moscow, 445–6, 450
Mulgrave, Lord, 298
Murat, Marshal, 126, 444–5, 450
Murman, 392
Mutiny, 21, 82–92, 98–101

Nantucket, 468
Naples, 71, 142, 146–7, 152, 273, 361
Napoleon I., 59, 67–8, 71–2, 124–8, 138, 141, 143, 150–2, 193, 211–8, 221–9, 243, 249–50, 257–8, 263–7, 273, 298–9, 301, 308–15, 319–23, 325–7, 331–4, 339–40, 343–4, 406–11, 414, 427–8, 440–51, 492–504
Narragansett Bay, 464
Naval stores, 54 and n., 172, 191, 326
Navigational conditions: Abonkir Bay, 132–4; Arctic Ocean, 370, 392; Baltic Sea and approaches, 174–84, 189, 372–4, 393–5; Bantry Bay, 44–7; Bay of Biscay, 237–8, 357–9, 436–9; Brest approaches, 44, 160–7, 235–6, 303; Caribbean Sea, 110–1, 375–6, 395; North American coast, 463–6, 478–9; English Channel, 28 and n., 29 and n., 39–40, 42, 49, 104–6, 160, 162–3, 195, 229, 231–5, 361–4, 366–9, 435; North Sea, 56, 93–4, 96–7, 195–6, 328–30, 341–2, 428–9; Straits of Gibraltar, 272; Thames estuary, 91, 194; Toulon approaches, 239–41, 343 n., 431. See also Trade Winds
Naze, 108, 171, 374
Neale, Rear-Admiral Sir Harry, 430, 437
Neilly, Rear-Admiral, 31, 33
Nelson, Vice-Admiral Lord: action with Ça Ira, 62–3; detached service, 64, 68, 71–5; action off Cape St. Vincent, 75–81; advanced station off Cadiz, 98; detached squadron in Mediterranean, 100, 124, 149; second-in-command, Baltic fleet, 173–89; Commander-in-Chief, 189–92; 'particular service', 194–7; Mediterranean station, 220, 239–42, 247–8; pursuit of Villeneuve, 253–7; re-appointed to Mediterranean command, 267–73; action off Trafalgar, 273–86; news of death received in England, 288–91; funeral, 291–4
Nepean, Sir Evan, 158
Neutral rights, 121–2, 170–3, 191, 310, 452–3, 484, 491, 502
New Brunswick, 419
New England, 120, 310, 453, 455, 462, 473–4
New Orleans, 481–2
New South Wales, 421
New York, 322, 461, 463, 465–7, 478–9
New Zealand, 421–2
Newfoundland, 102, 111, 396–7, 418, 462
Newhaven, 367–8

Ney, Marshal, 494–5
Niemen, R., 444, 447
Nile, 139–41
Non-Intercourse Act, 322, 410, 452
Nore, 88, 90, 194
Norfolk (Va.), 465
North Cape, 370, 392
North Sea, 55, 174, 319
Nova Scotia, 418

Occa Bay, 296
Oder, R., 447
Onslow, Vice-Admiral Richard, 56, 96
Orders in Council, 310, 319, 322, 413, 452–3
Orkney Islands, 55, 370, 374
L'Orient, 42
Ortegal, Cape, 237, 287
Owen, Captain Sir Edward, 195–6, 449

Pakenham, Major-General Sir Edward, 481–2
Palermo, 147–8, 300–1, 316
Pampeluna, 356
Paris, 214, 451, 493
Parker, Captain George, 323
    Admiral Sir Hyde, 173–7, 179, 184–7, 189–90
    Admiral Sir Peter, 291
    Richard, 88–9, 91–2
    Captain William, 33–4
Pasajes, 356–8
Pasley, Vice-Admiral Sir Thomas, 33
Passage du Raz. See Navigational conditions: Brest approaches
Patapsco, R., 476–7
Patrol system of commerce protection, 116 and n., 383–6
Patton, Rear-Admiral Philip, 83
Pegwell Bay, 224
Pellew, Vice-Admiral Sir Edward: action off Prawle Point, 25–6; action with Droits de l'Homme, 47–8; blockade of Ferrol, 221, 237–8; East India station, 378–82, 398; Mediterranean station, 431, 450
Penmarck Point, 48, 260
Perroud, Jacques, 379–80
Perry, Commander Oliver, 456, 469
Pevensey Levels, 224, 367
Philadelphia, 467
Phillip, Captain Arthur, 421
Pitt, William, the Younger, 16–20, 39, 52–7, 73, 85, 90, 124, 138, 141, 171–2, 246, 248–9, 266, 291, 298

Plattsburg, 480–1, 483
Plymouth, 18, 86, 219–20, 499; sound, 157
Poland, 311, 492
Pole, Admiral Sir Charles Morice, 192
Pondicherry, 116
Popham, Rear-Admiral Sir Home, 119, 262–3, 351–3, 358, 416, 419
Port Jackson, 421
Port Louis, 57, 380–1
Port Mahon, 145, 331
Portland Bill, 114
Porto Ferrajo, 71, 74, 498
Portsmouth, 22, 38, 84–8, 219–20, 245, 262, 265, 269, 396, 485–9
Portugal, 306, 309, 313–4, 338–9, 347–50, 352, 356, 360, 413
Potomac, R., 475–6
Prawle Point, 25, 106
Press-gang. See Manning of the Fleet
Prevost, General Sir George, 480–1
Privateers: American, 460–3, 470–4, 483; Danish-Norwegian, 325–6, 370–5, 393–4; French, 54, 102–15, 307, 361–9, 375–81, 383–6, 411; Spanish, 110, 375–6
Prussia, 20, 54, 191, 308, 447–51, 491–6, 503
Pym, Captain Samuel, 399
Pyrenees, 332, 350, 352, 356, 450

Quebec, 111

Raffles, Sir Stanford, 421
Ragusa, 346
Rainier, Admiral Peter, 57, 111, 114, 376–7, 390
Red Sea, 199
Reduction of hostile bases, 57, 116–7, 383, 400–1
Refitting, 125, 142, 155, 159, 205, 233–5, 239–40
Reggio, 314
Reval, 189–91
Reynier, General, 127, 300–1
Reynolds, Rear-Admiral Robert, 328
Rhine, R., 214, 450
Richery, Admiral Joseph de, 102
Riou, Captain Edward, 179–81, 183–4
Rochefort, 51, 262, 337, 430
Rodgers, Commodore John, 456, 460, 466
Romana, Marquis de la, 323
Rosas Bay, 344

Rosen, Count, 407, 410
Ross, General Robert, 475–7
Rostock, 361, 407
Rotterdam, 442
Rowley, Captain Josias, 381, 400, 450
Royal Sovereign shoal, 105
' Rule, Britannia ', 88, 290
Rule of 1756, 121, 191
Rum, 240, 423, 433–4
Running ships, 116, 403–4
Russia, 21, 55, 152, 170–2, 188–91, 216, 248–9, 267, 273, 311–2, 314, 318, 323–7, 407, 410, 440, 443–8, 450–1, 499–500, 503

St. Cyr, General, 242, 273, 298–9, 335
St. Helena, 397, 489, 502–4
St. Helens, 49, 84, 87–8, 291, 489
St. Lawrence, R., 418, 480
St. Lucia, 53
St. Malo, 104, 106 n., 307
St. Petersburg, 445, 448
St. Pierre, 116
St. Vincent, Cape, 75
St. Vincent, John Jarvis, Earl of: West Indies, 53; Mediterranean station, 64–81, 98–101, 107 n., 124–6, 130, 140, 142–6; Channel fleet, 153–60, 163–9; First Lord, 218, 229, 239, 241, 245–6, 266; Channel fleet, 302–8
Salamanca, 352, 356
Saldanha Bay, 57
Salem, 120, 475
Salonika, 416
Saltholm, 373
San Sebastian, 351, 355–6, 358–9
San Domingo, 215, 296
San Fiorenzo Bay, 61, 65, 73
Sandheads, 113, 121
Sandy Hook, 465, 479
Santander, 352–4, 355–6
Santona, 351, 358
Saumarez, Admiral Sir James: action off Cape Barfleur, 26–7; advanced station off Brest, 165–7; actions off Algeciras, 203–8; Baltic fleet, 323–8, 372, 374, 393–4, 407–10, 428
Saxony, 492
Scania, 324
Scheldt, R., 18, 82, 216, 337, 340, 342, 490–1
Scilly, Isles of, 106, 114
Scylla, 314
Sea-Fencibles, 194

Sea power, Influence of, 69, 141, 208, 212–3, 243, 295, 359, 440, 444, 470, 497, 501–2
Seaford, 367, 384
Seamanship: American, 456–8, 461–2, 471–2, 479; British, 25, 28 n., 30 and n., 31, 34, 47–9, 62, 65–9, 77–8, 119, 125, 133–4, 138, 148, 159–60, 163–9, 179–82, 187, 200–3, 230–2, 235–9, 247–8, 257, 274–5, 287, 297, 303–5, 328–9, 334–5, 341, 386, 397, 400, 428, 435–9, 463, 479; French, 36, 44–7, 103–5, 111–4, 248, 362–4, 426–7; Spanish, 53, 72, 77
Secret Expedition, 248–9, 251–6, 267
Senegal, 416
Seychelle Is., 416
Sheerness, 90–1
Sheffield, 198, 423
Shelburne, Lord, 416, 501
Ships, Principal references to: Achille (Fr.), 34–5, 286; Active, 315 n.; Adamant, 89–90; Africa, 373–4; Agamemnon, 19, 59, 62–3, 182, 262, 273, 282, 297; Aggerhuus (Dan.), 185; Aigle (Fr.), 280, 285; Ajax, 200–1, 282; Alexander, 125, 128, 132; Alexander (Fr.), 296; Algésiras (Fr.), 279, 284; Alphaea, 384; Amazon, 47–8, 179–80, 254; Amphion, 254, 317, 346; Anacreon (Fr.), 107; Anson, 51; Aquilon (Fr.), 134; Ardent, 96, 234, 237; Argonauta (Sp.), 285; Argonaute (Fr.), 280; Atalanta, 231 and n., 233; Atlas, 159; Audacious, 126, 128, 134, 181 n., 334; Bacchante, 348; Bahama (Fr.), 279, 285; Barfleur, 303; Beaver, 503 and n., 504; Belle Poule (Fr.), 379; Belleisle, 254, 279–80; Bellerophon, 37, 41, 83–5, 87, 125, 135, 276, 279–80, 284, 296–9, 496–9; Bellona, 181–3; Bellone (Fr.), 108, 379–80; Blenheim, 78, 379; Bombay Castle, 74; Boadicea, 400; Britannia, 63, 68, 282; Brunswick, 35–6, 41; Bucentaure (Fr.), 281–3; Ça Ira, 62, 69; Caesar, 34, 204–6, 303; Caledonia, 431; Cannonière, 379; Canopus, 254; Captain, 68, 75, 78–9; Caroline, 401; Caroline (Fr.), 381; Cartier (Fr.), 113; Censeur (Fr.), 62; Chasseur (Am.), 472; Cherub, 474; Chesapeake (Am.), 453, 468–9; Childers, 15; Clarisse (Fr.), 113; Cléopatre (Fr.), 25–6; Colossus, 280,

Ships, Principal references to—*cont.*
285; *Commerce de Paris,* 315; *Confiance* (Am.), 480–1; *Confiance* (Fr.), 113; *Congress* (Am.), 466; *Conquérant* (Fr.), 134; *Conqueror,* 254, 282–4; *Constellation* (Am.), 466; *Constitution* (Am.), 456–60, 466, 475, 478; *Contre Amiral Magon* (Fr.), 385–6, *Courageux,* 73; *Crescent,* 26–7; *Cressy;* 328; *Cruizer,* 385–6; *Culloden,* 77–8, 126, 128, 135; *Dannebrog* (Dan.), 182, 184–5; *Defence,* 285, 328–9; *Defiance,* 183, 187, 280; *Derwent,* 358; *Desirée,* 183; *Dessaix* (Fr.), 204; *Diadem,* 78; *Dictator,* 330; *Donegal,* 254; *Dreadnought,* 280, 284–5, 430; *Droits de l'Homme* (Fr.), 47–8; *Edgar,* 175, 182; *Elephant,* 177, 179–81, 184–7; *Elven* (Dan.), 185; *Endymion,* 479; *Essex* (Am.), 474; *Euryalus,* 267, 269, 274–5; *Exallent,* 78–9, 300; *Formidable,* 304; *Formidable* (Fr.), 204, 207; *Fortune* (Fr.), 378; *Foudroyant,* 147 and n., 148, 200, 232; *Fougueux* (Fr.), 277–8, 280, 283; *Franklin* (Fr.), 135–6; *Fraternité* (Fr.), 44; *Généreux* (Fr.), 137, 147; *Gernershe* (Dan.), 185; *Glatton,* 182, 187; *Goliath,* 70, 77, 126, 128, 132, 134; *Guerrière,* 457–8, 460; *Guerrier* (Fr.), 134–5; *Guillaume Tell* (Fr.), 137, 147–8; *Hannibal,* 204; *Hector,* 159–6; *Hermenogildo* (Sp.), 206–7; *Hero,* 329–30; *Heureux* (Fr.), 135–6; *Hibernia,* 302; *Hirondelle* (Fr.), 111; *Hjælperen* (Dan.), 185; *Hoche* (Fr.), 51–2; *Holstein* (Dan.), 183–4; *Hornet* (Am.), 459–60, 479; *Impérial* (Fr.), 296; *Impérieuse,* 336, 338; *Impétueux,* 36, 167, 231 and n., 232, 236; *Impregnable,* 428, 489; *Inconstant,* 61–2, 68, 70; *Indefatigable,* 44, 47–8, 338; *Indomptable* (Fr.), 47, 204; *Intrépide* (Fr.), 282, 286; *Isis,* 183; *Java,* 458–9; *Junon,* 475; *Jupiter* (D.), 97; *Leander,* 128, 135–6; *Leviathan,* 254, 282; *London,* 85–6, 101, 174–5; *Macedonian,* 458, 478; *Macedonian* (Am.), 465; *Magicienne,* 399; *Magnificient,* 437–8; *Majestic,* 126, 128, 135, 478; *Malartic* (Fr.), 113; *Manche* (Fr.), 381; *Marengo* (Fr.), 377, 379, 398; *Marlborough,* 36–7, 100; *Mars,* 41, 280, 285, 303; *Medusa,* 194; *Mercure* (Fr.), 135,

137; *Minerva,* 75; *Minotaur,* 126, 128, 134, 146–7, 200, 330; *Monarca* (Sp.), 279; *Monarch,* 96, 177, 182–3, 187; *Montagu,* 74; *Montague* (Fr.), 34–6; *Mucius* (Fr.), 36; *Neptune,* 164, 275, 277, 281 n.; *Neptune* (Fr.), 281–3, 286; *Nérèide,* 399; *Neufchatel* (Am.), 472–3; *Norge,* 488; *Northumberland,* 296, 436–7, 496, 499, 502; *Nyborg* (Dan.), 185; *Nymphe,* 25–6, 474; *Ocean,* 297, 344; *Orient,* 135–6; *Orion,* 33, 78, 118, 125, 128, 131, 134, 282, 285; *Osprey,* 385 and n.; *Peacock,* 459–60; *Peacock* (Am.), 473, 479; *Penelope,* 148; *Penguin,* 479–80; *Peuple Souverain* (Fr.), 135; *Phoebe,* 474; *Picque,* 386, 475; *Piémontaise* (Fr.), 379–81; *Plantagenet,* 232; *Pluton* (Fr.), 280; *Polyphemus,* 285; *Pomone,* 479; *Pompée,* 204–5; *Porcupine,* 315 n.; *President* (Am.), 456, 466, 474, 478–9; *Prince,* 49, 159–60, 234; *Prince George,* 234, 304; *Principe de Asturias* (Sp.), 77, 280, 285; *Prövestein* (Dan.), 182–4; *Queen,* 37, 118, 297; *Queen Charlotte,* 34–9; *Ranger,* 394–5; *Rattlesnake* (Am.), 472; *Real Carlos* (Sp.), 206; *Redoutable* (Fr.), 281–3; *Réunion* (Fr.), 26–7; *Revenant* (Fr.), 380–1; *Revenge,* 285; *Rover,* 358; *Royal George,* 49, 87–8; *Royal Sovereign,* 41, 232, 254, 275, 277–9, 282, 284–6; *Russell,* 95; *St. Antoine* (Fr.), 207; *St. George,* 99, 177, 190, 328–9; *Salvador del Mundo* (Sp.), 78, 80; *San Agustin* (Sp.), 286; *San Domingo* (Sp.), 488; *San Ildefonso* (Sp.), 285; *San Isidro* (Sp.), 78; *San Josef,* 233, 304; *San Josef* (Sp.), 78–9; *San Juan Nepomuceno* (Sp.), 280, 284; *San Leandro,* 279; *San Nicolas,* 78–9; *Sandwich,* 88, 92; *Santa Ana* (Sp.), 278–9, 282, 284; *Santissima Trinidad* (Sp.), 78–80, 283–4; *Saratoga* (Am.), 480; *Shannon,* 466, 468–9; *Scipion* (Fr.), 287; *Scoupion,* 386; *Scourge* (Am.), 472; *Sirius,* 273; *Spartan,* 315 n., 347; *Spartiate* (Fr.), 134–5; *Spencer,* 254; *Standard,* 346; *Superb,* 205–7, 254, 264, 296; *Surveillante,* 353, 358; *Swiftsure,* 126, 128, 132, 135, 200, 254, 280; *Swiftsure* (Fr.), 280; *Téméraire,* 277, 281–3; *Tenedos,* 466,

Ships, Principal references to—*cont.*
475, 479; *Theseus*, 126, 128, 134; *Thunder*, 373; *Thunderer*, 37, 285; *Tigre*, 200, 254, 488; *Timoléon* (Fr.), 137; *Tonnant*, 237–8, 284, 303, 474; *Tonnant* (Fr.), 136–7; *Triumph*, 96; *Turbulent*, 373; *Unité*, 346; *United States* (Am.), 456–8, 465, 474, 478; *Vanguard*, 125–6, 128, 130, 134, 136; *Venerable*, 86, 89, 92, 95–7, 204, 206–7, 236 n., 351, 353, 435; *Vengeance*, 108; *Vengeur de Peuple* (Fr.), 34–5; *Vénus*, 400; *Vénus* (Fr.), 381; *Victory*, 19 and n., 27, 66, 75–9, 219, 240, 254, 265, 269, 271–2, 275–8, 280–3, 285–6, 293, 328, 334, 394; *Ville de Paris*, 98, 159–60, 164, 235, 334, 344–5, 431; *Vrijheid* (D.), 96–7; *Warrior*, 95, 159, 343; *Wasp* (Am.), 459, 473; *Windsor Castle*, 159; *Wolverine*, 396; *Zealand* (Dan.), 183; *Zealous*, 73, 126, 128, 131, 134, 137, 334
Sicie, Cape, 431
Sicily, 266, 299–301, 314–7, 343
Signal Book, 34, 184–5; stations, 367–8, 384, 387–8
Sickness, 21, 53, 55–6, 156, 233, 254, 341, 432–4, 446–7
Simon's Bay, 56–7 and n.
Skagerrak, 328, 393
Skaw, 174
Smuggling, 384 and n.
Smyrna, 102, 121
Sotheron, Captain, 300
Souchet, General, 150
Soult, Marshal, 335, 339, 352–3, 356
Sound, 175–8, 318, 325, 372, 395
South America, 318, 321–2, 411, 414, 418–20
Spain, 54, 71–2, 247, 321–2, 335–6, 356
'Spanish ulcer', 441–2
Spencer, Lord, 39, 54, 81 n., 83–5, 87, 89, 94, 124–5, 128–9, 138, 140–1, 143, 145, 148–9, 155, 165, 168
Spithead, 84, 96, 248, 265, 488–9
Start Point, 114
Stephen, James, 170, 310
Stewart, Captain Charles, 456, 465–6, 478
— Colonel Edward, 178, 180, 184–5, 187
Stirling, Rear-Admiral Charles, 258, 261–2
Stockholm, 410

Strachan, Rear-Admiral Sir Richard, 287, 295, 303, 315–7
Stralsund, 361
Strategy: British, 29–33, 40, 42, 48–50, 54, 56–7, 61–3, 65, 71–3, 92–5, 128–9, 141–3, 145–6, 151–2, 157–69, 175–9, 188–91, 199–203, 223, 229–43, 248–50, 252–3, 256–65, 272–4, 295, 299–301, 310–4, 323–7, 331–60, 439–440, 469–70, 480–1, 483; French, 31–3, 37–8, 102–3, 110–1, 126–8, 221–3, 229, 247, 249–50, 299 n., 308–10, 318–9, 340, 361, 426–7, 443–4, 493–4. *See also* Blockade, Conjunct operations, Convoy, Patrol system of commerce protection, Reduction of hostile bases, ' Ulterior objects '
Stuart, General Sir Charles, 141, 301 n.
Suckling, Captain Maurice, 194, 252
Supply. *See* Victualling
Surcouf, Robert, 111–3, 376, 380–1
Sveaborg, 323
Sviatoi Nos, Cape, 370, 392
Sweden, 170–2, 189–90, 312, 317, 323, 326–7, 407–8, 410, 449, 500
Sydney Smith, Captain Sir William, 59, 143, 150, 202, 301–2, 313
Symonds, Vice-Admiral Sir William, 429

Table Bay, 56, 57 n.
Tactics: American, 457–9, 470, 479; British, 26–7, 34–6, 41, 47, 61–2, 77–9, 96–7, 131–6, 148, 181–5, 268, 270–1, 275–8, 280–4, 377–8, 468–9; Danish, 178; French, 27, 37, 132–3, 276–7, 283; Spanish, 77–8, 206
Tagus, R., 74, 306, 347–8
Talavera, 339
Talleyrand, 217, 257, 491
Tariffa, 369
Tarragona, 350
Telegraph, Manual, 87, 219, 262, 390
Telegraphic signal code, 263, 268–9
Teneriffe, 81, 140
Texel, 55, 82, 151, 261
Thames, R., 17, 103, 194, 501
Thornbrough, Vice-Admiral Sir Edward 167, 314, 331
Thornton, Richard, 401
Tides, as factor in naval warfare, 15, 39, 94, 104–5, 162–3, 195–6, 222, 224, 227, 236, 261, 264, 305, 338, 357, 372, 437

Tilsit, 311–2, 324 and 325 n.
Timber crisis, 244–7
Tippoo Sahib, 420
Tonningen, 311
Torbay, 29, 155, 160, 220, 295, 435, 498
Tor Quay, 29, 155
Torre Abbey, 168
Torres Vedras, 348–9
Touche-Tréville, 193
Toulon, 21, 59, 64–5, 68, 72, 125–6, 144–5, 204, 239–41, 247, 297, 315–7, 331, 343–4, 431
Trade Winds, 254, 376, 395
Trafalgar, 140, 275–87, 295, 416, 443–4, 497
Tras-os-Montes, 354
Trekroner Battery, 178–80, 183–4, 187
Trieste, 320, 346
Trincomali, 57
Tristan da Cunha, 479, 503
Trolloppe, Captain Henry, 95–6
Trotter, Dr. Thomas, 28, 433–4
Troubridge, Rear-Admiral Sir Thomas, 19, 65, 70, 77–8, 126, 128, 135, 137, 147–8, 153, 173, 196, 245, 378–9, 398
Tucker, Benjamin, 65, 164, 304
Turkey, 141, 143, 150, 199–200, 215, 242, 299–302, 314–5, 317, 343

Ulm, 298–9
' Ulterior objects ', 44, 243, 250
United States, 311, 318–9, 410, 418
Ushant, 29, 50, 144, 157–64, 164–6, 230–1, 234, 236, 262, 303–6, 496, 498

Vado Bay, 61, 64
Valetta, 127, 198
Valladollid, 332–3
Valmy, 20
Vansittart, Nicholas, 175
Vanstabel, Rear-Admiral, 31, 38
Vashon, Captain James, 164
Venice, 346, 426
Victualling, 22, 56, 68, 71, 74, 94–5, 98, 155–7, 188, 191–2, 233, 297, 304–5, 344–5, 429, 432–4
Vienna, 267, 300, 340, 410, 490–2
Vigo, 334
Villaret-Joyeuse, Rear-Admiral, 21 n., 31, 33, 37–8
Villeneuve, Admiral, 126, 247, 250–1, 253–67, 273, 275, 281 n., 283, 285

Vimiero, 332
Vinegar Hill, 51
Vinga Sound, 328–9, 374, 394
Vistula, R., 447
Vittoria, 356

Wagram, 340
Walcheren, 341–2, 429
' War Hawks ', 453
Warren, Vice-Admiral Sir John Borlase, 51–2, 167, 295, 379, 455, 457, 463, 466, 468, 474
Washington, President George, 122
Waterloo, 494–5
Watt, James, 198, 415
Wellesley, Sir Arthur. See Wellington, Duke of
   Marquis, 376, 420
Wellington, Duke of, 268, 332, 338–9, 347–9, 353–6, 358–9, 450, 483, 491, 493–5
Weser, R., 191, 406, 449
West India station, 27, 53–4, 65, 109–11, 115–6, 118, 212, 215, 247, 249–51, 253–7, 295–6, 375–6, 383, 391, 395–6, 415–8, 455, 460, 462, 471–2
West Indies, 53–4, 109–10, 212, 215, 247, 249–51, 253–7, 295–6, 337, 375–6, 417–8, 455, 471–3
Western Approaches, 25, 31–2, 397, 462
Western Squadron. See Channel fleet
Whitshed, Rear-Admiral Sir James, 157–8
Winds, as factor in naval warfare, 39, 92–5, 97, 118, 127, 129, 133–4, 144–5, 159–67, 173, 176–81, 189–90, 201, 204, 230, 239, 253–6, 259, 264, 272–5, 277, 303, 329, 334–5, 357–9, 362–3, 372–3, 394–5, 401, 457, 478–9, 481, 496. See also Gales
Windward Passage, 110–1
Wielingen Channel, 196, 342
Willaumez, Rear-Admiral, 295–6
Woodforde, Rev. James, 139, 197, 210
Wynter, Admiral de, 94–7

Yarmouth, 86, 173–4
Yawkins, 195–6
Yeo, Captain Sir James, 470, 481
Young, Admiral Sir William, 306, 428–9

Zuyder Zee, 55, 429